THE WORLD'S GREATEST
UFO & ALIEN
ENCOUNTERS

Merry Christmas
Jillan

Lots of Love for
Mun
2007
XXX

CHANCELLOR
PRESS

The material in this book has previously appeared in:
The World's Greatest Alien Conspiracy Theories
(Chancellor Press, Bounty Books, Octopus Publishing Group, 2002)
The World's Greatest UFO Sightings
(Chancellor Press, Bounty Books, Octopus Publishing Group, 2002)
The World's Greatest UFO Encounters
(Chancellor Press, Bounty Books, Octopus Publishing Group, 2002)
The World's Greatest Alien Encounters
(Chancellor Press, Bounty Books, Octopus Publishing Group, 2002)

First published in Great Britain in 2002 by Chancellor Press,
an imprint of Bounty Books, a division of
Octopus Publising Group Ltd.,
2–4 Heron Quays, London E14 4JP

Reprinted 2003 (twice)

ISBN 0 7537 0614 8

Printed in Great Britain by Mackays of Chatham

Contents

Alien Encounters

Close Encounters of the Third Kind

Adamski

In ancient times, humans had contact with beings that came down from the heavens. But the first well-documented contactee of modern times – that is, since the age of the flying saucer which began in 1947 – was a Polish American named George Adamski, who chronicled his adventures with the 'space people' in several books. A self-made man with interests in astronomy and oriental philosophies, Adamski took six friends out on a picnic in the Mojave Desert in California on 20 November 1952.

The purpose of the expedition was to spot and photograph flying saucers. They were not disappointed. Shortly after a light lunch, a gigantic cigar-shaped craft glided silently into view. It was chased away by military jets – but not before it had ejected a silver disc which landed some distance away. Adamski and two of his friends drove off into the desert after it, hoping to get a closer view and perhaps even take some photographs. At the end of a dirt road, they stopped. Adamski set up his tripod-mounted portable telescope and took a number of photographs of the silvery craft through it. Then he ventured alone out into the desert to get some close-ups.

Before he reached it, the alien craft shot skywards and soared out into space. A few minutes later, a second, smaller, saucer-shaped craft appeared. It was gliding between two mountain peaks some way ahead of Adamski. He watched and photographed the craft as it landed about four hundred yards away. A figure got out and beckoned to him. At first Adamski thought the figure was a man.

'But the beauty of his form surpassed anything I had ever seen,' Adamski recalled later. The humanoid was short, about 5 feet 3 inches. He had smooth, tanned skin and long blond hair, and he was dressed in a brown one-piece suit with a broad belt, and red shoes.

Adamski put out his hand to shake hands with the being, who was plainly familiar with the gesture. But when palm-to-palm contact was established, the two began communicating using telepathy, though sign language was needed to clarify some points. The creature's name was Orthon. He came from Venus, where he and his fellow Venusians lived a pure, spiritual and God-fearing way of life. He had come to Earth, he said, to warn humankind about the dangers of nuclear energy and pollution. He refused to be photographed, then stepped into his craft and shot off back into space. First contact had been made. There were no photographs of the alien, but the encounter had been witnessed by Adamski's friends, who had been standing a few hundred yards away.

George Adamski had been born in Poland on 17 April 1891. In 1893, he emigrated to New York with his family. In 1913 he joined the US Army, serving in 13th US Cavalry, K Troop, until 1916. In 1918 worked as a government painter and decorator at the Yellowstone National Park. He also served with the National Guard, stationed at Portland, Oregon, and received an honourable discharge in 1919.

After that, things get a bit murky. It is now thought that, during Prohibition, which began in 1920, Adamski worked as a bootlegger. In 1926 he settled at Laguna, California, where he began lecturing on oriental philosophy, though he had no formal training. In 1940 he moved to Valley Center, California, where he established a cult movement known as the Royal Order of Tibet. As its spiritual leader, Adamski became a self-styled professor of philosophy. It was there, on 9 October 1946, that Adamski claimed to have seen a 'dirigible-shaped mother ship' flying over his home, a full nine months before Kenneth Arnold's legendary flying saucer sighting. It was a sign. Adamski took his followers on a trek across California. The cult settled on the southern slopes of Mount Palomar, famous for the astronomical observatory that sits on its peak. From there, he set out to make contact with the aliens that were plainly visiting the Earth. Soon, the quietly spoken Polish immigrant achieved world-wide celebrity status as the world's first alien contactee.

The incredible tale of the world's first face-to-face extraterrestial encounter is recounted at great length by Adamski in *Flying Saucers Have Landed* in 1953. It was the first of many meetings with Venusians. Adamski lectured widely and his cult following grew. Those who came to hear him were told of strange journeys to distant worlds. The Venusians had taken him home to Venus and, with them, he had visited the Moon and Mars. He supported his claims with photographs of alien craft allegedly taken through his telescope. A month after his first alien contact, he photographed a 'Venusian scout craft', thirty-five feet in diameter, hovering above his home in Palomar Gardens, California. And in 1951 Adamski snapped the cigar-shaped 'mother ship' hovering there, ready to take him on an interplanetary jaunt. He also supplied detailed drawings of the interior. The newspapers around the world lapped it up. And Adamski was widely billed as a professor from the Palomar Observatory, which was not altogether untrue. Before he came to fame, he ran a hot dog stall in its grounds.

When *Flying Saucers Have Landed* was published in 1953, it became an instant best-seller. Two years later his new adventures reached a world audience with *Inside the Flying Saucers*. This recounts his experiences on board the Venusians' ship, another first in UFOlogy. The reader is given a fascinating account of what it is like to travel though space, and Adamski describes in great detail life on the still-to-be-explored Moon. There were forests, lakes, wooded valleys and snow-covered mountains on the lunar landscape, and citizens of the Moon 'strolled down the sidewalks' in lunar cities, just as humans did in Earth cities, he said. The aliens also informed Adamski that the Earth was being visited by beings from the solar system and beyond.

Some dismissed his tales of planetary excursions as the ramblings of a troubled mind. Nevertheless, he managed to attract a band of illustrious supporters. *Flying Saucers Have Landed* was co-written by Desmond Leslie the British author, Winston Churchill's cousin. He was dubbed the 'Saucerer Royal'. Queen Juliana of the Netherlands received Adamski at her palace in Amsterdam and it was said that Pope John XXIII granted him a private audience on 31 May 1963 – though the Vatican has denied the claim.

After one of Adamski's trips into space, two people who had witnessed his departure through binoculars signed affidavits backing his story. In an effort to discredit Adamski, UFO researcher Thomas Eickhoff tried to sue in the Federal Court so that he would get an opportunity to cross-examine them. The US government blocked the case. This was no accident, Adamski said. Washington sanctioned his efforts. Indeed, document requests under the Freedom of Information Act show that Adamski was in contact with the FBI. They contacted him to warn him to stop 'inferring that the FBI cleared his material on space travel'. Other FBI memos denounce Adamski as a Communist and say that he was 'mentally disturbed'.

In his defence, even sceptics were impressed with Adamski's apparent sincerity. Science journalist Robert Chapman wrote of a meeting with the great man in *UFO – Flying Saucers Over Britain*, 'Adamski was so damnably normal and this was the overall impression I carried away. He believed he had made contact with a man from Venus, and he did not see why anyone should disbelieve him. I told myself that if he was deluded he was the most lucid and intelligent man I had met.'

Adamski's third book, *Flying Saucer Farewell*, was published in 1961. But, by then, he was being greeted by a more educated and sceptical audience. On 12 September 1959 the Soviets had managed to hit the moon with their probe Luna 2 and, on 4 October 1959, Luna 3 orbited the moon and sent back pictures of the far side. There were no forests, lakes, wooded valleys and snow-capped mountains to be seen. Nor were there any cities. The lunar surface was a barren stretch of rocks, dust and craters. When asked to explain this, Adamski accused the Soviets of falsifying the pictures to deceive the Americans.

Adamski died on 23 April 1965, aged 73, as a series of new probes, both Soviet and American, were heading for the moon to further undermine his story. At best, it can be said that Adamski made wild exaggerations, which certainly destroyed any reputation he may have had. Today, he is largely dismissed as a fraud. However, when he died he left behind a huge collection of photographs and film footage, much of which has still not been discredited. True his photographs of 'mother ships' and their 'scout craft' may seem too good to be true. Critics have compared them variously to part of a vacuum cleaner, a chicken feeder and a bottle cooling machine made in Wigan, Lancashire, which intriguingly turned out to have been designed after the photographs were released. But while sceptics have mocked them, no one has proved them to be fakes.

On 26 February 1965, just months before he died, Adamski was staying with the Rodeffers at their house in Silver Spring, Maryland. That afternoon, Adamski and Madeleine Rodeffer saw something hovering through some trees. A car drew up and three men told Adamski: 'Get your cameras – they're here.' Then they drove off. Adamski grabbed the Rodeffers' cine camera and produced some 8mm colour footage which is among the most convincing UFO footage ever. Despite rigorous analysis, this film has stood the test of time.

NASA claims that the film shows a three-foot model. However, Adamski was neither an accomplished model maker, nor was he well-versed in special effects. Optical physicist William T. Sherwood, former project development engineer for Eastman-Kodak, spent a great deal of time examining the film and found that it had not been tampered with. The image, he says, shows a craft around twenty-five feet across. As it flies through the frames, it becomes distorted. Veteran aeronautics engineer Leonard Cramp says that this was caused by a powerful gravitational field produced by the craft.

Others around the world who had never heard of Adamski have sighted identical objects to the craft the film depicts. One of them was a schoolboy named Stephen Darbishire who, with his cousin, took two photographs in Coniston, Lancashire one day in February 1954. Cramp used a technique called orthographic projection to prove that the object depicted in Darbishire's and Adamski's photographs were proportionally identical.

Prominent UFOlogist Nick Pope also believes that Adamski's film is authentic and refuses to dismiss Adamski.

'My own intensive investigations over several decades have led me to the conviction that, even if some of his claims are nonsensical, others are legitimate,' Pope says. And he has other reputable backers. Adamski was the first to claim that contact had been established, at a 'restricted' level, between the Venusians and the scientific community, and the aliens were providing assistance in the space programme. This was confirmed by Dr Hermann Oberth, a senior rocket scientist who worked with NASA in the late 1950s.

There is other high-powered corroboration. On his first trip into space, Adamski said he observed 'manifestations taking place all around us, as though billions upon billions of fireflies were flickering everywhere'. This is not something that would readily emerge from the imagination to be included in a space yarn. When US astronaut John Glenn became the first American to orbit Earth on 20 February 1962, he said: 'A lot of the little things I thought were stars were actually a bright yellowish green about the size and intensity as looking at a firefly on a real dark night... there were literally thousands of them.' Russian cosmonauts have seen the same thing. They turned out to be billions of reflective dust particles. How could George Adamski have known?

Welcome to the Universal Confederation

After Adamski, aliens seemed to be queuing up to chat to humans. They first contacted Richard Miller by short-wave radio in 1954. They told him to go to an isolated place near Ann Arbor in Michigan, where after fifteen minutes a disc-shaped craft appeared and landed nearby. This spaceship, he learned later, was called 'Phoenix'. A doorway opened in the base of the vehicle and a staircase descended.

A young humanoid dressed in a brown one-piece space suit stood at the top of the stairs. He beckoned Miller to enter the ship, which he did. He found himself was standing in a large hallway which seemed to encircle the whole craft. The alien said nothing but the creature radiated a kind of friendliness that put him at his ease.

Miller was taken to the control room of the ship where he met the alien commander. His name was Soltec and he greeted Miller in perfect English. He explained that their home planet was Centurus of the Alpha Centauri system. It belonged to the 'Universal Confederation', a group of some 680 planets which earned the right to membership by their evolutionary progress.

Miller was told that, before Earth could become a member, mankind would have to awaken to higher spiritual values.

'When love of your fellow man becomes established, then will the "Sons of Light" appear and the Kingdom of your God will reign on Earth,' Miller was told. The 'Sons of Light', it was explained, were what the Bible called 'angels'.

Richard Miller's contacts with the extraterrestrials continued for over twenty years and he meticulously recorded all his contacts in a library of writings and tapes.

Independence Day

In 1954 Daniel Fry, a scientist at the White Sands Missile Range in New Mexico, claimed that he had been in contact with aliens for some time. On 4 July Fry missed the bus taking employees into town to see the Independence Day fireworks display and decided instead to take a walk in the desert to enjoy the cool night air. As he looked up he noticed that the stars were being blocked out by something descending.

It was a metallic object, oblate spheroid in shape, and it landed on the desert floor about seventy feet away from him. He approached the sphere, and heard a voice warning him not to touch the craft as the hull was still extremely hot. Fry was so shocked he fell over a root, and the voice attempted to calm him. According to Fry, the alien was up to speed on all the latest American slang. The voice belonged to an extraterrestrial called 'A-Lan' who was communicating with him telepathically. He had come to Earth to collect air samples.

A-Lan invited Fry to enter the ship. Once he was on board the craft took off and travelled to New York City and back in half-an-hour. This would have meant that it was travelling at a speed of over eight thousand miles an hour, yet Fry felt nothing except a slight motion. He was released back into the desert with the promise that there would be further contacts. Fry was given the task of preaching the aliens' philosophy of understanding to human society. A-Lan claimed that his race were the descendants of a previous Earth civilisation that had emigrated into space thirty thousand years ago.

Fry produced clear daylight photographs of the UFO to support his story. One, taken in 1965, shows two alien spacecraft hovering over a Joshua tree in California. He also founded a quasi-religious group called 'Understanding' to pass on the words of A-Lan. He published his claims in a book, which came out shortly after Adamski's. This gave him high-profile media coverage and earned him vociferous public support. However, he agreed to take a lie detector test live on television and appeared to fail – though the results are open to debate. But it is difficult to dismiss him as a hoaxer. As a scientist with a well-paid job, he risked destroying his career.

Like Adamski, Fry and a number of high-profile contactees said that the aliens that had spoken to them had come to warn humankind about the proliferation of nuclear weapons. After the Soviet Union exploded its first atomic bomb in 1949, this was plainly a concern to everyone on the planet. The beginnings of the space race also focused mankind's attention on the mysteries of the universe.

Hoaxers?

Many early contactees were completely discredited both by scientists and UFOlogists, eager to winnow out hoaxes. Dr J. Allen Hynek, scientific consultant to Project Blue Book – the US military's UFO monitor – denounced the early wave of contactees as 'pseudo-religious fanatics' of 'low credibility value'. Nevertheless many contactees enjoyed celebrity status.

In 1962, after being interviewed by the Air Ministry, fourteen-year-old British schoolboy Alex Birch became a minor celebrity on TV, radio and the lecture circuit after photographing five saucer-like craft. Ten years later, Birch admitted that the photographs had been faked. After that, Britain's UFO Research Organisation laid down guidelines for assessing photographic evidence. All negatives had to be submitted, along with the original film. Pictures should contain other objects, such as houses or trees, as a point of reference so estimates of size and distance could be made. Ideally, there should be an independent eyewitness to any encounter.

Despite his official role, even Hynek conceded that some UFO encounters were genuine. Twenty-three per cent of Project Blue Book's sightings – which ran from 1951 to 1969 – remain unexplained. He went on to found the Center for UFO Studies in 1973.

Danger UFO

Not all contact was benign. On 20 May 1967, Stephen Michalak saw a UFO land at Falcon Lake in the US. He managed to get close enough to touch it. As he did so, he said that a burst of intense light came blasting out of one of the spacecraft's 'exhaust panels', setting his shirt on fire and giving him first-degree burns. An investigation of the landing site found fragments of silver that had been exposed to great heat and a high level of radioactivity.

After his encounter, Michalak became ill. He suffered from dizziness, nausea, swollen joints and skin infections. In an effort of get his condition diagnosed, he visited twenty-seven doctors. None of them offered an explanation for his ill health.

Supplies from the Skies

Some aliens come to Earth for more down-to-earth reasons. One such visited Joe Simonton, a farmer, on the morning of 18 April 1961. Simonton noticed a bright, saucer-shaped object land near his farmhouse in Eagle River, Wisconsin, and went to check it out. It was about thirty feet across and twelve feet high. To his astonishment, a hatch opened and an alien climbed out. The figure was humanoid, about five feet tall and dressed like a human. The alien had no great message to communicate. Instead he waved an empty jug about. Simonton took this to mean that he wanted water and went to fetch it. When he returned, he found that the hospitable alien had set up a barbecue inside the craft and was cooking. The alien gave Simonton a 'pancake' in return for the water, then the alien closed the hatch and flew away. The pancake was analysed by a US Food and Drug Administration laboratory. No extraterrestrial ingredients were found, though there was a distinct absence of salt.

Pit Stop

On 24 April 1950 Bruno Facchini saw sparks near his home in Abbiate Buazzone, in Italy. At first he thought they were being generated by a storm, but when he went outside to investigate, he saw a dark UFO hovering just above the ground some two hundred yards away.

Nearby, a figure seemed to be working on the object, perhaps making repairs. Other entities were also seen near and around the object. They were dressed in tight-fitting clothes and were wearing helmets, but their faces were concealed behind masks that were connected to the craft by flexible pipes.

During the encounter, Facchini offered to help, but the entities fired a beam of light at him that blasted him along the ground for several yards. Shortly afterwards, when the repairs had apparently been completed, the object took off, making a heavy buzzing sound.

The following day Facchini returned to the site, where he found circular imprints and patches of scorched grass, and recovered metal fragments. There were a number of other witnesses to the event but they preferred to remain anonymous.

Contact Kentucky-style

One of the most famous alien contact stories occurred at Sutton Farm, Hopkinsville, Kentucky on the 21 August 1955.

At around 7 p.m., Billy Ray Taylor went out to fetch some water from the family well. While there, he noticed a large shining object land close to the farm. When he told the other family members inside the house they all laughed and failed to take him seriously.

Some time later, they heard their dog barking wildly outside, and Lucky and Billy went out to investigate. They had walked a few yards from the front door when they saw a small three-foot creature walking towards them. They described the creature as having large yellow eyes, a long thin mouth, large ears, thin short legs, and claws for hands.

One of the men then fired a shot from his .22 rifle. The creature, obviously hit, ran quickly into the woods.

When the men returned home – but before they had a chance to tell their incredible story – the house came under siege by a group of similar looking creatures. The eight adults and three children in the house at the time were all terrified as creature after creature appeared at windows around the house and the men loosed off another round whenever they got a clear shot at a creature.

The siege lasted around two hours before the family decided to make a run for the family pickup truck. They drove down to the local police station to report the event. When police officers turned up at the farm they could find no evidence of the strange creatures. However, there were gunshot holes in the windows and walls.

Police officers later admitted to seeing strange lights coming from the vicinity of the Sutton farm, but they did not bother to report them at the time.

Many people believe this to be a complete hoax. But the family made no money from the incident and shunned publicity. They had to make extensive repairs to the house, which cost a considerable amount of money. And all eight witnesses told the same story.

Alpine Encounters

Some bizarre stories have been told by those who have been visited by extraterrestrials, but none can match that related by the one-armed Swiss farmer Eduard 'Billy' Meier. Throughout the 1970s and 1980s he was in regular contact with the 'Pleiadians', as his alien contacts were called, who visited from a far-off galaxy. They not only passed on their all their secrets and whisked him around the universe, they took him back in time to meet Jesus and into a mystical realm where he photographed the 'Eye of God'.

Despite his outlandish claims, Meier could back what he said with the most comprehensive body of evidence any contactee has ever come up with. He had a thousand photographs of his many meetings with aliens and twelve films of alien spaceships. He also logged his conversations with the visitors and had reams of notes on the technical and spiritual knowledge passed to him by the Pleiadians. He also had a variety of mineral and rock samples, and over forty independent eyewitnesses said that they had seen him make contact with alien spaceships.

This huge body of evidence made Meier's story a landmark case in UFO history. It split the UFO lobby in two. Those who saw him as a fake attacked him with unprecedented hostility. But his supporters remain vehement in his defence.

Meier probably had his first encounter with UFOs in 1975, when he was a happily married man and the father of three children. They appeared to him in the woods behind his farm in Hinwil. But later, he recalled that when he was five, he saw a 'large circular craft' flying over the local church. For some reason, the aliens had picked him out as their chosen contact on Earth. Soon afterwards, he started receiving telepathic messages from the extraterrestrials. They urged him to mug up as much as he possible on the Earth's various religions and prepare himself for later visitations.

This preparation took Meier to many unusual places. He travelled extensively through Europe and India. He supported his quest by working as racing car driver and a snake charmer. He also spent time in the French Foreign Legion and, during his time as an industrial worker, he lost an arm in an accident. His travels exposed Meier to many different ways of life, broadening his mind and preparing him spiritually. 'His soul could understand ideas communicated to him better than our souls could,' says one supporter.

By the mid-1970s he was plainly ready. Between 1975 and 1978, he had over 130 well-documented meetings with visitors from the Pleiades, a cluster of stars about four hundred light years from Earth. The contacts followed a set pattern. Meier would feel a gentle breeze on his forehead, then he would receive telepathic instructions telling him where the starship would be landing. The meetings would begin with a photo call. Normally the aliens' spacecraft were invisible, but for the purposes of terrestrial photography they would be made visible by generating special cloaks of visibility around them. The Pleiadians made their craft visible and encouraged him to take photographs so that he had evidence of their meetings. He had pictures of numerous different types of craft, demonstrating the wide range of their technology.

Encounters would usually take place in various spots around southeast Zurich. He was invited to bring friends along, though they were never actually allowed to meet the Pleiadians. However, a number of them testified to seeing the lights of the visiting craft at dusk or dawn. After the initial photo session was over, Meier was transported instantly on board the alien craft. Some of his friends saw him beamed on board. They also photographed the landing sites after Meier's meetings, showing the marks of the alien craft in the grass.

During his many lengthy conversations with the Pleiadians, Meier discovered that they came from a planet called Erra, which had a population of some 127 billion. Pleiadians were similar to humans but, 'benefiting from greater time, and greater knowledge', they boasted that their civilisation was some three thousand years ahead of ours. They had come to Earth to make humankind aware of extraterrestrial life. And they told Meier that he and other contactees had been selected as the conduit for this knowledge. The Pleiadians picked candidates for contact using the technology that recorded 'soul patterns' they had developed. This had led the Pleiadians to choose Meier as their principal contact.

The Pleiadian Meier met most often was a female named Semjase. He first met her on 28 January 1978. Although she was 344 years old, she was pretty and had smooth fair skin – not a wrinkle in sight, apparently. From the photograph Meier took of her, she seems indistinguishable from an Earth woman, though she had with slightly longer earlobes. On her home planet of Erra, she was considered a demi-goddess and had learnt a lot about Earth from her father, 770-year-old Ptaah. He held the title 'King of Wisdom', and ruled over three inhabited planets, including Earth, dispensing help and advice when it was needed. It was Semjase's grandfather Sfath who had first made contact with Meier in 1942. Sfath had come to Earth in a silver spacecraft and taken the five-year-old Meier for a flight on board. He also educated Meier in Pleiadian ways through the medium of telepathy.

While most contactees had little in the way of evidence to support their claims, Meier had a surfeit of it. To some, this alone was suspicious, and they claimed that Meier had pulled off an impressive hoax. Others claimed that Meier was the butt of a bitter campaign to discredit him. They formed themselves into a support group called Genesis III. A leading member is retired US Air Force colonel Wendelle Stevens, who maintains that Meier's story was not a hoax and his evidence is impressive.

'The pictures were super fantastic,' Stevens says. 'I had never seen anything like them before.'

The book *Light Years* details Gary Kinder's three-year investigation of the Meier case. Kinder is convinced of the authenticity of Meier's photographs, films, sound recordings and the mineral samples given to Meier by a Pleiadian astronaut called Quetzel. Analysis of the soundtrack recording of a Pleiadian 'beamship' – made while it was hovering invisibly – proved conclusive to Kinder's ears. Quetzel's mineral samples were handed over to the scientist Dr Marcel Vogel for analysis. Most were of perfectly ordinary terrestrial material, though one possessed properties that were 'not immediately explainable'. It must be said that producing the number of models required to fake all the photographs would be difficult for a one-armed man and would have cost large sums of money – far beyond the means of a poor farmer. Kinder says that if Meier is not telling the truth, then he must be one of the finest illusionists the world has ever known.

Another investigator, Kal Korff, is convinced that this is the case and calls Meier story 'the most infamous hoax in UFOlogy' and set about trashing the photographic evidence. Stevens and Genesis III claimed that Meier's photographs had been subjected to computer analysis, which proved that they had not been tampered with and no 'paste-ups' or double exposures were used. But that did not rule out the use of models. Indeed Meier admitted making models of the Pleiadan craft he had seen, but only as an aide memoire.

Korff points out that, in the photographs, the shadows on the saucers rarely matched those on the landscapes. Often the craft were in too sharp focus to have been photographed in front of a real landscape. Many of them are at exactly the same angle to the camera, though Meier claimed to have taken them at different times and in different places. One photograph shows a Swiss fighter aircraft in the background, but the pilot had no recollection of seeing a UFO. In 8mm colour film of one of Meier's meetings, an alien craft is shown coming to a halt. As it does so, it wobbles back and forth as if on a fishing line. Korff also interviewed Meier's wife Kaliope – also known as Popi – who supported her husband during the 1970s and 1980s. But following their divorce she now says that his photographs were fakes.

Korff presented his damning evidence in his book *Spaceships of the Pleiades*. This did such a good job in undermining Meier's credibility that most leading UFOlogists in Europe and America rejected him as a charlatan. As Meier's reputation declined, the Pleiadians took him off to ever more outlandish destinations. On a Pleiadian time machine, he travelled back to prehistoric times where he photographed a pterodactyl with a pyramid in the background and snapped the 'Eye of God', which, judging by the photo, was winking at the time. More recently, he met Muhammad and Jesus, who made him a disciple. He also travelled into the future and watched the San Andreas Fault open up and swallow San Francisco. The Pleiadians also gave him a 'laser gun' – though, sadly, he has not used it to zap his critics.

The Pleiadians also gave him their most precious gift of all – their wisdom. This amounted to little more than the teachings of Jesus and could by summed up as: 'Do unto others as you would have them do unto you.'

'It was a very basic wisdom,' scoffs Korff. But it was enough to win Meier a following in the New Age movement.

However, Meier's bizarre claims undermined his credibility further among UFOlogists. Astronomers say that all of the five hundred stars in the Pleiades cluster are fiercely hot and the chance of life surviving on planets orbiting them is negligible. Meier is now widely regarded as a hoaxer, though he still has more evidence to back his claims that any other contactee.

A Meeting in Mexico

It was Mexican photographer Carlos Diaz's lucky day, when early one January morning in 1981, he pulled into a deserted car park at the top of a hill, in Ajusco Park near Mexico City. He was on assignment for a magazine, and had arranged to meet a journalist there. The journalist had not turned up and as Diaz sat in his car and waited, he prepared his camera for the job.

He soon grew impatient. Even though it was early in the morning, humidity was already uncomfortable. Diaz began to look at his watch. But then he became conscious of a strange yellow glow. At first he thought it was a forest fire on the slopes below the car park. Then he saw a large, orange, oval UFO, rising up from the valley below. It stopped, hovering about thirty yards in front of his car.

Diaz knew a photo opportunity when he saw one. He grabbed his camera and, with it resting on the steering wheel, he began firing off shots. Suddenly the whole car began to shake violently. So Diaz leapt out of the vehicle, getting two more shots before the craft soared vertically into the sky. Three shots came out perfectly. His amazing pictures have been examined by a range of experts. All have concluded that they are genuine.

Mexico City had long been a UFO hotspot and Diaz's encounter was almost run-of-the-mill. But the sighting had made a profound effect on Diaz. He kept returning to Ajusco Park in the hope of getting more pictures. For two months, his visits were fruitless visits. But then, on 23 March, his tenacity was rewarded.

This time he went roaming through the forest. It was a foul night, but through the fog and rain, Diaz saw an orange glow. Scaling the walls of a valley, he managed to get within fifty yards of the object. The source of the bright orange light was a dome-shaped craft with a smooth ring around its middle. This was covered with a series of small domes, each around three feet in diameter.

Diaz hid behind some rocks to watch the craft. Suddenly, someone behind him grabbed him by the shoulder. Diaz passed out. When he awoke, it was dark and the mysterious craft was gone. Despite the heavy rain, he found that his clothes were completely dry. It was then that he realised something very strange had happened.

When he returned to his car, he found that he was not alone. A humanoid entity with fair hair was waiting for him. The creature told Diaz that if he wanted to know more about what had happened, he should come back at noon the next day. He did and the humanoid was sitting on the grass waiting for him. The being explained that he had come from inside the craft Diaz had seen and that it was he who had grabbed Diaz's shoulder the previous day. He said no more, but promised Diaz that he would gradually recover his memory of what had happened.

Over the next few months, Diaz's memory returned, little by little. He recalled that he had seen the craft hovering directly over his head. As he reached up to touch it, his hand passed through its yellow aura and he seemed to meld with it. Then he recalled seeing the craft parked on a platform inside a giant cave.

'It was full of stalagmites, some of which were carved into what appeared to be Mayan sculptures,' Diaz said. 'I saw many "people" in the cave, some of whom waved to me and, in a state of shock, I waved back.'

The humanoid Diaz had met in the park was with Diaz outside the cave and told him that his extraterrestrial race had strong connections with both the Mayan and Aztec civilisations, which they had been visiting for millennia. Indeed, Diaz's hometown, Tepoztlan, is named after Tepoztcom, the son of the Aztec god Quetzalcoatl who, according to legend, descended from the heavens to bring knowledge to the Aztec people. The area around Tepoztlan has been considered sacred for hundreds of years.

His alien contact then took Diaz to another smaller cave. This contained seven glowing, egg-shaped orbs. Diaz was invited to step into one of them. Inside, Diaz found himself bathed in yellow light. But then this turned into an image of a forest.

'I could see all the details of the forest as if I was walking through it,' Diaz said. 'I couldn't touch anything, but I could feel the temperature and moisture. I could see and experience everything, yet I wasn't physically there.'

According to his guide, these orbs were data storage systems. While he was inside, certain information had been imparted to him. Puzzling though this was, it was only the first of a series of contacts. Each time he was taken to the orbs. Inside he has 'travelled' to different regions of the Earth's ecosystem – forest, desert, jungle, shoreline and even Arctic areas. Through his alien contacts, Diaz has become deeply aware of the interconnectedness of all life and the need to protect the environment. These claims may appear far-fetched, but Diaz is considered a highly reliable source, and can back his claims with photographic evidence.

Mexican TV journalist and UFOlogist Jaime Maussan, who became a leading UFO investigator since the Mexican wave of sightings in 1991, came across Diaz's UFO photographs and says they are among the best he has seen. He took Diaz's photographs to Jim Dilettoso, an image-processing expert at Village Labs, in Tucson, Arizona, who ruled out any possibility of a hoax.

Maussan then gave the transparencies to Professor Victor Quesada at the Polytechnical Institute of the University of Mexico for examination.

'We were shocked to discover that the spectrum of light from the object was unlike anything we had ever seen,' said Professor Quesada. 'It broke all pervious parameters and did not match anything in out data banks. The light was extraordinarily intense. There was no evidence of superimposition or a hoax. We estimate the object to be around thirty to fifty metres in diameter.'

The photographs were also analysed by Dr Robert Nathan at

NASA's Jet Propulsion Laboratory in Pasadena, California. A notorious UFO sceptic, Nathan admitted defeat. He could find no evidence of a fake. One picture, the first Diaz took, is the most impressive. It was shot through the windscreen of the car. It shows the light from the object reflected off the bonnet of the car and off the metal crash barrier at the side of the road. Experts say that this would be almost impossible to fake.

Satisfied that he was not dealing with a con man or a nutcase, Maussan visited Diaz at his home in Tepoztlan, Mexico, and tracked down a number of other witnesses who claimed to have seen the same type of UFO in the area at the time.

Maussan give Diaz a video camera and asked him to film the UFO when it next appeared. A few weeks later, Diaz awoke at 5 a.m., grabbed the camera and went outside and waited. Minutes later, the glowing spacecraft appeared, hovering about the house, and Diaz videoed it. Maussan was impressed, but he asked Diaz if he could get closer next time. Two months later, Diaz managed to video the craft hovering directly above him. Even more spectacular footage was to follow. On a third occasion, Diaz set the video camera up on a tripod in a field and locked it off. He filmed himself walking to the end of the field waving a torch. Suddenly the craft appeared directly above his head. It hovered there motionless for half-a-minute before disappearing. This is universally acknowledged as some of the best UFO footage ever shot.

Other UFOlogists have investigated the case and both German UFO author Michael Hesemann and alien abduction expert Dr John Mack have concluded that Diaz's story is credible.

'The Carlos Diaz case is the most important case of documented alien–human contact to have emerged in modern times,' says Hesemann, who first interviewed Diaz in 1994. 'Not only is he contacting these beings through encounters on the ships, but he also claims to be meeting these beings socially, since he believes some of them are living among us.'

Diaz says the beings are reluctant to fully disclose their origins.

However, they did explain that they have been visiting Earth for thousands of years, and are particularly interested in our evolution which, compared to their own, has happened at a much faster rate. They are trying to learn why.

In his book *Passport to the Cosmos*, John Mack, Professor of Psychiatry at Harvard Medical School, says: 'Out of all the experiencers I have worked with, it is Carlos Diaz who seems to have developed the richest understanding of the interconnected web of nature. Diaz's experience of connecting with living creatures is so intense that he seems literally to become the thing he is describing.'

Diaz's experience, Mack claims, constitutes an 'awakening', a process that involves the evolution of consciousness. This is something that Mack regularly finds in abductees. A deep passion for ecological responsibility and an awareness of environmental matters are key to this spiritual transformation, Mack says. Indeed, Diaz told Mack that his contact with the aliens has given him a renewed ability to enjoy the beauties of the plant and a burning desire to protect the environment. This has become a driving force in his life and he makes passionate pleas for the environment at UFO conferences.

For Diaz's visiting extraterrestrials, these warnings come from the heart – if they have such an organ. Their civilisation was destroyed by an environmental catastrophe. If humankind carries on, on its current course, it is heading for total extinction, the aliens say. Because of his environmental predictions, Diaz has assumed the status of a visionary both in UFO circles and his hometown of Tepoztlan. But Diaz says he is no visionary, merely 'a messenger', and he has recently opened a UFO centre in Tepoztlan to inform visitors about UFOs and his experiences as a contactee.

Maussan thinks that Diaz's encounter and the new wave of Mexican sightings that began in 1991 might be connected to the Mayan prophecy found in the Dresden Codex. This says that the 'Fifth Sun', which began with the solar eclipse in 1991, would be heralded by catastrophic environmental changes.

Whatever the validity of Diaz's environmental message, few alien encounters come with photographic evidence that has stood up to such rigorous scrutiny.

Global Encounters

Although sightings of UFOs are common, contact with aliens is still comparatively rare. But on 15 September 1994, two close encounters of the third kind occurred – on opposite sides of the globe.

The previous day, 14 September, the residents of the town of Ruwa in Zimbabwe had been treated to a massive pyrotechnic display in the sky over the northern part of South Africa. The celestial event was so powerful that, far to the north, MUFON co-ordinator for Africa Cynthia Hind heard a loud explosion that evening as she worked in her study in Zimbabwe's capital, Harare.

Soon after, Hind was swamped with reports of unusual aerial activity. A Russian satellite launch had taken place that day, and many of sightings, she discovered, were due to the ejected nose cone, which had re-entered the atmosphere over Africa. However, other reports, describing 'a brilliant cigar-shaped light moving at tree top level and changing direction,' could not be explained so easily.

This is what a group of young children from the Ariel Primary School in Ruwa saw the following day, 15 September. They spotted a cigar-shaped object hanging low in the sky. Suddenly the object disappeared. The children were puzzled, but soon forgot about what they had seen. But they were to receive an incredible reminder on the morning of 16 September.

At 10 a.m., it was break time and the children rushed out of their classrooms into the playground. That morning they would be unsupervised. The school's headmaster, Colin Mackie, and the thirteen teachers stayed inside for a staff meeting. Suddenly, there was a purple light flashing in the sky. Moments later, a large disc-shaped UFO appeared and began slowly descending into an empty field next to the school.

When the children were interviewed by Cynthia Hind several days after the event, their descriptions of the craft varied widely. Some were sure that there was only one craft. Others saw one main craft with three smaller ones. Eleven-year-old Guy had described it as 'multi-coloured with black, green and silver stripes', while ten-year-old Fifi said it had a 'golden glow that was so bright it was difficult to see'.

The German UFO researcher Michael Hesemann interviewed forty-four of the children in 1997 and believes that the discrepancies do not mean that the children were making it up.

'Given the number of witnesses and the shock of the event, you would expect the descriptions to vary,' he says.

Piecing together the consistent parts of the witness reports, investigators concluded that what had landed in the field was a large glowing disc, with a flattened dome on top. It was surrounded by yellow lights or portholes and extended a three-legged landing gear.

As the craft landed, balls of light, or perhaps miniature discs, appeared and flew around for a short while. Some children began screaming and ran back to the school building; others stood their ground, transfixed. In all, some one hundred children witnessed the landing. Some of the braver children even edged forward. They stood on logs to get a better view of the craft, which was about 220 yards away.

To the children's amazement, three beings emerged. They were humanoid and wore shiny, black, tight-fitting, one-piece suits. One remained near the craft, while the other two approached the children. They moved in what the children described as a 'slow-motion wobble'. Those closest said the aliens were about four feet tall. One had long black hair; the other two were bald. Their faces were dark and they had small noses and mouths. And some of the children said they had metal bands around their heads.

But the key feature that struck the children was the creatures' large black eyes. They said, they looked like 'cat's eyes' and several of the children said they received 'messages' after looking into the creatures' eyes. This method of communication is frequently reported by abductees. Abduction investigator Dr David Jacobs says that aliens use their eyes to implant ideas in the minds of humans. And looking deep into a human's eyes also allows the aliens to perform what one alien abductee called a 'mindscan'.

'When I looked into their eyes it is like they can see into my soul,' she told Dr Jacobs.

In Ruwa, Hesemann believes that the aliens used this procedure to implant an important ecological message. He says: 'The children who were not afraid and who managed to stare directly into the eyes of the beings began to hear a voice inside their head. Instantly, they got the thought that the ETs had come because humans were destroying the planet and that the children should participate in an effort to stop this.'

One of the children, eleven-year-old Carry Evans, said: 'I was afraid they wanted to attack us because we did something wrong, or destroyed something precious to them. I believe that the aliens came to warn us because the Earth is going to be destroyed by us.'

Headmaster Colin Mackie said that whatever the aliens had done seemed to work. All the children who reported receiving the telepathic communication from the extraterrestrials later became actively involved in ecological projects.

Once the beings had imparted their message, they went back to their ship, which began to flash. Then it was gone in a burst of light. The entire encounter had lasted about three minutes.

Several of the children who ran back to the school tried to inform the teachers, but they were still in the staff meeting. The only adult nearby was Alyson Kirkman, who was on duty at the tuck shop.

'Come quickly and see, ' begged one of the children. 'There's a little man running around in a one-piece suit with a band around his head.'

She laughed and said: 'Pull the other one.'

By the time the staff meeting was over, the alien ship had disappeared. At first, none of the teachers believed what the children were telling them. Some were hysterical. All of them had plainly been affected by some extraordinary event and it slowly began to dawn on the staff that the children's fantastic stories might be true. It was then that the UFO investigators were called in.

Whatever happened at the Ariel School that day, the events certainly had a profound impact on the children, especially those who claimed to have interacted with the 'alien' beings. The Ruwa children were left deeply changed by their experience.

Several thousand miles away in Mexico, it was still 15 September 1994. Between 8 p.m. that evening and 1 a.m. the following morning, air traffic controllers in Mexico reported UFO activity over the town of Metapec to the west of Mexico City. Soon, reports began rolling in that hundreds of people had seen a UFO hovering over the rooftops.

Among the witnesses were two sisters, Sara and Erika Cuevas. They had been driving back to their home in Metapec at the time of the sightings. As they approached the town, they saw a reddish disc in the sky, which they estimated to be about seventy feet in diameter. Eager to make a record of the event, when they arrived home, Sara rushed inside to get her video camera, but she soon discovered that the camera was not working, and nor were any of the electrical appliances in their home.

The two sisters went up to the roof for a better view of the UFO, which was still in plain sight in the sky. As they stood watching, two smaller red objects shot out of it and descended into the field next to their house. Two hours later, this extraordinary display was repeated. This time seven smaller discs ended up darting around on the ground. As they moved about in the field, they flattened the stalks of maize – without any physical contact, witnesses said – forming a large geometric pattern. Sudden, one of the discs exploded. Hundreds of tiny balls, resembling 'eyes', appeared, said one witness. This caused alarm and panic among the spectators.

The next day, UFO investigator and TV journalist Jaime Maussan, along with dozens of other reporters, arrived to interview witnesses. The investigators also charted a helicopter to film the strange pattern in the field. Despite this media circus and the numerous witnesses around the town, Sara Cuevas' husband refused to believe her when she told him what she had seen. Annoyed by his scepticism, she vowed to stay up all night, video camera in hand, in case the UFO returned.

Her sister Erika volunteered to wait with her, but they were to be disappointed. There was no sign of the craft. However, in the middle of the night, the sisters saw a mysterious glow in the field. There appeared to be a light about thirty yards away, but when they moved to get a better view, they realised that it was not a light at all it was a glowing figure who was standing in the middle of the crop pattern that had appeared the previous night.

Sara lifted her video camera and pressed record. This time the machine worked. She recorded three minutes of videotape, showing the figure standing still, shrouded in brilliant luminescence. On the soundtrack you can hear the reaction of the sisters. Sara says: 'What is it? That's horrible. Oh my God... Erika, it's so ugly.'

Then, suddenly the creature simply vanished.

A computer analysis of the Cuevas sisters' video was performed by Professor Victor Quesada at the University of Mexico's Polytechnical Institute. He estimated that the figure was about four feet three inches tall and some twenty-five yards from the camera. From its shape, he concluded that it was not human. According to Quesada, the light came from the creature itself. It was too bright and too evenly illuminated to be a mannequin. Computer enhancements revealed a large, terrifying insect-like head with a small stalk-like proboscis or antenna. And a similar enhancement of the lower part of the body revealed it was carrying some kind of instrument in its hand.

Jaime Maussan and another Mexican UFO researcher, Mario Torres, made an analysis of the soil and plants in the field. Anomalies were found in both. The temperature of the soil was found to be much higher than the surrounding ground. Radiation levels were 350 per cent above the background and strange cellular changes had occurred in the leaves of the pumpkin plants there. Unfortunately, investigators at Metapec discovered nothing else to shed any light on what the sisters caught on video that night.

The children in Zimbabwe did not have access to a video camera, so the two cases could not be compared. The best they could do was some interesting drawings of the benign creatures they had met.

Interestingly, there is a correlation between the heavenly gods in Aztec myth and the myths of Zimbabwe. When Dr John Mack began investigating the Ruwa case in 1994, he asked the advice of an African *sangoma*, or medicine man, named Credo Mutwa, whose knowledge of African myth is renowned throughout the continent. Mutwa explained that for thousands of years, local people had spoken of 'star people' who came to Earth in 'magic sky boats'. The creatures, with large, black, 'cat-like' eyes are what the Zulu called *mantindane*. The Australian aborigines called them *wandinja* and often depicted them in rock paintings. In Zulu culture, the *mantindane* are the bringers of knowledge – Quetzalcoatl – though they also spread disease and confusion among humankind. But Mutwa says that they are not extraterrestrials at all. They are the future descendants of humankind coming back in time.

But what was the significance of the encounters in Zimbabwe and Mexico occurring at the same time? UFOlogists speculated that it might be part of an increasingly intrusive pattern of alien visitations.

Monster on the Moor

In 1987 ex-police officer Philip Spencer made contact in the unlikely setting of Ilkley Moor in Yorkshire. On 1 December, he left his home in the town of Ilkley at around 7:15 a.m. He was planning to visit his father-in-law in the village of East Morton on the far side of the moor. History does not record whether he was wearing a hat, but he did take with him a compass, for navigation, and a camera with which he hoped to photograph some panoramic views from the moor tops.

It was a still, winter's day. The moor was empty and peaceful that morning, but he was conscious of a mysterious humming sound as he climbed a hill towards a group of trees. Ignoring it, he continued on his way. As the path he was following skirted an old quarry, his attention was attracted by something moving below him. Further along the path he came upon a small green creature standing just ten feet away. It was not like anything he had seen before. Apart from being green, it was short and hunched over, with massively long arms. It waved dismissively at him with one of them, before scuttling off.

Although he was dumbstruck, Spencer had the presence of mind to fumble for his camera and photograph the creature before it disappeared behind an outcrop. Then he pursued it, only to be confronted by a silver disc-shaped flying saucer hovering in front of him before soaring away into the sky and disappearing into the clouds.

Dazed and bewildered, Spencer decided to head back to Ilkley. On the way he noticed that the compass he was carrying had been affected by the encounter. The needle now pointed south instead of north. From the distance he had travelled, Spencer reckoned that he had been away from home for no more than an hour. It should have been no later than 8.15 a.m. when he got back to Ilkley. To his surprise, the streets were already bustling with shoppers and the church clock said it was 10 a.m. There was an hour and forty-five minutes he could not account for.

He began to wonder if the encounter had been a bizarre dream. But there was one way he could find out. He jumped on the next bus into Keithley, where there was a shop with a one-hour film processing service. Within an hour, he had confirmation. Exposure number ten showed a clear image of a small green alien being.

When he eventually returned home, Spencer showed the picture to his wife. She did not know what to make of it. But Spencer could not leave it there. He needed to contact someone with expert knowledge. As an ex-policeman he was concerned about his reputation. So using a Post Office box number to protect his identity, he wrote to top British UFOlogist Jenny Randles.

Randles was sceptical of his account but forwarded Spencer's letter to fellow UFOlogist Peter Hough. He too was unconvinced. After some discussion, both eventually agreed that they should pursue the matter. While Randles and Hough were dithering, Spencer had found the number of paranormal investigator Arthur Tomlinson listed in a directory in Ilkley library. Tomlinson interviewed Spencer and then, seeking a second opinion, sent an account of the meeting to Hough. Hough instantly recognised the case, and the two of them decided to collaborate.

On 3 January 1988, Hough went to see Spencer and accused him of making the whole thing up. 'What would you say to someone who said: "Come on, you've built a dummy, taken it up on the moor and photographed it?"' he asked.

Perhaps because of his police training, Spencer was not fazed by this line of questioning.

'I'm not particularly interested in what other people think,' he replied. 'I know what I saw, and if people don't believe me, that's up to them. I've got nothing to gain by doing that. I don't see the sense, I've got better things to do with my time.'

Impressed by Spencer's sincerity, Hough began conducting a thorough scientific investigation of this story. An examination of the place where the encounter occurred turned up nothing. The levels of radiation in the area were normal. There were no magnetic anomalies there either. So what could have affected Spencer's compass?

Hough turned to Dr Ed Spooner, head of the Department of Electrical Engineering and Electronics at the University of Manchester Institute of Science and Technology (UMIST). He carried out some tests on a compass identical to Spencer's and found that strong magnets had no permanent effect on the needle. However, a pulsed field, or one switched on and off again rapidly, did. This effect could be produced using mains electricity or even a car battery. But it was a dangerous procedure and required specialist knowledge. In 1990 powerful industrial magnets from Japan were found to cause the same effect, but they were not available in 1987 when the polarity of Spencer's compass was reversed.

Hough's investigation then focused on the 35mm camera that Spencer had used. It had a light meter, but it had been broken for several years. It would have been hard to produce a convincing fake with such an inadequate piece of equipment. Nevertheless, Hough sent the negative of Spencer's alien image to Kodak photographic expert Peter Sutherst, who said that the film had not been tampered with. However, he reported: 'It is underexposed by at least two stops. It is usual for these films to produce grainy pictures when underexposed.

The negative shows a degree of camera shake, making it difficult to decide what the small figure might be. Identification is made even more of a problem because of underexposure.'

This underexposure raised doubts. It was hazy that morning and Spencer had set the shutter speed at around 1/60th of a second and opened the lens to its widest aperture. The camera had also been loaded with 400 ASA film, which should have been almost impossible to underexpose. Others point out that the sky is too bright. It would have taken around half-an-hour to reach the place where the encounter had taken place. That would have made it around 7:45 a.m. Dawn didn't break until a couple of minutes before 8:00 a.m. that winter morning in West Yorkshire.

Hough looked into the possibility of computer enhancement of the image. But Sutherst pointed out that image enhancement was a costly exercise. He doubted its benefits in this case. 'The size, distance of the subject, camera movement and underexposure mean that there is insufficient detail available to enhance,' he said. Since then attempts to enhance the image in Britain, the US and Japan have all failed.

The only other place to look for clues was in Spencer's mind. Spencer was troubled by the missing time he had experienced and Hough arranged a meeting with clinical psychologist Jim Singleton, who practised regressional hypnosis. This is a technique used to recover lost memories.

Under hypnosis, Spencer relived his conscious memory of walking up the path towards the trees. But then a new chunk of memory emerged. The transcript of the session read: 'I'm walking along the moor. Oh! It's quite windy. There's a lot of clouds. Walking up towards the trees, I see this little something, can't tell, but he's green. It's moving towards me. Oh! I can't move. I'm stuck. He's still coming towards me. And I still can't move... I'm stuck, and everything's gone fuzzy. I'm... I'm floating along in the air... I want to get down! And this green thing's walking ahead of me, and I don't like it.'

Apparently, as Spencer drew level with the trees, he stopped, aware through the early morning haze that something was coming down the hill towards him. He froze as a green being with large eyes and pointed ears approached. Then he said: 'I still can't move. I'm going around the corner and this green thing's in front of me. Oh, God, I want to get down. There's a.... there's a big silver saucer thing, and there's a door in it, and I don't want to go in there! Everything's gone black now...'

Spencer wanted to escape, but found he was paralysed. The alien started walking back up the hill. Spencer found himself levitated, helplessly following the creature. It was then, in the quarry, that he first saw a silver disc. There was a door in the disc, then darkness enveloped him. He awoke to find himself in a small room illuminated by a bright light. A voice in his head told him not to be afraid. He was put on a table and a beam of light scanned the contours of his body. There were a number of creatures in the room.

'The creatures seemed part of a team,' he said. 'They weren't acting as individuals, but more like bees, as if they were doing what they were programmed to do.'

Spencer also gave a detailed description of one of them: 'He's quite small, about four foot. He's got a nose and only has a little mouth. His hands are enormous. He's got three big fingers, like big sausages and his arms were long. He's got funny feet – they're like a V-shape, like two big toes.'

Although Spencer referred to the alien as 'he', he gave no reason for deciding that the alien was male. He gave no information about primary or secondary sexual characteristics. But one thing that struck Hough was that the aliens Spencer had seen had cloven hooves.

Spencer then felt a strange sensation up his nose and he was accompanied out of the room by one of the several creatures present. In the corridor, Spencer looked out through a window to see the Earth below. It was only then that he realised he was in outer space. A door opened in the wall of the corridor, and he was led out onto a gantry that ran around the walls of a large room. In the middle of the room, there was a spinning ball. His camera and the compass that were hanging by cords around his neck were drawn towards the ball as if my magnetism.

In another room, he was shown a film depicting a polluted Earth where billions were starving. After that he was engulfed by blackness again. He had no further memories until he found himself back on the moor with no recollection of the abduction. What Hough and Singleton found particularly impressive was that, even under hypnosis, he expressed surprise at seeing the creature and taking its picture.

An examination of the historical records also proved fruitful. It seems that 1987 was not the first time that little green men had paid a visit to the area. In 1851 one famous incident had taken place at White Wells, just three hundred yards from where Spencer's encounter had taken place. The health spa there is built around a natural spring. One morning the caretaker, William Butterfield, arrived to open up, only to find that his key spun around in the lock by itself. Inside he found a bath full of aliens.

'All around the spring, dipping into it, were a lot of little creatures dressed in green, none more than eighteen inches, making chatter and jabber,' Butterfield said. 'They seemed to be taking a bath with their clothes on. Soon, however, one or two of them began to make off, bounding over the walls like squirrels. Then the whole tribe went, helter skelter, toppling and tumbling, head over heels.'

Butterfield ran after them. They disappeared up the path that Philip Spencer followed 172 years later.

No satisfactory explanation has been given of what happened on Ilkley Moor that day – any more than there is of the day Philip Spencer walked up that path. Although doubts have been raised about the photograph, it has resisted all attempts to expose it as a fake. As Spencer says himself, he had nothing to gain from carrying out a hoax. He is certainly not seeking publicity or even attention. Throughout, he has insisted on using the name 'Philip Spencer', which is a pseudonym. He is not after money either and has turned down several lucrative offers from newspapers and   television companies to go public. He has never sought to capitalise on his encounter and has insisted that his real identity be protected throughout. Otherwise, he says, 'it would ruin me both socially and professionally.'

Israeli Encounters

A wave of alien encounters that has taken place in modern Israel also have ancient resonances. In biblical times, beings fell from the heavens and later became the mortal enemies of the Hebrew nations. They were called *nefilim*, which means the 'fallen ones', and the giants that appear in the Bible were their descendants. Since the late 1980s, these giants have returned to Israel. And they are not shy about their presence. They have allowed their craft to be filmed. They chose to contact unimpeachable witnesses and have left abundant physical evidence.

Israel's new UFO age began on the evening of 28 September 1987, when twenty-seven-year-old auto mechanic Ami Achrai was driving down a road near the sea just south of Haifa. He saw what he took to be a helicopter hovering just above the sands of Shikmona Beach. It appeared to be in difficulties. He stopped his car for a better look. It was then he realised that the hovering craft was no helicopter. It was a disc-shaped flying saucer which gave off a bright red flash, then disappeared.

Achrai reported the sighting to the police, who referred him to UFOlogist Hadassah Arbel. Two days later, they returned to the site and discovered striking evidence that a UFO had been there. It seems the blinding red flash emitted by the craft had burned a fifty-foot ellipse in the sands of the beach. And the image of the spacecraft's pilot at his controls was imprinted in nearby vegetation, which remained otherwise undamaged.

Seven years later, samples of the burnt sand were sent to the US television show *Sightings* by UFOlogist Barry Chamish. Under the heat of the studio lights, the burnt sand seemed to melt. The reason for this, a laboratory later discovered, was that the sand particles were coated in a hydrocarbon material with a low melting point. But the laboratory could offer no explanation as to why the sand was coated with this substance.

On 6 June 1988, the image of another ellipsoid craft was burned into the sands of Shikmona Beach, a few yards north of the first site.

Then on 27 April 1989, two teenagers saw a UFO explode over Shikmona Beach. It disintegrated into thousands of shards that were strewn across the beach. When Israeli UFOlogists investigated the sighting, they found fragments of a strange glowing white metal that was cool to the touch. The fragments even glowed under water. But when they were picked up, they turned into a white ash. Analysis revealed that they were made from a very pure form of magnesium. Scientists from the Technion Institute of Technology in Haifa also found that the levels of magnetism at the site were six thousand times higher that in the surrounding area.

The site itself has some biblical significance. About six hundred feet above Shikmona Beach is a shrine called Elijah's Cave. The prophet Elijah was said to have preached there. Inside there is the drawing of a saucer-shaped craft that bears a distinct resemblance to those seen over Shikmona Beach in modern times. Elijah has some other extraterrestrial connections. According to the Bible, in the nearby Carmel Mountains, Elijah challenged the Canaanites to a battle of Gods. Two bulls were tethered out in the open. Baal, the god of the Canaanites, was called upon to roast one of them, while Elijah called upon the Israelite god Yahweh to roast the other. The Canaanite god failed, but Elijah's god sent down a ray of light from the heavens that cooked the bull on the spot. Could this have been a death ray, and could a similar beam have been used to burn the sands of Shikmona Beach thousands of years later?

After the UFO exploded over Shikmona Beach, there was a lull in UFO sightings. But activity started again five years later. This time, it was focused on the small Israeli town of Kadima. On the morning of 20 April 1993, Tsiporet Carmel woke up to discover her house bathed in a strange glow. Outside she saw a strange craft on the ground. As she looked, it appeared to grow in size before her eyes. Some ten yards from the spacecraft, she saw the figure of a giant. It was about six feet seven inches and was clad in a one-piece metallic suit. On its head, it wore a helmet, which Tsiporet compared to a beekeeper's hat.

Unafraid, Tsiporet went outside and spoke to the creature.

'Why don't you take off your hat so I can see your face?' she said. The creature's reply was delivered telepathically.

'That's the way it is,' it said.

The story of Tsiporet Carmel's encounter with the alien hit the newspapers. There had never been a publicised close encounter in Israel before and Tsiporet risked ridicule. Fortunately, the alien had left some physical evidence to back her story. A crop circle, some fifteen feet in diameter, was found where she had seen the alien spacecraft. Shards of a strange material were discovered inside the circle. On analysis this was found to be a very pure form of silicon. Ten days later, two more circles appeared just outside her back garden. They were soaked with a red liquid. The National Biological Laboratory in Ness Tziona analysed the liquid and found that it was composed mostly of cadmium. It was also found in other crop circles subsequently discovered in the area.

Two other residents of Kadima reported similar encounters. In May, the town treasurer, Shosh Vahud, claimed to have met a giant alien, which visited her bedroom. She woke to see a six feet seven inch, round-faced creature in a silver jump-suit circling her bed, as if 'floating on his shoes'. Telepathically it assured her that it meant her no harm and she relaxed. After a few minutes, the creature floated out through the wall. Shosh dismissed the encounter as a dream until she spotted a fifteen-foot crop circle outside her window the next morning. UFOlogists found both cadmium and silicon within the circle.

In June, the giant alien turned its attention to the village of Burgata, about three miles away. Hannah Somech was working in her kitchen one day when she saw her dog go flying across the room and crash into a wall. Outside she saw a six feet seven inch being clad in metallic overalls examining her pickup truck.

Like Tsiporet, Hanna was a tough Israeli woman. She marched right up to the alien.

'What did you do to my dog?' she demanded.

Again the reply came telepathically.

'Go away,' the creature said. 'I'm busy. I could crush you like an ant if I wanted to.'

Again, after the incident, a fifteen-foot circle was found in Hannah's back garden. The grass in the circle was soaked with the same red cadmium liquid as in Kadima.

In December 1994 the village of Yatzitz, twelve miles east of Rishon Letzion, played host to another giant. Herzl Casatini, the village security chief, was visiting his friend Danny Ezra when they heard a massive explosion. Ezra's house shook to its foundations. Herzl rushed to the door to find out what was happening. But when he opened the door, he found himself face to face with a giant, again clad in a metallic one-piece. This one was over eight feet tall and its face was obscured by a strange 'haze'. Discretion being the better part of valour, Herzl slammed the door in its face and called the cops.

When the police arrived, they found boot tracks. Some of the tracks had sunk in over a foot in the hard mud. This meant whatever had made them must have weighed over a ton. The creature seemed to 'walk' on its toes, as the heel was rarely indented more than two inches. Always on the alert for terrorist activity, the Israeli army arrived on the scene. The military trackers were equally puzzled. They followed the tracks for over five miles. In some places the distance between boot prints was over ten feet. They could only speculate that the tracks had been left by an unknown cult. But UFOlogists made the connection between the tall aliens the various witness had seen and the giants of ancient times. According to the Bible, King Og of Bashan had to have a bed that was thirteen feet long. Bashan's kingdom included the Golan Heights, home to a mysterious monument called the Gilgal Refaim, or 'circle of the giants'. It consists of five concentric rings of stone – the outermost is 522 feet in diameter. Like other such monuments it has celestial connections. Openings align with the solstices and the rising of Sirius in 3000 BCE. Otherwise archaeologists are puzzled. It predates the pyramids by five hundred years and no other structure in the Middle East remotely resembles it. The indigenous people of the area at that time were nomads who did not involve themselves in building megaliths. However, according to the Bible, a bunch of outsiders did visit the Golan Heights back then. And they were giants.

After Yatzitz, the modern-day giants spread out, visiting many other Israeli towns. Then in 1995, they returned to Kadima, with horrifying results. One morning in January, Amos and Rachel Gueta woke to find their livestock killed and mutilated. Sheep, chickens and even their farm dog were found dead. The heads of the sheep had been shaved and there were holes in the skulls that appeared to have been made by a drill. No satisfactory explanation has ever been offered.

In 1996 over a dozen UFOs were filmed over Israel. In August one flying saucer with distinctive square vents was filmed on three successive nights, hovering over the Israeli town of Hatzar. And Yugoslav immigrant Spasso Maximovitch managed to film two UFOs colliding over Rosh Haayin. MUFON's Jeff Sainio has examined the film and declared it genuine.

'The acceleration, light, size, and explosion are not explainable in any conventional way that I know of,' he says. 'This case remains unidentified.'

The following November, what looked like a 'flying brain' was filmed hovering over Tel Aviv. No one has yet been able to explain what it was.

Giants are not the only aliens to visit Israel. In December 1996, a Netanya household reported regular contact with small 'Greys' – the first time this species of alien had been seen in the Middle East. Physical evidence was produced to support this story, including stones that can melt ice although they have no known energy source.

It is noticeable that the giants were very selective about who they visited. All the contactees were women. They were all middle-class – making them, in the eyes of the authorities, credible witnesses – and they were all in their late thirties. When Tsiporet Carmel and Shosh Vahud appeared on TV, Clara Kahonov from Holon, south of Tel Aviv, came forward saying that she, too, had been visited by a giant. In Rishon Letzion, just twelve miles from Holon, Baya Shimon claimed that she had seen more than one. In early July 1993, two huge, bald beings beamed themselves into her seventh-floor apartment. As they floated around her apartment, they told her, telepathically, not to be afraid. They spent a few minutes dusting her shelves with a foul-smelling yellow powder, then disappeared the way they had come. At 3 a.m. the following night, a dozen of then turned up the same way.

Seven of the cases have been particularly well documented. In two cases, the contactees reported unexpected pregnancies. Three contactees have been haunted telepathically since. Although none of the women knew each other, they all reported seeing the same thing. Each independently described meeting six feet seven inch, round-faced giants. And in each case, the visitor left physical evidence of its presence. It seems that giants are roaming Israel today, just as they did thousands of years ago.

Abducted

First Contact

From the first sighting of flying saucers in 1947, there was a puzzle. What were the aliens doing here and why did they not make contact directly? It was only when UFOlogists began investigating the phenomenon of alien abduction that it became all to frighteningly clear what they were doing here and, it seemed, in their own sinister way they had been contacting us all along.

The first well-documented alien abduction took place on the night of 19 September 1961. Forty-one-year-old child-welfare worker Betty Hill and her thirty-nine-year-old mailman husband Barney were returning home to Portsmouth, New Hampshire, after a vacation in southern Canada. Having crossed back into the US near Colebrook, New Hampshire, at around 10 p.m., they took Interstate Route 3, which winds through the mountains to the east of the state. Out on the dark, lonely road, the Hills were puzzled by a strange, large 'white star' that seemed to be following them. Barney told his wife that it was probably a plane heading for Montreal.

There was little traffic on the highway and the Hills decided to stop to let their dog Delsey out of the car for some exercise. While Betty walked the dog, Barney got out his binoculars to take a   closer look at the strange light. When Betty and Delsey came back to the car, they drove off again. But a few minutes later, Barney felt an urgent and irrational need to stop the car and get out. By now they were at an isolated spot called Indian Head. Barney seemed completely hypnotised by the light in the sky. He ignored Betty's pleading to get back into the car and walked off in the direction of the light, disappearing into the undergrowth at the side of the road.

Studying the strange light through his binoculars, it became clear to Barney that they were being followed by a strange craft. It was banana shaped, with pointed tips and windows. Through large windows, Barney could see figures.

'I don't believe this!' he yelled as his yanked the binoculars from his eyes. 'They're going to capture us!'

In panic, he fled back to the car and they sped off southwards. The panic did not last. Instead, a strange feeling of detachment seemed to come over them. This is a phenomenon know to UFOlogists as the 'Oz Factor', which often accompanies encounters. The Hills remember an electronic beeping sound, followed by a bump. In no time at all they found themselves just seventeen miles from Portsmouth. The UFO had disappeared and the couple drove home without further incident.

The following day, the Hills noticed some peculiar blotches on the car. The paint had been removed to show the bare metal underneath. Betty's sister took a look. She had seen a UFO herself four years before, and had taken an interest in the subject. The patches, she suggested, might be magnetised. She had heard that UFOs generated massive magnetic fields that could stall car engines. Barney was sceptical but the Hills checked it out and they found that, when they passed a compass over the bodywork, the needle swung wildly over the blotched areas.

Realising that their encounter had been closer than they thought, the Hills called nearby Pease Air Force Base to report their UFO sighting. They were told nothing at the time but records released since under the Freedom of Information Act show that there had been UFO activity in the area at the time. At 2:15 a.m. on the morning of 20 September, a UFO flying in the vicinity of White Mountains had been tracked on military radar.

Even though the Hills had no idea that the military had also seen the UFO, they decided to write to a national UFO group and on 21 October 1961, astronomer and UFOlogist Walter Webb visited the Hills in their home.

During the interview Barney revealed other worrying details he had noticed after the encounter. His shoes were scuffed as if he had been dragged along the ground and he had a pain in his back that he could not account for.

Betty had also been badly affected by the incident. On 30 September, she began a series of disturbing nightmares. For several nights, she dreamed of strange creatures with horrible faces and cat-like eyes who were out to kidnap her and her husband.

One peculiar fact emerged from their account. They had no recollection of the thirty-five miles from Indian Head to the point where they were just seventeen miles from Portsmouth. Both their watches had stopped and when they got home it was much later than they thought. Two hours seemed to have gone missing. Both the 'interrupted journey' and 'missing time' are now recognised as classic features of alien abductions.

With no logical explanation of what had happened to them that night, the Hills began to fret. Betty was tormented by her dreams and Barney was becoming paranoid. The following spring things got so bad that they sought medical advice. Their doctor referred them to a number of specialists who were of little help. Eventually they found themselves in the Boston office of psychiatrist Dr Benjamin Simon, a

Harvard-trained expert in stress management.

Dr Simon listened to their UFO story and Betty told him about her dreams. A medical man, he tended to reject the idea of a paranormal explanation. Nevertheless he recognised that something to do with their fateful journey was disturbing the Hills and he recommended regressional hypnosis to get to the bottom of it.

Betty and Barney were regressed separately, but a number of images that surfaced from their unconscious memories were strikingly similar. Reliving the experience caused considerable stress and they sometimes reacted with terror. On more than one occasion Dr Simon had to get staff to help him hold down Barney while he relived the events of that night and fought to escape from the ghouls that were plaguing him.

After six months of hypnosis, Dr Simon was coming to realise that he had a unique case on his hands. No matter what he did he could not shake the Hills' story. They were not making up what they saw and they could not be sharing a single delusion. Their stories dovetailed together so perfectly that he could come to only one conclusion – what they were telling him was real.

According to the story they revealed under hypnotic regression, the light that they had seen in the sky was indeed a UFO. It had landed beside the road and somehow rendered the Hills semi-conscious. The couple were then forcibly taken on board the spacecraft by small beings with whitish skins and large cat-like eyes, like the ones Betty had seen in her nightmares. These are the 'Greys' that are now so frequently reported in abductions.

Once on board, the couple were separated. A voice in their heads told them not to be afraid and they were given medical examinations. Betty had a long needle inserted into her abdomen. This, she was told telepathically, was a type of pregnancy test. Meanwhile Barney had his penis inserted in some sort of suction device and semen was extracted. The alien's inordinate interest in our genetic make up became another standard feature of abductions.

Other samples were taken from the Hills during their abduction –

notably clippings of their nails and hair. New to the Earth, apparently the aliens were particularly bemused by the differences in the couple's skin colour. Betty was white; Barney, who was Ethiopian by birth, was black.

After these tests, the aliens showed Betty around the UFO. At one point, she was shown a 'star map' which, she was told, showed all the star systems that the aliens had visited on their travels. Some stars systems were joined by solid lines. These indicated regular trading routes. Other were joined by dotted lines, indicating the routes of occasional expeditions.

Under hypnosis, Betty made a sketch of her recollection of the map. It was sent to astronomer Majorie Fish. She plotted the location of all the stars systems within fifty light-years of Earth that were likely to contain habitable planets. It matched. From this, Fish was able to work out that the alien's home planet orbited the star Zeta Reticulli.

Before Betty left the spacecraft, she asked her alien captors for a memento to prove that she and Barney had really been on board. The aliens' leader agreed, and Betty chose a large book which contain tightly packed columns of characters that she likened to hieroglyphics. But just as the couple were about to leave the ship, the alien who had said that Betty could take the book changed his mind. Betty said it appeared as if his decision had been overruled by the other aliens. Despite her protests, Betty had to leave without it. Eventually the Hills were led back outside and lost consciousness. They woke up again inside the car, some distance from the site of the abduction, and the UFO was gone.

Under hypnosis, Barney sketched the alien craft, while Betty's description of the aliens themselves was drawn by local artist Dave Barker. The drawing he produced shows what we now know as the classic 'Grey'.

Betty and Barney Hill's abduction has become a landmark in UFO history. Boston journalist John Fuller wrote the Hill's story up as *The Interrupted Journey,* which was serialised around the world. It was later made into the 1975 TV movie called *The UFO Incident.* It is a key case in UFOlogy and established the use of regressional hypnosis in the field. The case also fired the public's imagination, and the threat of alien abduction suddenly gained credibility.

However, Betty Hill is sceptical about many of the abduction claims that have been made since she and Barney were taken.

'Real abductions are rare and they are all different,' she says. 'Ours did not involve anything sexual. And today almost all investigators are using suggestive hypnosis rather than the medical hypnosis Dr Simon used with Barney and me.'

Betty believes that she and Barney were abducted because of their behaviour – 'stopping the car, looking though binoculars, waving and shouting. We were showing curiosity, and maybe this made them curious of us,' she said.

At the time, the couple found that their alien abduction story was widely accepted. But since then, Betty feels, all the talk of a sexual motive for the abductions – 'weird fantasies,' she says – has turned the public off. However, she also thinks that the US government knows a great deal more about UFOs than it is letting on. 'What little they release is done to test the public's reaction,' she says.

Lurid Tale

One of the most lurid abductions occurred before the Hills' abduction case hit the headlines. It happened to a young Brazilian farmer named Antonio Villas-Boas, but the sexual nature of the story meant that it could not be published in the 1950s.

On 5 October 1957, Villas-Boas was in his room after a party. When he look out of his window, he saw a bright fluorescent light hovering just above the tree line of a nearby wood. He called his brother Jaoa who also witnessed the sighting. Neither of the men could explain what they saw and the object soon disappeared.

Then on the night of 16 October 1957, Villas-Boas was working late in his field when he observed a strange circular object coming towards him. He tried to drive away in his tractor but the engine cut out and lights went out. He was paralysed as the object started to land just a few feet away from him.

As the UFO approached the ground, it deployed three telescopic legs, which it settled on. He was still recoiling in shock when he felt several hands grabbing him. He shouted for help but no one came and, before he knew what was happening, he was being led inside the space ship.

Inside he was taken into a large, brightly lit room, which had a metal pole running from the floor to the ceiling. The creatures talked among themselves in a strange growling language. They stripped him naked and anointed him with some strange oily fluid. Then he was left alone in the room.

Villas-Boas found himself becoming very tired and he lay down on what he took to be a couch. Soon after that the door opened and a naked woman came in. She was more beautiful than any woman he had ever seen before and was indistinguishable from a human female, except for her bright red pubic hair. Without a word, the creature indicated that she wanted to have sexual intercourse with him. He obliged. After he had ejaculated the woman got up to go. But before she left the room, she pointed to her stomach and then to the sky. He took this to mean that she was going to have his baby somewhere out in outer space.

He was then given a brief tour of the ship. The aliens did not talk to him but, rudely, continued to talk among themselves. During the tour, he tried to steal a piece of alien hardware as proof of this abduction and he managed to grab a 'clock-like instrument'. He had almost smuggled it off the ship with him but a keen-eyed alien spotted it and took it from him. Then the aliens pushed Villas-Boas unceremoniously out of the craft into a field. The ship took off and soared away into the sky at a tremendous speed.

It was several weeks before he told his mother and brother what had happened and it was a further two years before he sought professional help. He was later interviewed by many UFO researchers, the first of which was Dr Olavo Fontes, Brazilian representative of the Aerial Phenomena Research Organisation.

Every investigator who has interviewed Villas-Boas subsequently has been impressed with him as a witness. His story never changed and when he cannot answer a question he never tries to embellish. He was seen as a man of low intelligence but his story is too full of detail and strangeness to be made up by such a simple person. He is regarded as genuine and has never made any money from his experience.

The Voice of God

Following the airing of *The UFO Incident*, telling the Hills' story, there was a sudden surge in the reporting of alien abductions. Jumping on the bandwagon, the *National Enquirer* offered $1 million for definitive proof of extraterrestrial life and up to $10,000 for the best UFO story. One of the stories that was sent in came from Betty Andreasson of Ashburnham, Massachusetts.

On the night of 25 January 1967, Betty was deeply perplexed. Her husband had been involved in a major car accident and was in hospital seriously ill. A devout Christian, Betty Andreasson was at home, praying hard for his recovery.

At around 7 p.m., she thought that her prayers had been answered. The family home was plunged into darkness, and a diffuse pink light shone in through the kitchen window. But when Betty's father looked outside, he saw what looked more like emissaries of the devil. In the yard was a group of small creatures that looked like 'Halloween freaks'. One of them turned to meet his gaze. The creature's eyes made him feel 'kinda queer' and he blacked out.

When the lights in the house came back on, Betty Andreasson saw her parents and her seven children standing their motionless, as if frozen. She, too, was rooted to the floor in terror. Four creatures, wreathed in haze, entered the house through the back door, which was locked. They were about four feet tall and were dressed in skin-tight blue uniforms. The heads were bulbous with almond-shaped eyes. When the family finally snapped out of their trance, they discovered that they had been unconscious for about three hours and forty minutes. Only Betty and her father had any recollection of anything at all that had happened. Even their memories were dim. It was only ten years later, when Andreasson was undergoing a session of regressional hypnosis that, the full story came out.

Based on what she had learned under hypnosis, Betty Andreasson wrote up the story and sent it to the *National Enquirer*. Although it would later be seen as one of the greatest UFO abduction stories on record, the *Enquirer* did not follow it up.

Undeterred by the *Enquirer's* rebuff, Betty Andreasson later responded to a newspaper article written by the scientist Dr J. Allen Hynek, founder of the Center for UFO Studies. In the article, he had appealed for contactees. There was a huge response right across the US and it was many months before investigator Jules Vailancourt turned up in Ashburnham. He was immediately interested in the case as there was a corroborating witness – Betty's father. Vailancourt decided that it merited further investigation and called in a regressional hypnosis expert, Henry J. Edelson. In fourteen sessions with Edelson between April and July 1977, Andreasson's amazing story unfolded.

It seems that, once the aliens had entered her home, the rest of her family were put into a deep trance. Only Betty remained conscious. The tallest alien, who called himself 'Quazgaa', asked her to accompany them. Andreasson was told that they had come to help the human race, which was in danger of destroying itself – the same message that contactees had been given before. It is not clear whether Andreasson gave her consent to go with the aliens. But they did not have to use force on her. There was no resisting them. Together they floated outside to the backyard, where an odd-looking, oval craft with a raised central console was waiting.

Once she was inside the craft, aliens began their examination. They used a machine that seemed to be a cross between a camera and an eye. It had a probe like a needle that was inserted into her navel. This was quite painful and Quazgaa laid his hand on her forehead to comfort her. The aliens seemed puzzled that some of her body parts were missing – she assumed that they were referring the hysterectomy she had recently undergone.

The alien's evident disappointment was later explained by UFOlogist Budd Hopkins. He believes that aliens are involved in widespread genetic sampling and are even possibly manipulating the development of humankind. Abductees frequently report sexual encounters with aliens. There are also mysterious pregnancies. Hopkins investigated the case of Kathie Davis, who had a phantom pregnancy in her teenage years. Under hypnosis she recalled that she had been abducted by aliens. Years later she had been abducted a second time and was introduced to a little girl who looked like 'an elf or an angel'. She realised that this was her baby, the half-alien, half-human hybrid that she had carried in her womb.

In another case, Collette Davis found that she was being abducted and impregnated with human–alien hybrids so often that she had a hysterectomy to protect herself from further interference.

When Betty Andreasson asked her abductors about this, she was told: 'We have to, because as time goes by, humankind will become sterile. They will not be able to reproduce.' Others believe that it is the aliens who are unable to reproduce without the involuntary assistance of humans.

During the examination, a tiny spiked ball was removed from her nostril using a long, thin instrument. For some time, this remained a puzzle. In later hypnotic sessions it emerged that Betty had been abducted before and this was some kind of device they had implanted in her.

After the examination was over, she was taken into a round room where there were eight seats that looked like armchairs. The aliens got her to sit in one of the seats and pipes were pushed into her mouth and nostrils. A clear canopy dropped down over her. The rim connected to the edge of the seat so that she was completely encapsulated. The space around her was then flooded with grey liquid. Under normal circumstances, this would have panicked her, but Andreasson was fed a spoonful of thick fluid through the pipe that went into her mouth and it seemed to have a tranquillising effect. The entire contraption began to vibrate in what she described as a very pleasant way. Then she felt herself being pushed down into the seat as if the ship were accelerating away from Earth.

When she was let out of the capsule, her clothes were sopping wet. Two hooded humanoids escorted her down a series of dark tunnels. The three of them floated along a black track. The only light was that given off by her escorts' suits. At the end of one of the tunnels she could see a mirrored wall in front of them and feared they were going to smash into it. She closed her eyes and braced herself. But there was no crash. When she opened her eyes again she found herself bathed in a vibrating infrared radiation. They passed a number of thin, lemur-like creatures that clambered on strange-looking buildings that had no glass in their windows. The creatures had suckers instead of fingers and they had two large eyes on the end of stalks that swivelled around as she passed.

The track then passed through a circular membrane and they travelled into a place that was green and beautiful like Earth. Overhead there were elevated walkways criss-crossing the sky and, in the distance, she could see cities with huge domes. Then she saw a large object silhouetted against a bright light directly ahead. As they approached it, she could see that it was a statue of an eagle, about fifteen feet high. Then, as she and her escorts stood before it, it was engulfed in flames.

When the statue had burned down to ashes, a thick, grey worm appeared in the embers. It communicated telepathically with her. She heard the words 'You have seen and you have heard. Do you understand?' in her mind. She replied that she was completely confused. But the voice spoke in her head said simply: 'I have chosen you... I have chosen you to show the world.' As a deeply religious person, Betty Andreasson believes that the voice she heard was the voice of God.

The worm then gave her a message to take back to humankind. But it was in an alien language. She was then returned to the alien ship and taken back to Massachusetts. She was still puzzled about the message that the worm had given her, but Quazgaa translated it for her. The worm had warned that humankind was following a perilous course, love was the answer and humans needed to seek out wisdom through the spirit. As they parted, Quazgaa told Andreasson that other humans had similar messages locked in their minds.

Sceptics have dismissed Andreasson's story as a hallucination brought on by the stress of her husband's hospitalisation and filtered though her own religious convictions. But that does not account for what her father saw. Later, her daughter Becky also went through regressional hypnosis and recovered memories of her mother's abduction. She said that after the aliens arrived in their home she managed to shake off the trance for a few moments. The strange visitors she saw were hairless, with pear-shaped heads and almond eyes. Their noses and ears had no external structures and the mouths were simply slits. These features are typical of Greys. She also noted that their skin was clay-like, rather than scaly, and that they had three thick fingers on their club-shaped hands. Then she lapsed back into unconsciousness.

After her hypnosis, Andreasson underwent psychiatric tests to make sure that she was not suffering from any sort of mental disorder. She also passed lie-detector and voice-stress tests. Like some other abductees, Betty Andreasson found that her life changed for the better after her experience. She became a talented artist and produced detailed drawings of what she had undergone at the hands of the aliens. Then, in 1987, she discovered a strange indented scar on her calf. Just over a year later, Raymond E. Fowler, the man who had been documenting her case, found a similar scar on his leg. Such marks are commonly found on abductees. Budd Hopkins says that they are due to cell sampling performed by aliens.

Betty Andreasson has had other encounters with aliens. During one powerful encounter, her husband John reported that mysterious black helicopters passed over their house. They were unmarked and seemed to shimmer in and out of reality. Calls to nearby airports and military bases drew a blank.

Spacenapping

Alien abductions hit the headlines again after a bizarre 'spacenapping' on 5 November 1975. That evening, Mike Rogers and his crew of six forestry workers were heading home to Snowflake, Arizona. They were heading down a track in the Heber forest when Alan Dalis, one of the crew, spotted a strange glow through the trees. As the truck moved closer, they noticed a ball of light hovering about twenty feet above the ground.

'When we got around the trees, we all saw the source of the light – boom – less than hundred feet away, a metallic disc hovering in the air, glowing,' forestry worker Travis Walton recalled.

As the truck screeched to a halt, Travis Walton jumped out to investigate. While his more cautious friends remained in truck, the impetuous Walton approached the mysterious object. The light appeared to be about twenty feet across and was hovering in an unsteady, wavering manner, and giving off beeping and rumbling sounds.

The object was casting a circle of light on the ground. Walton stopped at the edge. He was standing almost directly underneath the object when his nerve snapped. As he turned to run back to the truck he heard a crackling sound and felt what he described as 'a numbing shock... like a high-voltage electrocution'.

Mike Rogers, the crew boss, who was still in the trunk, saw a blue-green 'bolt of energy' flash from the object and zap Walton on his back.

It picked him up and flung him back down on the ground. At this point, Rogers panicked. He floored the accelerator and drove away. A short distance down the road, he regained his composure. The other men persuaded Rogers to drive back to pick up Walton, who they had left for dead. They got there just in time to see the spacecraft rise rapidly into the sky and disappear. Walton was nowhere to be seen.

The crew reported the events to the authorities in Heber. A search revealed nothing and the police suspected that Walton had been murdered by his workmates. The men were asked to take a lie detector test to clear their names. The first polygraph test was inconclusive, but a second confirmed they were telling the truth about what they had seen.

After five days and a massive police search, there was still no sign of Walton. Then suddenly, on 10 November, Walton's brother-in-law received a phone call from him. He went to collect Walton and found him naked in a phone booth a few miles outside town. Walton was seriously dehydrated, delirious, dazed, distraught and half-dead. It was only after months of rehabilitation that he was able to remember fragments of what had happened. He remembered being hit by the bolt of lightning and knocked out. When he regained consciousness, he found himself inside some sort of spaceship.

'I was lying on a table,' he said. 'I saw several strange creatures standing over me. I became completely hysterical and flipped out. I knocked them away, but I felt so weak I collapsed. They forced me back on the table, placed a mask over my face and I blacked out.'

The aliens were 'foetus-like', about five feet tall with domed, hairless heads, large dark eyes, tiny ears and noses, a slit for a mouth and marshmallowy skin. And they performed various experiments on him. He saw a humanoid entity, who showed him around but did not answer his questions. They visited a control room where he could see out through the exterior of the craft and gaze at the stars. Afterwards he lost consciousness again and when he came to he was lying on a country road near Heber.

What is significant about the Travis Walton case is that it is one of the few abductions observed by independent witnesses – his workmates saw his initial encounter with the UFO. It is also unusual because Walton was missing for five days. In most contemporary cases, the abduction experience lasts for only a few hours.

Over the years, sceptics have tried to debunk Walton's claims. The rarity of abduction reports in the 1970s meant Walton and his friends were subjected to years of ridicule and accusations of trickery. Yet all the men subsequently passed more lie-detector tests and the case has withstood years of rigorous investigation.

Walton recounted his abduction in the book *Fire in the Sky*, which was made into a TV film of the same name. Since the film Travis has passed two more lie-detector tests, but he has refused to be hypnotically regressed as he fears it will bring out too many disturbing memories.

Researchers are certain that Travis Walton was not suffering from any mental illness when he was abducted. It is also unlikely that all six of Walton's colleagues would have had hallucinations of the same kind at the same time. And the lie-detector tests show that they believed they saw Walton being zapped by a UFO.

More than twenty years later Walton is still clear about what happened to him.

'Something like that doesn't just disappear with the years,' he says. 'You can still remember the emotions. You can still remember the fear. When you try to cope with something like that you try to take a positive element from it. But I would rather it had not happened to me.'

To cope, he has avoided studying other cases. But he believes that some are definitely not genuine.

'I find this frustrating as it detracts from the legitimate case,' he says.

French Farce

One of the most troubling alien abduction cases took place in France on 26 November 1979. That Monday, eighteen-year-old Franck Fontaine, a street trader from the Parisian suburb of Cergy-Pontoise, disappeared in the early hours of the morning. Two of Fontaine's friends, Salomon N'Diaye and Jean-Pierre Prevost, rang the police and told them he was missing – and that they had seen a UFO shortly before he vanished.

Under interrogation, they told the whole story. On the night of the abduction, the three friends had slept for just a few hours at Prevost's high-rise flat in Cergy-Pontoise. In the morning, they planned to sell clothes in a Paris street market. The market was busy and you had to get there early to get a stall. So that morning they got up 3:30 a.m. and started loading their car.

Their ageing Ford Taunus was not the most reliable of cars. After they had brought the first load of clothes down from the flat, they decided to bump-start it. When the engine was running, they left Fontaine at the wheel to make sure it did not stall, while N'Diaye and Prevost went back up upstairs to get the rest of the gear.

While N'Diaye and Prevost were up in the flat, Fontaine spotted a bright, cylindrical light in the sky. He pointed it out to his friends when they returned to the car. There was a ready market for UFO pictures and N'Diaye reckoned that could sell a photograph to the local press at the very least. N'Diaye and Prevost went back up to the flat to find a camera, leaving Fontaine at the wheel of the car outside.

But when the two men reached the apartment, they heard the sound of the car driving away. They ran to the window and saw Fontaine drive up the road. Then, the engine cut out and the car came juddering to a halt.

N'Diaye and Prevost ran back downstairs. When they reached the street, they saw the back end of the car enveloped in a ball of glowing mist. Then a beam of light appeared from nowhere. It grew into the cylindrical shape they had seen earlier. The ball of mist then entered the hovering cylinder, which shot into the sky and vanished.

N'Diaye and Prevost ran to the car to see whether their friend Fontaine was all right. But when they reached the vehicle there was no sign of Fontaine. They looked up and down the road and searched the cabbage field beyond, but there was no trace of him. At this point Prevost grew concerned for Fontaine's safety and N'Diaye called the police. Local police made a thorough search, but neither hide nor hair of the missing Fontaine was found.

The police were more than a little bemused by Prevost and N'Diaye's story. They contacted the gendarmerie, the branch of the French police force charged with investigating UFO sightings. Meanwhile, the story leaked to the media and TV crews, and newspaper reporters from around the world descended on Cergy-Pontoise, eager to get the low-down on the latest UFO abduction.

Inside the police station, the pair were subjected to repeated interrogations – both by the local police who could not rule out the possibility of foul play, and the gendarmerie, who handled it as an alien abduction case. Eventually, Commandant Courcoux, head of the Cergy gendarmerie, emerged to tell the waiting newshounds that there were no grounds for disbelieving the two men's story. There was no doubt that something strange had happened, he said. But he had no idea what it was.

When N'Diaye and Prevost were finally released, they were besieged by reporters. Over the course of the next week, they told their story over and over again. But the constant retelling gave no new clue to Fontaine's whereabouts. And as time went by the mystery deepened.

On 3 December, seven days almost to the minute after his disappearance, Fontaine reappeared to find himself in the middle of a media circus. He had no idea that he had been missing for a week and had no recollection of what had happened to him. He thought he had simply fallen asleep for a few hours and was amazed to find himself the centre of media attention.

The story had been hot news, not just in France, but around the world. The British tabloids did not take it seriously, of course. They treated it like something straight out of a science-fiction comic. But even *The Times* carried the story. On the day after Fontaine's return, it ran the headline: 'Frenchman Back to Earth with a Bump.' The story, too, was slightly jokey. No one, it seemed, was quite sure whether to take it seriously or not.

Fontaine's reappearance failed to shed any further light on the mystery. He had woken up in the cabbage field next to the road, which both his friends and the police had searched thoroughly. He assumed that he had fallen asleep and his friends had left him. He went to Prevost's apartment, but found no one at home. Then he went to N'Diaye's place. When he rang the bell, a drowsy N'Diaye opened the door. It was N'Diaye who, to Fontaine's amazement, told him that he had been missing for seven whole days.

When they informed the police that Fontaine had returned, they took him in for questioning. But, as Fontaine had no recollection of what had happened to him, there was no way that they could progress the investigation. And, as no crime had been committed, they dropped the case. The papers soon grew tired of the story too. However, the interest of UFO groups had been tweaked and their investigations had only just begun.

The first group was the *Institut Mondial des Sciences Avancés* (World Institute of Advanced Sciences), run by French science-fiction writer Jimmy Guieu. Author of two books about UFOs and facinated by the Cergy-Pontoise case, Guieu took the three men under his wing. He whisked them off to a secluded spot, sat them down and started piecing together the definitive account of Fontaine's abduction. With four months later, Guieu's book, *Cergy-Pontoise UFO Contacts*, was on the bookshelves. It was an instant bestseller.

Guieu had taken the three friends away so that other UFOlogists could not question them, so he was accused of hogging the case. In a mixture of jealousy and pique, other UFO groups criticised Guieu's book, saying it was far from objective. While the *Institut Mondial des Sciences Avancés* found no flaws in the story told by Fontaine, N'Diaye and Prevost, a rival French UFO group called Control began to pick up on inconsistencies. The group produced a fifty-page report damning the book.

Most complaints were trifling. Although the three men said that they had been alone in Prevost's apartment on the night of the abduction, Control's Michel Piccin and other researchers discovered that Prevost's girlfriend Corrine had also been present, along with Fabrice Joly, another friend. Control also discovered that no one else in the block at night had heard the UFO, although they had heard the car being bump-started at around 4 a.m. and they had heard its engine running outside for the next few minutes. Residents returning home in the early hours had seen two people in the Ford Taunus, when Fontaine said that he had been alone. They also picked holes in the three men's chronology of the events of that night.

The account of Fontaine's return also seemed to be riddled with inconsistencies. Control said that, from the published accounts,

N'Diaye seems to have been in two places at one time. But some of these apparent contradictions could just be the result of a faulty memory, and, without access to the three principal witnesses, Control had no opportunity to clear them up.

However, the major problem with the book, as far as most readers were concerned, was its lack of a first-hand account of what had happened to Fontaine during the week he had been missing. Despite Guieu's pleading, he stubbornly refused to undergo regressional hypnosis.

The rivalries between the three friends then surfaced. Prevost began writing his own account of the abduction and underwent regressional hypnosis, only to discover that it was he, and not Fontaine, who the aliens were after. After Fontaine's abduction, he had been contacted by the aliens independently. Shortly after Fontaine's return, Prevost had been visited by a mysterious 'salesman' who had taken him on a trip of Bourg-de-Sirod, a village near the Swiss border that Prevost has visited as a child. Prevost was taken to a disused railway tunnel, which led to a secret alien base. In the base, he met a group of people from every country in the world. An alien being named Haurrio told the group that they had been chosen to spread the philosophy of the aliens on Earth. They were then given a tour of the base by a beautiful female alien. Prevost slept at the base that night, but whether he slept with the alien he is too discreet to say. The next day the mysterious 'salesman' took him home.

Prevost published his account in *The Truth About the Cergy-Pontoise Affair*. He claimed that he has been chosen as the channel though which alien contacts would be made. Few people could take Prevost's fantastical claims seriously and they began to undermine the credibility of the original story.

Fontaine struck back. Although he had refused to undergo regressional hypnosis, some memories of what had happened during his week as an abductee began to seep back into his conscious mind. It all seemed like a strange, disturbing dream, but he remembered being taken into a large room and being told to lie on a small couch. The walls were lined with machinery, and two glowing spheres talked to him about the problems confronting the Earth and their solutions. Sadly, he could remember none of the details. So Fontaine decided to arrange another meeting with the aliens. On 15 August 1980, a group of UFO enthusiasts gathered in Cergy-Pontoise for the encounter. But, sadly, no one had informed the aliens and they did not turn up.

By 1983, Prevost was the leader of his own UFO group and was giving lectures on the abduction across the country. In an effort to snooker Fontaine, Guieu and the *Institut Mondial des Sciences Avancés*, he confessed that Fontaine's abduction had been a hoax. The three young men had simply concocted the story as a money-making exercise, he said. But there was a problem with this. Neither Prevost, nor anybody else, has been able to explain where Fontaine had been during the missing week.

Nor has anyone been able to explain why the first policemen on the scene had also reported seeing some kind of 'mist' surrounding the Ford Taunus. How had Prevost, Fontaine and N'Diaye created this elaborate effect to corroborate their story?

Respected French UFOlogist Jacques Vallee, who has written a number of well received books on UFOs, has put forward another theory altogether. He says that, as part of an exercise in social control, the French military snatched Fontaine, drugged him and kept him 'in an altered state of high suggestibility' for a week. The aim was to create a religion based on UFO visitations. The programme has since been dropped, but its existence had been confirmed by Vallee's contacts inside the French Air Force, he says. Unfortunately, Vallee has not been able to offer any more corroboration, but to UFOlogists this story is all too familiar. UFO researchers in the UK and US have often found ties between the UFO phenomena and the military and intelligence communities. It is not beyond the realms of possibility that the same thing is happening in France. In that case, Prevost's confession cannot be taken at face value, but rather should be seen as part of a cleverly orchestrated campaign of disinformation.

Even though the Cergy-Pontoise abduction case has muddied the waters, the gendarmerie continues to play a central role in UFO cases. Its officers are used as preliminary investigators in the field. They are trained in how to carry out UFO investigations, paying particular attention to details that might be of interest to scientists, the effects felt by witnesses and any anomalous behaviour by wildlife in the area. When UFOs land, all traces left by the craft and samples of soil and vegetation from the area are collected and sent for analysis. The police also check the site for radioactivity and take aerial photographs of the area using a helicopter equipped with infrared cameras. The French government also funds a small UFO research programme that employs a number of top scientists.

'By virtue of the gendarmerie's presence throughout the whole territory of France,' writes Captain Kervendel in the international journal *Gendarmerie,* 'its knowledge of places and people, its integrity and intellectual honesty and the rapidity with which the gendarmerie can be on the spot, they are well place indeed to serve as a valuable auxiliary in the search for the truth about UFOs.'

Abducted From Birth

Jason Andrews seems to have been selected for alien abduction from birth, on 2 July 1983. Even as a baby, he seemed to be in the power of some strange external force. His mother, Ann, would find him on the floor under his cot when he was far too young to climb out of it. Once, she found him behind the bedroom door on the other side of the room. It was a heart-stopping moment.

The only reasonable explanation was that his three-year-old brother Daniel was responsible. He denied it and there were several occasions when Jason was moved and Daniel was not even in the house. Then, after a few months, the strange events stopped and Ann soon forgot about them. But then they were to return with a vengeance.

On Jason's fourth birthday, Ann and Jason's father, Paul, were at home with the children in their small cottage in Kent. Late in the evening, they were disturbed by a loud banging. At first it seemed to come from the doors, then from the windows, then the whole house seemed to be wracked by it. Paul though that someone was playing a practical joke on them. He opened the front door and looked out, but there was nobody there. Growing increasingly disturbed, he tried to call the police, but the phone was dead. Then a violent thunderstorm broke. Frightening though this was, it did offer some sort of explanation. But with the first crack of thunder Jason, who had been asleep on the sofa, sat bolt upright and began reeling off a series of numbers in a strange mechanical voice.

And it was not just numbers. He spewed out complex mathematical expressions, making references to pi and binary numbers – even though he had trouble counting up to ten in his picture books. Then he got up and walked to the door.

'They're waiting for me, I have to go,' he said.

Paul stopped him. It was a struggle. Jason seemed to be in a trance and was hell bent on going outside. Eventually Jason snapped out it and, when he came back to normal, he remembered nothing about his strange behaviour. Soon after, the phone began to work again. Ann and Paul called the police. But when they arrived at the house, they could find no trace of anything untoward. After the storm the cottage was surrounded by a sea of mud. If someone outside had been playing a practical joke, they would have left footprints, the police reasoned. There were none to be found.

The mysterious events of Jason's fourth birthday heralded a spate of strange new occurrences. Jason was apprehensive at bedtime. When his parents put him down for the night, he told them that small creatures came for him in the hours of darkness. In the morning, he woke tired. Often, inexplicably, he was covered in mud. And sometimes he had small scars and marks on his body. These mysteriously disappeared in a few hours.

He suffered mysterious stomach pains and was rushed into hospital twice. Once a doctor asked Ann about an operation Jason had had. She said that he had never been operated on. The doctor gave her a strange look. There was a fresh surgical scar on Jason's side. The following day it had disappeared.

At home, Ann and Paul would overhear Jason babbling in a strange language while he was alone in his bedroom. More worrying was the continued disturbance to his sleep. In the mornings, they would find him sleeping in odd places around the house. Once, they found him lying flat out on the kitchen worktop. Another time, they found him outside in the garden shed. Bafflingly, all the doors and windows of the house were locked and the shed door was bolted from the outside.

Other strange events began to plague them. Bright lights were seen over their farm, and strange figures were seen in the surrounding fields and woods. They became convinced that someone was watching the house. Then things took a more sinister turn. Their cattle died mysteriously. The vet blamed a virulent outbreak of salmonella. One of the horses on the Andrews' farm had a neat flap cut into its flank. It was a huge wound, but there was very little blood. The horse seemed docile and unconcerned. When the vet arrived, he said that the animal must have been tranquillised, and managed to sew up the wound without an anaesthetic.

The farm cat was found dead, stretched out on a bale of hay in the barn. It had a round hole bored in its head. Again, there was no blood around the wound. A few months later, a fox was found in the fields with similar hole in its head. Then four dead mice were found lined up by a farm gate, each with a small hole in its forehead and other surgical mutilations.

It was only in the autumn of 1995, when Jason was twelve, that they found out what was going on. One evening the family was watching television together. A man came on talking about how he had experienced a period of 'missing time' in his life. He told of how a thirty-five-minute journey had mysteriously taken over three hours. Since then he had suffered from uncontrollable mood swings, depression, and an irrational fear of the dark. In his efforts to find a cure, he visited a hypnotherapist who helped him to recover his memory of the lost time. At this point, Jason leapt to his feet, grabbed an ornament and threw it at the TV. The man was stupid to want to find out, he shouted. He knew what was going on, he said, and he wished he didn't.

When his parents managed to calm him down, he told them that he was being abducted by aliens. Despite the TV show, neither Paul nor Ann would accepted this. They thought Jason was simply having bad dreams. Although they were sceptical, they thought it would do no harm to look into it. They bought a few books on alien abductions and quickly realised that Jason's behaviour exactly fitted that of an abductee. For Jason, this was a breakthrough. At last, his parents believed him.

They turned for professional help to Tony Dodd, the Director of Investigations for Quest International, a body set up to investigate UFO activity. As an ex-police sergeant, Dodd was well trained to investigate such a case. He came to the conclusion that Jason was indeed an abductee, but he was unusual in that he had a conscious memory of the abductions. In most cases, the memories surfaced only under regressional hypnosis. As Dodd's investigation continued, Ann began to recover memories of abductions of her own. Like Jason, she had a memory of being in a crowd of humans who were being shown images on a large large screen of the Earth blowing up. This is a recurrent theme in abduction cases. One of the reasons, it seems, that aliens have come to Earth is to teach abductees about the destructive nature of humankind.

In the next three years, more memories came flooding back. Both Jason and Ann had memories of aliens carrying out weird medical examinations on them. A miscarriage she suffered in August 1989, she believed, was the deliberate abduction of the foetus from her womb by the aliens. On the night of the miscarriage, Ann was in such a deep sleep that Paul feared for her life.

But the aliens' interventions are not always so sinister. Jason says they are with him at other times – like when he is riding a horse or a bike – as if they are trying to share his emotions. Once, when he was thrown by a horse,he said that they hated the pain he suffered.

Dodd pointed out that Ann and Jason were reporting two common aspects of alien interest in the human race, according to the literature.

They seemed to be carrying out genetic experiments on humans, perhaps harvesting human DNA. But they were also fascinated by human emotions. Observing more than one generation on the same family is also a familiar pattern.

Jason was visited by various types of aliens. His mother made a sketch from his description of those who regularly came to abduct him. Her picture shows a classic Grey, with large, black, almond-shaped eyes and a bulbous head. Other alien visitors hid themselves under hoods and cloaks, while some were humanoid. Although Jason continued to be frightened at night when he felt they were coming for him, he coped much better after his parents accepted the situation. The aliens did not seem to wish him any harm and they always returned him in the morning.

However, Jason's abductions left him tired. This resulted in behavioural difficulties at school and attracted the attention of the authorities. The social services were called in. But when the family were seen by social workers, they accepted that Jason was loved and well cared for. He was referred to a psychiatrist, who saw him for over a year and declared that he was not suffering from delusions. Others have suggested that Jason was suffering from some strange sleep disorder. But this would not explain how a small boy got out of a locked house and threw the bolt on the outside of a shed door when he was on the inside.

Ann and Paul were not people inclined to flights of fantasy. They made very credible witnesses. Their major concern was the wellbeing of their child, and supporting his abduction story, if they did not believe it to be true, would not be in his best interests.

It is hard to see what Jason would have to gain from making up such a story – and sticking to it. It attracted teasing and name-calling at school. When he confided in friends, he was called 'ET' and 'spaceboy'. What is more, there was physical evidence that supports his abduction story – the strange lights over the farm, the scars and the animal mutilations.

Experienced UFO investigator Tony Dodd was convinced.

'Jason began reporting these even when he was very young, far too young to have picked up ideas from TV or newspapers,' Dodd said. 'His parents are good witnesses. Although Ann has also been involved, Paul has no personal experience and is by nature a sceptic. But he has seen so much evidence that he accepts that his family are telling the truth.'

Dodd knows only too well the difficulties that abductees experience in getting themselves believed.

'At one time, people who said they were being abducted were regarded as cranks. But more and more people are reporting experiences similar to Jason's. They can't all be making it up. I believe the aliens are interested in studying DNA and using our genetic material in breeding experiments. They are certainly monitoring us – they may even be responsible for the Earth being inhabited in the first place.'

At fifteen, Jason was still suffering regular abductions. They came in waves, perhaps three over a couple of weeks, then nothing for two or three months. The longest break between them was six months. They follow a familiar pattern. He wakes to hear all the family's dogs barking. It is always about 3 a.m. – he checks the time on his digital clock. Suddenly the dogs fall silent, as if they have been switched off. Then a tall alien rises up at the end of Jason's bed, as if he has come up through the floorboards. Several smaller aliens are standing around the bed, but Jason does not see where they come from. Then he blacks out. He does not remember anything until he is in a strange room. He is lying on a cold, hard surface, like a marble slab. There is a bright light, although he cannot see the source. The aliens are all around him and the tall one usually has a long, thin probe in his hand. The next thing he remembers is waking up at home.

On other occasions he has played with small aliens. He wants it to stop, but has never thought that they would leave him alone permanently. In the mean time, he has learned to be stoical.

'Perhaps I have been chosen,' Jason said. 'Perhaps I am special, and maybe one day I will understand, but right now I would just like it to stop. I want them to leave me alone. I want them to let me be ordinary.'

If Jason has been chosen, he is not alone. When he was fifteen, he was contacted by nineteen-year-old James Basil. A fellow abductee, Basil was discovered to have an alien device implanted in him. They had a lot to talk about.

A Night to Remember

Although some abduction victims can supply corroborating evidence, rarely has an abductee been able to photograph the alien craft that abducted him. But that is exactly what Amaury Rivera managed to do on 8 May 1988. What's more, his photograph provided proof that the US military were involved in the UFO phenomenon.

At 4:40 a.m. that night, Amaury Rivera left a nightclub in his home town of Jabo Rojo in Puerto Rico. Some musician friends had been playing there and he had taken a camera with him to photograph the band in action. As he drove home afterwards, he found himself swathed in a dense fog. He cut his speed. Even so, he lost the road and found himself in a cattle pasture. Fearing that he might hit one of the animals, he slowed to a snail's pace.

He was practically at a standstill when he heard a strange noise. Looking towards the source of the sound, he saw two strange beings approaching him. They were identical and both about three feet tall. Their skin was white and they were hairless with huge black eyes.

He tried to escape, but in his panic he hit the brake instead of its accelerator. By then, the creatures were standing directly in front of his car. The car door began to open of its own accord. Terrified, Rivera wet himself, then lost consciousness.

When he came round, he found himself still inside his car, but the car itself was inside a strange room, which had bright grey surfaces. There were several other cars parked next to his.

'I was really confused,' said Rivera. 'I thought I was in some kind of garage and I looked around for an exit sign.'

But the two small creatures he had seen in the field reappeared. They placed their hands on his forehead and he passed out again.

When he came to, he found himself in a room with fourteen other people, all sitting on benches.

'Some looked like they had come straight from a party,' said Rivera. 'Next to me was a teenager without any shoes or shirt. At this point, I still didn't believe I had been abducted by aliens. Because of my Catholic upbringing, I thought the little beings were devils and I had been in a car accident, died and gone to hell.'

A tall humanoid then came into the room. He had long black hair and his skin was dark and swarthy. He was accompanied by the two smaller beings. 'He introduced himself to us, saying he was a man like us,' Rivera said, 'but he came from another planet in a distant solar system. He spoke "verbally" in accent-free Spanish.'

During the speech, Rivera found that he could not move, but he did not know whether this was through fear or if he was restrained or otherwise paralysed. Rivera began to feel uneasy and was sure that the others felt the same. But the alien reassured them that there was nothing to be afraid of. He then told them that they had been chosen because it was necessary to share some information with them. The creature then showed them a series of three-dimensional holographic projections, which warned of the terrible fate that awaited the Earth if humankind did not mend its ways.

The first projections showed a comet colliding with the Earth. It hit the Caribbean near Puerto Rico with such force that it devastated the planet. A second showed what happened to the world after this cataclysm – there would be a single world government on an artificial island in a black polluted sea. When the show was over, Rivera was rendered unconscious a third time. This time, when he awoke, he found himself back in his car, outdoors, some distance from where the abduction had begun. Next, he heard the roar of jets overhead. On looking up, he saw three jet-fighters chasing a disc-shaped UFO.

In a flash of inspiration, he remembered that he had his camera in the car. Grabbing it, he leapt out and started shooting away. Although there were three jets in pursuit, only one appears in Rivera's photographs.

'The jets would take turns circling around the UFO so that one would always be near to it,' explains Rivera. 'That is why you only see one jet with the UFO in the pictures I released.'

But Rivera had been lucky to get any pictures at all. Within seconds, the UFO took off at a fantastic speed, leaving the jets standing. Rivera was hardly able to believe the evidence of his own eyes. Fortunately, he had captured the scene on film. And a few days later, after he developed the film, he had proof that what he had seen was real.

He took the pictures to Jorge Martin, editor of the Puerto Rico's leading UFO magazine, *Evidencia OVNI*. Martin was impressed. Not only was Rivera's tale convincing – with evidence to back it up – the pictures suggested that the US military knew about UFOs, as UFOlogists had suspected.

'The Rivera case is a very impressive one because of the evidence,' said Martin. 'He was able to take pictures of the disc and include the jet interceptors. These jets have been identified as F-14 "Tom Cat" fighters, which are used by the US Navy. Many witnesses have also reported seeing the same type of jets attempting to intercept UFOs over different areas of Puerto Rico on other occasions. When you see the pictures, it is obvious that the government has been lying for decades about their involvement.'

Puerto Rico has been a UFO hotspot since 1987. The centre of the activity is Laguna Cartagena, near Cabo Rojo where Rivera was abducted, and a small mountain ridge called Sierra Bermeja. A number of witnesses had seen UFOs flying in and out of the waters of Laguna Cartagena. Indeed one local witness, a Mrs Ramirez, said that she had seen flying saucers entering the lake since 1956.

'At first, they were bright and luminous,' she said. 'As they came out you could define their shape more clearly. They were disc-shaped, with a translucent dome on top and you could see people or figures inside the domes.'

It is no coincidence that there are a number of US military establishments in Puerto Rico. More than two-thirds of the nearby island of Vieques has been occupied by the US Navy for fifty years.

Despite protests from the inhabitants, they refuse to hand it back. The US government has also sealed off the area around Laguna Cartagena.

Jorge Martin says that there have been other cases of UFOs being pursued by jet fighters over Puerto Rico. On 16 November 1988, Yesenia Valasquez saw a huge ball of yellow light hovering over the town of San German. With other members of her family, she witnessed two jet fighters intercept the object and fly around it.

'Then, all of a sudden, they seemed to enter the object from below and disappeared,' she said. After that the UFO emitted two balls of light, which streaked away into the distance. The UFO followed.

Luminous pyramid-shaped craft are often seen over Puerto Rico. One of these appeared over the town of Barranquitas near the centre of the island on 18 November 1995. It hovered over the local radio station, Radio Procer, and played havoc with their electronic equipment. It was seen by numerous witnesses, but the authorities denied that anything unusual happened that day.

Because of the massive US military presence on Puerto Rico and the US government's secrecy, some UFOlogists have concluded that there is an alien base on the island, where extraterrestrials and US scientists perform secret experiments.

Rivera's photographs were sent for professional analysis. Professor Victor Quesada of the University of Mexico and Jim Dilettoso, whose Village Labs in Arizona uses state-of-the-art computer imaging technology in its consulting work for NASA, both examined the pictures and said they could find no evidence of fraud.

Their analysis showed that the disc-shaped craft and the jet were about two to two-and-a-half miles away from Rivera's position. The jet was moving at some speed, while the disc was standing still or moving slowly. In all four pictures Rivera took, the ambient light conditions were correct. This ruled out the use of models, paste-up, montages and all known forms of technical manipulation. Nothing in them contradicted anything Rivera said about what had happened when he took the photographs. As a result, they concluded that the pictures were genuine.

Jorge Martin found a fisherman named Andreas Mandolano who had also been abducted. His story exactly matched Rivera's experience. 'He told me various things like the name of the alien and other points that Rivera had only revealed to me,' said Martin. 'This, on top of the fact that the two men had never met or discussed the case, provides good corroborative evidence for Rivera's claims.'

During his investigation, Martin tracked down four people who described being abducted by the same creatures that Rivera had seen. 'It appears as if this alien has been contacting people from all around the area of Puerto Rico,' said Martin.

But according to Rivera, there were fourteen other abductees with him in the room on the alien craft. Where were the other ten? Rivera went on TV and asked for them to come forward. Several hundred people responded. Out of this group, Rivera managed to find seven who were in that room with him on the same night. Martin and Rivera are still trying to locate the other three.

The case attracted the attention of veteran American UFOlogist Wendelle Stevens. In his thirty-six years of UFOlogy, he had come to specialise in alien contact cases that involve the delivery of information. Like other investigators, Stevens was impressed by the emotion that Rivera displayed when recounting his experience – something that researchers believe is difficult to fake convincingly.

'At first, when he started to talk about his experience, he would turn pale and shake and you could see he was genuinely frightened,' says Stevens. 'You could tell he was still deeply affected by what had happened to him. He has now processed his experience sufficiently to be able to talk publicly without a high degree of trauma and with more confidence. From the evidence I have seen, there is no doubt in my mind that what he described really happened to him.'

What is more, he has four unimpeachable photographs and eleven other abductees to back his story. With such impressive evidence, it is not surprising that Amaury Rivera attracted the attention of the 'Men in Black'.

Shortly after his abduction, Rivera was visited by three black-suited men at his home in Cabo Rojo.

'They said they were from the CIA and showed me papers which had a CIA letterhead,' Rivera says. 'But I was so nervous that I wasn't able to read what was written on them. They told me it would be easier if I just gave them the photographs and negatives.' This was before Rivera and Martin had released the pictures to the press.

Rivera told them that he did not know what they were talking about, but they said they had a warrant to search his house.

'I told them "go ahead, be my guest", says Rivera. 'They searched but didn't find anything. I had hidden them far too well.'

UFOs at the UN

It is hard for the general public to believe that human beings are being abducted by aliens, and UFOlogists have long hoped that a case backed by irrefutable proof and unimpeachable witnesses would come up so that they could prove their case. And at the first Alien Study Conference at the Massachusetts of Technology on 13 June 1992, one case that had the potential to be just such a clincher was put forward.

The researcher on the case was Budd Hopkins, the New York-based artist and sculptor turned UFOlogist. It involved a woman, a New York housewife, known pseudonymously as 'Linda Cortile', who lived in an apartment block on the Lower East Side, just two blocks from the Brooklyn Bridge. In December 1989 Hopkins received a telephone call from an emotionally distraught Cortile. While she lay in bed on the night of 30 November 1989 about 3 a.m., the forty-one-year-old Italian-American had been approached by a 'small, grey-skinned alien'. In the presence of this creature, she felt her body became completely paralysed. She had only a vague recollection of what happened next, but she recalled lying on a table and being examined.

Mrs Cortile was so distressed that it was plain something had to be done urgently. So on 2 December 1989 Hopkins organised a session of regressional hypnosis, which he tape-recorded. Under hypnosis, Cortile provided a full account of her experience.

She began: 'Behind the drapes. There's something there. There's someone in the room... Ooh, I can't move my arms anymore. Now one, two, three, there's four and five. They're taking me outta bed. I won't let them. I won't let them take me outta bed.'

Hopkins asked her to describe the visitors.

'They're short. They're white and dark... Their eyes. Very intense eyes... Black. They shine.'

Realising that he was dealing with classic 'Greys', Hopkins asked what happened next.

'They lift me up and they bring me to the living room... They took me to the window. And there was a bright light. Blue-white. [Inaudible] right outside. I'm outside. I'm outside the window. It's weird.'

The aliens had floated Cortile out through her twelfth-storey window, even though it was locked and covered by a metal child-guard fence. She hovered there, suspended above the street. Then the creatures levitated the helpless woman up into the belly of a waiting spaceship. Inside she found herself lying on a table where they began examining her back and her right nostril. She was then questioned about her family. Afterwards they allowed her to leave the examining table. She remembered heading for the door, but the next thing she remembered was being back in bed in her apartment.

By Mrs Cortile's account, there was nothing exceptional about her case. It was just one of thousands of similar abductions reported to UFO researchers the world over, and may just have rated a footnote in one of Hopkins' books. But fifteen months later, Hopkins discovered something that would make this case very different indeed – the abduction itself had been witnessed.

In February 1991, two police officers who identified themselves only as 'Richard' and 'Dan' wrote to Hopkins. Although no details of the Cortile case had been made public, in their letter, Richard and Dan recounted witnessing an abduction that matched Mrs Cortile's precisely. They said that, at 3:30 a.m. 'in late November 1989', when they sat in their car, they saw 'a strange oval hovering over the top of an apartment building... its lights turned from a bright reddish orange to a very whitish blue. It moved out away from the building and lowered itself to an apartment window just below.'

Next they saw a woman floating in mid-air in a bright beam of bluish-white light. She was followed by three ugly little human-like beings who sprang out of the window one by one, in the foetal position, before straightening out. Then, with one above her and two below, they escorted her up to the waiting UFO. Once she was on board, the oval craft turned reddish-orange again and whisked away. 'It then plunged into the river behind us, not far from pier 17, behind the Brooklyn Bridge,' they said.

The two police officers ended their letter by saying that they wanted to retain their anonymity due to their professional standing. They also mentioned that they might try to contact the female they had seen.

In *Witnessed,* Hopkins' book about the case, he wrote: 'My astonishment at reading this letter was all the more profound because I was almost certain that I knew the woman.'

Although to those outside the UFO community, the Cortile case might appear absurd, the fact that it had been observed by two unimpeachable witnesses, who had nothing to gain by coming forward, proved to any reasonable standard that it had actually happened. The problem was that Hopkins had no return address for Richard and Dan. Nor did he know their full names. So there is no way he could contact them. However, they had mentioned in their letter that they might try to contact the woman they had seen being abducted.

Hopkins was concerned that meeting them without any prior warning might have a bad effect on Mrs Cortile. So he contacted her and told her about the two men. Together, they planned what to do should Richard and Dan contact her. Two weeks later, on 19 February 1991, the two men knocked on the door of her apartment.

Although Hopkins never got to meet Richard or Dan, Mrs Cortile met them on several occasions. During their first meeting, Richard and Dan questioned her closely about her abduction, and apologised for not coming to her assistance. Mrs Cortile sympathised. The two men seemed to have been badly shaken by the event. It seemed that they could still hardly believe that it had happened and needed confirmation.

Hopkins had asked Mrs Cortile to ask the two men to contact him – or at least prepare a written or taped account of what they saw. They should do this before she said too much. In this way, he would have their account on record before it was influenced by what she told them. They agreed to do this, and left.

The following month, Hopkins received an audiocassette from Richard and Dan. It confirmed that they had witnessed an alien abduction on 30 November 1989 and spelt out everything they had seen in great detail. As police officers they were trained in observation and presenting detailed witness testimony in court. Next, Hopkins set himself the task of tracking down the two men and confirming their identities. This was made more difficult by Richard and Dan's next letter, which explained that they were not quite who they had said they were – and that a third witness, a VIP, had been present that night.

Although Hopkins met with the so-called 'Third Man' at an airport in 1993 and received a package containing information on the case from him, he has never revealed his identity. But other UFOlogists have come to believe he was the then UN Secretary General Javier Perez de Cuellar. The clue comes from Mrs Cortile's regressional hypnosis. During her abduction, she recalled seeing a car carrying diplomatic registration plates being parked near her home. Mrs Cortile also believes she saw Dan standing next to Russian premier Mikhail Gorbachev during a newscast from the United Nations in December 1988. When Hopkins located the clip, she said she was '150 per cent sure' that man was Dan.

Piecing together the story, it seems that Richard and Dan were no ordinary patrolmen, but officers assigned to guard diplomats and other VIPs. They had been driving de Cuellar through New York late at night when their car came to a mysterious halt on Franklin D. Roosevelt Drive not far from the exit to Brooklyn Bridge. It was then that they witnessed Cortile's abduction. Hopkins has suggested that the abduction was 'a deliberate performance' put on for the benefit of a man of international standing. What better witness could you have?

But that was not the end of the story. On Monday, 29 April, Hopkins got another call from Mrs Cortile. She was very agitated. She had just been abducted again. Not by aliens this time, but by Richard and Dan.

'They forced me into their car and drove me around for about three hours just asking me questions,' she said. During this interrogation, Richard and Dan apparently accused Mrs Cortile of working for a government agency. They said she was an alien, and insisted on seeing her naked feet. On a second occasion, Dan alone abducted Mrs Cortile, took her to a beach on Long Island, and forced her to wear a night-gown similar to the one she had worn that night. He said he did this to check whether it really was Mrs Cortile he had seen on the night of the abduction. She said he also attempted to rape her. In a letter to Hopkins in September 1991, Dan explained that the Third Man had suddenly recalled being on a beach with Mrs Cortile seconds after they had seen her being abducted. Hopkins concluded that all three men had been abducted too. Apparently, the aliens were using Mrs Cortile – who they referred to as the 'Lady of the Sands' – to explain to the 'leading politician' the damage that humankind was doing to the environment. Mrs Cortile's subsequent hypnotic regressions confirmed this. And Richard had proof. The aliens had been collecting sand samples for analysis and he had managed pick up some of it while aboard the alien craft. On 20 May 1992, Richard sent Hopkins two small bags of sand. He had taken one sample from a 'contraption with metal-like pipes or tubes inside it,' Richard said. The other, contained sand he had found in his shoe. Afterwards he had put the samples away in a drawer and forgot about them.

Hopkins sent the samples to the University of Nevada for analysis. Chemically the samples were almost identical, though an electron microscope revealed that they differed considerably in grain size. The sample from the machine also had a slightly higher lead content. Hopkins could not figure out what this meant. The researchers at the University of Nevada were puzzled too. They could not figure out what they were supposed to be looking for.

Then Hopkins discovered that Richard and Mrs Cortile had both been abducted together all their lives, and that Richard may have been the father of Cortile's son. Dan apparently went insane. This made him 'an official problem' and he disappeared. This spooked Mrs Cortile, who hired a private detective to protect her.

On 20 October 1991 Mrs Cortile woke to find her face and pillow covered with blood and concluded that she had had a nosebleed during the night. She called Hopkins to tell him about it. In passing she mentioned that a week before, her niece, a chiropodist, had taken an X-ray of her head because, since childhood, she had a lump on her nose and scarring inside her nasal cavity that doctors could not account for. However, an examination of the X-ray provided the answer. There was a tiny, cylindrical object lodged up her nose. A second X-ray was taken, which showed no such object. Hopkins deduced that Mrs Cortile had been abducted again and the object had been removed – hence the nosebleed. Further hypnosis revealed that, when she had been abducted in 1975, an alien had used a long needle to insert a similar object up her right nostril. When she was regressed again in 1992, she recalled that an alien had entered her apartment on the night of the nosebleed and removed an object, which it had called a 'regulator'.

No matter how bizarre things became, more witnesses came forward to verify Mrs Cortile's abduction in November 1989. Nevertheless, sceptics still pour scorn on the case. They point out that, over the years, no one but Mrs Cortile and her family have ever seen Richard and Dan. All their communication with Hopkins has been via letter or tape. Hopkins has failed to prove that the two men exist to the sceptics' satisfaction. Perez de Cuellar has denied being in a stalled car on the night in question. And he has not admitted that he was involved in an alien abduction.

Sceptics also point out that if Mrs Cortile had been abducted by a huge illuminated UFO hovering over FDR Drive, even at 3:30 in the morning, there should have been thousands of witnesses. The freeway would have been littered with stalled cars, but the event did not even make the newspapers. Neither the workers at the nearby loading bay of the *New York Post* nor the 24-hour security staff at Mrs Cortile's apartment block reported seeing a UFO.

Hopkins' integrity is above question. No one would suggest that he would fake a case. So the sceptics have no choice but to point the finger of suspicion at Mrs Cortile, and Hopkins is merely being a dupe. UFO sceptic Philip Klass says: 'Hopkins does not consider the possibility that the Dan and Richard letters were authored by Mrs Cortile herself.' But Hopkins sympathises with witnesses like Richard and Dan who are reluctant to go public 'especially when you get someone like Philip Klass waiting in the wings to pounce when they come out; it's witness harassment… blatantly dishonest and cruel'.

Klass was also suspicious that each new revelation by Richard and Dan was immediately confirmed by Mrs Cortile under hypnosis. But Hopkins points out that there is not a shred of evidence of a conspiracy. If Mrs Cortile was the lynch pin of a huge hoax, her co-conspirators would have to have included her young sons, Stephen and John, and her husband Steve, who all met Richard and could describe his physical appearance. Somehow she would also have had to co-opt 'Janet Kimball', the pseudonym of another eyewitness who claimed to have seen the abduction, and Lisa Bayer, her niece, the chiropodist who took the X-rays of the alien implant found in her nose, and a number of other friends and neighbours.

'The basic rule for a scam is you don't have a cast of thousands,' says Hopkins. 'Besides, how could it be maintained for so long?'

The Third Man, whoever he was, also plied Mrs Cortile and her family with expensive gifts – which had to be paid for. A hoax would also have required detailed planning, Oscar-winning acting and the ability to memorise complex narratives and descriptions.

As Mrs Cortile points out: "It would take Bobby Fischer [US chess grandmaster] to come up with this hoax. Only one per cent of people have a Bobby Fischer mind, so I should take it as a compliment.'

She accuses her denigrators of being not sceptics but debunkers. 'If a person is intelligent but has a closed mind, they can't learn anything.

That makes them a moron,' she says. On the other hand, 'this isn't something anyone wants to believe – especially me.'

'Scepticism is fine,' says Hopkins. 'I approach all my new cases as a sceptic – but most sceptics will hear fifty pieces of supporting evidence but look at the fifty-first and find something about it that makes them sweep the rest of the evidence away.'

Mrs Cortile's abductions stopped in 1993. She thinks this was because she was getting older and no longer has the eggs that her abductors were looking for. By that time she was no longer convinced that the UFO that abducted her was manned by extraterrestrials. She had come to believe that her abduction could have been a military experiment and points out that there is a military base not far away on Governor's Island. This was where the 'Third Man's' car was headed, she thinks.

Communion

It is the night after Christmas Day 1985. Before going to bed, a man sets the alarm and locks the doors of his house in the country, a couple of hours' drive north of New York City. He retires for the night earlier than usual, but in the small hours of the morning a disturbance wakes him. He sits up in bed, but the panel in the bedroom shows that no burglar alarm has been tripped.

He wonders whether to get dressed and take a look outside. The snow-covered grounds around the house might show footprints. But he finds himself stricken with fear. Sleep seems out of the question, but he relaxes and gradually begins to drift off. Suddenly he is awoken again by a strange noise. He senses a presence in the room. In panic, he reaches for the light switch. As he moves, he sees a shape flying towards him at incredible speed.

The freezing temperature outside brings him around, but he still feels as if he is in a dream. There are strange creatures all around him. Suddenly he feels a tremendous sensation of acceleration and sees the forest floor receding below him. Then he blacks out again.

Next time he awakes, he finds himself in a small, foul-smelling circular room. A strange being – hairless, thin and about five feet tall – appears. There is barely a trace of a nose or a mouth, but its eyes are mesmerising. They are bulging, slanted and as black as night.

Without warning, a needle is inserted into the man's brain. A cut is made in his forefinger and he is given by a painful anal probe. The next thing he knows, he is all alone in the forest in the morning sunlight.

Is this story familiar? It should be. It is an account of the abduction of Whitley Strieber, whose book – and subsequent film – *Communion* made him the world's most famous abductee. In the book, he claims to be the victim of multiple abductions. In fact, his whole life is plagued by little bug-eyed aliens stomping around his home at night and whisking him off for proctology practice.

Strieber was born in San Antonio, Texas, the son of a wealthy lawyer. As a child, he was fascinated by the space race and once, as a joke, his school friends painted him green. He was always talking about little green men. He graduated from the University of Texas and went to film school in London. Then he moved back to New York where he worked in advertising, though he spent much of his free time studying witchcraft and mysticism.

In his thirties, he decided to become a writer and in 1978 he published *The Wolfen*, which was about a pack of super-wolves who roam Manhattan, ripping people's throats out. It was made into a movie. The book was followed by *The Hunger* about a romance between a couple of high-school vampires. He continued in the vein of horror-thriller with supernatural overtones. In one book, *Cat Magic*, the female protagonist is abducted by fairies – small humanoids who have 'sharp faces with pointed noses and large eyes'. They take great delight in examining her both physically and mentally.

Another trend in his fiction was the claim that his books were true stories, though related by fictional characters. But in the futuristic book *Warday*, which Strieber co-wrote with James Kunetka, the two authors wrote as themselves, only fictionalising their future experiences in the book. So the line between fact and fiction had become well and truly blurred.

Then it happened. On 4 October 1985 Strieber, his wife Anne and their son Andrew, along with their friends Jacques Sandulescu and Annie Gottlieb, who were both writers, went to stay in the Striebers' cabin in upstate New York for the weekend. That night, it was foggy and Strieber lit the stove. He woke to find a blue light shining on the ceiling. He was frightened. The cabin was out in the woods and he could not see the headlights of passing traffic. In his sleepy state, it passed through his mind that the chimney might be on fire. Then he fell back into a deep sleep.

Later he was awoken by a loud bang. It woke his wife and he could hear his son downstairs shouting. When he opened his eyes he found the cabin was shrouded in a glow that extended out into the fog. He cursed himself for falling back asleep. Now the roof was on fire. He told his wife that he would go and get their son. She should wake the others. But before he could get downstairs the glow suddenly disappeared. In the morning, Jacques Sandulescu mentioned that he had been bothered by a light the night before, but nothing more was said.

Later that week Strieber found himself increasingly disturbed by the incident. Then he suddenly remembered seeing a huge crystal, hundreds of feet tall, standing on end over the house. It was emitting the strange blue glow. His wife thought he was crazy.

Slowly, in Strieber's mind, the cabin became a dark and terrible place. New York City also seemed dangerous and he decided to move back to Texas. Strieber and his wife went down to Austin in November. But when he saw the house that they intended to buy, he became paranoid. The huge Texas sky, he thought, was a living thing. And it was watching him. He cancelled the plans to move to Texas. His wife was furious. If he did not pull himself together, she said, she would leave him.

Strieber put aside his fears until they went up to the cabin again at Christmas. The night of 26 December 1985 was the night it happened. He awoke, he said, to hear a peculiar sound, as if lots of people were running around downstairs. Suddenly a small figure flew at him. He lost consciousness. Next, he got the impression that he was being carried. He awoke to find himself in a small depression out in the woods. He was paralysed and someone was doing something to the side of his head. The next thing he knew, he was travelling upwards high above the forest. He found himself in a circular room. It was messy and he was terrified. Small creatures were scurrying around him. They inserted a needle into his brain. Then they examined his rectum with a probe, possibly to take a sample of faecal matter, but leaving Strieber with the distinct impression that he was being anally raped. Then they cut his forefinger.

Strieber awoke back in his bed in the cabin. He felt a distinct sense of unease. He read a report in the newspapers about a UFO being sighted over upstate New York that night. His brother had bought him a book about UFOs for Christmas. He tried to read it but, for no reason, it frightened him. He ploughed on though. Finally he got to the chapter about alien abductions and everything began to make sense.

Back in New York City, he got the number of UFO abduction researcher Budd Hopkins from the telephone book and phoned him. Hopkins suggested that he investigate the events of the night of 4 October, as then he had witnesses. His wife remembered being awakened by the bang, but did not remember the glow. Jacques Sandulescu remembered the light, but neither of them could come up with an explanation for it. Strieber's son had the most interesting recollection. When he had heard the bang, he had been told that it was okay because his father had just thrown a shoe at a fly. 'Told by who?' he was asked.

'A bunch of little doctors,' he said. He had dreamt that a bunch of little doctors had carried him out on to the porch. They had told him telepathically that they were not going to hurt him. The boy said it was the strangest dream because it was 'just like real'.

At Hopkins' suggestion, Strieber went to see a therapist. He had been feeling suicidal. He also suggested regressive hypnosis. After a couple of weeks, Strieber dropped the therapy, but kept on with the hypnosis.

At the first session, Strieber was regressed to 4 October. He recalled seeing something flash past the window. Then came the light. He saw a goblin wearing a cloak in the corner of the bedroom. It rushed at him and struck him on the forehead with a wand. At this point, Strieber screamed so hard that he came out of the hypnotic trance. When he was put under again, he saw pictures of the world blowing up.

'That's your home,' the goblin said.

Then he saw his son in a park, an image that Strieber associated with death. The goblin said that he would not hurt Strieber. But he took a needle and lit the end. It exploded and Strieber began to think of the house burning down. It was as if the goblin had implanted the image. Then he came out of the trance again.

He went under once more to find out what happened. This time he saw his son dead in the park. Then he saw his father dying. He was sitting in an armchair choking while his mother watched. This was not the scene as his mother described it.

In a later session, Strieber was regressed to 26 December. He recalled being dragged naked from his bedroom by aliens in blue overalls. They dragged him out into the woods and sat him on a chair, which, with a whoosh, propelled him hundreds of feet in the air. Next he was on a bench in a room. There was a female alien there in a tan suit. She stuck something resembling a penis up Strieber's backside and told him that he was 'the chosen one' in a flat Midwestern accent. He scoffed. Then she tried to get him to have an erection. But he could not, fully. He did not fancy her. She had leathery yellow skin and a mouth like an insect, and besides, the atmosphere was rather intimidating. The next thing he knew, he was naked on the living room couch. He went upstairs, put his pyjamas on and went to bed.

Further hypnosis revealed more bizarre abductions. One time, he was in spaceship and saw his sister in her nightie sprawled on an examination table. His father, paralysed, stood beside her. On other tables were soldiers in uniform, unconscious. He was even invited to give a lecture on the evils of the British Empire. Another time, he awoke to find a group of hybrids around his bed. The aliens seemed to be tinkering with his mind, showing him symbols and images that evoked thoughts and memories in his mind.

Outside hypnosis, Strieber's life became more and more bizarre. He woke up one night, paralysed, convinced that a probe had been shoved up into his brain via his nose. He developed nosebleeds. So did his wife and son. Strieber began to smell the odour of aliens around his apartment. Symbols the aliens had shown him appeared on his arm. He suffered the sensation of missing time regularly. He was plagued with bizarre memories and strange phone calls. His stereo began speaking to him. He became so afraid of his apartment that he moved to Connecticut. But when Connecticut proved scary too, he moved back to New York.

Numerous psychological and physical tests were run on him and no-one could find anything wrong. The answer, Strieber concluded, must lie with UFOs. Hopkins plugged him into the UFO network, but he managed to alienate Hopkins' contacts with his eccentricities. Strieber became paranoid about reporters, fearing that, if news of his abduction experiences came out, he would be held up to ridicule, which might damage his career.

Strieber began to feel that he was all written out anyway. His last book had not done well and his abduction experiences were making it impossible for him to work. He decided to confront his fears and write about the abduction itself, though he was not sure whether his experiences were real or whether they were memories from a former life. Nevertheless he produced the manuscript of a book he called *Body Terror*. But one night, when his wife was asleep beside him, she spoke to him in a strange deep voice. She warned him that he should change the title to *Communion*, otherwise he would frighten people.

Strieber circulated the manuscript. According to Hopkins, it came across as something in Strieber's horror-thriller genre, rather than a factual account. In one place, the female alien leads him around by the penis like a dog on a lead. He persuaded Strieber to tone it down a bit. Once he had done this, Strieber secured a million-dollar advance on the book. It was published in 1987, as *Communion: A True Story*. It sold millions worldwide. Strieber has since published four more books in his 'Communion' series.

The Dark Secret of Dulce

In the late 1980s UFO investigator Paul Bennewitz received a report of an alien abduction in New Mexico. At first it seemed to fit the classic abduction pattern. The majority of abduction cases begin with unaccompanied people seeing strange lights in the sky. Before they know it, they are face to face with a creature from another world. Then they are taken aboard a spacecraft, where they undergo an intimate physical examination. Afterwards, they are returned to the place they were taken from, somewhat shaken. Often they have no memory of what has happened. The only clues that something strange has occurred are mysterious marks on their bodies and the discovery that there was 'missing' time that they could not account for. And the only way what happened can be revealed is through the controversial technique of regressional hypnosis. However, when Bennewitz read further into the case, he started to suspect that the abduction was only a small part of a far greater mystery.

The abductee, Christa Tilton of Oklahoma, said that she had been kidnapped in July 1987 by two small 'Grey' aliens. Regressional hypnosis revealed that she had been forced into a saucer-shaped spacecraft. But then her story began to differ from the regular pattern. The alien craft took her to a secret hillside location. There she was handed over to a man wearing a red military-style one-piece suit. He took her down a tunnel lined with security cameras. She passed through computerised check-points, then she was put on transit vehicle which took her to another area. There she was made to stand on a device that looked like a weighing machine, though instead of a dial it had a computer screen.

Tilton was issued with an identity card, and told that she had just entered level one of an underground facility. As the ordeal continued, the terrified abductee was taken down to level five, where she saw more of the strange grey creatures that had abducted her. The facility also housed a number of spacecraft like the one that had brought her there.

In another enormous chamber she saw a series of large tanks. They smelled of formaldehyde and were linked up to computerised gauges. She had no idea what was in the tanks, but later she was able to make drawings of them. It was these drawings that impressed Paul Bennewitz. He had seen them before. Just a few months earlier, he had seen an almost identical series of sketches. These had been part of a document entitled *The Dulce Papers*, which was put together by former Dulce Base Security Officer Thomas Edwin Castello, explaining what he had seen at the top-secret facility.

Theories Galore

The Starchild Theory

There is a theory that aliens are conducting some genetic experiment on earth. They are taking women and impregnating them with starchildren. A typical victim is a woman, Helen, who had been having terrible encounters with UFOs and aliens for years. They had come at night since she was a child. She tried to convince herself that her nocturnal visitors were merely vivid dreams, but the time she spent in a cold room being prodded by small, grey-skinned, hairless creatures with strange, slanting eyes who probed her with strange instruments felt terribly real.

Then, one day in 1989, something different happened. Again she had been abducted at night and taken to the same cold room; this time one of her captors held a tiny baby, perhaps just a few days old. Helen took it and, when she examined it closely, she saw that it seemed to share both human and alien features. Normally she would have found its appearance repellent. Instead she was overcome with maternal feelings.

She felt like a new mother being shown her child for the first time. And as she cuddled it close, the aliens close by watched in fascination.

Helen was the latest in a long line of women used by aliens in strange reproduction experiments. Men too have had semen samples taken during abductions. Some UFOlogists believe the alien visitors are trying to breed a race of hybrids – half human, half extraterrestrial.

The first clue to this came in October 1957, when the Brazilian farmer Antonio Villas-Boas was led aboard a UFO by several small, humanoid creatures, before being seduced by a beautiful female alien with bright red pubic hair. Afterwards she pointed to her belly and to the sky in a gesture that he interpreted to mean that she was going to have his baby up somewhere in out space.

Villas-Boas was rather embarrassed by the tale, and spoke of it at length only to a doctor in Rio de Janeiro, who found he was suffering from mild radiation sickness. The story was not published in Brazil for many years, but it was logged with the British UFO journal, *Flying Saucer Review*, which eventually published it in 1964.

Three weeks after Villas-Boas was abducted, a related encounter occurred in England. There was a flash of light that left scorch marks on an old newspaper in the Birmingham home of a young mother, Cynthia Appleton, and an alien with long, blond hair materialised. During this visit, and several others over the coming months, the alien told Mrs Appleton about the dangers of atomic energy. In later visits, some of which were witnessed by Mrs Appleton's daughter, the alien gave up its flashy entrances and arrived in an old-fashioned suit and a dark car, as if it were a Man in Black.

On one of these visits he told Cynthia she was pregnant. It was a boy. He would be a fair-haired boy. The alien told her when the baby would be born, the birth weight and the name he should be given. Mrs Appleton dashed to her doctor, who confirmed that was indeed pregnant and that she had conceived around the time of the alien's first visit. After that, the blond-haired alien made one last visit to assure Mrs Appleton that, though her son was the product of the alien race, he had been fathered by her husband. Mr Appleton's reaction has not been recorded.

It was later discovered that Cynthia Appleton's pregnancy was not the first time that the aliens had brought a little bundle of joy to Earth. In 1950, in the town of Anthony, Kansas, a young farming couple were awoken by a UFO. They went outside to investigate and encountered a glowing figure. It announced that the woman was pregnant with a baby 'sent' by the aliens and that the child would grow up to spread the word of their presence.

The woman was indeed pregnant and had a baby daughter, but the couple decided that it was best not to tell the child of their encounter. The girl's name was Donna Butts. She grew up unaware of her alien ancestry, married and had a family of her own, but her extraterrestrial heritage could not be denied. In November 1980, while driving with her family outside Topeka, Kansas, they got stuck behind a truck. Suddenly the sky was filled with a beam of light. The next thing anyone knew, they were driving into Topeka itself. The miles in between seemed to have vanished miraculously.

When Donna told the story to her parents, they told her about her conception. Under regressional hypnosis, she remembered being abducted by Greys. They had told her that human civilisation was entering its 'end times' and that she was one of the alien emissaries on Earth who would help guide humankind into the new millennium. Since then, she has met up with other 'starchildren' who are the progeny of the alien's hybridisation scheme. We do not know whether Cynthia Appleton's son was one of these.

The type of blond-haired Nordic-type aliens that brought Cynthia Appleton her little surprise appeared in Latin America and confessed. On 7 August 1965, at San Pedro de los Altos, thirty miles south of Caracas in Venezuela, two businessmen and a gynaecologist were visiting a stud farm when there was a brilliant flash of light. A spherical craft drifted to the ground making a soft humming noise. Two Nordics in silver suits then got out. The men were terrified, but the aliens told them, telepathically, to be calm. They explained that they were from Orion. They had come to Earth to study the psyches of humans and adapt them to their own species and to check out the possibility of 'inter-breeding to create a new species'. What better place to start than at a stud farm?

They also explained that, while they were pretty well disposed towards human beings, there was another race of aliens – Small Greys – visiting Earth who were less benign.

The aliens' genetic agenda has in fact been plain from the outset. In the first publicised alien abduction case – that of Betty and Barney Hill in the White Mountains of New Hampshire in September 1961 – sperm samples were taken from Barney and what was termed 'a pregnancy test' attempted on Betty. After that there was a tidal wave of alien contacts, all of which involved intimate examinations and genetic experimentation.

In December 1967 a highway patrolman, Herb Schirmer, had a close encounter at Ashland, Nebraska. The aliens had told him they were undertaking a 'breeding analysis programme', but they did not go into details. On 3 May 1968 nineteen-year-old nurse's aide, Shane Kurz, was abducted by a UFO. Afterwards, she found a red ring around her abdomen and stopped menstruating. A gynaecologist was baffled by her case and a hypnotist was called in. It was then discovered that the aliens had extracted ova from her, telling her that she had 'been chosen to have a baby for us'.

In October 1974, an entire family was abducted from their car on a quiet road in Essex. Inside the UFO were two types of being: tall humanoid entities that seemed to be in control and small squat Greys that conducted medical tests – an all too familiar aspect of these abductions. However, in this case, the family was also given a tour of the craft and shown a series of films. These told of the aliens' genetically barren home world. The aliens said that they had come to Earth to ensure we did not go the same way as they had done, explaining: 'You are our children. You are part of an experiment.'

Meanwhile, in Rawlins, Wyoming, in 1974, a hunter was abducted – only to be rejected by the aliens because he had had a vasectomy. Elsie Oakensen was abducted by a dumb-bell-shaped UFO near

Church Stowe in Northamptonshire, only to be rejected because she was too old. She was given healing powers as a consolation prize. The aliens then abducted three young women from nearby Preston Capes. And on 15 October 1979, a postmenopausal concert pianist, Luli Oswald, was abducted while driving down a coastal road in Brazil. She was given a gynaecological examination, but rejected. However, her companion, a twenty-five-year-old student, was accepted into the alien programme.

In 1980, aliens removed eggs from a Finnish abductee's ovaries using a long tube. Again she was told her that their race was genetically sterile, but that they had found within humanity an unexpectedly rich gene pool. This was helping them keep their species alive.

Female abductees often find themselves pregnant after an encounter. One Lancashire woman was shocked to find herself pregnant – she did not even have a boyfriend at the time. However, she had been abducted a few days before and gynaecologically examined by a female alien. After a few weeks, she miscarried, losing a large amount of blood. By then she was convinced the aliens had impregnated her, then taken the foetus which continued its development elsewhere.

In a study of fifty British abduction cases, it was found that four women became unexpectedly pregnant immediately after their encounter, then had a mysterious miscarriage within three months. One case involved a young woman called Karen. In 1979 she and her boyfriend had taken a holiday job in Cornwall. One night, Karen had a close encounter with a strange and blinding light. When she return home to Cheshire she found herself pregnant, but she was plagued with strange dreams. In them, she would have the baby, but it would have an odd appearance and preternatural intelligence. But three months into her pregnancy, Karen awoke to find her bed covered in blood. She was no longer pregnant, but instead of feeling bereft, because of the dreams, she felt relieved. This, in turn, brought on a terrible sense of guilt. But this was by no means the end of the matter. Karen went on to have a number of other strange encounters with UFOs and aliens. Then, in early 1987, she awoke in the middle of the night to find herself holding the hand of a small child. A ball of light rose upwards through the ceiling and the child vanished. It was a brief encounter, but it brought her comfort. She felt that the child she had lost to the aliens had returned briefly to show her that it had survived and was flourishing in some other realm.

There is some physical proof of the 'starchild' theory. It was unearthed in the 1930s, when a teenage American girl was taken by her parents to visit relatives in a small rural village about a hundred miles south-west of Chihuahua in northern Mexico. There were numerous caves and mine shafts in the area and, for her own safety, her parents told her not to go near them. But she was a teen ager and a warning was not going to stop her.

One day, while exploring a disused mine shaft in the hills, she found a human skeleton lying on the ground. The skeleton's hand was holding a malformed skeletal hand that was sticking up out of the ground beside it. The girl scraped away the dirt to find a shallow grave. The malformed hand was attached to another complete skeleton. This was smaller than the first and terribly deformed.

As her parents had forbidden her to explore the caves and tunnels, she could hardly tell them about her find. But she took the two skulls and kept them for the rest of her life. When she died, they came into the possession of an American couple, who knew something of the story of their discovery. They had read researcher Lloyd Pye's book *Everything You Know Is Wrong – Book One: Human Origins* and, in February 1999, they went to see him to discuss the skulls. In particular, they wanted his opinion of the smaller of the two skulls which, although clearly humanoid, was like nothing they had ever seen before.

'I nearly fell from my chair when they handed it to me,' he said. 'It was precisely how I imaged a "Grey" skull might look, and I felt strongly from the first moment that it was at least partially alien.'

The couple hoped that Pye would arrange to have a scientific study performed on the skull to determine if it belonged to a poor, misshapen human child, or something else entirely. Pye was happy to oblige and began talking to various anthropologists, pathologists, dentists, ophthalmologists, paediatricians, radiologists and anyone else with specialised knowledge who might help.

The couple were not rich and Pye had no funding for the research but various experts in the field examined the skull as a favour. The larger skull had a confusing mixture of cranial features, but in general it looked more female than male. It had cheekbones that could belong to either sex. But it had the slender brow ridge of a female and it was small and light compared with human norms. All but one of the teeth, a rear molar, were present. The cusps of the teeth were worn flat, and the dentists guessed that it would require no less than twenty years of eating grit-laced food to cause such cusp wear. The consensus was that the skull belonged to a female in her late twenties.

The upper jaw had become detached from the other skull. Technically it could not be considered part of the other skull without expensive DNA matching, but it was of the right size and carried a similar pattern of staining. It seemed a sure bet that it did belong to the skull, though. It carried the only two teeth of the smaller skull. These were milk teeth and were about to be replaced by adult molars. It was concluded that the second skull belonged to a child of five or six years old.

However, not all the experts agreed. Some pointed to a cranial suture between the lower left parietal area and the upper left occipital bone on the left rear quadrant of the head. Here, there was a three-inch line of small 'islands' of bone. These grow to fill in gaps appearing in suture lines during periods of rapid, sustained growth – such as those that take place during adolescence. Those islands made the skull appear much older than five years – it could have belonged to a fifteen year old.

Pye then began to consider the details of how the skulls were found. Unfortunately, the girl who had first discovered the skeletons years before was not alive and could not be questioned. He was particularly interested in the malformation of the smaller skeleton, but there was no way that this could be determined. But details of how they had been found intrigued him. One skeleton being above the ground with its hand holding that of the buried skeleton led him to postulate that the two individuals had died in some kind of murder suicide pact, with the older one killing the younger and burying it before taking her own life.

During his investigation, Pye discovered that there was a legend concerning 'Star Beings' throughout the whole of Latin America. This legend concerns extraterrestrials – types we now call Greys – who impregnate native women. The offspring would be allowed to stay with their mother until the age of six or so, then they would be repossessed by the aliens.

Pye realised that the 'Star Being' legend tied in perfectly with his murder–suicide scenario. Imagine a woman in her late twenties who had been impregnated by an alien. She gave birth and had raised the hybrid child to the age of around six, when the pick-up time was approaching. Then she somehow received word that the aliens were coming to retrieve her child. But she was not willing to give it up. Instead of letting the aliens take it away to some unknown fate, she took it into a mine shaft, killed it and buried it in a shallow grave, leaving one of its hands sticking up out of ground. Then she held onto her child's hand as she poisoned herself and lay down beside the child's body to die.

The woman concerned would have to be in some kind of state to do such a thing and Pye found evidence of a blow to the larger skull's left parietal bone above and to the rear of the left ear not long before death. This would have caused concussion, just the sort of brain-addling injury that might have caused a loving mother to put such a lethal scheme into action, he reckons.

During Pye's investigation, he was contacted by Mrs Karen Scheidt. She had a photograph of similar 'starchild' skulls, which she had taken while holidaying in Cholula, northern Mexico in 1975. The guide told her that the two skulls belonged to 'gods' that had come down from the sky centuries before to teach the local people astronomy, mathematics and how to live in harmony with nature. These gods were planning to return to their home in the heavens. Before they could do so, another bunch of gods turned up. There was an almighty battle and the two gods were killed. They were buried in a small shrine near the main temple at Cholula, which became a place of pilgrimage for the local people.

New Religion

So is the modern-day belief in UFOs really a new religion that mirrors the needs and beliefs of those who live in the new scientific age? Certainly people had seen things flying around in the sky before 1947 when Kenneth Arnold inadvertently dubbed them 'flying saucers'. Indeed, Christ was seen to ascend into the sky after his 'death' on the cross.

Consider this for an alien encounter. At a time of great upheaval in the world, a humanoid being appeared to three witnesses and announces that it is 'from above'. For the next six months, they have traumatic visions. When the being leaves, an estimated 50,000 to 70,000 people see what they called the 'Dance of the Sun'. The shining disc descends through the clouds, spins and dives towards the Earth in a flash of light and heat. This would normally be considered a first class alien encounter report. Only it is the story of the so-called 'visions at Fatima' where the Virgin Mary appeared to three young girls in Portugal in 1917.

In ancient times all heavenly objects had a religious significance – whether they came from God or Satan. However, with the retreat of religion at the end of the nineteenth century, few admitted to seeing flying angels. Objects seen in the skies were just one of many mysteries that were subsequently called 'Fortean', after writer and investigator Charles Fort (1874–1932). Fortean investigators simply referred to such anomalous bodies as 'objects seen floating'. But, after Kenneth Arnold, flying saucers acquired a status of their own.

The explosion of interest in UFOs and the mythologies that surround them have led many to compare it to the founding of a new religion. UFOs and their alien occupants live in a sphere far higher than that occupied by mere terrestrials. Although Kenneth Arnold reported his sighting because he believed that what he had witnessed might be Soviet military hardware, the idea that anomalous objects and lights in the sky were aliens visiting from outer space caught on very quickly.

Because of the birth of aerial bombings, the development of ballistic missiles and the dropping of the atomic bomb, people naturally had their eyes on the skies. These unprecedented technological advances also spawned the idea that there was a great deal more in the scientific world that we did not understand. But maybe, there was someone out there who did. Certainly the impossible manoeuvrings of UFOs suggested that there was.

It was some time before reports of the 'beings' that pilot flying saucers emerged. UFO research groups tried to suppress the accounts of contactees. However, when they did speak out about their encounters it seemed that the aliens had a message for us. George Adamski encountered an alien 1952, who warned him that Earth must learn to control its use of nuclear energy. Coincidentally, Adamski met his 'Venusian' just three weeks after America exploded the first hydrogen bomb.

Adamski made no secret of the religious dimension of his testimony. Many saw him as a modern-day prophet. He was an emissary of some heavenly force bringing higher wisdom to humanity whose folly risked bringing down the apocalypse. It is not difficult to see how such ideas could have taken hold.

From the beginnings of the scientific revolution in the West, a belief system based on religion had been replaced by scientific reason and logic. In 1843, John Stuart Mill published *A System of Logic*, which was closely followed by Charles Darwin's *On The Origin of Species* in 1858. These writings undermined organised religion. With other works, they set out 'the scientific principle', which rejected as 'unreal' anything that was not amenable to reason or scientific experiment.

Science brought with it tangible benefits – the automobile,

electric light, the aeroplane, everything that was modern and new. It also brought with it the mechanised slaughter of the First and Second World Wars. By the 1950s, the dream of science was becoming a little tarnished. The shadow of the 'Bomb' that hung over world affairs brought widespread disillusionment with the very real achievements of science. Scientists were portrayed as 'Frankensteins' who had created the monster that would destroy civilisation, humankind and the planet. However this did not halt the decline of the old religions. What was needed was something new.

It was into this world that Erich von Däniken launched his book *Chariots of the Gods*. The book contained the radical proposition that humanity had, in the past, been seeded by extraterrestrials whom our ancestors later mistook for gods. The book became an instant bestseller and turned von Däniken into a world-wide celebrity. He had hit the mood of the moment, and his later books became enormously influential.

His book emerged at a time when many were desperate for something to believe in. The old religions had been largely discredited by science, and science itself was tainted. What von Däniken did was give his readers the best of both worlds. His 'gods' were tangible and real and, if you will, scientific. They brought to Earth the wisdom of the heavens. What's more, unlike the gods of the old religions, von Däniken's were, like scientific theories, open to testing. The existence of his 'gods' could be proved – if you proved that flying saucers existed.

Although science has set its face against UFOlogy, in the same way it attacked the old religions, the UFO phenomenon exists within the realm of science itself. Its extraterrestrial 'gods' are not metaphysical beings but scientists – only they are better than our terrestrial scientists because they can fly effortlessly among the stars.

Until cast-iron proof of the existence of alien visitors is produced, the idea of extraterrestrials should be considered a myth. But why do we need myths? They seem to be vital to human life. No culture we know of has ever existed that did not have a mythology. 'Myth is a dramatic shorthand record of such matters as invasions, migrations, dynastic changes, admission of foreign cults, and social reforms,' said scholar of mythology Robert Graves. In other words, myths are the metaphors through which we make sense of the world in which we live. So modern myths must encompass the awesome power of technology, a distrust of government, the need for wisdom and knowledge from a source that is untainted and the desire for salvation in a world where God has all but been destroyed. UFO mythology involves all of this. Not only are extraterrestrials more technologically advanced than we are, they are able to control technology in a way that we have yet to achieve. The fact that governments are deemed to be withholding UFO secrets speaks volumes about our alienation from the political process. Extraterrestrials bring wisdom and they offer us transportation into a higher realm. They fulfil the emotional and spiritual needs that science and rationalism have failed to provide for and have given us the gods back again, but this time, as scientifically acceptable gods. In *The Republic*, Plato pondered whether one myth could be constructed that would be believable and meaningful to the whole world. Perhaps that it what UFOs provide.

Heaven's Gate

The quasi-religious UFO theories of Marshall Applewhite, leader of the Heaven's Gate cult, had lethal consequences for his followers. His belief that a UFO was heading towards Earth in the wake of the Hale–Bopp comet to take his followers to the 'Next Level' led to the biggest mass suicide in North America.

It became clear that something was terribly wrong when, on 25 March 1997, Federal Express delivered a package of videocassettes to the San Diego, California, home of ex-cult member Richard Ford. The tapes were from Marshall Applewhite. When Ford played the cassettes, he found that they were essentially videotaped suicide notes, with cult members giving what they termed 'exit statements'. Ford showed his employer the tape and they went to the cult's headquarters at Rancho Santa Fe, a secluded mansion on the outskirts of San Diego.

Inside, they found the bodies of thirty-nine cult members – eighteen men and twenty-one women – in various stages of decomposition. Death had been caused by a lethal cocktail of vodka and phenobarbitol, a powerful sedative.

There was no sign of rush or panic. It was plain the mass suicide had been rigorously planned. All the victims were dressed in the same dark outfits and wore new trainers. They had their hands by their sides and they were staring at the ceiling through a three-foot square of purple silk, folded into a triangle pointing downwards. Many of the corpses were neatly arranged in their beds, which suggested that the suicides had been carried out in shifts. Their bags were packed and they carried identification details in their shirt pockets. It seemed inexplicable that so many people had gone to their deaths without putting up a struggle.

Many more people – over nine hundred – had died at Jonestown but some had struggled and others escaped. The cult was facing a Congressional enquiry and, basically, the game was up for cult leader Jim Jones. More died at Waco, but the eighty-one Branch Davidians who perished there died during a shoot-out with the FBI. Some seventy members of the Solar Temple died believing that they would be reincarnated on Sirius if they died a fiery death on Earth. However, some were murdered by their leaders, who were under investigation for fraud. The Heaven's Gate deaths were different. They was no confrontation with the authorities and, seemingly, no coercion. Applewhite and his followers had gone peacefully into the arms of death.

They had made no secret of their plans. From 1993 onwards, Heaven's Gate had promoted itself as the 'last chance to advance beyond human'. They had taken advertisements in the national press and ran a website announcing their intention to leave this Earth. However, Applewhite promised his followers that they would taken aboard a UFO. For that reason, Heaven's Gate had been dubbed the 'UFO cult'.

Born in Spur, Texas on 17 May 1931, Applewhite was the son of a

Presbyterian minister. He attended Austin College in Sherman, Texas, and it was thought that Applewhite would follow his father into the seminary. Instead, he decided to pursue a career in music. A talented singer, he took the lead in the college productions of *Oklahoma!* and *South Pacific*. He later sang at the Houston Grand Opera, then became music professor at a Catholic college in Houston. In the 1950s, he married and had two children and led a conventional life. Then a string of homosexual affairs over a period of three years at the end of the 1960s ruined his marriage, and he was sacked from his college post after a scandal involving the daughter of a trustee. In 1971 Applewhite booked himself into a mental hospital in Houston, Texas, and begged to be 'cured' of his homosexuality.

There, he met Bonnie 'Lu' Nettles, a psychiatric nurse who, like Applewhite, came from a deeply religious background. Nettles abandoned her family and she and Applewhite went on the road as New Age gurus, while wandering around the US under a variety of names, including 'Brother Sun' and 'Sister Moon', 'Him' and 'Her', and 'Bo' and 'Peep'.

Applewhite and Nettles claimed to have been sent to Earth by a spaceship to teach humans how to attain a level beyond Earth. Together they set up a cult called Human Individual Metamorphosis (HIM) in California. Followers had to give up their names and their property and become celibate. However, HIM fell apart after various prophecies failed.

For a while, Applewhite and Nettles supported themselves by stealing cars and credit card fraud. Then in 1973, Applewhite had a revelation that they were the biblical 'Two Witnesses' who would rise from the dead before ascending to heaven in a cloud. A year later, the cloud became a UFO. By this time, Nettles and Applewhite, now referring to themselves as 'The Two', had begun to attract devotees and they organised them into a new UFO cult. They moved back to Texas, where Applewhite took out a full-page advertisement that invited people to join. The cult used the names Total Overcomers Anonymous and Higher Source. Those who responded were sent a video showing Applewhite and two zonked-out followers who appeared to hang on every word that issued from the guru's lips. As with all such cults, their philosophy centred around total acceptance of the leaders' ideas, no matter how bizarre.

Yet, far from alienating potential members, it was the cult's more extreme ideas concerning UFOs that actually drew in new recruits. Indeed, when, in the mid-1970s, this mythology was propounded in a series of public lectures, the result was to bolster the cult's membership and considerably increase its media profile.

UFO Magazine published a feature on the cult. In it, Applewhite referred to himself as Do and Nettles as Te. It is thought that these were taken from the notes played to signal the aliens in the film *Close Encounters of the Third Kind*. However, there may have been another influence. Do – who also called himself Father John Doe and even King Do – had a special affection for *The Sound of Music*. Te in that film was, like the poison the suicide cult took, a 'drink with jam and bread, which takes you back to Do'. Other cult members were called Re, So and Fah. This may sound ludicrous, but Applewhite was painfully serious. He and some of his senior lieutenants had themselves castrated so that they could more easily live up to Applewhite's requirement that they should be totally celibate.

With media interest came paranoia. 'The Two' were plagued by the fear of assassination and throughout the late 1970s and into the 1980s the group became a shadowy entity, adopting several different names and living in a series of camps across Arizona, California and Montana. This did nothing to dent Applewhite and Nettles' growing cult status and, in 1982, they were made the subject of a TV film entitled *The Mysterious Two*. Afterwards, Applewhite outlined his beliefs in a screenplay called *Beyond Human: Return of the Next Level*. The American TV network NBC expressed interest.

Nettles' death from cancer in 1985 was a blow. But Applewhite soon decided that she had merely left for the 'Next Level'. He then declared himself to be the 'expected Messiah'. The cult all but disappeared, only to resurface five years later in 1990 with a new name.

The cult moved into a $1.3 million mansion in San Diego County which had once been the home of Douglas Fairbanks Jr. Set in three acres on a hilltop, the lavish retreat was leased to the cult by its owner Sam Koutchesfahani, a convict fraudster who had run a scam that involved bribing colleges to enrol students from the Middle East who had already entered the US illegally.

When the cult members moved in, they had no contact with their millionaire neighbours. They slept on bunk beds. They were not allowed to drink or smoke and they had to cut off all contact with their families. To earn money, they turned to the internet, designing websites. This was highly profitable. The mansion was packed with computers. Their own website advertised their wares.

'Higher Source is very much "in tune" with the current pulse and future direction of technology,' they boasted. What's more, their leaders 'had worked closely together for over twenty years. During those years each of us has developed a high degree of skill and know-how through personal discipline and concerted effort. We try to stay positive in every circumstance and put the good of a project above any personal concerns or artistic egos. This crew-minded effort, combined with ingenuity and creativity, has helped us provide advanced solutions.'

The cult's website also preached Applewhite's paranoid concoction of UFO fantasies and apocalyptic Christianity. Anyone receiving one of Applewhite's e-mail sermons could not help but understand that, for Heaven's Gate, the 'End' was at hand. He made it clear that only by leaving their bodies behind could he and his followers join the ethereal spacecraft that would take them to the 'evolutionary level above human'. In 1996, over the Internet, the cult gave notice of its imminent departure to join the 'Next Level mothership'.

On the night of 22 July 1995, the comet Hale–Bopp had been discovered independently by amateur astronomer Thomas Bopp of Phoenix, Arizona, and Alan Hale, head of the Southwest Institute for Space Research in New Mexico. Then in November 1996, amateur astronomer Chuck Shramek announced on UFOlogist Art Bell's popular radio show that he had seen a strange, unidentified object, which seemed to be travelling alongside the approaching Hale–Bopp comet. Pictures were posted on the Net and prominent UFOlogists such as Whitley Strieber speculated that it might be an alien spaceship. It did not take long for Applewhite to decide that this was the long-awaited shuttle to the 'Next Level'.

Within months the comet was nearing its closest approach to Earth and cult members were finalising their plans to 'shed their containers' (bodies) and 'ascend to the Next Level'. In early March 1997 the cult's website declared their intentions clearly: 'Hale–Bopp's approach is the marker we've been waiting for,' it said. 'We are happily prepared to leave this world.'

One of the cult's clients was the San Diego Polo Club, which asked Higher Source to do some more work for them early the next year. They got an e-mail back saying that Higher Source could not do any work after that Easter, owing to a 'religious festival'.

Cult members wore badges saying they were the 'Heaven's Gate Away Team'. They were an 'away team' in the *Star Trek* sense – a group of crew members that has beamed down to the surface of a planet to visit alien life-forms there. Members thought of themselves as caterpillars. Their bodies were 'vehicles' or 'containers' they could leave behind. The comet Hale–Bopp was 'the sign we've been waiting for'. Following unseen behind it would be 'the spacecraft to take us home'.

Their departure was again announced on the Internet. 'RED ALERT – Hale–Bopp brings closure to Heaven's Gate,' their home page said. By way of explanation, Applewhite added: 'I am in the same position in today's society as the one that Jesus was in... If you want to go to Heaven, I can take you through that gate – it requires everything of you.' The approach of Hale–Bopp meant: 'Our twenty-two years of classroom here on planet Earth is finally coming to conclusion – "graduation" from the Human Evolutionary Level. We are happily prepared to leave "this world" and go with [the spaceship's] crew.'

The website also contained a warning: 'Planet about to be recycled – Your only chance to survive – Leave with us.'

The cult prepared for their departure by sending videos explaining what they were going to do to former cult members.

'By the time you get this we'll be gone – several dozen of us,' said a note accompanying the video that Richard Ford received. 'We came from the Level Above Human in distant space and we have now exited the bodies that we were wearing for our earthly task, to return to the world from whence we came – task completed.'

'We couldn't be happier about what we're about to do,' said one cult member on the video.

'Maybe they're crazy for all I know,' said a woman cultist. 'But I don't have any choice but to go for it, because I've been on this planet for thirty-one years and there's nothing here for me.'

Another female follower, who apparently believed – groundlessly – that Applewhite had terminal cancer, said: 'Once he is gone... there is nothing left here on the face of the Earth for me... no reason to stay a moment longer.'

All thirty-nine of the suicide victims appeared on the tape. They all had their hair cut short, leading the police to believe that they were all young men. In fact, their ages ranged from twenty-six to seventy-two and twenty-one of them were women.

In a second tape, Applewhite gave a long and rambling explanation of their beliefs.

'We came for the express purpose to offer a doorway to the Kingdom of Heaven at the end of this civilisation, the end of the millennium,' he said. 'Your only chance to evacuate is to leave with us. I guess we take the prize of being the cult of cults.'

The videos despatched, the thirty-nine members of the cult went out for a final meal in a local restaurant. They then split themselves into three groups and committed suicide in shifts over the next three days. Applewhite had kindly written out suicide instructions for each member: 'Take pudding or apple sauce and mix it with the medicine' – phenobarbitol – 'drink it down with a vodka mixture and relax.'

This was plainly ineffective. Most of the cult member died of suffocation and the last two suffocated themselves by putting plastic bags over their heads.

When Ford and his employer found the bodies, they called the police. The first two deputies who turned up were rushed to hospital. A Hazard Materials team was sent in to test for poisonous gases. The noxious fumes were discovered to have come from the victims' bodies. These were removed using a refrigerated lorry and a fork-lift truck.

With their containers disposed of by the San Diego Mortuary Department, the cult members' spirits reached the spaceship which took them home – well, no one can tell them that it didn't happen.

Afterwards, the police were on the alert for copycat suicides. Two more followers did indeed try to follow Applewhite in May 1997 even though, presumably, they had missed the ship. Acting on a tip-off from a CBS journalist, police went to a hotel some five miles from Rancho Santa Fe. There they found Wayne Cook from Las Vegas, apparently unconsious after taking an overdose. With him was Chuck Humphrey from Denver, also in a sorry state. Both were dressed in the regulation black with new trainers and had packed their bags for the trip. Purple shrouds to cover their faces were at hand. They had been members of the cult, but had left before the final send-off. They were rushed to hospital and both pulled through. They had survived, ironically, because they mis timed the despatch of their 'goodbye' videos.

Applewhite – 'Do' – left a chilling message for the world on the Internet, which remained there long after their deaths. It read:

Do's Intro: Purpose – Belief
What Our Purpose Is – The Simple 'Bottom Line'
Two thousand years ago, a crew of members of the Kingdom of Heaven who are responsible for nurturing 'gardens,' determined that a percentage of the human 'plants' of the present civilization of this Garden (Earth) had developed enough that some of those bodies might be ready to be used as 'containers' for soul deposits. Upon instruction, a member of the Kingdom of Heaven then left behind His body in that

Next Level (similar to putting it in a closet, like a suit of clothes that doesn't need to be worn for awhile), came to Earth, and moved into (or incarnated into), an adult human body (or 'vehicle') that had been 'prepped' for this particular task. The body that was chosen was called Jesus. The member of the Kingdom of Heaven who was instructed to incarnate into that body did so at His 'Father's' (or Older Member's) instruction. He 'moved into' (or took over) that body when it was 29 or 30 years old, at the time referred to as its baptism by John the Baptist (the incarnating event was depicted as '...the Holy Spirit descended upon Him in bodily form like a dove' – Luke 3:22). [That body (named Jesus) was tagged in its formative period to be the receptacle of a Next Level Representative, and even just that 'tagging' gave that 'vehicle' some unique awareness of its coming purpose.]

The sole task that was given to this member from the Kingdom of Heaven was to offer the way leading to membership into the Kingdom of Heaven to those who recognized Him for who He was and chose to follow Him. 'The Kingdom of Heaven is at hand' meant – 'since I am here, and I am from that Kingdom, if you leave everything of this world and follow me, I can take you into my Father's Kingdom.' Only those individuals who had received a 'deposit' containing a soul's beginning had the capacity to believe or recognize the Kingdom of Heaven's Representative. They could get to His Father only through total reliance upon Him. He later sent His students out with the 'Good news of the Kingdom of Heaven is at hand,' and His followers could then help gather the 'flock' so that the 'Shepherd' might teach others what was required of them to enter His Father's House – His Father's Kingdom – the Kingdom of Heaven – in the literal and physical Heavens – certainly not among humans on Earth. Leaving behind this world included: family, sensuality, selfish desires, your human mind, and even your human body if it be required of you – all mammalian ways, thinking, and behavior. Since He had been through this metamorphic transition Himself from human to Level Above Human – under the guidance of His Father – He was qualified to take others through that same discipline and transition. Remember, the One who incarnated in Jesus was sent for one purpose only, to say, 'If you want to go to Heaven, I can take you through that gate – it requires everything of you.'

Our mission is exactly the same. I am in the same position to today's society as was the One that was in Jesus then. My being here now is actually a continuation of that last task as was promised, to those who were students 2000 years ago. They are here again, continuing in their own overcoming, while offering the same transition to others. Our only purpose is to offer the discipline and 'grafting' required of this transition into membership in My Father's House. My Father, my Older Member, came with me this time for the first half of this task to assist in the task because of its present difficulty.

Looking to us, and desiring to be a part of my Father's Kingdom, can offer to those with deposits that chance to connect with the Level Above Human, and begin that transition. Your separation from the world and reliance upon the Kingdom of Heaven through its Representatives can open to you the opportunity to become a new creature, one of the Next Evolutionary Level, rightfully belonging to the Kingdom of Heaven.

Why It Is Difficult To Believe or Accept Us

We don't know if you believe in the real existence of negative or 'lower' forces. If you do, then you may be able to understand or relate to some of what we are about to say. It seems that how your 'programming' permits you to see or identify those forces, determines the limit of your acceptance or understanding. Many believe that there are 'evil' acts or even 'evil' individuals, but would draw the line before they would believe in evil spirits, evil discarnates, negative influences, malevolent space aliens, 'Luciferians,' or Satan and his fallen angels.

The generally accepted 'norms' of today's societies – world over – are designed, established, and maintained by the individuals who were at one time 'students' of the Kingdom of Heaven – 'angels' in the making – who 'flunked out' of the classroom. Legends and scriptures refer to them as fallen angels. The current civilization's records use the name Satan or Lucifer to describe a single fallen angel and also to 'nickname' any 'evil presence.' If you have experienced some of what our 'classroom' requires of us, you would know that these 'presences' are real and that the Kingdom of God even permits them to 'attack' us in order for us to learn their tricks and how to stay above them or conquer them. The space aliens, or Luciferians, use the discarnate spirits (the minds that are disembodied at the death of a body) as their primary servants – against potential members of the Kingdom of God. These 'influences,' or discarnates, are constantly 'programming' every human 'plant' (vehicle or body), to accept a set of beliefs and norms for behavior during a lifetime. From our point of view, this 'programming' finds that body, and the vast majority of all human bodies, barely usable by students of the Kingdom of Heaven.

As the above example can serve to testify, the 'lower forces' would – through their 'norm' concept – what is 'socially acceptable,' what is politically correct – have you not believe in spirits, spirit possession, negative space aliens, Satan, etc. They would have you believe that to even dabble in these ideas is of the 'occult,' satanic, or at the least, giving credence to 'fringe' topics. That's where they would also categorize any mental search of Eastern religions, astrology, metaphysics, paranormal, UFOs, etc., etc. In other words, they (these space aliens) don't want themselves 'found out,' so they condemn any exploration. They want you to be a perfect servant to society (THEIR society – of THEIR world) – to the 'acceptable establishment,' to humanity, and to false religious concepts. Part of that 'stay blinded' formula goes like this: 'Above all, be married, a good parent, a reasonable church goer, buy a house, pay your mortgage, pay your insurance, have a good line of credit, be socially committed, and graciously accept death with the hope that 'through His shed blood,' or some other equally worthless religious precept, you will go to Heaven after your death.'

Many segments of society, especially segments of the religious, think that they are not 'of the world,' but rather that their 'conversion' experience finds them 'outside of worldliness.' The next statement that we will make will be the 'Big Tester,' the one that the 'lower forces' would use to clearly have you discredit or disregard us. That statement is: Unless you are currently an active student or are attempting to become a student of the present Representative from the Kingdom of Heaven – you ARE STILL 'of the world,' having done no significant separation from worldliness, and you are still serving the opposition to the Kingdom of Heaven. This statement sounds – to humans who have been so carefully programmed by the 'lower forces' – arrogant, pompous, or egotistical at the least – as if by taking this stand we had something to gain – as if we were seeking recognition as 'Deity' or as self-appointed prophets.

That Luciferian programming has truly been effective, for we don't even want to voice to you the statement in question. However, believe it or not, it is only for your sake – the sake of prospective recipients of the Kingdom of Heaven – that we must 'tell the truth,' openly identify to you as Representatives of the Kingdom of Heaven, well aware of the 'fallout' of that position.

The hard facts or bold statements in a nutshell, that are so difficult to accept or 'digest' – come down to: If you want or ever expect to go to Heaven – here is your window. That window opportunity requires: 1) an incarnate (as human) Representative of the Kingdom of Heaven; 2) that all who hope to enter Heaven become active students of that Representative while the Representative is present; 3) those who endure the 'transition classroom' until it ends (adequately bonding or 'grafting' to that Representative) will go with that Representative – literally LEAVE the human kingdom and Earth as He is about to do. Staying behind, for any significant period, could jeopardize that 'graft.' That window to Heaven will not open again until another civilization is planted and has reached sufficient maturity (according to the judgement of the Next Level).

We can't blame you for 'buying into' the 'Luciferian' program. What else has been available during those periods when no Representative was present? Almost nothing – save some warnings in the Scriptures, i.e., Luke 20:34-36, Luke 21:23, Mark 12:25, and Mark

13:17-19. Check these out.

Another fact is that what someone is into during the time a Representative is not present really doesn't matter that much, except that they are found unprepared when One comes – the only time when the Kingdom of Heaven can be offered to you.

The dilemma is we are here and most humans are thoroughly 'hooked' to humanity. However, the same 'grace' that was available at the end of the Representative's mission 2000 years ago is available now with our presence. If you quickly choose to take these steps toward separating from the world, and look to us for help, you will see our Father's Kingdom.

It is clear to all of us, that to the Anti-Christ – those propagators of sustained faithfulness to mammalian humanism – we are, and will be seen as, their Anti-Christ. This is certainly to be expected, and it will not delay our return to our Father's Kingdom. It might even accelerate that return.

We will, between now and our departure, do everything we can for those who want to go with us. But we cannot allow them to interfere with or delay our return to Him.

The Present Representative

Do

If you are convinced by that and feel the urge to shed your container, remember that Heaven's Gate is closed. Hale–Bopp is on its way back out into the farthest corner of the solar system and it won't be coming back near Earth until 6210 – and you are going to be dead by then anyway.

In the aftermath of the suicides, the cult's history and the events leading up to the suicides were dissected minutely in an effort to understand what drove these people to take their own lives. Many commentators pointed to the strict regime Applewhite had imposed on his followers and claimed that the deaths, like those at Jonestown and Waco, were the result of powerful mind-control techniques by which followers became lost in the paranoid personality of their leader.

Others, however, focused on the UFO side of the story, claiming that the cult's destructive fantasies had been fuelled by figures in the UFO community suggesting that the unknown object said to be accompanying the Hale–Bopp comet might be an alien spacecraft. To many, the only difference between Heaven's Gate and other 'doomsday cults' was their choice of metaphor, with talk to UFOs and the 'Next Level' standing in for the more familiar sermons on Jesus, the Second Coming and the Kingdom of Heaven.

As it was, the comet Hale–Bopp had passed within a mere 156 million miles of Earth and could be seen plainly in the night sky. The object that Chuck Shramek said was accompanying it, and that some prominent UFOlogists speculated might be a spaceship, was never identified.

A Timeless Myth?
So are UFO and alien encounters really just modern-day fairy tales? There are certainly many parallels between folklore and modern alien encounters.

For example, in the 1857 book *Cumberland and Westmoreland Ancient and Modern,* author Jeremiah Sullivan recounts a tale, involving a man named Jack Wilson. One evening, when returning home, he noticed a ladder reaching down from a cloud and around the bottom of it was a large group of fairies. As he approached, the fairies spotted him and ran up the ladder. They drew it up after them, then 'shut the cloud' and disappeared.

These days we would not hesitate to dismiss such a fanciful tale. But there is no denying that it has strong parallels with the UFO encounter of patrolman Lonnie Zamora in New Mexico in 1964. Zamora saw an egg-shaped craft land in a desert gulch and two small aliens standing close by it. When the aliens spotted him they jumped back into her spacecraft and took off. The craft actually left physical evidence in the form of scorch marks.

Those who do not believe in UFOs claim that what Zamora had actually seen was a plasma ball whose electromagnetic field induced a hallucination. The same thing could be true of the fairies seen by Jack Wilson. On the other hand, it could be that both witnesses actually encountered alien beings, but that their experiences were interpreted differently due to the prevailing ways of thinking of the time during which they took place.

Another powerful example of the similarity between folkfore and modern-UFO reports can be found in the Celtic traditions of Ireland. One of the central features of Celtic myth is a fabled supernatural realm. This is located within the Sidhs, or burial mounds, of the early people buried there. According to folklore, this otherworld is a place of perfection where there is plenty of food and no illness or unpleasantness. The gods sometimes come into our world and invite mortals into their realm, though sometimes they take humans there by force. These are the Celtic equivalent of alien contacts and abductions. And occasional contactees and abductees are taken to a similar world of utopian perfection.

In her book, *Beyond the Light Barrier*, contactee Elisabeth Klarer reported how, in 1956, she had taken a flight in a flying saucer with an alien called Akon. They visited Akon's idyllic home-planet, Meton: a world free of war, politics and illness.

In Celtic tradition, once within such worlds, a mortal would experience time distortion. One minute spent there could be the equivalent of several years in the physical world and, similarly, years in the otherworld might pass in an instant of mortal time. Alien abductees regularly report the phenomenon of 'missing time'.

In his book *The Science of Fairy Tales*, Edwin S. Hartland relates the story of a Welshman who went to tend his cattle and came back three weeks later, thinking that he had only been gone three hours. During this period he said that he had been surrounded by little people who mesmerised him with their dancing and singing. Although these Welsh little people sound much nicer than their modern 'Grey' counterparts, many of the elements are otherwise the same as a modern-day alien abduction.

There is another bit of Celtic folklore that has a modern

comparison. Fairy folk would often ask for pure water from their human contact. In return they would offer food, though it never contained salt. Compare that to the tale of Wisconsin farmer Joe Simonton, who saw a UFO land near his home in Eagle River in April 1961. When he went to check it out, he found an alien on board who appeared to be having a barbecue. He asked Simonton for some water. When he returned with it, the alien gave him a pancake. When it was analysed, it was found to contain no salt.

In ninth, century France a number of men were captured descending from an 'airship'. According to their captors they came from 'a certain region called Magonia, whence ships come in the clouds, and which bear away the fruits of the Earth to that same country'. Their captors asked Agobard, the bishop of Lyons, for permission to stone them to death. He refused as he did not believe the story.

The biblical tale of Noah and the ark is familiar in other guises around the world. In Mesopotamian mythology, the flood was planned by four gods. But a fifth, named Ea, told a man named Ut-Napishtin that he should build a boat and, like Noah, be saved. In 1997 Marshall Applewhite committed suicide along with thirty-eight of his followers because he thought the Earth was about to be recycled and a ship was coming to save then. Contactee Marian Keech also marshalled her followers on the top of a hill, convinced that the Earth was about to be engulfed by a flood of biblical proportions and a flying saucer was on its way to save them. Sadly, her group broke up when neither saucer nor flood put in an appearance.

Legends of cloud ships with trailing anchors are also rife. In the tenth century it is said that a cloud ship's trailing anchor caught on the porchway of St Kinarus's church in Cloera, Ireland. One of the ship's occupants had to climb down and cut the rope, leaving the anchor behind. In March 1897, during a wave of phantom airship sightings seen across North America, Robert Hibbard claims to have been abducted when he was caught on a trailing anchor. It carried him for some distance before releasing him.

Another idea that has become central to UFOlogy is the idea that aliens are visiting Earth on a programme of genetic manipulation, designed to create human–alien hybrids. This idea also occurs in Greek mythology, where the god Zeus took several mortal women as his concubines and had children. With Niobe, for example, he had the hybrid son Argos.

Greek mythology has been particularly influential in Western culture and aspects are mirrored in the UFO phenomenon. The Greek location of the afterworld is a good example. In Homer's *The Odyssey*, the afterworld is said to be placed 'at the extremity of the Earth, beyond the vast Ocean'. At that time the River Ocean was thought to encompass the whole of the Earth. But later, when ships sailed the oceans and found more land beyond the horizon, the afterworld had to be relocated somewhere more distant and less accessible. It became the 'Kingdom of Shadows' and was placed at the centre of the Earth, where it could be reached only by the perilous journey into deep caverns, or by certain rivers that flowed down into the earth and on to the mystical realm.

The parallels here with the claims of the contactees are clear. In 1952, the home of the aliens who contacted George Adamski was Venus, still believed by some to be a paradise sister world of Earth. Since then probes have reached the planets and proved that it is one of the most inhospitable places in the solar system, and the location of the aliens' 'afterworld' has subsequently moved out of the solar system to planets orbiting distant stars or into other dimensions altogether.

In Greek myths, the gods often allowed some particularly noble or heroic individuals to break all the rules and inherit some god-like powers. This also happens in UFOlogy. Abductees often find they have been endowed with special powers after their abduction.

Of course, these parallels work both ways. While they can be used to argue that UFO and alien encounters are simply imagined to fulfil the human need for myths, they can also be used to demonstrate that aliens have been intimately involved with humans since the dawn of time.

Identified Flying Objects

So if UFOs are not alien spacecraft visiting Earth, what are they? Certainly some very funny things do go on in the atmosphere, not all of them are explainable, even by conventional science.

One case in point occurred at the beginning of June 1996, when a factory full of workers at a packaging factory in Tewkesbury in Gloucestershire, England, saw a ball of white light the size of a tennis ball burst through the roof of the factory and buzz erratically around the ceiling girders. Then the fizzing, sparking ball fell to the floor, giving the staff electric shocks and damaging equipment. Finally, it hit a window. Then the mysterious ball popped noisily like a soap bubble and vanished completely, leaving workers speechless.

But they were not the first to see the ball of light; shortly before the incident an aircraft passed through the heavy thunderclouds overhead and the crew had seen an anomalous ball of pure energy materialise as if out of nowhere next to the fuselage. It was this that fell to Earth and buzzed around the packaging works below.

But what exactly was this UFO? Perhaps it was one of the foo fighters that had been seen so often during World War II. Or was it something more mundane that had perhaps been overlooked by science?

The object in question was, it now appears, ball lightning. But for years, mainstream science had been saying that this meteorological phenomenon did not exist. However, dogged research on this fringe topic has produced an overwhelming weight of evidence – including photographs – that has finally forced science to accept that ball lightning is a real phenomenon.

This demonstrates just how blinkered scientific thinking can be. It also highlights that our knowledge of the skies is far from complete. It should be remembered that in 1770s the father of modern chemistry Antoine Lavoisier famously announced that meteorites were a myth. His reasoning was impeccable. In an address to the French Academy of Science in the 1770s, he pointed out that, as rocks did not live in the sky, they could not fall out of it. Despite the great man's wise words, meteorites do exist and the scientific community was eventually forced to accept the fact.

Today, meteorites and ball lightning are reported almost as commonly as flying saucers. However, it is generally assumed that over ninety per cent of UFO reports can be explained as the result of natural or technological occurrences. Consequently, it is assumed, quite falsely, that the other ten per cent can be explained that way too.

One of the first UFO debunkers to assume that there was a large degree of mistaken identity in UFO sightings was Dr Donald Menzel, the former Professor of Astrophysics at Harvard University. At the American Association for the Advancement of Science in 1969, Menzel presented his list of 'identified flying objects', claiming that they would eventually explain every flying saucers report.

Menzel divided his IFOs into categories:
- Material – aircraft, balloons, fireworks
- Immaterial – cloud formations, meteorological phenomena
- Astronomical – misidentified stars, planets, comets, meteorites
- Physiological – eye problems, after-images burned on to the retina
- Psychological – hallucinations, mass hysteria
- Photographic – double exposures, processing defects
- Radar anomalies

And then there were the hoaxes.

Admittedly, UFOlogy did need something of a more rigorous scientific approach at that time, but Menzel began to dismiss perfectly reliable UFO sightings by suggesting that the witnesses had actually seen spiders' webs, insects, soap bubbles or cigarette butts. As a result, his debunking backfired. It left UFO eyewitnesses looking more credible than the scientists debunking them. And, after a re-evaluation of many of Menzel's cases by Dr James McDonald, a former Director of the University of Arizona's Institute of Atmospheric Physics, many of Menzel's proposals were 'quantitatively absurd'. Even so, sceptics continue to go out of their way to find a rational explanation, even if none exists.

Take the classic case of RAF Intelligence Officer J.B.W. 'Angus' Brooks. In 1967, while walking his dog across Moigne Downs in Dorset, Brooks saw a long, thin, almost translucent craft flying towards him. As the object neared him, two more pieces of fuselage emerged from its side. They formed a perfect cross, roughly 170 feet wide, which then climbed into the morning sky and vanished.

Brooks was a trained RAF observer who had witnessed a UFO that could not have been mistaken for any conventional aircraft. It was less than three hundred yards away, in good light, just before midday. His credentials and experience could not have been bettered. But Ministry of Defence investigators and RAF psychologists decided that all he had seen were dead cells floating in the vitreous humour of his eyes.

Close Encounters of the Cinematic Kind

There was no implicit connection between the objects Kenneth Arnold saw in flight over Washington State in 1947 and the idea of aliens from outer space. Yet, in no time, the idea that flying saucers flown by extraterrestrials were visiting Earth was widespread. Some claim that the popular culture of the time was already set up to accept the reality of aliens.

From the beginning of the twentieth century, science-fiction writers had toyed with the notion of extraterrestrial races, and by the 1920s, there were numerous comic books and magazines pumping out wild ideas on the form extraterrestrial life might take. In 1936, aliens had made their celluloid debut in the series *Flash Gordon*, which created a cult following around the world.

But Arnold's sighting itself was the inspiration for a rash of science-fiction movies depicting alien invaders. They invariably came in saucer-shaped craft. Even in the 1953 movie *War of the Worlds*, the Martians attacked Earth in saucers – though, of course, H.G. Wells published the book in 1898.

Undoubtedly, eyewitness reports such as Arnold's have influenced the movies. But then movies have also influenced eyewitness reports. In the influential 1951 movie *The Day the Earth Stood Still*, a humanoid alien named Klaatu and his giant 'policeman' robot Gort arrive on Earth in a saucer-shaped spacecraft to warn humanity not to stray into outer space until it has cleaned up its nuclear act – a message often echoed by contactees and abductees. However, even some of the film's minor details would later find echoes in real-life accounts of alien contact. For example, Klaatu's silver suit clearly came from the same tailor as the one worn by the Venusian that George Adamski encountered the year after the film's release.

What's more, the interior of Klaatu's ship was strikingly similar to the description given a decade later by abductees Betty and Barney Hill. It came complete with platform beds for the medical examinations that have become a staple of the abduction phenomenon ever since.

In the 1953 movie *Invaders from Mars*, the aliens hid in secret underground bases, as they did in the 1955 movie *This Island Earth*. By the 1980s the notion of underground installations containing extraterrestrials and their technology lying beneath Area 51 in Nevada and the town of Dulce in New Mexico was widely accepted among UFOlogists.

Many of these early films also portrayed the extraterrestrials as hostile, emotionless and robot-like. Typical are the aliens that can adopt human form at will in the 1953 movie *It Came from Outer Space*, and the human replicants that grow in pods in *Invasion of the Body Snatchers* in 1956. The abductees still talk of their abductors as cold, emotionless automatons.

After the glut of science-fiction movies of the 1950s, there was a lull in the 1960s. But, interestingly, UFO sightings and alien encounters did not go away. So by the 1970s, a new generation of moviemakers had numerous new accounts of alien encounters to call on. Science fiction gave way to fact with full-on reconstructions of the accounts of prominent UFO eyewitnesses. *Hangar 18* told the story of the crash retrievals, while the story of Betty and Barney Hill's

121

abduction was told in *The UFO Incident.*

In 1962, the year after the Hill's abduction, the TV puppet series *Fireball XL5* featured Grey aliens with large bald heads in an episode called 'Robert to the Rescue'. These aliens could take over a human's will and switch off their memory – just like the creatures the Hills had encountered.

In 1977, the UFO movie went big budget with *Close Encounters of the Third Kind.* This drew on numerous accounts from UFO eyewitnesses, contactees and abductees and wove them together into one storyline, then added the latest in special effects to bring the subject to a much wider audience than ever before. There were 550 more UFO sightings reported in the year following the movie's release than in the previous twelve months.

Soon a lot of details of *Close Encounters* began turning up in UFO and alien encounter reports. Naturally, Hollywood had pushed things over the top. The budget for the encounter at the climax of the movie stretched to a truly massive spacecraft, a first for Hollywood. After that, the spacecraft seen by UFO eyewitnesses got noticeably bigger. In one case, the pilot of flight JAL 1628 reported seeing a walnut-shaped object over Alaska, twice the size of an aircraft carrier.

Interestingly, although for years *ET,* released in 1982, was the top grossing movie of all time, it prompted no rash of similar sightings.

Hybrids have found their way into *Star Trek,* first with Mr Spock, the half-human and half-Vulcan, while in *Star Trek – The Next Generation,* Counsellor Troi is half-human, half-Betazoid, and Tasha Yar comes back after her death, through a complicated time-travel story, as half-human, half-Romulan. Meanwhile, back on Earth, there are people who claim to be the progeny of a one-night stand between an alien and a human.

Star Trek – The Next Generation also features a Holodeck, an artificial environment where real people undergo experiences that they can barely distinguish from the real thing. In the UFO literature this has several eerie forerunners. On the night of 30 May 1974, two people were driving towards Beit Bridge on the border of South Africa and what was then Rhodesia (now Zimbabwe). They spotted a UFO that kept pace with their car. Then they realised that they did not recognise the landscape round them. The road was straight, when it should have been windy. When they arrived at Beit Bridge, they discovered that they had used no petrol – when the journey should have used at least half a tank. Nor did the tyres show any wear. The two concluded that they had been transported to Beit Bridge on board the UFO in a room especially constructed to look like the real environment.

The movies and UFO reality intersected again in 1996, when the film *Independence Day* was launched on the 'ET Highway' outside Area 51 in Nevada. Many believed that it would smooth the way for the US government to reveal what it knew about the alien technology there. It was not forthcoming. Nevertheless, audiences across America rose cheering to their feet when the White House got zapped in the movie.

Plainly there is some kind of 'feedback loop' between science fiction and UFOlogy. Some have used this to suggest that all UFO accounts are fictitious, and simply inspired by what people see in the movies, while others claim that it is the real-life experiences of UFO eyewitnesses and abductees that are finding their way onto the silver screen.

The Hollow Earth

One of the wackiest theories in UFOlogy is that of the 'hollow Earth'. It's proponents point out that any environment that could support intelligent life is so far from Earth that meeting an extraterrestrial is about as likely as meeting Elvis in the local supermarket. Consequently, aliens must come from somewhere closer to home. And there is only one place that their home could be – beneath our very feet.

Hollow-Earth theorists maintain that there is a world within our world, where an environment exists not very different from our own. It has its own inner landscape and its own life forms that have evolved separately from those on the outside. Its higher creatures are more advanced than we are, and they are the aliens we see visiting our outer world.

The idea that the Earth is hollow is not a recent invention. Myths that an underworld exists stretch back to the dawn of time. Usually it is the home of the souls of the damned, demons, trolls, elves and other supernatural beings.

However, in 1692, astronomer Edmond Halley speculated that within the Earth there is another concentric innermost sphere. A luminous atmosphere provides light to this inner world and allows creatures to live there. The aurora, or northern lights, that we see are in fact, some of the luminous gases escaping from the interior, Halley said.

In 1812 former US army officer John Cleves Symmes began a lecture tour of America, setting out his theory that the Earth is made up of five spheres, one within the other. He said that it was habitable within, and that the oceans, flowed in and out of openings at the poles. His ideas were popularised in the 1820 novel called *Symzonia* by Adam Seaborn, which may have been a pseudonym adopted by Symmes. He pledged to explore this new inner world and, in January 1823, he petitioned Congress, requesting that the government organise an expedition to claim the lands of the Earth's interior for the United States. But sadly Congress refused to fund this harebrained scheme, and Symmes died in 1829 without putting his theory to the test.

But the hollow-Earth theory did not die with Symmes. After his death a full exposition of his theories was give in *The Symmes Theory of Concentric Spheres, Demonstrating that the Earth is Hollow, Habitable Within, and Widely Open About the Pole,* written by one of his sons. Although the scientific community refused to take the idea seriously, it may have prompted America's exploration of the polar regions between 1838 and 1842.

Cyrus Teed then came up with an even more bizarre hollow-Earth theory. He claimed that we were actually living on the inside of a hollow sphere – just 750 miles in diameter and 25,000 in circumference – which contained everything in the visible universe. The Moon, he said, was around half-a-mile across, while the Sun was less than three feet in diameter. The light curved in such a way to make them look bigger. This bending made it look like the Earth fell away from us, so that we could only see part of it. It also made part of the central region invisible and celestial bodies were seen to set and rise by passing by in and out of this region. The idea was, of course, a religious one. Instead of the Earth being an insignificant rock in a vast universe, it became all there is. Teed changed his name to Koresh (note the similarities with the Waco incident) and, with his followers, established a community of believers at Koreshanity in Florida.

Jules Verne published *Le Voyage au centre de la Terre* in 1864, which was translated into English as *A Journey to the Centre of the Earth* in 1874. Then in 1906, William Reed published *Phantom of the Poles,* in which he predicted that the interior of the hollow Earth could 'be made accessible to mankind with one-fourth the outlay of money, time and life that it cost to build the subway in New York City.' However, in 1909 Robert Perry reached the North Pole and two years later Roald Amundsen reached the South Pole – and neither reporting seeing any giant openings there.

Undeterred, hollow-Earth theorists re-evaluated their position, and in 1913, Marshall B. Gardner published *A Journey to the Earth's Interior, or, Have the Poles Really Been Discovered?* In it, he dismissed Symmes' fanciful idea that there were five concentric spheres within the Earth. According to Gardner, the Earth was simply hollow, warmed by an inner sun some six hundred miles in diameter. There were openings at the poles, however, which were over a thousand miles across. Speculation was rife about what sort of creatures lived down there.

The theory suffered another setback with Richard E. Byrd's flights over the North Pole in 1926 and over the South Pole in 1929. On these flights, no openings were seen. Still, the hollow-Earth theory was far from dead.

In a 1945 issue of *Amazing Stories* Ray Palmer published the tales of a fictional character named Richard Shaver, who described the activities of a race of subterranean beings called the Deros. And in 1957 Palmer launched a new pulp magazine, *Flying Saucers from*

Other Worlds, in which he claimed that flying saucers originated in the interior of the Earth.

Since then every inch of the Arctic and Antarctic have been flown over, and the whole of the Earth has been surveyed by satellites. But the hollow-Earth theorists would still not give up. In June 1970 Palmer printed of a satellite photograph that showed a dark hole around the north pole.

The photograph was taken by the satellite ESSA-7 on 23 November 1968. It showed the whole of the northern hemisphere bathed in sunlight with a dark circular region centred on the pole in the middle. The accompanying story said: 'Although, surrounding the polar area, and north of such areas as the North American continent and Greenland and the Asian continent, we can see the ice-field – eight-foot thick ice – we do not see any ice fields in the large circular area directly at the geographic pole. Instead we see a hole.'

The picture was genuine. However, it was not a snapshot. It was a picture compiled throughout the day, so all the continents are shown in daylight, while the dark 'hole' in the centre was the region in perpetual polar winter night.

Undaunted, in 1979 Raymond Bernard published *The Hollow Earth: The Greatest Geographical Discovery in History.* According to Bernard, the Earth is a hollow shell eight hundred miles thick. The inner surface is illuminated by an inner sun six hundred miles in diameter. The aurorae are its reflection in the clouds.

Seismic data demonstrate clearly that the Earth is not hollow. However, Bernard also claims that other celestial bodies are also hollow. He says that the bright polar regions of Mars, thought by scientists to be ice caps, are the light of the planet's inner sun shining out. This cannot be disproven, though it is thought unlikely.

And still, the hollow-Earthers cling on tenaciously. They say that the polar openings are being concealed by the advanced technology of the inner-Earth dwellers. Indeed, the openings are not three-dimensional ones but exist in some higher dimension. In 1995 a hollow-Earther corresponding with an Internet discussion group wrote:

'The Earth is hollow in the fourth dimension... There are two "entrances", and these are reflected in the physical world as the north and south magnetic poles.'

Hollow-Earth theorists point out that explorers have reported that north winds get warmer nearer the poles, suggesting that they are warmed by air emanating from the Earth's interior. They also say that tropical plants have been found in the melt-waters of icebergs. Surely this misplaced flora came from within the Earth.

There is, of course, a government cover-up concerning the hollow Earth. American polar flyer Richard E. Byrd did, in fact, discover the polar openings, but was forced to pretend otherwise. A document that purports to be Byrd's diary was made public by his grandson and appeared on the Internet. It is dated 1947; Byrd went to the Arctic in 1947 to search for sources of uranium ore. According to the 'diary', Byrd took off from his Arctic base on 19 February. After three hours of normal flight the magnetic and gyro compasses went crazy. After another hour, he was flying over a valley with lush green vegetation and saw a mammoth on the ground. Later, his controls went dead. His plane was taken over by disc-shaped craft with swastika markings, which escorted him to the ground.

Byrd was taken by German-speaking Nordics to meet one of their leaders in a crystalline city. This, he was told, was 'the domain of the Arianni, the Inner World of the Earth'. A great storm was coming to ravage the world, Byrd was told. But he was not to worry. A new world run by the inner-Earth beings would emerge from the ruins of the human race. Byrd told the Pentagon all he had learned but was ordered to remain silent. As a naval officer, he did what he was told.

Visits From a Higher Dimension

One of the theories that has become popular among UFOlogists is that UFOs are visitors from 'other dimensions'. This theory acknowledges the idea of the existence of 'alternate realities' – which would explain not just UFOs, but many other paranormal phenomena. Although these ideas seem as if they have been plucked from the furthest reaches of science fiction, they are actually under serious consideration by the world's leading theoretical physicists.

To some UFOlogists, the idea that UFOs exist in other, higher dimensions would explain their elusiveness. If an object did exist in a dimension beyond our ordinary realm of space and time, when it did show up in our dimensions, it would appear very alien indeed.

Imagine, for example, that you saw a shape appear from thin air, hanging there in space. Before your very eyes it grows larger, rotates slowly, then shrinks and vanishes without a trace. You would naturally call your local UFO society and report that you have seen an extraterrestrial craft. And they would file your sighting with thousands of similar reports they have collected over the past fifty years. But what you have just visualised is what would happen if a four-dimensional object passed through our three-dimension world. At any one moment you would merely be glimpsing a cross-section through a reality that you could not possibly visualise as a whole.

The idea that we live in three-dimensional space has been around since 300 BC, when the Greek mathematician Euclid wrote his famous textbook on geometry, *Elements*. However, in the early part of the twentieth century, Albert Einstein realised that some of the anomalous properties of electromagnetic radiation and gravity could be explained if we lived in four-dimensional space–time. He and German mathematician Hermann Weyl began to develop the idea that space and time were combined in a single, four-dimensional 'continuum'. The idea of this 'space–time continuum' is widely accepted in the world of science. However, the idea that there may be other dimensions is now a topic of hot debate in scientific circles.

It is very difficult for us to think in higher dimensions. However, Edwin A. Abbott came up with a useful analogy in his 1884 novel *Flatland*. In the book, the inhabitants of Flatland are squares, lines, angles and pentagons that are confined to a world that has just two dimensions. They are extremely thin and can move in any direction across the surface, but they have no concept of the third dimension of space that exists at right angles to their world. The book describes what happens when three-dimensional objects pass through their flat world. To us, who are used to living in a three-dimensional world, everything that happens seems ordinary and readily understandable, but for Flatlanders it seems spooky and mysterious.

For example, if a sphere passes through Flatland, it appears first as a single point that appears out of nowhere. This is where the surface of the sphere touches the plane of the flat world. As it passes through, Flatlanders would see the point turn into a circle this is the sphere's cross-section. It would grow slowly and reach a maximum size when the sphere is halfway through. Then it would shrink back down to a point before disappearing again.

So three-dimensional objects passing through a two-dimensional world appear to perform impossible tricks, just as UFOs seem to when they appear and disappear, change shape and perform impossible manoeuvres in our world.

To many UFOlogists, the idea that UFOs are glimpses of things that exist in higher dimensions is a good deal more credible than the extraterrestrial hypothesis. Even our cursory exploration of our own solar system has pretty much ruled out our neighbouring planets as a home for intelligent life. And if extraterrestrials lived on the planets of other stars, they would be faced with travelling impossible distances to visit us. But if UFOs existed in other dimensions, they would not have to inhabit a planet in our solar system. Nor would they have to tear holes in the fabric of space–time to get herof the universe. They could exist right here with us, but in a dimension that is normally imperceptible to us. The appearance of a UFO would then be the intersection of a higher dimensional object with our three dimensions of space. And when it left those dimensions, it would disappear.

There are problems here though. The main scientific theory to deal with other dimensions is known as 'string theory'. According to string theory, when the universe was born in the Big Bang, some 15 billion years ago, it had not four, but ten or eleven dimensions – scientists can't make up their minds. But as the universe expanded, three space dimensions and one dimension of time 'unrolled' and grew to their present vast extent, while the other dimensions remained 'rolled up'. They are so tiny that they play virtually no role on the scale of the universe as we know it. Unfortunately, this has little to offer the world of UFOlogy.

What Do They Want?

For over fifty years now UFOs have been visiting the Earth. Aliens have been seen around the globe. So what have they come for? Are they concerned space brothers who want to save us from ourselves? Are they evil aliens planning to conquer Earth and wipe out humankind? Or is it just our genetic material they are after?

In trying to work out exactly what the alien agenda is, researchers have come up with a bewildering array of theories. The task is complicated by the wide variety of aliens reported, ranging from different types of biological extraterrestrials to non-physical entities referred to as 'ultraterrestrials'. Then we have the problem of seeing things through exclusively human eyes, which define alien behaviour as benevolent or malevolent and slot everything into a convenient moral framework. This is no small matter. As we are on the threshold of developing technologies that will take us to the stars, the question of who is out there and what they want with us is becoming increasingly important. The information we have on the alien agenda comes from two main sources. One is observation of the activities of extraterrestrials when they interact with Earth and its population. The other is from direct contact with extraterrestrial intelligence, from what they do and what they say.

In the early days of UFO visits it was generally assumed that extraterrestrials were necessarily hostile. Early UFO sightings often involved pilots or military personnel. They were trained to see any uninvited intrusion into a nation's air space as an act of hostility. UFOs were pursued and often fired on by intercept aircraft. There is some evidence to suggest that the real motive behind building particle beam weapons for use in the Strategic Defense Initiative was not simply to protect the West from Soviet missiles, but to fire at alien spacecraft.

That equally applies to the new National Missile Defense system. In his book *UFOs: The Secret History,* German researcher Michael Hesemann describes how two spacecraft were shot down by Brookhaven National Laboratory on Long Island using SDI weaponry in 1989 and 1992.

However, although there are numerous reports of the military attacking alien craft, there are very few examples of the aliens responding in anything but a defensive mode. This alone suggests that they are tolerant and non-threatening.

They may be here merely to observe and even guide us. The UFO archives are crammed with reports of alien craft monitoring human technology – space shots, military bases, nuclear installations and missile silos. Documents released under America's Freedom of Information Act revealed that, in the 1970s, a number of Intercontinental Ballistic Missile sites were visited by UFOs. Again the aliens showed no hostile intent. Instead the missiles' seven-digit launch codes were scrambled, rendering the system harmless. As the aliens did not use America's defencelessness as an opportunity to attack, one can only assume that they were trying to protect us from our own self-destructive drives.

There has also been some direct intervention with human space technology, which shows that the extraterrestrials want to curtail certain human activities in space. In his book *Alien Agenda*, Jim Marrs shows that the aliens are imposing a selective space quarantine on us. They sabotage certain military payloads and disable probes that may discover alien bases throughout solar system. Marrs cites the loss of both Russian and American Martian probes. The Russian *Phobos 2,* he points out, photographed a disc-shaped object gaining on it just before it malfunctioned. According to Marrs, the US Army has trained teams of remote viewers who use their psychic abilities to examine distant events and objects. They have described small multifaceted objects in the upper atmosphere that are responsible for numerous set-backs in space launches, including the 1993 Titan and 1996 Mars rocket launches.

But if the alien agenda is largely benevolent, how does alien abduction fit into that pattern? Veteran UFO researcher David Jacobs insists that abductions are a fundamental violation of human free will and are a prime example of one highly advanced species exploiting another. But Dr John Mack disagrees. He sees abduction as a form of benevolent biological intervention. Extraterrestrials are creating a hybrid species to preserve human DNA because humankind faces extinction by our wilful destruction of the environment, he says.

'Evidently, what we have been doing to the Earth has not gone "unnoticed" at a higher, cosmic level,' he writes in his book *Passport to the Cosmos*. 'Some sort of odd intervention seems to be occurring here. We are not, apparently, being permitted to continue our destructive ways without some kind of "feedback".'

Dr Joe Lewells concurs, but sees the alien intervention as part of a larger pattern. In his book *The God Hypothesis* he recounts the tale of an abductee called Rebecca Grant. She maintained contact with insectoid extraterrestials who told her why extraterrestrials would not intervene directly to prevent human destruction of the environment. 'If ETs were to repair the Earth without making any changes in our behaviour, we would simply undo all the good they had done,' she said. 'We might survive long enough to find an even grander way to destroy ourselves, one that could harm worlds other than our own. These beings feel that, by saving the human race, they would be condemning themselves to a violent confrontation with us in the future.'

Grant said that several groups of extraterrestrial were trying to stimulate a higher consciousness in the form of psychic abilities and paranormal powers in abductees. Numerous abductees have discovered undreamed of physic abilities after an encounter. Brazilian abductee Vera Rubia is a good example of this. After encountering humanoid extraterrestrials in her home in the town of Valencia, she was able to diagnose a person's illness simply by thinking about them. Doctors who investigated her abilities found her to be accurate ninety-nine per cent of the time.

Aliens also give abductees lectures on the environment and the dangers of destroying it. Carlos Dias, abducted in Ajusco Park near Mexico City in 1981, said that the aliens impressed on him the interconnectedness of things.

'All the things I saw made me realise about the interaction between the smallest particle and the biggest,' he said. 'Each has a specific duty.' His abduction triggered in him a profound reverence for life, a need to get involved in conservation and a renewed wish to 'enjoy a beautiful living planet'.

If the information given to abductees by extraterrestrials is taken at face value, humankind seems to have reached a crisis point in its evolution. It is at a dangerous point of transition where our activity is becoming a cause of concern to a wide range of extraterrestrial civilisations. They are worried what we may do to ourselves and presumably, the galaxy around us. But, by and large, they are here to help.

This is also the conclusion of Dr Steven Greer, the director of the Center for the Study of Extraterrestrial Intelligences. His comprehensive survey of documents and case studies has led him write a list of the aliens' principal activities. These are:

- General reconnaissance of the Earth and its civilisations.
- Observation and assessment of our military and nuclear capabilities.
- Studying human psychology.
- Assessment of human development.
- Assessment of human technology.
- Monitoring the space programme, with particular interest in parts directed towards establishing colonies in space.
- Limited interaction with humankind to pass on information about themselves and accustom us to their presence.

Greer believes that all the aliens' aims are entirely benevolent, especially when you consider how much more technologically advanced they are. They regard us with the compassion a mature species would reserve for a fledgling one and are trying to guide us through this difficult stage in our development.

The Nightmare Begins

But what happens if the aliens really are hostile? There are still those who suggest that it is only a matter of time before the Earth is visited by an alien aggressor. Surely the aliens have been observing the Earth for over fifty years in preparation for just such an invasion. So what are the chances of survival for the human race? Unfortunately, the prognosis is bad – very bad.

While we know very little about the aliens, they know a great deal about us. SETI –the Search for Extraterrestrial Intelligence – is beaming out messages into the sky. They tell anyone out there who cares to listen the position of our solar system in the galaxy and the position of our planet within the solar system. Along with that there is information on the total population of the Earth, the average height of a human being, the structure of our DNA and the atomic numbers of carbon, hydrogen, oxygen, nitrogen and phosphorus – the elements we are made out of. No invading force in history has been given such vital intelligence.

American astronomer Frank Drake came up with an equation to estimate how many inhabitable planets there may be out there. He takes the lowest reasonable assumptions for the relevant factors. For example, he assumes that only one per cent of the billion stars in our galaxy have planets orbiting them – we already know this is a vast underestimate – and that one per cent of that one per cent are capable of sustaining life as we know it. Taking as a model the way that civilisations were eventually established on Earth, he worked out that, at the very least, there are forty planets in our galaxy with technology that is similar, if not vastly superior, to our own. And it would be those with a superior technology that would turn up on our doorstep – otherwise they would not be able to get here. They could, of course, be peaceful, fun-loving people. But think of the various civilisations that have grown up on this planet. The ones that flourished and took over the world were universally warlike. And what happened when they came across peoples who were less technologically developed? They ruthlessly exploited and dominated them. Millions of people in both North and South America died because of their contact with a handful of technologically superior Europeans.

It goes without saying that any invading alien force that actually managed to reach the Earth is bound to possess technology far in advance of our own. Even in the unlikely event that they came from a planet orbiting the nearest neighbouring star, they would have travelled many billions of miles to get here. By comparison, the furthest the human race has managed to go is the half-a-million miles or so to the Moon and back.

The invaders will have had to master the fundamental forces of nature to get here. They will have some form of power that is beyond the imagination of humankind's finest minds. And they will be tough enough, physically and mentally, to survive a journey of billions of miles across the hostile environment of space. If it came to a shooting war, it would be no contest. Our puny weapons would be pitted against a technology that we could not even begin to understand.

Even if the aliens did not wipe us out on the first day just for the fun of it, or because they were so advanced that they considered us nothing more than lice on a disused planet, our governments would have no choice but to capitulate. There would, of course, be a few brave pockets of resistance, a handful of heroes who would rather live in freedom for one more day than face a lifetime of slavery. But they would not stand a chance. Humankind would have to accommodate the demands of the invaders or die. But what might those demands be?

We know that water is important. Although we know nothing of its existence outside the solar system, we known that it is a rare and precious commodity here. Liquid water exists in only one place that we know of – right here on planet Earth. Mercury and Venus are so hot that water boils instantly. There may be some ice around the Martian poles, but generally Mars has insufficient mass to hold water at its surface. The other planets are too cold, being made up mostly of huge balls of assorted gases orbited by a few lifeless rocky moons. But without water, life as we know it cannot exist. The aliens, when they get here, are likely to be very thirsty, so humankind could be in for a drought such as we have never experienced in history.

The invaders might also come to plunder the Earth's mineral deposits. The planet is still a rich storehouse of coal, gas and oil along with an abundant supply of diamonds, gold and other metals that aliens are likely to prize. Alien technology would make mining in places that were previously inaccessible a possibility. But they may need a workforce. That, unfortunately, is where we would come in. After all, to them, it would be simply a matter of pressing animals into service the way we do with horses, asses, oxen, elephants and water buffalo. In fact, these are the very animals the aliens might use. Humans are physically weaker, have greater difficulty following instructions and are generally more troublesome.

However, it might worth keeping some of the fitter and compliant humans alive to use as slave labour. There is nothing so alien about that. Until the beginnings of the fight again slavery at the end of the eighteenth century, every civilisation practised it. And in the twentieth century slave labour was used with ruthless efficiency in the Nazi and Soviet labour camps. Auschwitz survivor Primo Levi can give us some idea of what to expect. In his harrowing book, *If This Is a Man*, he writes: 'In less than ten minutes all the fit men had been collected together in a group... of all the others, more than five hundred in number, not one was living two days later.'

Alien
Conspiracy
Theories

This Alien is Deceased

The Roswell Incident

The most famous UFO encounter in history occurred on 2 July 1947. On that day, a flying saucer crashed near Roswell in a remote part of New Mexico. News reached the newspapers on 8 July. But having proof positive that aliens were visiting Earth so scared the American authorities that, later that day, they denied it had ever happened. This was the start of a UFO cover-up that exists in every country in the world to this day.

The headline of the *Roswell Daily Record* of 8 July 1947 could not be clearer. 'RAAF Captures Flying Saucer on Ranch in Roswell,' it said in sixty-point type. Other newspapers carried equally unambiguous headlines: 'Army Finds Air Saucer in New Mexico' and 'Army Declares Flying Disc Found' were two of them. And they were not making it up. The story came from the horse's mouth – the Army itself. News of the UFO crash at Roswell was given to the world in press release issued by Lieutenant Walter Haut, Press Officer at the Roswell Army Air Field (RAAF). UFOlogists, with some justification, say that this was the most important press release of the twentieth century.

When it came to the cover-up, the timing of the press release proved crucial. It was issued at noon Mountain Time. This meant that it was too late for most morning papers. However, it did just catch some evening editions on the West Coast. Newspapers called the base at Roswell to check out the story. They were happy to expand on the press release. The sheriff's office and local newspapers were also inundated with queries. Then suddenly, without any warning, the Air Force killed the story. They said that what they had found was not a UFO after all. It was just a weather balloon.

The headlines the next day effectively buried the story: 'Reports of Flying Saucers Dwindle; New Mexico "Disc" is only Weather

Balloon.' Local papers carried pictures of the wreckage. And that was the end of it.

Over thirty years later nuclear physicist and UFOlogist Stanton Friedman went to a TV station in Louisiana for an interview about his UFO work. Before he went on, Friedman was chatting with the station manager, who told him that he ought to go and talk to a man named Jesse Marcel who lived nearby in Houna, Louisiana. Marcel, the station manager said, 'handled pieces of one of those flying saucers you're interested in when he was in the military'.

The next day, Friedman tracked down Marcel and discovered that he had been the intelligence officer at the RAAF. He told Friedman that sometime after World War II a flying saucer was supposed to have crashed near Corona, New Mexico, just seventy-five miles north-west of Roswell. Marcel had been ordered to collect the crash wreckage and deliver it to Wright Field in Dayton, Ohio, where the US Army stockpiled captured enemy equipment. Marcel was on his way to Ohio, when Haut issued his press release. But later that day, when the brass in Washington heard about the incident, it was decided to hush everything up and a second statement was issued to the press, this time saying that the wreckage was that of a weather balloon.

Unfortunately, Marcel could not remember exactly when this had happened, but Friedman and fellow UFOlogist William Moore began an investigation. They got lucky. British TV personality Hughie Green had been in Pennsylvania at the time and had heard a report of the downed UFO on the radio. Though he never discovered any more, his story was carried in the very first edition of *Flying Saucer Review*. Green's account narrowed the date of the crash down to late June or early July 1947.

Moore trawled through the newspaper archive of the library of the University of Minnesota Library and found editions from 8 July 1947 covering the Corona–Roswell event. The papers gave the name of the rancher who owned the land where the crash had occurred, the local sheriff and the RAAF personnel involved. By 1980, Friedman and Moore had interviewed sixty-two people involved with the event, including neighbours who had also handled some debris – such as Loretta Proctor, and Jesse Marcel's son, Jesse junior – and Bill Brazel, son of the rancher who found the wreckage. Amazingly, Walter Haut, the Press Officer who released the story, still lived in Roswell. He had a copy of the base yearbook and was helpful in tracking down people and filling in details. And he was adamant that the debris he had seen at Roswell Army Air Force base was not the wreckage of a weather balloon.

'Anyone with any experience in the Air Force would be able to tell you the difference between a weather balloon and a flying disc,' he said. 'I'd seen them go up over the base – you'd look at them and say: "It's a weather balloon." A balloon is a balloon is a balloon.'

His boss Colonel Blanchard must have been convinced too. He authorised Haut to issue the press release.

The story of the Roswell crash began on the night of 1 July 1947. There was a thunderstorm that night over the small town of Corona, seventy-five miles north-west of Roswell. In the middle of it, there was a huge explosion. The following morning, Mac Brazel, a sheep farmer who operated the Foster Ranch twenty miles south-east of the town, went out to check on a water pump. On his way, he discovered an area over half-a-mile long strewn with debris. The pieces he picked up were made of a material he had never come across before. When he folded it several times, it spontaneously unfolded. There were also pieces of I-beam, which was as light as balsa wood but could not be broken or bent. Inside the 'I' of the beam, there were unusual symbols in a lavender-coloured pigment.

Brazel did not know what to do with the wreckage, so on Sunday, 6 July, he made the long cross-country trip to Roswell with some of the debris in the back of his pickup truck. He took it to the office of Roswell Sheriff George Wilcox. Wilcox, in turn, called the Army Air Force base. He was put through to the intelligence officer Major Marcel. When Marcel checked out the material, he concluded that it was unlike any debris seen during his service in World War II. And Marcel was experienced in these matters. He was the intelligence officer for the world's then one and only atomic-bomb unit. Roswell was home to the 509th Bomb Group, which, in 1945, had tested the first atomic bomb at the nearby White Sands Missile Range.

Marcel reported the find to Roswell base commander, Colonel William Blanchard. He instructed Marcel and counter-intelligence officer Sheridan W. Cavitt to go back to the ranch with Brazel and collect the rest of the debris.

'When we arrived at the crash site, it was amazing to see the vast amount of area it covered,' Marcel said. 'It was nothing that hit the ground or exploded on the ground. It's something that must have exploded above ground, travelling perhaps at a high rate of speed... It was quite obvious to me, familiar with air activities, that it was not a weather balloon, nor was it a plane or a missile.'

The two officers collected as much debris as their vehicles could hold, but they had to leave a lot of it behind when they set off back to Roswell. On the way back to the base, Marcel could not resist stopping off at his home to show the wreckage to his wife and their son, Jesse junior.

'My father was so excited about the debris that he drove by our house to show my mother and me the material before delivering it to the air base,' says Jesse Marcel Jr. 'There were several boxes of it in our car but we emptied the contents of just one of these boxes on our kitchen floor. He wanted to see if he could piece some of the fragments back together.'

According to Jesse Jr., the debris contained a lot of metal foil. It looked like aluminium, although its surface was not so reflective.

'I didn't try to bend it,' he says, 'nor did I witness the "metal with a memory" that some have described. I do recall my dad saying a colleague had tried to bend one of the larger pieces with a sledgehammer without denting it.'

Jesse Jr. said that the most striking parts of the material were the beams.

'The one I remember best was about twelve to eighteen inches and was made from a very lightweight material. When I held it up to the light I could see what appeared to be symbols printed or embossed along the length of the beam,' he says. 'They looked at first like hieroglyphics, but on closer scrutiny appeared to be geometric designs.'

The next morning, Colonel Blanchard had the Corona crash site sealed off. The military police and a large body of soldiers were sent to the Foster ranch. They were making a detailed search of the area when, back at the Army Air Force base, press officer Lieutenant Haut issued the famous press release. The news appeared in the evening editions of the local papers and was quickly picked up by the radio stations.

By this time, Major Jesse Marcel and the wreckage were on board a B-29 on their way to Wright Field (which is now known as Wright–Patterson Air Force Base) in Ohio. On the way, they stopped at Fort Worth, Texas, headquarters of the Eighth Air Force.

By this time, General Clemens McMullen, the Acting Director of Strategic Air Command (SAC) in Washington, had heard about the press release and taken immediate action. He contacted the Chief of Staff at Fort Worth, Colonel Thomas Jefferson DuBose, and told him to invent a cover story. Given the sensitive nature of the incident, base commander General Roger M. Ramey was put in charge.

Colonel DuBose later explained why the cover-up was put into action. 'We had just gone through a World War, then came this flying saucer business,' he said. 'It was just too much for the public to have to deal with.'

When Marcel touched down at Fort Worth, he was met by General Ramey. 'Don't say anything,' Ramey ordered. 'I'll take care of it.'

The weather-balloon cover story had already been dreamed up. The base's meteorologist Irving Newton provided some home-made wreckage – a mangled radar reflector made of foil and a few wooden sticks. Marcel posed by the 'wreckage' and the press was told that a mistake had been made. What had crashed to Earth in New Mexico was not a flying saucer, but a radar reflector. After the photo-call, Major Marcel was sent back to Roswell where he was forbidden to speak to anyone. When he returned home, he told his wife and son not to talk about the crash to anyone, either strangers or friends.

The cover story hit the newswires at about 5 p.m. Central Time. It was too late for the newspapers, except the last edition of the *Los Angeles Herald Express,* which added to their flying saucer story the subheading: 'General Believes it is Radar Weather Gadget.'

When Lieutenant Haut heard about the cover-up he was appalled, but there was nothing he could do.

'A balloon may have crashed, but it certainly had nothing to do with the downed saucer,' he says. 'What most people don't realise is that, back then, you didn't ask questions – you did whatever your superior told you. Today, there'd be a lot of questions, or even a Congressional hearing, but it was a different era then.'

The military moved in on the Foster ranch. After two days, the main body of the saucer was found not far from the ranch house. The search for debris was then expanded and, just over a mile from the craft, the bodies of two dead aliens were found. Over the following week, the military cleared up the debris and surrounding area.

Not all the debris may have found its way to a top-secret cache. On 24 March 1996, a visitor marched into Roswell's International UFO Museum and handed over a fragment of metal which he said he had got from a retired serviceman who had been involved in the clean-up of the crash debris. Under police escort, it was taken to the New Mexico Bureau of Mines and Mineral Resources where it was examined by metallurgist Chris McKee. X-ray fluorescence analysis showed that the fragment was 69 per cent silver and 31 per cent copper, and McKee concluded: 'There was nothing associated with it to suggest an exotic origin.' The fragment is still under investigation and remains under police protection.

Friedman and Moore published six papers about the crash at Roswell and, eventually, in 1986, Friedman persuaded the producers of NBC's *Unsolved Mysteries* to do a segment about Roswell in their TV show. By this time Friedman and Moore had tracked down ninety-two people involved in the case, but in his role as a consultant to the production he continued investigating the case. It was then that he got to the bottom of a mystery that had been bugging him since he had first talked to Marcel in 1978 – what had happened to the aliens?

In August 1989, while NBC were filming in Roswell, Friedman met retired mortician Glenn Dennis. He had worked for the Ballard Funeral Home, which had had a long-standing arrangement with Roswell Army Air Field, providing mortuary services. Glenn told Friedman about strange goings -on at the hospital on the base in the summer of 1947. The Army asked his advice on how to deal with 'small bodies'. The next time he turned up at the hospital he had been forcibly ejected, but a nurse at the base told him about 'very smelly' bodies she had seen being autopsied by two doctors. The corpses had brownish-grey skin and big heads with no hair. They had slits or holes for nose, ears and mouth and each hand had four slender fingers but no thumb. After several meetings with Dennis, the nurse suddenly disappeared. He had been told that she had moved to England but, when he tried to write to her, his letters were returned, stamped 'deceased'.

The episode of *Unsolved Mysteries* on the Roswell crash was aired in September 1989. It was seen across the US by twenty-eight million people. There followed a great wave of books and TV shows about Roswell.

In 1990 another witness who had seen the alien bodies came forward. An Army Air Forces photographer – who wished to be known only by the initials FB – approached Friedman, claiming to have seen the aliens' bodies recovered from the field in Corona. FB had been stationed at the Anacostia Naval Air Station, Washington, D.C, at the time. In July 1947, he and another photographer were ordered to fly to Roswell. When they arrived at RAAF, the two photographers were driven out to a tent in a field and told to photograph its contents.

'There were four bodies I could see,' FB says. 'They were not human; their heads appeared much too large for their tiny bodies.'

Friedman and others have come to believe that a second UFO had crashed around that time, on the plains of San Augustin, New Mexico, based on the testimony of two witnesses. One, Gerald Anderson, had contacted Friedman after seeing a 1990 re-run of the *Unsolved Mysteries* show. The other witness, Grady 'Barney' Barnett, had died by this time, but he had told the story to two friends, LaVerne and Jean Maltais, and they passed it on to Friedman independently.

The two stories matched. Both men said that alien bodies had been discovered in or around saucer debris. According to Anderson, one of the aliens survived the crash. Sadly, as Barnett was dead by then, he could not be questioned about this. As a result, a certain amount of doubt surrounds the San Augustin crash.

However, the details of the crash at Corona crash are now almost universally accepted. By the time Friedman's account *Crash at Corona* (co-written by aviation science writer Don Berliner) was published in 1992, most of the blanks in the story had been filled in.

In 1994, New Mexico Congressman Steven Schiff asked the US General Accounting Office to look into documents relating to the Corona–Roswell incident. When the Air Force heard about the GAO's investigation, they quickly issued their own twenty-five-page report admitting that they had lied about the weather-balloon story. In fact, what had crashed at Corona was a top-secret Mogul balloon designed to detect Soviet nuclear tests. However, the pro- ject was soon scrapped and declassified – so why did it take them so long to own up?

Lieutenant Haut has no time for this story either.

'Colonel Blanchard [the base commander who authorised Haut's press release] would have known about any secret experiments, or at least not to panic if anything odd fell from the sky,' he says. 'Why would he have authorised me to announce the story to the press? It just doesn't make sense.'

When the GAO's report was published in 1995, it reported that files relating to the crash had gone missing or been destroyed – to the point where the GAO could find no evidence of the crash at all. In response the USAF published *The Roswell Report: Truth Versus Fiction in the New Mexico Desert*. This was a simply an updated version of their first report, which makes no mention of the missing or destroyed files. However, it claims that the 'aliens' observed in the New Mexico desert were life-like test dummies, which had been dropped from a high-altitude balloon, and that the unusual military activity in the area at the time was simply the Air Force's attempt to recover them.

UFOlogists have universally discounted the USAF's explanation. However, some debunkers have come up with even weirder terrestrial explanations. It has been suggested that it was one of the nine thousand 'FUGO' balloons released by the Japanese in 1945. These were paper balloons that carried explosives. The idea was that they would drift over the Pacific and explode when they landed in America. But no one has been able to explain what it had been doing for the two years since the end of the war.

Some researchers have suggested that a rocket the US military were testing at the nearby White Sands Missile Range had gone astray. That might have fooled Mac Brazel, but surely the Army personnel at Roswell would have recognised a missile. The space programme – what there was of it at the time – was still under military control and some researchers claim that the 'alien bodies' were those of rhesus monkeys used in experiments to see how humans might cope with space travel.

In 1997, another reliable witness went public. A retired army officer, Philip J. Corso, had been a major in 1947. In early July, he had caught a corporal off-limit. The man was lurking in the shadows at the doorway of a warehouse on the base. His face was deathly white. The man was plainly frightened. He had disobeyed orders and was expecting to face severe discipline. He had been detailed to guard some crates that had been sent over from the army base at Fort Bliss, Texas. They were marked top-secret. Breaking every rule in the book, he had opened some of the crates to take a look. What he had seen had scared him even more than the punishment he faced.

'You won't believe this,' he told Major Corso.

'What are you talking about?' asked Corso. There was no need for a reply. Inside the open crate, he saw the body of a strange creature.

'At first I thought it was a dead child they were shipping somewhere,' said Corso. 'It was a four-foot, human-shaped creature with bizarre-looking four-fingered hands... and a light-bulb shaped head. The eye sockets were oversized and almond-shaped and pointed down to its tiny nose, which didn't really protrude from its skull.'

Among the paperwork that accompanied the crate, Corso found an army intelligence report. It said that the creature had been recovered from a spacecraft that had crashed at Roswell, New Mexico, two days earlier. In the warehouse, there were over thirty other wooden crates that were part of the consignment. Major Corso slipped the lid back on and covered the crate with a tarpaulin. Outside he told the corporal: 'You never saw this and you tell no one.' Corso himself tried to forget what he had seen. But when the Roswell story broke, it brought it all back.

Corso is an unimpeachable witness. He spent twenty-one years in the army, serving alongside General Douglas MacArthur in Korea and later under President Eisenhower on the National Security Council, and was decorated nineteen times. After he left the service in 1963, he worked as an advisor on the staffs of US Senators Strom Thurmond and James Eastland and came to public attention when he testified to the House National Security Committee on the fate of US prisoners of war held in North Korea.

But not only has he testified to the fact that he saw a dead alien in 1947, he was to come across those mysterious packing cases again.

Crash in Arizona

Another UFO crash took place in Paradise Valley, Phoenix, Arizona, in 1947. A craft thirty-six feet in diameter was retrieved, along with two humanoid bodies.

Former businessman and pilot Selman E. Graves witnessed part of the recovery operation with two friends during a hunting trip.

'There were some mine shafts – what you might call an outcropping – and a small hill, and we went up there and the three of us could look back and see everything that was taking place,' said Graves. 'There was a large – I can best describe it as a large aluminium dome-shaped thing there, which was roughly the size of a house – it was measured to be thirty-six feet in diameter.

'We could see that there were pitched buildings – tents – and men moving about. We at that time didn't have any idea what we were looking at. We thought it might be an observatory dome, except why would they have it down there on that piece of ground?'

Another informant named Silas Newton told Frank Scully, author of *Behind the Flying Saucers,* 'Supposedly there were a couple of small humanoids – about four-and-a-half feet tall – that were reported to be there.'

The Aztec Incident

Author Frank Scully also reported a crash that occurred near Aztec, New Mexico, in 1948. More dead aliens were retrieved. Most of Scully's information came from a 'Dr. Gee', who was in fact a composite of eight different people.

The disc that landed near Aztec was nearly a hundred feet in diameter and its exterior was made of a light metal resembling aluminium but was so durable that no amount of heat or diamond drilling had any effect. The craft was made from large rings of metal, which revolved around a central stabilised cabin, using an unfamiliar gear ratio. There were no rivets, bolts, screws or signs of welding. Investigators were eventually able to gain access to the craft by pushing a knob with a long pole through a porthole, which caused a hidden door to open. The craft was found to be assembled in segments using a complex system of grooves and pins. It was undamaged, having landed under its own guidance.

Sixteen small humanoids, ranging in height from thirty-six to forty-two inches, were found dead inside the cabin, their bodies charred to a dark brown colour. The craft and bodies were flown to Wright–Patterson Air Force Base.

In 1987, researcher William Steinman found some further evidence to support Scully's claim but refused to divulge his source. Steinman said that the crash had occurred on 25 March 1948 and was detected by three separate radar centres. It was the radar apparently that caused the craft to crash. In Steinman's version, only fourteen humanoid bodies were recovered and not sixteen as Scully had claimed.

Crash at Laredo

Another UFO crashed in Laredo, Texas, in the late 1940s. It was unearthed by Todd Zechel, of Ground Saucer Watch, who usually works with UFO documents he has obtained under the Freedom of Information Act. But in this case he got his information from an air force technician who was based at Carswell Air Force Base and chooses to remain anonymous.

The source says that on 7 July 1948, he had been involved in cordoning off an area near the town of Laredo. A ninety-foot disc had been downed in the area and was recovered. Radar operators and pilots witnessed the object as it flew over Albuquerque at an estimated speed of two thousand miles an hour.

Further evidence came from Leonard Stringfield, who learnt from other witnesses that a hairless four-foot entity had died in the crash and its body had been recovered. A US Navy officer also witnessed the wreckage being loaded onto trucks at the site.

Years later a photo was released of the dead 'alien'. However, this was quickly dismissed as a hoax. It showed a dead human pilot severely burned. Unfortunately the hoaxers did not realise that the photo also showed the dead man's sunglasses.

Government papers since released indicate that the Air Force were experimenting with modified Nazi V2 rockets at the time. The 'alien', it is said, was a monkey.

Alien Autopsy

While the USAF continues to deny that a UFO crashed at Roswell, there is evidence that yet another UFO may have been downed in New Mexico that year. Since 1995, television stations in over thirty countries have broadcast portions of what is said to be an alien autopsy. The alien in the film appears to match the eyewitness descriptions and sketches made by Roswell mortician Glenn Dennis from what his contact, the Air Force nurse, had told him. London-based film producer Ray Santilli, who claims to have bought the film from the cameraman, says that several military personnel involved in 1947 have confirmed that the alien is the creature recovered from a saucer crash in New Mexico. However, the cameraman claimed to have taken the footage on 31 May 1947, near Socorro, New Mexico, three days before the crash at Roswell.

The film was first aired in America on 28 August 1995, when ten million television viewers watched the documentary, *Alien Autopsy: Fact or Fiction*, on the Fox Network. It comprised a series of grainy, black-and-white film segments, which were said to be archive footage from 1947. In the footage, pathologists are shown carefully dissecting what appears to be an alien life form.

The film begins with a military officer showing pieces of debris to the camera. Unfortunately, neither his face nor any insignia that would identify his rank or unit are shown. Next the staircase and doorway to the autopsy room are shown. The camera then sweeps around the naked body of an alien lying on a table. It is bald and hairless, with a rounded stomach and no evidence of genitals. The pathologist then enters, wearing a biohazard suit, and begins his grisly work.

Deep incisions were made in the neck and chest. The skin was then drawn back and the creature's internal organs removed. Then the skin was removed from the top of the head. The skull was sawn open and the brain removed. During the autopsy, a figure can be seen behind an observation window. Santilli maintains that this is President Truman.

Santilli says he discovered the autopsy footage when he had been researching a music documentary. In the summer of 1993, he came across some previously unseen Elvis Presley footage in Cleveland, Ohio. After arranging the cash to buy the Presley film, the cameraman offered Santilli some other footage that he shot during his time in the forces. Santilli was told that the film was 'valuable' and a screening was arranged. He was impressed. The film showed a UFO crash site, and the autopsy of the extraterrestrials who had died in the crash. By November 1994, Santilli had raised another $150,000 to buy the film.

Back in Britain, Santilli took the film to the British UFO Research Association and showed it to Philip Mantle, BUFORA's director of research. Mantle was convinced by what he saw.

'The footage is unique,' he said. 'It is the only known instance of aliens on film.' On 26 March 1995, BUFORA issued a press release. In it, Mantle said: 'We have had the film checked out by Kodak who confirm it is fifty years old... we now plan to have it examined by film experts at Sheffield.'

However, some people in the UFO community smelt a rat. The editor of *UFO Magazine* Graham Birdsall phoned Peter Milson, a senior manager with Kodak in England. Milson knew nothing of BUFORA's press release claiming that Kodak had verified the date of the film. Birdsall began ringing round other Kodak offices. None of them admitted carrying out any tests on the alien autopsy film. After four months, Birdsall found a salesman at Kodak's Copenhagen office, who had been approached by someone on Santilli's behalf. He asked whether the film-edge markings, a square and triangle, meant the year of manufacture was 1947. The salesman checked back through Kodak's film logs and confirmed that this was correct. However, the salesman did not realise that the same edge markings also appeared on film manufactured in 1927 and 1967. Kodak's Peter Milson then went to great pains to point out to Santilli that 'the date of manufacture does not confirm the date when the film was shot or processed'.

Kodak could confirm the date of the film and offered to do so. What they would need were two frames of the autopsy sequence. But when the alien autopsy footage appeared on TV in August 1995, Kodak said that no frames had been forthcoming.

Santilli insists that Kodak had tested the film and confirmed the age of the footage. However, Kodak's motion-picture specialist Tony Amato, who would have directed the authentication process, says that, despite promises from Santilli through a US intermediary, Kodak has never received a single frame of the alien autopsy film.

Other UFOlogists expressed their concern that the film was doing their case more harm than good. They were particularly concerned that UFO researchers with established credentials in the Roswell crash were not being given access to the film. Nor were they being given the facts behind the story.

Undeterred, German UFO researcher Michael Hesemann began his own investigation and published his findings in *Facts v Polemics in the Alien Autopsy Footage Debate*. According to Hesemann, two three-frame segments were submitted for tests to the editor of the photography magazine *Shutterbug*, Bob Shell, who had been a photographic consultant for the US legal system and for the FBI.

Shell made a careful chemical analysis of the film's make-up and confirmed that it had been manufactured before 1956. The film was Super XX-Panchromatic 16mm Safety Film, an indoor, high-speed film, which was unstable. It had a life span of no more than two years. So the film had to be shot and developed before 1958. That meant the film could well be genuine. The problem was that the segments Shell tested did not show the alien, so some doubts still hung over the film's authenticity.

Meanwhile, attention turned to the cameraman who had taken the film. He did not want his identity revealed, but under the pseudonym 'Jack Barnett' he issued a statement explaining how he had come to shoot the film. In the summer of 1947, 'Barnett' was stationed in Washington, D.C., when he received orders to make his way to New Mexico to film the crash site of a Russian spy plane. On the way, he stopped off at Wright Field in Ohio to pick up the equipment he would need. From Wright Field he flew to Roswell, then travelled by road through the desert to the crash site. In his 1995 statement, Barnett was vague about the location of the crash site, but later he led Michael Hesemann to a site near Socorro, New Mexico. And he said that the crash had occurred on 31 May 1947, not in July 1947 when the UFO had crashed at Corona.

Kent Jeffrey, head of the International Roswell Initiative, a UFO research group, was also on the case. He noted that Barnett's statement was full of British expressions, not the sort of language that an American would have used. He tracked down a number of retired combat cameramen who had been in the service in 1947. They included retired Air Force Lieutenant Colonel Daniel A. McGovern, a motion-picture project officer for the Air Force, who filmed the devastation of Nagasaki after the atomic bomb was dropped on it in 1945 and was stationed in Washington, D.C, in June 1947 when the cameraman of the alien autopsy was there, and Bill Gibson, who filmed the B-25 bombers taking off from the aircraft carrier *Hornet* to make the famous 'Doolittle raid' on Japan in April 1942. All of them had worked on top secret projects. They said it made no sense to fly a cameraman from Washington to New Mexico to film the crash site. There were qualified cameramen with high-level security clearances stationed across the country. If a UFO had crashed in New Mexico, combat cameramen would have been despatched from Roswell Army Air Field itself.

McGovern had filmed a number of conventional autopsies during his career. He maintained that all medical procedures were routinely shot in colour. The alien autopsy was shot in grainy monochrome. The hand-held film is shaky and out of focus. The veterans say that the quality of the camera work is appalling, well below the standard required in the military.

'If anybody in my unit shot film in that manner, he'd be back scrubbing pots in the kitchen,' said Joe Longo, President of the International Combat Camera Association.

Colonel McGovern offered to check out the cameraman. He was prepared to do this in conditions of the strictest confidentiality. However, he would need the cameraman's full name and serial number to access his military service file in the Air Force Records Center. However, Santilli, respecting the cameraman's right to privacy, said: 'I can state quite categorically that the last person the cameraman is going to place any confidence in is an ex-military serviceman... in the present climate the cameraman will be doing himself and his family a disservice by going public… However good his credentials, he will be torn limb from limb.'

Critics claim that Santilli is deliberately obstructing their efforts to find out the truth. But given the media feeding frenzy that accompanies any fresh development in the Roswell case, it seems quite reasonable that the cameraman should want to protect his privacy. Those who take the footage at face value point to attacks on its authenticity as another example of the authorities covering up the facts about UFOs by discrediting genuine evidence and credible witnesses with a campaign of smear and disinformation that ultimately turns public attention from the issue.

However, whether the alien autopsy film is genuine or a hoax, it did do one valuable thing. It revived interest in the whole issue of UFOs. What's more, there are plenty of UFOlogists who stick up for the film.

'We've got surgeons saying that the creature in the film was flesh and blood,' says Philip Mantle of BUFORA. 'We've got military personnel who recognise the alien as the same thing they saw in 1947. It fits.'

Survivor?

While researchers were arguing about the authenticity of the alien autopsy film, evidence emerged that not all the alien astronauts had perished in the 1947 UFO crashes. At least one, it seemed, survived long enough to be interviewed. Another remarkable piece of footage showing an alien being interrogated surfaced. Just under three minutes long, it was said to have been smuggled out of the Nellis Air Force Range and Nuclear Test Site – the home of the secret establishment known as Area 51. The footage clearly shows two men cross-questioning an ailing extraterrestrial.

Area 51 first came to the attention of the public in 1989, when Robert 'Bob' Lazar, a physicist who had worked there, claimed that the US military were building nine flying saucers there, based on downed craft in their possession. His revelation produced a vicious backlash from the authorities, though they subsequently admitted that Area 51 actually exists.

The alien interrogation footage was stolen from the Groom Lake complex by a man known as 'Victor', who also worked there. He said that the film was a clipping from hundreds of hours of interview footage showing the many different species of extraterrestral held at Area 51.

A few seconds of the tape were aired in April 1997 on the US TV show *Strange Universe*. This provoked a massive media reaction and reawakened public interest in Area 51. But the question in everyone's mind was, was it true?

The film was first shown to TV network executive Robert Kiviat, who made the documentary *Alien Autopsy: Fact or Fiction*. He turned it down on the grounds that he had already had his fingers burnt in the row over the authenticity of the alien autopsy film. Other producers were equally wary. However, Rocket Pictures Home Video of Los Angeles were making a documentary investigating claims that the US government were employing extraterrestrials on top-secret technology projects at Area 51. Rocket's president, Tom Coleman, stepped in and bought the footage. Independent producer and UFO enthusiast Jeff Broadstreet was called in to make a show around the three-minute clip. He lined up a group of experts to view the film. Among them were distinguished UFO researchers and writers Whitley Strieber, Sean Morton and Major Robert Dean, along with two leading Hollywood special-effects men.

The alien interview footage had been shot through a pane of glass and there was no sound. It showed an interview taking place in a darkened room that was lit with an eerie greenish glow. It is possible to make out the silhouettes of two men, sitting with their backs to the camera at one end of a long table, which was covered with microphones and wires. One was wearing a military uniform. There appear to be stars on the epaulets of his jacket. The other man was more casually dressed and occasionally rubbed his forehead with his hand.

At the other end of the table sat a small, beige-skinned creature with black eyes and a bulbous head – 'the likes of which haunt the nightmares of thousands of unwilling abductees,' said Sean Morton, who was amazed by the footage.

The creature appeared to be unwell. It seemed to be hooked up to medical monitors. One was blinking erratically, as if it were monitoring a very sickly heart. Its bulbous head looked purple and bruised, and it bobbed and jerked involuntarily. Towards the end of the footage, the creature suffers some form of seizure. Its mouth snapped open and closed rapidly as some kind of fluid dribbled from it. The heart monitor went wild, and two medics rushed in. One of them cradled the alien's head and pointed a pen-light into its eyes. The other put his fingers into its mouth, apparently in an attempt to help it breathe. At this point, the footage comes to an abrupt end.

In August 1997, Rocket released their documentary *Area 51: The Alien Interview*. It showed the footage and a discussion between the expert witnesses.

'Rocket tried to make a balanced documentary,' said producer Jeff Broadstreet, 'and so have contrasted the comments of Morton and Dean, who both believe the footage to be genuine, against two of Hollywood's leading special-effects experts, who both thought the video was a hoax and that the ET was either digitally created or a mechanical puppet.'

This left Broadstreet sitting on the fence. 'Personally, I don't know if it's real or not,' he says. And he does not believe the matter is ever going to be settled one way or the other. 'I mean, who's going to be able to authenticate whether the footage of a live ET is real? Even if the government had footage of a live ET, do you think they are going to admit it?'

The documentary sparked a debate about the authenticity of the footage. Like the cameraman of the alien autopsy, Victor is publicity shy. In the documentary he appeared only in silhouette.

'He won't tell us his real name,' says Broadstreet. 'He won't tell us in what official capacity he worked at Area 51, only that he was definitely there. He told me that his biggest fear is if the authorities discover his identity and he wants, at all costs, to avoid the trouble Bob Lazar attracted.'

Although the original video had a soundtrack, Victor removed the soundtrack from the tape before going public to hide the identity of the two men interrogating the creature. Victor said that the man in the military uniform was 'some kind of aide', while the civilian was a government telepath.

Victor thought that the alien died later from its injuries, though he was not sure. He did know that it was not interviewed again. Victor also said it was not the only alien at Area 51. He had seen them on other occasions but he does not know, or cannot say, whether they had been captured from crashed UFOs or were working at the base voluntarily.

Unfortunately, the original videotape was not available for examination as Victor had smuggled the footage out of Area 51 on a computer disk, after converting it into digital format. Nevertheless, computer image analyst Jim Dilettoso examined the footage frame by frame. He believes that it was not shot on video, as Victor had claimed, but on film stocks, as no interference patterns were shown on the monitor in the shot. But he admits that this could also be explained if the interview was videoed 'under very low lighting conditions'.

The two Hollywood special effects technicians called in thought the footage was a hoax and said that they could have done much better. Four-time Oscar winner Rick Baker said: 'It's definitely a puppet and not a very well done one either. It's very much like a guy's got his hand inside the thing, manoeuvring it... It looks like they took a great deal of effort to hide as much of the anatomy as possible. I'd be willing to stake my reputation on this being a hoax. It's a fake.'

However, John Criswell does have some doubts.

'Just when I was sure it was some kind of puppet, it would start to lift up, jerk or move in such a way that would be very difficult to fake,' he says.

Whitley Strieber, author of *Communion and Transformations*, who claims to be a multiple abductee, also believes the tape is a fake, but was distressed by the way the creature – fake or not – was being treated. It invokes memories of his own abductions.

'It is very difficult to watch this,' he said, 'because somebody who made this knows something about the way they move.' He never wants to see the footage again.

Morton was 'utterly amazed' by the footage and was very concerned by the condition of the alien. He was particularly interested in the time code that appears on the video. It is prefaced by the letters DNI. Morton believes that Area 51 is run by the Department of Naval Intelligence. This had been the conclusion of George Knapp, who had spent a year investigating the claims of Bob Lazar. Lazar's pay cheques had had the letters DNI printed on them and his tax statement for 1989 showed that he was employed by the Department of Naval Intelligence.

But the video's most enthusiastic supporter was Colonel Bob Dean, generally regarded as one of the most important UFO researchers from the military.

'I was quite prepared to see a hoax,' he said, 'yet what I saw took me completely by surprise. It had a profound emotional impact on me. I became convinced that this was the real thing.' He, too, reacted angrily to the way the alien was being treated.

Dean says the alien in the interview video 'matches with other photographs of ETs I have seen'. Dean also believes that the alien autopsy film is genuine because the creature depicted looks exactly like pictures he had seen of alien bodies recovered from UFO crashes he had privileged access to in the military.

'I happen to know the autopsy film is real,' he says, 'because the footage sold to producer Ray Santilli was released over twenty years ago to our military allies in the South East Asia Organisation. He also believes that the release of the autopsy film was no accident. It was part of a CIA plan to gauge and manipulate public opinion.

'I know that the level of classification on this kind of material is so far beyond top secret that you can't imagine how tightly the government sits on it,' he says.

Nevertheless, he can quite understand why other UFOlogists are sceptical about the alien interview video, and he compares it to the reaction of people when they first saw the extraterrestrial in the autopsy film.

'Just because it didn't look like a "typical Grey", or whatever it's expected to look like, they immediately thought it was fake,' says Dean. 'The alien creature in the interview video is not one of the typical-looking Greys either, but people don't realise we are not dealing with one but several different species.'

The sceptics are lead by UFO researcher Michael Lindemann.

'There is no compelling reason to consider it real,' he says. 'Therefore it has to be a fake. I know of a number of people who have seen the entire tape, who have said that it's a hoax.'

Lindemann saw the 'same stupid three seconds on *Strange Universe* as everyone else' and was so angry at the show's lack of balance that he called the producers and complained.

'I think the whole character of Victor is highly dubious,' Lindemann said. 'There's not even a hint of authenticity when he was interviewed. I believe Rocket Home Video are looking for a quick killing.'

This serves to highlight the problem that controversial evidence, such as the alien autopsy and the alien interview, poses for UFOlogists. If they are shown to be fake, it dents the credibility of the whole phenomenon. And where alien footage is concerned, the allegation can always be made that they have been cleverly faked in the hope of making money.

The Kingman Crash

The New Mexico, Arizona and Texas crashes of 1947 and 1948 were not the only times that UFOs have come to Earth. According to US scientist Fritz Werner, a UFO crashed just south of the Grand Canyon national park at Kingman, Arizona, in 1953. Werner had first-hand knowledge of the crash because he was one of the
scientists sent to investigate the wreckage. At the time, Werner was part of a top-secret team of scientists working in the deserts of Nevada.

Their assignment was to make a scientific assessment of blast damage caused by a nuclear test.

On 20 May 1953, Werner was called aside by the physicist incharge of the research group. He was to catch a special flight to Phoenix, Arizona. At the airfield, he was picked up by a large bus with blacked-out windows. There were fifteen other passengers on board, and they were ordered to remain silent during their journey out into the desert.

The bus arrived at their destination on the evening of 21 May. When the passengers alighted they were escorted to a canyon where huge arc lights illuminated a large disc that was guarded by a detachment of soldiers. The disc was around thirty feet in diameter. It was embedded into the sandy soil and stuck out of the ground at an angle.

Werner was told to calculate the impact speed of the object. He did this and reported his findings, and then he was told to go back to the bus to await transportation back to Nevada. On the way, he managed to sneak a quick peek inside a tent. Inside, to his amazement, he saw the body of an alien. It had brownish skin and was about four feet tall, and it was dressed in a silver one-piece suit complete with skull-cap.

Werner was told that the disc he had seen was a highly classified US jet fighter that had crashed in the desert. He did not believe this. As the years passed, nothing remotely like it went into service, and in 1973, although Werner had signed a declaration of secrecy, he contacted eminent UFOlogist Ray Fowler. Unfortunately, as no-one outside the military knew anything about the crash at Roswell at the time, Fowler could shed no light on what Werner had seen. However, four years later, Fowler's colleague Leonard Stringfield heard an account from another witness that seemed to corroborate Werner's story.

The second witness was a former National Guard pilot who wished to remain anonymous. In the 1950s, he had been stationed at the Wright–Patterson Air Force Base in Dayton, Ohio. Between 1948 and 1969, Wright Field was the home of the US government UFO research project. It also housed the Foreign Technology Division. The job of FTD specialists was to unravel the mysteries of enemy technology that had fallen into US hands. Usually this meant examining the wreckage of the latest crashed Soviet MiG jet and working out enemy capabilities, but there were rumours that the technicians there also worked on technology collected from more exotic sources. A secret US Air Force intelligence document outlined Project Moon Dust, which was responsible for collecting any Soviet space debris that fell to Earth. It also mentions that, as part of these 'FTD Projects... qualified field intelligence personnel' were to be posted on 'a quick reaction basis to recover or perform field exploration of Unidentified Flying Objects'.

One day in mid-1953, some crates were delivered to Wright–Patterson containing items retrieved from the Arizona desert, the airman said. Inside there was wreckage from a crash. The airman said that some of it had strange writing on it in symbols that resembled Sanskrit. Other crates contained the bodies of three aliens, packed into dry-ice containers to preserve the tissues. They were about four feet tall, with large heads and parchment-like skin – almost identical to the one Werner had seen. And they had come from Arizona.

A data file hacked from the mainframe at Wright–Patterson contains a description of the aliens by Dr Frederick Hauser. He said that the creatures were 'eerily human-like' though 'smaller than average in size, and completely bald. No eyebrows or eyelashes. No body hair at all.'

Another scientist who has examined alien remains recovered from a downed UFO is Dr Robert Sarbacher. In 1986, he said that their bodies were extremely light 'constructed like certain insects we have observed on Earth, wherein, because of the low mass, the inertial forces involved would be quite low'. This would explain how the creatures survived high-G aerial manoeuvres. It also matches the descriptions given by many eyewitnesses who have come face-to-face with aliens.

Crash at Kecksburg

Another UFO crashed in 1965 near Kecksburg, Pennsylvania. At 4:45 p.m. on the afternoon of 9 December 1965, a fiery object was seen flying across the skies above the Great Lakes on the US–Canadian border. Numerous witnesses saw it and reported what they had seen to the authorities. They said they had seen an orange mass with smoke trailing from it and pieces falling off it. Some mistook what they saw for an aircraft that was on fire, though their accounts more accurately resembled meteorite breaking up high above the earth – an explanation often given for UFO sightings.

However, later the same evening, a loud sonic boom was heard in the area of Kecksburg and a powerful tremor shook the ground as something crash-landed in a nearby wood. It left behind it a thick trail of smoke that remained in the sky for twenty minutes. This could be seen from Pontiac, Michigan, some two hundred miles away, where it was filmed.

It was certainly not a meteorite. Scientist Ivan Sanderson collected the sighting reports and found some extraordinary anomalies. According to eyewitnesses, the UFO took six minutes to cover a few hundred miles. Meteorites travel much faster than that. By plotting the sightings on a map, it was possible to show that the object veered to the east before it crashed. Meteorites cannot change direction. If the object that crashed into the wood was not a meteorite, perhaps it was a piece of space junk. Sanderson discovered that a Soviet rocket, Cosmos 96, had indeed re-entered that day. But NORAD, the early warning system in Colorado, reported the re-entry thirteen hours before the crash at Kecksburg.

The local emergency services rushed to the crash site, expecting to find the wreckage of plane. Instead, the firemen saw a strange, cone-shaped object. But the military soon arrived and took over, so they assumed that the object was part of a crashed military jet.

The military claimed that they had found nothing in the forest that night and dismissed the UFO sighting reports that had been made in the area. However, in 1980, Kecksburg fire chief Robert Bitner told local UFO investigators Clark McClelland and Stan Gordon what he had seen. On the evening of 9 December 1965, Bitner and assistant fire chief James Mayes had entered the woods, expecting to find a scene of devastation left by a plane crash. Instead, they found a conical craft – about ten or twelve feet high – embedded in the ground.

The flying saucer had crashed into the woods at an angle of about 30 degrees. It had knocked the tops off trees and flattened the undergrowth. Despite the evidence of the severity of the crash, it had not caught fire and was virtually intact. There was a circle on the base of the craft. On it there were what looked like symbols or some form of writing. Bitner and his team had had plenty of time to examine the craft, before the military arrived and escorted them out of the woods. They knew what they saw.

Assistant fire chief Mayes also talked to McClelland and Stan Gordon and confirmed what Bitner had said. According to Mayes, a flat-bed truck had left the site later that night. It was carrying a large object covered with a tarpaulin. Mayes has no doubt that the US military removed the strange object they had seen, then denied that they had found anything in the woods as part of a cover-up.

Later, an officer at Lockbourne Air Force Base near Columbus, Ohio, which is about 150 miles from Kecksburg, told researchers that a flat-bed truck carrying a large conical object, covered by a tarpaulin, arrived at Lockbourne before dawn on 10 December 1965. The truck entered by a little-used back gate where the officer had been posted. He was ordered to shoot anyone who tried to get near the truck. At 7 a.m., the truck and its mysterious load left for Wright–Patterson Air Force Base – home of UFO research project and the FTD unit. The officer was never told what was under the tarpaulin. But are there reasons to believe that it was an extraterestrial craft?

Mysterious Cargo

Another mysterious cargo had turned up at Fort Riley, Kansas, exactly a year earlier. On 10 December 1964, a guard on duty in the motor pool and three other men were ordered by a senior officer to make their way to a remote corner of the base.

When they arrived, they noticed a large military chopper shining a large searchlight on a strange object which was resting on the ground.

The object was already surrounded by other military personnel. The guard was given orders to stop any civilians who tried to get near it. He was told to 'shot to kill' if necessary. He was also warned not to tell anyone about the incident.

The object looked something like a giant hamburger, forty foot by sixteen foot, with a dark line along its rim and a small tail-fin stabiliser. The guard noticed that the air near the craft was very warm despite it being a bitterly cold night.

Some time later, UFO researchers managed to obtain some corroboration of his story. Another guard reported that on the next morning, he saw a large flat-bed truck with a roundish object covered with canvas sheets being driven out of the base under high security.

The Port Ness Monster

UFOs do not only crash in America. At 4:10 p.m. on 26 October 1996, a bright light, trailing smoke and fire, was seen moving across the sky from the Port of Ness at the northern tip of the Isle of Lewis in the Outer Hebrides. Suddenly it exploded over the sea. Eyewitnesses saw two large pieces of debris spiral down towards the water, leaving a trail of smoke. As they hit the water, they exploded again, so violently that the surface of the sea was ablaze for several minutes.

The coastguards at nearby Stornoway were alerted, and lifeboats were quickly dispatched to the scene. Transatlantic airline routes pass over Lewis, and the authorities feared that a plane had crashed. It was quickly established that no planes, military or civilian, were missing. Nevertheless, an RAF Nimrod was sent to join the surface craft searching the dark waters. The search was wound up the next day, without result. 'It has been a fairly massive search, but a complete blank has been drawn,' said an RAF spokesman. 'We remain puzzled by what could have caused this.'

However, it was only the public search that was over. Civilian vessels were quickly moved out of the waters around Lewis. The official reason for this was that a naval exercise was taking place in the area. The fact that it began the day after a UFO had been downed was purely coincidental, of course. A fleet of military aircraft, ships and submarines converged on the area. Later, fishermen saw a naval frigate hauling wreckage up from the ocean floor. Apparently something had been found.

Four months later, in April 1997, an unidentified substance, possibly a fuel residue, washed up on Tangusdale Beach on Barra, at the southern end of the Outer Hebrides. Local seamen confirmed that, given the currents and prevailing winds, this substance could well have taken that long to have been carried down from the northern tip of Lewis.

Downed in Nebraska

It is not even as if UFO crashes were new. On 6 June 1884, a blazing object fell from the skies above Dundy County in southern Nebraska. Seeing the object hit the ground, local farmhands ran to the scene. They found a large area of scorched vegetation and that the ground had been fused into glass. In the middle of devastation was a mass of smouldering metal. One man got too close. His skin blistered in a way reminiscent of radiation burns. It took several days before the wreckage was cool enough to touch. The debris, it was found, was as strong as brass, but incredibly light. It seemed to have the characteristics of aluminium alloys, unknown in the 1880s. The local press at the time speculated that the strange craft had come from outer space.

The Bodies From Brazil

The alien seen in the alien interview video may not have been the only extraterrestrial to survive a crash. In 1996, two aliens were captured in Brazil. Despite medical care they do not seem to have survived and their remains, like those of other extraterrestrials, seem to have ended up in the hands of the American government.

The story began at 8 a.m. on the morning of Saturday 20 January 1996, when the fire department of Varginha – a city of 180,000 inhabitants in the Minais Gerais state of Brazil – received an anonymous telephone call. The caller had seen a mysterious creature in a park in the northern suburb of Jardim Andere. In Varginha, it was not unusual for dangerous wild animals to wader into populated areas, and the fire department was responsible for dealing with such incidents. They were, in no great hurry. Two hours later, a fire truck eventually arrived at Jardim Andere and parked on the brow of a hill overlooking the park. A number of journalists were already on the scene, interviewing eyewitnesses.

The five fire officers were expecting to deal with a wild animal so, equipped with nets and cages, they made their way down the slope into the park. In the woodlands there, they found a small biped crouching in the trees. It was three foot tall with strange oily-brown skin. The strange creature had three raised humps on its forehead, blood-red eyes and a small opening for a mouth. It also gave off a strange buzzing sound, like a swarm of bees, and it appeared to be injured.

The fire-fighters were ill equipped to deal with an injured alien. The officer called the local army base. The commandant, General Sergio Coelho Lima, despatched troops who sealed off the area, but builder's assistant Henrique Jose saw what happened next from the rooftop of a nearby house. Four firemen trapped the creature in their nets. Then they transferred it to a wooden crate, which they handed over to the military. Everyone seemed pleased with the efficiency of the operation.

What no one had realised was that there was not just one alien on the loose in Varginha, but two. Later that day, local UFO investigator Ubirijara Franco Rodrigues – who was unaware of the first incident – began getting calls reporting another bizarre sighting. These led him to interview three girls who had stumbled across a strange creature crouching outside a building on Benevenuto Bras Vieira Street in the Jardim Andere district, near to where the first creature had been captured. They had seen the creature at around 3:30 p.m. on their way back from work as housemaids.

The girls – Liliane Fatima Silva, sixteen, her sister Valquira, fourteen, and a friend Katia Andrade Xavier, twenty-two – told

Rodrigues that the creature they had seen looked like the devil, with three raised humps on its forehead. They ran screaming from the scene.

'It was not animal or human,' Katia said. 'It was a horrible thing.'

Harvard psychologist Dr John Mack interviewed the three girls later and was convinced they are telling the truth. 'If I am wrong,' he said. 'I will tear up my diploma.'

The three girls ran as fast as they could to the house of Luisa Silva, the mother of two of the girls. The news spread like wildfire. Soon terrified residents were calling the fire department reporting a second creature on the loose.

'The witnesses are very reliable,' said Rodrigues. 'There are signs of emotional trauma caused by the strange meeting with the alien.'

The second creature also appeared to be injured. The authorities moved more quickly this time. Again fire officers netted the unfortunate creature, and the army whisked it away. But this capture took place on the street and they could not prevent a crowd gathering to watch.

Soon Ubirijara Franco Rodrigues hooked up with a fellow UFO researcher, Rodrigues e Pacaccini, who was investigating the morning sightings, but knew nothing of the second incident. At first there was some confusion, but the two UFOlogists eventually realised that they were investigating two separate, though connected, alien sightings and decided to pool their resources. The first thing they needed was more witnesses, so they began distributing flyers.

Although Varginha is three hundred miles from Rio de Janeiro, rumours that the authorities had captured two aliens soon reached the Brazilian UFO publications there. Every UFO researcher in Brazil beat a path to Varginha to investigate. The local press also appealed for witnesses. Public meetings were held. Soon over sixty eyewitnesses had come forward – and a substantial proportion were in the military. From the beginning it was plain that two extraterrestrials had indeed been captured. But what the investigators wanted to know was, what had happened to them. As the eyewitness accounts were pieced together, a clear picture began to emerge.

It appears that the first creature was taken to the School of the Sergeant at Arms – a military school – at Tres Coracoes, south east of Varginha. The authorities then refused to say what happened to it afterwards. However, investigators discovered that a policeman who had been involved in its capture on Saturday night had been injured. Two days later, he died in hospital. The cause of death was given as pneumonia but, when the dead man's family pushed for more details, the hospital authorities refused to discuss the matter further.

Rodrigues and Pacaccini established that the second creature had been taken to Varginha Regional Hospital, late on Saturday afternoon. Either that day or the following morning, the creature was transferred to Varginha's Humanitas Hospital two miles away. The doctors there were apparently better equipped to deal with its injuries. Nevertheless, the creature died in Humanitas Hospital at 6 p.m. on Monday, 22 January. According to a military source, the alien's autopsy was performed there. At least fifteen doctors, military, police and fire officers crowded into the room to see the creature laid out in a wooden casket. Apparently, one of the doctors prised open the alien's tiny mouth, pushed a pair of forceps inside and pulled out its tongue, which was black. When he let go, the tongue sprang back.

Those who saw the corpse said the creature had three fingers and three raised humps on its forehead. It had no navel, no nipples and no sexual organs. Its skin was brown and oily in texture, matching other eyewitness descriptions. And its legs, which appeared to be jointed, were grazed and wrinkled.

When the lid to the casket was screwed down, two military figures wearing face masks and gloves wrapped the coffin in black plastic sheeting, then placed it on the back of a truck. Early the following morning, a convoy of army trucks headed out of Varginha. The indications are that alien's body was taken to the University of Campinas, Unicamp, two hundred miles south-west of Varginha. Nothing more is known about what happened to the creature.

Pacaccini interviewed a Brazilian Air Force radar operator, who told him that, before the incidents in Varginha, the Brazilian Armed Forces had been alerted by the US. They were tracking a UFO that was entering Brazilian airspace. The Americans gave details of the craft's trajectory, but they could not say whether the UFO was intending to land or was about to crash.

In the days leading up to 20 January, Varginha had been a hotbed of UFO sightings. Hundreds had been reported in the area. Aliens had also been seen. Farmer Eurico de Freitas and his wife had been woken in the early hours of the morning by the sound of disturbed farm animals. Looking out from their bedroom window, they saw a grey object, emitting 'some kind of smoke', move silently across the fields about sixteen feet above the ground, before disappearing into the night.

Pacaccini did not discount the possibility that the two creatures in captivity might have been human in origin – maybe the result of a military experiment that had gone badly wrong. But if the creatures captured in Varginha were genuine extraterrestrials, where was their spacecraft? Pacaccini's efforts to trace the wreckage have been stonewalled by the military, and he claims there has been an official cover-up. He has also received countless death threats by anonymous callers. If anyone in the military so much as mentions his name, they risk an immediate ten-day detention. General Lima ordered a security clamp-down as leaks from the military provoked what the local papers called 'ET mania'. He issued an order banning anyone under his command from speaking to any Brazilian UFOlogist. But this has not prevented further details about the case being leaked to researchers.

It has since come to the investigators' attention that an American was present on the morning of 20 January when the first creature was captured and loaded on to the military truck. And a C-5 or C-17 US Air Force transport plane was seen later that day at Sao Paulo International Airport. Two days later, an American transport – probably the same plane – appeared at Campinas Airport, which is close to the university where the second creature was taken after its autopsy. The indications are that the creatures – one possibly still alive, the other dead – were flown to the US in the care of the American military.

In that case they may have missed a third creature on the loose. In

February 1996, a local van driver was driving round a curve when his headlights picked out a strange creature some fifty-five yards away. The driver screeched to a halt. He saw the creature raise its arms to cover its 'blood-red eyes' and run off into the night. The driver said that it had either four or three fingers on each hand.

Two months later, on the evening of 21 April, sixty-seven-year-old Mrs Terezinha Gallo Clepf was dining at the restaurant in Varingha Zoo when, at 9 p.m., she went outside for a cigarette. She came face-to-face with a creature matching the description of the others seen in the area. This immediately spawned speculation that more extraterrestrials had arrived in Varginha and were looking for their friends.

Also in April 1996, Luisa Silva, mother of two of the girls who first witnessed the second creature, got a visit from the 'Men in Black' – though, this being Latin America, they were men in white. Four strangers – none of whom were Brazilian – wearing white or cream Armani suits turned up at her home. They offered her 'a large sum of cash' to persuade her daughters to deny what they had seen. Mrs Silva refused and the men drove off in a blue 1994 Lincoln Continental car. They promised to return.

Since the incident in Varginha, Brazil's leading UFO magazine has discovered that the office phones have been bugged.

'We have received confirmation of this from a reliable source,' says editor A.J. Gevaerd. 'We have always condemned the worldwide cover-up surrounding UFOs, and the Roswell case. But there isn't a single article in the Brazilian Constitution that prohibits UFOlogical research – and that's enough reason for us to continue.'

Despite the dangers, Gevaerd continues investigating the aliens of Varginha.

'It has been a breakthrough in Brazilian UFOlogy,' he says. 'To our happiness, it happened right in Varginha. I think it will be the first step towards a global change of consciousness regarding the subject of UFOs.'

Russia's Roswell

In the closing months of 1998, some footage emerged that proved that extraterrestials were visiting Earth. Not only that, it showed that a crashed alien spacecraft and some dead aliens were in the possession of a superpower. But this time the extraterrestrials had not fallen into the hands of the US. The Soviets had got them.

A series of segments of colour film have been found in the files of the KGB and were aired on the US cable channel TNT on 13 September 1998. The footage shows a disc-shaped alien spacecraft that had crashed into the Sverdlovsk region of Western Siberia some time in March 1969. In one segment, Russian military personnel and KGB officers are shown inspecting the crash site. In the foreground, a large fragment of disc juts from the frozen Soviet soil. Another segment shows the autopsy of a badly mutilated creature recovered from the wreck. Three men in surgical garb are shown setting to work on its headless torso and arm.

In the KGB films the surgical work on the unfortunate extraterrestrial was frighteningly realistic. This time it was in focus and, unlike the American alien autopsy movie, the faces of the people in the footage can be clearly made out. However, although these men can be identified, tracking down former military personnel in the former Soviet Union is no easy task. Although the film has passed all sorts of tests, UFO researchers are reluctant to attest to its authenticity, just in case.

Alien Grave

One of the strangest cases involving a crashed UFO occurred more than a hundred years ago in the town of Aurora, Texas. The year was 1897, during which the US was plagued with hundreds of sightings of strange airships.

The story goes that on 19 April 1897 a strange airship appeared over the town of Aurora. The craft then apparently crashed into a windmill tower and exploded. Some of the material recovered had strange hieroglyphic symbols on it. The townspeople recovered from among the wreckage the body of an 'alien', which they buried in the local cemetery.

Several UFO researchers have tried to uncover some supportive documentation with varying success. Between 1966 and 1977, some went down to Aurora and discovered that a few witnesses were still alive and they confirmed that the story was essentially true. Researchers located the grave where the alien was buried several years ago and tried to get the body exhumed. The request was denied by the authorities.

Technology Uncovered

Welcome to Area 51

There is a part of the United States the size of Switzerland that appears blank on every map. It lies in the Nevada desert north-west of Las Vegas. Don't go there. Photography is prohibited and signs warn that it is unlawful to enter the area without permission. Ignore the signs and you will find yourself handcuffed, put in leg irons and strip-searched. Trespassers are known to have been fined $6,000 or jailed for up to a year. And they were the lucky ones. The signs say: 'Use of deadly force authorized.' The airspace over the area is restricted too.

Although nothing is shown on the map, there is plenty there. Along with mountains and creeks, there are roads, buildings, bunkers and a massive runway six miles long. At night the Groom Lake area is a blaze of light. The closed area is known officially as Nellis Air Force Range and Nuclear Test Site. It is home to Area 51. That was a name given to one section of the base on old government maps. And it is generally agreed by UFOlogists that, if the government did have a UFO or a batch of aliens, this is where they would keep it.

The base began in 1954 as a top-secret site where the Lockheed Aircraft Corporation could develop spy planes for the CIA. Since then, the US military's most futuristic technological projects have been developed there. The Stealth bomber and other unconventional aircraft were tested at Nellis. Its very existence has always been shrouded in secrecy. The US Air Force only admitted that Area 51 existed at all in 1994, after Soviet spy satellite footage of the facility was shown in evidence during a court case. The reason for the secrecy, the US government says, is that Nellis is home to the cutting edge of military technology. But the technology is not American. Nor are the technicians working on it. They are from outer space.

Ever since Area 51 was established, it has been the centre of UFO sightings. The authorities issued regular denials. But they found they had egg on their faces when one of their own men said that, not only were there UFOs flying in the airspace above Area 51, but that the USAF was developing alien technology in an underground plant there.

The man's name was Robert 'Bob' Lazar. A child prodigy, he developed a hydrogen-fuelled car and made a jet-powered car and motorbike that had a top speed of 350 miles an hour. At the age of twenty-three, he was employed as a scientist, working on the Strategic Defense Initiative – 'Star Wars' – at the National Laboratory at Los Alamos, New Mexico. Then, in December 1988, he was given a new government contract and sent to work at Area 51. He was shocked and frightened by what he saw and he felt that the American people had a right to know what was going on there. In May 1989, he went on television and revealed that the US government had nine flying saucers in Area 51 and was secretly developing alien technology to its own ends. Knowing the sensitivity of what he was saying, he used the alias 'Dennis'. He was filmed only in silhouette and had his voice electronically distorted. This did no good. Both he and his wife had already received death threats.

After his car was shot at, Lazar realised that he would be safer if he came out into the open and, in November, he gave details of the top-secret 'S4' site, where the alien craft were stored. It was next to

Papoose Lake, one of the many dry lakes inside Area 51. An underground complex, it occupied the inside of the whole of Papoose mountain range. Lazar had worked there as part of a team of twenty-two engineers who were employed to work out how the crafts' propulsion systems worked.

Lazar and his colleagues were told little. At first he thought he was working on advanced man-made technology. But when he entered one of the discs, he realised that it was nothing that the Soviets had come up with.

'It has no physical seams, no welds or bolts or rivets,' Lazar said. 'Everything has a soft, round edge to it... as if it's made out of wax and heated for a time and then cooled off.'

Its form and dimensions did not appear to be man-made. Its portholes, arches and tiny chairs were only a foot or so off the ground. Plainly it was designed for creatures a good deal smaller than humans. The propulsion unit, which Lazar and his colleagues worked on, was the size of a baseball. It produced an anti-gravity field which was directed along a hollow column that ran vertically through the centre of the craft. Lazar became convinced it came from another world.

When Lazar got down to work, his suspicions were confirmed. The briefing papers he read were full of UFO information. Among them there were pictures of little grey beings with large hairless heads undergoing autopsies. The briefing papers said the aliens were from the Zeta Reticuli, a star system frequently mentioned as the home of aliens. All this left no doubt in Lazar's mind that he was working with an alien craft built in alien materials by aliens.

Lazar also believes that there were aliens working in S4. One day, as he was passing a room, he saw two men in white lab coats 'looking down and talking to something small with long arms.' He only caught a glimpse. 'I don't know what on earth that was,' said Lazar. But it made sense that it was an alien. And it made sense that it would be kept under lock and key. The briefing papers had mentioned an incident in 1979 where the aliens had killed security guards and scientists at the base.

Although these seem incredible claims, they don't come without corroboration. Since Lazar spilt the beans on TV, over a dozen people have come forward to support his story, though they are afraid of the consequences if they go public. TV journalist George Knapp videotaped one man who ran several large military programmes out at Nellis. He said that the government have had extraterrestrial technology and extraterrestrials themselves since the 1950s. But he will only allow the tape to be screened after his death.

Another journalist tracked down an electrical engineer who had worked at Area 51. He had seen flying saucers there and was willing to say so on TV. But he changed his mind when he found black-suited men parked outside his home day and night. Another witness was threatened more directly. 'We know you do a lot of travelling,' she was told. 'We'd hate an accident to happen to you or your family.'

However, some witnesses have been prepared to talk outside the United States. In 1995, a German film company released a video called *Secrets of the Black World*. In it, a number of witnesses give testimonies that support Lazar's story and prove that something is going on in Area 51. Even more fantastically, the video includes a clip of grainy film, shot inside S4, showing a roomful of canisters where the bodies of dead aliens were stored.

The video also shows UFOs being tested over the base. This was confirmed by the dogged Norio Hayakawa of Nippon TV who camped out outside Area 51 for nights on end. Eventually his patience was rewarded. He caught a fleeting glimpse of a mysterious light rising from the base and filmed a glowing object as it disappeared over the mountains. 'It seemed to "skate" through the sky,' he said. State-of-the-art computer analysis of Hayakawa's film has shown that the object was 'definitely no conventional aircraft'.

Other films shot in the area show the same thing – a bright object that hopped through the sky at incredible speeds and performed impossible manoeuvres. One of these objects actually buzzed an NBC-TV crew, leaving them with radiation burns.

On 28 February 1990, UFO researcher Billy Goodman

photographed another UFO over Groom Lake, where it was thought that alien craft were being tested. Freedom Heights, which overlooks Groom Lake's six-mile runway, has been off-limits to the public since April 1995. The idea that something unworldly is going on there has also percolated into the public consciousness. Highway 375, which runs past Groom Lake, was renamed 'Extraterrestrial Highway' in 1996.

There is no doubt that something strange is going on in the Nevada desert. In 1987, Robert Frost, a worker at Area 51, came home screaming in pain and fear. His symptoms were attributed to a mysterious chemical fire, but he was dead two years later. Other victims sued. It was this case that forced the USAF to finally admit that Area 51 existed.

According to aviation journalist Jim Goodall, there are at least eight 'black programs' flying out of Area 51. These black programs are ultra-secret government projects that cost the American taxpayer $35 billion a year. According to those in the industry, they include the production of fast and highly manoeuvrable unmanned probes that could easily be mistaken for flying saucers.

But Goodall believes there is more to it. Reliable witnesses have seen some of these silent and incredibly fast craft. One flew out of Area 51 and was later tracked by the Federal Aviation Administration Center travelling at over ten thousand miles an hour. That is some thirteen times the speed of sound, well beyond the capability of any known human technology.

Former President of Lockheed Advance Development Ben Rich told Goodall that he was a 'firm believer' in UFOs. Goodall also tracked an ex-Lockheed worker who said, 'We have things flying in the Nevada desert that would make [*Star Wars* director] George Lucas drool.'

Many dismiss such statements as government-orchestrated disinformation designed to cover-up what really is going on. Naturally there has been a well-organised campaign to discredit Lazar. This is led by the physicist and UFOlogist Stanton Friedman, who does not believe that Lazar worked at Area 51. Nor does he believe that Lazar has the scientific credentials he claims.

'Not one shred of evidence has been put forward to support this great story,' says Friedman. 'No diplomas, resumes, transcripts, or memberships of professional organisations.'

Lazar claims to have Masters degrees from the California Institute of Technology and the Massachusetts Institute of Technology. Friedman says that they can find no record of him. What's more, he doubts Lazar's practical background.

'Bob is not a scientist,' says Friedman. 'He failed to answer all scientific questions put to him.'

The US government deny that Lazar worked at Los Alamos from 1982 to 1984, as he claimed. But when George Knapp checked this out, he found Lazar's name in the internal phone directory at Los Alamos. Strangely, the government never denied that Lazar worked in Area 51 – and a salary statement was issued by the US Department of Naval Intelligence.

Lazar's motives have also been questioned. He has sold the movie rights to his story and his drawings of the extraterrestrial ship have been used to merchandise a model of the craft. He made the story up, it is implied, to make money. But Lazar is clear that he went public because the secrecy surrounding the activities at Area 51 is an insult to science and to the American people. However, since he lost his job at Area 51, he has had money troubles. A divorce in 1990 left him bankrupt and, in April 1990, he was arrested for his business links with a Las Vegas brothel. He was sentenced to six months probation and 150 hours community service.

But on camera, Lazar is a convincing witness. He is cool, calm and unpretentious. He has always told the same story – something unusual among fantasists and false witnesses. And he claims no expertise in fields where he has none. One particularly convincing detail that surfaced in his televised testimony is that Lazar said workers at S4 wore badges carrying the letters MAJ. This plainly refers to Majestic-12, a top-secret flying saucer research group set up by the President

Truman in 1947.

What's more, those in a position to know agree with him. Dr Edgar Mitchell, the sixth astronaut to walk on the moon and founder of the Institute of Noetic Studies, a think-tank, said: 'There is strong evidence that a covert group within the US government is engaged in the back-engineering of alien spacecraft.'

And he is concerned about how things are going.

'I am extremely worried this is no longer a government operation, but one run by private parties that are unaccountable – and use billions of dollars in black budget funds.'

Landing at Area 51

One of the most intriguing UFO reports to have surfaced over the years is a report of a crash – or perhaps a landing – that occurred in Nellis, Nevada in 1962. For many years this case was thought of as nothing more than a rumour amongst UFO researchers. However, reports and statements from many eyewitnesses slowly emerged, and there was enough for researchers to start digging for more information.

The object was first spotted over Oneida, New York, and was heading in a westerly direction. There were also reports of the object in Kansas, Colorado and Eureka, Utah. The object was then seen over Reno, Nevada, and was seen to turn and head towards Las Vegas. On the way it disappeared into Nellis. The object was also tracked at several radar sites.

The object was reported by over a thousand people, most of whom assumed that the object was a meteorite. Various news- papers covered the story the following morning, although most of them concluded also that it must have been just a very spectacular meteorite. The object was also seen at various times by several commercial airline pilots who reported that the object was below them, which is unusual for a meteorite. And the Air Defence Command, after watching the object for several hours, scrambled several fighters – not something that they normally do for meteorites.

More remarkably, on its way to Nellis, the object seems to have touched down near Eureka at the same time as the town experienced a total blackout. When it took off again, the power came back.

The official USAF explanation was that it was a meteorite. However, this does not explain why fighters were scrambled, how it changed direction or why the object appeared to land and then take off again.

Sudden Breakthroughs

In 1947, Major Philip J. Corso had seen the corpse of a dead alien. It was one of the creatures that had been killed in the crash at Roswell on 2 July. The alien had been in a wooden crate, one among some thirty stored in a US Army warehouse. Fourteen years later he was to come across those crates again.

By 1961, Philip J. Corso had risen to the rank of Lieutenant Colonel. He had been posted to the Pentagon, where he was in charge of the Foreign Technology desk in the US Army's Research and Development Division. His job was to evaluate enemy weapons systems and other foreign technology. Typically his work involved stripping down captured Soviet MiGs to find out why they were so much better than American fighter planes.

In 1961, Corso's commanding officer and close friend General Arthur Trudeau offered him a top-secret assignment. Corso was to report on the contents of a number of crates. They turned out to be the same crates he had seen in the warehouse fourteen years before.

The crates were wheeled into his office. Then he locked the room and started to open them. He was relieved to find there were no bodies in them this time. However, what he did find was just as mysterious – or so it seemed at the time.

He found a set of strange filaments that were clear and flexible, and made of something like glass – though he had never seen glass that bent before. As he examined them, he noticed that when he pointed a strand towards a source of light, the other end lit up. The filaments seemed to conduct light along their length. Next he came across wafer-thin squares of material. They appeared to be made from some form of plastic and were covered in tiny intricate patterns that had somehow been etched into their surface. After studying the squares for some time, Corso realised that he was looking at some form of electrical circuit, like that on a printed circuit board. But this circuitry was far more intricate and there were no holes where electronic components could be soldered in position.

Then he found some dull, greyish, fibrous material, which resembled aluminium foil. But Corso found he could not tear the material. Nor could he fold or bend it. Whatever he did to it, it simply sprang back to its original shape. It was exhibiting a physical property that would later be called 'supertenacity'. This property is well known now, but it was unheard of in 1961.

A file had come with the crates and Corso sat down to read it. It said that a set of dark, elliptical eyepieces had been found attached to a creature that had been found in a crashed UFO. They were as thin as human skin but exhibited the magic property of illuminating images in low-light conditions, allowing the wearer to see in the dark.

In the file, he also came across a description of a device that contained a power source and looked like a stubby torch. But the beam it produced was so intense that it could burn its way through solid material. When Corso read later about bizarre cattle mutilations associated with UFOs, it seemed to him that this device had been used on the unfortunate livestock – it was plainly a surgical cutting tool.

The growing incidence of cattle mutilations formed a vital part of the conclusion of Corso's chilling report to General Trudeau. From what he had seen, Corso deduced that the aliens in the crashed UFO were genetically altered humanoids. They were cloned biological entities who were harvesting biological material on Earth for their own experimentation. Their technology was clearly superior to our own and they were a clear danger to humankind. The American government had only one option: it had to prepare for a possible conflict. Corso's recommendation was that they begin 'reverse-engineering' – that is attempting to re-create the alien technology recovered at the crash site in order to find out how it worked. General Trudeau accepted Corso's report and endorsed his plan, but they had to find trustworthy scientists and technicians to carry out the work.

The Cold War was at its peak in the early 1960s, and secrecy was paramount for the US military. However, the McCarthy hearings of the 1950s and the investigations of the House Un-American Activities Committee had convinced Trudeau and Corso that the military was too full of leaks to be given the job of back-engineering the alien technology. The last thing they needed was for the Soviets to get hold of it. Trudeau said that the only people they could trust were themselves. So they labelled the alien artefacts as 'foreign technology' and treated them as if they were parts of a captured Soviet MiG fighter.

'Foreign technology was the absolute perfect cover,' said Corso. 'All I had to do was figure out what to do with the stuff I had.'

Trudeau and Corso had access to the most eminent army scientists of their day but, more than anything, they feared that the security of their project would be compromised. Scientists talked to each other and were likely to put two and two together. Instead, they decided to farm the alien devices out to various trusted figures in the business world. Commercial companies rarely talk to each other and have every reason to guard their secrets. Over the next two years, Corso delivered the aliens' devices to the research divisions of many defence contractors, including leading engineering and telecommunications firms. The army funded the back-engineering by paying 'research costs', while the companies benefited by filing patents on their 'discoveries'.

UFOlogist Stanton Friedman goes along with this theory, though he believes that the programme began before Corso got his hands on the contents of the crates.

'An example would be the transistor by Bell Labs,' he says. 'Bell has close ties with Scandia National Laboratory in Albuquerque – one of the trio of high-security US nuclear weapons manufacturers. The official birthday of the transistor is given as 23 December 1947 – six months after Roswell.'

Throughout the 1960s, these companies claimed responsibility for a number of 'miracle breakthroughs' – fibre optics, integrated circuit chips, night-vision goggles, lasers and supertenacity fibres –all of which had come from Corso's crates. Once US companies had perfected the technology, it became part of the arsenal of the US military. The 'seeding' of these new super-technologies has also spawned numerous civilian applications. Anyone that has used a CD player, operated a modern computer or made a transatlantic phone call has been benefiting from alien technology.

Dulce, New Mexico

Area 51 in the deserts of Nevada is not the only place where aliens are assisting the American military with their technology. There is another secret base in the north of New Mexico, near the town of Dulce and close to the Jicarilla Indian Reservation. Dulce has a population of just nine hundred. It is an out-of-the-way and otherwise unremarkable place. However, UFO researchers have discovered that it is home to the most incredible and sinister facility. Under the desert plains nearby is a secret underground base. The vast complex is home to a joint US government–alien biogenetic laboratory, which carries out hideous experiments on both humans and animals.

The base came to light when Security Officer Thomas Edwin Castello spilled the beans in a document known as *The Dulce Papers*, which he circulated in the early 1980s. By then the project had been going on for a considerable time. Castello had taken the documents from the Dulce underground facility, and he backed them with a videotape and over thirty black-and-white photographs. He had worked as a security officer at the Dulce base until 1979, but by then he had had his fill of what was going on in the complex and decided to part company with his secretive employers. But before he left, he stole some documents and removed a security videotape which showed various views of the underground complex from the base's control centre. He made five copies of the documents, and hid the originals. The copies were then distributed to the UFO community via intermediaries.

Realising that what he had seen at the base was extremely sensitive, he knew that he and his family would be in danger. They had to go into hiding. But when he went to pick up his wife and children, government agents were waiting for him. He fled and never saw his family again.

Castello was in his mid-twenties when he first joined the service and was given training in photography at a top-secret underground facility in West Virginia. He stayed with the US Air Force for seven years, leaving in 1971 to work for the Rand Corporation – America's military think -tank – in Santa Monica, California. By 1977, he was considered trustworthy and he was transferred to the secret Dulce facility. He bought a home in Santa Fe, and commuted to work from there five days a week via a shuttle system that ran deep underground. In the hallway of the tube stations hallway, he saw a sign that read: 'To Los Alamos'. The tracks, he believes, also led on to the underground base in the Nevada desert that is known as Area 51.

The work force at Dulce was strange, to say the least. Castello estimates that there were over 18,000 small 'Grey' aliens on staff, along with hundreds of reptilian humanoids known as the 'Draco'. The underground facility was so large that it had seven sub-levels. The aliens lived on level five and worked on levels six and seven.

All sorts of bizarre experiments were going on there. The aliens were doing research into hypnosis, telepathy and dreams. Another area of interest was human auras. This had paid dividends, Castello said. The aliens were able to separate the 'bioplasmic body from the physical body', and place an 'alien life-force' within a human body after removing the human's 'soul'.

Level six of the complex was known as 'Nightmare Hall'. This was where the aliens did hideous genetic experiments on all forms of terrestrial life – fish, seals, mice, birds and, of course, humans. There was a storage area for the results of these experiments. Tanks contained multi-armed and multi-legged humans, while cages housed tall, humanoid, bat-like creatures. There were 'row upon row of thousands of humans, human-mixture remains and embryos of humanoids kept in cold storage,' Castello says.

But worst: 'I frequently encountered humans in cages. Usually they were dazed or drugged, but sometimes they cried and begged for help. We were told that they were hopelessly insane, and involved in high-risk drug tests to cure insanity. We were told never to speak to them at all.'

Despite these grisly experiments, it seemed that the aliens had no hostile intentions. Both the Greys and the reptilian aliens seemed to have been on Earth for thousands of years. Humans   didn't bother them. They were far more concerned about other space-faring races. The aliens didn't seem to be interested in the land, minerals, fuel or water that Earth could offer them either. Their primary concern was the magnetic power of the Earth. The aliens have learnt to harvest this energy in a way unknown to terrestrial science. Magnetic energy was used to control the elevators and supply heat and power to the base.

The Dulce Papers show that the aliens were working hand in hand with the US government. Castello can reel off a list of US government agencies who maintained a presence at Dulce. They included the Department of Energy, the National Institute of Health, the National Science Foundation, the Howard Hughes Medical Institute and the Department of the Environment. Castello himself was recruited through his government service.

Security was super-tight at the Dulce facility. Visitors were weighed, naked, before being allowed to enter. Their weight was recorded, then they were given a one-piece suit and an ID card that could be used to access the various level. There were scales scattered throughout the complex. Everyone's weight was recorded every day and a gain of more than three pounds would lead to a thorough physical examination, including an X-ray. Everyone who worked there was under the surveillance of the security guards at all times. No one was allowed to carry anything into sensitive areas. Everything was delivered by conveyor belt and X-rayed before being distributed.

Since Thomas Castello went public with his story, he has become a regular speaker at a number of UFO conventions. Although he comes over as a highly plausible witness, some have chosen to dismiss his accounts. But it has not derailed Castello, who says that there are other alien bases scattered throughout the solar systems. There are similar facilities on the moons of Saturn and Jupiter.

Along with the photographic and documentary evidence Castello has presented, circumstantial evidence that something strange is going on at Dulce had been accruing. Between 1976 and 1978, Dulce was the centre of a string of cattle mutilations that left local ranchers mystified. Senseless and unexplainable attacks on livestock became so frequent that research teams from all over the world converged on the tiny town. In July 1978, scientist Howard Burgess discovered that many Dulce cattle were covered with strange markings that only showed up when they were placed under ultra-violet light. A glittery substance was found on the right side of their necks, on the right ear and on the right leg. Analysis of the substance revealed that is was rich in magnesium and potassium. Dulce is also a Mecca for UFO sightings, many of which occurred around the same time the mutilated cows were found. And following up on Castello's story, a research team took soundings of the ground in the area. It revealed a complex of deep cavities under the mesa.

Naturally, the US government refuses to acknowledge the existence of any military installation around or under Dulce, New Mexico – just as they denied the existence of Area 51. However, they will have to pit their wits against legions of UFO researchers determined to unearth the town's dark secret.

Bugging Dulce

One UFO researcher, Paul Bennewitz, claimed some success in finding out what was going on in the base at Dulce. Not only did he photograph UFOs over Dulce, he made contact with the aliens in the facility. After two years of tracking the craft, he managed to establish constant video reception from the alien motherships and their underground base. And he could communicate with them via computer using hexadecimal code. Subsequent photographs he received showed landing pylons and ships on the ground, along with aliens on the ground riding around in vehicles powered by static electricity. They also used static electricity to charge their beam weapons.

His constant interaction with the aliens gave him a clear picture of alien psychology. Although he never met them directly, he understood their logic and ways of thinking and got an insight into their intentions. Every night, he discovered, they were abducting people, cutting them and implanting devices into them, though he is not sure that the implants are totally effective. However, he estimates that over 300,000 people have been implanted in the US and over two million world-wide.

Then things began to go wrong. In 1985, he suffered a nervous breakdown. According to colleagues, this was cause by a government disinformation campaign designed to subvert his activities and ruin his reputation. It succeeded.

What UFOs Can Teach Us

There is nothing intrinsically wrong with what is going on in Area 51. Humankind has every reason to try and learn from aliens and alien technology. After all, they are plainly much more advanced than we are. Simply look at the astonishing flight characteristics of UFOs: they can accelerate instantly to enormous speeds – measured at over 10,000 miles an hour – then come instantly to a halt. They can do high-speed right-angle turns without slowing, or hover motionless in the sky with no visible means of support. Clearly they do not operate on the same principles as a conventional aircraft. Indeed, they seem to violate the laws of physics at will.

Even to reach the solar system from a distant star system in a reasonable length of time means that they would have to travel faster than the speed of light. This is one reason why many scientists choose to dismiss the subject of UFOs altogether. However, it is a violation of the principles of science itself to ignore observations that are in favour of an established theory. It is a fundamental principle that laws of physics should be modified to reflect the data, not vice versa.

With this philosophy in mind, a handful of scientists have tried to explain the extraordinary behaviour of UFOs using the normal laws of physics to see what advances can be made. By studying the thousands of detailed reports that have been provided by credible witnesses, they have attempted to discover the science and technology utilised by alien spacecraft. Leader in the field is physicist Paul Hill, who worked with NASA for twenty-five years.

Hill set to work on the most credible reports from the 1950s, 1960s and 1970s. He avoided the fruitless speculation about whether UFOs are real or not, and accepted the reports at face value and analysed them as he would any other scientific data. His first conclusion was that UFOs do not defy the laws of physics. This finding has subsequently been confirmed by scientists working in a new field of physics called 'breakthrough propulsion'. Their aim is to develop propellantless propulsion systems. The result would be craft that emulate the flight characteristics of UFOs.

To appreciate how radical UFO propulsion systems are, you need to understand how conventional aircraft work. An engine is bolted to an airframe. This engine produces thrust which pushes the aircraft and pilot forward. According to Newton's first law of motion, a body continues in a uniform state of motion – that is, travelling at a constant speed in a straight line – until a force acts on it. This gives rise to the concept of inertia, the property of matter that resists charges in speed or direction. When an aircraft makes a turn, say, the atoms of the plane and the pilot want to continue in a straight path. To overcome their inertia, a force must be applied. This is provided by banking the plane so that the lift provided by the wings, instead of pushing directly upwards, is angled and pushes the plane around the turn.

Newton's third law of motion states that, for every action there is an equal and opposite reaction. So when the air under the wings pushes the plane around the turn, the wings push on the air with an equal and opposite force. This force is felt by the pilot as the G-force that pushes him down in his seat. The faster or more violent the turn, the higher G-force created. Even high-speed manoeuvres in a plane can produce G-forces that will result in the unconsciousness or death of the pilot. G-force can even tear the airframe apart. Hill has calculated that UFOs regularly pull an astonishing 100 G. This is more than enough to kill any human being and tear apart any plane that has been built. The question is, how do UFOs overcome the effects of inertia?

Hill has an answer. A UFO would have to generate a force field to power and steer the craft. In conventional physics, only three such force fields have been discovered outside the atomic – electric, magnetic and gravitational. So which are UFOs using?

To answer that question, Hill again turns back to eyewitness testimony. One case provides a clue. A farmer in Missouri was confronted by a flying saucer, fifteen feet in diameter, hovering just above the ground. In an attempt to scare it off, the intrepid soul threw a rock at it. But instead of clunking into the structure of the craft, the man observed the rock bounce off an invisible force field some fifteen feet from the hull itself. From this, Hill concludes that the field is gravitational – electric or magnetic fields would have no effect on a non-magnetic substance such as rock.

Somehow UFOs generate a localised repulsive force field. This could be characterised as an anti-gravitational field or negative gravity. A craft that could generate anti-gravity could counteract the attractive force of Earth's gravity. It could hover or fly vertically into the sky at will. And, by angling the anti-gravity field, it could produce thrust in any direction. Flying saucers are not usually seen to have external propulsion components. This would account for that. The anti-gravity field produced by a propulsion unit inside the craft would have permeated the hull without affecting it. That means that the hull would be impervious to gravity, thus it would be effectively weightless. It would also have no inertia. It is also a basic law of physics that gravitational fields travel at the speed of light. This would mean that the craft would have limitless acceleration and deceleration, and incredible speed.

Although all this sounds inconceivable, there is nothing new about the idea. It was first proposed by Professor Hermann Oberth, the father of Germany's wartime rocket programme, who, after World War II, headed the US government commission on UFOs. 'UFOs are directed by intelligent beings of a very high order, and are propelled by distorting the gravitational field, converting gravity into usable energy,' he said.

But Hill has worked this out in more detail and, theoretically at least, discovered how an anti-gravity field could be used to rid the craft and those inside it of inertia. As well as directing the field outside the craft for thrust and manoeuvring, the field would also envelop the physical mass of the ship and, for that matter, the atmosphere surrounding it. The force is generated uniformly around the craft, and does not originate from a single point such as a jet or rocket; the ship effectively becomes its own centre of gravity. So if the field wants the craft to make a right turn, then all the atoms on or in the craft and the occupants, would turn together. There would be no G-forces caused by one part pushing on another. It would be as effortless as falling down a lift-shaft. Effectively there would be no inertia. Such a means of propulsion would explain all of the observations of UFO activity that have so puzzled scientists.

The fact that the anti-gravity field also acts on the atmosphere surrounding the UFO would explain why UFOs – unless they are crippled and about to crash – are able to exceed the speed of sound without creating sonic booms. In a conventional aircraft, the air in front of its surfaces has to be pushed out of the way. But the fastest air can move, normally, is the speed of sound. Consequently, as the aircraft's speed increases, air builds up in front of it. When the plane reaches the speed of sound, it is facing a solid wall of air. If the speed is increased, this wall of air is blasted apart, producing a shock wave, or sonic boom. Using wind-tunnel studies and computer simulation, Hill has shown that supersonic flight can easily be achieved by UFOs without sonic booms. All it has to do is use its force field to keep the airflow around the craft at subsonic speeds. No matter how fast the ship is travelling, the airflow over its surfaces remains the same.

Another advantage of this is that small objects such dust, rain and insects would not hit the hull of the craft, causing damage. It would also explain how UFOs avoid burning up from enormous heat caused by air friction when flying at enormous speeds and why they have been observed to emerge from the sea without getting wet.

Key to manoeuvring a UFO is the ability to direct the force field. Hill notes that witnesses often report that discs tilt down when moving forward and tilt up when stopping. They also exhibit a characteristic 'falling leaf' wobble when descending. Using advanced mathematics, Hill has been able to show that these are exactly the movements that would be produced if some kind of repulsive force field was being used. Hill also has a theory on what sort of mechanism is used to guide this field energy.

'In a saucer, the power focusing or driving link, is comprised of a bladed mechanism located in the ringed area just within and below the rim,' he says. He bases this on a series of close-up observations made by witnesses who saw movable plates in UFOs shortly before they took off.

One of those accounts came from Ray Hawks. On 11 August 1960, he saw a strange craft drop vertically out of a cloud over Boulder, Colorado, and hover about a hundred feet above the ground. It looked like two convex discs joined at the perimeter. Hawks says it was dull grey in colour. A little way from the rim, he saw a series of shiny plates. These were separated by small radial gaps. They appeared both on the underside, which he could see quite clearly, and on the upper surface, which came into view as the craft wobbled to a halt. One of the plates was giving off blue smoke, but it tilted, retracted inside the craft and was replaced by another one, which gave off a click as it fell into place. The craft then shot off back into the clouds.

A similar sighting was made on 2 March 1965, in Weeki Wachee Springs, Florida, when John Reeves came upon a flying saucer in a clearing in a wood. It was above twenty to thirty feet in diameter and sat on four legs. He managed to get within a hundred feet of it and saw around the rim of the saucer a series of blades. These were standing out so that he could see through them and into the saucer itself. After a short time, the blades closed, the rim began to rotate and the UFO lifted off into the air.

Developing a gravity field such as those used by UFOs is well beyond our current technological capabilities. Indeed, there is no single theory within the known laws of physics that can explain how a field propulsion system that nullifies or manipulates gravity would work. However, there are two main schools of thought. One operates within Einstein's space-time theories. It speculates that the gravity field produced by UFOs warps the fabric of space-time and allows the craft to travel along the contours of warped space without incurring inertia.

The other falls into the realms of the as-yet incomplete Grand Unified Theory, which is attempting to unify the four known forces that regulate the universe – the nuclear strong force, nuclear weak force, electromagnetic force and gravity. Gravity is unique among all the forces as it has no known opposing force; it only attracts and does not repel.

The Grand Unified Theory postulates that the four forces of the universe are in some way related. This has led some physicists to speculate that UFO propulsion systems somehow harness the electromagnetic force, say in such a way that gravity is neutralised or redirected. It would work by generating a continuous stream of antigravitons – antiparticles of gravity. These would bounce back and forth between the craft and the source of the gravitational field affecting it, and nullify its gravitational force.

Hill rules out the possibility of the field being electromagnetic in nature, but he admits the possibility that electromagnetic forces could be used to generate such a field, in a way that is currently not understood. UFOs sightings often report effects similar to those produced by large electromagnetic fields – and interference with electrical systems, car engines cutting out, guidance computers on aircraft failing. Even the chemical changes found in soil where UFOs have landed could be caused by microwave radiation.

This would also explain why UFOs are often invisible to radar. If the electromagnetic field operating the anti-gravity propulsion system was sufficiently strong in the microwave section of the spectrum it would simply absorb incoming radar waves. This was confirmed by a USAF electronic countermeasure plane that was tailed by a UFO. The onboard equipment measured the UFO's microwave output at over one megawatt.

Some faltering steps have already been made in the field of antigravity. In the 1950s, American scientist T. Townsend Brown worked on electromagnetically induced antigravity, or electrogravitics. He built a disc-shaped capacitor that exhibited a propulsive force in the direction of the positive electrode. The higher the charge, the greater the electrogravitic force. Using a charge of several hundred thousand volts, he could fire a three-foot disc at speeds of several hundreds of miles an hour.

And in 1992, at Tempere University in Finland, two physicists – R. Nieminen and E. Podkletnov – tried a different approach when they noticed strange antigravitational effects on smoke when it moved up a column above a series of rapidly rotating superconducting ceramic discs. Small weights suspended on a strain gauge above this contraption showed a weight loss of two per cent.

It seems that human technology is just not up to the task yet. So if propellantless propulsion has been developed already – and sightings at Area 51 show it has – it would have to be back-engineering from crashed or captured alien technology. In that case, it would be of paramount economic importance to keep its development totally secret. Introducing a propulsion system that was much more efficient than jets or rockets and does without chemical or fossil fuels would have a devastating effect on the global economy.

Nevertheless, there is talk in the scientific community of 'breakthrough propulsion physics'. If UFO-style propulsion was introduced in ten or twenty years, the world economy would have time to adjust.

Secrets of the Nazi Saucers
The American scientists at Area 51 are not the first to work on flying

saucers. It seems that German scientists were well down that track towards the end of World War II.

At that time the Third Reich's aeronautical engineers were far ahead of those of the Allies, who had invested most of their technical expertise in developing the atomic bomb. In the dying days of the war, Hitler had an extraordinary array of 'Vengeance' weapons, with which he hoped to reverse the course of the war. Only two of them, the V-1 pilotless aircraft and the V-2 ballistic missile, were actually used.

But by 1945, German engineers had developed over 130 types of rockets and missiles. The ME-110 jet fighter was equipped to carry twenty-four air-to-air missiles and the prototype of a jet-powered flying wing was being built by Walter and Reimar Horten. Even more futuristic was the delta-shaped Horten DM-1, which some have compared to the B2 Stealth bomber.

But that was not the half of it. When the Third Reich was finally overrun and its secret weapons bases captured, the Allies realised how sophisticated some of Hitler's terror weapons were. Among the discoveries in a research facility deep underground was the existence of a programme to build a disc-shaped flying craft, the V-7 – the Nazis' own flying saucer.

As with other German research programmes, the technology and the personnel were co-opted into secret Allied projects at the end of the war. Some researchers believe that the V-7 project provided the technology for America to develop its own man-made UFO.

Even after all these years, it is difficult to make out what exactly was going on in Germany's underground bunkers. The Germans destroyed many of their underground bases as they retreated, and anything captured by Allied troops was immediately classified. However, some of those who worked on the V-7 and other top-secret projects have come forward to reveal what they knew about Germany's flying saucers.

In the spring of 1941, Luftwaffe aeronautical engineer Dr Rudolf Schriever designed a prototype disc-shaped craft called 'The Flying Top'. Schriever later collaborated with two other German engineers,

Habermohl and Miethe, and an Italian named Giuseppe Belluzzo. However, Belluzzo claimed that he was the one who came up with the idea for a man-made 'flying saucer' and the idea was later taken up by the Germans.

Whoever first thought of it, it is generally agreed that Schriever, Habermohl, Miethe and Belluzzo designed a series of flying discs for the Nazis and the first prototype was ready for test flights in June 1942. The first models were powered by gas turbines. Later the craft were modified to make use of the new advanced jet engines that the Nazis had developed. Schriever and Habermohl's design for a jet-powered disc showed a fixed, cupola-style cockpit with a wide-surface ring rotating around it. This ring incorporated movable wing surfaces that could be reconfigured for take-off, landing and level flight.

Blueprints of Schriever's disc have been declassified, but many UFO researchers claim that they have been doctored. Even so, the designs show a fifty-foot diameter disc that sits on four legs. This concept was very advanced for the time, but is now familiar from UFO sightings. Although the details are missing from the plans, the craft was said to have been equipped with radar, lasers and 'electromagnetic turbines' – possibly of the type Paul Hill speculates about.

Another disc-shaped craft was designed by Dr Miethe. It was an amazing 140 feet in diameter and powered by jets with swivelling nozzles, later seen on the Harrier jump jet. The craft had phenomenal performance, reaching speeds of nearly 1,250 miles an hour and climbing over 32,000 feet in under three minutes, easily outperforming any aircraft of its time. Miethe's saucer made a test flight on 14 February 1945. It was only when a design finally became operational that it acquired its V number. Miethe's craft became V-7. Interestingly, Miethe's disc had twin cockpits above and below the body of the disc and twin jet pipes at the rear. Its design is strikingly similar to the B2 Stealth bomber.

If Miethe's designs have been recycled in the Stealth programme, how much else of the flying saucer technology developed by the Germans during World War II has surfaced in top-secret American projects? Rudolf Schriever, for one, believes that a lot of it found its way into use. Much of the UFO activity reported after the war, he believes, were sightings of craft built by the Americans from his designs.

It is known that Miethe was recruited by the Allies to continue the work he had done earlier in Germany, just as Werner von Braun, designer of the V-2, was recruited by the Americans to work on the rocket programme. Henry Stevens, head of a research group devoted to exploring the Nazi disc programme, unearthed a declassified US project from 1955 to build a jet-powered saucer capable of reaching Mach 3.4 (3.4 times the speed of sound) at 80,000 feet. It was to be built by a Canadian company called A.V. Roe. Stevens found that one 'Miethe – Designer 1950' was listed on their personnel roster.

There was also the *Feuerball* – or 'fireball' – project unearthed by Dr Renato Vesco. This was a sophisticated, radio-controlled anti-aircraft weapon that was able to jam enemy radar and attack enemy aircraft using a 'multi-batteried blower cannon'. A flat disc, it was powered by a special turbojet engine that was developed by scientists at the aeronautical establishment in Wiener Neustadt. It actually saw action towards the end of the war when one was seen to attack a squadron of American Liberator bombers. One burst into flames after the *Feuerball* 'emitted a bluish cloud of smoke'. According to Vesco, the principles of the *Feuerball* were used to develop a larger supersonic craft called the *Kugelblitz*, or 'ball lightning' fighter, at the underground facilities at Kahla, in Thuringia, central Germany. The *Kugelblitz* took to the air in February 1945, three months before the end of the war in Europe.

A mysterious aspect of the V-7 weapons' story is the involvement of the Thule Society – an occult group that restricted its membership to high-ranking German Army officers and the professional classes. It perpetuated German racial myths and provided Hitler with much of his Nazi ideology. Even the Swastika was originally the symbol of the Thule group.

The Thule Society, which even claimed kinship to a race of alien beings who lived inside the earth, were said to have mastered a new form of energy, called 'Vril'. American UFOlogist Colonel Wendelle Stevens says that the breakthrough was made at the University of Vienna before the war. A group that called itself the Vril Society found ways to manipulate forces underlying the physical universe. This knowledge was later combined with other new energy technologies. It seems to have influenced the work of Victor Schauberger, an Austrian who invented machines operated by 'inward spiralling' – power was generated from implosion, rather than explosions as in the internal combustion engine.

Schauberger applied the principle 'understand nature, then copy nature' to all his work. After observing the spiralling motion of water, he developed the concept of an engine powered by implosion. His theory was: 'If water or air is rotated into a twisting form known as a "colloidal", a build up of energy results, which, with immense power, can cause levitation.' When the Nazis took over Austria in 1938 Schauberger was arrested and, with his family under threat of execution, he worked on his energy-generating device for the Germans. He developed a flying disc for the Nazis and used 'liquid vortex propulsion', a technology that nullified gravity. It was test flown, but both the prototype and his plans were destroyed by the retreating Nazis. Schauberger was taken to America, where he worked on a secret project for the US government. An oath of secrecy he signed prevented him from ever writing or talking about his inventions. On his deathbed, he said: 'They have stolen everything from me, everything. I don't even own myself.'

The Vril Society also experimented with other exotic technology. These included a device, designed by Hans Kohler, which was called the Kohler tachyon magneto-gravitic drive, or, alternatively, the Thule tachyonator. Wendelle Stevens says that these exotic devices developed under the auspices of the Vril Society were used to construct the so-called Vril discs. These were highly advanced flying discs that were thirty foot in diameter and designed to be used as fighter interceptors. Stevens claims that the electromagnetic field propulsion technology they used was later incorporated into the seventy-five foot diameter Haunebu discs that were successfully tested in 1941. Haunebu discs, he says, were used to attack and destroy Allied bombers attacking the ball-bearing factories at Schweinfurth in 1943. SS blueprints and photographs of the Vril and Haunebu discs were published in Germany in the book *Die Dunkle Seite des Mondes* ('The dark Side of the Moon') by Brad Harris.

Although the Vril craft did not tip World War II in favour of the Nazis, there are suggestions that the technology was spirited away before the fall of Berlin to await the call of the Reich at some future time. According to author W.A. Harbinson, under the influence of the Thule Society, Hitler began seeking a foothold in Antarctica. In 1938 German expeditions mapped an area of Queen Maud Land, the area of the Antarctic directly south of Africa. Although the plateau there is covered by an ice sheet up to one-and-a-half miles thick, there were several sections free of ice where rocky peaks pierce the ice caps. The Nazis was renamed it Neu-Schwabenland. Throughout the war, the Nazis ferried materiel there to build a huge underground base. Once it was complete, the Vril discs were secretly installed.

In 1947, the US Navy carried out a huge exercise called Operation Highjump off Neu-Schwabenland. According to Harbinson, the exercise was a cover for an operation to root out any Nazis surviving in the secret base. It ended badly for the Americans when they encountered Germans armed with flying Vril disc technology. The US had no weapons that could match them and were forced to withdraw. After this defeat, the US pulled out of the Antarctic for a decade and began to develop its own disc techno logy, based on what they had managed to salvage from the Nazi facilities they had overrun. So America had every reason to continue the work begun by Schriever, Miethe, Habermohl, Belluzzo, Schauberger and others, and develop their own V-7.

Animal Mutilations

The Slaughter Begins

Alien abductions have been closely associated with the disturbing phenomenon of animal mutilations. They began in the 1960s. The victim of the first documented case concerned a young horse called Lady, who was being raised on a farm near Alamosa in the San Luis Valley, Colorado. Every night she would turn up at the ranch house for her food and water. Then on 8 September 1967, for the first time, she did not show up.

The next day, Lady's owner Berle Lewis went out to try and find the horse. He found her dead with her flesh stripped from the neck upwards. The case was so unusual that a pathology examination was ordered. The pathologist Dr John Altshuler was shocked to find that Lady's brain, spine and internal organs, including the heart, had been removed with incredible precision. Some of the cuts were as clean as a surgeon's scalpel. It was a professional job. Even more baffling was that the mare's body had been completely drained of blood without so much as a stain on or around the corpse. Dr Altshuler also took tissue samples. When he examined them under a microscope, he found even more disturbing evidence.

'There was a darkened colour as if the flesh had been opened and cauterised with a surgical cauterising blade,' he said later, 'almost as if it had been done with a modern-day laser.'

Although lasers had first been developed in the early 1960s, surgical laser technology capable of causing such wounds was not available in 1967. The possibilities of the technology were widely known, but what lasers there were, were vastly expensive research tools confined to university and industrial laboratories. They were not the sort of thing you toted about on the prairies of Colorado.

Several explanations were given, ranging from the horse being struck by a bolt of lightning to her being attacked by Satanists.

However, there had been no storm the night before and there were no tracks – vehicular, human or animal – anywhere near the carcass. The only prints found were the colt's hoof-prints, and these ended about thirty yards from its body. This was a mystery in itself. However, some strange exhaust marks were found on the ground nearby which contained higher than normal levels of radiation. This provided a clue. Many local people had reported seeing strange lights in the sky and Berle Lewis's mother had seen a large craft passing over her cabin the day Lady disappeared.

The mutilation of Lady was not an isolated case. It was the first of a spate of animal mutilations in Colorado. Later that year, it spread to Pennsylvania. These were followed by a wave of mutilations in Alabama, Iowa and Texas. In the 1970s in the US alone, over ten thousand cattle were discovered with organs surgically removed and corpses drained of blood. Hundreds of mutilations occurred in some areas. Since then cattle have been found dead and mutilated in forty-nine out of the fifty states and reports have come in from around the world.

What's more, strange cases of animal mutilation are not just a recent phenomenon. Accounts of unexplained sheep mutilations in Britain and Australia also occurred in the nineteenth century. The earliest known account that links UFOs to mutilations comes from an edition of the *Farmers' Advocate* published in Yates Center, Kansas, on the 23 April 1897. Local farmer Alexander Hamilton made a sworn statement describing how he had been woken by bawling cows. He looked outside to find 'an airship slowly descending on my cow lot about 40 rods [220 yards] from the house'. It was a cigar-shaped craft around three hundred feet long and it turned a beam of light on him. The ship made a buzzing noise and rose up to about five hundred feet, taking one of his heifers with it. Next day he was told that the head, legs and hide of the cow had been found.

A famous encounter that occurred in May 1973 may hold a clue to why this is happening. It happened when Judy Doraty, Judy's daughter Cindy Doraty, Judy's mother and Judy's sister-in-law were driving near Houston, Texas. The women suddenly saw a strange light hovering in the sky. They stopped the car and got out to take a closer look. Eventually the object disappeared. They then returned to the car and went on their way.

Later Judy began to experience anxiety attacks and severe headaches. Several doctors examined her and drew a blank. Finally she was referred to UFOlogist Dr Leo Sprinkle.

Under hypnosis she described what she had seen: 'It's like a spotlight shining down on the back of my car. And it's like it has substance to it... I'm looking up. I can see an animal being taken up into this... I can see it squirming and trying to get free. And it's like it's being sucked up. It's taken into some sort of chamber and I get nauseated watching how to excise parts. It's done very quickly, but the calf doesn't die immediately. The calf's heart isn't taken... and then I can see the calf being lowered and when it's on the ground I can see it's not moving...'

When asked how the animal was being cut up, she said: 'With instruments... they are like a knife but with different handles... the tissue is laid out flat and smooth and there are needles in it, or probes with tubes connected to them. The same thing is happening with the testicles and eyes.'

And she was not alone: 'I feel the presence of things, but I can't see them... It appears to be two little men... Their hands have long claw nails... very large hypnotic eyes, but they don't blink... I did not see a mouth...they talk, but not with their mouths... they said I wasn't supposed to be here... they project that it was necessary this be done and that it is for the benefit of mankind – and that they are watching us.'

She then went on to mention seeing her daughter Cindy on an 'operating' table.

'They don't listen, they just ignore me,' Judy went on. 'They go about their work as if it's nothing. They don't seem to have any emotions. They don't seem to care. They just take some samples from her.'

Later Cindy was also hypnotised and recalled events which clearly backed up her mother's accounts. She described two 'mantis-like' creatures that moved 'mechanically like robots'. She recounted seeing a calf being raised into a spaceship by a yellow beam.

'It acts like it's bawling,' she said, 'but you can't hear it.'

This case provided the first link between animal mutilations and alien abductions. However, alien abduction was still a relatively poorly understood phenomenon at the time and this connection only fuelled the controversy.

Even so, the subject of animal mutilations could not be lightly dismissed. There was another outbreak in Colorado in the early 1980s and another in the Deep South in the early 1990s. In between, isolated cases have occurred across America with similar reports coming from Puerto Rico, Canada, Mexico, Central and South America, Australia, Russia and parts of Europe.

Mutilation UK

British UFO researcher Tony Dodd has amassed a huge file of animal mutilations that have occurred in the UK. They exhibit the same hallmarks as the US cases: the 'surgical removal' of internal organs along with tongues and eyes; bloodless wounds; jawbones stripped of flesh and rectums cored out. Following a spate of cat mutilations in Texas in 1991, where moggies had been drained of blood and subjected to intense heat, cat killing spread to the UK. In 1999, numerous cats were found decapitated or disembowelled.

Since 1990, Dodd has found that wild animals – deer, badgers, foxes, seals and birds – have been mutilated as well as livestock. There was a particular outbreak in North Yorkshire in 1998, where spinal cords, optic nerves, digestive systems and brains were removed. However, both the Nation Union of Farmers and the National Veterinary College deny all knowledge of mutilations. But Dodd says that individual vets have frequently told him that they have found dead sheep with their organs missing and their bodies drained of blood. British cases also report a small hole bored in the cranium.

And Dodd is convinced that there is a connection between these mutilations and alien intruders.

'There have been reports of dead animals falling from the sky, often coinciding with UFO sightings,' he says.

Alien Sushi

Mutilation cases have also been reported in Japan. On 29 December 1990, a farmer in the Saga Prefecture was woken by the loud and continuous barking of his dog. He went out to see what all the fuss was about. When he entered the cow shed, he found a twelve-month-old cow lying on the floor with its tongue missing and the nipples from its udders removed.

Then on 4 January 1993, his dog began barking again. This time he rushed out to the cow shed and was just in time to observe a small white object floating in the air next to a cow. The object quickly moved outside and disappeared. The second cow, however, was more fortunate. It only suffered a broken leg.

Prize Bull

One of the most famous animal mutilation cases of recent times, was discovered on 5 August 1999. It was a bright and sunny morning when cattle rancher Milo Hauck went out to start work on his farm in Menno, South Dakota. He began, like every other day, with a check on the cattle. But when Hauck went to visit his 350-pound prize bull, he was confronted with a sickening sight. The prized animal was lying face down in the mud, its lifeless body strangely mutilated. Its genitals had been removed by a circular, bloodless incision and its rectum had been neatly cored out.

Hauck looked around for some clue to who could have done such a thing. But, even though the ground was muddy, there were no tracks. Even more puzzling was that there was no sign that the fit and aggressive bull had put up a struggle.

Running back to the ranch house, Hauck called the police. When Sheriff Jack Holden arrived, he could offer Hauck little help. Holden was as mystified as Hauck by the bizarre mutilation. But one thing that he did notice was that the barbed wire fence of the bull's pen was underneath the dead animal. For this to have happened, the bull must have fallen on it from above. And judging by how deeply the carcass was embedded in the ground, it must have fallen from quite some height.

Case Studies

Most mutilations involve cattle, although sheep, goats, horses, domestic pets and even wild animals have occasionally been victims. And the vast majority of cases follow a remarkably similar pattern. Usually, there is no trace of a struggle. Even in muddy or snow-covered ground, no tracks or footprints are found near the carcass. However, there are sometimes indications that the animals have somehow been lifted off the ground and dumped where they are found from the air. Generally, the internal organs, eyes, ears, tongues, rectums and genitalia, along with flesh from the jaw, have been surgically removed and are missing. Bloodless incisions – often deep and circular or oval in shape – are also found. Many of the carcasses are completely drained of blood. Again, these incisions are made with surgical precision.

Microscopic analysis of the tissue has shown that some of the cuts are made by a scalpel. But others appear to have been made without a knife. In some cases the incision seems to have been made by cutting between the cells, without tearing them – which would be impossible using any normal technique. Sometimes there are traces of 'cooking', which a pathologist's report said was 'consistent with a heat-induced injury' as if the flesh has been cut with a laser. However, none of the carbon deposits normally left by lasers have been found. Nevertheless, the wound was 'consistent with a specimen collected via electrosurgical excision'. So are the aliens here taking medical samples?

The phenomenon left pathologist investigators unfamiliar with alien abductions baffled. Experienced ranchers and sheriffs who have been called to cattle mutilations for decades are convinced that they could not possibly be the work of indigenous predators, such as mountain lions, wolves or coyotes. They would leave messy wounds when they ate their prey. The clean and precise wounds on the carcasses show that something else is involved. But what? Since the 1970s, cattlemen's associations have posted rewards for information – to no avail.

In exhaustive undercover operations, US and Canadian state authorities investigated the possible involvement of satanic cults. They have failed to find any link between occult activity and these mutilations. And no one could explain what kind of strange diabolical ritual involved the use of bulky medical lasers and helicopters – or what kind of sect would have access to such things.

However, mysterious, low-flying black helicopters were often seen in the area immediately before or after the discovery of a mutilated carcass. They were often silent and carried none of the identification numbers required by Federal regulations. On several occasions, the helicopters were seen spraying the area where mutilated animals were subsequently found. This gave rise to speculation that livestock was being used for testing chemical and biological weapons by covert government agencies.

Government Involvement

Another explanation comes from former police officer turned   cattle-mutilation researcher Ted Oliphant, who investigated a spate of mutilations in the small town of Fyffe, Alabama, in the 1990s. He believes that the mutilations are part of a massive US government experiment, using helicopters and cutting-edge technology to monitor the spread of infectious diseases, especially Bovine Spongiform Encephalopathy (BSE) or 'mad-cow disease'. Oliphant insists that such apparently clumsy, dangerous and clandestine methods are the only way to monitor the spread of disease across a wide territory.

During his investigations, a large number of unmarked helicopters were spotted in the area where the cattle had been mutilated. One case that linked the helicopters to the mutilations occurred in February 1993, when farmer Keith Davis was woken by a helicopter. In the morning, he found that his cattle had been horridly mutilated. Oliphant submitted the victims' tissue for laboratory analysis. This found a cocktail of human pharmaceuticals, including synthetic amphetamines, anti-coagulants, barbiturates and other chemicals that had no place in a cow. 'Military personnel in helicopters are doing one of three things,' says Oliphant. 'They may be conducting the mutilations themselves. They may be using helicopters to investigate the mutilations once they have been carried out by another, possibly extraterrestrial, source. Finally, they may be tampering with existing mutilations to imply that the military was responsible.'

US military and intelligence agencies have consistently denied any involvement in animal mutilations. And the Federal Aviation Authority has denied the very existence of these strange helicopters. Witnesses who have photographed these helicopters have found themselves threatened by men wearing black uniforms without insignia.

Although the official explanation for animal mutilations has always been natural causes, the FBI bowed to public pressure in 1979 and began investigating the phenomenon. Its 279-page report was published the following year. Again natural causes were cited as the culprit. The cause of death could be linked to parasites, the report said. Official government autopsies cited showed that the lack of blood was consistent with the length of time the dead animals had been left undisturbed. It largely sided with those who believed that the mutilations were the work of animal predators. Outraged ranchers complained that the report was a whitewash. They formed vigilante groups and shot at any low-flying helicopters crossing their fields.

Strange Harvest
Award-winning documentary film-maker Linda Moulton Howe began investigating the phenomenon. She had already won Emmies for her documentaries on medical, environmental and scientific subjects when, in October 1975, she got a call from her brother who was a helicopter pilot stationed at the ICBM silo at Malmstrom, Montana. He

had seen an 'orange glowing disc the size of a football field' hovering over the silo. It cast a 'light brighter than daylight'. The following day, it was discovered that the missiles' targeting systems had been scrambled and eventually, the missiles had to be replaced. What initially sparked Linda Howe's interest was the fact that several ranchers discovered mutilated animals in the same area. The veterinary surgeon who examined the carcasses reported that he had seen a cow with its lips removed in precise 'bevelled' cuts. The animal's blood had been drained from its body so completely that the tissue was left a pinkish white.

She produced her first documentary on animal mutilations, *A Strange Harvest*, in 1980. Since then she has become an authority on the subject. In 1989, she wrote *An Alien Harvest*, following its success with *Glimpses of Other Realities* in 1993.

In 1993, in some cases in Alabama, she showed that even the mutilated animals' capillaries – as well as their arteries and veins – had been drained of blood. This could not have occurred had the livestock been attacked by predators. Besides, what predators would be so particular as only to take the genitalia and other specific organs? Carnivores, humans included, go for the meat – that is, the muscle; the very thing the mutilators leave behind.

She believes that this points to the fact that the mystery assailants are extraterrestrial in origin. Since her 1980 documentary *A Strange Harvest* first brought the cattle mutilation phenomenon to international attention she has amassed a huge body of evidence which, she claims, points strongly towards alien intervention.

Like other investigators, in the course of her research, she has noted that mutilations always conform to a repeated set of characteristics.

'An eye and an ear are often missing,' she says. 'Flesh from the jaw is stripped off on one side only, bones are cut cleanly without a trace of bone chippings, indicating a saw was not used. The tongue is always severed with a vertical cut deep in the throat... The animal's rectum is always cored out, and various internal organs are removed. The cuts are usually bloodless.'

In many cases Howe investigated the bodies of the animals have been completely drained of blood. This is often done via a small hole punched in the jugular vein. The evidence indicates that the animals are still alive when this is done. This has led Howe to speculate that advanced technology is being used in this procedure. She cites one case, which occurred in Arkansas, in March 1989, where five pregnant cows were mutilated and an unborn calf was removed through an incision while still in its embryonic sac. Under forensic examination it was shown that the fluid inside the sac had evaporated completely. This indicated the presence of a searing heat. This theory gets some corroboration from the work of Dr John Altshuler, who has undertaken a number of private investigations since being involved in the Lady case. His microscopic examination of tissues taken from the incised areas of mutilated animals has shown that some had been exposed to temperatures of over 350°C. Even more mysteriously, it was found that the cells surrounding the incision were individually parted and not damaged or split, as would occur if a knife had been used. To Howe and others, this indicates that the cutting is done using highly sophisticated technology, possibly a laser-like instrument not of terrestrial origin.

FBI Involvement

Although the FBI had officially stated that animal mutilations could be put down to natural causes, they had good reason to believe otherwise. UFO author Timothy Good obtained a secret 1976 FBI report which contains the testimony of Officer Gabriel Valdez of the New Mexico State Police. After being called to an animal mutilation, Valdez discovered a series of strange depressions in the earth. Each indentation had a diameter of sixteen inches and the marks formed a series of equilateral triangles. To Valdez, this strongly suggested that a 'suspected aircraft' had landed, then taken off again, followed the cow and landed again where the cow was killed. An oily yellow substance was found at the landing sites. The grass there was scorched and radiation levels at those sites were considerably higher than the surrounding area.

When this report saw the light of day, it confirmed what UFOlogists had long suspected. State investigators and ranchers became convinced too. The chief investigator of mutilations for the District Attorney's office in Trinidad, Colorado, Lou Girodo, said plainly: 'We were dealing with creatures not from this planet.'

The UFO Connection

Lady's mutilation, in September 1967, had coincided with a wave of UFO sightings and reports of strange lights in the San Luis Valley. Each subsequent outbreak was heralded by a new wave of UFO sightings. Some UFOlogists speculate that there is a connection between the UFO sightings and the helicopters. A few believed that the UFOs disguise themselves as helicopters.

It is not surprising that animal mutilations occur at the UFO hotspot Dulce, New Mexico. A curious feature of the mutilations there was the presence of fluorescent paint – visible only under ultraviolet light – on the hides of some of the victims. In another case, a putty-like material was found in a cow's ribcage. Analysis showed that substance was chemically related to paint – though researchers are still puzzled about how it got inside the animal.

In her 1989 documentary, *Alien Life Forms,* Linda Moulton Howe interviewed farmers who had witnessed extraterrestrials engaged in the abduction of animals. But she was warned off this line of investigation.

'That documentary you did about cattle mutilations upset some people in Washington. They don't want mutilations and UFOs connected together,' USAF special agent Richard Doty told her.

No doubt the authorities in Washington were doubly upset when they heard from the numerous eyewitnesses whose accounts made a direct link between UFOs and cattle mutilations. One such came from Dwain Wright, a UCLA graduate, who found a cow suspended in the branches of a tree in Sands Springs, Oregon, in 1979. A year later, Wright was in the vicinity again and met a cowboy who told him of a wave of UFO sightings in the area. The cowboy then showed Wright a dead bull that was half-buried in mud as if it had been dropped from a great height. The animal had been mutilated and its genitals removed. The cowboy later told Wright how he had seen cattle being floated off the ground and into glowing discs in the sky.

A more spectacular incident was witnessed by Timothy Flint, a medical assistant from Portland, Oregon. On the evening of 29 August 1987, Flint had retired for the night and was about to go to bed when he, quite inexplicably, found himself standing in a field in the dark. Then he saw a strange craft. It sent a beam of light down, which levitated a cow.

'The cow was still eating,' said Flint. 'It don't know this dome-shaped thing was there. All of a sudden this light beam came down from a blue base of a round lighted object in the sky... It came down, surrounded the cow and started to levitate it.'

Flint described how the cow was taken up to the top of the beam where it came into contact with something that emitted a sound like a power saw. The animal was mutilated while floating high in the sky and then dropped earthward.

Then in July 1993, Ron and Paula Watson were standing on the porch of their ranch in Mount Vernon, Missouri, when they saw something strange happening at the far end of their pasture. With a pair of binoculars, they saw a cow lying on its side. It looked like it was paralysed. Two small creatures with large white heads, dressed in silver suits, were standing over the stricken animal. They waved their arms over the cow and it began to float. They raised it until it was over six feet off the ground, then steered it up a ramp into their cone-shaped spaceship. The Watsons had not spotted the ship before because its mirrored surface reflected the surrounding foliage, making it practically invisible. Once the carcass was on board, the aliens followed it up the ramp. The ramp was then retracted, and the ship took off, and vanished into the sky at incredible speed.

The question remains, if the mystery assailants are indeed extraterrestrial in origin, what is the reason for their interventions?

Alien Abductions

Many UFO researchers believe that the key to this question lies in the connection between animal mutilations and alien abductions. Indeed, it has been suggested that both cattle mutilations and abductions are being conducted by the same extraterrestrial group, and for similar reasons.

Dr John Mack, Professor of Psychiatry at Harvard Medical School, is a researcher who has performed long-standing work with abductees. He says those who have direct contact with aliens are told at least part of the agenda behind their abductions and the related phenomenon of animal mutilations. From abductees' accounts, Mack has discovered that humankind's environmental destruction of the Earth has stimulated the intervention of various groups of alien intelligences. Both mutilations and abductions are a wake-up call to humankind, warning of an impending environmental crisis, he says.

Mack also believes that some alien groups have a problem with reproduction and they have carried out abductions and mutilations as a means of extracting human and animal DNA. Their aim is to fuse it with their own in order to advance their evolution.

His view is supported Linda Howe. In her book *Glimpses of Other Realities,* she recounts the case of Jeanne Robinson, who is in telepathic communication with an alien intelligence. During one exchange, the extraterrestrial explained why they were performing the mutilations.

'We use substances from cows in an essential biochemical process for our survival,' it said. 'The material we use from cattle contains the correct amount of protein needed for biochemical absorption... While we respect all life, some sacrifices are made for the preservation of other species.'

Another link between alien abductions and animal mutilations is the presence of 'Greys' – small aliens with bulbous heads, big black almond-shaped eyes and claw-like hands. Linda Howe has information from various 'confidential sources' – including people in the military and intelligence agencies – confirming the involvement of Greys in animal mutilations. 'One of these Grey groups has some kind of survival problem,' she has been told, 'and at least one of the reasons for animal mutilations is to gather enough fluid, I guess from haemoglobin and the plasma, to make some kind of essential bio-chemical ingredient that these creatures need.'

But why would a technologically advanced species, capable of travelling billions of miles across space to visit Earth, need our livestock to cure their medical problems?

Goat-Suckers

Greys are not the only species of aliens who mutilate animals. In Caribbean countries and Latin America, witnesses have seen a strange breed of extraterrestrial lizard, which is thought to be responsible for the attacks. The mutilated animals are usually found with a number of small holes bored into the neck or head. In many cases, all the blood has been drained from the body. For this reason, the local population has named this strange creature *El Chupacabra,* or the 'Goat-sucker'.

Sightings began in early 1995 on the Caribbean island of Puerto Rico. One of the first reliable eyewitness reports was made by a police officer who went to investigate the mutilation of a sheep. While he was inspecting the carcass, he became aware that something was observing him from the shadows. When he turned around, he saw a strange creature. It was about five feet tall, with dark skin and orange-yellow eyes. As it made off, he tried to pursue it, but he quickly developed a throbbing headache, was overcome with nausea and collapsed.

A more detailed description was provided by Luis Guadaloupe, a resident of the town of Canovanas. In October 1995, he walked into the police station there and reported his encounter with a bizarre creature, which he had seen flying through the air while he was out walking.

'It was really ugly, like a demon,' Guadaloupe said. 'It was around four to five feet tall, with huge, elongated eyes. It moved like a kangaroo by jumping from powerful back legs. It had a long pointed tongue, which moved in and out of its mouth.'

Its skin was mainly grey, but its back seemed to change colour, and it gave off a foul sulphurous stench.

Normally, such a story would have been dismissed by the police. But they took Guadaloupe's sighting seriously because there were so many similar sightings already on file. Some people had reported that there was a series of spines, about ten inches long, down the creature's back. These, it seemed, were responsible for the colour change. They also made a buzzing sound. Other witnesses said it smelled like animal urine or battery acid, rather than sulphur – but anyway, nothing pleasant.

Since 1995, there have been numerous other sightings of this creature. It has been linked to the grisly slaughter and mutilation of animals. By 1997, well over 2,500 had fallen victim. Throughout the island, farmers have lost all sorts of livestock, including cattle, sheep and goats, as well as cats, dogs, rabbits, rats and birds. Examination of their mutilated bodies shows that the blood has been sucked from them through small holes bored in the head and neck – hence the local name for creature, 'Chupacabra', or goat-sucker. The incisions are clean, as if made by a surgical instrument. The owner of some livestock killed in Puerto Rico on 12 August 1998 said: 'The animals were sucked dry and appeared as if cut by a double-edged surgical knife.'

The teeth or claws of a predator would leave a ragged wound and signs of a struggle. Vets also point out that if a wild animal grabs another creature by the neck, its teeth cause wounding to both sides of the neck. This does not occur to victims of Chupacabras.

Other bizarre findings include strange triangular wounds in the liver of a sheep that had been drained of blood and mutilated sheep on the farm of Radames Marin in Yuco; Puerto Rico, that showed no signs of rigor mortis.

ABEs and UFOs

Jorge Martin, editor of the magazine *Evidencia OVNI* and Puerto Rico's leading investigator into the Chupacabras phenomenon, prefers to call the creatures Anomalous Biological Entities (ABEs). He believes there is a link between ABEs and UFO activity, as UFOs are often seen hovering over the area where the mutilated remains of animals are found. Reports from investigators and eyewitnesses suggest that ABEs or Chupacabras are unlike any known species. This has led a number of researchers to conclude that they are of extraterrestrial origin. Another faction say that the Chupacabras are the product of some hideous covert genetic experiment conducted by the US military. The allegation is that the military is using the off-shore island as an experimental 'playground' for testing illegal weapons. In the past, a variety of top-secret pro jects, involving everything from Thalidomide and Agent Orange to radiation weapons, were based on the island. These practices have gone on for years.

In 1932, the Rockefeller Institute's chief pathologist said: 'The Puerto Ricans are the dirtiest, laziest, most degenerate and thievish race of men ever inhabiting this sphere... all physicians take delight in the abuse and torture of these unfortunate subjects.'

Many people on the island have been given cancer or infected with fatal diseases to further US research. As late as the 1980s, male prison inmates on Puerto Rico were being injected with female hormones as part of an experiment.

'At first I believed these animals were the result of some genetic or bionic experiment, but I now believe that they are not terrestrial in origin,' says Martin. 'Over twenty per cent of people who see this strange creature also report witnessing some sort of aerial phenomena. These witnesses – separated socially as well as geographically – give remarkably similar UFO descriptions. I don't think this can be ignored when trying to understand the Chupacabra problem.'

Puerto Rico has been a centre for UFO activity for many years. Many Chupacabra witnesses report seeing luminous pyramid-shaped craft, and reports of animal mutilations invariably increase the day after these sightings.

Martin published an artist's impression of a Chupacabra, based on a number of eyewitness descriptions, and widely considered to be the most accurate. It shows a lizard-like creature, although it has a stockier body and longer legs. Significantly, it has large, dark, almond-shaped eyes.

Hundreds of people all over Puerto Rico have seen similar creatures, though there are significant differences in the descriptions they give. This has led researchers to believe that there may be a number of different species on the island. Some are hairy; others have scaly skin. Some, like the one Guadaloupe saw, can fly. Another witness saw a creature with vestigial wings, perched in trees. It then launched itself from the branches and glided down on to its prey.

'We are telling people to keep the women and children locked up inside at night,' one villager told the local TV station. 'No one really knows what it is.'

Martin spoke for many of the local population when he expressed his anger at the lack of official action. Whether the creatures were terrestrial or alien, valuable livestock was being slaughtered.

'Right now, I would say the situation is out of control,' Martin said in 1996. 'It's happening everywhere, and government officials who are elected by us to solve our problems are not doing this at the moment.'

Official Reaction

The authorities tried to dismiss the sightings as hysteria and blamed the mutilations on human mischief. However, public pressure forced them to arrange for government veterinarians to conduct an official autopsy of twenty mutilated animals in front of an audience of invited journalists to establish the facts.

After this public examination of the mutilated animals, the head of the government's Agricultural Department of Veterinarian Services Dr Hector Garcia was still prepared to dismiss the possibility of attack by Chupacabras as the cause of death.

'The autopsy revealed a variety of causes of death, including parasites,' he announced. 'I believe the attacks are most likely due to feral dogs or a rhesus monkey imported to Puerto Rico for scientific experiments.'

And Angel Luis, a veterinarian at the island's Gardenville Clinic, said: 'It could be a human being who belongs to a religious sect, even another animal. It could also be someone who wants to make fun out of the Puerto Rican people.'

These statements were greeted with ridicule, and investigators accused the government of conducting a cover-up. They point out that the official explanations, such as attacks by predators or hoaxers, make little sense when you take into account the huge number of animals being killed. The authorities made no attempt to explain the strange mutilations and the physical evidence on the victims. Nor did they take into account the numerous eyewitness accounts.

Jorge Martin accuses the authorities of ignoring the evidence rather than admitting their ignorance. But he says that something may be going on behind the scenes.

'I have confidential sources that have informed me that two Chupacabras have been captured by the authorities here, and are being studied in conjunction with US investigators,' he says. 'So, while animals are dying and the farmers are panicking about their livelihood, there is a possibility that someone, somewhere, knows exactly what is going on.'

To Catch a Chupacabra

The noted UFO researcher Professor G. C. Schellhorn has investigated a number of reports from people who have tried to kill or capture Chupacabras. In one case, Canovanas policeman Juan Collazo shot at one at point-blank range. He hit the creature – to no apparent effect. A fire chief managed to scare a Chupacabra away by shooting at it. Afterwards, he discovered what he believed to be Chupacabra hair caught on a barbed wire fence.

Another case occurred in the town of Gurabo, when a man named Jesus Sanchez found the bodies of his rabbits dead in his backyard. Suspecting that a Chupacabra might be responsible, he mounted a vigil and wait for the creature to return. A few days later, when the Chupacabra came back at 4 a.m., Sanchez was ready. He dazzled it with a powerful torch and tried to kill it with two blows of his machete.

'It sounded like I had struck a hollow drum,' he told Schellhorn. Apparently unharmed, the creature escaped.

The situation in Canovanas became so serious that, despite official opposition, the town's mayor, former police detective Jose Soto, got involved. After examining the evidence of mutilation, he had no choice but to take people's fear of the Chupacabra seriously. He organised a number of expeditions to try to capture a Chupacabra. With the help of the local civil defence unit, he assembled two hundred heavily-armed volunteers and laid traps around the jungles of El Yunque in the Cubuy region of Puerto Rico, an area which has long been a hot spot for paranormal and UFO sightings. So far they have come up empty-handed.

Soto is furious that his pleas to the island's governor and the police chief have largely been ignored.

'Whatever it is,' he said, 'it's highly intelligent. Today it's attacking animals, but tomorrow it may attack people.'

Soto feels that he has no choice but to take the matter into his own hands.

'I am engaged in a search for this creature,' he said. 'If I can capture one of them I will make it public at once. I won't allow anyone to come and take it away.'

In the mean time, Puerto Ricans are exploiting the situation for all it is worth. They have developed quite a Chupacabra industry – along the lines of the Scottish exploitation of the Loch Ness Monster. You can buy posters, key rings, tee-shirts and golf bags, all with the image of a Chupacabra on it.

'This is not a joking matter,' says Martin. 'Whatever is killing these farm animals is seriously affecting the economy. Some people may laugh at the Chupacabras, but people here stay inside at night and lock their doors.'

Sightings Spread
Although Chupacabra sightings began around the town of Canovanas, they spread to forty of Puerto Rico's seventy municipalities within four

months. In 1997, a spate of new attacks were reported from the town of Utuado, forty miles south-west of the capital San Juan. Some forty-two rabbits, a number of chickens and a duck were found dead on farm on 20 November. All of the animals had twin, triangular perforations on their bodies, mostly in the region of the stomach. Researcher Scott Corrales was called in.

'One rabbit had its stomach split by an incision so precise it could only have been made by a surgical instrument used by an expert surgeon,' he said. 'No trace of blood remained in any of the dead animals.'

On 12 August 1998, residents of Barrio Playa near San Juan found a number of dead animals in their back yards. Police officer Rogelio Orsini reported that a total of seventeen rabbits, four guinea hens, two hens, four chicks and one rooster were found dead – 'victims of a strange Chupacabra-like assailant'. According to his report: 'The animals presented perforations on their necks or stomachs and were completely bloodless.'

A trained criminal investigator, Officer Orsini concluded: 'This is not the handiwork of a dog or an ordinary animal, given the number of animals killed and the strangeness of the circumstances. The animals have two perforations made with some kind of sharp object and have no blood in them. This is strange, very strange.'

Reports were soon coming from all areas of the island, which has led Professor Schellhorn to conclude that the creature is very mobile or is breeding extremely rapidly.

Mexican Mutilations

Chupacabra attacks are now no longer an exclusively Puerto Rican problem. They are now being seen in Florida, Texas, California and, particularly, Mexico. On 19 August 1998, Chupacabras struck at a small farm on the outskirts of Monterrey. A peasant farmer, so scared by the attack that he would be identified only by the name 'Rodrigo', reported that two of his chickens had died mysteriously. Examining one of the bodies, he was shocked to find that its internal organs were gone and its blood had been removed.

Mexican TV journalist and UFOlogist Jaime Maussan turned his attention to Chupacabra sightings.

'There have been hundreds of attacks in Mexico,' Maussan says. 'In some cases more than sixty animals were killed. All of them have been found with circular holes, usually in the neck. I don't know if it's of ET origin or a genetic experiment, all I know is it's real.'

In Puerto Rico, Chupacabras activity has been limited to animal mutilation, but Maussan has investigated several cases in Mexico where people have been attacked. He has interviewed people who shake with terror and begin to sob. Maussan is in no doubt that they are telling the truth. 'Believe me, it's a very scary experience,' he says.

In Puerto Rico too, Chupacabras are sometimes threatening. On 9 November 1995, Ada Arroyo, the assistant director of the Mount Sion Nursing Home near Barrio Turabo Arriba in Caguas, had a nervous breakdown after seeing a Chupacabra. At around 7 p.m., Senora Arroyo heard screams 'like those made by a lamb being slaughtered'. When she went outside to investigate, she saw a 'strange hairy figure, greyish in colour, covering its body with a pair of wings'. It had 'a flattened, vulpine face with enormous red eyes'. The creature held her gaze with its hypnotic eyes before spreading its wings and soaring into the air.

It is unclear how the Chupacabras got from Puerto Rico to the mainland. The island are separated from Florida by over a thousand miles of water, but there are reports there of bizarre creatures that match the descriptions of the Chupacabras seen in Puerto Rico. They have spread across the south and are now emerging in California.

In 1998, British cryptozoologist Jonathan Downes and colleague Graham Inglis travelled though Mexico, Puerto Rico and Florida in search of Chupacabras. Their first stop was the state of Puebla in Central Mexico. There, with local vet Soledad de la Pena, they went to visit the smallholding of a farmer named Dom Pedro. In July 1996, Soledad had been called to Dom Pedro's farm after he had found three of his sheep mysteriously mutilated. Downes and Inglis found the walls of many of Dom Pedro's village daubed with crosses. This, Dom Pedro explained, was *'por protectione de vampiros'*. In Mexico, people call Chupacabras *'vampiros'*. Despite the crosses, the church has refused to get involved.

Dom Pedro's case was of particular interest to Downes because, unusually, at least one of the three sheep in question had remained alive for some time after the attack. Soledad had arrived at Dom Pedro's some twelve hours after the attack and had videoed her examination of the victims. The video shows Soledad putting her gloved hand through an enormous hole in the chest of one of the sheep and into the thoracic cavity itself. But when she withdrew her hand, the glove had no more than tiny traces of blood upon it. According to Soledad, the animal been completely drained of its blood.

Although there were two massive holes in the animal's body – one drilled completely through the bones of the rib cage – and some of its internal organs were missing, somehow the animal was still alive. Soledad had no medical explanation for this.

Downes and Inglis then travelled to the village of Tlaloxitcan, about a hundred miles to the south, to investigate another series of reported attacks. These had taken place on the same night as the mutilation of Dom Pedro's sheep. An elderly farmhand named Juan volunteered a description of the attacks. That night, ten households in the village had been attacked simultaneously. Early in the evening they had seen strange lights in the sky. Then, at about midnight, people from the ten households were woken up by the pitiful cries of their goats and sheep. The animals were being attacked by an unknown predator. In all, thirty animals – three from each household – had been mutilated. All of them had been completely drained of blood. Here, though, the blood of the victims splashed across the ground, which is unusual in Chupacabra attacks. There was another key difference. This was an Indian village – Dom Pedro's village was peopled by descendants of the Spaniards.

In Downes' book *Only Fools and Goat-suckers – the Search for the Chupacabra,* he hypothesises that the phenomenon somehow mirrors the religious background of the local people. Where there are

Catholics, who believe that blood of Christ is consumed during Holy Communion, the blood of the Chupacabra's victims is also consumed, whereas in Tlaloxitcan, which is inhabited by the descendants of Aztecs who gloried in the ritual spilling of blood, the Chupacabra follow suit. Downes does not know why this should be, but it clearly indicates that there is an intelligent force behind the Chupacabra attacks.

From Downes' research it is clear that there was a connection between Chupacabra attacks and UFO activity. However, he was unable to pin down the precise nature of the Chupacabra itself.

'Confusing the issue is the wide variety of eyewitness reports,' Downes says, 'many of which describe creatures with vastly differing morphologies, and all of which have, at one time or another, been identified as the "true" Chupacabra. The creatures described have ranged from ape-like animals and bizarre winged creatures, to flying cat-like animals and archetypal bipedal, kangaroo-like creatures with a row of spines along their backs.'

However, an intriguing photograph has come to light. It originally appeared in the 25 September 1996 issue of the *De Quincy News*, in De Quincy, Louisiana, under the headline 'What is it?' The picture had been taken by a woman named Barbara Mullins and showed a strange-looking creature covered with thick woolly hair, which she had found dead at the roadside. The creature was the size of a very large dog, Mullins said. The animal also had the general appearance of a dog, except for the face, which looked like a baboon's. In October 1998, veteran investigator Loren Coleman show the picture to students at a US veterinary school. They concluded that the animal was, indeed, a dog.

'The canine has manicured toenails, not claws, is petite footed, not webbed, as perhaps would be found on an expensive show quality dog,' they said. 'It looks as if it was also recently groomed as the muzzle and paws have been shaved in typical poodle and Pomeranian styles.'

This was a case of mistaken identity. But it will come as no comfort to the farmers in Mexico and Puerto Rico who continue to lose their livestock, and their livelihood, on an almost nightly basis.

More disturbing is the strange connection that has been made between the flying Chupacabras that have been seen and the phenomenon of airborne 'rods'. Recently a number of Mexican newspapers have reported that a strange airborne creature resembling 'a flying manta ray' was videotaped by Jose Eriverto Lopez de la Garza over Monterrey, where Santiago Ytturia first filmed rods. According to the reports, the creature 'can be seen in a number of slow-motion frames of the video recording'. Again, this was how rods were first identified. The creature's skin is greenish and it has a membrane that connects its arms to its thorax – something commonly reported by those who see Chupacabras.

Conspiracies of Silence

All the President's Men

In December 1984, the mailman delivered a package to Hollywood movie producer and UFOlogist Jaime Shandera. Inside there was a roll of undeveloped black and white 35mm film. There was no letter accompanying it. The package carried no return address, though the postmark said Albuquerque, New Mexico.

Shandera had the film processed. It showed an eight-page government document dated 18 November 1952 and a briefing paper for the then president-elect Dwight Eisenhower, who would be sworn in the following January. The first page said: 'This is a TOP SECRET – EYES ONLY document containing compartmentalised information essential to the national security of the United States.'

Page two listed the twelve top US intelligence experts, military leaders and scientists involved in its preparation. Then, on page three, what the paper was about was revealed. It said explicitly that in July

1947, a 'flying disc-shaped aircraft' had crashed near Roswell, New Mexico, and 'extra-terrestrial biological entities' had been recovered by the military.

Attached to the briefing paper was a copy of a memorandum, dated 24 September 1947. It was from President Eisenhower's predecessor, Harry S. Truman, to James Forrestal, the Secretary of Defense in the Truman administration. In it, Truman instructs Forrestal to proceed with 'Operation Majestic-12'. Read in conjunction with the briefing paper, it became clear that Majestic-12 was a twelve-man committee set up by Defense Secretary Forrestal to handle the possibility of an alien invasion at Roswell. Its members were the high-flyers listed on page two. The briefing paper also made the national security implications clear. The final paragraph stressed the need to 'avoid a public panic at all costs'. This, the UFO lobby say, is where the government cover-up started.

Leading UFO sceptic Philip Klass, along with researchers Armen Victorian and Kevin Randle, dismissed the documents as clever fakes. But Jaime Shandera and fellow UFOlogist Stanton T. Friedman, who has dedicated over ten years to investigating Roswell, believe they are genuine. They believe that the Majestic-12 papers had been sent to Shandera by one of the many military contacts he had made while researching a 1980 UFO movie.

Other evidence of the activities of Majestic-12 has been pushed through the letter boxes of researchers over the years. A postcard from New Zealand delivered to Bill Moore in 1985 suggested that he take a look through some files at the US National Archives that had recently been declassified. When Moore and Shandera did so, they found a memo confirming the existence of Majestic-12 (also known as MJ-12, or MAJIC). It was addressed to the US Air Force Chief of Staff Nathan Twining and had been written by Robert Cutler, Special Assistant for National Security in the Eisenhower administration.

Between 1992 and 1996, other documents referring to Majestic-12 dropped onto the doormat of Tim Cooper. He sent copies to Friedman. Although several proved to be hoaxes, Cooper and Friedman believe two single-page documents are genuine. One was a memo to President Truman, dictated by US Secretary of State George C. Marshall to his Executive Secretary, R. H. Humelsine. There is no direct mention of MJ-12 in the memo, but the reference code reads: 'MAJIC EO 092447 MJ-12'.

The other was a brief instruction to General Nathan Twining – an MJ-12 member according to the 1952 briefing paper. It concerned his activities during a July 1947 trip to the saucer's crash site in New Mexico.

In 1994, an anonymous informer sent science writer and long-time UFO investigator Don Berliner a roll of film through the post. It carried photographs of twenty-three pages of a 'Majestic-12 Group Special Operations Manual', dated April 1954. The instruction manual was entitled: 'Extra-terrestrial Entities and Technology, Recovery and Disposal.'

Sceptics point out that, as these MJ-12 documents were supplied on film, their veracity cannot be checked by analysing the ink and paper. However, when investigators have found MJ-12 documents in the files, they were printed on onionskin paper of a type supplied in bulk to the US government between 1953 and 1970. There are also numerous factual details that can be checked out. So investigators set about checking out the background of the twelve committee members and the dates of their meetings. They compared the style and format of the MJ-12 documents to other government correspondence and authenticated the signatures.

The Majestic Twelve

The membership of MJ-12 comprised the cream of the military, scientific and intelligence communities. Along with Secretary of Defense Forrestal, there were the secretary of the Army, three generals – two army, one air force – the first three Directors of the Central Intelligence Agency and five of America's top scientists. If you had to pick a top-secret government committee to investigate a UFO crash, this would be it. The members were:

• James V. Forrestal, the first US Secretary of Defense to sit on the cabinet. During World War II he had been in charge of navy procurements. In 1949, he resigned and was hospitalised suffering from depression. Soon after, he committed suicide by throwing himself from his hospital window.

• Gordon Gray, Assistant Secretary of the Army. He became National Security Advisor and Director of the CIA's Psychological Strategy Board.

• General Hoyt Vandenberg, Chief of Military Intelligence during World War II and Director of Central Intelligence from 1946 to 1947.

• Major General Robert Montague, head of the Special Weapons Project at the Atomic Energy Commission at Albuquerque, New Mexico.

• General Nathan F. Twining, Commander of Air Materiel Command at Wright Field. During World War II, he played a large part in directing the war against the Japanese. In 1957, he was appointed Chairman of the Joint Chiefs of Staff.

• Rear Admiral Roscoe Hillenkoetter, Director of Central Intelligence from 1947 to 1950. In 1960, he acknowledged that there was a UFO cover-up.

• Rear Admiral Sidney Souers, the first Director of Central Intelligence in 1946.

• Dr Vannevar Bush, who was President Truman's scientific advisor and Chairman of the Joint Research and Development Board from 1945 to 1947. During World War II he had been a key player in the development of the atomic bomb.

• Dr Detlev Bronk, a biophysicist who was head of the National Academy of Science and the Chairman of the Medical Advisory Board of the Atomic Energy Committee.

• Dr Lloyd Berkener, Executive Secretary of the Joint Research and Development Board. He became a member of the CIA-funded UFO committee in the 1950s.

• Dr Jerome Hunsaker, Chairman of the National Advisory

Committee on Aeronautics and famous aircraft designer.
• Dr Donald Menzel, professor of astrophysics at Harvard and science writer.

But one thing bothered the investigators. All the MJ-12 members had top-level security clearance with the exception of Donald Menzel. He was a well-known UFO sceptic who had written numerous papers debunking flying saucers and three anti-UFO books. However, in April 1986, Stanton Friedman got permission from Menzel's widow and university officials to go through Menzel's papers in the archives at Harvard. In them, he discovered that Menzel had 'Top Secret Ultra' clearance from the CIA and had a thirty-year association with the National Security Agency. He advised the government on numerous classified projects, did highly classified consulting work for many major US corporations and had close connections with the other scientists who sat on MJ-12. He was not just any old astronomy professor and UFO sceptic. In security terms, he was of equal calibre to the rest of the committee. What's more, Menzel made a number of trips to New Mexico during 1947 and 1948, at government expense.

The other alleged members of the group also checked out. All had worked on top-secret projects and were members of various government research and development boards.

Silent Witnesses

The last member of the committee died just three months before Jaime Shandera received the film, so none of them could be questioned. However, their comings and goings could be traced from telephone logs, minutes from meetings, correspondence and other papers which by that time were on open access in the Library of Congress and various presidential libraries.

The earliest documented reference to Majestic is in the 24 September 1947 memo sent by Truman to Secretary of Defense Forrestal. The memo mentions the president's science advisor Vannevar Bush. Records show that Truman had a meeting with Bush on 24 September – it was the only day between May and December that year they met. Bush also had a meeting with Forrestal on that day.

That same day, a secret memo was sent to the Pentagon by General Twining, Commander of the Air Materiel Command. Its subject was 'flying discs' and in it Twining said: 'The phenomenon reported is something real and not visionary or fictitious.' And a flight log from July 1947 records the fact that Twining had flown to New Mexico on 7 July. According to Eisenhower's briefing paper, that same day 'a secret operation was begun to assure recovery of the wreckage... for scientific study'.

Forrestal, Bush and Twining were all members of MJ-12. But Joe Nickell, writer for *Skeptical Enquirer* magazine and expert in document analysis, is not convinced.

'It is not what is correct that matters nearly so much as what is wrong,' he says. 'Even a novice forger can be expected to get some things right.'

Nickell's examination of the format and presentation of the documents brought to light a number of serious problems. Although Truman's signature on the memo to Forrestal matches those on other documents that Truman signed and that are known to be authentic, Nickell points out that it is positioned wrongly on the page. The typefaces, date formats, and style of language used in the MJ-12 papers does not match those in comparable documents from the same sources.

'The many anomalous and suspicious elements detected in the MJ-12 papers clearly demonstrate the documents are forgeries,' Nickell concludes.

Critics also point out that Eisenhower was Army Chief of Staff at the time of the Roswell incident, so he would not have needed to be briefed on the crash. However, the preparation of such briefing papers is common practice in the White House when the administration changes.

Stanton Friedman dismisses such niggles. His ten years of research have led him to conclude that the papers are genuine.

'Frankly, I consider this ensemble of documents [to be] the most important classified documents ever leaked to the public,' Friedman says. 'I have yet to hear a convincing argument against MJ-12.'

Copies of the MJ-12 documents were sent to British UFO expert Timothy Good. However he became suspicious because Truman's signature on the Forrestal memo was almost identical to one on a memo known to be authentic. No two signatures are the same. Good examined the signature more closely and found a nick on the top of the T that had been whited out. However, he does not dismiss the documents completely.

'There's definitely something to the documents,' he says. 'If you look at the evidence, there's so much historical [evidence] that's been proved accurate.'

In his 1996 book, *TOP SECRET/MAJIC*, Friedman lists over thirty details not known by anyone outside the government before the film arrived at Jaime Shandera's Hollywood home. Good's conclusion is that they had been written by a well-informed insider.

'There is such a thing as positive disinformation. These documents could well be that,' he says.

The argument is that even if the documents are fakes they had to be written by someone with inside knowledge who is trying to get the truth to a wider public. Either way the documents prove that the government knows the truth about UFOs and is deliberately covering up.

Canadian Confirmation

The existence of MJ-12 has been alluded to by others in a position to know. In 1950, a Canadian government memo written by defence project engineer Wilbur Smith says: 'Flying saucers exist. Their *modus operandi* is unknown but concentrated effort is being made by a small group headed by Dr Vannevar Bush.'

Former Chairman of the Institute for Defense Analysis Dr Eric Walker recently said that he had known of the existence of MJ-12 for forty years and had attended meetings at Wright–Patterson Air Base in

Ohio concerning the recovery of flying saucers. However, former commander of Wright–Patterson Air Base Brigadier General Arthur Exon said he knew nothing of a group called MJ-12. However, he confirmed that there was a top-secret group set up to control access to classified UFO reports. It was called 'The Unholy Thirteen'. UFO enthusiasts have speculated that this was MJ-12 plus one: the President.

Huff and Puff

More information about Majestic-12 came from West Point graduate Bob Huff. After retiring from the US military, he worked as an expert in information technology in companies that were contracted to work for the Federal government and the intelligence community. He has also been investigating the military involvement in the UFO phenomenon for decades.

During the course of his work he was introduced to a former Majestic-12 contractor, whom he calls SARGON, who spilled the beans on the organisation's covert operations. According to Huff, MJ-12 is a government programme that interacts with at least one species of extraterrestrial, either through radio or live interactions. It started in 1947, after the Roswell incident. MJ-12 missions are designed to manage our interactions with the aliens and to exploit reverse-engineering technology for national purposes. Although it acts autonomously, MJ-12 ultimately reports to a joint committee whose members include the directors of both the CIA and the NSA. Boeing, Lockheed, TASC and TRW are all MJ-12 contractors. MJ-12 also has a unique system of identifying potential employees and tracking their careers.

Birdland

The existence of Majestic-12 was again confirmed during the course of a US television documentary aired in October 1988 called *UFO Cover-up? Live*. Two US intelligence agents, whose faces were hidden and whose voices were electronically manipulated to protect their identities, talked openly about its function as a policy-making group on UFO activity. The government knew far more about alien visitations than they were letting on, they said. Then they dropped the bombshell. They revealed that the US government had captured extraterrestrials and learned to communicate with them. One of them, a mechanic from the Zeta Reticuli star system, had even learnt to speak English.

If viewers were unconvinced by this, they filled in all the details. They explained how the aliens love strawberry ice-cream and 'Tibetan-style music'.

The two agents were known only as 'Condor' and 'Falcon' and their story can be traced back to 1979 or 1980. It was then that a 'well-placed individual within the intelligence community' made contact with former Air Force Office of Special Investigations agent and UFOlogist Bill Moore. Moore's shady contact asked him to befriend UFO researcher Paul Bennewitz. Bennewitz was something of an electronics whiz. He lived near Kirtland Air Force Base at Albuquerque, New Mexico – home of the Scandia National Laboratories where military scientists keep watch on the skies using the Starfire laser telescope – and had been attempting to intercept radio signals from it that he believed contained information about UFOs and aliens.

Moore monitored Bennewitz's activities and reported back to his intelligence contact. Meanwhile his intelligence contact gave him information about aliens to feed to Bennewitz. Although Moore denies it, some of this appears to have been disinformation so that, if Bennewitz published anything he had learnt from his intercepts of Kirtland's communications traffic, he could easily be discredited. What Moore got out of the deal is unclear, but many UFOlogists believe that it was copies of the famous Majestic-12 papers.

Moore maintained communication with his mysterious contact, who began leaking him details of official UFO research. Soon the leak became a flood. It was more than Moore could handle alone so, in 1982, he turned for help to fellow UFOlogist Jaime Shandera. It became clear to Shandera that, if they were to con- tinue to use

Moore's contact, they had to use a codename to protect the man's identity. The codename they chose was Falcon.

While Shandera and Moore tried to verify the material Falcon was feeding them, they came across a number of other intelligence insiders who were willing to leak information on the government's involvement with crashed saucers and extraterrestrials. Each was given a bird's name and soon Shandera and Moore were referring to this dissident group of insiders as the 'Aviary'.

Shandera and Moore have never revealed who their contacts were, but other researchers believe they can identify the members of the Aviary. One of them was Bruce Maccabee, an optical physicist and laser weapons expert from the US Naval Surface Weapons Laboratory at Maryland, who used the codename Seagull. Mind-control operations specialist John Alexander, a former colonel from the US Army Intelligence and Security Command and expert in non-lethal weapons, was Penguin. And the CIA's Deputy Director for the Science and Technology Division – the so-called 'weird desk' – Ron Pandolphi was Pelican.

However, a growing number of UFOlogists believe there is more to the Aviary than a random selection of government insiders who want the truth about UFOs and alien encounters to be available to the public at large. And it is thought that Shandera and Moore are pawns in larger game.

Conspiracies Within Conspiracies

Many of the members of the Aviary are senior individuals with extremely high security clearances who have been involved in the UFO investigations on the inside since the early 1970s. They are involved in a political struggle against Majestic who, because of the secrecy surrounding the UFO issue, have formed a government within the government. There is even some overlap between the Aviary and Majestic as MJ-12 have infiltrated the Aviary to keep it under control, or possibly the other way round.

In the meantime, Richard Boylan, author of *Labored Journey to the*

Stars, believes that Aviary members are pooling their information in an attempt to 'see the big picture about UFOs and ET contacts with Earth, and to use this privileged information pool to gain access to additional secret data [and] to understand the policies of the elite, hypersecret... group'.

Boylan also believes that there was a split in the Aviary caused by a disagreement between 'lower' level associates who wanted to make UFO information public and the MJ-12 members who wanted to keep it under wraps.

But the conspiracy goes deeper than that. Some of the Aviary members are involved in 'black ops' – projects that are so highly classified that they have no official budgets and are, consequently, not open to Congressional scrutiny. Conspiracy researcher Armen Victorian believes that Aviary members involved in 'black ops' secretly manipulated the group's lower ranking members. They also created alternate levels of UFO cover stories and counter cover stories to cloak their black operations in a mantle of disinformation. According to Victorian: 'Hoaxed and bogus documents suddenly flooded the UFO field and gullible researchers entered into lengthy arguments among themselves, allowing the main proponents behind this well-organised disinformation campaign to further their original work unhindered.'

Certainly members of the Aviary are in key positions and are closely interconnected. For example, Christopher 'Kit' Green – Bluejay – became chief of Biomedical Sciences. Before that, he was the CIA liaison officer for a remote viewing project where he worked with Stanford University's Harold 'Hal' Putholf – Owl – who moved on to the Institute of Advanced Research in Austin, Texas. Another Aviary member, psychic warfare expert Albert Stubblebine – Heron – later headed up the military side of remote viewing. Green also manned the 'weird desk' at the CIA's Division of Science and Technology, the post taken over by Pelican, Ron Pandolphi. Pandolphi also worked at the White House on a project funded by the Rockefeller Foundation to oversee the release of UFO information to the public. That project also involved Commander C.C. Scott Jones – Hummingbird – a retired US Navy officer who served in the Office of Naval Intelligence and went on to become President of the Human Potential Foundation.

Penguin, John Raven, is another key player in the psychic spies projects and was also involved with psychotronic and mind-control research, as was Jack Vorona, who is thought to be Raven – though other candidates include Henry Kissinger, former National Security Advisor Brent Scrowcroft, and Eward Teller, father of the hydrogen bomb.

Then there is Ernie Kellerstraus – Hawk – who has security clearance to handle classified UFO material, worked at Wright–Patterson AFB during the 1970s, and reputedly lived with an ET; Rosemary Guiley – Mourning Dove – director of the US crop circle research group; Barry Hennessy – Bird Colonel – former head of AFOSI; and Jaques Vallee – Partridge – US Defense Department computer expert, former UFO investigator for the French government and prolific writer on UFOs.

Condor is USAF Captain Robert Collins, a former special agent at AFOSI who has been engaged in high-level UFO intelligence operations. No one knows who Falcon is. But there are two candidates: one is Richard Doty – also know as Sparrow – formerly with AFOSI and who went on to become a state policeman in Dulce, New Mexico. The other is Hummingbird, Scott Jones.

Innocent Explanation

Scott Jones freely admits that there was such an organisation as the Aviary, which tried to encourage the US government to come clean on the UFO issue. But he said that there were no formal meetings as such. He used to meet with other guys who found out that he had a bird name, but he never saw it as an institution.

He was picked to be a member of the Aviary because he had worked in Naval Intelligence for fifteen years and the organisers thought that that would have brought him closer to the truth. However, he never saw any documents relating to the UFOs.

Either they did not exist, or he was denied access to them. The evidence he has seen from other, public sources does not impress him, though he believes that extraterrestrial intelligence is impinging on us.

The others in the Aviary, he says, are also keen to get their hands on the evidence. But he can see why the government would be covering up. If they have spent over fifty years since Roswell trying to back-engineer a flying saucer and have still got nowhere, that would be an embarrassment. The Aviary, he says, has not met up for years, though some old friends have stayed in touch.

The Golden Age Dawns

The Majestic-12 committee set up a programme for the systematic study of UFO activity. It began as Project Sign in 1947. Its codename was changed in 1949 to Grudge, then to Blue Book in 1952. The third phase, Blue Book, shut up shop 1969. By and large, the US government's investigations have been secretive and desultory. However, during that time, there was a golden age of UFO investigation. It was sparked by an incident that occurred at the Army Signal Corps radar centre in Fort Monmouth, New Jersey, on 10 September 1951.

A group of officers were making an inspection of the facility, when a student radar operator picked up an anomalous blip on his radar screen. The contact appeared to be around seven miles to the south-east of the radar station. It was travelling northwards up the coast – and it was travelling too fast to be tracked automatically by the centre's radar, so the operator switched to manual.

The officers watched over the student's shoulder for about three minutes, until the blip disappeared from the screen. It was travelling in a north-easterly direction at an estimated range of 15,000 yards. The operator estimated that it was travelling at more than seven hundred miles an hour, faster than the fastest jets in those days.

Twenty-five minutes after the radar sighting, Lieutenant Wilbert S. Rogers, in a T-33 Lockheed trainer, pursued as best he could a silver-coloured disc, flying at around nine hundred miles an hour. Rogers and his instructor, Major Edward Ballard, dived down at the object from 20,000 feet, but still could not match its speed. It was a classic flying saucer, round and flat and between thirty and fifty feet across. They watched helplessly as the saucer streaked twenty miles up the coast, before making an extraordinary 120-degree turn and vanishing over the sea.

The next day, Fort Monmouth radar station tracked two more high-speed contacts – one at 10:50 a.m., the other at 1:30 p.m. But it was overcast that day, and there were no planes up to make visual contact.

In the annals of UFOlogy, the Fort Monmouth radar contacts were unexceptional. However, a report found its way to the office of Major General Charles Cabell, head of Air Force Intelligence at the Pentagon. Cabell was intrigued. He ordered a thorough investigation and insisted on being briefed personally on the findings. Cabell's request landed on the desk of Lieutenant Jerry Cummings at the Air Technical Intelligence Center in Dayton, Ohio. He had recently been appointed director of 'Project Grudge', the Air Force agency assigned to check out UFO reports. When Cummings started to prepare his briefing, he was gratified to discover that the Monmouth case had already been 'solved' by his team.

'The whole outfit [at Monmouth] were a bunch of young impressionable kids and the T-33 crew had seen a reflection,' the Grudge file said. The problem was that analysts had concluded that without ever leaving their desks in Ohio.

Cummings knew that this was not going to satisfy General Cabell and turned to his boss, Lieutenant Colonel N. R. Rosengarten, chief of ATIC's Aircraft and Missiles Branch, for help. In a matter of hours, they were on their way to New Jersey. The two of them interviewed everyone involved, including Rogers and Ballard. They said that what they had seen was no 'reflection'. They were convinced that it was 'intelligently controlled'. The next morning, Rosengarten and Cummings turned up at the Pentagon to brief Cabell.

When the briefing was over, Cabell wanted to know how Project

Grudge was handling its investigations in general. Cummings reported that his men seemed to consider every report as huge joke. This was because the head of ATIC, General Harold Watson, had ordered the staff of Project Grudge to do everything they could to 'degrade the quality of the reports'. Cummings said: 'The only analysis consists of trying to think up new and original explanations that hadn't been sent to Washington before.'

Cabell was furious and complained that he had been lied to. And Rosengarten and Cummings were sent back to Dayton with orders to completely reorganise Project Grudge. Anyone without an open mind, Cabell said, was to be sacked.

Cummings himself was a victim of the reorganisation. He became a civilian and was sent to work on another top-secret government project.

Project Blue Book

Captain Edward J. Ruppelt took over. Project Grudge was redesignated 'Project Blue Book', and given a higher security classification. Channels were established for military personnel to report their UFO sightings directly and more staff were taken on to handle the vastly increased workload. Reports came in so thick and fast that there were never enough people to handle them all. However, high priority cases were routinely investigated in person for the first time. Analysts would no longer be desk-bound debunkers as they had been in the 'Dark Ages'. Under Ruppelt, Blue Book would work like any other military intelligence operation.

To change his staff's thinking on the subject, Ruppelt even coined the term 'Unidentified Flying Object', or 'UFO'. The term 'flying saucer' was open to ridicule, while a UFO was a serious phenomenon. It was during this period of openness that the Washington flap occurred.

For three consecutive weekends in the summer of 1952, the airspace above Washington, D.C., was buzzing with UFOs. Lights in the night skies were seen by numerous ground and airborne observers, both civilian and military, and contacts filled the capital's radar screens. The

Pentagon's switchboards were jammed with calls from the public and ordinary military communications ground to halt. The sightings captured headlines, and the Pentagon held its largest press conference since World War II. In fact, the whole of 1952 was the busiest in Blue Book's history. That year, its analysts investigated over 1,500 cases and 303 cases – some 20 per cent – were designated 'unidentified'.

However, the Washington flap put the wind up the US government. If they could not control the airspace over the capital, what could they control? This was the height of the Cold War; the UFOs presented a clear threat to national security. It undermined the American people's faith in their government. The CIA feared that some foreign power might manipulate the situation to its own advantage. Already, the population of Washington was on the verge of mass hysteria. So they set up the Robertson Panel. It was named after its chairman, the physicist H.P. Robertson, who was head of the Defense Department's Weapons System Evaluation Group and who was also on the CIA's payroll. He recruited other distinguished members, including physicist Samuel A. Goudsmit from the Brookhaven National Laboratories, the winner of the 1968 Nobel prize for physics Luis Alvarez, and astrophysicist Thornton Page, who was deputy director of the Operations Research Office of Johns Hopkins University. They were all prominent sceptics.

They met for two days in Washington in January of 1953 and, instead of calling for a comprehensive and impartial investigation of the phenomenon, they recommended that a programme of serious debunking begin. The media was to be used to strip flying saucers of their mysterious and threatening status. One suggestion was to call in Walt Disney to assist in this, though there is no evidence that he was recruited. The CIA also proposed infiltrating the groups of flying saucer enthusiasts that had sprung up – in case they became the Trojan horse for some foreign power.

The first victim of the new attitude in Washington was Ruppelt. The Cold War was not the right time for open-mindedness, and Ruppelt got his marching orders. When he left the service, he wrote an account of his experiences, *The Report on Unidentified Flying Objects,* which became a classic in the field of UFOlogy.

After Ruppelt, Blue Book was starved of funds. It returned to making desultory desk-bound investigations, half-hearted analysis and debunking. Headed by die-hard sceptics such as Major Hector Quintanilla, it was forced to resort to 'outsourcing', which was handled via the Robertson Panel. A civilian think-tank was instituted to handle a statistical study at the Battelle Memorial Institute. It was codenamed 'Project Stork' and its activities classified. Photographic evidence was handed over to the US Navy Photographic Interpretation Laboratory and the US Air Force Photo Analysis Division. But despite spending anything up to a thousand hours on some images, they came up with no very firm conclusions.

In 1966, the Air Force handed over its investigation of UFOs to the University of Colorado. Then on 17 December 1969, Blue Book was closed for good. During the two decades of its existence, it had logged 12,618 reports, 701 of which – five per cent – remained unsolved. But in the Ruppelt years, things were very different. In December 1952, Ruppelt briefed the Air Defense Command on 1,021 cases. Some 20.1 per cent could not be accounted for and hoaxes were proved in less than two per cent.

Blue Book was started up again in 1989 as a civilian operation, dedicated to furthering the investigation of the 701 'unidentified' cases.

The Condon Committee

In 1966, the Condon Committee was set up at the University of Colorado by the USAF, under Dr Edward Condon. The Committee comprised a hand-picked bunch of sceptics whose job was to take over the scientific investigation of UFO reports from Blue Book. In 1967, it made its only investigation of an alien abduction case. They did not usually bother with such cases, but were forced to take this one seriously because it involved a police officer.

On 3 December 1967, at around 2:30 a.m., Herbert Schirmer, a patrolman in Ashland, Nebraska was on his way to investigate a livestock disturbance. When he reached a junction, he noticed what at first appeared to be the red taillights of a truck. But when he took a closer look, the truck turned out to be a metallic, flying saucer that was hovering around eight feet above the road. The red lights were coming from portholes around its rim. After a moment, the space ship gave off a fiery glow and shot up into the clouds.

Schirmer returned to the police station thirty minutes later and noted in the station log that he had seen a flying saucer. But when he came to write down the time of the incident, he found that he was unable to account for twenty minutes.

Over the next few days, a red mark appeared on Schirmer's neck. He suffered from splitting headaches and a buzzing in his ears kept him awake at night. These symptoms, he believed, were associated with his encounter.

As the incident was reported by a police officer, it was referred to the Condon Committee. Psychologist R. Leo Sprinkle of the University of Wyoming was also called in. Under regressional hypnosis, Schirmer relived the encounter. This time he recalled that, while he had sat looking mesmerised at the UFO, strange beings approached his car. A green gas had enveloped the car. Then he had passed out. When he came to, Schirmer was being led aboard the spacecraft. It was a friendly enough encounter. He was shown around by a 'grey-skinned being', then he was led back to his car and told to forget all about the encounter.

Sprinkle believed that there was more to it, but although they probed Schirmer, the Condon Committee made it clear that they did not believe a word of it. Schirmer found the stress of the situation too much to handle and quit his job. The Committee promptly dismissed all the evidence that emerged under hypnosis and none of it appeared in their report.

'Unidentified'
One of the very last cases reported to Project Blue Book that was

labelled as 'unidentified' occurred in Meridian, Mississippi. Philip Lanning was driving south of town on the evening of 10 July 1967, when his car coasted to a halt and the radio faded. Lanning got out and started to look at the car engine, when an enormous object flew over his head about three hundred feet in the air. The object was silent and moving to the east.

Lanning thought the object was about to crash, but just before the object reached a group of nearby trees, it tilted upward, turned right and then accelerated at great speed straight up into the low-lying clouds. The object was described as being 'like a cymbal on a drum set and was a dirty metallic grey in colour on the underside'. Lanning saw no portholes or hatches and said that it appeared to the size of house.

Lanning was not sure who would be interested in the report, but he felt that it should be sent to someone in the government, so he forwarded it to a friend in Naval Intelligence. It was handed on to the Air Force. Blue Book eventually received it and began an investigation.

They were impressed with Lanning as a witness, as he was a former military officer who was trained in observation. After extensive research and interviews the Air Force were unable to find any conventional explanation and were forced to label this sighting 'unidentified'. This was one of the very last reports in Blue Book to receive that tag.

The Missing Report

Project Blue Book's findings were published in a series of thirteen Blue Book Special Reports. Their overall conclusion was that UFOs did not exist, and that there were no such thing as flying saucers. Sightings could be accounted for in other ways and extraterrestrials were not paying flying visits to Earth. More specifically: 'No UFO reported, investigated, and evaluated by the Air Force has ever given any indication of a threat to our national security... There has been no evidence indicating that sightings categorised as "unidentified" are extraterrestrial vehicles.' This was the result of the millions of dollars the US government had spent on its official investigations into UFOs.

UFOlogists were naturally disappointed by these conclusions, but that was not the end of the story. Indeed. The Blue Book reports actually posed more questions than they answered. Indeed, one aspect of the publication of the reports themselves cried out for an explanation. If there were thirteen Blue Book reports, how was it possible that the last one was entitled Blue Book Special Report 14? The one before it in the series was Blue Book Special Report 12. What had happened to number thirteen?

The official reason that there was no Special Report 13 was the same reason that American skyscrapers often don't have a thirteenth floor – or that Britain's Ministry of Transport no longer issues car registration plates bearing the number 666, the 'number of the beast'. It is considered bad luck. But surely the people who ran Project Blue Book were rational men who went about their job of examining the evidence for UFOs using scientific methods? These were not the type of people to suffer from triskaidekaphobia – the irrational fear of the number thirteen.

It soon became clear, however, that Blue Book Special Report 13 contained explosive material that the US government did not dare publish. It was, in fact, a repository for all the material that would have caused panic if it had been allowed to get inti the public domain. Then, in the early 1980s, the once water-tight Special Report 13 sprang a leak.

Special Forces

The hole in the dyke came in the form of the tape-recorded testimony of former US Special Forces officer William S. English, the son of an Arizona state senator. In May 1970, he was serving with the Green Berets in Vietnam when he and his A-team were sent on a peculiar mission. They were to make an illegal incursion into neighbouring Laos, locate a Boeing B-52 Stratofortress bomber that had been downed in the triple-canopy jungle there and, if possible, rescue its crew. What was peculiar about this mission was that the B-52 had not been downed by enemy fire. It had crashed after coming off worst in a hostile encounter with a UFO. In tapes of the crew's last Mayday call, they identified their attacker simply as a 'large white light'.

The A-team went into Laos by helicopter and located the B-52. It had not crashed in the normal way, slicing a swathe through the trees on its way down. Instead it lay there, English said, 'like a great big giant hand had grabbed it and just set it down'. The aircraft itself was undamaged. Its bomb load was intact. And there was no damage to the vegetation around it. All the crew were still on board, strapped in their seats. They were all dead and hideously mutilated – but there was no sign of blood. English photographed the grisly scene. Then, following standard army procedures, the team took dog tags from the corpses and buried them in temporary graves, hoping to recover them later. The code books were removed and then the aircraft was blown up.

The mission had spooked English's men. His unit was ambushed in the jungle a few weeks later and most of them were killed. English himself was taken prisoner, but he managed to give his captors the slip and fled into the jungle where he was rescued by US forces some time later. With the American withdrawal from Southeast Asia in 1973, English left the Army. However, he did not leave the service altogether. In 1976 he began working as an intelligence analyst at the major USAF/NSA electronic listening post at RAF Chicksands in Bedfordshire. Chicksands is the home of the USAF's 6950th Electronic Security Group, which monitors and analyses military communications across Europe using the so-called Elephant Cage – a massive ring of radio aerials.

As part of his duties, on 29 June 1976 he was given a 625-page document to assess. It was entitled Grudge/Blue Book Report 13. English says that the report seemed incredible. It contained reports of alien encounters and described the captured extraterrestrial craft, detailing their armaments. There were also autopsy reports on dead aliens. It was unbelievable, except for one incident. Among the close-encounter reports was the report of the downed B-52 English had investigated in Laos. It contained the photographs English himself had taken six years earlier, showing the mutilated crew. This convinced English that the report was genuine. He submitted an assessment saying that, and got on with other work.

English does not know if he had been given the report by accident, but a few weeks later he was summarily dismissed. On the orders of the base commander, Colonel Robert Black, he was shipped back to the US that very day. Bewildered, he found himself dumped back in his hometown, Tucson, Arizona. English could only conclude that his dismissal had something to do with the Blue Book report he had read. This tweaked his interest in UFOs and he went to a lecture given by the well-known UFOlogist Stanton Friedman at Pima Community College. After the lecture, English approached Friedman, who was intimidated at first.

'English is a big man, physically imposing,' says Friedman. 'He looked anxious, like he didn't want to be in one place for too long. Initially he was quite scary until he trusted that I was taking him seriously.'

Then he told Friedman what he had seen. So there could be no dispute later about what he had said, his testimony was tape-recorded, and he told Friedman and the tape recorder all he knew.

English began working as a researcher for the Aerial Phenomena Research Organisation, then one of the top UFO groups, which was based in Tucson. Through APRO he met the astronomer J. Allen Hynek, who had been an advisor to Blue Book and whose hand-written notes were scattered throughout the report. In a private conversation, Hynek confirmed that the report English had evaluated was the missing Grudge 13 report. But Hynek said he would deny this if English went public.

Four years later, Colonel Black and his staff sergeant turned up in Tucson. They told English that they had also been kicked out of the USAF because of the Grudge 13 report. The three men were aggrieved and swore to do something about it. Colonel Black knew just what they should do. He told English that a large alien craft was buried on the White Sands Missile Range in New Mexico. They should mount an expedition to find it. To finance this, English sold the leather-goods business he had started in Tucson to support himself. They bought a van, which they filled with cameras, video recorders and other equipment. Armed with infrared-sensing devices, gravitometers, magnetometers and sound detectors, the intrepid trio broke into the highly restricted White Sands Missile Range.

Naturally, the authorities were not too thrilled about having their security compromised by renegade UFOlogists. When their infiltration was detected, the military sent helicopters, which fired rockets at the van. The van was destroyed and Colonel Black and his staff sergeant, who were in it, were killed. Luckily, English was about half-a-mile away on foot. He managed to escape and headed for the Tucson home of fellow UFO researcher Wendelle Stevens. His own home was under surveillance and English had himself smuggled out of Tucson. Eventually, he settled Lynchburg, Virginia, where he worked for a few years as a TV cameraman.

But the authorities would not leave him alone. In September 1988, he decided that he had nothing to lose by going public. In December 1988, English posted his story on the Internet. It detailed the fifteen attempts that had been made on his life because of his knowledge of Grudge 13. In one attack, two men had raked his Lynchburg home with machine gun fire for fifteen minutes. They fired at least two thousand rounds at the house. The local police precinct was only two hundred yards away, but no came to his help.

As well as government assassins, English has also been the target of debunkers. They point out that, according to Pentagon records, no B-52 was lost in Southeast Asia between July 1969 and July 1972. If a B-52 was downed in the Laotian jungle in April or May 1970, it had been expunged from the official records. A B-52 Stratofortress is a large and costly aircraft, and it is hard to lose one without it being noticed. The histories of all of the B-52s made by Boeing between November 1951 and October 1962 exist. Each one can be accounted for, officially. But it must be remembered that the Vietnam war was fraught with misreporting – overestimating the enemy's body count while under-reporting US loses. As Congress had given the administration no permission to bomb Laos, overflights by fully laden B-52s were illegal and the loss of a B-52 there would have been covered up.

It has also been said that English was, in fact, too young to have served in Special Forces in 1970. Records show that English did serve in the US Army but as a telephone technician with the rank of Spec 4, or corporal. However, Friedman has checked his military credentials and believes that he has the necessary credentials to see government records on UFO activity.

However, it is unlikely that he served in Southeast Asia in that capacity. The British Home Office has no record of the deportation of a William S. English in 1976, though this would have been a military matter. Records also show that the American base commander of RAF Chicksands from September 1974 until August 1976 was Colonel James W. Johnson Jr. and not Colonel Robert Black. However, if there is a cover-up, the records would be easy to falsify.

Joint Venture

Former Green Beret William English was not the only one to come forward. Milton W. Cooper was a Petty Officer in the US Navy in 1972 when he too saw Grudge 13. He says that it was not released because it details the co-operation between the US government and the aliens. In a joint venture, they are constructing a base on the moon. The aliens are providing the technology while the US government are providing the manpower, in the form of human slaves. The elite are going to start a human colony there after the destruction of the Earth which will happen 'by or soon after the year 2000'.

According to Cooper, another colony is being secretly planned on Mars. He says that on 22 May 1962 a probe landed on the red planet and confirmed the existence of an environment that could support life. This does not even convince fellow UFOlogists. Stanton Friedman said: 'If Cooper told me it was raining, I'd go and put a pair of shorts on.'

However, although Friedman does not trust Cooper, he does believe that Grudge 13 exists. He finds English's story plausible and says that his description of the report matches that given to him by a military colleague that he won't name. This convinces him that it is real and that it is not being released because the information it contains is explosive.

Disinformation

The existence of Grudge 13 has always been denied by the USAF, who say that the material originally intended for Blue Book Report 13 – the findings of an investigation known as Project Stork – was incorporated in Blue Book 14. Assuming this to be true, some UFOlogists have come up with theories about what was in the Grudge/Blue Book Report 13 that English and others claim to have seen.

'I am not questioning the good faith of their testimony,' says Vallee. 'The documents in question may have been nothing more than fabrications designed by their superiors to test their abilities to screen disinformation. It would only have been natural to test their degree of gullibility and their analytical skill, to thrust under their noses a document that mixed some element of reality with some preposterous claims, as any good piece of good disinformation art would. If that was the case, they certainly did not pass the test.

But then one could accuse Vallee of being part of the disinformation campaign too. Friedman says that certain journalists and researchers ridicule English out of hand because he makes fantastic claims with little evidence to back them up. But the critics have little evidence either, says Friedman: 'This, in itself is the perpetuation of disinformation.

National Security

The USAF has been involved with the UFO phenomenon, and naturally they involved military intelligence. Then in 1952 the CIA got involved, in case the agents of foreign powers infiltrated the UFO community, provoked mass hysteria or simply used sightings to jam the switchboard at the Pentagon. However, another far more shadowy agency was also taking an interest in UFOs.

Of America's thirteen intelligence agencies, the biggest and most secretive is undoubtedly the National Security Agency. While the CIA was set up by Congress and is answerable to the legislators, the NSA was established by Presidential fiat and is answerable only to the chief executive himself.

Founded in 1952, its headquarters are in Fort Meade, Maryland, where it has a staff of 50,000, mainly seconded from the military. It also maintains listening posts in the UK and Japan and other parts of the world. The NSA has two main responsibilities. It is charged with maintaining the security of communications within the US government and protecting them 'against exploitation through interception, unauthorised access, or related technical intelligence threats'. To do this, it is in charge of code making and polices the flow of information in and out of the country.

Its other task involves communications intelligence – COMINT – and electronic intelligence – ELINT. It intercepts telephone calls, faxes and e-mails world-wide and breaks codes. It also monitors the military communications of other nations and eavesdrops on radar and electronic warning systems. Of greater interest to UFOlogists is its role in collecting signals intelligence, known in the military as SIGINT.

Listening in to the entire electromagnetic spectrum, if alien spacecraft were anywhere near the Earth, the NSA would pick up their messages and any signals given off by their control systems. Even if some other agency received the first communication from aliens, it would be handed to the NSA. The agency is in the business of code breaking. It employs the world's top mathematicians, linguists, cryptologists and supercomputers. These would be dedicated to decoding and translating any alien information. So if anyone knows about UFOs, it is the NSA.

Freedom of Information

When the Freedom of Information Act was passed in 1974 in the wake of the Watergate scandal, UFOlogists attempted to use it to force classified UFO information out of America's intelligence agencies. The key player was attorney Peter Gersten, a UFO researcher and legal counsel for Citizens Against UFO Secrecy (CAUS). He discovered that UFO documents given to him by the CIA referred to other files held by the NSA. Then on 9 November 1978, he was given notice that a number of the CIA documents he was after had been sent to the NSA prior to declassification. UFOlogists believe that the CIA was, in fact, leaking the information that the NSA were involved in UFO monitoring. However, when Gersten filed an FOIA request with the NSA, the agency refused to open their files on grounds of national security. But, in doing so, they tacitly admitted that they were holding UFO data in the first place.

On 23 January 1980, CAUS made an another attempt to get the material released. When the NSA refused, CAUS took the case to federal court. On 18 November 1980, Federal Judge Gerhard Gesell upheld the NSA's refusal. So CAUS appealed the following January. This also failed. CAUS then petitioned the Supreme Court in Washington, D.C, but on 8 March 1982, the justices announced their decision not to hear the case.

But during this judicial process, the NSA had to explain to the courts why they had to withhold the information. To do this, the NSA's Director of Policy, Eugene Yeates, issued an *in camera* affidavit to Judge Gesell. This is a sworn affidavit that is lodged with the court in a closed session and its contents themselves are classified. The affidavit outlined the contents of the NSA's classified UFO files and explained why they could not be released to the public. But the only people allowed to read the affidavit were the judge and the NSA's lawyers.

This gave CAUS a new avenue of attack. They filed an FOIA request for 'all or any portion' of Yeates' affidavit. Again, they had to jump through hoops. But in May 1982, they eventually succeeded. The NSA released the affidavit, though 412 of the 582 lines of type handed over had been blacked out by the censor. And the page numbering showed that eleven pages were missing entirely. Plainly the NSA were hiding something.

The remaining 170 lines of the affidavit released explained that: 'The COMINT reports being withheld... are all based on intercepted foreign communications. The disclosure of these records would identify the communications that had been successfully intercepted and processed for intelligence purposes. No meaningful portion of any of the records could be segregated and released without identifying the communications underlying the communications intelligence report... Disclosing them would permit foreign intelligence officials to draw inferences [and] to take countermeasures... to defeat the capabilities of NSA's intelligence gathering techniques.'

Even the least paranoid of UFO researches who normally had no truck with conspiracy theories believed that the NSA were hiding something and they were refusing to release documents, not for reasons of NSA procedure but precisely because of their UFO content. Meanwhile, the NSA continued their blanket denials.

'Regarding your enquiry about UFOs, please be advised that the NSA do not have any interest in UFOs in any manner,' one NSA information officer told UFO researcher Robert Todd, even though the declassified affidavit revealed that the NSA had 156 classified UFO files.

Stanton Friedman took to waving the blacked-out affidavit about at his lectures and on TV appearances, calling the NSA's cover-up a 'Cosmic Watergate'. Meanwhile, other researchers became convinced that the NSA was refusing to release the documents because they proved that the US government was in contact with aliens. Even sceptics were unhappy about the NSA's handling of the situation. It seemed to have been playing into the hands of the most radical in the UFO community.

Declassification

In late 1996, the NSA decided to change its stance. It released a less censored version of the blacked-out affidavit lodged with Judge Gesell. Only 30 per cent of the original affidavit was readable; now only 25 cent was blacked out. The agency also began to declassify many of the 156 files it had withheld in 1982. Interestingly, among the first to receive copies of the declassified material was veteran UFO debunker Philip Klass. In January 1997, he published selections in his *Skeptics UFO Newsletter.*

The documents were, of course, innocuous. They were intercepts of Soviet air defence messages transmitted from radar stations sent between 1958 and 1979. These would obviously have been of interest to the USAF's Strategic Air Command. They still contained blacked-out sections, but these seemed to hide the locations of the installations, the names of agents and clues to the NSA's intercept capabilities. So a typical report reads:

'[censored] unidentified flying object (UFO): (A) 0028-0325, four UFO (probably balloon) moved slowly from SE of [censored] towards SW and passed [censored]. (B) 0325-0515, one UFO (probably a balloon) moved slowly from [censored] toward west, passed [censored] and faded [censored]... (D) 1355-1630, 19 UFO (probably balloons) moved from [censored] and [censored] towards west and faded [censored] and [censored], alt 69,000-79,000ft. [censored]'

According to the NSA, the UFOs mentioned in these reports are – like all sightings in the UK and US – probably balloons. NSA analysts say that the Soviets attached radar reflectors to balloons and released them secretly to check their height-finding radars and their radar operators' performance. The groups of figures – such as 1355-1630 – refer to the time during which contact with UFO remained on the screen. The slow progress of these objects confirms that they are balloons, the NSA say. It can, of course, be argued that the NSA had fourteen years to collect innocent intercepts to release – and why were they not released immediately after the collapse of the Soviet Union in 1991?

Insider's Story
Former NSA agent Thomas P. Deuley was working in the

communications section of the NSA when the CAUS FOIA request arrived. He had been working there for about two years and, as a UFO enthusiast, he had collected about two-thirds of a file drawer full of material. He photocopied it all and sent it to the NSA's FOIA office. However, he says that only some of it was actually classified. He did not have the signals intelligence data. What he had were largely clippings of magazines and newspapers and sightings reports. He does not know of any other material, though he does believe that there have been a few genuine UFO incidents, but he is sure that the government is not involved and does not know how they would keep such a thing hushed up.

Cuban Crisis

There is one genuine incident that the NSA was involved in, which took place in 1978. It is mentioned in the NSA papers, though many of the details are heavily censored. According to Stanton Friedman, the full story is that an intelligence analyst from the USAF's 6947 security squadron intercepted a message from a Cuban radar station, saying that it had picked up a UFO flying at 750 miles an hour at 98,000 feet. Two MiG-21 jet fighters were scrambled. They made visual contact and reported seeing a 'bright metallic sphere with no visible markings or appendages'. They tried to hail it by radio but failed to make contact. Then they were ordered to destroy it. The flight leader got his weapons system locked on to the object, but before he could fire his aircraft disintegrated. The NSA had all tapes and reports of the incident shipped to Fort Meade and made an official note that the Cuban MiG had been lost 'due to equipment malfunction'. When confronted with the details of this case, the NSA can only answer lamely: 'The factual circumstances of the incident reported in this record... are considered to be fictitious.'

Soviet Sightings

Even in the Soviet intercepts released by the NSA, the evidence of extraterrestrial activity comes through. One report says: '[censored] sights UFO [censored] sighted a UFO described as spherical or disc-like in form with no established color, brighter than the sun, with a diameter of one-half the visible size of the moon. At the time of observation, object was at the upper edge of the clouds on a true bearing 120 degrees, azimuth 080 degrees travelling north.'

Another says: '[censored] sight three unidentified flying objects [censored] at 1915 [censored], three luminous objects were seen in the western part of [censored]. The first object was shaped like a horseshoe and was white in color. The other two were round and yellow in color.' So they are out there.

Ignorance is Bliss

While the Americans have developed all sorts of sophisticated conspiracies to cover up what the government knows about their extraterrestrial involvements, the British are altogether more amateurish. Take, for example, the incident that occurred on 5 November 1990. That day a squadron of Royal Air Force Tornadoes was flying over the North Sea on its way back to base. Suddenly, a high-speed UFO streaked past them. The pilots were amazed at its speed and none of the trained observers was able to identify the craft. Nevertheless, the squadron signalled the Ministry of Defence with a report of the encounter.

However, when they landed they were not met with intelligence officers eager to debrief them about what they had seen. Nor were they visited by the menacing 'Men in Black'. No one told them to keep quiet about the incident, nor were they threatened with prosecution under the Official Secrets Act if they opened their mouth about it down the pub that night. Instead, the MoD used its tried and tested way of dealing with awkward UFO sightings. It sent the pilots' signal to the division in charge of investigating UFO reports. There the report was marked 'Object unexplained: case closed'. Then this was filed along with all the other sighting reports. And that was the end of the matter.

The British have not always been so blasé about UFOs. An official report of sorts was prepared in 1951. It has since disappeared, but there is a reference to it in a letter dated 9 August 1952 from the Air Ministry to Prime Minister Winston Churchill. He had asked for the study to be carried out. Its conclusion, it seems, was that all UFOs could be explained in conventional terms. However, how much original work went into the study is not known. It certainly relied heavily on the information that had been amassed by the USAF's Projects Sign, Grudge and Blue Book since 1947.

Captain Edward J. Ruppelt, who headed Grudge and Blue Book between 1951 and 1953, was contacted by the British. In his 1956 book *The Report On Unidentified Flying Objects*, Ruppelt revealed that he had been visited by two RAF intelligence officers. They arrived at the headquarters of Project Blue Book with six sheets of questions. The answers Ruppelt gave provided the basis for their report and its seems very likely that no other work was done before an answer was given to Churchill.

Although Churchill had some interest in UFOs in 1912, in the 1950s he was more concerned that the sightings of high-speed flying craft were a new type of Soviet aircraft that was being used to probe Britain's air defences. The Cold War was at its height and the British military were more interested in enemies invading their airspace than extraterrestrials. Extraterrestrials represented a negligible threat, compare to the massed nuclear-armed strike force of the Soviet Air Force. Alien craft were a distraction. There was no point on wasting over-stretched manpower on them. So sightings were filed and forgotten. Not only were the files closed, the minds were closed, too.

The attitude the British government adopted was revealed in a letter dated 24 June 1965. The letter was a reply to an enquiry by the Department of the Air Force in Washington, D.C. In it, the MoD outlined their policy. It was 'to play down the subject of UFOs and to avoid attaching undue attention or publicity to it'. The British establishment took a conservative view and regarded investigating UFO sightings as a huge waste of time.

Not all the military are total sceptics though. Lord Hill-Norton, Admiral of the Fleet and Chief of the Defence Staff from 1971 to 1973, is convinced that UFOs pose a potential threat. As a member of the House of Lords' All-Party UFO study group, he pressed the military establishment to take the threat seriously.

Along with other government documents, UFO files are subject to the thirty-year rule. Unless the government feel that the information is particularly sensitive, all government files are open for viewing at the Public Record Office in Kew after thirty years. It is clear from the documents that have been released that there have been numerous UFO encounters in British air space. They have been seen by military witnesses and detected on radar. In many cases, RAF jets were scrambled to intercept the UFOs, usually unsuccessfully. Some ten per cent of sightings remain unexplained, and the MoD has acknowledged that these cases defy explanation, even in the rare case that there has been a rigorous investigation. But by and large these secret files reveal that, in most of these cases, no further action was taken once the encounter itself had been reported – even when jet fighters had been scrambled to intercept the intruders.

This lack of follow-up is exactly what happened in the well-attested Rendlesham Forest UFO incident in December 1980. Lieutenant Colonel Halt submitted a remarkable report to the MoD about UFO activity near the military bases of RAF Bentwaters and RAF Woodbridge. The report told how abnormally high radiation readings had been taken at a site where a small, metallic UFO had been seen to land. However, the MoD never even acknowledged that it had received Halt's memorandum and certainly nothing was done about it. The MoD's policy, like that of the British government as a whole, is that it is better to keep your head in the sand, and they reply to all enquiries by saying: 'To date, no evidence of any threat to the United Kingdom has been found.'

Rudloe Manor

There are some that believe that the attitude of the British government is not just driven by incompetence and indifference. In his book *A Covert Agenda*, Nick Redfern points to the involvement of the Provost and Security Services, a wing of the RAF that deals with security vetting and counter-intelligence. While the MoD have consistently denied that they have any role in UFO investigation, Redfern unearthed a document in the Public Record Office from 1962 that proved otherwise. And he got a letter from Group Captain Rose at RAF Rudloe Manor in Wiltshire confirming it.

Many British UFOlogists believe that Rudloe Manor is the centre of secret UFO research. UFO researcher Timothy Good was arrested by military policemen when walking around the perimeter of the base. Later he was encouraged to telephone in a UFO sighting report to Rudloe Manor by Ralph Noyes, former head of Defence Sectretariat 8 – the forerunner of Secretariat (Air Staff) 2a. Noyes is now a leading authority on UFOs and crop circles and he wanted to see if staff at Rudloe Manor would accept the sighting report. They did – though nothing further happened.

Redfern believes that the MoD do realise that something very strange is going on, but they don't know what to do about it. If they admit that they don't have all the answers, they appear foolish and vulnerable – the last thing you want from the military. They are powerless, Redfern says, so they have no choice but to cover up.

Police Business

Although it is the military that is officially charged with investigating UFO sightings, it is often the police who make first contact with UFO eyewitnesses or aliens themselves. Unfortunately, official scepticism is also rife in the police – even when it is a police officer who had the encounter.

At 5:45 p.m. on the afternoon of Friday, 24 April 1964, Patrolman Lonnie Zamora was hot on the heels of a speeding black Chevrolet near Socorro, New Mexico. It was sunny day. Suddenly Zamora saw a flame in the sky and heard a loud roaring noise. The patrolman thought that a miner's dynamite shack had blown up. He broke off the chase and headed instead towards the mysterious flame to see if anyone was hurt.

As Zamora turned off the highway, down the rough gravel road towards the dynamite shack, he noticed a shiny, metallic object in a gulch some 250 yards to the south. He stopped his patrol car and got out. The object looked like an overturned car. Next to it he saw two small figures in white cover-alls, which he took to be children, and he assumed they were responsible.

Zamora got back into his patrol car and drove towards the scene. As he did so, he reported back to the sheriff's office in Socorro by radio, giving them the location in case he needed back-up. He pulled up about thirty yards away. As he opened the car door to get out, he heard another loud roar. It was then that he realised that the metallic object was not a car at all. Flames belched from underneath it and the object rose slowly, vertically, into the air. The object was egg-shaped and aluminium coloured, with red markings around its middle that looked like some sort of insignia. It had no windows, doors or other external features. However, it did seem to have slanted legs on the underside, which Zamora took to be landing gear.

As the strange craft rose higher, Zamora could see a blue and orange flame spewing from a port in the middle of its underside. It produced no smoke, but the exhaust kicked up dust in the immediate area. As the roar increased, Zamora feared the object might blow up and he ran for safety behind a hillock. But, before he got there, he noticed that the roaring had stopped, so he ducked down behind a bush. The craft had risen some fifteen feet, and it then shot off horizontally, narrowly missing the dynamite shack. Zamora watched as it headed off south-east.

He ran back to his car and radioed in, keeping an eye on the UFO as it flew away.

'Look out the window and tell me what you see,' he told the police radio officer Ned Lopez.

'What am I looking for?' asked Lopez.

'It looks like a balloon,' said Zamora. But by that time the object had climbed to an enormous height and soon disappeared into the distance.

New Mexico State Trooper Sergeant M. Samuel Chavez was

despatched to assist Zamora. As he waited, Zamora made a sketch of the insignia he had seen on the side of the UFO. Then he went back down to the scene where the brush was on fire in several places.

When Chavez arrived, he noted that Zamora looked pale and sweaty.

'You look like you've seen the devil,' he said.

'Maybe I have,' said Zamora.

He told Chavez what had happened. Then the two officers looked around the gulch where Zamora had seen the object on the ground. They found that the earth was scorched and a bush was still smouldering. Chavez also found four wedge-shaped imprints in the middle of the burned area. Being a sceptic by nature, Chavez later took a surreptitious look in Zamora's car, searching for implements that Zamora might have used to fake these landing marks. He found nothing.

Undersheriff James Luckie and State Policeman Ted Jordan turned up to photograph and search the scene. At 7 p.m., Zamora and Chavez returned to the precinct. FBI agent J. Arthur Byrnes happened to be there on other business. He heard about the incident on the police radio and waited to talk to the two men. Byrnes then called the local army base and spoke to Captain Richard T. Holder. Twenty minutes later, Holder arrived at the station and sat in while Byrnes formally interviewed Zamora. When he had heard Zamora's story, Byrnes told Zamora that it would be better for all concerned if he did not mention the two small figures he had seen dressed in white, as no one would believe him.

Then, with a team of Socorro police officers, Byrnes and Holder visited the site. Concerned by what he had seen, Holder called in the military police. They roped off the scene. It was now dark so, with the aid of flashlights, they collected samples and made measurements. It was 1 a.m. before Holder completed his report and sent it to Washington. Then he waited.

Later that morning Holder got a call from a colonel from the Pentagon war room of the Joint Chiefs of Staff. Over a scrambled line he asked Holder to give him a personal briefing. The Air Force investigation began immediately. There was no time to lose. The story had already hit the newswires. Reporters were calling Major Hector Quintanilla, then head of the Project Blue Book, non-stop, though he refused to speak to them.

Quintanilla flew to New Mexico and had the site checked for radioactivity, but there were no unusual readings. Blue Book investigators checked the radar records, but found no unusual contact in the area at the time. Meanwhile, the soil samples Holder had taken were sent to the Air Force Materials Laboratory for spectographic analysis. No traces of non-terrestrial materials were found. The investigation was getting nowhere, so Quintanilla sent for Project Blue Book's scientific consultant, astronomer J. Allen Hynek.

Hynek flew to New Mexico. At Socorro, he got Zamora to take him to the site of the encounter and talk him through the whole incident. He then examined the site for himself but found no new evidence. Hynek deduced that, if the encounter was a hoax, Zamora must be in on it. So he cross-questioned Zamora again, hoping to find something that would invalidate his testimony. But he could not shake the patrolman's story.

Hynek announced his conclusions at a press conference.

'It is my opinion that a real, physical event occurred on the outskirts of Socorro that afternoon,' Hynek said.

Quintanilla was furious at Hynek for adding fuel to the fire, but he too believed that Zamora had seen a real physical craft that afternoon. However, he believed it was man-made. He checked out nearby Holloman Air Force Base, but they were testing no new equipment there that might account for Zamora's sighting. He later thought that a lunar lander might fit the bill. He contacted NASA and asked whether they were testing them in the field.

The concept of the lander had been developed in late 1962. NASA signed a contract with the manufacturer on 14 January 1963. Over the next three months, the design of the prototype was drawn up. Testing was planned for New Mexico. But as it turned out, the lunar landing modules were not operational in April 1964, when Zamora made his sighting. Besides, the lunar lander was distinctly not egg-shaped. It had no reason to be streamlined as there is no atmosphere on the moon. Reluctantly, Quintanilla was forced to conclude that the case justified the label 'unidentified'.

Independent Enquiries

UFOlogists were already suspicious of the military's debunking of UFO cases so, on Sunday, 26 April, Jim and Coral Lorenzen of the Aerial Phenomena Research Organisation in Tucson, Arizona, drove to Socorro to conduct their own investigation. The first thing they did was look at the marks that had been left on the ground. The UFO's legs, they found, had left wedge-shaped impressions, three to four inches deep. The span between them was around ten feet. They also found four circular depressions, some three inches deep and four inches in diameter. These, they assumed, had been left by the ladder that the small alien figures Zamora had seen used to get in and out of the ship. And on the exact spot where Zamora had seen the small figures standing, they found four small prints with a little crescent shape in the middle. They could only conclude that these were the aliens' footprints.

But the Lorenzens did not have the field to themselves. On Tuesday, 28 April, Ray Stanford, a psychic who has seen UFOs many times himself, turned up. He was an investigator for the National Investigations Committee on Aerial Phenomena, a high-profile UFO group based in Washington, D.C, and run by retired Marine Major Donald E. Keyhoe. He talked to Zamora and discovered that Captain Holder had told him not to mention the insignia he had seen on the side of the craft, except to official investigators, and FBI agent Byrnes had told him not to mention the two small figures he had seen. He later discovered that Byrnes had asked to have his name removed from the case.

When he examined the site, he found metallic scrapings on a rock in one of the depressions in the soil where the object had stood. He collected these and sent them for analysis at the Goddard Space Flight Center in Greenbelt, Maryland. Stanford was told initially that the scrapings were of a zinc-iron alloy unknown on Earth. This proved that the object that Zamora had seen at Socorro was of extraterrestrial origin. However, the scientists who did the analysis subsequently said the samples were simply sand.

Standford was later told by James McDonald, a senior atmospheric physicist at the University of Arizona, that a radiological chemist working for the Public Health Service in Las Vegas had analysed other material collected at the site. This included vitrified sand collected at Socorro. However, the chemist's notes and samples were confiscated by the Air Force. USAF personnel had also taken State Patrolman Ted Jordan's photographs. When he asked for them back, he was told that the film had been ruined – apparently it had been irradiated.

However, this did not take the investigation much further forward. Work on it effectively ended right there. Local people in Socorro thought that the object Zamora had seen was probably a secret experimental device. The flame from its engine made it seem very much like a terrestrial object. The regular excuse, that the object was a hot-air balloon – there was a balloon race in the area at the time – was trotted out. And UFO debunker Donald Menzel said that Zamora was the victim of a prank.

But Zamora is clear in his mind what he saw that day. It was not some secret experimental craft, a vertical take-off and landing aircraft, or a hot air balloon.

'I know what I saw,' he says, 'and it wasn't any of those.'

The Socorro incident remained as Project Blue Book's only 'unidentified' case that involved the sighting of a UFO and its occupants on the ground, though Quintanilla felt that the real 'solution to this case could very well be lying dormant in Lonnie Zamora's head'. And for the UFO community, it is the first solid case of a close encounter of the third kind.

The year after the Socorro encounter, the scientific community began looking for a site to build the VLA – Very Large Array – the world's largest radio telescope. In 1972, they decided to build it, of all places, at Socorro. In 1975, the first dish-shaped antenna was erected. It would be the first of twenty-seven arranged in a huge Y shape over twenty miles across. This VLA has been used by SETI – the Search for Extraterrestrial Intelligence – and is the very place that the first alien communication is received in Carl Sagan's ground-breaking novel *Contact*.

Lavender Vandals

The following year a similar sighting took place in France. In 1965, Maurice Masse, a farmer living in Valensole, France, was having problems with his lavender crop. Over several weeks he had found bare patches in the crops which he could not account for. Then one morning in July at around 6 a.m., he noticed what he thought were two boys playing in the field. He immediately concluded that he had found the culprits who were responsible for destroying his lavender crop.

As he made off after them, he noticed a strange craft which he took to be a peculiar sort of helicopter. The 'boys' were making towards it. As Maurice caught up with them he realised that they were not boys at all. In fact, they were not human, but instead strange looking beings, with large bald heads, pasty faces and huge slanted eyes. They wore one-piece cover-alls, and one had a tube-like instrument by his side.

The alien lifted this tubular device, pointed it at the advancing Maurice and shot a ray of light at him. This knocked him to the ground and he lay there paralysed for several minutes. When he was able to move again, he saw the craft shoot vertically up into the sky at a tremendous speed.

When he was later shown an artist's impression of the craft that Lonnie Zamora had seen at Socorro, he said: 'Someone else has seen my UFO.' The lavender has never grown back on the spot where the UFO landed.

The Long Arm of the Law

Aliens do not have run-ins with the law only in the United States. At

261

3:15 a.m., on 13 March 1997, local policemen Anerilton Neves and Moacir Pereira dos Santos were driving through the deserted streets of the Nations Park district of the city of Americana near Sao Paulo, Brazil. It was a quiet night and the two officers were on their way to the precinct. Then, as they reached the intersection of Malaysia Street and United States Avenue, they saw a dazzling light appear in the skies ahead of them.

They pulled over and got out to take a closer look. The light came from an object hovering about six hundred feet above the road. It was oval, with red, blue and yellow lights around it. As the two officers watched, the UFO moved noiselessly off over an area of wasteland. Dos Santos ran back to the patrol car and flicked on the car's emergency lights. Immediately, the UFO shot away into the night sky. As it disappeared, they could see that its lights formed a triangle.

A few moments later, local taxi driver Henrique Moretti pulled up. He and his terrified passenger had just seen a UFO. It was about fifteen feet across and hovered some five hundred feet above the cab, before shooting off noiselessly in the direction of the nearby town of Nova Odessa.

Neves and dos Santos called Americana Police Central Control and requested assistance. When more policemen turned up at the scene, they laughed at Neves and dos Santos's stories. Their eyes had been playing tricks on them. But when Moretti and his passenger said that they had also seen the UFO, the laughter stopped. It soon became clear that they were not the only ones to have seen it. Numerous reports of sightings came in from all over the city. Indeed, two other policemen had seen it, along with a radio announcer and a photo- grapher who had managed to photograph it. When the case was investigated, the Brazilian Air Force reported that they had not been airborne that night and the Brazilian National Institute of Space Research said that no meteorological experiments involving balloons or any other airborne objects had been undertaken on the evening of the sighting. The case remains officially 'unresolved'.

The Police in Force

On 17 April 1966, Deputy Sheriff Dale F. Spaur and his deputy, Wilbur Neff, were out on night patrol in Portage County, Ohio. At 4:45 a.m., they were sent to visit a woman who lived in the west of the county. She had reported seeing a bright object, 'as big as a house' fly over her neighbourhood and she was highly agitated.

Puzzled, Spaur and Neff set off to investigate the case. The woman had little to add and the patrolmen set about a routine inspection of the area. While they were investigating a car parked illegally nearby, Spaur noticed a strange object hovering over the neighbouring woods. It was so low that the patrolmen did not see it until it was practically on top of them. The only sound it made was a slight hum, but the light it gave off was so intense that the patrolmen looked down at their clothes to check if they were on fire. The huge cone-shaped UFO hovered over them for some time before moving off to the east.

Back in the patrol car, Spaur radioed in his sighting of a 'bright object' in the sky and received orders to shoot at it. So Spaur and Neff flicked on the siren and gave chase.

Fellow officer Wayne Huston, who was patrolling some twenty-five miles to the east, saw the UFO streak past at a speed of around fifty miles an hour. Huston described it as 'shaped like an ice cream cone with a sort of partly melted down top'. When Spaur and Neff came down the road after it, Huston fell in behind. They headed off on a fifty-mile chase at speeds of up to eighty miles an hour.

Over the border in Conway, Pennsylvania, Officer Frank Panzanella was heading down Second Avenue at 5:20 a.m. when he saw a bright shiny object flying by. He got out of the car and was looking at it when Spaur and Neff's, and then Huston's, black-and-whites pulled up. All four officers then watched agog as the object stopped, rose up, flew off to the left of the moon and vanished. Another officer, Gerald Buchert, saw the UFO and managed to photograph it, but he was forbidden to publicise his pictures.

Despite this incredible story, Major Hector Quintanilla, then head of the Air Force's Project Blue Book, dismissed the eyewitness testimony of five police officers. He concluded that they had first seen a satellite, then transferred their gaze to the planet Venus. But Blue Book's scientific consultant J. Allen Hynek disagreed.

'A more lucid example of the disregarding of evidence unfavourable to a preconceived explanation could hardly be found,' he said.

Bobbies on the Beat

At around 2:30 a.m., one January morning in 1978, Sergeant Tony Dodd and Police Constable Alan Dale were driving near the town of Cononley, North Yorkshire, when the dark country lane in front of them was suddenly lit by a mysterious light. As they travelled towards it, they experienced heavy static on their police radio. When they stopped the car to investigate, they looked up and saw a bright white, glowing object, moving silently at around twenty-five miles an hour some hundred feet above them.

Dodd and Dale got a good look at it as it passed right over their heads. It was about a hundred feet in diameter, saucer-shaped, with an elongated dome on top that had flashing lights, dark portholes and three large spheres protruding from it. Under the dome was a skirt of brilliant coloured lights that seemed to dance around it. They watched it for about three minutes altogether. As the UFO moved away, it seemed to land in a forest on a nearby hillside.

Shocked and scarcely believing the evidence of their own eyes, Dodd and Dale continued on into town. But before they got there they met another police car coming the other way. The driver stopped. He had seen the huge UFO too. Like all police officers, they were trained observers. Dodd had also been in the RAF before joining the police force and knew a lot about military aircraft.

'The object we saw made no sound at all when it moved,' he said. 'I've never known of any terrestrial craft that can move at any speed without generating some noise.' However, despite the credibility of the witnesses, there was no official investigation.

Men in Black

The Sinister Men

On 30 November 1987, former policeman Philip Spencer had an encounter with a strange 'entity with a green cast' on Ilkley Moor. He also managed to photograph it. Puzzled by what he had seen, he sought out UFO researchers Jenny Randles and Peter Hough, who began investigating the case.

About six weeks later, Spencer was paid an unexpected visit by two men, who introduced themselves as Royal Air Force Intelligence Officers. They flashed ID cards at him and said their names were Davis and Jefferson. They did not beat about the bush; they were there to get the photograph he had taken on Ilkley Moor. The strangers left empty-handed. Spencer no longer had the picture. He had given it to Hough.

It was only after they had gone that Spencer began to wonder how the two strangers had known of the photograph's existence. He had hardly broadcast the fact. As far as he knew, only his wife, Jenny Randles, Peter Hough and another researcher named Arthur Tomlinson had any knowledge of it.

Hough was intrigued too. He contacted RAF Intelligence to find out, but he was told that they had no officers called Davis and Jefferson. What's more, none of their staff had visited Spencer. It was then that Hough realised that Spencer had come up against what American eyewitnesses were already referring to as the 'Men in Black'.

As part of the investigation, clinical psychologist Dr Jim Singleton ran a series of tests on Spencer and confirmed that he was telling the truth 'as he believed it'. And Spencer's experience was far from unique. UFO researchers around the world tell tales of sinister Men in Black, who call on witnesses seemingly with the intention of stealing any physical evidence they might have of the encounter or terrorising them into silence. This sinister cover-up is now so familiar that the perpetrators are known simply as MIBs and they have even had a Hollywood movie made glamorising their activities.

The MIBs first made an appearance in 1947, when a mysterious black-clad stranger turned up in a black Buick sedan car at the home of Harold Dahl, the morning after the Maury Island encounter. The MIB knew what had happened the previous day and invited Dahl out for breakfast. He warned Dahl that he had best keep quiet about what he had seen. 'Silence is the best thing for you and your family,' he said. Dahl was naturally intimidated.

In 1953 when Albert Bender, the founder of the Connecticut-based International Flying Saucer Bureau, was investigating the case again he was visited by three MIBs. They told him to stop his research and threatened his family. He closed down the IFSB just eighteen months after it started. He did, however, make a drawing of one of the men who had visited him and circulated it in the UFO community.

Then in 1988, after Amaury Rivera was abducted by aliens in Puerto Rico, he was visited by three black-suited MIBs in his home in Cabo Rojo. They said they were from the CIA and told him to hand over the photographs he had taken. But Rivera had hidden them and, again, they went away empty-handed.

In May 1964, firefighter James Templeton took a photograph of his daughter at a remote marsh near Carlisle, Cumbria. When the film was developed, it showed a man in a silver spacesuit floating in mid-air behind the little girls. Soon after, two men in black suits turned up at the Templeton home in a black Jaguar car.

'They were very strange,' said Templeton, 'asking peculiar questions about the weather and the behaviour of animals.'

They claimed to be from the government but never referred to each other by name, just by numbers. Templeton drove them out to the marsh where the photograph had been taken, but they grew angry when he said he had not seen anyone there that day; he only saw the space-suited man in the photograph after it had been developed.

'They drove away, stranding me alone to walk five miles home,' Templeton said. 'I never heard from them again.'

Who are the MIBs?

Although accounts vary widely, MIBs usually turn up unannounced shortly after a UFO sighting or an encounter with an extraterrestrial. They usually appear in pairs or groups of three. They are dressed in black military uniform with no insignia or in plain black suits, which are always immaculately pressed, white shirt and black hats. And they often arrive in an old-fashioned black car that is in mint condition. Most MIBs produce ID cards and claim to come from a government deparment, a military intelligence agency or a UFO research group. But when their names are checked out, the organisation they say they work for denies all knowledge of them.

MIBs also have an uncannily detailed knowledge of the case, even when the details have not been publicised, and they warn that terrible consequences will ensue if witnesses talk to anyone about their encounter. What makes this all the more unsettling is that they also have detailed information of the victim, often relating things about the victim or the incident that only they could verify. Because the visit often takes place within hours of the UFO incident, victims are left wondering how they acquired this knowledge so quickly.

It stands to reason that the only people with instant access to this kind of information are government intelligence agencies. It is plain that they also have the access to phone calls, faxes and e-mails that would give them the most thorough-going details of any case right away. This would also explain why the organisations they purport to come from deny all knowledge of them. This is standard practice in the intelligence community. The CIA and MI5 will never confirm or deny that any particular individual is working or even has worked for them.

UFOlogists believe that these shadowy strangers are involved in a campaign of disinformation to conceal the true nature of covert government operations, possibly top-secret military programmes, or they could be part of a government-organised conspiracy to prevent the truth about UFO and alien encounters becoming public knowledge.

Are MIBs Aliens?

The phenomenon of 'Men in Black' took an even more sinister twist after the alien abduction of two men at the height of UFO activity in the Maine in October 1975. Nearly a year later, on 11 September 1976, Dr Herbert Hopkins, a psychiatrist who was investigating the abductions, was working alone at home when he got a telephone call from man who said he was UFO researcher. The stranger said he was interested in the case the doctor was investigating and asked if he might visit. Hopkins agreed. But he did not expect that, less than a minute after he had put the phone down, the stranger would appear at the back door.

'I saw no car,' said Hopkins, 'and even if he did have a car, he could not have possibly gotten to my house that quickly from any pay phone.' This was before the days that everyone had a mobile phone.

The strange visitor advised Dr Hopkins to destroy all his records on the abduction case. Then when the conversation turned to the general topic of UFOs, the visitor's speech began to falter. The stranger stood up shakily and stumbled towards the door.

'I must go now,' he said, excusing himself. 'My energy is running low.'

Once the stranger had left, Dr Hopkins began to realise that there was something very odd about his visitor's appearance. Although he wore an old-fashioned black suit, it looked brand new. He had no eyebrows or eyelashes and was completely bald. His skin was strangely wan and he appeared to be wearing lipstick. Some have suggested he was an extraterrestrial in disguise.

MIBs, All in the Mind?

Some MIB encounters have a distinctly surreal feel to them, not unlike the dream-like – or nightmare-like – quality of some alien abduction stories. And it has been suggested by those who are convinced that MIBs are extraterrestrials that the two phenomena are in some way related.

Others have looked for a psychological explanation of the MIB phenomenon. American UFO researcher Dr Alvin Lawson has drawn attention to the fact that the alien figures seen in alien encounters and the strange 'foreign-looking' MIBs both correspond to the archetypes that psychologist Carl Jung discovered lying buried in everyone's unconscious. Lawson believes that something triggers the victim's imagination to draw upon this well of imagery.

'I myself feel certain that accounts given by witnesses reflect what their senses have reported – that, is they do actually perceive humanoids,' he says.

After all, MIBs have been around for some time. Thomas Jefferson, the man who wrote the Declaration of Independence and went on to become the third President of the United States, is said to have received the first idea for the Great Seal of the United States from a mysterious Man in Black who turned up at his home in Virginia. And in his book *The Mothman Prophecies*, veteran UFOlogist John Keel says that Julius Caesar, Napoleon Bonaparte and Malcolm X, among others, were all visited by MIBs – who could well have been aliens.

Running counter to this argument is the fact that government bodies and intelligence agencies are slowly admitting that they have been investigating UFO sightings. Although they still deny that they employ 'Men in Black', some government agencies, including Britain's Ministry of Defence, admit that they have sent out officers to interview witnesses – though they do not say whether they wear black suits or not.

UFOlogist Peter Hough has investigated a number of MIB cases. 'My feelings are that, in some cases, we are dealing with undercover agents, possibly from the Ministry of Defence,' he says. 'But the overwhelming number of MIB cases seem to tie in with UFO phenomena. To my mind, the likeliest possible explanation is that

MIBs are intruders from another dimension who have somehow found a way of manifesting in ours. But the whole thing seems to be a charade. There are often comical features about them and they frequently ask trivial questions that have nothing to do with UFOs. The most sinister thing is that they appear to know what's in our minds and then play up to it.'

The Men From the Ministry

Peter Hough's colleague, British UFOlogist Jenny Randles, has unearthed information that the 'Men in Black' are indeed government investigators. The new evidence comes from a small story that broke in the UK's national press on 3 March 1966. It concerned the close encounter of twenty-eight-year-old PC Colin Perks in the English town of Wilmslow, Cheshire. The story made no great waves among the population generally, but UFOlogists recognised that it was a very impressive case – an unidentified craft had been seen at close quarters by a reliable witness.

PC Perks had his encounter with a UFO at 4:10 a.m. on 7 January 1966.

'It was about the length of a bus and an estimated twenty feet wide,' he said. 'It was elliptical in shape and emanated a greenish-grey glow which I can only describe as an eerie colour.'

It made a mechanical humming noise, but was stationary for about five seconds before it shot off at incredible speed 'in an east-south-easterly direction'. Very quickly, it disappeared from view.

Being a police officer, Perks made his sighting report by the book. He phoned air traffic control at nearby Manchester Airport, gave the information to the staff of the radio telescope at Jodrell Bank and sent a report to his superintendent. The police report then got passed up the chain of command. Eventually it reached the desk of the Deputy Chief Constable of Cheshire, who decided to endorse it, and on 12 January 1966 he sent it to the Ministry of Aviation, part of the Ministry of Defence. As the report was forwarded to them from such a high-ranking official, the MoD was forced to take the matter seriously. They investigated PC Colin Perks and his encounter, and compiled an impressive twenty-page report. A brief mention did surface in the press nearly two months after the original sighting, but then the Perks case disappeared into the files. It languished there for three decades. But in early 1997, under the thirty-year rule, the report was sent to the Public Record Office at Kew, along with hundreds of other UFO reports sent to the Ministry in 1966.

However, the file on the PC Perks case contained a major surprise – documented proof that the British government maintained a covert UFO investigation unit, though they had long denied it. Agents from that unit had been directly involved in the Perks case. Here at last was documentary evidence of the 'Men in Black'.

On 13 January 1996, PC Perks' sighting report arrived on the desk of the deputy controller of aircraft research at the Ministry of Aviation. The following day he forwarded it to the UFO desk, then designated S4f, at the MoD. In doing so, he noted that 'the controller of aircraft in this ministry has seen the reports and considers that some experts should speak to the constable'. So far, so good.

On 18 February 1966, a report classified as 'restricted' about Perks' encounter was sent to S4f by a Flight Lieutenant J.P.H. Mercer of DI (Defence Intelligence) Unit 61e (Air). But the distribution codes on the document show that it was also forwarded to another department. This was DSTI Tech Int (Air). DSTI is the Directorate of Scientific Technical Intelligence – the overall intelligence division of which DI 61e was a part.

In the report Mercer says that someone from DI 61e (Air) went to Wilmslow on 1 February and interviewed PC Perks. The file also includes the plans of a dome-shaped craft drawn up by Perks. The agent also visited the site of his encounter and made a search of the area. During the course of the investigation, DI 61e discovered that a 'glass like substance was found on the adjacent car park... on the morning of the sighting'. But Mercer said he did not think this was unusual. His unit had not connected it with the sighting, nor had they bothered to send it for analysis. Checks with radar stations had not uncovered any unidentified contacts in the area that coincided with Perks' sighting. However, other people in the area also saw a UFO that night. One report came from a Wilmslow woman who had returned home from a dance at around 4 a.m. on the night of 7 January. She reported seeing a green object streak across the sky, in clear view from her bedroom window. S4f also passed her sighting report on to DI 61e (Air).

What is important about the Perks' case is that the British government had always vehemently denied that there was any special intelligence unit that investigated UFO sightings beyond the S4f desk at the Air Ministry. The Mercer document proved there was – DI 61e (Air) – and a forty-five-year-old government cover-up had finally been uncovered.

History of a Cover-up

British government interest in UFOs dates from July 1952, when Prime Minister Winston Churchill wrote to his Air Minister, Lord Cherwell, asking him to look into the reality of UFO activity in the wake of the wave of reports of flying saucers being seen over Washington. In due course, an official report was prepared that concluded that most UFOs reports were a case of mistaken identity and flying saucers were 'no perceived defence threat'.

Events conspired to contradict this official position almost straight away when a NATO exercise called Operation Mainbrace, underway from 19 to 21 September, was infiltrated in daylight by UFOs. RAF planes chased other anomalous objects over North Yorkshire, and a US aircraft carrier in the North Sea was 'buzzed' by a flying saucer. Under the circumstances, the British authorities were forced to reconsider. On 13 January 1953, a memo bearing the code FC/S.45485/Signals was sent to all RAF station chiefs informing them that there was a new policy on UFOs. This was spelt out in a restricted document dated 16 December. The memo ordered senior staff to report all UFO sightings to the Air Ministry.

'All reports are to be classified "restricted", and personnel are to be warned that they are not to communicate to anyone other than official persons any information about phenomena they have observed,' it said.

This was clear evidence of a flying saucer cover-up. Classification meant that UFO sighting reports were now to fall under the aegis of the Official Secrets Act and people were warned not to talk. At the same time, 'sympathetic' journalists were employed both in the UK and US throughout the 1950s and 1960s to ridicule UFO witnesses and generally debunk the idea that aliens were visiting Earth.

When asked about UFOs, the MoD has replied with a form letter. It reads: 'The Ministry of Defence has no full-time organisation investigating or studying UFOs. Its interest in UFOs is limited to the defence aspects and the department does not undertake to pursue its research, other than for defence implications, to a point where positive correlation with a known object is established.'

After the Perks' file became public the letter was amended, adding that 'secretarial support staff receive sightings via airports, coastguard stations and RAF commands, but do so only as a minor part of their routine work'. This is a tacit admission that there are people working on UFO sightings. But the 'Men in Black' who visited Perks, Spencer and others were not 'secretarial support staff'. Nor are they the medium-grade clerical staff at Air Staff 2A – the current designation of the so-called UFO desk that files sighting reports, speaks to the media and reassures the public that UFOs are being taken seriously by the MoD. Air Staff 2A does no real research, and it never sends people to visit witnesses. Its staff have limited security clearance, so could not read highly classified UFO reports anyway. AS 2A is merely a shop-window. The real work takes place at the back of the store. This is where you find the science and technical staff of the DSTI and defence intelligence units such as DI 55/DI 61e (Air). The Perks case proves that agents from these units do visit UFO witnesses. Some say that these mysterious Men in Black flourishing MoD credentials are sometimes responsible for more intimidating visits. They confiscate physical evidence and cajole witnesses into silence. Since Perks was visited by a DI 61e (Air) agent on 1 February 1966, he has said nothing more about his sighting.

UFO
Sightings

Lights in the Sky

Encounters with Flying Triangles

Flying saucers have developed a lot since they were first spotted in 1947. In the aftermath of that incident nearly all UFOs seen were saucer shaped. Later, cigar shapes became more common. Although both disc-shaped craft and cylindrical UFOs are still around, the latest batch, seen since the 1980s, are three-sided craft. These Flying Triangles were responsible for the biggest mass sighting in history.

The first major wave of sightings of Flying Triangles occurred in the Hudson Valley area of upstate New York and Connecticut in March 1983. Witnesses reported seeing 'V-shaped' UFOs, and often referred to them as 'flying wings'. They were extremely large, over three hundred feet in length. One eyewitness said the unidentified craft was 'so huge it filled up the entire sky', and others described them as being larger than a football field but with multicoloured flashing lights.

They only appeared triangular when viewed from the ground. Seen in profile from the air they were flat, some reports described them as being wedge-shaped or shaped like a boomerang – though some mistakenly said they were circular. Nevertheless most witnesses reported sightings of solid objects made up of some type of very dark, gun-metal grey material. Such objects have been seen by at least five thousand witnesses worldwide, including police officers and scientists. All indicate that these UFOs, which are often the silent, slow-moving type, were like nothing they had ever seen before.

One distinctive feature of these craft is the three red lights mounted on the underside. There is one light at each corner, though many witnesses report a fourth bright white light in the middle of the configuration. Unlike aircraft identification lights, the Flying Triangle's lights do not appear to flash.

A flash in the sky often precedes the appearance of Flying Triangles and they sometimes project a beam of light onto the ground. They can accelerate and decelerate more rapidly than conventional aircraft and change direction in an instant, and they are silent, apart from a low humming sound. Electrical disturbances are also associated with their appearance.

Between 1983 and 1987, hundreds of people saw these triangular craft in the Hudson Valley area. However, UFO sightings are so common in the US that few people outside UFO circles took any notice. It was only when Flying Triangles began appearing over Belgium in 1989 and 1990 that the world took them seriously.

The Belgian wave of sightings began on 29 November 1989. At dusk on that evening, two Sergeant Majors of the Belgian Gendarmerie were on patrol, travelling down the road from Eupen to Kittenis in the Hautes Fagnes region of eastern Belgium, when they noticed something strange, two hundred yards away to one side of the road. A slowly moving object was hovering, around a thousand feet above a field next to the road.

Both policemen noted that it was a dark triangular craft with three powerful lights shining from its underside onto the ground below. In the centre, it had a coloured light that changed from red to orange and back again.

Suddenly the object turned towards them and passed directly over their vehicle. As it did so, it illuminated the whole area. When directly above them, its triangle form was all the more obvious. They also noted that the craft appeared almost completely noiseless, except for a very soft humming sound.

It travelled slowly towards Eupen, then stopped motionless, hovering above the dam at Gileppe for a period of forty-five minutes. After that it moved away in the direction of Baelen and Spa, where it disappeared.

The two gendarmes contacted the Royal Belgian Air Force base at Bierset, which, like the radar stations at Glons and Butgenbach, had already detected an anomalous blip on their radar screens. These radar reports were positive readings made by skilled operatives, who would not have misinterpreted reflections from thermal inversions. Nor would they have misinterpreted ghost contacts from unusual electromagnetic interference or signals from other radar. The air bases at Aachen and Maastricht were notified and an AWACS – airborne warning and control system – aircraft was sent to the area from its home base at Gelsenkirchen.

By that time the Flying Triangle had been seen by another nineteen gendarmes who had been attending a social event near Eupen. Other witnesses from Liége, Eupen, Plombiéres, Kittenis, Baelin, Verviers, Jalhay, St Vith, Andrimont, Lontzen, Voeren, Battice and Herbesthal, called the gendarmerie to report seeing a UFO. The descriptions from the witnesses tallied, and there was no doubt that they were all seeing the same object. The sightings cover a period of some two-and-half hours.

Some fifty-five minutes after the first sighting, the same two gendarmes saw another Flying Triangle – but this time it was much larger. It appeared almost at ground level from behind a small wood. It made a climbing turn while slowly rotating in a horizontal plane. Its speed was relatively slow, about forty miles an hour, and it followed the course of a nearby main road.

The first few sightings passed without reaction even though they were seen not just by gendarmes and the general public but also by trained observers from the Belgian military. These are not the type of people who are likely to confuse a conventional object with a UFO. However, in December 1989, the Royal Belgian Air Force was inundated by hundreds of calls from terrified citizens who had seen large triangular craft hovering at an altitude of around 350 feet. It had a light at each corner and gave off a 'light humming noise'.

Over the next few months the Belgian Air Force was scrambled several times, but the alien craft were to fast for even NATO's fastest aircraft. As a member of NATO, Belgium had a squadron of F-16 jet fighters permanently on standby. Throughout the Cold War, NATO jet fighters regularly had to see off Warsaw Pact planes probing Western defences. Soviet MiGs were easy to pick up on radar, but the Russians liked to show off the superiority of their aircraft in a deadly game to check NATO reaction times. But while the Belgian Air Force could handle themselves well enough against the Soviets, they were not up to handling aliens. The F-16 had a top speed of well over 1,250 miles an hour but, no matter how fast they scrambled, by the time they got aloft they were too late to find anything. Witnesses had seen the triangular craft make off at incredible speeds. Despite their lack of success, the Belgian air ministry were not about to dismiss the matter. It drew up plans to deal with future incursions into its airspace. Nothing, not even a UFO, was allowed to enter its Belgian jurisdiction without official clearance.

The next time a Belgian F-16 was sent aloft it found something. What people were reporting as a UFO was the light from a laser display. After that, the Belgian Air Force command decided that its fighters would only be scrambled if a visual sighting was matched by a radar contact or could be confirmed by the local police. On the night of 30 March 1990, and in the early hours of the following day, these new criteria were put to the test.

The preliminary sightings were focused on the Wavre region of central Belgium, around fourteen miles south-east of Brussels. At around 11 p.m., the phone of the Wavre gendarmerie began ringing. On the other end of the line was a witness who claimed to have seen a huge triangular UFO hovering in the night sky. The night sky was clear and the man said that the lights at the corners of the craft shone more brightly than the stars. There was no doubt in the witness's mind that what he was seeing was a UFO. A Wavre gendarme ran outside, then ran back to the phone to confirm the sighting. He noted that the UFO had the same massive triangular shape with the same lighting configuration as seen at Eupen four months earlier.

The police called the radar station at Glons near Tongeren in north-east Belgium for confirmation. Glons radar confirmed the sighting of an unidentified object at an altitude of ten thousand feet. The NATO radar station at Semmerzake confirmed the Glons finding and passed its confirmation onto the Belgian Air Force. The radar scans were compared with the previous Eupen radar sightings at Semmerzake and

Glons and were found to be identical. By this time the phones were red hot. Worried witnesses were reporting sightings of three lights flying in a perfect triangular formation. Many people clearly saw that these lights were on the underside of a huge, triangular craft.

Colonel Wilfred de Brouwer, chief of the operations section of the Belgian Air Force, said, 'Because of the frequency of requests for radar confirmation at Glons and Semmerzake – and as a number of private visual observations had been confirmed by the police – it was decided that as these parameters had been met, a patrol of F-16 aircraft should be sent to intercept an unidentified object somewhere to the south of Brussels.'

As a result, two F-16 aircraft of the Belgian Air Force, flown by a captain and a flight lieutenant, both highly qualified pilots, took off from Bevekom. Guided by the radar station, the pilots soon located the object. Their on-board radar made contact at a height of two thousand feet. By this time, the UFO was hovering menacingly over the suburbs of Brussels. As the F-16s tore towards the intruder, they locked their weapons system on to it when they were still around seven miles away. From this point, any missile they fired would have hit the target – if the target was a conventional aircraft.

'I've got lock on,' reported one of the F-16 pilots. 'Repeat. I've got lock on. Approaching target now. Wait. Target beginning to move. Trying to follow. I've lost it. Repeat. I've lost it. Target has moved, target has moved. Attempting to lock on again. I have it. Closing in... closing... closing... It's gone. The target has gone.'

Then things got strange. Initially, the radar contact had been oval in shape. Suddenly, it changed to a diamond shape on their radar screens, and increased its speed instantly to 625 miles an hour. Over the next few minutes, the two F-16 pilots – who were among the most highly trained in NATO – managed to lock on to the target another six times. Three times they managed to lock on simultaneously. Each time, however, the craft simple shrugged them off by pursuing a violently erratic course at impossible speeds and losing its pursuers.

According to one of the pilots, the target was 'jumping around the radar screen like a dancing bee'. Two F-16s with locked-on missiles could have blown any known aircraft out of the sky, but in this case the pilots never got the chance to let loose a single warhead. Although its evasive action suggested that the craft was under intelligent control, the acceleration produced by the manoeuvres it made would have killed any living pilot. The photographic record of the on-board radar of the F-16s recorded a descent from 2,000 feet to 750 feet in two seconds, a rate of 1,125 miles an hour. The same photographs show an unbelievable acceleration rate of 175 miles to 1,125 miles an hour in a few seconds. According to Professor Leon Brenig, professor of physics at the Free University of Brussels, this would represent an acceleration of 46G – 46 times the force of gravity we experience on the surface of Earth – and way beyond the endurance of any human pilot. The maximum the human body can stand is around 8G. At the end of this descent the UFO came to an abrupt halt, which would have left any human pilot splattered over the instrument panel. Nevertheless, the craft moved off again as if nothing had happened. In spite of these incredible speeds and acceleration times, there were no sonic booms.

The movements of the UFO were described by the pilots and radar operators as 'wildly erratic and step-like' as it took a zigzag course over the city of Brussels with the two F-16s in pursuit. By this time, the pilots of the F-16s were alarmed. They realised that they were up against an infinitely superior craft and were, effectively, defenceless against it. But the UFO showed no hostile intentions. It dropped to just six hundred feet above a suburb of Brussels, then vanished from the radar as it disappeared into the lights of the city below. The pursuit had last over an hour.

'Immediately after the operation, the pilots said they had never seen anything like it,' said Colonel de Brouwer. 'Certainly the flight pattern and echo on their screens was in no way that of a conventional aircraft.'

Meanwhile, on the ground, all hell broke loose. Every military base, police station, TV and radio station saw its switchboard light up as some three thousand eyewitnesses from Eupen, Wavre, Liége and

Brussels called in to report what they had seen – amazing if you consider that in the UK an average of two hundred eyewitnesses report UFOs a year. Over 2,600 statements were made to the police and the flight of the amazing craft had been captured on film and video. The whole country was in panic.

The Rodberg family had managed to film the craft from a distance of two hundred feet. One of the videos of the Flying Triangle came from Professor Brenig himself, who had observed the UFO through binoculars.

'It was like a triangular platform,' he said, 'with three very large lights on the base. There was also a smaller light in the middle. This was red and pulsating, while the other lights were yellow-white in colour. The thing flew slowly from north to south then, when it was almost overhead, rotated horizontally, spinning on its centre. Then it started to fly perpendicular to its original course.'

It was this rotation that convinced Professor Brenig he was seeing a UFO. 'The object did not incline like a normal aircraft,' he said. 'It was an unconventional shape and moved in an unconventional way.'

The Royal Belgian Air Force sent up more F-16s to search for the intruder. Belgium has around seventy F-16s in service and the skies were abuzz with activity. But despite this flurry of activity, the Belgian Air Force realised it had one big problem. What was it going to do if one of its planes located the elusive UFO?

Later, the Belgian Air Force was quizzed about the events of 30 March 1990 and co-operated with a Belgian UFO research group carrying out a detailed investigation. Attempts were made to find some rational, or at least comforting, explanation for what occurred that night. The standard explanation for a UFO sighting is that it is a weather balloon, especially when it is seen to hang in the air. But weather balloons are usually round, not triangular, and no weather balloon has ever pulled 46G in a dive.

Another standard explanation for UFO sightings is that they are secret tests of military aircraft. But the Belgian government is not in the business of developing new aircraft, and a quick check of the air ministry's records revealed that no foreign government had requested permission to make test flights over Belgium on that date. Why would anyone test a top-secret military aircraft on a clear night over a well-populated city rather than in some deserted area, anyway?

Claims that the Flying Triangles must have been the US testing a new type of Stealth aircraft are disproved by the fact that the UFO appeared on both ground-based and airborne radar. The whole point of Stealth planes is that they are invisible to radar. The amazing manoeuvres of the Belgian Flying Triangle could not be explained as a holographic projection on the clouds. On the night of 30 March 1990 the sky over Belgium was entirely free of cloud – that is why some three thousand people saw the UFOs.

The Belgian Air Force chief of staff went on record to express the military's consternation.

'The Air Force has arrived at the conclusion that a number of anomalous phenomena have been produced within Belgian air space,' he said. And he conceded that the UFO that had penetrated Belgian air space without authority on 30 March 1990 was a solid, structured craft.

Major Lambrechts of the Royal Belgian Air Force prepared an official report that reveled just how seriously the Belgian authorities took the matter.

'Since early September 1989,' it said, 'strange phenomena were regularly witnessed in Belgian air space.' It went on to dismiss some of the possible explanations that had been offered. 'The presence of and/or tests with B2 or F-117A [Stealth planes], remotely piloted vehicles... and AWACS at the time of the happenings can be excluded.'

The lights on the UFOs, Lambrechts reported, 'were very clear, as if they were signals; this enables [us] to distinguish them from the stars.' The report also admitted that 'contact was observed by different sensors [radar] of the Air Force' and concluded: 'This report is based on eyewitness accounts by police officers on duty whose objectivity and common sense is beyond doubt.'

Colonel de Brouwer, Air Force chief of operations that night, concluded: 'Even if until now there has been no threat, one must accept the fact that for the past six months the Belgian skies have experienced extraordinary phenomena.' And the Belgian Minister of Defence said in parliament that 'the government did not know what they were'.

This is quite an admission in view of the fact that officialdom the world over routinely denies the existence of UFOs.

The Triangle Returns

Three years later, the Flying Triangle put in an appearance over the UK. Most of the sightings occurred in the early hours of 31 March 1993. Nick Pope, who manned the desk at the Ministry of Defence that handles UFO sightings, recalled: 'Calls came in all morning from people, many of them police officers, saying they had seen these huge triangular craft.'

The descriptions were similar to the Belgian and Hudson Valley sightings. Many witnesses reported three lights moving in perfect formation. Others who had been closer said that the lights simply marked the corners of a huge, triangular craft. Witnesses also reported that the craft gave off a deep humming sound. A family in Staffordshire in the Midlands reported seeing a UFO hovering over their house. Again it made a low humming noise.

Along with reports from the police came sightings by military personnel guarding bases. One came from RAF Cosford in Shropshire. There, an entire military guard patrol reported seeing the UFO pass directly over the base. They checked with duty air traffic controllers, but drew a complete blank. According to the logs, there were no aircraft in the area.

Having heard about the UFO sighting at Cosford, the meteorological officer at RAF Shawbury, only a few miles away, went outside to see if he could see anything. What he saw was a triangular craft flying directly towards the base. It was emitting a low humming sound. He estimated the size of the object as being only a little smaller than a 747. Others said it was the size of a Hercules transport plane –

but neither jumbo jets nor Hercules can hover. Shawbury's met officer reported that the UFO came to a halt and shone a beam of light on the ground. The beam swept from side to side, as if the craft was looking for something. Then the light went out and the UFO passed slowly over the base, almost directly overhead.

The Ministry of Defence launched a full investigation. Officially the MoD has always maintained that UFO sightings were 'of no defence significance', so it needed to discover a mundane explanation for the sightings. The problem here was that a number of their own personnel had reported seeing an unidentified triangular craft flying, unhampered, directly over two key military establishments.

At least ninety per cent of UFO sightings have a conventional explanation, so the MoD began checking on aircraft activity, airship flights and weather balloon launches. Again, it found nothing in the area at the time. So it then checked with the Royal Observatory to see if there might be an astronomical explanation, such as unusual meteorite activity. The observatory reported that a Russian rocket had re-entered the Earth's atmosphere. This had been responsible for the appearance of strange lights at high altitude for a few minutes at around 1.10 a.m. But the UFO the RAF personnel had seen was low down and the sightings happened over a period of several hours. The sightings at Cosford and Shawbury could not be explained by the rocket's re-entry and this theory was discounted.

Again, the theory that the Flying Triangle might be some sort of secret, prototype craft was investigated. For years, there had been rumours of a hypersonic replacement for the Lockheed SR-71 Blackbird, called Aurora. The Belgian Air Force had investigated similar possibilities, but both the Belgian and British authorities were given categorical assurances by the American government that no US aircraft were involved. Besides, it is hardly likely that a secret aircraft would be tested in heavily defended air space without proper diplomatic clearance. The MoD had no choice but to reject the theory that the UFO was an American prototype aircraft. 'Flying Triangle clearly behaves in a way that is beyond the cutting edge of our technology,' said MoD UFOlogist Nick Pope. So, like the Belgian government before it, the British government were forced to admit that they could find no explanation.

However, there is one interesting connection between the sightings in Belgium and the UK. Both occurred late at night on 30 March, and in the early hours of the next day. If these UFO stories were reported in the media, the stories would have appeared on 1 April – April Fool's Day? Is this just a coincidence? Or does it point to an elaborate hoax? Or perhaps, the aliens who built and fly the craft have a sense of humour.

But this is no laughing matter. In both Belgium and the UK, the UFOs were observed by military personnel. From their observations it is clear that NATO could do nothing to stop the uninvited intruders. And, whatever the authorities say, that has national security implications.

RAF Cosford

This is not the first time RAF Cosford has played host to a UFO. On 10 December 1963, two RAF personnel saw a strange domed object sweeping the airfield there with a strange green beam. As they ran to get help, it crashed behind a hanger. When they returned, it was nowhere to be seen.

The two men were then subjected to a rigorous interrogation, but their story could not be shaken. However, a couple of days later, a very large transport plane landed. This was an extremely unusual event at Cosford. A large object hidden under tarpaulins was loaded up and flown off.

Mexican Sightings

Sceptics often ask why UFOs and aliens always appear to lonely people in the back of beyond. But that is not true. On the afternoon of 11 July 1991, a UFO appeared over the world's most populous metropolis, Mexico City, where it was seen by millions of people. And it did not turn up on just any old day. It appeared on a day and at a time when the inhabitants of Mexico's capital would inevitably be turning their attention to the skies. It was the day of an eclipse of the sun, which would turn day into night in Mexico City for over six minutes. Spectacular though the eclipse was, it was upstaged by an extraterrestrial craft that managed to steal the attention of tens of thousands of spectators.

At 1:22 p.m., just as the eclipse was starting, a shiny metallic object appeared in the sky. It hovered silently near the eclipsing sun, floating there for a half an hour. In that time, not only thousands saw it, but at least seventeen different people in various locations around the city had filmed it on video. For the next few months, Mexico was in the grip of 'UFO fever'. One of those caught up in it was one of country's most respected TV journalists and host to the popular news programme *60 Minutos*, Jaime Maussan. Previously Maussan had had no interest in UFOs.

'I am a journalist and, as such, I only wish to deal with the facts,' he said. 'However, since I became involved with this, along with the rest of Mexico, I have seen overwhelming evidence which convinces me that my country is being visited regularly by a huge number of extraterrestrial craft. There is no other explanation.'

Soon after the eclipse, Maussan made an appeal on TV, asking the public to send in any footage they had shot of the UFO. There was an overwhelming response. The TV company was inundated with spectacular video footage which showed the unidentified craft spinning on its own axis. But it did not stop there.

'Since the eclipse, there has been a UFO flap – people, almost daily, are witnessing the most intense manifestation of the UFO phenomenon,' said Mexican UFO researcher Santiago Yturria Gorza. And the public continued to send in videotapes of UFOs spotted since the eclipse.

On the day of the eclipse, a UFO also appeared over the town of Puebla. A disc-shaped craft was filmed moving slowly and silently through the sky. It was seen by thousands of Mexicans who had lined the streets to watch the eclipse. A UFO had also been filmed in the area four days before. Then in January 1996, streaks of light appeared in the night sky over Puebla. These were seen by dozens of witnesses. Examining film taken of them, astronomers initially dismissed them as comets, but later analysis showed that they were too low and too slow to be comets.

On 5 May 1994, a pulsating craft in the sky above the district of Juarez in Chihuahua was filmed separately by two neighbours, Senora Rosi Uribe and Francisco Javier. Known to UFOlogists as the 'plasma ship' because of its internal pulsating light, similar craft have been seen over Mexico on numerous occasions since 1991. Carlos Dias, a professional photographer, had photographed them regularly. One even put in an appearance on Mexico's Independence Day in 1991, seemingly observing a Mexican air force fly-by. It turned up again in 1993, passing through a helicopter formation.

In collaboration with American husband-and-wife private-detective team Lee and Brit Elders, Maussan produced a series of three remarkable documentaries called *The Messengers of Destiny*. These have been widely acclaimed throughout the UFO community for showing some of the best UFO footage ever shot. In the eyes of UFOlogists, the video evidence collected by Maussan demonstrates that, whatever UFOs are, they are not the product of any technology known to humans. One video showed a UFO flying through cloud. Sceptics say that the object could be a plane, a meteorite, or even a bird. But computer analysis of the sequence clearly demonstrated that it was a solid, metallic, disc-shaped craft. Computer enhancement of the image also revealed two other, smaller craft flying just below the main structure that were otherwise invisible to the naked eye.

Dozens of videos showed a single UFO that slowly split into two separate craft. On one tape, a UFO could be seen splitting into five distinct entities. Computer analysis also revealed the incredible manoeuvrability of these craft. They were seen accelerating at rates that would kill any human pilot and moving at seemingly impossible speed across the sky. One UFO zoomed out of sight in the space of a single video frame – it had disappeared from a clear sky in under a sixtieth of a second.

The Mexican sightings have provided a huge amount of solid evidence to support the idea that UFOs are extraterrestrial in origin. The video footage went way beyond the fleeting glimpses of UFOs seen before, and analysis of their aerial activity confounds any terrestrial explanation. The regular explanations of UFO sightings – that they are the planet Venus, weather balloons or meteorites – could easily be dismissed in this case, and UFO sceptics have studiously avoided studying Maussan's video material.

With the Mexican evidence for the presence of UFOs unrefuted, the question remains: why had the aliens chosen the skies above Mexico City to reveal themselves? Jaime Maussan believes that its inhabitants have been chosen to test human reactions towards the arrival of extraterrestrials. He thinks the aliens are being so open about their presence that this must herald something else.

Other researchers point out that more than a thousand years ago the Maya, who occupied southern Mexico before the Spanish conquest, predicted the birth of the 'sixth sun' in the period following the eclipse of the sun in 1991. Then the 'Masters of the Stars' or the 'Messengers of Destiny' would return. The Mayans were accomplished astronomers and could calculate eclipses with extraordinary accuracy. According to the Dresden Codex, a stone table that depicts Mayan cosmology: 'In the era of the sixth sun, all that is buried will be discovered, truth shall be the seed of light and the sons of the sixth sun shall be the ones who travel through the stars.'

Although their purpose has yet to be revealed, the strange objects in the skies above Mexico continue to be seen and videoed. Subsequent footage showed UFO fleets of several craft flying in a formation that resembled the constellations. This may be an attempt at communication. However, there may be a more sinister interpretation. In 1995, security camera tapes from Nellis Air Force Base in Nevada, home of America's secret research establishment Area 51, fell into the hands of UFO researchers. They showed a pulsating metallic craft climbing through the sky. When compared to Maussan's footage by researchers from the US TV programme *Sightings* the following year they proved to be identical.

The Nellis footage has been authenticated by a handful of American defence analysts, including leading Stealth-technology researcher Bill Sweetman. Could it be that the US military are testing a secret weapons programme in Mexican air space?

Encounters at Gulf Breeze

The small holiday resort of Gulf Breeze, which lies on a peninsula in north-west Florida, has fewer than ten thousand residents. Otherwise unexceptionable, in the late 1980s it became one of the great hotspots of UFO activity. The sightings began on 11 November 1987, when building contractor Ed Walters claims to have seen and filmed one of the most dramatic UFO encounters ever to be recorded. Although Gulf Breeze has since become a Mecca for UFOlogists and numerous other sightings have been made there, the Walters' case remains the best documented. Walters claims to have a ninety-eight-second videotape of his UFO encounter, along with some forty genuine photographs of the craft. More sinisterly, he also claims that the UFO tried to abduct him.

Walters' first encounter took place on the afternoon of 11 November. He was working at home, when his attention was drawn to a strange light outside. It appeared to be coming from behind a thirty-foot pine tree in his front yard. The glowing object was partially obscured by the tree, so Walters left his home office to investigate. But when he opened the front door, he saw, a large, glowing, bluish-grey craft floating silently above the ground. With amazing presence of mind, Walters ducked back inside the house, grabbed his Polaroid camera and started snapping.

The excitement made him foolhardy and Walters rushed outside to get a better view. The extraterrestrial craft, which was now directly above him, emitted a pulsing beam of blue light from its underside.

'I stared at the object hovering over my front yard then... Bang! Something hit me all over my body,' he said. An energy beam paralysed Walters, lifted him three feet in the air and held him there for around twenty seconds.

'I tried to lift my arms to point the camera,' he said. 'I couldn't move them. I was in a blue light beam. Then my feet lifted off the ground and as I began to scream a deep computer-like voice groaned in my head, "We will not harm you." But it was in my head, not in my ears.'

Walters also managed to capture the blue beam descending from the glowing underside of the portholed, disc-shaped craft on film.

Initially, Walters sent the photographs anonymously to his local paper, *The Sentinel*. When they published them, a number of other witnesses contacted the paper. They reported seeing a similar craft at around the same time and their descriptions matched his photographs.

Walters continued seeing strange silent objects hovering in the sky, backing his claims with more photographs and video footage. On 12 January 1988, he photographed the alien craft hovering over his truck. Five 'beings' from it landed on the road in front of him, but he did not manage to photograph them. Walters has no idea why the aliens are visiting him.

'I don't even know if these "beings" are alien,' he said. 'I have not idea what they are.'

The wave of sightings in Gulf Breeze attracted national attention and the small town became the centre of a media circus. Then MUFON – the Mutual UFO Network, a grassroots organisation of private citizens who have taken it upon themselves to get to the bottom of the UFO phenomena – turned up. Key to their investigation was the authenticity of the Walters' photographs and video footage. Several experts were called in. The most prominent among them was the optical physicist Dr Bruce Maccabee. A former US government researcher, he is widely respected among the UFO community for his unbiased scientific approach. Maccabee began by inspecting the site of the encounters. Then he conducted a series of detailed, personal interviews with all the witnesses. The photographs were analysed using state-of-the-art computer equipment. At the end of his rigorous investigation, Maccabee could find no evidence of a hoax. The photographs, he said, were authentic images of 'unconventional aircraft'. But the video footage proved harder to authenticate.

'With enough time, money, luck and skill – anything can be faked,' says MUFON's video analyst Jeff Soinio.

However, the Gulf Breeze sightings also attracted the attention of the sceptics. Philip Klass, author and well-known UFO debunker, claimed that Walters' photographs were clever double exposures. He said that models had been photographed under clever lighting conditions, then combined with photographs of the sky to provide the background. A model bearing a remarkable similarity to detailed sketches Walters made of the craft he saw was found in the attic of his previous home. He claims that it had been planted to discredit him.

To rebut Klass's allegations, MUFON gave Walters a sealed four-lens stereo camera, which is practically tamper-proof. The new pictures Walters took with this camera, UFO enthusiasts claim, provided conclusive proof of his sightings. But the sceptics were still not convinced. Among them, surprisingly, was Barbara Becker, a MUFON member herself and keen amateur photographer of twenty years, standing. The photographs may be genuine, she conceded, but the UFOs themselves she claimed were ingenious fakes.

'The fact that Walters took more than forty excellent photographs is enough to arouse suspicions,' she said. 'Ed loves to tell a good story – so much so, that he couldn't restrain himself from embellishing his accounts of the incidents in his books.'

In fact, Walters has written three books about his encounters. One, called *UFOs Are Real: Here's The Proof*, was co-authored with Dr Bruce Maccabee.

However, Barbara Becker's position was soon contradicted by a flurry of new sightings. In the following six months, more than a hundred witnesses reported other UFO sightings in the Gulf Breeze area, and they produced more photographs and video footage to back their claims. To most people, this vindicated Walters. However, some of the die-hard sceptics investigating the case claimed that the entire population of Gulf Breeze was involved in the hoax.

The inhabitants of Gulf Breeze took being called liars amiss, so, with the residents of nearby Pensacola, they organised surveillance teams to monitor the air space of western Florida day and night, calling themselves the Skywatchers. In a matter of weeks, they saw a bright red and amber light zigzagging across the sky, before it finally disappeared. Several more UFO sightings followed. Usually these involved small points of light in the sky that changed size rapidly, moved at odd angles, travelled at unimaginable speeds and accelerated at rates thought to be impossible, all without making a sound. However, these new sightings were hard to substantiate. In the immediate area of Gulf Breeze, there were three major military bases, all of which generated extensive air traffic. MUFON investigator Gary Watson said that the military was always asked whether aircraft were in the air when the Skywatchers made a sighting. On each occasion, they confirmed that no aircraft were aloft at the time.

In 1991, Gulf Breeze MUFON president Art Hufford photographed an unexplained source of light in the night sky, which suddenly disappeared after ten seconds. It was witnessed by over thirty people. One of the luckiest UFO watchers in the area was photographer Bland Pugh. In 1991, he captured two UFOs in one shot. One orange-coloured UFO left an extraordinary corkscrew trail across the sky, while seeming to drop a white UFO from its belly. Nicknamed 'Bubba', the object has been seen by residents a number of times and MUFON member Bruce Morrison managed to capture this particular event on video.

Then in 1993, Pugh photographed what looked like a white light in the sky. But when it was enhanced, a black craft appeared above it. And in 1996, Pugh snapped a pulsating orange 'doughnut', similar to the glowing ring Walters said he saw on the underside of the UFO that visited him in 1987.

It has become increasingly hard for debunkers to deny that something odd is going on in the skies above Gulf Breeze, though sceptics remain convinced that Walters is a publicity-seeking con man.

Meanwhile, the UFO community point to the overwhelming evidence Walters has presented and the fact that for years after the Ed Walters story broke the sightings continued.

'There will always be people who choose not to believe, whatever the evidence suggests,' said Walters. 'Some simply refuse to accept that UFOs exist, so ultimately they brand me a hoaxer.'

Rendezvous Français

On the afternoon of 8 January 1981, Renato Nicolai – an Italian living in Trans-en-Provence, a small village in the south of France – was building a concrete shelter for the water pump he had recently installed behind his house. Renato had hoped to finish the work before nightfall, but at 5 p.m. he heard a strange noise coming from above. As he looked up he noticed a strange object descending onto a nearby hill.

'I was startled by a light whistling,' he said. 'The noise was unusual, so I turned round and lifted my head. Above the tall pine tree at the bottom of my land I saw a craft descending towards the ground without rotating.'

The object he described was small, only a few feet in diameter, like 'two bowls turned one on of top of the other'. It was metallic grey in colour and had small 'landing' legs on its base. It was some two hundred feet away.

Intrigued, Renato walked over to it to take a closer look. He assumed that it was a military craft in distress – there was an air base not far away at Canjuers – and the craft looked more like it was falling than making a controlled descent.

The UFO hit the ground with a thud. Discretion being the better part of valour, Renato stopped behind a hut next to the small field where the UFO had come to rest. From there, he was just thirty yards from the craft with a clear field of vision.

'It stood on some sort of small feet and measured 1.8 metres in height by about 2.5 metres in diameter,' he said. 'In the centre, there was a kind of metal crown separating the two bowls.'

The craft sat there, inert.

'There were no flames or smoke,' he said. 'There wasn't even any light.'

After a couple of minutes, Renato came out from behind the hut and walked over towards the craft. But as he approached the object it suddenly started to make a very high-pitched whistling noise, then shot away vertically at an amazing speed.

Renato followed the path of the UFO with his eyes, as its strange whistling sound resonated in his ears. As the UFO shot skywards, he could see an opening underneath the craft, but he saw no flames or smoke came out of it. Renato recalled something else strange about the craft.

'As it left the ground,' he said, 'it picked up a small amount of earth.'

Once the UFO had disappeared behind the trees, Renato approached the landing site and he saw clear marks on the ground where it had stood. That evening, when his wife came home, he told her what he'd seen. She did not believe him so, the following morning, he took her out into the field and showed her the marks on the ground. She phoned neighbours, who came round to have a look. Then they notified the police.

On Friday, 9 January 1981, the Draguignan gendarmerie received a call reporting a UFO sighting. They went to investigate. When the gendarmes reached the site, they examined the marks. According to their notes, these consisted of two concentric circles, one 2.4 metres in diameter and the other 2.2 metres inside it. The edges showed evidence of scraping, as if whatever made them had been skidding or spinning on its axis. Another mark could be seen on a low wall near by. The object had plainly crashed into the wall before skidding to a halt in the field.

The gendarmes then took the witness's statement and collected a number of samples of plants and soil from the site. These samples were sent for analysis in Toulouse. The police then announced that they could find no logical explanation for the sightings and handed over the case to the government agency responsible for dealing with UFO cases.

At that time, the agency charged with investigating unidentified aerial phenomenon in France was the *Groupe d'Etude des Phénoménes*

Aérospatioux Non-identifiés (GEPAN). This group was more than capable of investigating such a case. It had the expertise of a number of scientific experts – physicists, biologists and psychologists – to call on. However, the police report on the incident arrived at GEPAN headquarters on Monday, 12 January, but their investigators did not turn up at Trans-en-Provence for over a month. By then, the evidence in Renato's field had disappeared.

However, GEPAN could not overlook the samples that the police had sent to various labs, or the detailed measurements the gendarmes had made of the marks at the site. Eventually GEPAN had to release a highly censored technical report – though the names of all the people, places and laboratories involved were deliberately removed. The report stated that the gendarmes' description of the marks left in Renato Nicolai's field showed the earth had been crushed. A very heavy object had stood at the site. The soil samples showed that the ground had been heated to a temperature of between 300 and 600°C. Various materials had been deposited at the site, principally iron and phosphates along with residues from the combustion process. Unusually high levels of zinc were also found. And the plants in the area were found to have been bleached of fifty per cent of their chlorophyll. The vegetation samples passed on to professor of biochemistry Michel Bounias showed signs of senescence, a biochemical ageing of the leaves that can only be explained as a result of artificial processes.

'One thing's for certain: we know nothing of the nature or the origin of the phenomenon,' said biochemist Michel Bounias. 'And this is where the real problem starts, because I've never come across anything like it on the planet.'

Renato was interviewed by psychologists who concluded that he was telling the truth and he had hard evidence to corroborate his story. But still GEPAN investigators tried to find some logical explanation for the sighting: helicopters, weather balloons, stray shells. So far they have come up with nothing that can explain what happened on 8 January 1981 in Trans-en-Provence. Meanwhile, Jean-Pierre Petit, head of the French Centre for Scientific Research, offered his expert opinion on the case:

'In order to back the "case for UFOs" with something of real consequence, you need to produce hard evidence that cannot easily be reproduced by humans,' he says. 'The Trans-en-Provence case offers this kind of objective proof, which, in this instance, comes in the form of a significant alteration in the environment.

'Biochemists agree that the pigmentary structure of the plants is not only stable, but also difficult to modify. Moreover, Michel Bounias carried out a parallel study on the samples in order to quantify the radioactive source that had affected them. The results suggested gamma rays as high as one megarad in intensity, a level of exposure capable of killing all bacterial life and sterilising food stuffs.

'Radioactivity specialists will tell you that, given the area affected, exposure to such a high level of gamma radiation for thirty seconds represents a significant quantity of energy. So this is not exactly the work of a DIY enthusiast. Even if the Atomic Energy Commission had wanted to pull such a stunt, it wouldn't exactly have been a piece of cake.

'In this case... the hypothesis of some kind of vehicle must be considered, simply because it is the most plausible. Were the "case for UFOs" subject to a judicial inquiry, the investigating magistrate would be forced to admit the Trans-en-Provence incident as evidence.'

The Amaranth Case

Another remarkably similar case occurred the following year in France. On 21 October 1982, an egg-shaped UFO was seen flying over a French garden. It came to a halt and hovered over an amaranth bush for twenty minutes, before shooting skywards. It was seen by a prominent metallurgist, who managed to get within two feet of it and, at one point, managed to touch it. He said that the craft was about 80 centimetres in height and 1.5 m in diameter. The upper half was marine blue, the lower half gun-metal grey.

Once it had gone, the bush was left a dark brown colour. Its centre had been dehydrated. The seeds had ripened spontaneously and some of their heads had burst. Again GEPAN was called in to investigate.

'The fact that the leaves had dried out and the husks of certain fruits had burst could have been due to the corona effect of an electric field,' said their report.

As in the Trans-en-Provence case, Michel Bounias concluded that: 'It would be useful to compare our observations with the effects of other physical agents, such as electromagnetic field generators.'

Down Under

The Knowles family were driving across the great limestone plateau of the Nullarbor Plain in southern Australia on the night of 20 January 1988, when they experienced one of the southern hemisphere's most famous UFO encounters. The Knowleses were travelling from Perth to Melbourne to visit family. Sean Knowles was driving. Also in the car were his mother Faye Knowles, his two younger brothers, Patrick and Wayne, and the family's two dogs.

At about 1:30 a.m. they were heading east along the Eyre Highway towards Mundrabilla, when the car radio began picking up strange interference. Then it packed up. Some ten or fifteen minutes later, Sean saw something on the road ahead of him. At first he thought it was a truck with only one headlight. As it approached, he could see it was indeed a truck. But the light he'd seen was not a single headlight. It came from a strange glowing ball that hovered above the vehicle. What's more, the truck was driving erratically down the wrong side of the road. Sean swerved to avoid a collision, narrowly missing the wayward truck.

A little later, the Sean saw a car with a similar ball of light hovering above it. Sean was determined to find out what was going on. He turned around and began to follow the car and its glowing companion. The he woke up Patrick who was asleep in the front passenger seat beside him.

'Look at that Pat,' he said. 'There's something in front of us. I think it's a UFO.'

As they approached it, they saw it was now hovering over an old station wagon. And it was coming at them. They swerved to avoid it, ending up on the other side of the road. Then the ball of light doubled back again and started following them. Quickly Sean turned around again and made off. By this time, everyone in the car was in a desperate panic. Faye and the children were screaming, but it was too late. They could not outrun it. The glowing object quickly caught up with them and landed on the roof of the car with a loud bang.

'The next thing we knew, the object was on the roof and had picked the car up off the ground,' said Patrick.

Bright beams of light bathed the car's interior. The dogs went crazy and everyone thought they were going to die. Patrick said he felt as if his brains were being sucked out of his head. Sean was still trying to escape the light. He had not noticed was that the car was not on the ground at all. Under the influence of the UFO, it had been drawn up into the air. With his foot flat to the floor, Sean estimated that his speed was over 125 miles an hour.

In a state of panic, Faye, who was in the back, wound down her window. She reached up out of the window and touched the object. It felt warm and spongy, like some form of suction pad, she said. The sensation made her recoil violently. Pulling her hand back in, she found it was red, swollen and cold. Seeing this, she began to scream and became hysterical.

Patrick rolled the front window down. The inside of the car was suddenly covered with a black, ash-like substance that smelt of 'decomposing bodies'. Everyone's hair stood on end and their voices became distorted, as if everything was happening in slow motion. Suddenly the alien craft released them. The car dropped back onto the road, bursting one of the rear tyres. It was only then that Sean realised that the car had been flying through the air.

He now jammed on the brakes. When the car came to a stop, the family got out and ran for cover. They hid in some nearby bushes. The UFO was still in the vicinity. It hovered above, shining a searchlight down on to the ground as if it was searching for them, while they watched, petrified, from the undergrowth. The object, they said, resembled 'an egg in a cup' and emitted a low humming sound. The craft kept circling the area but, when the sun began to come up, it vanished.

Sean changed the tyre and, for about a quarter of an hour, their voices remained strangely distorted. Things were just getting back to normal when they saw that the UFO was coming back. The family jumped in the car and Sean hurtled off in the direction of the Mundrabilla Roadhouse, which was about twenty-five miles away. On the way, they hit a kangaroo, which dented the wing, but the car stayed on the road. They continued at a frantic pace and it was only when they were in sight of the service station that the UFO stopped following them and mysteriously disappeared again.

When they arrived at the Mundrabilla Roadhouse, the family told two truck drivers what had happened.

'I thought at first they were trying to be funny when they were telling me about their experience,' said the service station attendant. 'They were excited and scared. When I got near the car, I noticed an odour similar to that of hot insulation.' He also noticed that the family were visibly shaken. Faye's hand was still badly swollen and the dogs had started to lose hair in clumps.

The Knowles encounter was investigated by Paul Norman of the Victorian UFO Research Society (VUFORS). He caught up with Knowleses ten days later, on 30 January, in Adelaide and began his investigation by inspecting their car. He found that the radio that had malfunctioned during the encounter was now working fine. However, marks on the roof correlated with the family's account of what had happened.

During the encounter, Sean had said that he had been driving at over 125 miles an hour. According to the manufacturers, the model of Ford Telstra the Knowleses were driving was incapable of such a speed. However, in a TV documentary on the encounter by Australia's Channel Seven, the car was tested with its front wheels off the floor and it was shown that the car could, in fact, reach such speeds.

301

The dust that had covered the inside of the car during the encounter was tested in Adelaide and was found to be mostly iron oxide, which is often produced by worn brake pads. But one of the truck drivers the family had talked to at the Mundrabilla Roadhouse, a Mr Henly, was also a keen racing driver. He said that the dust looked like silicon. It had an incredible feel to it, and it was nothing like brake dust. And the first police officer to arrive after the incident also said that the dust he found in the Knowleses' car was not from the brakes.

To check this out further, Norman sent a sample to a NASA lab in California. Their analysis showed that it was made up mainly of silicon, carbon, oxygen and potassium and could not have come from the brake pads. The sample also carried a trace of astatine – a radioactive chemical that can only be produced synthetically. Its half-life is only a few hours, so even a large amount should have disappeared long before the investigation got under way. Nevertheless the radiation was there and would help to explain Faye's swollen hand.

Norman also investigated the blown-out tyre. Normally, when a tyre blows out at the speed the Knowleses were travelling, it would have split apart like a peeled mandarin. But the Knowles tyre had blown in a very unusual way – it had ripped all the way around the circumference.

Despite all the evidence to the contrary, the Nullarbor case has generally been dismissed as a hoax. Philip Klass, the America's most famous UFO debunker, claims that marks on the car's roof were actually caused by a roof rack. The Knowleses say that no roof rack had ever been attached to their vehicle. Klass also says that the UFO encounter had been invented for insurance purposes, that Sean Knowles fell asleep at the wheel and came off the road, hence the damaged tyre. The Knowleses vehemently deny this. Other sceptics say that the family saw a meteorite or, more preposterously, the sun rising. Other 'scientific' explanations include that they encountered a stray missile from Woomera Test Range in the Great Victoria Desert, that they were gripped by an unusual form of electrically charged tornado or that they were suffering a collective hallucination caused by driving for long hours in the desert at night.

However, a dispassionate evaluation of the evidence suggests that something mysterious did happen on the Nullarbor Plain that night, and the case still intrigues members of the UFO community around the world. Certainly for the Knowles it was a very real experience.

Wide Load

Gary Wood was driving home from work with his friend Colin down a motorway in Scotland one night around 10:30 p.m. As they were going around a corner, Colin pointed out of the windscreen at something hovering above the road. They were about a hundred yards from it.

'As we got closer, I could see the object in great detail,' said Gary. 'It was a black, circular object, about thirty-five feet wide, and was in three parts, with pieces hanging underneath.'

They began to panic. Gary was too scared to stop the car, but jammed it into second gear and accelerated hard underneath it. Colin was shouting and screaming. Just as they headed under the object, a curtain of light descended. Suddenly Gary found he was plunged into complete blackness. He was looking about for Colin but could see nothing. He tried to grab the car door, but it was not there. He had the sensation that he was not in his car any longer and thought he must have died. Then, suddenly, he was back in his car as it dropped back onto the road, damaging the bottom of the car. It ended up on an embankment. Later he discovered that he was missing two hours and, although the car was just one year old, it inexplicably began to rot away.

The Bonnybridge Triangle

Some places seem to attract more UFO sightings that others. These are so-called 'window areas'. One such is the area around Bonnybridge. It is so popular among UFOlogists that the Comfort Inn in Falkirk, in the middle of the so-called 'Bonnybridge Triangle', stages official UFO weekends. These have proved a great success, even attracting enthusiasts from the US and Japan. They come hoping to catch a glimpse of the strange lights in the sky that are seen and filmed regularly in the vicinity.

The idea of the Bonnybridge window began in 26 September 1992, when the newspaper *The Scotsman* carried an article written by Albert Morris. It was headlined 'Where on earth did the Martians go?' and its intention was to show that UFO sightings were falling. However, by accident, it drew attention to the fact that Scotland had two of the UK's five most prominent 'window areas'. The result was a media circus.

The other newspapers picked up on it, along with radio and TV. The *Glasgow Herald* claimed that 'Scotland was the top hotspot for UFOs', while the *Aberdeen Press* said that the skies above Scotland were teeming with aliens.

Into this furore stepped Malcolm McDonald, the Falkirk district environmental health officer. He had met a prominent local businessman who claimed to have had an encounter with a UFO. The council set up an investigation, in the course of which it became clear that the small Scottish town of Bonnybridge was the centre of a spate of encounters that had started the previous spring. The council's conclusions were published in the local press that November, and Bonnybridge took its place as a major new UFO hotspot. Council member Billy Buchanan was appointed UFO officer and, encouraged by the newspaper publicity, eyewitnesses began beating a path to his door.

Buchanan discovered that a wave of sightings had begun in March 1992, when a huge blue light, making a whirring and rattling sound, came out of some roadside trees, scaring three people who were walking down a back road to Bonnybridge. Buchanan called for more witnesses and, within a week, twenty-two cases were on record. Councillor Buchanan announced gravely that 'too many people have sighted UFOs for it to be dismissed lightly'. According to the *Glasgow Mail*, 'terrified townsfolk [were] scouring the sky at night, seeking UFOs'. Something had to be done. So Buchanan called in local UFO expert Malcolm Robinson to handle the situation. The media were soon calling Bonnybridge 'the UFO capital of the world', while Buchanan and Robinson set up a UFO hotline.

Sceptics point out that a plaque to commemorate a local UFO sighting erected in nearby Livingston had become something of a tourist attraction. While nobody was accusing the inhabitants of Bonnybridge of making up their sightings, many UFOlogists felt that the town council was skilfully manipulating the media attention the sightings had brought.

However, Malcolm Robinson went on record to say that many of the cases that had been reported were valuable and that something significant was really going on in Bonnybridge. Councillor Buchanan was singled out for praise. He responded like a true politician, organising open meetings in the town hall and sending letters to the Prime Minister, demanding government action to bring the truth about the Bonnybridge UFOs to light.

UFO Alley

However, Bonnybridge is far from being the UK's premier window area. Although it topped the sightings table in the early 1990s, there were few UFO encounters in the area before that time, and study a of fifty years' sighting statistics carried out for a TV documentary showed that, over the long term, UK UFO activity centred on a small area of northern England. The analysis found that around one tenth of all encounters in the UK occurred in a narrow, moorland region in the Pennine hills. The majority happened in a triangle that fell between the outer suburbs of the cities of Sheffield, Leeds and Manchester. It was found that the area that the local press had dubbed 'UFO alley' was a corridor between the small towns of Bacup and Todmorden, straddling the border between Yorkshire and Lancashire. Amazingly, one eighth of all alien contacts and abductions in the UK occurred within ten miles of this remote spot.

What further differentiated this window from Bonnybridge was that sightings of strange lights in the heavens stretch back to the days when horses and carts rather than cars and trucks, plied the Pennine roads.

Strange encounters took place there even before the idea of flying saucers was invented. Local names link certain areas with supernatural encounters. Balls of light have been seen since medieval times over the Devil's Elbow, a desolate track in nearby Derbyshire. Near the town of Bacup is Pendle Hill, which was once believed to be home to 'demons', and those accused of being witches were put to the test by rolling them down its slopes. At the beginning of the twentieth century, a local constable reported seeing a strange 'airship' floating over Pendle Hill. Then in 1977, a car was stopped dead in its tracks by a UFO hovering in the mist on it summit.

All this has led UFOlogists to conclude that the Pennine window area is undoubtedly something real, while the one at Bonnybridge is actually a creation of media interest and speculation. UFOlogists point out that a similar 'window' opened in the London overspill development of Milton Keynes in Buckinghamshire in the 1970s. The sighting reports soared from practically nothing to dozens a year. However, when the statistics were analysed, it was discovered that this was because the population of the new town was soaring and there were simply more people around to report sightings.

The Pennine Triangle

On the 24 February 1979, Mike Sacks and his wife observed a strange orange object through the downstairs window of their home in the town of Bacup, one corner of the Pennine triangle. It lit up the room as it fell slowly and silently from the sky over Rossendale Valley. They observed the object as it descended, then it stopped, hovered for a bit, then changed course and shot off.

Sacks thought the object had landed in a nearby quarry and went out with his camera to investigate. When he got there, he heard a strange voice in his head that kept saying 'Portakabin, Portakabin'. As he looked down into the quarry he could see a set of lights which resembled those of a Portakabin. The next day when he returned to the site there was no Portakabin nor any other building that would have accounted for the lights.

Other people in the area, including two policemen, also reported seeing the strange object at around the time in question. Another witness, Alf Kyme, saw a dome-shaped mass surrounded by red rings descend into the quarry. A local taxi driver chased the object for a short while before losing it in the vicinity of the quarry.

The Ministry of Defence claimed that the sightings had been that of a 'special exercise' that had been taking place that night. However, Colonel Shrihofer, base commander at Upper Heyford, after checking his records said that there had 'definitely not' been any Air Force activity that night.

The last witness to see the UFO claimed that he saw the object while on Blackpool pier, and that he noticed an RAF jet chasing the object. The object then appeared to enter the sea and disappear. When the jet had disappeared, the witness claims that he saw the object rise from the sea and shoot off vertically.

UFO researchers will have to wait until the year 2009 before they can obtain any documents on the case, as the UK government hold all such documents for thirty years.

Silent Running

On 30 October 1975, military personnel at the Wurtsmith Air Force Base, Michigan, reported seeing what appeared to be running lights of low-flying craft. The craft hovered up and down and performed erratic zigzag manoeuvres.

The base received several calls from outside personnel who had also seen this strange object. All of them reported that they had seen the same craft and they said that it was completely silent in operation.

A pilot in a KC-135 tanker reported seeing the object as he was preparing to land. The pilot was ordered to change course and try to observe what the object was. Several times as the KC-135 approached to within a mile or so of the object it would suddenly shoot away at a tremendous speed; this happened three or four times before the pilot had to return because of a shortage of fuel. The pilot later estimated that the object had flown at over a thousand knots.

A Freedom of Information Act request managed to turn up the following entry in the NORAD log: 'Alerted by NCOC of a helicopter sighted over Wurtsmith AFB Wpns storage area, a tanker sighted same and pursued it 35° SE over Lake Huron. Upon request of NCOC – Gen Wainwright and concurrence of Gen Taylor – contacted 379BW CP and offered assistance. Also advised ML, LH and JL alert of possibility of a scramble.'

There were also several reports from civilians in nearby towns who had also witnessed the object that same night.

Down Under, Again

In the early morning of 30 September 1980, near Rosedale, Victoria, an Australian cattle rancher was awoken by the sound of his frightened cattle. When he went outside, he saw a domed disc with orange and blue lights gliding about ten feet above the ground. It rose slightly in the air, hovered briefly above an open ten-thousand-gallon water tank, and then landed fifty feet away.

The rancher jumped on his motorbike and sped towards the object, which was making a 'whistling' sound. Suddenly an 'awful scream' sounded as a black tube extended from the UFO's base. With an ear-splitting bang, the strange craft rose into the air. A blast of air knocked the rancher down.

The sounds ceased as the object slowly moved to a position about thirty feet away and eight feet above the ground. Hovering briefly, it dropped debris – stones, weeds, cow dung – from underneath it, then flew away, disappearing in the east.

A ring of black flattened grass thirty feet in diameter marked the place where the disc had landed. When he examined it in the daylight, the witness discovered that all the yellow flowers within the circle had been removed. Only green grass remained. But even more bizarre, the water tank was empty, with no evidence of spillage. Only the muddy residue at the bottom of the tank was left – and it had been pulled into a two-foot-high cone shape. The witness was sick with headaches and nausea for more than a week afterward.

A similar ring of blackened grass was found the following December at Bundalaguah, not far from Rosedale. The water in a nearby reservoir was also mysteriously missing.

Red Light

On 13 August 1960, near midnight, while driving east of Corning, California, state police officers Stanley Carson and Charles Scott saw a lighted object drop out of the sky. Fearing the imminent crash, they slammed on the brakes and jumped out of their car.

The object continued to fall until it reached about one hundred feet, at which point it suddenly reversed direction and climbed four hundred feet, where it stopped and began to hover. Carson wrote in his official report:

'At this time, it was clearly visible to both of us. It was surrounded by a glow, making the round or oblong object visible,' he said. 'At each end, or each side of the object, there were definite red lights. At times about five white lights were visible between the red lights. As we watched, the object moved again and performed aerial feats that were actually unbelievable.'

The two officers radioed the Tehama County Sheriff's Office and asked it to contact the nearest Air Force Base, which was at Red Bluff. Radar confirmed the object's presence.

The UFO remained in view for more than two hours. During that time, two deputy sheriffs and the county jailer made independent sightings.

'On two occasions the object came directly towards the patrol vehicle,' said Carson. 'Each time it approached, the object turned, swept the area with a huge red light. Officer Scott turned the red light on the patrol vehicle towards the object, and it immediately went away from us. We observed the object use the red beam approximately six or seven times, sweeping the sky and ground areas. The object began moving slowly in an easterly direction and we followed. We proceeded to the Vina Plains Fire Station where it was approached by a similar object from the south. It moved near the first object and both stopped, remaining in that position for some time, occasionally emitting the red beam. Finally, both objects disappeared below the eastern horizon.'

Carson also noted that each time the object came near they experienced radio interference. No one has ever explained this sighting.

Encounters in Michigan

On 20 March 1966, near Dexter, Michigan, farmer Frank Mannor and his son watched a car-sized, football-shaped object with a central porthole and pulsating lights at each end of its brown, quilted surface rise from a swampy area on his farm, hover for several minutes at a thousand feet, and then then depart.

The following day, eighty-seven women students at Hillsdale College in Hillsdale, Michigan, their dean and a civil defence director all claimed to have watched, for four hours, a glowing football-shaped object hovering above a swampy area several hundred yards from the women's dormitory. At one point, the object flew directly towards the dormitory, then retreated. On another occasion the object appeared to 'dodge an airport beacon light'. Its glow would diminish when police cars approached, and it 'brightened when the cars left'.

The Michigan sightings made nearly every newspaper. Even the *New York Times* – which normally declined to run 'flying saucer' stories – gave it several inches. Major Hector Quintanilla, head of the US Air Force's Project Blue Book, which investigated UFO sightings, sent Blue Book's scientific consultant astronomer Dr. J. Allen Hynek to Michigan to investigate.

'By the time I arrived,' Hynek later wrote, 'the situation was so charged with emotion that it was impossible to do any serious investigating. I had to fight my way through reporters to interview witnesses. Police were madly chasing stars they thought to be flying saucers. People believed space ships were all over the area.'

Hynek spent a week interviewing witnesses; he even pulled on a pair of hip boots to wade through farmer Frank Mannor's swamp. Pressure mounted for an explanation, and on 27 March Hynek held the largest press conference in the Detroit Press Club's history. Hynek later described the gathering of television reporters, newspapermen, photographers and others, all 'clamouring for a single, spectacular explanation of the sightings,' as 'a circus'.

Hynek provided 'what I thought at the time to be the only explanation possible... I made the statement it was "swamp gas".' This is a faint glow caused when decaying vegetation has spontaneously ignited. He went on to emphasise he could not prove this in a court of law and that there was another explanation, but the press had picked up the words 'swamp gas' even before he had finished and that was what was reported. Naturally Hynek's 'swamp gas' explanation met with ridicule and hostility, and increased suspicion that the government was engaged in a cover-up.

Victor Alert

On the 1 July 1977, the NATO base at Aviano, Italy, which was closed for flying because a parade was being prepared, had a close encounter. At about 3 a.m. a USAF guard observed a strange object hovering above an area known as 'Victor Alert', which housed two secret jet fighters in a large hanger. The object was described as a large spinning top, 150 feet in diameter and hovering very low above the hangar. The upper surface was domed and had white, red and green lights emitting from its surface.

The USAF guard reported the incident and a team of military guards were sent to the hangar. The guards surrounded the area and radar personnel were contacted to see if they could pick the object up on their equipment. However, when they tried to access the radar consoles, the base was hit by a mysterious power-cut.

The incident was reported all the way up to NATO headquarters in Brussels, but it was later dismissed as the moon shining off some low clouds.

Soviet Sightings

During the Cold War, little of what happened on the other side of Iron Curtain was known in the West. There was the lingering suspicion that UFOs were in some way linked to the titanic struggle between the Communist bloc and the Western democracies. Sightings were often dismissed as secret weapons developed either by the US or by the Soviets.

It was not until the summer of 1991, and the so-called 'Second Russian Revolution', when Mikhail Gorbachev was toppled and Boris Yeltsin began dismantling Soviet Union itself, that UFOlogists in the West got their first hint that the Russians had been plagued with similar encounters. Then, as the KGB opened up, files detailing UFO sightings that had taken place between 1982 and 1995 were released.

One of the most recent encounters had occurred on 3 February 1995. Private Schepin and Private Zhabanov of the Russian Army were on guard at a fuel-oil depot near the settlement of Guzev in the Burg region when they saw a luminous dot, flying parallel to the ground at no great height, for several minutes.

'Between 2200 and 2400 hours I was in charge of Post Two guarding the south-eastern side of the depot,' says Zhabanov in his official account. 'At about 2400 hours, while patrolling the prescribed route from the observation tower to the Post One border, I heard a faint click, similar to the sound of a cigarette case being closed. On hearing this faint click, I turned around to check if everything was OK, but as I saw nothing suspicious I decided to walk on.

'Having taken a few steps, I felt a bright light above me... What attracted my attention was a luminous dot of a greenish colour similar to a signal flare, with a tail like it was a comet. It moved at an altitude of about 18-20 metres from the ground parallel to the perimeter. I observed this – let's call it an object – for only a few seconds. Since the moment that I first saw it, it had flown some distance.'

Zhabanov was unable to make any realistic estimate of the distance the 'object' had travelled before it suddenly separated into two parts.

'One part seemed to go out when it separated from the main [body] and descended. The second, larger part, having flown a certain distance, also began to burn out, and, having turned into a small dot, then disappeared from sight.'

The following morning, two soldiers guarding another post at the depot saw something similar, although they said the object was blue. One of them, Warrant Officer Yarosh, described a ball of light flying above the depot. Interestingly, he also said that a similar series of events had occurred at the depot in December 1983. He had reported these incidents to his superior officers at the time, but they had been unable to come up with any explanation. They said that as far as they knew there were no experimental aircraft on manoeuvres in the area at the time.

Another incident was recorded in 1983. This time it was witnessed by a more high-ranking officer and Communist Party official. Colonel Skrypnik was the duty officer at a top-secret installation. Its exact whereabouts are still classified, as its name had been deleted from the document when it was released. However, it is clear that it was somewhere near the city of Kursk in central Russia.

Interviewed seven days after the event took place, 'Col. Skrypnik recounted that at 6 a.m. on 17 October [1983], Major Kiselev... reported a visual contact with a UFO that was sporadically moving, changing its altitude and brightness, and periodically emitting a beam of light directed downwards. The UFO was of a round shape with a bright halo around it and a darker centre. The UFO was moving randomly and had no definite direction. Observers sighted the appearance of periodic light beams directed towards the earth. On its closest approaches to the ground, the UFO looked like a polyhedron, invariably with a shining halo around it.

'A P-12 radar... did not manage to pick up the object and produce any valuable data. By means of a geodetic level sited at Kursk, the UFO was visually fixed, illuminated by the rays of the rising sun, at an elevation angle of about 30–50° above the horizon...

'All the UFO observers are positive that the object they watched was not identical to any star in the observation sector. This was proved by the UFO's random movement, with altitude and brightness variations, and the periodic light beam directed towards the earth. The UFO was sighted at sunrise, when no stars are visible.'

But it was not just Skrypnik, Kiselev and their comrades who had seen it. According to the report, the object was observed from several cities. The names and ranks of the people who made the sightings were given and the KGB worked out by triangulation that the UFO must have been hovering above the city of Voronezh, three hundred miles south-east of Moscow. Attached to the report are the statements of twelve eyewitnesses, apparently stationed there, that confirm this. Indeed, sightings of UFOs were a regular occurrence in Voronezh. In 1989, schoolchildren there said that a UFO had landed in one of the city's parks and contact was made, according to a report from the Russian news agency Tass on 9 October. The case was investigated by Vladimir Lebedev and Dr Henry Silanov. According to Silanov's report: 'In the period between September 21 to October 28 1989, in the Western Park, six landings and one sighting (hovering) were registered, with the appearance of walking beings. We have collected a wealth of video materials with eyewitness accounts, particularly from pupils of the nearest school. We have no doubt that they are telling the truth.'

Inspection of the landing site revealed 'incredibly high levels of magnetism'. Imprints found in the ground indicated that an object weighing around eleven tonnes had landed there.

On 23 May 1985, a UFO crashed into the forest at Khabarovsk in south-east Russia. The report says: 'The next day at 04:00 an anomalous phenomenon was observed for 10–12 minutes at the Litovoko bombing range... by the [censored] regiment senior navigator programmer Major V.V. Kudriavtsev and meteorological section engineer Senior Lieutenant V.V. Maltsev. The ellipsoid object with light beams leaving it upwards and downwards was of a dull white colour. The intensity of the lower beam was much greater than that of the upper one. The object was moving at a high altitude and a high speed.'

Another sighting came from the industrial town of Khabarovsk on the night of 5–6 May. Lieutenant Colonel Kornienko reported the encounter to the KGB:

'Between 01:20 and 01:26, I sighted a strangely "behaving" object in the north-eastern part of the sky at a fairly large distance from where I was standing. The object, the shape of a cigar or an ellipsoid, was flying fast in a vertical attitude. Sectors of light – I cannot call them beams – were leaving the bottom part of the object.'

A number of other Soviet UFO sightings took place near to military installations, where there were trained military observers. However, as during the Cold War any information about these bases would be highly sensitive, the files are distinguished by their poverty of detail. But nothing could be done to disguise a cigar-shaped object that was seen flying over the slopes of Mount Aj-Petri in the Crimea in September 1983. A flying 'silver ball' had been seen there five years before. These sightings remain officially unexplained. A large saucer-shaped UFO was photographed hovering over a church in Yaroslavl near Moscow in 1983. And in 1991, seventeen-year-old Alexandr Pavlov photographed a UFO flying over the Volga near the town of Tver in Central Russia. He was too far away to tell how big it was but said, as he watched, it changed in shape from a disc into a ball.

One of the most intriguing UFO sightings in the KGB files happened on 12 November 1985; when Hasan Kayumovich Rakhimov was on guard duty at a military installation inside the USSR known cryptically as 'Post Seven'. According to his account, 'a ball of yellow-blue colour, the size of a football, suddenly appeared... about 30–40 metres from where I stood'.

The UFO was initially spotted when it was thirty to fifty feet above the ground, but it seemed to bounce up and down as it hopped across the base. 'Having made three or four hops of 50–100 metres,' Rakhimov said, 'it moved towards the dog-breeding quarters and disappeared.'

This may sound like a ball lightning phenomenon, a common feature of Russian encounters. However, another UFO sighting that occurred a few weeks earlier in the same area punches a hole in this theory. On that occasion, two civilians were out hunting when they saw a UFO that could not be explained as ball lightning.

'At 20:30 on 3 November 1985, I returned to my motor boat and started the motor to warm it up,' one of the men reported. 'Then I caught sight of a UFO moving at high speed from the north to the south at an altitude greater than that of an aeroplane. The UFO was a little bit larger than a star, and had a searchlight beam leaving it at an angle of 5–10 degrees. The weather was clear, and the UFO was clearly visible against a starry sky.

'The light beam covered about a quarter to a fifth of the distance from the object to the ground. The beam did not hit the ground, but scattered. When the UFO came closer, the motor on the boat suddenly stopped. I thought that the jolting might have caused the lever to slip into reverse. I pulled the starter cord after I had checked the fuel and opened the throttle. The motor started at once, but as it was running I saw a glow coming out of the ignition coil sockets. Having run for five to seven seconds, the motor stopped again. And it stopped abruptly, without slowing down. The UFO at that time was overhead.

'After the UFO flew south in the direction of Vladivostok we saw a satellite above it. The UFO and the satellite moved with the same speed and in the same direction. Having flown for some time more, the searchlight was switched off and the UFO was no longer visible.'

According to the KGB documents, a large number of UFO sightings occurred over the far east of Russia. In 1986, a huge flying saucer was photographed over Iturup, the largest of the Russian Kuril Islands. The Kamchatka peninsula in the far eastern corner of the mainland of the Russian Federation was home to other sightings in 1987 and 1988. Personnel at the Kura Missile Range regularly reported 'the overflights of ball-shaped unidentified flying objects'. Private Kolosov and Senior Lieutenant Vasilevski at Telemetry Instrumentation Site Three saw a UFO that resembled 'climbing lights changing their colour from red to white'.

In a military report, Senior Lieutenant Vasilevski pointed out that sightings of the UFOs are correlated with the scheduled launch times of heavy missiles,' claiming that 'when the times were slipped, the objects would not appear'. Others did not make that connection. In mid-December 1987, two privates and a warrant officer saw an orange ball of light moving from the north to the south. Similar objects were seen on two other occasions that same month and at intervals over the following year. On the night of 9–10 September 1988, a silver ball emitting a cone-shaped beam of light down towards the earth was sighted five minutes before a missile launch. The UFO appeared to be the size of the moon when viewed from the earth.

Vasilevski's encounters were reported from three different locations and sightings lasted from thirty seconds to three minutes. The UFOs were also seen by officers stationed on the top of Lyzyk mountain, near the range's missile site. The testimony of these two officers is more important because they were trained observers. And as senior personnel, they had more to lose.

The sighting of UFOs over Russia and Soviet Central Asia continued in the final years of the Soviet Union. On 22 September 1989, in the south-west Russian city of Astrakhan, half-a-dozen individual witnesses saw a glowing, red 'drop-shaped' UFO near Koxhevaya railway station. Three other witnesses said the object was yellow, but had seen it on and off for forty-five to fifty minutes.

Six days later, near the runway of a nearby air base, two 'luminous, violet and red dots nearly a metre in diameter' were seen by several witnesses. A month later, another 'red drop' was seen by a large number of civilian and military witnesses near the village of Burkhala in the Yagodinski region.

Nine months before the Soviet Union collapsed, a handful of witnesses saw bright white flashes in the sky over the town of Aleksandrov, not far from Moscow. They reported seeing them anything from four or five kilometres up to just a few metres off the ground. Their estimates of the speeds of these objects and descriptions of their flight patterns also varied widely. One was seen over the eternal flame in the Tomb of the Unknown Soldier in Karabavano. It seems that the UFO emitted a flash of light that momentarily lit up the monument.

Flying Triangles were also seen over the Soviet Union in March 1990. One was even photographed over the Russian town of Tagresk. Speculation was – as in the West – that it was some kind of experimental aircraft. But that would not explain why one attacked a radar station at Kuybishev, Samara, near the Tarta province in Russia on 13 September 1990. It was witnessed by Corporal S. Dudnik.

'I watched the approaching flight of a big, black triangular craft, each side about fifty feet in length,' he said. 'It landed after coming down vertically, rather slowly and making a rattling noise. The flash of light, which shattered the radar antennae behind me, came out of the middle of the object. I could see no opening there, but it seemed to be aiming at its target and I found myself directly in its line of fire. Oddly enough, nothing happened to me, but the antennae collapsed and began to burn brightly.' The team who inspected the collapsed radar antennae could not explain how the steel parts could have been melted by a beam of energy fired from 160 yards away.

On 3 March 1991, a diamond-shaped craft was photographed over the Tevare military base by a gang of local youths. It hovered menacingly before disappearing. Another strange diamond-shaped craft was caught on video by Nikolai Yegorov over the Crimean city of Sevastopol in August 1993. It shows the UFO accelerating from ground level to a high altitude, and disappearing within the space of a minute.

It is clear from these reports and others in the KGB files that the UFO sightings reported in the West throughout the years of the Cold War also occurred behind the Iron Curtain – and the Soviet authorities were just perplexed by them as their counterparts in the West. The question remains for UFOlogists: Is this apparent lack of interest in UFOs by the authorities in the former Soviet Union and in the West simply because they do not believe in such things, or because they already know what they are and are not saying?

Certainly the KGB files contain little by the way of analysis and the

Soviet authorities seem to have made little effort to follow up on the sightings. They do seem to take them seriously, though. The man charged to investigate them was the president of the State Security Committee, Commander Popovitch. A letter from Popovitch in the file outlines the official position.

'The State Security Committee [SSC] has never been engaged in systematic gathering and analysis of information on anomalous phenomena (the so-called Unidentified Flying Objects). At the same time the SSC of the USSR has been receiving statements from a number of persons and agencies on cases of observations of the above phenomena. We forward you copies of such statements. At an earlier date the same material was sent to the Central Machine Building Research Institute in the town of Kalingrad.'

The investigation went no further.

Encounter in Rendlesham Forest

East Anglia has been home to a great deal of UFO activity, especially during the Cold War, when a large number of Air Force personnel, both British and American, were stationed there. In 1980, an incident occurred in Rendlesham forest that became one of the most intriguing cases in the annals of UFOlogy. Rendlesham is a vast pine forest that lies to the east of the county town, Ipswich. It runs across Suffolk, hitting the coast at a spit called Orford Ness, which is just down the coast from the nuclear power station at Sizewell. The Ness is known for its lighthouse, but it is also home to other mysterious buildings. Although officially they were home to research on over-the-horizon radar, at the time it was thought that the US's largest and most secretive intelligence, the National Security Agency – America's equivalent of Britain's GCHQ – was conducting top secret experiments known as 'Cobra Mist' there, involving prototype 'Star Wars' weapons. Also in the area were the twin NATO air bases of Bentwaters and Woodbridge, which were rented from the RAF by the US Air Force and, during the Cold War, were manned exclusively by USAF personnel.

On the night of Christmas Day 1980, a UFO was spotted over Rendlesham forest by Gordon Levett, who lived in a remote cottage near the village of Sudbourne. He was out in the garden with his dog. When the dog began barking, Levett looked up to see the UFO flying towards him. He said it was shaped like an upturned mushroom, glowing with a greenish-white phosphorescent light. It stopped briefly and hovered directly above him, at about rooftop height. Then it glided silently on in the direction of RAF Woodbridge.

Shortly after Levett's sighting, in the early hours of 26 December, the Webb family were returning home from a Christmas party. They were driving down the B road that snakes gently through the woodland between the villages of Woodbridge and Orford. Suddenly they spotted a huge white light over the trees. Aircraft activity was common in the area. Both American Chinook helicopters and A-10 Thunderbolts regularly disturbed the peace, but this strange light appeared to be very different from normal air traffic. For one thing it was silent. The Webbs were puzzling what it might when it suddenly plunged into the woods.

US Air Force security patrolmen Budd Parker and John Burroughs were at the east gate of RAF Woodbridge that night. They saw the light in the sky which, they said, looked like a Christmas tree. When it crashed into the forest, they assumed that an aircraft had been downed. Then they realised something odd was going on. The object had not simply plunged earthwards. It drifted downwards, as if under control. There was no explosion as it hit the ground. Now was there any sense of impact. All they could see in the forest was a mass of flashing coloured lights.

Burroughs phoned base HQ. It was 2 a.m. and he was told that no aircraft should have been in the area at that time. Nevertheless, base security despatched Sergeant Jim Penniston to investigate in a jeep driven by Herman Kavanasac.

As the UFO had flown over, David Roberts and his girlfriend had been enjoying a few moments of tenderness out on the grass under the trees. They had been hoping that the midwinter darkness would protect them from the prying eyes of any late-night passers-by. But suddenly the cloak of darkness was snatched from them as the sky filled with light. Then the earth moved for them as something heavy crashed into the ground less than half-a-mile away. They had barely had time to compose themselves when a military jeep came hurtling down the forest trail towards the crash site. Its lights were flashing and its sirens blaring. Something serious was going on. The romance of moment was lost and they fled.

Outside the east gate, Penniston and Kavanasac saw strange-coloured lights flickering through the trees. Penniston assumed command. He told Parker and Burroughs that this was an emergency. A plane had gone down in the forest and was burning furiously. But they were not convinced. As far as they were concerned, whatever was in the wood had landed, not crashed.

Penniston led Burroughs and Kavanasac out into the forest to investigate, leaving Parker manning the gate. As they made their way deeper into the wood, they found that radio contact with the base began to break down. Their communication was swamped with static as if they were in the presence of a massive electric field. So Penniston told Kavanasac to station himself at the edge of an access route, where the radio still worked. From there, he could act as a communications relay.

Penniston and Burroughs continued on into the woods. Penniston was convinced that they would find an aircraft ablaze in the forest but, as they approached a clearing, the air crackled with static electricity. The two men's skin began to tingle and their hair stood on end. In the clearing they saw, not tangled wreckage, but a strange craft. It was conical and, Penniston said, it hovered about a foot above the ground on beams of light, though other witnesses said it had legs. There were strange black markings on the side in some alien script and the whole object was bathed in a glowing aura.

'The air was filled with electricity,' said Penniston, 'and we saw an object about the size of a tank. It was made of moulded black glass and had symbols on it... It was definitely not in the Jane's Book of World Aircraft.'

Although he could not readily identify it, it was Penniston's job to

321

find out what it was. So after a few moments gathering his thoughts, Penniston tried to approach the craft. But he and Burroughs found themselves in the grip of a force field. They said it was like trying to wade through molasses. They went through the motions of walking but could not seem to get any closer to the object.

Then suddenly there was a flash of light and the craft shot skywards. With this, the sleepy forest became alive with birds fleeing their roosts and deer bolting for cover. All the airmen could do was stand open-mouthed as they stared into the sky.

The morning after Penniston and Burroughs' close encounter in Rendlesham Forest, tangible evidence of the presence of a UFO was found. The tops of the trees had been smashed off, leaving a huge swathe through the forest as if something heavy had crashed from the sky. Gordon Levett's dog was found shivering in its kennel, terrified to come out. It became ill and the vet was called. He could only speculate that the dog had been poisoned. There was nothing he could do and, within a couple of days, the dog was dead.

An A-10 fighter flew over the site at dawn and detected a high level of radiation in the area. In the frozen soil at the landing site, three indentations were found. These matched the location of the beams or legs seen under the mysterious craft the night before. The area was surveyed in detail and plaster casts taken. However, the police showed little interest, dismissing the indentations as rabbits' holes. The Ministry of Defence made no effort to investigate. According to MoD UFO investigator Nick Pope, this was ruled out by the US authorities.

However, this was not the end of the matter. The following evening, there was a party for officers at RAF Bentwaters. Base commander Ted Conrad was about to make an after-dinner speech when acting night security commander Lieutenant Bruce Englund burst in to report that a security patrol near the Woodbridge road had seen strange lights floating in the sky over the forest. 'It' was back. Conrad ordered his deputy, Lieutenant Colonel Charles Halt, to make a thorough investigation. Halt quickly assembled a team of skilled airforce personnel and equipment. Halt grabbed a portable Dictaphone to take notes. Englund commandeered some gas-powered arc lights to illuminate the forest, and Sergeant Nevells of the 'Disaster Preparedness' unit carried a Geiger counter to measure radiation. John Burroughs also turned up to join the group.

Halt established a security cordon around the perimeter of the wood. The strange lights the security patrol had seen were no longer visible. Although he could not see the UFO, Halt had no doubts that it was still there. Just as Penniston and Burroughs had reported previously, radio communications – both between members of the team and with the base – were swamped with static and the security cordon had to serve as a relay. Halt also had trouble with the 'light-all' arc lights he had brought. They kept cutting out and he sent back to base for new ones.

In the gloom, there was nothing visible except for a few stars and the beam of the Orford Ness lighthouse and the Shipwash lightship to the south. Halt and his men knew the area well enough not to confuse these lights with UFO activity. Without any further sighting to go on, Halt began an accurate record of the situation and began making notes on his Dictaphone.

'One-hundred-and-fifty feet or more from the initial – I should say suspected – impact point. Having a little difficulty. Can't get the light-alls to work... Meanwhile we're gonna take some readings with the Geiger counter and, ah, chase around the area a little bit, waiting for another light-all to come out.'

In the background on the tape, the clicks of the Geiger counter could be heard soaring. The radiation levels rose to ten times the normal background level. This was significant, but just short of danger level, so Halt continued with his investigation.

The team began taking samples of tree bark and soil, and photographed the damage they found in the area. An infra-red night vision detector picked up heat or some form of energy. This activity went on for more than an hour.

Then, at 1:48 a.m., a group of men who had ventured deeper into the forest, including Burroughs and Sergeant Adrian Bustinza, spotted something. Bustinza described it as a glowing light resting on a pillar of yellowish mist and split in the middle like a rainbow produced by a prism. On the tape, Halt can be heard telling his men to 'slow down' and be careful. He, too, had seen the light.

'There's no doubt about it,' he said on the tape. 'There's some type of strange flashing red light ahead… It appears to be moving a bit this way. It's brighter than it has been. It's definitely coming this way. There's no doubt about it. This is weird.'

The light grew and changed shape. It began to look like a large eye with a dark pupil at its centre. Initially, Halt said he thought it must be a mirage or atmospheric phenomenon such as a temperature inversion. But as it moved through the forests he became convinced that this was no earthly phenomenon.

Halt and his group of airmen chased the light through the woods, across a farmer's field and over a small brook. For more than an hour they followed it, with Halt recording details of the encounter on tape: 'Zero three fifteen – now we've got an object about ten degrees directly south.'

Suddenly, without warning, the object soared into the air. After a moment of silence, Halt's quavering voice can be heard saying: 'Now we observe what appears to be a beam coming down towards the ground – this is unreal.'

By this time Halt's team were tired and wet. Some of them had forded a stream. So, with the strange lights still visible above RAF Woodbridge, they turned for home. As they reached the perimeter fence, they saw laser-like beams shining down into the security area. One beam hit the ground so close to Halt that he thought they were under attack. And it was not just the military personnel on the base who saw the beams. Local residents witnessed them too. Sarah Richardson, whose bedroom overlooked the air base, said she saw 'bands of rippling colour' in the night sky.

The military tried to hush the story up. But rumours began to circulate among radar officers at RAF Watton after USAF intelligence staff commandeered their radar record for the 1980 Christmas period.

The reason given was that a UFO had crashed into forest. Senior USAF officers had witnessed the event and they had even seen extraterrestrials floating in beams under the alien craft. Three days later, USAF intelligence officers collected the records from RAF Neatishead. On the night of 26 December, the radar there had also detected an unidentified flying object. It had created a furore in the control room when it returned no identification and seemed to outperform NATO's best planes. When it disappeared off the screen at phenomenal speed it prompted a major investigation.

The story of the Rendlesham forest encounter leaked to the world of UFOlogy when, in January 1981, local paranormal researcher Brenda Butler was contacted by an American friend who was a USAF security police officer at Bentwaters and Woodbridge. He claimed that in the early hours of 26 December, he and two other guards had been sent into Rendlesham forest. There had been reports of a flying light crashing into the woods. When the men arrived they found a disc-shaped craft on tripod legs resting on the ground. They radioed back to the base for back-up and over the next couple of hours senior personnel came out to the site. But Butler's friend also reported that several small aliens, about three feet tall with grey skin and large heads, were seen floating around the craft as if making repairs. He also claimed that one of the senior officers tried to communicate with the aliens using sign language.

Together with UFO researchers Jenny Randles and Dot Street, Butler started collating eyewitness evidence and testimony. The three of them put together a book on the incident called *Sky Crash*. Its publication opened the floodgates. New witnesses came forward. One of the witnesses was a forestry worker, who stumbled onto the crash site a day after the crash. He said he reported the damage to the trees and the indentations on the ground to the local authorities. But when he returned the next day, the entire site had been cleared. The trees had been felled and the ground dug up.

The publication of *Sky Crash* alerted American UFO researchers, who eventually managed to obtain a secret memo on the incident through the Freedom of Information Act. The memo was written by Lieutenant Colonel Charles Halt. The circulation codes showed that it had been sent to Britain's Ministry of Defence as early as 13 January 1981 – although the MoD had told Jenny Randles that no such memo existed.

Halt's memo detailed three separate events. The landing of a small craft on the first night, the discovery of ground traces with excess radiation readings and another sighting the following night, which Halt himself had witnessed.

There is no doubt that Lieutenant Colonel Charles Halt was an extremely reliable witness. A professional soldier, he had been stationed in Japan and served in Vietnam. Soon after the Rendlesham incident, he was promoted to full colonel. Later, as commander of Bentwaters air base, he oversaw the deployment and, later, the decommissioning of cruise missiles there. He then took a staff job in the Pentagon before retiring in 1992 to take a job in the aviation industry.

The Halt memo also mentions a second document about the case. This has not been cleared for release to UFO researchers on the grounds of 'national security'.

Gordon Levett came forward with the tale of his sighting and the death of his dog. And a radar operator from the tracking station at RAF Watton told researchers that two days after the incident, USAF personnel came to the tracking station and removed all radar recordings for the previous two nights. These were never seen again.

All this new information, along with a transcript of the tape recording made by Halt on the night of the encounter, were put together by Jenny Randles in a second book, *From Out of the Blue*.

The other USAF airmen involved in the incident – Penniston, Burroughs, Bustinza and others – have since left the service and have spoken out. One of them was Larry Warren, a USAF security policeman who had been posted to England on 1 December 1980, just weeks before the incident.

'I was taken off my post to the forest,' he said, 'with a number of other personnel who were bringing lighting equipment out used to illuminate large areas, but it wouldn't work because of some mechanical malfunction. We still had no idea what we were up to.'

It was then that Warren saw a light moving through the forest.

'A dim red light, opposite the Orford lighthouse, stopped over a strange mist on the ground. It quickly transformed into a triangular object approximately thirty feet high. It had a solid structure, with a rough surface.'

Warren said that some men ran away. He, and others, stayed put. He said he could not move, but does not know whether that was because of shock or some external force.

'It was very dreamlike... I think time was distorted and perceptions were intentionally affected by this intelligence. There was one reality and in front of you was another. I felt slower on that night. Everything was on half speed and something was wrong; something was out of place.'

In all, some thirty military personnel, including senior officers, were all sent out into the forest to investigate. They all report witnessing something remarkable. Whatever they saw, they are convinced that it could not have been a plane crash or a secret aircraft downed in the woods, as it hit the forest then took off again. It was also seen to perform manoeuvres that seemed to defy the normal laws of physics. Some of the witnesses even claimed that they saw beams of light pass through jeeps and trees as if they were transparent.

So was the object in the forest a craft from another world? The witnesses do not rule out that possibility, but they say they cannot prove it. Was the craft under intelligent control? Some feel that some fantastic energy force, of unknown origin, might have created a natural UFO. A few think that a portal to a different dimension might have opened briefly under the influence of some natural earth energy.

Clifford Stone, a former US government intelligence agent, came up with a more intriguing theory. He claims that the Pentagon considers the Rendlesham forest incident presents some of the most persuasive evidence that we are not alone. He believes that the aliens that were seen 'did not originate on earth' and they were 'intruders from a parallel dimension – coming through a breach in the quantum basis of matter.'

On the other hand, sceptics, such as astronomer Ian Ridpath, says that all the witnesses saw was a bright meteor that crossed the skies of East Anglia around 2:50 a.m. This had lured the security personnel into the forest. Once there, the American airmen, who were unfamiliar with Suffolk surroundings, mistook the beam from the lighthouse on Orford Ness four miles away for a UFO. Ridpath maintains that the Rendlesham case is 'a ghastly embarrassment to UFOlogy'.

A bright meteor did indeed fly across south-east England on the night of 26 December. It was seen by numerous observers. But both the sighting report by Penniston and Burroughs and the testimony of the civilian witnesses show that they saw the UFO well before the meteor flew by at 2:50 a.m. Indeed, it has been suggested that the 'meteor' might even have been the UFO departing. Both Penniston and Burroughs say they saw the lighthouse as well as the UFO. They had been posted to the area for some time. Burroughs, particularly, liked to picnic in the woods and was familiar with the lighthouse.

Eyewitness Charles Halt also rejected Ridpath's theory. 'A lighthouse doesn't move through a forest,' he said. 'It doesn't explode, doesn't change shape, doesn't send down beams of light.'

Nevertheless, Ridpath was joined by other critics, including psychologist Nicholas Humphrey. In a Channel Four documentary and the pages of *New Scientist* magazine, he argued that what the witnesses saw was actually the flashing light on a police car that was called into the forest to investigate the crash. The problem was that the police car went to the forest in response to the airmen's sighting and, consequently, arrived after them.

Other sceptics say that the airmen saw a Russian rocket that re-entered the earth's atmosphere that night. Astronomer John Mason confirms that a 'brilliant natural fireball' caused by the rocket burning up was seen by many in south-east England. Others say that a Soviet satellite fell to earth over East Anglia that night and that it may even have been shot down by the Star Wars weapons being tested at secret establishments in the area.

The possibility has been raised that there was some nuclear accident at one of the airbases and the military cooked up the UFO story to cover their tracks. At the time, the MoD denied that there were nuclear weapons at RAF Bentwaters, but more than ten years later admitted that there were.

However, this does nothing to explain what Penniston and Burroughs saw. They say they came very close to a craft that was like nothing they had ever seen before – and Halt and others saw the same thing the next night. Burroughs does not claim to have any answers, but insists: 'I do not know whether this was some kind of machine under intelligent control or a fantastic natural phenomenon – some rare kind of energy. What I do know is that it was nothing mundane. There are no words that can adequately describe the wonder of what we saw.'

Neither Burroughs nor Penniston were told the results of the investigation into the incident. Within hours, they were out of the loop. Halt discussed the case with his RAF liaison officer, Squadron Leader Donald Moreland. After that meeting, there was a publicity clampdown. Soon top-secret flights were landing at the air bases, bringing in personnel from America's covert intelligence agencies.

Retired Chief of Staff at the Ministry of Defence Admiral Lord Hill-Norton questioned the Defence Minister Lord Trefgarne about the incident and was told simply that there were no defence implications to the case. Similarly Michael Heseltine, Minister of Defence in the Thatcher government, said: 'There is not a grain of truth in the allegation that there has been a cover-up about alleged UFO sightings.'

However, Ralph Noyes, former under-secretary at the Ministry of Defence who headed the division that investigated UFO sightings, said that that was exactly what had happened.

'We now have the evidence – I blush to say about my own Ministry of Defence – that they have lied about this case,' he says. 'They have covered up.'

Sky Serpents

Even stranger things can be seen in the sky. In the early months of 1994, Santiago Ytturia had seen numerous UFOs in the skies over his hometown Monterrey in north-east Mexico and he was determined to capture one of them on film. So on 19 March 1994, Santiago Ytturia set up his video camera in the garden of his home and waited.

He kept his eyes on the skies but, after more than an hour of waiting, nothing happened. He was just about to give up, when his vigil was rewarded. Suddenly, a flashing light appeared in the sky. But as fast it had appeared, it disappeared again, leaving Ytturia bewildered. He waited for it to re-appear. He waited and waited, in vain. Eventually, Ytturia took down his camera. Then he went inside and replayed the video, just to see if he had captured the fleeting sighting. Sure enough, on reviewing the footage carefully, frame by frame, he saw the image of the glowing UFO. But as he checked the rest of the tape he found something even more intriguing.

A few frames after the fleeting appearance of the UFO, Ytturia noticed a brief but distinctive image. It was a long, spear-shape object, which flew across the screen at incredible speed. Analysing the footage a frame at a time, he calculated that the object was moving much too fast to be an insect or bird. Indeed, it could only be seen at all when the video was reviewed using stop frame. Ytturia was quickly convinced that he had captured something unique on film. What it was, he did not know. Nor did he know how it was linked to the recent UFO activity.

The phenomenon that Ytturia captured on video has since been dubbed a 'rod'. On careful analysis of other footage, similar anomalous objects have been discovered on videos filmed all around the world and a number of leading UFOlogists have turned their attention to the study of rods. One of the key figures in the investigation is Jose Escamilla. The owner of a video production company, Escamilla and his team of independent investigators have obtained spectacular footage and photographs of rods from countries around the world, including the UK, the US, Mexico, Canada, Sweden and Norway. Although they are usually seen flying through the air at incredible speeds, Escamilla also has film of rods underwater.

Despite the copious footage, the appearance of rods is so fleeting that little is known about them. However, what researchers have agreed upon so far is that rods are organic. These UFOs are living creatures and not just some new form of alien craft.

As sightings of rods have regularly coincided with UFO activity, some researchers believe that they are some sort of extraterrestrial life form. Others believe that they may be an as-yet undiscovered type of terrestrial life. Naturally, sceptics have dismissed the sightings as stray insects, birds, lens flares or even camera trickery.

Detailed examination of the video footage has revealed several consistent features. The creatures are cigar-shaped and range in length from approximately four inches to about ten feet. Amazingly, they travel at speeds of up to 190 miles an hour, propelled by a solid, undulating membrane along each side of their body which vibrates extremely rapidly.

Jim Peterson, the Assistant State Director of MUFON in Colorado and another rods investigator, says: 'Rods are very hard to see with the naked eye. Usually, they are so fleeting and so fast that the brain just filters them out of your vision. Consequently, they have been virtually invisible until the recent advent of camcorders, where their presence has generally been captured accidentally.'

Even with thirty frames per second (fps), state-of-the-art video cameras still have difficulty in capturing detailed pictures of rods because of their enormous speeds. Within just a few frames they are gone. Even in the frames where they appear, their fantastic speeds mean that they appear as little more than a blur, so it is impossible to work out the details of their morphology. So far, it has not been possible to make out whether they have a head or eyes. Escamilla plans to obtain a special camera that can shoot 500 fps, rather than the 30 fps. At that speed, you can freeze the motion of a speeding bullet, so investigators should be able to determine more about the creatures' structure.

However, Escamilla has already been able to dismiss the cavils of critics. Rods can easily be distinguished from lens flares, he says, and lens flares do not manoeuvre around the frame when the camera is static. He has also shot rods footage that has insects, birds and rods all in the same frame. With a shutter speed of 1/10,000th of a second, he points out, the flight of an insect or bird is frozen, so you can easily make out what it is. But the flight of rods is so fast that the shutter can't freeze their motion and all you get is a blurred streak. However, it is just possible to see the undulating membranes that run down each side of rods' bodies. Escamilla says that these establish that, whatever these creatures are, they are not any known biological organism. His problem is to find out just what they are.

One extraordinary piece of video footage shows just how fast rods can fly. It was shot at a military gunnery range in Sundsvall, Sweden. A tank was filmed loosing off eight rounds in three seconds. As the tank fires, the shell casings are ejected through the top of the turret. A rod flashes through the frame and is gone before the first casing hits the ground.

The best video footage showing rods was shot by TV cameraman Mark Lichtle. In 1996, he was filming base jumpers parachuting into a deep ravine in Mexico. As in most cases involving rods, no one noticed them at the time. It was only when he ran the video back in slow motion that Lichtle saw swarms of rods darting in and out of the frame. They flew around the base jumpers as they free-falled into the ravine. In one shot, a rod is seen veering away at the last second to avoid colliding with one of the jumpers.

Lichtle's footage was examined by optical expert Dr Bruce Maccabee, who also analysed the Gulf Breeze UFO footage. He calculated that the objects were between six and twelve feet long – far too large to be either an insect or a bird.

In 1997, Escamilla presented his selection of footage to zoologists and entomologists from the University of Colorado. 'They were totally baffled by what they saw,' he says. 'All they could say was that it was unlike anything they had ever seen and that it deserved further study.'

Because there were so many rods in the ravine, Escamilla believes that it is some form of habitat for the creatures and, consequently, the ideal place to film and study them. Biologist Ken Swartz took up the challenge and has been investigating the phenomenon since 1998.

'Rods appear to be biological,' he says, 'but without a physical specimen it is difficult to say anything conclusively. They seem to be amphibious, as they have been seen entering and leaving water. Perhaps they are born in the sea and emerge into the air?'

Swartz has discovered some eyewitness testimony of people who claim to have seen them on the ground. This seems to indicate that they have some similarities to the family of creatures known as cephalopods. 'There have been descriptions of them expanding like a balloon and rapidly deflating,' he says, 'so they could be using a mechanism similar to a squid, which sucks in water and jets it out for propulsion.'

What puzzles Swartz most is the creatures' enormous speed. This would mean that it would have to have a phenomenal metabolic rate. 'Even a hummingbird's incredibly rapid metabolic rate would still be nowhere near as fast as that of a rod,' he says. 'I estimate it would have to consume its own weight in food every day.'

Another problem is that, if they are biological entities, how come no one has found the body of a dead one? The video footage indicates that they are quite common, yet not a single dead body has been discovered on the ground. 'One feasible explanation,' says Swartz, 'is that, like a squid, they have no hard body parts and so could decompose without a trace.'

Undeterred by the lack of physical evidence, Swartz has turned to the evolutionary record for clues. 'If you look at the fossil record,' he says, 'there is only one creature that ever lived that had the rod mode of locomotion, and this was the dominant predator of the time called anamalocaris, which lived in the sea during the Cambrian evolutionary expansion four hundred million years ago.' According to Swartz, the creature propelled itself by a row of plates or fins that vibrated in a similar manner to the membranes seen on rods. From this, he concludes: 'It is possible that anamalocaris is the evolutionary ancestor

333

of rods.'

Another evolutionary theory has been floated by British entomologist Dr Steven Wooten. He worked with palaeobiologists to create a theoretical reconstruction of original ancestors of modern-day insects. The creature they came up with was related to the now-extinct anamalocaris and is called a protopterygote. 'This creature looks amazingly like a rod,' says Jim Peterson. 'It is possible then that rods originally evolved from anamalocaris through this ancestor of insects and then took its own evolutionary path.' As yet, no one is sure.

Another remarkable piece of footage was shot on 3 May 1999, by meteorologist Garry England, when he was filming a tornado in Oklahoma for the local TV channel News Nine. When he reviewed the tape, he saw a rod flying towards the tornado at a height of around three thousand feet. It was about ten foot long and was seemingly unaffected by the 450-miles-per-hour wind. 'If these creatures are alive, they must be incredibly durable,' said England. 'The wind did not even slow it down.'

Near Misses and Encounters

Near Misses

The end of its routine two-hour flight from Milan on 6 January 1995 took British Airways flight BA 5061 though the UK's UFO hotspot over the south Pennines. It was already dark as it began its descent into Manchester Airport. The time was 6:48 p.m. and the Boeing 737 was flying at about four thousand feet as it prepared to turn towards runway 24. First officer Mark Stuart was monitoring the instruments, while Captain Roger Wills battled a strong north-westerly wind at the controls. Neither were prepared for what happened next.

The UFO flashed by at high speed, missing the right side of the aircraft by as little as three feet. In less than three seconds it was gone. The ashen-faced first officer turned to the Captain and said, 'Did you see that?' Captain Wills had indeed seen the object. Fortunately, due to the restricted view from the small side windows, none of the passengers had.

'I saw something out of my peripheral vision,' said Stuart. 'My instinct was to grab the controls as it seemed to be coming towards us. But I was unable to move more than an inch before it was upon us and past us.'

The crew called the tower at Manchester airport and asked if there were any other aircraft in the vicinity. Air traffic control reported that they could see no other plane on the radar screen. When the plane landed safely at Manchester, the crew sat down to discuss whether they should file an 'air miss' report. They were in broad agreement about what they had seen and decided to go ahead. Their report says: 'The first officer... looked up in time to see a dark object pass down the side of the aircraft at high speed; it was wedge-shaped with a black stripe.'

The pilots also attached sketches of what they saw, drawn minutes after they landed. First Officer Stuart drew a silver wedge-shaped craft with streaks along the side. Captain Wills saw it more as a series of lights, but agreed that the UFO was wedge shaped. Now it was up to the Civil Aviation Authority to find out what had nearly knocked them out of the sky.

The story was leaked to the press and made front-page news, especially as the UFO had also been seen from the ground by Manchester student Mark Lloyd, who said it was 'the size of Wembley stadium'. Wills and Stuart declined to give interviews, while the CAA struggled to come up with some plausible explanation. But with no reasonable answers to hand, eventually, even the CAA began speculating about UFOs – this is thought to be the first time an official air miss report mentioned 'extraterrestrial activity'. However, the CAA refused to go too far down that alley, saying: 'Fascinating though it may be, it is not within the [air miss] group's remit and must be left to those whose interest lies in that field.' But the fact that the CAA even mentioned the possibility of UFOs caused a storm in the tabloids. It was taken to mean that the plane had actually encountered aliens.

There could, of course, have been other explanations. The crew of BA 5061 might have encountered a bright fireball meteor, known as a bolide. Or it could have seen a piece of space debris falling back into the earth's atmosphere and burning up. These often cause strange lights high in the atmosphere.

But it may be that BA 5061 had a narrow escape that night. On 24 August 1984, a Britten-Norman Trislander operated by Kondair was on a cargo flight from London Stansted to Amsterdam when it was struck by an unidentified flying object with such force that it lost an engine. The aircraft managed to fly on to Schiphol, where it was forced to make an emergency landing. Once safely on the ground, the plane was examined. There was a large hole in the tail fin where something had passed right through. It was not a bird strike, as anomalous metallic fragments were discovered there.

The civil aviation authorities in the UK and Holland could come up with no explanation. The Ministry of Defence was brought in, in case some sort of military technology might have been involved, but they were equally baffled. Again there was speculation that the plane had been hit by space debris re-entering the atmosphere, but that would have been a billion-to-one freak event. But something had hit the aircraft. Although it had survived, next time a plane might not be so lucky.

There has been a long history of aerial sightings that cannot be easily explained. Until World War II, the skies were virtually empty. But with the war there were suddenly thousands of aircraft in flight over Europe and the Pacific on bombing raids and reconnaissance missions every night. Soon there were numerous reports of strange lights that appeared to tail Allied aircraft. These mysterious lights – usually only a foot or so in diameter – littered the skies as if they were observing the great aerial battles, yet they never interfered. The US Army Air Force, as it was then, dubbed them 'foo fighters', after the euphemistic expletive use by the character Smokey Stover in a popular American newspaper comic strip. It was only after the war that they discovered German and Japanese pilots were seeing foo fighters too.

Even after the end of the war, American military aircraft continued to report encounters with foo fighters, though they soon became known as UFOs. On 24 July 1948, two experienced Eastern Airlines crew members, pilot Clarence S. Chiles and his co-pilot, John B. Whitted, while en route from Houston to Atlanta, encountered a one hundred-foot-long, wingless, finless, cigar-shaped object with two rows of large, square windows that emanated a bright, glowing light from within.

On a seeming collision course with the UFO, Chiles threw his DC-3 airliner into a tight left-hand banking turn, and the object, with a forty-foot orange red flame flashing from its tail, shot past not more that seven hundred feet away. The object was tracked on radar and no explanation of the sighting has ever been given.

In 1952, there was a spate of anomalous sightings. On 14 July, two long-serving Pan American pilots encountered UFOs as they flew over Washington, D.C. They reported that the craft behaved in a controlled manner. Then, between 19 July and 26 July, the D.C. area was invaded by numerous UFOs, which were picked up on radar screens. Because of the possibility of a security threat to the Pentagon and the White House, a full investigation was ordered. When the news reached British Prime Minister Winston Churchill on 28 July, he wrote to the Secretary of State for Air, Lord Cherwell, asking, 'What does all this stuff about flying saucers amount to? What is the truth?' He was about to find out.

Military Encounters

Between 19 September and 21 September 1952, the NATO manoeuvre Operation Mainbrace over England was intercepted by UFOs and, in the North Sea, an aircraft carrier carrying nuclear weapons was buzzed by a strange disc.

One of the most compelling cases occurred on the first day of the exercise, 19 September 1952, when two RAF officers and three aircrew at RAF Topcliffe observed a strange object which appeared to be following a Meteor jet. In a written statement, Flight Lieutenant John Kilburm wrote:

'The Meteor jet was crossing from east to west when I noticed the white object in the sky. This object was silver and circular in shape, about ten thousand feet up some five miles astern of the aircraft. It appeared to be travelling at a lower speed than the Meteor but was on the same course.

'I said "What the hell's that?" and the chaps looked to where I was pointing. Somebody shouted that it might be the engine cowling of the Meteor falling out of the sky. Then we thought it might be a parachute. But as we watched the disc maintained a slow forward speed for a few seconds before starting to descend. While descending it was swinging in a pendulum fashion from left to right.

'As the Meteor jet turned to start its landing run the object appeared hung in the air, rotating as if on its own axis. Then it accelerated at an incredible speed to the west, turned south-east and then disappeared. It is difficult to estimate the object's speed. The incident happened within a matter of fifteen to twenty seconds. During the few seconds that it rotated we could see it flashing in the sunshine. It appeared to be about the size of a Vampire jet aircraft at a similar height.

'We are all convinced that it was some solid object. We realised very quickly that it could not be a broken cowling or parachute. There was not the slightest possibility that the object we saw was a smoke ring or was caused by the vapour trail from the Meteor or from any jet aircraft. We have, of course, seen this, and we are all quite certain that what we saw was not caused by vapour or smoke. We are also quite certain that it was not a weather observation balloon. The speed at which it moved away discounts this altogether. It was not a small object which appeared bigger in the condition of light. Our combined opinion is that it was something we had never seen before in a long experience of air observation.'

This, along with other reports during 1952, caused the RAF to recognise UFOs officially.

On 3 March 1953, USAF Captain Roderick Thomspon was flying a F-84 strike aircraft during combat manoeuvres over Luke Air Force Base in Arizona. He and two student fliers saw a crescent-shaped UFO leaving a vapour trail. He attempted pursuit but could not catch it, but he did manage to capture it on his gun camera. The footage was only released in 1978 under the Freedom of Information Act.

On 23 November 1953, a USAF F-89 Scorpion was scrambled from Kinross Air Force Base to intercept a UFO. At 11:35 p.m. the plane intercepted the intruder. The two radar blips merged into one and the airbase lost radio contact with the plane. Then the radar blip disappeared too. Eventually the air controller had to file an accident report. An extensive land and water search found no trace of the craft or the two men aboard, pilot Lieutenant Felix Moncla, Jr, and radar observer Lieutenant R.R. Wilson.

Later, after aviation writer Donald E. Keyhoe broke the story in his 1955 best-seller *The Flying Saucer Conspiracy*, the Air Force insisted that the UFO had proved to be a Royal Canadian C-47. They claimed that the F-89C had not actually collided with the Canadian transport plane, but that something 'unspecified' had happened, and the interceptor crashed.

In 1958, a leaked Air Force document made it clear that officials considered the Kinross incident a UFO encounter of the strangest kind. The document quoted the radar operator as saying: 'It seems incredible, but the blip apparently just swallowed our F-89.'

In August 1956, over the UK, there were two UFO encounters within a week. A USAF transport plane flying at five thousand feet over East Anglia saw a smudgy yellow light below them. Radar systems in the area also detected a strange object moving between the air bases at RAF Bentwaters and RAF Lakenheath. Two RAF Venom fighters were scrambled and intercepted the UFO above Ely where, the pilots say, it hung stationary in the sky. Even so, try as they might, their weapons systems could not lock on to it.

A few days later, Flight Officer Wilbur Wright was one of two Javelin pilots who were flying a practice mission over the sea between the Isle of Wight and Bournemouth. They were ordered to break off their manoeuvre and to intercept a target picked up by a secret radar site nearby. This time the pilots managed to lock on to the UFO. When they came within visual contact range, they saw a bright disc which reflected the sun. It appeared to be hovering there, waiting for them to fly right at it. As the two planes closed within a few miles, the UFO simply flipped on its edge and took off into the sky at an incredible speed. In the blink of an eye, it had completely disappeared.

A USAF F-106 intercepted a UFO over Masawa, Japan, in 1959. When the alien craft did not respond to his hails, the pilot was authorised to fire a warning shot. The pilot loosed a missile, then began screaming that it had no effect. He said that the UFO was now pursuing him and it was closing rapidly. His last radio message said that the UFO had turned some kind of beam on him. The radio fell silent. On the radar screen, the blips from the F-106 and his pursuer merged – and disappeared.

Many similar cases defy any rational explanation. In September 1976, a UFO was seen by many people over the outskirts of Tehran. An Iranian Air Force Phantom was scrambled to intercept it. As the pilot approach what he took to be a glowing light, he noticed a small object eject from it. Thinking that he might be under attack, he prepared to launch an air-to-air missile. But just as he pressed the button to fire, all power drained from his aircraft. The object he had seen returned into the UFO, then the Phantom's electrical system powered up again. An explanation is that the UFO was an intelligent craft with capabilities that far outstrip our own.

'They've tested our defences to see if we can withstand an invasion… at some time in the future we can expect UFOs to become increasingly hostile,' a CIA informant told a journalist.

Soviet Encounters

On 20 October 1982, a Soviet Illyushin-62 Airliner, flying from Moscow to Magadan on the Siberian coast, was forced to make an unscheduled stop at Petropavolovsk in Kazakhstan, as the weather had closed in at its destination. The plane was on its final approach, when the crew saw 'a shining object flying at head-on and parallel headings, and various speeds and flight levels.' The pilot, Captain Vasilievyh, and others on the flight deck watched the object for over twelve minutes. However, neither their radar nor that of air traffic control on the ground were able to detect the object. Vasilievyh said: 'We are observing flashes but there is nothing on the radar, but the light flashes with a ten-second period.' And he clearly identified the object as 'some alien flying object'.

Vasilievyh told Karikov, the air traffic controller at Petropavolovsk: 'At a flight level of about 7,200 metres I caught sight of two intermingling, bright blue lights, 45 degrees to port and below us. I thought that it was an incoming plane and flashed the lamps for it and then reported to the air controller that there was an incoming plane below me. The controller told me that the zone was clear and that no planes were present. After that I saw the shining object several times, but now it was of a light yellow colour which seemed to burn for about 25–30 seconds... first the object was moving towards me from the port, then it stopped and started moving away at 80 degrees off our heading.'

According to the files, eight minutes after the aircraft landed, Karikov 'saw due north, exactly along the projection of the runway, a burst of light resembling the flasher of an aircraft. He observed six bursts during three minutes; the colour of the bursts varied from pink-red to pink, first in the western and then in the north-western direction.' When the aircraft was given a routine inspection five days later, serious damage to the engine was found.

Another encounter involved an airliner flying from Volgograd to Tbilisi in Georgia on 14 December 1987. The crew reported a 'flying object on a head-on course, resembling an aircraft with retracted landing lamps burning'. Another airline crew said: 'The UFO was also observed by tail number 6352 which reported the sighting at about 23:20. The crew reported a fire train scattering sparks that was trailing the UFO.'

An unnamed witness phoned the air traffic controller at the local airport and reported seeing an object like a 'burning aeroplane trailing a tail of fire flying over the settlement. After a light-burst resembling an explosion – although there were no accompanying sound effects – the aircraft disappeared.' But the caller could see 'no debris or explosion after-effects'. There were no reports of any crash debris being found.

The KGB files carry the following conversion between the air traffic controller at Sochi Airport on the Black Sea and the aircrew of Flight 138 after the airliner had been buzzed by UFOs:

Air Traffic Controller: TWR Flight 138. Go ahead.

Flight 138: Request you observe two objects hanging on our port.

Air Traffic Controller: What altitude to your port?

Flight 138: Our altitude, 50 or 60 kilometres directly abeam.

Air Traffic Controller: You have head-on traffic. Do you observe anything to port?

Flight 138: There was one object, then another one appeared nearby. Now they are flying away from us. The distance is already about 80 kilometres.

Air Traffic Controller: What is their shape?

Flight 138: One is oblong, the shape of a dirigible. The other is kind of spherical.

Russian planes even got buzzed on the ground. In 1990, three UFOs flew low over an Illyushin-96-300 standing at an airfield near Moscow, leaving vapour trails. A witness, Nikolay Nilov, managed to photograph the mysterious objects, but the entire incident remains unexplained.

Aerial encounters were also reported by Soviet military aircraft. One KGB file says: 'On 23 May 1985, during the scheduled flights of the 27th Bomber Regiment over Khabarovsk, an unidentified flying object the shape of an ellipsoid was observed at 22:35 local time in the vicinity of the airfield. The pale orange UFO was moving from the west to the east at a speed of 500–600 kilometres an hour and at an altitude of 2–3 kilometres. A glow in the form of a halo was visible around the object.'

The report goes on to state that 'the object's movement was not accompanied by noise of any kind. No target bursts were observed on radar scopes. No adverse effects on personnel, hardware or environment were registered.' Although statements such as this are common throughout the KGB files, some UFOlogists have speculated that they imply that, on other occasions, 'adverse effects' on personnel, hardware or the environment were registered, but that these incidents have been suppressed.

These encounters are not without their dangers. In 1961, an Antonov AN-2P mail plane disappeared from the radar between Ekaterinburg in the Sverdlovsk region and Kurgan in western Siberia. A UFO was being tracked in the area at the time. A Red Army helicopter found the plane in a small clearing in dense forest. The plane was intact and it had not cut a swathe through the trees as it had come into land. It appeared to have been dropped there from above. There was no sign of the seven people who were on the plane. However, there was a scorched circle of grass a hundred feet in diameter, around a hundred yards from the plane.

Mexican Wave
During the wave of sightings over Mexico City in the 1990s, the Mexican government refused to make any official comment on the UFO question. This may be because UFOs buzzing Mexico City presented a clear danger to aeroplanes using the city's international airport and they did not want to cause panic among passengers. The danger was highlighted on the evening of 28 July 1994, when Flight 129 was making its final approach into Mexico City airport. The DC9 had 109 passengers on board. They had just settled back for a routine landing when the plane was hit by a unknown object.

'I've never felt an impact so strong,' said the captain, Raymond

Cervantes Ruana. 'When we checked the plane we discovered that one of the shock absorbers had been ripped off.'

Following the mid-air collision, Ruana had to make an emergency landing, but he managed to get the aircraft down safely. Once the passengers had been evacuated, Ruana rushed to the control tower. He was told that, as he was making his final turn, two UFOs appeared on their radar screens. Their paths crossed. This is when he had declared an emergency. The air traffic controllers also told him that there were no other military or civilian aircraft in the area at the time.

A month later, Flight 304 from Acapulco was coming in to land when the pilot had to take evasive action to avoid a catastrophe.

'A big silver object came out of a cloud,' he said. 'It was metallic and circular. We clearly saw the object. It passed directly under the plane and we were forced to make a very difficult manoeuvre to avoid a collision.'

Once safely on the ground, the captain confronted the air traffic controllers. Why had he received no warning, he wanted to know.

There were numerous other events involving UFOs and passenger aircraft, prompting a public outcry. And the Mexican Pilots Association asked Jaime Maussan to present two lectures about the UFOs to their pilots. This is a measure of how worried they were.

'They don't care if they are UFOs or identified flying objects, they just want to avoid an accident,' said Maussan. 'Can you imagine what would happen if there had been a head-on collision with a passenger jet over densely populated Mexico City? How would they explain an accident like this to the general public?'

One puzzle was that, despite the danger posed by UFOs – whether alien or not – appearing along civilian air routes, the Mexican air force has rarely scrambled its fighters to try to intercept them. Perhaps the Mexican government does not regard the UFOs as a threat. Some researchers claim that the government know exactly what the objects are and may even be welcoming them. Whatever the case, the authorities are unwilling to discuss the situation.

Encounters Worldwide

Around August 1984, a flurry of sightings were reported by aircrews over Tasmania, Brazil, France and Russia; doubtless there were many more unreported. Numerous airlines have been involved, but most prefer their pilots not to talk about these encounters for fear of undermining passenger confidence. But no one has yet worked out whether they constitute a physical threat.

On 17 November 1986, at 17:10, Japanese airline pilot Captain Kenju Terauchi, who was flying a 747 cargo plane, saw what he at first thought were lights coming from a military aircraft. During the next half hour, he and his crew realised that things of an unearthly nature had joined them in the skies.

The pilot, first officer and flight engineer saw two lighted structures which were, according to Terauchi, 'about the same size as the body of a DC-8 jet'. It was flying about one thousand feet in front of the cargo plane. Terauchi's radio communications to Anchorage flight control were strangely garbled, but enough got through that Anchorage urgently contacted a nearby Air Force radar station to see what they were picking up. At various times during the event the UFOs were tracked by the 747 on-board radar and by the USAF ground radar.

As the sky darkened, the UFOs paced the 747 and were finally lost over the distant horizon. Then a pale white light appeared behind the aircraft. Silhouetted against lights on the ground, it looked like an immense, Saturn-shaped object – the size, Terauchi estimated, of 'two aircraft carriers'. He thought it was a 'mothership' that had carried the two 'smaller' objects, themselves of no small size. The Anchorage radar was still recording the object's presence. For the first time the crew felt fear. By now the aircraft was running low on fuel, and the captain requested permission to land. The UFO vanished suddenly at 17:39.

Danger Aloft

Another British plane had a close encounter with a huge UFO on 3 February 1999. At around 5:30 p.m. over the North Sea, about sixty miles from the Danish coast, the crew of the Debonair BAel46, a UK-based charter jet flying a party of businessmen from Sweden to the UK, noticed that the plane's underside was immersed in 'incandescent light'. The light lasted for about ten seconds, during which time those on board the plane reported that the jet was buzzed by a 'cylindrical craft' with 'rows of square portholes'. It was 'the size of a battleship'; at least, that is what newspaper reports of the incident said.

Safely on the ground in the UK, the pilot told air traffic control what had happened. They confirmed that there had been no other air traffic in the area. The Debonair's crew filed a near-miss report with the CAA. They were not alone. Three other pilots had independently logged sightings of the UFO. And these could not be dismissed as the misidentification of a terrestrial craft. According to the CAA report, at one point, the UFO was seen to come to an abrupt halt. It then turned westwards and accelerated past the Debonair flight at 'thousands of miles per hour'. And it was no figment of the imagination. As it entered British airspace, it was tracked briefly by military radar.

The Debonair encounter is just one of numerous encounters that took place at the end of the last century. During the 1990s, around fifty such incidents were reported in British airspace alone. Hundreds more have been reported around the world.

Fearing that the UFO in the Debonair encounter might present a danger to other aircraft, Swedish UFOlogist Clas Svahn and British journalist David Clarke investigated. They concluded that, although the Debonair jet had probably encountered an extraterrestrial object, they did not believe it to have been intelligently controlled. Svahn and Clarke noted that there is no mention of a UFO the size of a battleship nor of a craft with rows of portholes in the Debonair crew's near-miss report. That only appeared in the newspapers later. The crew reported only that they had seen an 'unidentified bright light' underneath the aircraft for about ten seconds. Svahn and Clarke pointed out that the crew had not reported seeing a UFO at all, but rather an unidentified aircraft light. And three other pilots who reported the UFO described it simply as a 'flare of light'.

However, the object was tracked for some time by the Debonair's on-board radar. But Svahn and Clarke found this evidence too shot through with holes. The object was only detected some minutes after the visual sighting and it was several miles away. Besides it had been picked up on the plane's weather radar, which was designed to pick up mountains or thunderclouds, not other aircraft. Svahn and Clarke concluded that the radar picked up some surface reflection, unconnected with the UFO.

The nearest radar ground station at Copenhagen had picked up nothing and, although an object was tracked by a UK military radar station, there is some question as to whether it was the same object seen by the Debonair crew. Weighing up the evidence, Svahn and Clarke came to the conclusion that the UFO that buzzed Debonair BAel46 was actually a bright meteor or bolide. Professor Bertil Lindblad, a Swedish expert on these high atmospheric burn-outs, says that, when meteors enter the atmosphere, they disintegrate, producing a trail of ionised gas in their wake and this, in some circumstances, can create the impression of a UFO.

It is often though that most mid-air encounters have natural causes. Although pilots are skilled observers and make good witnesses, there are some things that happen in the sky that are so rare that even an experienced pilot will never have seen one. It is generally believed that the 'foo fighters' reported during World War II, when military pilots saw strange lights in the skies over Europe, were some form of atmospheric phenomenon. They had not been seen before the 1940s because never before in history had thousands of aircraft been in the skies at any one time. Foo fighters are no longer reported; however, small balls of light are often seen which appear to tail aircraft. No satisfactory explanation for these modern-day foo fighters has yet been given, but it is generally assumed that they are some kind of atmospheric or electrical phenomenon that home in on the metal in the same way that a bolt of lightning would.

Collision Course

Although Svahn and Clarke came up with a partial explanation of the Debonair encounter, not all mid-air sightings can be dismissed so easily. In recent years, dozens of aircraft have reported sightings of lozenge-shaped dark brown or black objects in their vicinity. They have been pursued by military fighters, and both commercial pilots and air traffic controllers consider them a threat to life.

On 15 July 1991, a UFO buzzed a Britannia Airways Boeing 737 flying from Crete to London Gatwick, coming within 100 metres of its right wing as it came in to land. In their near-miss report, the crew of the charter flight rated the risk of a collision as 'high'. The 737 was given a comprehensive inspection for possible damage, in case a minor impact had occurred.

According to CAA investigation, the 737 and the UFO had been tracked by Gatwick radar. The unidentified radar blip that crossed the path of the jet streaked away at over 125 miles an hour. All aircraft give off an electronic code signal that identifies them on the radar screen. This object did not, so it was definitely not an aircraft. Gatwick air traffic control were so concerned that they ordered the in-bound jet following the Britannia Airways flight in to land to change course to get it out of the path of the UFO. The unidentified craft then turned south abruptly and disappeared over the English Channel.

After a twelve-month investigation, the CAA concluded that the unidentified flying object was 'probably' a toy balloon. But it is hard to square this theory with the facts. Balloons cannot normally reach altitudes much above 6,000 feet. The UFO was at over 12,000 feet. And balloons certainly cannot travel at 125 miles an hour or change direction abruptly. By coincidence, a weather balloon was released from the nearby town of Crawley that same evening. The wind took it east, while the UFO was seen flying west and then south. The weather balloon reached a top speed of 45 miles an hour. On the face of it, the 737 narrowly missed a collision with something truly unexplained.

On 24 March 1968, the sixty people flying on the Cork-to-London shuttle on an Aer Lingus Viscount were not so lucky. Hit by an unknown object, the Viscount plunged into the Irish Sea. No one survived. The air-crash investigation concluded that the Aer Lingus shuttle hit another aircraft. 'The conclusion that there was another aircraft involved is inescapable,' the Irish Inspector of Transport, Richard O'Sullivan, reported in June 1970. But what aircraft? There were none in the area at the time and none were reported missing. However, the air-crash report had ignored the testimony of a number witnesses at Carnsore Point, Ireland, near where the Viscount was lost. They reported seeing a 'dark cigar-like object' in the sky earlier that day.

Another dark, cylindrical object flashed past the cockpit of an Alitalia jet crossing on its descent into London Heathrow in April 1991. It was tracked by radar. On 14 September 1992, a similar craft flew past Australian Airlines Flight 405 over Tasmania. A long, black lozenge crossed the path of a military helicopter near Brignoles, France, on 8 July 1992. And on 9 August 1997, a Swissair Boeing 747 flying from Philadelphia to Zurich encountered a 'long, dark, wingless' cylinder near Boston. The crew reported that it came 'dangerously close'. And these are just the tip of the iceberg. During the 1990s, UFOlogist James Sneddon monitored radio traffic between air crews and air traffic controllers and found that numerous encounters went unreported.

For example, at about 2 a.m. on 1 February 1997 he overheard the following conversation between Gilair 274P, flying from Belfast to Newcastle, and air traffic control:

Gilair: 'Ah, it's... been getting closer in the last sixty seconds. Do you have anything on radar?'
Air Traffic Control: 'Negative. Can you describe the object?'
Gilair: 'Red flamey object.'
Air Traffic Control: 'Ah... I have a primary object [on radar]... range about seven miles. It's more or less stationary.'
Gilair: 'It could be the same one... [it's] stationary, but it got bigger in the last sixty seconds.

Air Traffic Control: 'Okay. Just go left about 30 degrees to avoid this. It's been steady there [on radar] for the last two three minutes.'

The Gilair aircraft successfully avoided the UFO. When it resumed its normal course for Tyneside, the air traffic controller joked: 'Okay then, fine – that's one for the X Files.'

Details of this incident appeared in no CAA report. According to pilot Graham Shepherd, civil aircrew are asked to keep quiet about sightings for fear of damaging passenger confidence.

Dr Richard Haines of the Ames Research Center in California, who regularly works for NASA, has collated hundreds of reports of mid-air encounters over the past 30 years. He fears that modern aircraft, which rely so heavily on computer systems, are in danger from the electromagnetic fields given off by UFOs.

'Mid-air encounters that threaten lives happen almost every week,' he says, 'but very little money is being spent on them because of the term UFO.'

Shoot 'Em Up

While civilian pilots keep quiet to avoid scaring away passengers, military pilots are bound by oaths of secrecy. However, rather than just taking action to avoid UFOs, they often take them on.

On 16 April 1998, a Draken jet fighter of the Finnish Air Force was on a routine reconnaissance mission over the Russo-Finnish border when the pilot spotted five 'glowing orange objects' flying in formation south-east of Lake Inarijarvi over the frozen tundra. He reported back to the air base at Rovaniemi, 250 miles north of Helsinki.

His commander ordered him to intercept the alien craft. This was easier said than done. He chased them for some time, but was unable to gain on them. Then, when they broke formation, he asked permission to engage them in a dogfight. Granted permission to fire, the pilot locked on, but his weapons systems malfunctioned. The UFOs then regrouped and sped off in a north-easterly direction. The Draken jet turned home.

Back at Rovaniemi, all the aircraft's systems were checked and found to be in perfect working order.

One of our Pilots is Missing

Twenty-year-old Australian Frederick Valentich was a keen flyer. He was also a UFO enthusiast and an avid reader on the subject. On 21 October 1978 he decided to fly a hired Cessna 182 over the Bass Strait to King Island from his Melbourne home. That way he could combine his two passions. He knew that, in the previous week, there had been numerous reports of strange cigar-shaped UFOs spotted in the Bass Strait area.

At 6:19 p.m. he took off from Moorabbin Airport in Melbourne in the rented aircraft. He had filed a flight plan for a night flight to King Island over the Bass Strait, which separates the mainland of Australia from Tasmania. He said he was going to collect crayfish for the officers of the local Air Training Corps, and he expected to return to by 10 p.m. that same night.

Valentich was about halfway into his journey when he spottedsomething strange over the water. At 7:06 p.m., he contacted Steve Robey, an air traffic controller with the Melbourne Flight Service. 'Is there any known traffic below 5,000 feet?' he asked. Robey said no other aircraft were expected in that area. The taped conversation following Valentich's query reveal an extraordinary tale:

19.06
Valentich: There seems to be a large aircraft below 5,000.
Robey: What type of aircraft is it?
Valentich: I cannot affirm. It is four bright... it seems to me like landing lights.
19.07
Valentich: The aircraft has just passed over me, at least 1,000 feet above.
Robey: And it is a large aircraft, confirm?
Valentich: Er, unknown due to the speed... Is there any Air Force

aircraft in the vicinity?

Robey: No known aircraft.

Valentich: It's approaching now from due east towards me... he's flying over me two, three times at speeds I could not identify...

Robey: Can you describe the, err, aircraft?

Valentich: As it's flying past it's a long shape. Cannot identify more than that, it has such speed...

19.10

Robey: Roger, and how large would the, err, object be?

Valentich: It's got a green light and sort of metallic, like it's all shiny on the outside... It's just vanished.

Valentich then radioed that his engine was 'rough idling'. It was missing and spluttering, but Valentich informed Robey that he would try to reach King Island. Suddenly, sounding extremely distressed, Valentich suddenly reported: 'Ah, Melbourne, That strange craft is hovering on top of me again... hovering and it's not an aircraft!' These were the last words that Robey heard. There was a cry and loud metallic sound before all contact was lost. Valentich never made it to King Island and, from 19:12 on 21 October 1978, the young pilot and his plane were officially declared 'missing'. A full-scale land, air and sea search was launched. It lasted for the next five days, but no trace of Valentich or his Cessna was ever found.

The ensuing official investigation by Australia's Aviation Administration lasted four years. In May 1982, its report was published. The conclusions were hardly worth waiting for. The report merely stated that 'the reason for the disappearance of the aircraft has not been determined'.

In the light of the mysterious circumstances surrounding the disappearance, this left the field wide open for a multitude of theories to be put forward, all attempting to explain Valentich's fate. Naturally, the standard explanation – that, by billion-to-one odds Valentich's Cessna 182 had been hit by space debris – came up. This could easily be discounted: the length of the taped contact between Valentich and

Robey ruled it out.

Another theory was that Valentich had become disorientated and had flipped his aircraft over on to its back. In that case, the aircraft he had seen above him would have been his own reflection on the water below. This would also have explained why the engine began misfiring. In that attitude, it would have been starved of fuel. And if he had not righted himself before the engine died, he would have crashed. Again, however, the testimony of Robey, the last man to speak to Valentich, seemed to discount this. Valentich seemed far from disorientated during their conversation. Besides, if he mistook his own reflection in the water for an aircraft above him, what was it he saw below. Valentich's evident coherence during the radio exchange also excluded another possibility – that he was confused and mistook the Cape Otway lighthouse for aviation lights.

The Bass Straits are a route used by drug smugglers to smuggle drugs into Australia. Rumours circulated that Valentich was involved in, or had somehow stumbled into, some criminal venture. But if he was actively involved, how can the conversation with Robey be explained? And if he had just stumbled into it by accident, how can the lights of the craft he saw be explained? Surely drug smugglers would not advertise their activities in this way.

NASA psychologist Dr Richard Haines proposed the theory that Valentich may have fallen foul of a Strategic Defence Initiative programme. He says that, at the time of Valentich's disappearance, the US Defense Intelligence Agency and National Security Agency were using a top-secret facility called Pine Gap in the deserted Australian outback. Haines also claims that these agencies had been performing experiments to test the projection of high-intensity laser beams into the atmosphere, an early stage in the development of a 'Star Wars' weapon.

As incredible as this may sound, Haines' role at NASA gave him access to classified files that are still withheld from the public for 'national security' reasons. What's more, his theory ties in with the Rendlesham forest incident in England. An investigation revealed that the same US intelligence agencies were co-ordinating in the Rendlesham area a similar project to that at Pine Gap.

A more widely accepted theory is that Valentich was a hoaxer. He had just seen the movie *Close Encounters of the Third Kind*, which could have led him to fake his own disappearance. At Moorabbin air field, Valentich had filled the aircraft's fuel tank to capacity and, after his frantic calls to Melbourne, he could have flown on to Tasmania.

The fact that he never turned up in Tasmania has not discouraged proponents of this theory. They say that Valentich may subsequently have lost control of his craft and crashed into the sea. However, no wreckage was found and, once again, Robey, the last man to speak to Valentich, discounts this theory. 'I am convinced in my own mind that he saw something strange,' he said. 'Whether it was a UFO or not I just do not know.'

All these 'logical' explanations for Valentich's disappearance take no account of the events leading up to it. Investigators from the Victorian UFO Research Society (VUFORS) have confirmed that there were numerous reports of flying objects throughout southern Victoria on 21 October 1978, many of them similar to Valentich's. They continued for several days following Valentich's disappearance, then suddenly stopped.

At 2 p.m. on 21 October, the day Valentich vanished, a strange cloud was seen floating in the sky above King Island. Suddenly, a silvery-white object emerged from the cloud. It was said to be about a quarter of the size of the moon. It moved slowly out to the west towards the sea, stopped, then circled back into the cloud.

At 4 p.m., a number of independent witnesses saw two cigar-shaped UFOs, around the size of a jumbo jet, moving west to east across the state of Victoria, towards the Bass Strait. The last sighting was made at around 4:30 p.m. near Cape Otway, though the craft were said to have turned away north and disappeared.

Between 7:06 and 7:12 p.m., at the very time Valentich was having his last conversation with Robey, several people saw a green light over the Bass Strait – at exactly the same time as Valentich was reporting the same thing.

Three minutes later, a witness reported seeing a cigar-shaped arrangement of lights in the sky over the Ormond district of Melbourne. At the same time, two young boys playing with walkie-talkies in Melbourne say they saw a white star-shaped UFO hovering at a low altitude above their heads. The UFO emitted a pulsating hum that seemed to jam their walkie-talkies. Then it disappeared.

The UFOlogists also came up with some photographic evidence. About twenty-one minutes before Valentich disappeared, Melbourne resident Roy Manifold, who was holidaying on King Island, took some photographs. His 35mm camera was mounted on a tripod and set for twenty-second automatic sequencing. It took six shots out over the Bass Strait, two of which show a strange blur out near Cape Otway lighthouse. Although some UFO experts say they show alien craft, the Royal Australian Air Force was not convinced. They say that the photographs show cumulus clouds. However, Australian researcher William H. Spaulding has pointed out that for the clouds to appear within the time sequence of the photographs, they would have to have been travelling at over two hundred miles an hour.

Even so, a UFO encounter only partially explains how Valentich vanished from the face of the earth. Some have suggested that interference from the unidentified craft may have caused the engine failure that he reported in the radio conversation, causing him to crash into the water. If the craft he saw was, indeed, piloted by aliens, the theory goes that they may have 'rescued' Valentich and his Cessna in an emergency airborne abduction. This would explain why no wreckage was found. Alternatively, the plane and its pilot may have simply been lost in the depths of the Bass Strait.

When a young pilot, on his first solo night flight, disappears without trace, the obvious conclusion is 'death by misadventure', but the Valentich case is not as simple as that. Valentich's conversation with air traffic control suggests that he did encounter something that night. Even to this day no one is sure what happened to Frederick Valentich.

Two months later, the UFO activity was reported over New Zealand. On 21 December 1978, Captain John Randle and Captain Vern Powell were flying two Argosy cargo aircraft from Blenheim to Dunedin, in South Island. Both pilots independently reported encountering several UFOs. And there was tangible evidence to back up their sighting. The UFOs had been detected on radar and the contacts confirmed by a number of air traffic controllers.

Astronauts' Sightings

If anyone knows about UFOs it is NASA. After all, NASA is looking out into space, where aliens come from, and it is sending its people out there. And there is little doubt that NASA has much more evidence about extraterrestrials than it is letting on.

Since 1958, when the National Aeronautical and Space Administration was established, NASA astronauts and test pilots have reported having aerial encounters with UFOs and other craft of unknown origin. The first to go public with a sighting was Joseph Walker, who was the pilot of NASA's pioneering space planes, the X-15s. During a speech to the National Conference on the Peaceful Uses of Space Research in May 1962, it was announced that Walker had an aerial encounter with two disc-shaped objects the previous month. And he had filmed them. The following July, Major Robert White, another X-15 pilot, found himself flying in formation with a number of UFOs at 314,000 feet.

NASA pilots are highly trained. But despite these accounts from eminently reliable eyewitness, NASA refused to back its men and the film and photographs they had shot of these encounters were never released. The official line is that what the two men had seen had been identified as 'flakes of ice'. NASA has also consistently denied having any interest in UFOs. But this is not entirely true. Indeed, a NASA operations manual published in 1967 details the procedures NASA staff must follow when filing UFO sighting reports.

In 1965, the Federal Bureau of Investigation learned from a confidential source that a NASA member of staff was secretly leaking information the space agency had collected on UFOs. The information was being given to two individuals from Pittsburgh who were 'acquainted with the NASA employee' and, to quote the FBI, 'had personal interest in UFOs'.

'The source believes that the information may be classified,' says an FBI report dated 2 September 1965, which was purged of names before being released. 'The source said, for example, that [censored] had seen a motion picture film showing a missile separating and a UFO appearing on the screen. Prior to the flight of Gemini 4, [censored] said to watch out for something interesting because the spaceship had devices aboard to detect UFOs...'

The FBI's reference to a 'motion picture film' held by NASA showing a UFO in flight indicates that NASA does have information on UFOs, which it has kept from the public. The mention of Gemini 4 is particularly intriguing, as one of its astronauts, James McDivitt, has confirmed that he saw some form of unidentified flying object during that flight. McDivitt does not believe that the object was alien in origin, but he disagrees with the theory UFO sceptic James Oberg put forward, that the object he saw was merely the second stage of Gemini 4's Titan rocket. 'If this is the case, the only puzzle remaining is McDivitt's apparent failure to recognise his own rocket,' wrote UFO researcher Timothy Good in his 1996 book, *Beyond Top Secret*.

On Gemini 12, Edwin 'Buzz' Aldrin, later the second man to set foot on the Moon, photographed three glowing orbs. The fifteen shots he took in a three-minute period show clearly that the objects were moving at some speed. Both Aldrin and NASA deny they were of alien origin.

When, in May 1961, President Kennedy promised to put a man on the Moon 'before the decade is out', NASA went into overdrive. To achieve Kennedy's goal, an American spacecraft would have to leave Earth orbit, cosmologically our own back yard. It then would have to cross a quarter-of-a-million miles of hostile interplanetary space and land on an alien world. NASA scientists must have at least considered the possibility that its astronauts might encounter extraterrestrials. And when the astronauts of Apollo 11 finally took their first tentative steps on the surface of the Moon on 20 July 1969, no one – not even the most hardened sceptic – could have entirely discounted the possibility that they might meet some form of alien life.

As well as being a technical achievement, the Moon landings were a highly organised exercise in public relations. Even the words uttered by Neil Armstrong when he descended on to the lunar surface were written for him – though, in the event, he got them wrong. He should have said: 'That's one small step for a man, one giant leap for mankind.' Not: 'That's one small step for man, one giant leap for mankind,' which does not make sense. Otherwise, the astronauts were word perfect. At the press conferences when they returned they said that nothing unusual occurred, and Armstrong stated categorically: 'There were no objects reported, found, or seen on Apollo 11 or any other Apollo flight other than of natural origin.'

However, rumours soon circulated that, during their stay on the Moon's surface, the astronauts were never alone. On one occasion the following conversation took place between the Apollo 11 crew and Mission Control:

Apollo 11: What was it? What the hell was it? That's all I want to know. These babies were huge, sir... Oh, God, you wouldn't believe it...

NASA: What... What the hell's going on?

Apollo 11: They're here, under the surface.

NASA: What's there? Mission Control calling Apollo 11.

Apollo 11: Roger, we're here, all three of us. But we've found some visitors... They've been here for quite a while judging by the installations... I'm telling you there are other spacecraft out there. They're lined up in ranks on the far side of the crater edge...

This exchange was not broadcast and the tapes and transcripts were classified. But a former NASA employee, Otto Binder, claimed that the conversation was overheard by amateur radio enthusiasts eavesdropping on a confidential channel reserved for high security messages. Timothy Good believes that Neil Armstrong and Buzz Aldrin saw aliens on the Moon, but he says that this secret conversation between Mission Control and Apollo 11 astronauts was actually monitored by Soviet scientists. Russian physicist and Professor of Mathematics Dr Vladimir Azhazha said that the encounter occurred shortly after the lunar module landed, but that the astronauts' report was never heard by the public because NASA censored it.

Corroboration of this story came from a NASA communications expert Maurice Chatelain, who helped design the Apollo spacecraft and worked for NASA at the time. He stated publicly that the Apollo 11 encounter with the UFOs was 'common knowledge in NASA' and that all the Apollo missions had been observed by UFOs. In an interview given in 1979, Chatelain confirmed that NASA had built a time delay in the transmissions between Apollo 11 and Mission Control so that any information regarding extraterrestrial 'visitors' could be censored.

Photographs of the Apollo 12 mission released by NASA show anomalous streaks of light over the surface of the Moon. One photograph of a moonwalk, some UFO enthusiasts say, has been cropped to cut out a brightly lit alien craft hovering over an astronaut's head. The Apollo 12 command module Yankee Clipper photographed a bright disc that, on enlargement, was full of intricate detail. Another glowing disc was photographed from command module Odyssey during the ill-fated Apollo 13 mission. Other pictures from that mission showed anomalous streaks of light, a red cigar-shaped object and other foreign bodies in the skies. And as the Apollo 14's lunar module Antares flew over the craters Lansberg C and A, 'a large lighted object with windows swept into view'. NASA has refused to comment.

Chatelain said that from the beginning of the manned space programme astronauts had been given code words to use so, if they saw alien craft, they could talk about them over the airwaves. 'Walter Schirra aboard Mercury 8 was the first the astronauts to use the code name "Santa Claus" to indicate a flying saucer,' Chatelain said.

He also claimed that: 'All Apollo and Gemini flights were followed at a distance, and sometimes quite closely, by space vehicles of extraterrestrial origin. Every time it occurred, the astronauts informed Mission Control who then ordered absolute silence.'

This was confirmed by Mercury 7 astronaut Scott Carpenter, who said: 'At no time, when the astronauts were in space, were they alone; there was constant surveillance by UFOs.'

Chatelain said that UFO encounters were common knowledge at NASA, though no one ever talked about them. He believed that some of the alien craft originated on Titan, a moon of Saturn, pointing out that at on a least one occasion in the 1970s, when a NASA probe neared Titan, its photographic and radio equipment malfunctioned. NASA, Chatelain said, is involved in a conspiracy of silence.

NASA denied censoring Apollo 11's transmissions and scorn was poured on Binder and Chatelain, despite their outstanding credentials. Another NASA employee with impeccable credentials is Apollo 14's lunar module pilot, Edgar Dean Mitchell, who spentthirty-three hours walking on the surface of the Moon. He believes that UFO encounters are real and that there is a cover-up.

'I am convinced there is a small body of valid information,' he said, 'and that there is a body of information ten times as big that is total disinformation that is put out by the source to confuse the whole issue. The information is now held primarily by a body of semi- or quasi-private organisations that have kind of spun off from military intelligence organisations of the past...

'The danger is that they are still operating under a black budget, which has been estimated at over $30 billion a year. And nobody knows what goes into black budgets. The prime requisite is security first and everything else second... I would say, however, that if there was knowledge of extraterrestrial contact existing in the government, and we were sent out into space blind and dumb to such information, I think it is a case of criminal culpability. To send us up there into a what-if scenario? If the evidence is real, and we were led to believe that no such thing was possible – to me, that's criminal.'

He is backed by astronaut Colonel Gordon Cooper, who had once held the record for the longest space fight – thirty-four hours – and was one of the first Americans to orbit the Earth. In 1985, Cooper appeared before a United Nations panel chaired by Secretary General Kurt Waldheim and told them what he knew.

'I believe that extraterrestrial vehicles and their crews are visiting this planet from other planets, which are a little more technically advanced than we are on Earth,' said Cooper. 'I feel that we need to have a top-level programme to scientifically collect and analyse data concerning any type of encounter, and to determine how best to interfere with these visitors in a friendly fashion.'

Cooper claimed that he had not only 'been into the fringes of the vast areas of which "they" travel,' but also, 'I did have occasion in 1951 to have two days of observation of many flights of "them", of different sizes flying in fighter formation... they were at a higher altitude than we could reach.'

Aliens continue to observe man's puny attempts that space flight. Around 6:30 a.m. on 14 March 1990, Donald Ratsch, amateur radio enthusiast from Baltimore, Maryland, was monitoring the radio transmissions from Discovery when he heard the pilot say: 'Houston, Discovery, we have a problem. We have a fire.' Shortly after, Rasch claims an additional transmission was heard: 'Houston, this is Discovery. We still have the alien spacecraft under observance.'

However, NASA mission specialist Bob Oeschler, a former mission specialist with NASA, investigated and discovered that the second message did not come from the Shuttle at all. Instead, he says that the signal came from Fort Meade, Maryland – not far from Baltimore. Fort Meade is the home to America's National Security Agency, which has a longstanding involvement in UFO reports. Oeschler's conclusion was that the broadcast was 'an institutionally orchestrated hoax for subtle intelligence purpose'.

Oeschler was later informed by a senior NASA source that the Shuttle had indeed encountered a UFO around that time. The encounter, he was told, lasted for eight hours, and caused a major disruption of Discovery's electrical systems. It seems that NASA does indeed know about UFO and alien encounters. It is just not saying.

Sightings from the Past

Anomalous Airships

There is nothing new about UFOs. They have been seen throughout human history. Sightings of mysterious lights in the skies began long before the phrase 'flying saucer' was coined in 1947, when the idea caught on that flying objects may be craft from distant planets flown by aliens.

In ancient times, UFOs were thought to be flying chariots or some other sign of a heavenly presence. But in the nineteenth century, with the onset of the airship, it was conceded that UFOs might have earthly origins. Even today, many sightings spring from human activity in the air, but some early reports offer a tantalising taste of the mystery that was to come.

The first modern-day UFO 'flap' occurred in North America as the nineteenth century ended. In 1896 and 1897, there were numerous reports of 'airships' across the US and the prairies of Canada, even though, at that time, no airship had crossed the Atlantic. Between 6 and 7 p.m. on 17 November 1896, an intensely bright light, like an 'electric arc lamp', was seen moving over the housetops in Sacramento, California. Some of the hundreds of eyewitnesses claimed to have got a closer view of the craft. They said that it was an enormous, cigar-shaped object, apparently made of aluminium, held aloft by large wings. It was assumed to be one of the newfangled airships; a couple of witnesses said they heard a voice calling down, saying: 'We hope to be in San Francisco by tomorrow noon!'

In the following January, the *Omaha Bee* carried reports of a series of mysterious sightings in Hastings, Nebraska. 'Several Hastings people report that an airship, or something of the kind, has been sailing around in the air west of this city,' the papers reported. 'It was first noticed sometime last fall when it was seen floating in the air about five hundred feet above the ground, and, after standing still for about thirty minutes, it began to circle about and took a northerly direction for about two miles, after which it returned to its starting place and sank into oblivion.

'At first sight it had the appearance of an immense star, but after closer observation the powerful light shows [itself] by its color to be artificial. It certainly must be illuminated by powerful electric dynamos for the light sent forth by it is wonderful. At 9:30 last Monday night [25 January 1897], the large glaring light was seen to circle around for a few minutes and then descend for about two hundred feet, circling as it travelled at a remarkable speed... A close watch is being kept for its reappearance.'

In April, an 'airship' began making regular visits to Kansas. News spread east. On 2 April 1897, the *Evening Times* of Pawtucket, Rhode Island, carried a story saying: 'The mysterious airship seen often in Kansas during the past two weeks was seen again last night at Everest, Brown County, in the north-western part of the state... The ship was seemingly erratic in its movements. Instead of moving in a straight line, it rode up and down, now to the left, and again to the right, but always, apparently, under absolute control... when the ship has been seen, it has come from the north in the early evening and returned in the early morning. In all expectation that this programme will be repeated, a good number of the citizens of Everest will remain out all night, hoping for another glance at the mysterious visitor.'

In May 1897, the plague of airships seems to have moved northwards and new sightings began to come in from the other side of the Canadian border in Manitoba and British Columbia. These peaked in July and August. For example, on 14 August 1897, the *Vancouver Daily World* asked: 'Have you seen the light in the heavens? If not, you are not up to date. It has been hovering in the skies above Vancouver almost every night this week, and has been viewed by many. It was last seen on Friday evening and may be on view tonight, and again it may not. Last night the strange object in the skies was noticed to the north of the city... travelling in an easterly direction. The luminous ball of fire, or airship as some call it, was closely watched. It approached with great swiftness, paused in mid-air, then surrounded itself with flashes of colour and moved towards the north-east. At times it looked like a ball of fire, at others it had a dull lustre and small particles of fire would shoot from the great glowing mass.'

Perhaps some unknown American inventor had developed an airship independently. But why did all trace of him, and them, disappear after 1897?

Phantom Fliers

With the turn of the new century, UFOs seemed to turn their attention elsewhere. The earliest known UFO picture was taken over the Norwegian town of Drobach in 1907. The photograph is hazy, but the object is saucer shaped and could not be mistaken for the airships of the day.

A large numbers of cases have been documented in eastern Europe, though witnesses often interpreted them as if they were from an earlier age. This one, dating from 1904, is typical: 'In Romania's Transylvania a farmer was still in his fields with his cart long after midnight. Suddenly he saw a fiery wheel over the Muntii Apuseni [mountains], coming down to the ground. The wheel approached fast, turning as it did so, and the farmer stood by helplessly. When the fiery wheel was quite close to him it changed into the shape of a human being, who looked at the farmer for a long time without speaking.'

Meanwhile, back in the States, the sightings had started again. On 1 February 1908, a reddish cigar-shaped object was seen flying over the town of Kent in Washington state, between 7:00 and 9:00 in the evening. One witness described it as 'two or three times as bright as Jupiter'. The same object appeared again the next night. After that, it was never seen again.

New Zealand UFOlogist Murray Bott unearthed a wave of sightings the following year down under. On 27 July 1909, the Clutha Leader of Balclutha on New Zealand's South Island reported that 'some half dozen boys were playing on the beach at Kaka Point [when they] saw a huge illuminated object moving about in the air. It appeared as if it was going to alight at Kaka Point... The boys thought it was being attracted by their lantern and left it on the beach. The airship then glided around the rocks at the old pilot station and nearly came in contact with them. It shortly afterwards disappeared. The boys said it was as big as a house.'

Another encounter had taken place at Kelso on South Island just four days early. That time: 'A small group of schoolchildren and some residents reported that an airship came down and bobbed around in the sky over the school for a few minutes.' A reporter for the *Otago Daily Times* went to Kelso and interviewed the witnesses. 'All those scholars who saw the ship were interrogated singly and independently [and] were asked to draw an impression of what they had seen... The result was six drawings, the degree of resemblance and unanimity of which was nothing short of dumbfounding to all sceptics.'

Meanwhile, on the other side of the world, the 21 May 1909 edition of the *East Anglian Daily Times* carried the headline: 'Britain Invaded!' Its subheadings said: 'Airships in East Anglia, Wales, and Midlands. Phantom Fleet. Norwich and Southend Paid A Visit.' The body of the story reported: 'The airship fleet which is invading England had a busy night on Wednesday. We speak of a fleet because, according to correspondents, there must be not only one, but half a dozen mysterious cigar-shaped machines with quivering lights and whirring mechanisms flitting about the country by night. Wednesday night's observers report manifestations at such widely divergent points as: Southend-on-Sea, Birmingham, Norwich, Tasburgh, Wroxham and Pontypool.'

In the run-up to World War I another wave of airship sightings took place over western Europe. As the belligerents were eyeing each other up, it was assumed that the reports of unidentified flying were sightings of experimental enemy military machines.

In 1912, there was an epidemic of sightings in Britain. Questions were asked in the House of Commons and Winston Churchill, then First Lord of the Admiralty, issued a statement that an unidentified flying object had been seen on the night of 27 November 1912. Flares had been lit at the airfield at Eastchurch in anticipation of an aircraft landing. But nothing had descended from the sky. This was the first of a number of so-called 'scareships'. In January 1913, there were scareship sightings over Cardiff, Liverpool, Dover and Yorkshire. Witnesses said that the craft travelled very fast and left a cloud of smoke in their wake. One, according to a witness, circled, 'as if surveying something'. To this day, there has been no satisfactory explanation of these sightings.

Also in 1913, in Moravia –which was then part of the Austro-Hungarian Empire, but now in the Czech Republic – it was reported that: 'A 20 year-old boy was travelling from Brno to Zidence in clear weather at the end of the summer. Between 21:00 and 22:00 hours he saw six objects very high in the sky, like large fiery red stars, travelling soundlessly round a fixed point in a clockwise direction.'

UFOs also returned to North America that year. In 1913, a mysterious procession of glowing lights was seen by hundreds of witnesses above Saskatchewan. By this time the vogue for airships was waning and they were described as 'ghost aeroplanes'.

UFO sightings dropped off during the Great War, presumably because people were concentrating on what was going on on the ground. But wartime Europe did record the first occasion when an aircraft fired on a UFO. It occurred on 31 January 1916. The official record of the encounter says: 'At 20:45 hours, local time near Rochford, England, Flight Sublieutenant J.E. Morgan, flying at 5,000 feet saw a row of lights like lighted windows on a railway carriage with the blinds drawn. Thinking it was a German Zeppelin, he fired his

Webley Scott pistol. The light rose and rapidly disappeared.'

Following the war, with more aircraft aloft, sightings became more common. In the 1960s Francis (later Sir Francis) Chichester was a renowned single-handed yachtsman, but in 1931 he made the first east-west flight across the Tasman Sea from New Zealand to Australia in a Gypsy Moth biplane fitted with floats. On 10 June 1931, during the flight, he saw a 'flashing airship' and reported the incident in his book *The Lonely Sea and the Sky*, first published in 1932.

The following year, Lieutenant Tage Anderson and Lieutenant Peter Grunnet of the Royal Danish Air Force found that their plane was being tailed by a UFO off the coast of Greenland.

'It was nothing like the flying machines of that period,' said Grunnet. 'It was hexagonal, flat and seemingly made of aluminium or some other metal, with no breaks in the surface and no rivets. At the time, I had a spooky feeling. I can't explain it. It was as if I "felt" the presence of whoever was inside that craft and the feeling was hostile.'

Suddenly the whole of Scandinavia was swamped with sightings of 'ghost planes'. Witnesses said they had multiple engines and out-performed any known aircraft. They were flown by mysterious pilots wearing what looked like goggles.

Foo Fighters

Late in 1941 the Chiefs of the Imperial General Staff began to fear that the Nazis had developed a secret weapon. RAF aircrew had reported numerous unexplained sightings in the skies. Michael Bentine – who later found fame as one of the Goons – was an RAF Intelligence Officer during World War II. He debriefed Polish bomber crews who said they had seen a strange 'weapon' that flew

alongside their aircraft. Others would report strange lights that hovered close to their aircraft, often too close for comfort. Sometimes these lights would flash across the sky at tremendous speeds. They did not attack the aircraft directly, but they often disrupted the electrical equipment on board. Although the name had not yet been coined, they acted in the same way as what we call 'flying saucers'.

These lights were not seen only in Europe, nor exclusively from the air. One evening in September 1941, the SS *Pulaski*, an old Polish vessel that was being used as a British troop carrier, was steaming across the Indian Ocean when seaman Mar Doroba looked up and saw 'a strange globe glowing with greenish light, about half the size of the full moon'. Doroba estimated that the object was flying at an altitude of approximately 4,500 feet. It appeared to follow the ship for the next hour.

On 26 February 1942, seaman William J. Methorst made a similar sighting from a ship in the Timor Sea, off northern Australia. In 1957 he told Australia's Victorian Flying Saucer Society: 'While on watch for enemy aircraft just after noon, I was scanning the skies with binoculars when suddenly I saw a large illuminated disc approaching at terrific speed. After reporting it to the officers on the bridge, they were unable to identify it as any known aircraft. After keeping track of this object for about three to four hours, as it flew in big circles and at the same height, the craft suddenly veered off in a tremendous burst of speed and disappeared from sight.'

The logical explanation was that these sightings were an electrical phenomenon related to St Elmo's Fire, the glowing that occurs around a ship's masts or an aircraft's wings due to a build-up of static electricity. But as more reports came in, military intelligence began to fear that the Germans or Japanese might even have developed this effect into a weapon. When the attack on Pearl Harbor in December 1941 brought America into the war, United States Air Force pilots began to see these strange unidentified flying objects too, and they nicknamed them 'phantoms' or 'foo fighters', after one of the comic sayings of the popular cartoon character Smokey Stover. They were also seen from the ground. US Marine Sergeant Stephen J. Brickner saw a whole wing of them.

'The sightings occurred on August 12, 1942, at about ten in the morning while I was with my squad on the island of Tulagi in the southern Solomons, west of Guadalcanal,' he reported. 'It was a bright tropical morning with high banks of white, fleecy clouds. I was cleaning my rifle on the edge of my foxhole, when suddenly the air raid warning was sounded. I immediately slid into my foxhole, with my back to the ground and my face turned up to the sky. I heard the formation before I saw it. Even then, I was puzzled by the sound. It was a mighty roar that seemed to echo in the heavens. It didn't sound at all like the "sewing machine" drone of the Jap formations. A few seconds later, I saw the formation of silvery objects directly overhead.

'They were flying very high above the clouds... the formation was huge, I would say over 150 objects were in it... this formation was in straight lines of ten or twelve objects, one behind the other. The speed was a little faster than Jap planes, and they were soon out of sight. A few other things puzzled me: I couldn't seem to make out any wings or tails. They seemed to wobble slightly, and every time they wobbled they would shimmer brightly from the sun. Their colour was like highly polished silver. All in all, it was the most awe-inspiring and yet frightening spectacle I have seen in my life.'

But despite numerous sightings of foo fighters by both British and American pilots, over Europe and the Pacific, no one could decide whether they were natural or man-made or whether they were dangerous. Nor had anyone devised a counter-measure.

By 1943, the British had become so concerned about the potential threat of foo fighters that they set up a special study group. According to the official record, it was headed by a Lieutenant General Massey. However, there is no other mention of a General Massey in the military records. Nevertheless the Massey Project collected hundreds of first-hand accounts of encounters with foo fighters over the next few years.

One of the reports, from a C.J.J., was found buried in the files of British and American intelligence. (During World War II, documents were copied and shared.) He was a nose gunner with an anti-submarine squadron. This wing were patrolling over the Bay of Biscay one day in November 1942 when the tail gunner reported they were being followed. A 'massive' wingless object had suddenly appeared behind the bomber. C.J.J. climbed out of his nose turret to take a look. The whole crew saw it and C.J.J. examined it at close quarters from the waist gunners' position. It followed them for about fifteen minutes, before making an abrupt 180-degree turn and disappearing. Meanwhile another one of the bomber's crew, a Sergeant M.F.B., was busy photographing it with his K-20 camera. C.J.J. said that only one of the pictures came out, but it was a 'perfect print'. It has yet to surface.

Most witnesses reported shapeless lights. They appeared to lack any clearly designed form or substance. Also, the objects rarely showed up on radar. However, another photograph was taken of three UFOs following a US bomber over the Sea of Japan in 1943.

It seems that the foo fighters did not like this attention. Towards the end of 1943, all sightings of them mysteriously halted, but the following year they were back with a vengeance. From April 1944 to August 1945, reports of hundreds of sightings of foo fighters came in from around the world. When American troops hit Omaha beach on the morning of 6 June as part of the Normandy landings, a dark, cigar-shaped object was seen crossing the horizon by hundreds of witnesses. When the Allies reached Germany in 1945, thirty Allied soldiers in Darmstadt watched six or seven bright yellow-orange circular objects approach the autobahn from the west at an altitude of about 140 feet. Over Tawara, Japan, a 'bogey' blip on a radar screen was calculated to be moving at the incredible speed of 690 miles an hour, at a time when planes had yet to break the sound barrier. With the fall of Japan, the Allies occupied the country, and American and Japanese soldiers saw objects described as 'round, speedy balls of fire' streaking over Tokyo.

Serviceman Leonard H. Stringfield was on board an American C-46 plane on his way to Tokyo as part of the Allied occupation force on 28 August 1945. The plane was midway between the Pacific islands of Ie Shoma and Iwo Jima when an engine began to fail.

Stringfield recalled: 'As the plane dipped, sputtered oil, and lost altitude, I remember looking out through one of the windows and, to my surprise, seeing three unidentifiable blobs of brilliant white light, each about the size of a dime held at arm's length. The lights travelled in a straight line through the clouds, keeping pace and staying parallel with the C-46. When my plane pulled up the objects remained below and then disappeared into a cloudbank.'

Years later, when Stringfield became a prominent UFOlogist, he came across cases in which UFOs seemed to be responsible for electromagnetic disturbances in cars and planes. It was only then that he connected the C-46's sputtering engine with the anomalous blobs. He also recalled that it was the port engine that had failed and the UFOs had been on the port side of the plane. So the foo fighters were no secret weapon. The war was over, following the Japanese surrender on 10 August, two more weeks before Stringfield's sighting.

During the war, information about foo fighters was top secret. But with the war over, the truth could be told. In December 1945 *American Legion Magazine* published an article on the phenomenon. The author concluded that: 'the foo fighter mystery continues unsolved... and your guess as to what they were is as good as mine, for nobody really knows.' That is as true today as it was then.

The foo fighters turned up again during the Korean War. And, although they have changed their name with succeeding generations, they are still seen today. After the war they became known as 'ghost rockets', then 'flying saucers'. Now they are called UFOs and there are reasons to believe they are of alien origin.

Fireballs

It was only after the end of World War II that the Allies discovered that the Germans were indeed developing a revolutionary, top-secret weapons called the *Feuerball*, or 'fireball', which could have been mistaken for a foo fighter. According to researcher Dr Renato Vesco, a flat, circular flying machine powered by a special turbojet engine was developed by scientists at the aeronautical establishment in Wiener Neustadt and actually saw action towards the end of the war. Vesco also claims that the principles of the *Feuerball* were used to develop a larger supersonic craft called the *Kugelblitz*, or 'ball lightning fighter'. Built in the underground factories at Kahla, in Thuringia, central Germany, it took to the air in February 1945, three months before the fall of the Third Reich.

In 1975, when the papers of the deceased World War II Luftwaffe officer Rudolph Schriever were being sorted, they were found to contain the design of a large flying saucer, including numerous sketches and copious notes. Schriever's friends said that, up until his death, he claimed that post-war UFO sightings proved that his work had been taken seriously.

However, the Germans themselves were plagued by the foo fighters. In 1944, the German Wehrmacht set up an office to investigate sighting reports of anomalous flying objects. The Luftwaffe's Sonderburo ('Special Office') 13 went about its task thoroughly until it was shut down when Germany was overrun in April 1945. Although it was only in operation for a matter of months, Sonderburo 13 collected a vast amount of information.

The first sighting the Sonderburo studied came from a pilot called Hauptmann (Captain) Fischer. At 17:35 on 14 March 1942, Fischer was scrambled to investigate a strange blip on the radar of a secret air base in Banak, Norway. He intercepted the intruder at 10,000 feet and radioed a description back to base. What he could see, he said, was an 'aerial whale'. It was an enormous, streamlined craft around 90 metres long and 15 metres in diameter. This description sounds like a Zeppelin, but it was not. The craft, Fischer said, stayed horizontal for several seconds, then stood on end and soared away vertically at great speed.

Then, at 10:45 on the morning of 29 September 1944, a new Messerschmitt ME-262 Schwalbe jet was being put through its paces when the test pilot spotted two luminous points of light to starboard. He banked right at full speed and found himself face-to-face with a cylindrical craft about a hundred feet long. It had openings along its side and a long antenna at the front. Again, the description would have fitted an airship, but the pilot saw it take off at a speed of over 1,250 miles an hour.

Ghost Rockets

The division of Europe into Soviet and Western spheres of influence in 1945 and the beginnings of the Cold War meant that the military on both sides of the Iron Curtain were constantly on the alert for signs of open hostility. Following the use of V2 rockets by the Nazis and the development of the atomic bomb by the Allies, the stakes were now that much higher.

Everyone, it seemed, was afraid of the V1s and V2s that had devastated London only two years before. Both sides had seized German scientists who had built the V2, and they dedicated themselves to developing bigger and more long-range missiles that could carry nuclear warheads. The race to construct intercontinental ballistic missiles was on, and both sides were terrified that the other might get there first. Everyone's eyes were on the skies.

In the summer of 1946, just a year after the end of the war in Europe, mysterious missiles were sighted in the skies over Western Europe. They were first seen over Finland, Norway, Sweden and Denmark. Similar reports came in from Portugal, Italy and Greece, then from India and North Africa. Reports of sightings – many from reliable sources – talked of wingless, silver objects in the sky. Often they had a flame at the tail, and a trail of smoke. A frontline country in the Cold War, Sweden took these reports very seriously. In July 1946, the authorities there set up a committee of investigation, comprising leading scientists and engineers and representatives from the armed forces. An appeal for sightings brought a deluge of reports. When the mundane and easily explicable were winnowed out, the committee began investing those that exhibited what it termed 'high strangeness' – for example, unidentified flying objects that were estimated to be travelling at many thousands of miles an hour. It was, of course, only in October 1947 that Chuck Yeager broke the sound barrier in a Bell X-1 experimental rocket plane that topped six hundred miles an hour.

In Sweden these identified flying objects became known as 'ghost rockets', after the 'ghost planes' seen over Scandinavia in the 1930s.

The fear was that the new rockets, along the lines of V2s, had been developed by the Soviet Union and that they were straying or being fired deliberately into Swedish airspace from test sites inside the USSR.

When the Swedish government took the matter up in Moscow, the Soviet authorities denied all knowledge of the ghost rockets. But this denial was taken with a pinch of salt. No one really believed what the Soviets said. Clearly the Soviet Union was developing rocket-powered weapons, but why they would test them near the Scandinavian border rather than out in the broad plains of Siberia was a mystery. Nevertheless the Swedish sightings became news world-wide. Even the Prime Minister of South Africa, Jan Smuts, warned in a radio broadcast of the threat the Soviet rockets presented.

Russian rockets were of particular interest to the US. One of the staff of the US embassy in Stockholm saw a mystery rocket, and ghost rockets were a regular feature of the diplomatic traffic between the Swedish legation and the State Department at the time.

'My own source is personally convinced that some foreign power is experimenting over Sweden,' says one State Department memo of 1946, 'and he guesses it is Russia.'

The Pentagon became so concerned that it sent a Lieutenant General from the US 14th Army Air Force and General David Sarnoff from military intelligence to Sweden. Sarnoff was an expert on aerial warfare and he concluded that the ghost rockets seen over Norway and Sweden were 'real missiles'.

British radar experts were also despatched to Stockholm. Their reports were sent back to the director of Air Defence Intelligence, the legendary R.V. Jones. A scientist by training, Jones was known as the Sherlock Holmes of the War Office. During World War II, he had laboriously pieced together decoded German communications, air reconnaissance photographs and information gleaned from Allied spies, to work out what the enemy was up to. From the beginning of the Swedish flap, he doubted that the ghost rockets were coming from the Soviet Union. It made no sense. The USSR had vast tracts of lands to the east where it could test secret weapons. Why risk launching them where they could fly into the airspace of another – albeit neutral – country, where they would inevitably fall into the hands of the enemy?

And if these were test flights, how could they be carried out with so few mishaps? When testing the V2, Nazi scientists had experienced a failure rate of ten per cent. Assuming a failure rate a tenth of that, Jones argued that several ghost rockets would have crashed on Swedish territory. Yet none had been recovered. Nevertheless, the British authorities continued to take the sightings very seriously. One of Jones's colleagues in Air Defence Intelligence analysed a series of reports in which a similar object had been seen by several observers in widely separated parts of Sweden within a few minutes of each other. It seemed reasonable to assume that they had all seen the same object and, from the times of the sightings, the officer calculated that the object had zigzagged across southern Sweden, travelling at up to 2,000 miles an hour.

Jones rejected this theory. He agree that it was likely that all the observers had seen the same object, but he noticed that they had all seen it in the sky to the east. This would make sense only if the object was at a much greater height and distance than they had realised. In that case, what they were seeing was probably a daylight meteor or bolide. However, Jones's colleague point out that, if the object was a bolide high in the sky, all the witnesses would have seen the object at exactly the same time. But the sightings were spread over several minutes. Jones said there was no great mystery to why the witnesses had reported seeing the object a few minutes apart. Few people kept their watches set to exactly the right time, and besides, the witnesses would not necessarily have looked at their watches directly after they saw the object.

It seemed clear that progress could only be made if the investigators got their hands on a ghost rocket, or at least part of one. Then a report that a rocket had crashed into Lake Kolmjarv in Sweden came in. But when the crash was investigated, it could not be verified and, despite enormous effort, no debris was recovered. On another occasion, half a dozen irregularly shaped lumps of material, supposedly ejected from a ghost rocket in flight, were obtained. They were shipped to Jones in London, who forwarded them to the Chemical Analysis Section at Farnborough.

The next day a senior chemist telephoned him in a state of excitement. Analysis, he said, had revealed an unknown chemical in one of the samples. Jones was mystified. He telephoned the chief of the chemical laboratory and questioned him. It turned out that the chemists had been analysing the samples for metal and other minerals. If the ghost rocket was man-made it would almost certainly have been made out of metal, while meteorites are either stone or iron. However, Jones knew that some rarer types of meteorite contain a significant amount of carbon.

'No one had stopped to look at the material in an effort to get the analysis made quickly, and they had failed to test for carbon,' said Jones. When he pointed this out 'there was a gasp from the other end of the telephone as the penny dropped.'

As the ghost rockets seemed to have an innocent explanation, in August 1946, the Norwegian authorities instructed their news-papers not to report any more sightings. However, the Swedes went on looking, though the government banned any mention of the location where the rockets had been seen in case it was used by the rocket-builders to tell how accurate or otherwise their launches had been.

Meanwhile, the Swedish investigating committee continued to sift through the reported sightings, separating those that could be explained as weather balloons, misidentified aircraft, meteors, clouds, etc., from those of 'high strangeness'. In October 1946, the committee reported that, of some one thousand sightings, around 80 per cent had mundane causes. The remaining 20 per cent 'cannot be the phenomena of nature or products of the imagination, nor can [they] be referred to as Swedish aeroplanes,' the report said.

In their report, the investigators also said that, although they could not prove that the ghost rockets were not Soviet-built rockets, they thought it was unlikely. After this rather inconclusive end, reports of ghost rockets tailed off. The following year, the first 'flying saucers' were seen. But were these just ghost rockets or foo fighters under another name?

Spitzbergen

Even though interest in ghost rockets soon faded, especially after the firsts sightings of 'flying saucers' in America in 1947, Scandinavia continued to be a target for anomalous objects – and one may even have been captured. In June 1952, stories were beginning to come out in the German press about an alleged UFO crash on the island of Spitzbergen, off the northern coast of Norway.

The stories reported that six Norwegian jets were on an exercise flying over the Hinlopen Straits when radio contact was lost due to heavy static interference. At the same time the local radar post at Narvik was showing a distorted signal of the jet fighters, as well as the presence of a UFO.

While the jets were circling, the flight leader Captain Olaf Larsen spotted a large metallic disc in the snow, which looked as if it had crashed. He reported his findings and search and recovery teams were sent to the location.

When the teams arrived they found a craft, one-hundred-and-fifty feet in diameter, that was giving off radioactive emissions. The craft was silver in colour and had strange symbols written on the outside. The teams assumed that this was a Russian test aircraft that had flown out of control. It was shipped to Narvik where it was examined.

The results of the investigation were not released for two years. The German newspapers said that the report concluded that the craft was not of Russian origin and that it had not been built by any country on Earth. The material the craft was made from could not be identified.

Flying Saucers Cometh

Although strange phenomena have been seen in the skies around the world for centuries, in 1947 they were inadvertently given a name that captured the popular imagination. The man responsible was a thirty-two-year-old businessman named Kenneth Arnold.

Born in Minnesota in 1915, Arnold attended college on an athletics scholarship, but a knee injury dashed any hope of a career in American football. After he graduated, he set up his own business in Boise, Idaho, designing and marketing fire-fighting equipment. He sold his products across the north-western states and, to visit clients, he learnt to fly, took a pilot's licence and bought a small Callair plane. On 24 June 1947, Arnold clinched a deal in Chehalis, Washington state. His next stop was Yakima, which lay to the east, the other side of the Cascade mountains.

Arnold was also an official air rescue search pilot and he planned to spend some time over the Cascades, searching for a transport aeroplane that had been lost in the area some weeks before. A reward had been offered for finding the wreckage.

It was a clear, sunny day and Arnold spent about an hour searching the area around Mount Rainier. Finding nothing, he turned east for Yakima, flying at an altitude of around 10,000 feet. Suddenly, his plane was lit up by a bright flash. At first, he thought it was the sunlight reflected from a military jet buzzing him, but a visual scan of the sky revealed only a four-engined DC-4 freight plane to port and about fifteen miles behind him. Then he saw a flash in the direction of Mount Baker, 140 miles to the north of Mount Rainier.

Suddenly a formation of nine bright objects came speeding southward towards him. The flashes were sunlight from their metal surfaces, and the whole formation travelled with a strange undulating motion. Eight of the objects were boomerang shaped, but the leading object appeared to be shaped like two boomerangs stuck together.

Arnold turned his plane to get a clearer view. He opened a side window of the cockpit and watched the objects weaving among the peaks of the mountain range. An experienced pilot, Arnold was adept at estimating distance in the air. He estimated that the formation was a hundred miles away when he first saw it and he realised that they must be travelling at an incredible speed. He set about making detailed observations that would help him work out the size and speed of the objects. As the objects passed over a snow-covered ridge, he noted that lead object left the southern end of the ridge as the last one reached the northern end.

As the strange, undulating line of objects passed ahead of his little plane, he timed how long it took for the objects to cover the distance from Mount Rainier to the southern-most crest of Mount Adams, around fifty miles to the south-east. After that, they disappeared. They were travelling at such a speed that the whole sighting had lasted under three minutes.

Arnold was intrigued and excited. Seattle in Washington state was one of the great centres of aircraft design and he was convinced that he had seen the very latest jet aircraft. When he landed at Yakima, he told several people about what he had seen. Then he sat down with a map. Arnold found that the snow-covered ridge the formation had flown over – and hence the formation itself – was five miles long. Then he did some rough calculations based on the timings he had taken and worked out that the objects were travelling at some 1,200 miles an hour, twice the speed of sound, a feat that many still thought was impossible.

Later that afternoon, Arnold flew on to Pendleton, Oregon. There, to his surprise, he was greeted by a crowd of people, including a number of newspaper reporters. News of his mysterious sighting had been radioed ahead from Yakima. In Pendleton, Arnold sat down to check his figures. He obtained a more accurate distance between Mount Rainier and Mount Adams. And when he recalculate the speed of the mysterious objects he discovered that they were travelling at an astonishing 1,700 miles an hour. Even Arnold did not believe this and he cautiously continued to quote his previous figure to the press.

The next day, a man stopped Arnold in the street. He claimed to have seen similar objects just hours before Arnold had made his sighting. This convinced Arnold that he had seen something truly extraordinary. Perhaps it had not been the latest US jet at all, but something more sinister; the Soviets' latest secret weapon, perhaps.

And he decided to report the matter to the FBI. He went to the local FBI office, but it was closed. So Arnold went to the offices of the local newspaper office and told the full story to journalists there.

The newspaper ran the story, using Arnold's description of the sighting and quoting his estimate of the objects' speed. It was in that story that the term 'flying saucer' was invented. Arnold did not describe what he had seen as flying saucers. Nor did he say that he had seen something that looked like a saucer. However, he had used the word saucer: describing the objects, he said: 'Their flight was like speedboats on rough water, or similar to the tail of a Chinese kite that I once saw blowing in the wind. Or maybe it would be best to describe their flight characteristics as very similar to a formation of geese, in a rather diagonal chain-like line, as if they were linked together. As I put it to newsmen in Pendleton, Oregon, they flew like a saucer would if you skipped it across the water. They fluttered and sailed, tipping their wings alternately and emitting those very bright blue-white flashes from their surfaces.'

So it was their movement that was like that of a saucer, not the shape of them.

After the paper ran the story, it put it out on the Associated Press newswires. The newswire subtly changed the story. Their bulletin ran: 'Nine bright saucer-like objects flying at "incredible speed" at 10,000 feet altitude were reported here today by Kenneth Arnold, a Boise, Idaho pilot, who said he could not hazard a guess as to what they were.'

The story caught the media's imagination. It went around the world and, in the process, the term 'flying saucer' caught on. Arnold found himself besieged by the media. The following day he told the local radio station, KWRC: 'I at first thought they were geese, because [they] flew like geese, but [they were] going so fast that I immediately changed my mind and decided it was a bunch of new jet planes in formation... like I told the Associated Press, I'd be glad to confirm it with my hands on a Bible because I did see it, and whether it has anything to do with our army or our intelligence, or whether it has to do with some foreign country, I don't know. But I did see it and I did clock it, and I just happened to be in a beautiful position to do it, and it's just as much a mystery to me as it is to everyone else who's been calling me the last twenty-four hours, wondering what it was.'

Belatedly, the FBI got on the case. Their report says: '[Arnold]... would have to be strongly convinced that he actually saw something before he would report such an incident and open himself up for the ridicule that would accompany such a report.'

Arnold was also contacted by two US Air Force pilots, Captain E.J. Smith and his co-pilot Ralph Stevens, who claimed to have seen similar craft. The three men met up in Seattle in 1947 and compared notes.

There was yet another independent witness to Arnold's sighting. It came from a prospector named Fred Johnson who had seen the objects from the ground. He shied away from going to the news- papers. Instead, he contacted the US Army with his story.

He said that on the afternoon of 24 June, he had been prospecting in the Cascade mountains when a formation of flying objects had passed overhead at around 1,000 feet.

'Their speed as far as I know seemed to be greater than anything I ever saw,' he said.

Altogether he thought that there were five or six objects in the formation. He was carrying a telescope and turned it on one of them. It was oval, he said, with a pointed nose and tail that 'looked like the big hand of a clock and shifted from side to side'. The last he saw of the discs, they were standing on edge, banking away into a cloud. He also noticed that the needle of his compass swung about wildly while they were around. But once they had gone, it settled down.

A month after the sighting, Arnold was flying to Maury Island in Puget Sound, when he saw another chain of objects approaching him at high speed. This time there were twenty-five of them.

'I was a little bit shocked and excited when I realised that they had the same flight characteristics as the large objects I had observed,' he said.

He turned his plane to follow them, but they disappeared at high speed. He was sure that they could not have been birds – they travelled too fast. Later he discovered that local farmers had reported seeing an unusual flight of 'birds' that morning. Having already been in the centre of a media circus, this time Arnold refrained from telling the press or the authorities.

Arnold's interest in UFOs did not end there. He took to investigating other sightings and has been called the world's first UFOlogist. In 1952, he published *The Coming of the Saucers*, co-written by the publisher of *Amazing Stories*, Ray Palmer, who quickly founded *Fate* magazine, the first dedicated UFO publication.

In 1977, Arnold was the guest of honour at a UFO convention called to celebrate the 30th anniversary of this Mount Rainier sighting. Otherwise he kept his distance from enthusiasts. He did not believe that flying saucers were alien spacecraft, rather he thought that they were some kind of living creature that lived high up in the Earth's atmosphere. He died in 1984.

The Site of the Sighting

Since Kenneth Arnold's first encounter with flying saucers there in 1947, the Cascades have been a rich source of sightings, particularly in the mid-1960s. Sightings reached another peak in the 1970s when local firemen were alerted to glowing balls of light being observed in the Yakima Indian Reserve, just east of the Cascades. UFOlogist David Ackers was called in to investigate.

'There was one spooky one which just crept up on me,' he said. 'The object had the shape of a large brownish-orange ball which flickered slightly.'

Ackers concluded that there was UFO activity going on, but there was no conclusive proof that it was extraterrestrial in origin. Writer Paul Devereux, who is a leading proponent of the 'earthlight' theory of UFOs, points to the Cascades as a natural home for that phenomenon. According to the earthlight theory, glowing lights in the sky and other anomalies that are interpreted as UFOs are caused by electromagnetic fields generated by the build-up of strains in the Earth's crust. The Cascades are subject to just such geological disturbances. Geological surveys say there was a lull in seismic activity in the area at the time of Arnold's sighting. But Devereux says the geological stresses were building and there was an earthquake in the area in 1949.

However, Arnold was an experienced pilot and was trained in the observational skills required by a search pilot. Few can doubt that he knew what he saw. Despite the scoffing of sceptics, his sighting has stood the test of time and in all the years since he saw the first flying saucer no one has proved him wrong.

Island of Intrigue

After his first sighting over the Cascades, Kenneth Arnold saw another formation of UFOs flying over Maury Island in Washington state. He was not alone. On 23 June 1947, the day before Arnold made his famous 'flying saucer' sighting, Tacoma harbour patrolman Harold A. Dahl, his fifteen-year-old son, another crew member and the Dahl's dog set off by boat to patrol Puget Sound. The day was overcast. The sky was thick with grey clouds and it looked as if it was going to rain. Anticipating a storm, Dahl decided to take shelter in a bay on Maury Island, opposite Tacoma, which was about two miles away across the water. On the way, six doughnut-shaped UFOs appeared overhead. Dahl and crew were stunned. Then, menacingly, one of the objects began to descend.

The UFO was around a hundred feet in diameter and it had a hole in the middle. It appeared to be made of metal. On the outer rim there were two portholes but the inner side of the doughnut was lined with round windows. Dahl quickly beached his vessel, then climbed out and took four photographs of the UFO.

The UFOs seemed to take this amiss. Without warning, one of them sprayed the beach with molten metal. The red-hot shower hit the boat, killing the dog and severely burning the arm of Dahl's son. Then the UFOs rose into the sky and disappeared towards the Pacific.

Dahl reported the encounter to his superior officer, Fred L. Crisman.

The following morning, a mysterious black-clad stranger arrived at Dahl's home in a black Buick sedan car and invited him out for breakfast. Dahl was amazed when the man revealed that he knew about the encounter the previous day.

'Silence is the best thing for you and your family,' the man whispered conspiratorially. 'You should not have seen what you have seen.'

Dahl was a good, law-abiding citizen, and the meeting left him shaken and perplexed.

Although Maury Island is just twenty miles away from the Cascade Mountains, it is fairly cut off from the rest of the world and Dahl knew nothing of Kenneth Arnold's fateful encounter that day. However, *Amazing Stories*' publisher Ray Palmer heard of the sighting at Maury Island, and he offered Arnold $200 to investigate the case. $200 was not to be sniffed at in 1947 and Arnold plunged himself into what was to become one of the most contentious cases in the history of UFOlogy.

On 29 July, Arnold flew to Tacoma to start his investigation. He was on his way when he made his second sighting. When he arrived, he headed for the Winthrop Hotel and was surprised to find that a room had already been booked in his name, even though no one was supposed to know that he was in town. But Arnold put this down to a lucky coincidence and set about tracking down Dahl.

After his meeting with the man in black, Dahl was naturally circumspect. He refused to meet Arnold, saying the encounter had brought him nothing but bad luck. He even suggested that Arnold ditch the investigation and head back to Idaho where he belonged. But Arnold was persistent and eventually persuaded Dahl to come to his room at the Winthrop, where Dahl explained what he had seen.

Dahl turned up again the following morning at 9:30 a.m. Arnold was still asleep and he was woken by Dahl banging on the door. This time, Dahl was not alone. He was with Crisman, his command officer, and Crisman was doing all the talking. He said that he had been out to the island to check out Dahl's story. There was debris all over the island, he said.

Arnold naturally wanted to see the debris for himself, but first he decided to enlist some help. He called Captain E.J. Smith, one of the other witnesses to his Mount Rainier sighting, who he had recently met in Seattle, and explained the situation. Smith was eager to help and, on 30 July, Arnold went to pick him up in his plane.

That afternoon, with Smith now ensconced at the Winthrop, Dahl and Crisman returned to the hotel and told Smith their stories. After a thorough cross-examination of the pair, Smith asked Crisman and Dahl to supply samples of the debris. He also wanted to see Dahl's photographs. And he asked them to organise a meeting with Dahl's crewman and a trip to the island.

Later that evening, out of the blue, Arnold got a phone call from Ted Morello, a journalist from the United Press. Morello said that details of private conversations between Arnold and Smith had been leaked to him by an anonymous caller. Arnold suspected Dahl and Crisman, but Morello knew what had been said when Arnold and Smith had been alone in the room. Arnold then suspected that the room was bugged, but an exhaustive search of the room found nothing. Arnold was now beginning to regret that he had got himself involved.

Smith and Arnold's suspicions were further aroused the following day when Crisman, Dahl and his crewman arrived with samples of the debris as requested. Arnold noted that the fragments did not match Dahl's descriptions. They looked and felt no like ordinary aircraft metal. The photographs were not forthcoming either. Arnold attempted to apply pressure by telling Crisman that he was going to involve US Air Force Intelligence. Although this did not faze Crisman at all, Arnold was prepared. As good his word, he phoned Lieutenant Brown, an intelligence officer at Hamilton Field Air Force Base in California who had a history of investigating UFO reports. He agreed to lend his expertise to the investigation.

But even as he was making his call, Arnold saw Smith and Crisman rapt in a private conversation. He then began to believe that it was Smith that was leaking their private conversations. After all, he was an officer in the Air Force.

Later that day, Brown and a colleague called Davidson flew to Tacoma in a B-25. They came to the Winthrop. Crisman duly arrived and related both his own and Dahl's story. Arnold noticed that Brown showed little interest in Crisman's account, as if he had heard it all before. When Crisman had finished, Brown and his colleague immediately made their excuses and set off back to Hamilton Field with the box of the so-called 'debris'.

Events, already suspicious, now turned down right sinister. The following day, Arnold got a call from Crisman telling him that Brown's B-25 had crashed some twenty minutes after taking off from Tacoma. Both Brown and Davidson had been killed, Crisman said. Arnold could not believe his ears, but the report was confirmed by Smith who had verified the news with Brown's superiors.

Arnold then began to fear for his own life. He called Ray Palmer and told him what had happened to Brown and Davidson. He said he was quitting the investigation and heading home. Under the circumstances, Palmer advised Arnold not to take any remaining fragments with him on the plane home.

Before Arnold left, Crisman took him to see the boat that he said had been damaged in the encounter. But when Arnold saw it, it was obvious that it was not the same boat that Dahl had taken to Maury Island on 23 June. And Crisman still failed to produce the photographs. In despair, Arnold returned to the Winthorp. He was packing when got a call from Morello.

The anonymous informant had informed Morello that Brown and Davidson's plane was shot down. On 2 August, the *Tacoma Times* carried the headline: 'Sabotage Hinted in Crash of Army Bomber at Kelso.' The article speculated that the plane had been hit by a 20mm cannon to stop the Maury Island 'flying saucer debris' from reaching Hamilton Field Air Force Base. Morello also hinted that Arnold's aircraft would be shot at.

Arnold was now completely freaked. He and Smith went to find Dahl, who informed them that Crisman had left town. Morello confirmed that Crisman had embarked on an army bomber bound for Alaska. Smith had already received orders return to his post. As the entire investigation fell apart, Arnold was eager to make himself scarce too.

It was now too late to fly home and Arnold decided to stay on in Tacoma overnight. The following morning, he decided to say goodbye to Dahl before leaving. But when he arrived at Dahl's home he found the house derelict. And there was no sign of Dahl.

By then only thing that concerned Arnold was getting home in one piece. He took off from Tacoma in trepidation. Everything went smoothly until he made a refuelling stop in Pendleton, Oregon. After that, on the final leg of the journey to Idaho, his engine cut out. He was sure that he was going the same way as Brown and Davidson. But he was in small plane that could glide, and he had the skill to land the plane in one piece.

With Arnold out of the way, the investigation was taken over by an Army Intelligence officer from McChord Field. The case, he said, was a hoax and the associated deaths and disappearances mere coincidences. However, for those who understood the machinations of government, this pat explanation suggested a cover-up. Plainly, someone had gone to great lengths to sandbag the Maury Island investigation. They were willing to kill to prevent the truth coming out. But who were they, and why were they doing this?

Four years later UFOlogist John Keel claimed to have the answer. He reckons that Crisman had been in cahoots with Ray Palmer for years and, after Arnold's sighting in the Cascades had made headlines, they had dreamt up the Maury Island mystery. Crisman had recruited Dahl into the conspiracy, then tried to persuade Palmer to run the story in *Amazing Stories*. Lieutenant Brown showed no interest in Crisman's story because it was so plainly a hoax. According to Keel, Brown did not even take the debris on the plane with him back to Hamilton Field Air Force Base and the crash was merely a coincidence.

Strangely, although Keel is convinced that Crisman and Dahl's story was an invention, he believes that something strange did occur on Maury Island on 23 June 1947. Dahl's son's injuries and the death of the dog bear this out. The key, Keel maintains, lies in the strange molten metal deposited on the boat. Keel believes that this came from the Atomic Energy Commission plutonium processing plant in nearby Hanford, Washington. The Maury Island encounter, he reckons, was simply a case of the illegal dumping of radioactive waste dropped by plane in the sound.

Then we come to Dahl's mysterious black-clad visitor. According to Keel, he was simply a security agent of the AEC, who had traced Dahl from the records of his son who was then in hospital with radiation burns. The AEC hardly wanted evidence of illegal dumping of nuclear waste being published far and wide. That's why he had warned Dahl to keep quiet.

You may find Keel's argument is convincing. It may be the truth. But we will never know what really happened at Maury Island that night. Crisman and Dahl, the men who hold all the answers, have not resurfaced since their disappearance in 1947, so we will have to make do with the official findings.

On 27 April 1949, a report on UFO sightings entitled 'Project Saucer' was issued by the Air Materials Command at Wright Field, Dayton, Ohio. As part of its investigation, it published details of the analysis of the Maury Island debris. Its findings were that the crude material sample was magnetic and the debris contained minerals such as iron oxide; about 21 per cent of the sample was soluble in hydrochloric acid. The part of the residue that was insoluble was non-magnetic. Since there were obviously two different chemical components, they were tested separately. The acid-soluble fraction was 49.7 per cent iron with traces of the heavy metals molybdenum and cadmium. No copper, nickel or cobalt was found. The remainder of this faction was largely oxygen. The fraction that was acid insoluble contained manganese and manganese oxide, iron and iron oxide, calcium and calcium oxide, and barium and barium oxide. The report's conclusion was that all these substances were terrestrial in origin, implying that the Maury Island encounter was a hoax.

However, the debris samples have never been submitted to independent analysis.

History as We Know it?

Antique Astronauts

In the thirty years following World War II, humankind made its technological leap into space. At the same time flying saucers began buzzing the earth in ever increasing numbers and reports of alien encounters became commonplace.

But some people began to wonder if aliens had only just started visiting the Earth. We now saw their craft as spaceship and the aliens themselves as astronauts only because we had recently become familiar with these ideas. If they had been visiting us in ancient times, say, they would have been seen completely differently.

An early advocate of the idea was Desmond Leslie, who co-authored the best-selling *Flying Saucers Have Landed* with UFO contactee George Adamski in 1953. Leslie began looking for evidence that space visitors had come to Earth before. He turned to ancient literature. In the Vedic literature of India, written between 1,500 and 500 BCE, he found references to *vimanas* or 'airboats'. Leslie realised that the flying saucers seen in the 1940s and 1950s were only an interplanetary, more advanced, model of the ancient *vimana*. He also looked into Celtic myth and found ancient heroes such as Chuchulain of Ireland, who had at their disposal weapons that bore a striking resemblance to modern-day missiles and tanks. And hieroglyphics on the ceiling of the Temple of Abydos in Egypt, built over five thousand years ago, clearly shows modern military technology, including gunboats, a helicopter, a submarine, a plane and a gun.

Leslie deduced that a race of space people had come to Earth before the Flood and interbred with Earthlings. Their hybrid offspring founded what we now known as the civilisation of Atlantis. And he is not alone in this belief. Many people believe that alien intervention explains the great leap humankind made when our ape-like ancestors came down from the trees and suddenly spawned vast, complex civilisations.

It has also been suggested that ancient monuments, such as the pyramids, were built by ancient astronauts. Some five thousand years ago, it is said, a giant UFO swooped down over the desert at Gisa. Its energy beams cut and moved huge stone blocks into place while astonished desert nomads looked on. The craft then flew off leaving behind them three huge pyramids. The amazed onlookers would have had no words to describe what they saw. For generations, they would recount in their legends and their sacred texts that they had received a visit from god. After all, the ancient Egyptian god, Re, rides across the sky in a fiery chariot.

According to this theory, the ancient astronauts also intervened to build other, otherwise unexplainable ancient monuments – Stonehenge in England, the giant statues on Easter Island and the curious pyramids of Latin America. No one knows why these advanced alien civilisations would help the primitive indigenous people to build these huge structures. However, even the sceptics admit that these monuments have an astronomical significance. Perhaps they are gateways to the stars.

Alien Influence

Others believe that the alien visitors made no direct intervention in human history – just as they refrain from direct intervention now. But the mere presence of the aliens and their artefacts gave evolution a nudge – the most famous depiction of this is the opening scenes of Arthur C. Clarke's novel and the movie *2001: A Space Odyssey*.

None of these ideas are particularly new. The concept of advanced civilisations from the stars influencing human progress has been around since at least Victorian times, when members of the Theosophical Society, an occult group, imagined an alternative history for the human race. In 1888, the Theosophists' leader Madame Blavatsky published *The Secret Doctrine*, all 1,500 pages of it. It purports to have been based on the world's first book *The Stanzas of Dzyan* which, unfortunately, scholars down the ages have failed to unearth. The heavens, Madame Blavatsky said, are full of numerous universes, each containing countless solar systems. Each solar system had its own god. Beneath him are seven planetary spirits, each in charge of a phalanx of angels. They had all the characteristics of modern-day astronauts.

Evolution, she said, takes place by steps from mineral to vegetable to animal to human to the superhuman or spiritual being who could travel out into space. The first inhabitants of Earth descended from the residents of the moon and lived on a continent called the 'Imperishable Sacred Land'. Then came the Hyperborean race, also known as the Boneless or the Sweatborn. They lived at the North Pole. But as they did not have bodies, presumably, they did not feel the cold. Next came the Lemurians, who were the first to have bodies and reproduced by sexual intercourse. Their homeland is now at the bottom of the Indian Ocean – Atlantis again.

The fifth of these so-called 'root races' were the Aryans who spread south and west from Northern Asia. Apparently, we are still in the Aryan phase. Madam Blavatsky revealed that there will be two more root races. Then the cycle will be complete and humans will move on to another planet to start all over again. Meanwhile, individual humans progress from having physical bodies, through astral, mental and ethereal, in a series of incarnations. Progress is regulated by your karma. Obviously, those with the best karma have arrived at the highest ethereal state. These are the Masters, superbeings who visited Earth to vouchsafe wisdom to Madame Blavatsky.

Chariots of the Gods

These concepts made global headlines again the 1970s with the work of the Swiss author, Erich von Däniken. In 1968, he wrote *Chariots of the Gods*, which presented evidence for alien visitations in ancient times. After a slow start, it became a world-wide best-seller. Von Däniken followed up with further titles, which unravel all the ancient mysteries in terms of visits from ancient spacemen.

Central to von Däniken's concept is the remarkable consistency of the images and icons of ancient peoples – even though they were spread far and wide across the world. There is also a uniformity to their legends and the characteristics of their gods which could not be put down to chance. He picked up these ideas from his childhood reading of the Bible.

'I was intrigued by the references in the Old Testament which seemed to suggest God travelled by various means of sophisticated transport,' he says. 'After a lot of research, I found that many other ancient peoples recorded similar stories about god-like beings. I decided that the gods must therefore be extraterrestrials.'

There is a similarity in the creation myths and the accounts of visitations from the gods from sources as diverse as the ancient Egyptians, the Maya and the ancient Chinese, who would have had no contact with each other. Von Däniken dismisses the idea that the accounts of flying gods might only be symbolic.

'That's impossible,' he says. 'These "heavenly beings" gave mankind a lot of advanced knowledge – astronomy, for instance – at the dawn of civilisation. This is not symbolism, but fact.'

This memory of visitation by ancient astronauts exists not just in myth and sacred texts. The Kayapo Indians of Brazil – a tribe that has been in existence for over four thousand years – has a ceremony in which a figure appears in a bulky 'space suit' made from basketwork. The figure represents the 'teacher from heaven' and the ceremony commemorates the alien's visit to the tribe.

Von Däniken also turned to ancient Indian texts, in this case the *Mahabharata*, which was written slightly later than the Vedic texts, but borrows much from them. And, like Desmond Leslie before him, von Däniken draws attention to the detailed descriptions of the *virmanas* –

a word meaning 'flying machines'. In the text, the *virmanas* are often piloted by Indian gods and are sometimes used for military purposes. In one particularly striking passage, one of them unleashes an *agneya* weapon: 'A blazing missile possessed of the radiance of smokeless fire was discharged. A thick gloom suddenly encompassed the hosts. All points of the compass were suddenly enveloped in darkness. Evil bearing winds began to blow. Clouds reared into the higher air, showering blood. The very elements seemed confused. The sun appeared to spin round. The world, scorched by the heat of that weapon, seemed to be in fever.'

It is not hard to see that this is the description of a nuclear warhead exploding. There is no reason to believe that the ancient Indian civilisation – or indeed any ancient civilisation – had nuclear weapons, so it is easy to conclude that the *virmanas* were of extraterrestrial origin.

It is clear that the story of the destruction of Sodom and Gomorrah in the Bible was also caused by a nuclear blast. First two angels appeared to Lot, the only righteous man in Sodom. They told him to take his family and leave as the two cities were to be destroyed. As they were fleeing, 'the Lord rained upon Sodom and Gomorrah brimstone and fire'. Lot's wife stopped and looked back. She was turned into a pillar of salt. Von Däniken says that the two angels who appeared to Lot were clearly ancient alien astronauts.

According to the Bible, the Red Sea was parted to let the Children of Israel escape from Egypt and the Moses was led to the Promised Land by a pillar of light. These have been interpreted as more examples of alien intervention in human history.

Once ancient history is seen through these eyes, evidence of ancient astronauts is everywhere. Primitive man was obsessed with space-suited figures. Drawings of what look like astronauts are found in cave dwellings in the Americas, Europe, Africa, the Far East and Australia. A figure carved on the rocks of Val Camonica, Italy, is wearing headgear with some kind of aerial sprouting from it. Another helmeted figure appears in a rock carving at Capo di Ponte. Similar figures have been found carved into the ancient petroglyphs of the Toro Muerte desert in Peru. A weird rock art figure at Tassili in the Sahara was nicknamed 'the Martian' by archaeologists. Von Däniken says that it is plainly wearing a spacesuit. An ancient Australian Aboriginal cave drawing made some five thousand years ago shows the same thing.

A space-suited figure in a cave painting on the Russo-Chinese border, painted around 2000 BCE, is holding a disc-shaped communication device. The figure's helmet has two antennae on it and above it there is a flying saucer, emitting a plume of smoke.

Von Däniken also points out that the astonishing cementless masonry of Inca architecture, as well as the erection of the massive stone blocks found in megalithic monuments worldwide, could easily be achieved by alien anti-gravity technology or something similar. He has found Egyptian effigies that bear an astonishing resemblance to modern aircraft and an Aztec incense burner that is shaped like a jet engine. The handle of an Aztec ceremonial knife shows a flying god, and a pre-historic Colombian figurine shows a god wearing a space helmet, as does a Japanese Dogu sculpture, which is over five thousand years old. This figure is also wearing goggles – not a common item in Stone Age Japan.

A carving on the lid of a tomb in the ancient Mayan Temple at Palenque, Mexico, shows a seated figure, wearing a helmet, squeezed into small capsule, crammed with levers and other controls. This is plainly a space ship, though experts in Maya mythology insist that it shows the symbolic descent of a dead man's soul into the underworld.

A small sculpture showing a figure in a space capsule was unearthed at Toprakkale in Turkey. Although some have tried to dismiss it as a hoax, it is three thousand years old. The four-thousand-year-old Lolladoff plate from Nepal clearly shows a disc-shaped UFO and the figure of a classic 'Grey', as seen by modern abductees. Other flying saucers appear in a Neolithic cave painting in south-west France, painted five thousand years ago. It shows wildlife in a landscape, with disc-shaped UFOs hovering above. Curiously, a humanoid figure near one of the UFOs has a tail.

But more disturbing is the evidence of a deformed skull on show at the Museum of the Inca in Peru. It is three thousand years old, and its weird elongated head-shape is also seen in ancient Egyptian reliefs. Von Däniken maintains that the head was deliberately stretched to ape the head-shape of alien visitors. Others say that it is the product of some early genetic experiment.

The lost Ark of the Covenant, the gold-plated chest in which Moses put the tablets of stone containing the Ten Commandments, may hold another clue. No ordinary person can touch it, otherwise they would die. Von Däniken says that it was essentially a condenser and anyone who touched it would be electrocuted. The two gold cherubs on the top were antennae – the whole thing was a radio set, which allowed, Moses to communicate with the 'Lord' in the mothership above. But in *The Sign and the Seal,* journalist Graham Hancock maintains that it was a nuclear weapon and anyone who touched it would die from radiation sickness.

Von Däniken has also found one of the alien's landing sites. These are the so-called Nazca lines, a vast array of ancient lines and drawings on the Plain of Nazca in the Peruvian Andes, which can be seen only from the air. Because there is no rain and little wind on the Nazca plain, these lines have survived since prehistoric times, but they were identified only when people began flying over them in aircraft in the 1930s.

Orthodox archaeologists insist that the Nazca markings are ancient roads. The problem is that they lead nowhere, though there is now a theory that the cities some of the straight lines joined were subsequently destroyed. Others have said that the markings are some kind of ancient calendar. But in *Von Däniken's Proof* (1977), he points out, correctly, that the lines show no astronomical alignments. Along with the straight lines, there are markings that look like the parking bays for aircraft at a modern-day airport. Is this where ancient astronauts parked their spaceships? There are patterns – triangles, spirals, a bird, a monkey, a spider and flowers – all hundreds of feet long. They can be seen only from the sky.

Researchers in Britain and France say that ley lines – the lines that connect ancient monuments that are, again, clearly visible only from above – also hold a clue. Plotted on a map, UFO sightings fall into straight lines that correspond to ancient leys.

The biggest problem with the concept of alien visitation, ancient or modern, is the question of how aliens could travel vast interstellar distances to get here. As far as we can tell, there is no other inhabited planet in our solar system. So the nearest home for another civilisation most be at least 4.2 light years away – on a planet orbiting the nearest star to our sun. Even if a civilisation discovered a way of travelling at close to the speed of light – the theoretical limit – it would take them over eight years to make a round trip, so they would hardly be dropping by for a casual visit. Physicists are now grappling with ways to break this upper limit, possibly by travelling through worm-holes in space and time which join two very distance places. Another theory is that they travel through space relatively slowly on huge, self-sustaining motherships and those craft we see visiting Earth are smaller scout craft. In this scenario, the extraterrestrial race visited our forebears on Earth thousands of years ago and left their indelible mark on human history. Now they are coming back again.

The Offspring of Sirius

Another version of the ancient astronaut idea was outlined by Robert Temple in 1976 in his book *The Sirius Mystery*. In the book, Temple expands on the findings of two French anthropologists who studied the Dogon people of Mali. According to tribal folklore, the Dogon trace their origins to the Nommo, a race of amphibious creatures who come from a planet orbiting the star Sirius and landed in ships in Egypt five to six thousand years ago. Indeed, Sirius was central to ancient Egyptian cosmology. The brightest star in the sky, its first dawn rising each year coincided with the annual flood of the Nile, which was crucial to the agriculture that sustained Egyptian civilisation.

Every half century, the Dogon perform a unique ceremony called the Sigui. In it they celebrate Sirius's twin, a small, heavy star that orbits Sirius once every fifty years. Indeed the star Sirius does have a twin, Sirius B, but it is invisible to the naked eye. Neither the Dogon nor any ancient civilisations possessed the optics necessary to see it. The Dogon also knew that Sirius's companion was super dense, a fact known to modern science only in 1926, just five years before Western anthropologists first contacted the Dogon.

But that is not the limit of their knowledge of the Sirius system. Dogon priests have known details of the precise orbital period of Sirius B for many centuries. They also know of a third body in the system that has not yet been identified by modern astronomers. The knowledge has been handed down by a secret oral tradition, started long before Western astronomers even knew that Sirius B existed. Plainly, the Dogon could have got their information only from some extraterrestrial source. There is no other explanation.

The Dogon of Mali are an isolated tribe living in a remote area of West Africa. These days there are barely two hundred thousand of them. They live in villages clinging to the steep Bandiagara cliffs east of the Upper Niger River. While they cannot be described as 'primitive' – they have a sophisticated cultural life – they are not technically advanced.

In the late 1940s, two leading French anthropologists, Marcel Griaule and Germaine Dieterlen, spent a long period living with the Dogon. The two scientists eventually won the confidence of the priests, who divulged the secrets of their religious beliefs.

The Dogon's creation myth is tied up with a small star called Po Tolo, which means 'seed star'. The star is also named after the tiniest seed known to them, which they call 'fonio', and is know botanically as *Digitaria exilis*. The smallest seed, for the Dogon, means the beginning of all things. The Dogon believe that creation began with this collapsed star, which is companion of the brilliant Sirius A, or Dog Star. Known astronomically as Sirius B, it is a 'white dwarf' and is visible only through a powerful telescope. It gives off little light and is overwhelmed by Sirius A, which is ten thousand times brighter. Indeed, although Sirius A is 23 times more luminous than our own sun

– there are many stars that are far brighter – it is only 8.6 light years from Earth, making it the brightest star in the night sky.

The Dogon possess a startling wealth of astronomical detail about the Sirius system. They know that Po Tolo is massively dense – its weight is out of all proportion to its small size. This is a property of white dwarves, whose density is a million times that of water. Sirius B is 27,000 times denser than our sun. However, astrophysicists discovered this property only in the twentieth century. The Dogon believe that this is due to the presence of sagala, an extremely dense and strong metallic element unknown on earth. Indeed, matter compressed to that extent is metallic. The Dogon also show that the orbit of Sirius B around Sirius A forms an ellipse, with Sirius A at one focus. This idea only arrived in Western astronomy in the early seventeenth century, when Johannes Kepler overturned the idea that heavenly bodies moved in perfect circular paths.

The Dogon believe Sirius B takes fifty years to orbit Sirius A. Modern astronomy has put the actual orbital period at 50.04 years – close enough. The Dogon also say that Sirius B rotates on its own axis, with a period of one earth-year. Modern astronomy does not have equipment powerful enough to check this. Nor can modern astronomers confirm the Dogon claim that there is a third body in the Sirius system. They call this third object Emme Ya, or 'sorghum woman' (sorghum is the local grain). This is either a small star with a single planet orbiting it, or a planet with a large satellite – like the Earth and the Moon. This is said to be the home of their ancestors, the Nommo.

Griaule and Dieterlen published the Dogon's story for the first time in the book, *A Sudanese Sirius System*, in 1950. This piqued the interest of Robert Temple, a Fellow of the Royal Astronomical Society, who then set about investigating their extraordinary claims. As the Dogon have known this information for thousands of year, Temple argues that it must have been come from ancient astronauts.

This idea was not received with universal approval. Indeed, it was greeted with downright hostility by the late Carl Sagan, popular science writer, Ian Ridpath and others. They argued that people from Europe had been exploring Africa for the previous 150 years. Someone could have come across the Dogon during that time, given them the information about the Sirius system, and the Dogon incorporated it into their cosmology. However, the idea that Sirius might have a tiny companion was raised by F.W. Bessel only in Köningsberg, Prussia, in 1844. It was not until 1862, when Alva N Clark made a 45-centimetre lens for the Dearborn Observatory in Evansville, Indiana, that it was first seen and it was only photographed for the first time in 1970. The idea that there were such things as super-dense stars only came into currency in 1926. Even so, it was hardly the topic of casual conversation. Dieterlen has since shown that one Dogon model of the Sirius system is nearly five hundred years old. And there is plenty of evidence to show that the Dogon's astronomical knowledge is much older than that. According to conventional history, the Dogon are descendants of Greeks who colonised the part of northern Africa that forms modern Libya. The Roman historian Herodotus called them 'Garamantians', after Garamas, the son of the Greek earth goddess Gaia. Like their Greek forebears, the Dogon are preoccupied with numbers. During their time in Libya, they would certainly have been in an excellent position to pick up astronomical knowledge from the neighbouring Egyptians.

With the destruction of Carthage in 146 BCE, they began to move south. Centuries of slow migration brought the Dogon to the Upper Niger River where they settled and interbred with black Africans living there. According to the twentieth-century historian Robert Graves, the last remnants of this wandering tribe now live in a village called Koromantse, about fifty miles from Bandiagara.

During their travels, it seems improbable that the Dogon had access to astronomical instruments, or met people who had a sophisticated knowledge of the workings of the heavens. So it seems likely that whatever astronomical knowledge they have came from Egypt, at least nine hundred years before.

The Dogon themselves say that their remarkable knowledge of the complex astronomy of the Sirius system came from their distant ancestors, amphibian extraterrestrials, who they call 'Nommos' and who came from the vicinity of Po Tolo, or Sirius B.

The Dogon are very precise about this. They say the Nommos first arrived from the Sirius system in a vessel that spun, or whirled, during its descent, and made a loud noise like the roaring wind. They also recalled that the flying machine skipped as it landed – like a flat stone skimming across water. It churned up the surface of the ground with what the Dogon call 'spurts of blood'. Those who know the Dogon language say that this phrase could equally translate as 'rocket exhaust' and they could be describing the reverse thrust used to land modern spacecraft. At the same time, the Dogon say that a new heavenly body hovered in the sky at some distance. This could have been a 'mother ship' that remained in orbit while a smaller craft was sent down to the surface of the Earth – in the same way as, during the moon landings, the Apollo space capsule stayed in orbit while the lunar module landed on the Moon's surface.

The Dogon say that the Nommos are amphibians – Nommos in the Dogon language means 'associated with water' or 'finding drinking water is essential'. The Dogon say that they normally lived in water, indeed, they were 'masters of the water'. In Dogon art, they are shown as half reptile, half human.

And the Nommos are not entirely unknown elsewhere on Earth. Representations of the Nommos in Dogon ceremonial carvings bear a striking resemblance to the Babylonian fish-tailed 'demi-god' Oannes, the Akkadians' Nommos-like amphibians known as Ea, the Sumerian Enki and the depiction in some early Egyptian religious art of the goddess Isis in mermaid form. All these figures were supposed to be the progenitors of their particular civilisations.

While the Dogon's knowledge is preserved as a living tradition, much of the knowledge of the Babylonians, Akkadians and ancient Egyptians has been lost. However, it is known that Isis was associated with Sirius, and her consort Osiris was linked to the Dog Star's dark companion. In the temple to Isis at Denderah, the Chapel of the New

Year is constructed so that the light from Sirius is channelled down a shaft into the chamber within. This is reminiscent of the Dogon's Sigui ceremony, which is held in the village of Yougo Dogorou when Sirius is visible through a cleft of a rock. Osiris was also the god of the afterlife and Egyptians believed that their immortal souls would live in the heavens with him.

UFO
Encounters

Dangerous Liaisons

Protect Yourself

There should be a warning on the side of every UFO that reads: alien encounters can harm your health. And this is not simple paranoia. There are plenty of reports of people being harmed by extraterrestrials. Sometimes they suffer through exposure to the energy fields associated with UFOs. Then there are the more life-threatening episodes that occur during alien abductions – intrusive examinations, unwanted surgery and the embedding of 'implants' in the body. And sometimes there is outright hostile intent.

Even an innocent UFO sighting can result in psychological problems, including anxiety, mania, depression and post-traumatic stress disorder. In other cases, severe physical effects – burns, eyesight damage, radiation sickness and even cancer – have been reported. One consistent feature of reports of UFO sightings and alien encounters from across the globe is that they cast the human witness as a victim. Usually, there is little doubt that those involved in such episodes have experienced ill effects; the medical evidence is there for all to see.

Alien Aggression

The first hostile alien encounter took place two months after Kenneth Arnold had first reported seeing flying saucers over the Cascades. In August 1947, geologist Rapuzzi Johannis was climbing the Italian Alps above the village of Villa Santina when he saw a group of aliens. Johannes raised his geologist's pick in greeting, but his gesture misinterpreted. The aliens immediately fired a beam of light at him that knocked him down the mountainside. Fortunately, his fall was halted by some loose rubble. But the fall left him semi-paralysed and he faced a painful crawl home.

Another unprovoked attack occurred in France on 1 July 1965, when farmer Maurice Masse encountered a similar group of aliens near Valensole. The aliens pointed a 'stick' at him. Although he did not see what happened next, he found himself being flung to the ground. His muscles were paralysed, but he remained conscious.

Too Close for Comfort

On 20 May 1967, a UFO encounter left fifty-two-year-old Canadian engineer Stephen Michalak injured. Michalak's hobby was geology and he was out hunting for minerals near Falcon Lake, eighty miles east of Winnipeg. He heard the sound of geese cackling and looked upwards. He saw two disc-shaped craft hovering overhead. One flew away, but the other landed not far away. Michalak noticed that the object was changing colour as if cooling. He felt waves of heat coming off it. They carried with them a vile, sulphurous odour.

As Michalak approached the craft, a doorway opened in its side and a brilliant violet light spilled out. The doorway closed again as he got closer. In a foolhardy move, Michalak reached out his hand to touch the surface of the ship. It was hot and he immediately drew his hand back, but his glove had already melted. At that moment, the disc tilted and a blast of light from an 'exhaust panel' in the side hit Michalak in the chest, setting fire to his shirt. He tore off his burning shirt as the spaceship disappeared out of sight.

The two-mile trek back to the highway was agonising and Michalak vomited countless times. When he returned to Winnipeg he was treated for first-degree burns and released. Two days later he returned to the doctor suffering from a mysterious malady. The doctor prescribed pain-killers and sea-sickness tablets, which were of little help. For several days after the incident he was unable to keep his food down and he lost twenty-two pounds in weight. His blood lymphocyte count was down from twenty-five per cent to sixteen per cent. Medical reports also showed that he had skin infections and rashes. He suffered from nausea, diarrhoea, generalised urticaria and blackouts, and generally felt weak and dizzy. He also experienced numbness and chronic swelling of the joints. Then, in August 1968 – fifteen months after the encounter – a geometric pattern of burns appeared on his chest.

Over eighteen months, Michalak was examined by a total of twenty-seven doctors, at a cost of thousands of dollars, but none explained the cause of his symptoms. The case was also investigated by a number of government departments.

The Canadian Department of National Defense examined the encounter site. They found higher than normal background radiation, along with silver fragments that had been exposed to great heat. The full results of their investigations were never made public. A file itself was eventually released, but it was incomplete and contained so many deletions that it was not much use. However, a number of independent researchers have pointed out that Michalak's symptoms are reminiscent of radiation exposure. If this was the case, Michalak is far from alone in experiencing these symptoms after an encounter with a UFO.

Blinded by the Light

On the evening of 7 January 1970, two unfortunate skiers were out on the wooded slopes near the village of Imjarvi, Finland. The temperature was far below freezing that night and Esko Viljo and Aarno Heinonen had stopped briefly at the base of a slope to try and warm themselves when, suddenly, the air was filled with a strange buzzing sound. Then they saw a glowing light surrounded by mist, spiralling downwards into a clearing. The fog began to spread out through the woods and the sound increased in pitch. Then, through the mist, a strange figure appeared. The encounter was cut short by a silent but dazzling explosion of light. It blasted the mist apart, leaving Viljo and Heinonen shrouded in darkness.

The shock was too much for Heinonen, who had been closer to the explosion. He stumbled forward and collapsed. One side of his body was completely paralysed. Viljo helped him to his feet and, together, they began to trudge back to the village.

It was an arduous journey in their enfeebled state. On the way, Heinonen's condition worsened, and the two men were forced to abandon their skis. By the time they reached the village, Heinonen was seriously ill. He was vomiting frequently. His head was pounding and he found that his urine was discoloured. One doctor who examined Heinonen noted that he exhibited the symptoms of radiation sickness, but could find no obvious cause, and, eventually, the symptoms disappeared.

Although Viljo had been further away, he had not escaped unscathed. There were problems with his eyes and he suffered excessive tiredness. The both men suffered post-traumatic stress, which badly affected their memories. But gradually, some recollection of the small, wax-coloured alien they had seen inside the glowing mist came back to them. This, they were sure, was the cause of the medical problems.

One theory was that they had encountered some entirely natural phenomenon that, as well as causing their physical injuries, had triggered a vivid hallucination. Professor Stig Lundquist of the University of Uppsala in Sweden considered that option in the Heinonen and Viljo case. The incident occurred up in the region of the Northern Lights and he investigated local atmospheric conditions, but he concluded that these were unlikely to be the cause of the incident:

'I do not think that I can explain the phenomenon as being naturally occurring,' he said.

Cornish Contretemps

On 17 September 1977, Caroline Bond and Peter Boulter suffered a similar encounter. The young couple were doing some work on an old post-office in the village of Newmill in Cornwall. Caroline was astride her moped, about to ride off, when she felt her skin tingle. She looked around to see a strange green mist drifting towards her, a few inches off the ground.

She leapt off her moped and ran back inside the building, screaming that she had just seen a ghost. Peter could hardly take this seriously, but he could see her terror was very real. When he went outside to take look, he saw a strange light soaring away into the sky. It was travelling relatively slowly and took a long time to disappear. So he went back inside and watched it from an upstairs window. It was then he noted that the light was no longer alone. It now seemed to have smaller red lights alongside it.

Meanwhile, Caroline, who had recovered her composure, leapt back on her moped and set off in pursuit. On the way, she came across several other villagers who had also seen the strange light, though none of them had had her ringside seat.

Soon after the encounter, Peter and Caroline became seriously ill. They suffering aching muscles, pounding headaches, vomiting and other symptoms that had been reported in the Finnish case. Peter went though a series of exhaustive tests, but nothing could be found. Eventually the mystery illness cleared up without treatment. Caroline, who had been closer, was more seriously affected. The possibility of appendicitis was considered. She was operated on and her appendix removed although, on examination, it seemed perfectly healthy. After some weeks, she began to recover. Nevertheless, the trauma of the encounter remained with the two of them for many years even though they had not seen any aliens or even anything that they could identify as a spacecraft.

Attack in the Forest

Scottish forester Bob Taylor was another victim. While working in the woodlands outside Livingston in West Lothian on 9 November 1979, Taylor came upon a strange egg-shaped object about twenty feet across in a clearing. It 'faded in and out of reality', he said, as he watched. Then two dark objects around a foot in diameter with six legs, like old-fashioned sea mines, sped towards him. They were round with spikes. He was knocked to the ground and remembered feeling a strange pulling sensation on his legs. When he came to, Taylor was alone, but he found himself in a terrible state. His trousers were torn. His head was pounding and his legs felt like jelly. Partially paralysed, he had to drag himself home painfully along the ground.

The police were called in. A major inquiry followed and the site of the encounter was cordoned off like a crime scene while the forensic team went over it. They found mysterious triangular indentations in the ground. Taylor's trousers were sent away for forensic analysis. However, the police eventually reported that they could find no evidence of an alien force, even though the credibility of the witness and the physical effects that he suffered were undoubted. Like the previous victims, he eventually recovered.

Burning Ring of Fire

On 13 March 1980, a sub-contractor was driving home from Worcester to Stratford-upon-Avon. When he passed near the village of Haselor, he had a close encounter. A cigar-shaped white craft surrounded by a red glow flashed passed his car. It was so big it filled the windscreen. As it passed by, the steering wheel suddenly became unbearably hot – a burning ring of fire. He let go and the car swerved. His hands suffered serious burns.

Scientists have explained that fluctuating magnetic fields produced by the UFO induced electrical eddy currents inside the metal steering wheel, heating it up. Such an intense field could have caused all sorts of other health problems if the UFO had hung around longer.

The ABC of After-Effects

The after-effects of alien abductions can have serious long-term effects. American UFOlogist Jerome Clark divides them into three stages. The initial stage, which Clark calls 'immediate after-effects', usually involves physical problems, such as nausea, irritated eyes, an unusual thirst, scoop-like cuts in the legs and nosebleeds that can last days or weeks.

The second stage, 'intermediate after-effects', usually start a few weeks or even months after the abduction. It is then that the psychological difficulties begin. These include recurring nightmares, flashbacks, panic attacks and an irrational anxiety when returning to the area of the abduction – even though the victim may have no conscious memory of the event itself. Even so, this stage is often marked by the obsessive need to return to the site of the abduction, as if the victim is willing it to happen again.

The final stage in Clark's outline are the 'long-term effects'. These can occur years after the abduction and often involve changes in the personality and outlook of the abductee. Often these changes can be for the better. Some abductees have discovered hidden artistic talents or a previously unacknowledged spiritual side to their nature.

Stage One and Two

UFOlogist Leonard Stringfield encountered stage-one after-effects after Mona Stafford, Elaine Thomas and Louise Smith had been abducted by a UFO while driving down Route 78 in Kentucky on 6 January 1976. They wanted to keep their story a secret but information was leaked to the local press. Stringfield picked up on the story and persuaded them to meet him on 29 February.

'The effects of the close encounter were still painfully apparent,' said Stringfield. 'They looked drained and tense.' All three women had experienced severe weight loss, and Smith had what Stringfield described as 'a round, pinkish-grey blotch' on her body.

Smith also suffered second-stage effects, which lured her back to the site of the encounter, where she seems to have been abducted again. On 28 January she was in bed asleep when she was woken by strange voices. They urged her to get dressed and drive back to Route 78. Once she arrived at the site of the encounter, she stood there not knowing what to do. A feeling of terror came over her and she felt a pulling at her hands. Then she fled back to her car and drove off. She later noticed that three rings were missing from her hand – rings that normally required lubricating with soap before they could be removed.

Stafford, too, suffered second-stage effects. Disturbing mental images came and went. For a while she moved back in with her parents but, when she returned to her trailer, she was woken one night by 'mental voices'. A bright light came flooding in through the doorway and she saw a small being standing there.

411

Epilepsy

MUFON's Robert J. Durrant has suggested that encounters or abductions may cause temporal lobe epilepsy. Unlike normal epileptic attacks, when the victim suffers fits, convulsions and unconsciousness, TLE often produces hallucinatory effects. This is because the temporal lobe is not connected to any muscles that can convulse. Instead, it controls higher functions of the brain, such as memory and learning. Durrant has studied Whitley Strieber's autobiographical accounts of his abduction experiences, *Transformation* and *Majestic*, and says that all the symptoms of temporal lobe epilepsy are present in Strieber's writings. These include floating sensations, paranormal experiences, anomalous smells, enhanced imagination and episodes that seem to have intense personal meaning. However, Strieber has undergone two series of tests for TLE. Both of them proved negative. This has led to the suggestion that aliens communicate telepathically with their abductees through the temporal lobe, hence the similarities between TLE and abduction experiences.

Implants

One of the most obvious after-effects of abductions is the discovery of an alien object implanted in the body of the abductee. Chief of Abduction Investigations for the Houston UFO Network, Derrel Sims has spent twenty-five years investigating abductions, and has himself been abducted. Implants are his field. In 1995 he called in Dr Roger Leir to remove two objects from an abductee known as Mrs Connely. Although her abduction had occurred twenty-five years before, in 1970, until the implants showed up on an X-ray, she had no idea of their existence. The T-shaped objects were found in her toe. They were about a fifth of an inch in height and made from an ultra-hard, unidentifiable metal, which was highly magnetic. The implants were sheathed in a dense, dark grey membrane that could not be cut with a sharp scalpel. Mysteriously, they were attached to nerve endings in a part of the body where no nerves are known to exist. Mrs Connely's case might help to explain why scoop-like scars are frequently found

412

on the lower leg area ofabductees.

Unexplained Pregnancies

Perhaps the most disturbing of the after-effects of alien abductions are unexplained pregnancies. The evidence indicates that our extraterrestrial intruders are running a programme to create a human–alien hybrid. There are numerous reports of aliens abducting women, impregnating them, returning them home, then abducting them again a few months later to take the foetus. This has a devastating affect on the women involved.

One such is Indiana housewife Kathie Davis. One evening in 1977, at around 9:30 p.m., she saw a light about the size of a baseball floating around her backyard. She went outside to look for it. She spent no more than ten minutes looking for it then, finding nothing, went to a friend's house for a moonlight swim. But when she arrived it was already 11 p.m. More than hour of her life was missing. Later, when she returned home from the swim, she felt an inexplicable chill and a fogging of the vision. Later she recalled an abduction experience. Neighbours confirmed this. They had seen a flash of light and felt their house vibrate as if there had been an earth tremor.

Kathie recalled being given a gynaecological examination by aliens. Abduction expert Budd Hopkins believes that she was impregnated by the aliens. A few months, she was abducted again. This time, during a second examination, she reported feeling a terrible pressure inside her. Then, under hypnosis, she became disturbed and cried out: 'It's not fair. It's mine.'

Later, she began having disturbing dreams. In them, she gave birth to a weird-looking, super-intelligent hybrid. Other abductees also reported dreaming of giving birth to so-called wise babies. Later Kathie recalled having a phantom pregnancy when she was teenager. When she was abducted years later she was introduced to a half-alien half-human hybrid that she recognised was her daughter.

In November 1983 she was abducted once again. This time the aliens removed some of her ova. During an abduction in April 1986, she was shown two elf-like infants. She was told that these were her children, too. The aliens told her they had nine of her offspring altogether. Although none of Kathie's extraterrestrial pregnancies was confirmed medically, she was left with a series of unexplainable scars that had resulted from the experience.

Lethal Encounter

At around 11:30 p.m. on 17 March 1978, service engineer Ken Edwards left the M62 motorway at the turn off to Risley. He was on his way home from a trade union meeting in Cheshire. His route took him through a deserted industrial area, much of which was derelict. As he passed the vast Atomic Energy Authority complex, his headlights picked out a weird figure, standing alone at the top of an embankment. Edwards stopped his van to investigate.

The creature was over seven feet tall and did not look human. Its arms came out of the top of its shoulders. Its body was silver, but its head was black and shaped like a goldfish bowl. It held its arms out ahead like a sleepwalker, then start walking down the embankment. The odd thing was that it walked at right angles to the steep slope, but did not topple forward.

When it reached the road, Edwards noticed that it had no knee joints. Its legs articulated from the hips, making its movement rather stiff. Then the creature stopped. It turned its head towards Edwards. Two pencil-thin beams of light shot out its eye socket. The beams came straight through the windscreen and hit Edwards full on. The effect was immediate.

'My head was swimming with strange thoughts,' he said. 'There were hundreds of them, all racing through my mind at once. I also felt very odd. It was a sensation like two enormous hands pressing down on me from above. The pressure was tremendous. It seemed to paralyse me. I could only move my eyes. The rest of me was rigid.'

The creature then carried on across the road. It walked straight through a ten-foot-high security fence as if it was not there, and vanished into the trees beyond. At this point, Edwards' mind went completely blank.

The next thing he recalled was arriving home at around half-past midnight. He had no idea how he had got there. He walked into the house, where his wife Barbara was waiting for him. She was anxious and could have been angry, but she noticed the state he was in. When he saw his wife, he blurted out: 'I've seen a silver man.' This sounded crazy and his 'missing time' story sounded a bit thin. But when they noticed that his watch had stopped at exactly 11:45 p.m., she took it seriously.

The couple went to the local police station. The duty officer thought the story was crazy too, but Edwards' obvious sincerity impressed him. The police contacted the atomic plant and Edwards reluctantly agreed to go back to the scene of the encounter with them. They were met by a team of twenty-five AEA security guards who carried batons. When Edwards related his incredible story, not one of them so much as smirked. Then they made a cursory search of the area, but they refused to go into the trees where Edwards had seen the creature disappear.

It turned out that the AEA complex was a UFO hotspot. Eight sightings had been reported in the area around that time. And four local youths had seen a cigar-shaped craft flying over the plant on the day of Edwards' encounter. Two police constables, Rob Thompson and Roy Kirckpatrick, followed up several leads. They checked out nearby Warrington College in case the students there had pulled some stunt, but they were not holding a rag week at the time and no link was established. Edwards was not impressed by this line of investigation.

'I wish they could tell me how they did it,' he said. 'How they blew up my radio and walked through a fence, some stunt.'

The police also wondered whether Edwards had seen a fireman clad in a silver radiation suit. They took him to the AEA complex and, without warning, had a member of staff in a silver fireman's suit walk out in front of the car. Edwards was unfazed.

'It was nothing like it,' he said.

Unable to shed any further light on the matter, the police had no option but to close the case.

But the case was far from closed for Edwards. The 'missing' forty-five minutes between his watch stopping and the time he arrived home troubled him. He worried that he might have been abducted. But he could not simply put the matter out of his mind. He had physical proof that something had happened. The beams from the creature's eyes had damaged both him and his vehicle.

Where he had gripped the steering wheel, Edwards's fingers were bright red, as if badly sunburned. After the encounter he found that the van's two-way radio did not work. When an electrician examined it, he discovered that the circuit board was burned out. The probable cause of this, he speculated, was an enormous power surge through the aerial.

Then, less than a year after his strange encounter, Edwards fell ill. He lost all energy and began to suffer from stomach cramps. When he went to hospital, the doctors diagnosed cancer of the kidneys. In 1980, Edwards underwent major surgery. All seemed well but, after a couple of months, cancer cells appeared in his throat. The disease seemed unstoppable. Four years after the encounter with the silver-suited alien, Edwards was dead.

UFO investigators Peter Hough and Jenny Randles later discovered that unusual experiments were being carried out in a building near the AEA complex. But no one will say whether an experiment was underway that night.

Death Ray

The Edwards' case is reminiscent of another encounter when a victim was zapped in Brazil. On 13 August 1967, forty-one-year-old Ignacio de Souza and his young wife Louisa were returning to their ranch at Pilar de Goias, Brazil. The ranch had its own landing strip, but the couple were astounded to see that what had landed on it in their absence was no ordinary aircraft. What they saw was a spacecraft that looked like 'an upturned wash basin' on the runway. Near to it, were three alien entities wearing yellow ski suits.

De Souza loosed off a shot at one of them with the .44 carbine he

416

was carrying. The UFO fired back and he was hit by a green beam that came from the craft. Realising that their reception was far from friendly, the aliens then climbed into the spaceship and it took off. Until the encounter de Souza had been good health. But afterwards, he suffered from nausea and uncontrollable shaking. He was flown to hospital in nearby Goiana for tests. He had leukaemia and died two months later.

Grievous Bodily Harm
Probably the best-known UFO encounter that caused harm to humans involved restaurant owner Betty Cash, her friend Vickie Landrum and her grandson, Colby. The case received enormous media coverage worldwide because the victims sued the US government for $20 million.

The deadly encounter took place on the chilly night of 29 December 1980, when Betty, Vickie and Colby were driving down an isolated section of Highway 1485, which took them though a pine and oak forest near Huffman, Texas, some fifteen miles outside Houston. The two middle-aged women and the young boy had had their evening meal at a roadside restaurant in nearby New Caney and were now heading towards home in Dayton. At around 9 p.m., they had just rounded a bend in the highway, when ten-year-old Colby pointed out a blazing light in the sky. A huge diamond-shaped vessel loomed in front of them. It descended to tree-top level, straddling the road. They found their way blocked by a jet of fire that looked like the exhaust of a space rocket.

Cash, who was driving, stopped the car less than sixty yards from the mysterious object, which glowed so brightly that, in the surrounding forest, it could have been day. The three of them got out of the car to investigate, only to be met by a wave of tremendous heat. Colby became distressed and Vickie Landrum got back into the car with him. But Betty Cash continued to gaze mesmerised at the dazzling object, even though the intense heat was burning her skin and the bright light was damaging her eyes. It was only when the object began to move that Cash heard Landrum's pleas and returned to the car. But as Cash touched the handle of the car door, she found it was red hot and burned her hand. Her wedding ring also burned into her finger.

The craft then made a loud roaring noise. As it took off into night sky, some two dozen unmarked black helicopters swept into view. The three witnesses later identified them as CH-47 Chinook twin-blades, and they were either pursuing or escorting the mysterious craft. Cash set off in pursuit of the unidentified aircraft and the fleet of dark helicopters. After a mile or so they had to turn onto a larger highway. One of the helicopters turned back and buzzed the car, deafening the passengers with the roar of its engines. They got the message, turned off the highway and headed home.

All three of them were stunned and bewildered by the encounter. At first they thought it must have been a hallucination, but then they learned that, in the outskirts of Houston, residents had also seen bright lights and helicopters in the sky that night. Then there were the injuries that they had sustained from the strange encounter.

Cash's eyes were so swollen that she unable to see for a week. She suffered from vomiting and diarrhoea, various aches and pains, blistering of the scalp and temporary hair loss. Three days after the encounter, her condition deteriorated to the point that she checked into the emergency room of a nearby hospital. Betty did not tell thehospital doctors about her UFO encounter – they treated her as a classic burns victim, until Colby revealed what had happened. Vickie Landrum and Colby also exhibited burns, although to a lesser extent. Both had swollen eyes and suffered vomiting and diarrhoea, and Vickie had some hair loss. When the three of them were examined, it was discovered that their symptoms were consistent with exposure to ultra-violet, microwave and X-ray radiation. Later Betty suffered cataracts and developed breast cancer and had to have a mastectomy.

A few months later, Cash and Landrum sued the US government for $20 million in medical compensation for the injuries they had suffered, with the help of Peter Gersten, a lawyer who specialises in UFO cases. The lawsuit proved to be a long and drawn-out one. Although it was ultimately a futile exercise, officers from every branch of the services were dragged into court. They insisted that the US military was neither involved in or responsible for what had happened. Finally, in 1986, a judge dismissed the case on the grounds that Cash and Landrum could not prove the 'UFO' that had caused them injury was the property of the US government. However, this ignored the presence of the Chinooks.

While the US government is in full-scale denial of the facts, the UFO community has broken into four factions when it comes to the Cash–Landrum case. One faction believes that they saw a top-secret nuclear-powered US military aircraft with extraterrestrial connections. Another faction believes that they witnessed the test-flight of a US military spacecraft back-engineered by US scientists from their examination of alien wreckage. An anonymous US intelligence office apparently confessed: 'The craft was an alien craft piloted by military aircraft pilots.'

A third faction believes that what they saw was a UFO intruder being shepherded out of US airspace by the military, while a fourth say what the Texas trio saw was one of the many manoeuvres conducted by the ultra-top-secret alliance between the US government and an alien force. All four agree that the helicopters were there to seal off the area in the event that the mysterious craft was somehow forced to land.

Houston-based Boeing aerospace engineer John Schuessler, a thirty-five-year veteran of many UFO investigations, studied the case and concluded that what Cash and Landrum had seen was a UFO, which may or may not have been in difficulty. The US military had deployed a fleet of helicopters to follow it and Cash, Landrum and Colby suffered injuries as a direct result of their encounter.

He discovered the helicopters came from Fort Hood, in Waco, Texas, and from an aircraft carrier anchored in the Gulf of Mexico – a vessel he cannot name. Schuessler says that the military helicopters were on a monitoring mission. The aliens are now here in such force that, although the US government is in communication with them, it can do nothing to prevent their frequent sorties. Schuessler discounts

419

the idea that the aliens are here to create a new hybrid species using the terrestrial gene pool. Nor does he believe that the aliens are out to destroy us, although they are exploiting our resources in a number of mysterious ways. But the US government can do little more than keep tabs on their foraging expeditions – one of which was witnessed by Cash, Landrum and Colby.

Schuessler interviewed Air Force generals and congressmen, who gave him a lot of answers – but many of them turned out to be contradictory or downright lies. This convinced him that there was something to the story, or why would senior figures go to such great lengths to deny it? He pursued the matter through covert sources, who confirmed the story. But none of them would make any on-the-record admission. Nor could the government admit its impotence in court. However, a helicopter pilot came forward to give details of what had happened that night, but subsequently recanted. 'Obviously, his superiors shut him up,' Schuessler said.

Reviewing the witnesses' injuries, Schuessler said: 'Betty Cash's after-effects were the most drastic because she was out the car for the longest period of time and was exposed directly to the UFO. Within twenty-four hours, she had swelling, blisters on the face and sunburn. She was vomiting for weeks and, after three weeks, a large amount of her hair fell out. In the years that followed, she suffered twenty-five to thirty hospitalisations, many of them in intensive care. She developed cancer and a low red blood cell count, she had bone marrow problems and then, eventually, she had a stroke.'

He believes that her illnesses were cause by exposure to some kind of radiation.

'I am not saying it was ionising radiation,' he said. 'The electromagnetic spectrum has a wide range of radiation that one can be exposed to. At first, the doctors were totally baffled and the initial doctor she went to in emergency care actually consulted other doctors who understood UFOs. Her long-term doctor, who was an expert in the field of radiation sickness, felt that she had been exposed to ionising radiation because her skin had the texture and the feel of it. She couldn't have skin grafts on the burns because of the texture of her skin.'

He could not get any more out of the doctors, for fear of breaching patient confidentiality, but they believed that the injuries were genuine and not self-inflicted.

With no federal money to compensate them, Betty Cash, Vickie Landrum and Colby tried to rebuild their lives. After years of drifting, Cash returned to live with her family in seclusion in Alabama. Throughout this unsettled time, she was dogged by ill-health. She contracted cancer, which she was certain was induced her UFO encounter and also suffered a near-fatal heart attack. She said these illnesses, together with intrusion by the press and assaults by the government on her credibility in the years following her encounter, virtually destroyed her life. She died on 29 December 1998, eighteen years to the day after her UFO encounter.

Vickie Landrum has also suffered health problems since the encounter. Like Cash, she too drifted from place to place for years, before disappearing into a very private life.

Only Colby appears to have come through unscathed. He suffered no long-term ill effects from the encounter and held down a good job in Houston, Texas. However, he refuses to talk about his experience.

'Many people have been injured emotionally as well as physically by their encounters with UFOs and have had their lives devastated,' says Sue Pitts, Alabama assistant state director for the Mutual UFO Network. She tells the story of Falkville police chief Jeff Greenhaw who photographed and chased an alien in 1973.

'Folks thought Jeff was hoaxed or was himself lying,' says Pitts. 'He lost his job. His wife divorced him. For years he's lived in seclusion in Alabama, refusing interviews.'

The sad case of Betty Cash, Vickie Landrum and Colby is far from an isolated one. In the 1994 book *Taken*, author Karla Turner describes symptoms similar to those exhibited by Betty Cash that were suffered by a number of women abductees. Four of them reported waking up with badly irritated eyes. Two of them suffered inexplicable 'sunburn' and sudden hair losses. One, 'Beth', woke up the morning after her abduction with a pounding headache, aching muscles and dizziness. She felt extreme nausea and suffered from diarrhoea and repeated vomiting. He eyes were so badly swollen that she could not see. The parallels to Cash's symptoms are so close that some have suggested that Cash, Landrum and Colby were abducted.

Curiously, another of Turner's abductees, 'Amelia', reported lying in bed surrounded by light – she was not alone and this was witnessed by friends. The ceiling then opened. She looked up to see a helicopter with two aliens inside. She could describe the helicopter and the aliens, but her friends were dazzled by the light and saw nothing more.

Silver Linings

The effects of a UFO encounter, or an alien abduction, are not necessarily harmful. In some cases victims have reported that the experience has changed their life for the better. They have discovered hitherto unknown artistic talents, the development of psychic skills, a new awareness of environmental issues and profound lifestyle changes. Some UFOlogists argue that these beneficial transformations may actually hold the key to a true understanding of UFO phenomena as a whole.

One such transformation was experienced by Peter Holding. As a teenager, he had a number of UFO encounters including an abduction-like experience. In the middle of the night, Holding woke suddenly and experienced an overwhelming compulsion to go to the window. When he opened the curtains, he noticed that there was no glass in the window. In its place was a mesmerising bright light with colours swirling around it. The next thing he knew the image had disappeared and the window had glass in it again. Soon after, Holding developed a previously undetected artistic talent for painting and photography. His works often incorporate the swirling image he saw during the encounter. He found that he could sell his paintings. His photographs have been published and he won a bursary to study art. It eventually became his career, though he had no thought of becoming an artist until after the encounter.

Betty Andreason developed a talent for drawing after her abduction. A similar transformation was experienced by another witness known in the literature only as Bryan. He had had a lifelong history of UFO encounters and, during his adolescence, had a number of night-time visits from extraterrestrial entities. These encounters heralded a sudden explosion of artistic talent. He excelled at art school and went on to make his living by painting.

Psychic Powers

Many abductees have also shown a marked increase in their psychic awareness and abilities after their encounter. Dr John E. Mack, Professor of Psychiatry at Harvard Medical School, has come across several cases in his extensive work with abductees. One of his subjects was a woman named Eva. She had several UFO encounters. After an abduction, she developed telepathic contact with the alien entities. This has opened a gateway to a wide range of paranormal phenomena. She began to see ghosts and, during a near-death experience, she saw a doorway into another dimension.

One famous psychic who now attributes his astonishing powers to a UFO encounter is world-famous spoon-bender Uri Geller. One day when he was four or five years old and was living in Tel Aviv, Israel, he went into the overgrown garden across the road from the apartment block where he lived. He heard kittens crying and walked towards the sound. Then, suddenly, he felt something hovering above him. When he looked up, he saw a ball of light, not the sun, but a pulsating sphere of light in the air. Years later he could still remember this vividly.

'I remember all the sounds stopped, as if time itself had stopped,' he says. 'I looked at this thing for about ten seconds when, suddenly, a beam shot out of it and hit my forehead and knocked me back. It didn't hurt, it just pushed me back on to the ground.'

He suffered no physical after-effects, but soon afterwards, spoons started to bend in his hands. Geller is convinced that his experience was responsible. And he has a number of theories.

'My most bizarre theory is that the energy is coming from a higher intelligence, maybe extraterrestrial in form,' he says. 'Maybe a baby extraterrestrial that ran away from its parents is playing havoc with me and my life.'

Brazilian psychic Thomaz Green Morton, who is one of the world's most gifted paranormal practitioners, also believes that he got his prodigious powers from an extraterrestrial source. He was struck by a beam of light from a strange cloud while out fishing. Since then he has been able to perform psychokinesis and materialisation, and he has been investigated by numerous scientists, including NASA astronaut Dr Brian O'Leary.

Like Uri Geller, he can bend metal objects just by holding them. He can also transform a dollar bill into a bill made up of numerous other world currencies fused together. His favourite trick is to manifest perfume, which pours from his skin. In front of a camera and under the strictest scientific conditions, he can take a regular egg and materialise a chick inside it, which then breaks out of the shell.

Healing Powers

Other abductees have developed mediumship, dowsing abilities and healing powers after their encounters. In one case in 1978 Elsie Oakensen encountered a dumb-bell-shaped UFO while driving on a motorway in Northamptonshire. She was struck by the light of the object as it hovered above her car. Then quite spontaneously it disappeared. At the time, she thought it was just a brief encounter, but later she discovered that it had lasted a couple of hours. Within days, she developed spectacular healing abilities. She even cured her granddaughter, who was deaf, after doctors had suggested that no cure was likely. Oakensen was sure she had no such ability before.

Sometimes a UFO encounter has a more direct beneficial effect. Witnesses have reported miracle cures simply from seeing a UFO. In one striking case, an American law enforcement officer was pursing a UFO, when he was zapped by an energy beam at close quarters. Shortly before, a pet alligator had inflicted a painful bite on his hand.

After the encounter, the bite mark was gone. The wound had spontaneous healed. It is thought that the intense energy fields that UFOs generate could be harnessed in the same way that radiotherapy is now used.

Much the same thing happened to a famous French biochemist. He told the story of his miracle cure to French UFOlogist Aimé Michel, who was allowed to publish an account of the abduction, only provided that he did not use his name and identified him as 'Dr X'.

In 1968, Dr X was thirty-eight and was living with his wife and fourteen-month-old son in a house overlooking a valley in south-east France. On the night of 2 November 1968, he awoke to hear the cries of his son. There was a thunderstorm going on outside. His wife was sound asleep, so Dr X got up to attend to the child. He did so with some difficulty. A couple of days before he had been chopping wood and had slipped. The axe had struck his left leg, bursting an artery and causing extensive internal bleeding. The wound had been treated by a doctor, who had examined it again the previous afternoon.

He already had problems with his right leg. During the Algerian war, a mine had exploded, fracturing his skull. This damaged the left hemisphere of his brain, paralysing the right side of his body. The paralysis passed after a couple of months, but left the muscles of his right side permanently wasted. This cost him a career as a musician and he could not stand on his right leg alone. Even so, he managed to totter to his son's room.

The boy was standing up in his crib, shouting, 'Rho, rho'.

This was the word the child used for a fire in the hearth or any bright light. He was pointing to the window. Dr X assumed he was indicating the lightning flashes that were visible through the cracks in the shutters. He got the boy some water and settled him down again. He could hear a shutter blowing back and forth in the breeze. It was in an upstairs room. He went up and closed it, noticing, in his half-asleep state, that the room was bathed in a pulsating light.

After closing the shutter, he felt thirsty and went downstairs to get a drink of water. Still puzzled by the pulsating light, he went out onto the terrace to investigate. It was 3:55 a.m. by the kitchen clock, he noted. Outside, he immediately saw the source of the flashing light. It was being emitted by two disc-shaped silver UFOs that hovered over the valley. They had long antennae sprouting from them. These seemed to be collecting electricity from the storm clouds. A glow would start at the furthest end of the antenna, build up along its length, then discharge suddenly as a lightning bolt to the ground. The build up happened rhythmically and the discharge bathed the whole valley with a pulsating light.

The two craft merged into one and the pulsating ceased. The united object then moved up the valley towards him. Dr X saw the underside was covered with rotating dark bands, causing patterns that defied the laws of science and logic. When the craft got within five hundred yards of Dr X, he began to feel that it had noticed him. It turned a bright beam of light on him, which bathed the whole house in an intense glow. He raised his hands to protect his eyes. Then there was a loud bang and the craft shot skywards so fast that it appeared to be a single streak of light.

When Dr X went back inside it was 4:05 am. He did not think that he had been outside for one minute, let alone ten. He went back upstairs and woke his wife. He told her what he had seen. As he talked excitedly to her, he paced up and down, stopping every so often to make notes and draw sketches of what he had seen. Suddenly, his wife noticed that he was walking normally. He pulled up his pyjama leg. The axe wound had healed completely. This was impossible in such a short time. What is more, his withered right leg was functioning perfectly too.

However, the encounter seemed to have disturbed him psychologically and he experienced some form of amnesia. After Dr X went back to bed, his wife noticed that he was talking in his sleep. She noted down what it was saying. One of the things he repeated was: 'Contact will be re-established by falling downstairs on 2 November.'

She did not tell him about this. When he awoke at 2 p.m. the next day, she suggested that he should write to the UFOlogist Aimé Michel, who was a friend. Why should he do that, he asked. His wife then discovered that he had lost all recollection of the UFO sighting the previous night. When she showed him the notes and sketches he had made, he grew alarmed.

Later that afternoon, Dr X tripped and fell down the stairs. It was as if something had grabbed his leg, he said. He hit his head and suddenly total recall of his experiences the previous night flooded back into his head.

However, there were other worrying effects from a subsequent encounter. Twelve days later, he dreamed about seeing another UFO. It was not like the ones he had seen. It was bright, luminous and triangular. Three days after that, he felt an itching sensation on his stomach. The following day a red triangle appeared around his navel. The dermatologist was baffled and wanted to write a scientific paper about it. Dr X prevented him.

Dr X contacted his friend Aimé Michel, who discovered that there had been a rash of UFO sightings around the area the night Dr X had seen his flying saucers. He suggested that the red triangle might be psychosomatic in origin. Dr X agreed, only to find that a similar red mark had appeared on his son's stomach the next day.

The experience left Dr X depressed and confused. The triangle disappeared, but reappeared every so often. Gradually Dr X began to take an interest in ecology. Other injuries he suffered healed up miraculously. However he has become sensitive to poltergeists and ghosts in the house. Aliens also pay visits and take him on journeys over impossible distances.

Spiritual Fulfilment

Sometimes the after-effects are more subtle, such as an urge to find greater spiritual fulfilment. One of Dr Mack's subjects, named Lee, found that a classical, intrusive abduction spiritually transformed her life. She told Dr Mack that the encounter was 'a priceless opportunity for spiritual growth and sensitivity to all sentient beings, ranging from insects to those of other dimensions and planetary systems'.

Another of Mack's subjects, Catherine, said that her abduction had boosted her intuition and given her a 'greater sensitivity to other people's auras'. In his assessment of the case, Dr Mack said: 'The acceptance of the actuality of her experiences, whatever their source may ultimately prove to be, has permitted Catherine to deal more effectively with the powerful effects and bodily feelings that accompany them and to reach a higher, or more creative, level of consciousness.'

Debbie Jordan had a spiritual awakening of a more religious nature. She had suffered multiple abductions, beginning in childhood, and was once artificially inseminated by an alien. Even so, she has drawn spiritual nourishment from it.

'The experiences changed from being physical in nature to being more mental, psychological, psychic and spiritual,' she said in an interview in 1996. 'I have since become aware of being taught Hinduism and Eastern religions I didn't have any previous knowledge of at all.' Now she has no terror of further abductions. 'It's like going to school. It opens my mind. It's changing everything about me inside – the way I look at life and God and myself and my fellow man.'

Another abductee reported more practical results of this alien education. During her abduction she was interrogated by the aliens. If she answered their questions, the extraterrestrials said, they would answer some of hers.

'We went on like this for quite a while,' she said. 'Because I left school at fourteen, I never learned anything. Anything I did learn, I learned through these experiences. In fact, without these experiences, I would be illiterate. I wouldn't have any interest in maths or history or anything like that.'

Positive lifestyle changes are also reported. Abductees frequently convert to vegetarianism or give up smoking; others change their attitude to the work they do and change career as a result. This happened to Elaine and John Avis after they and their three children were abducted in 1974. Driving on the outskirts of London, the family saw a light in the sky. Their car was then engulfed in a green mist. Again, although they thought this was a momentary experience, they discovered later that it had lasted two hours. Regressional hypnosis revealed an abduction, during which the family members underwent a thorough medical examination at the hands of the alien. But instead of being traumatised, the family members acquired a new-found self confidence. New, different avenues opened up for each of them. John became intensely creative and began to write poetry, while the son, Kevin, who had previously experienced learning difficulties at school, became an A-grade student. John and Elaine gave up smoking and drinking after the encounter, and the whole family gave up eating meat and developed strong feelings on the subject of the environment.

Abductees frequently report that the aliens are here to warn us that humankind is about to destroy the planet with nuclear weapons or our assault on the environment. Such things have been reported by contactees.since the 1950s.

In all these cases the after-effects were real, but no one knows why they happen. Some suggest that the alien presence has had a direct effect on the brain or consciousness of the victim. Others point out that similar changes in people had been observed in the aftermath of harrowing wartime experiences.

Frying Tonight

UFO encounters are best avoided, according to French UFOlogist, Jaques Vallee. He points out that the phenomenon dictates that a large amount of energy must confined in a restricted space. Just how dangerous this could be to human beings was calculated by American physicist Professor Galloway, who saw a UFO while driving along a highway in Louisiana one night. As he grew closer, the light from the UFO became as powerful as a car's headlights. Knowing the energy emitted by headlights and estimating the distance to the UFO, he was able to work out that the light energy it was emitting was equivalent to the output of a small nuclear reactor.

Dr Edward Condon, who conducted the University of Colorado's UFO investigation for the USAF, checked the figures and confirmed his conclusion.

Duck and Cover

Aliens have also taken a more direct approach in helping humankind to save itself from itself by turning their attentions on nuclear weapons facilities. In the 1950s, when extraterrestrials first contacted humankind, they warned us about nuclear weapons. We took no notice. Since then, they have decided to take the matter into their own hands.

One attack came at the height of the Cold War. On 27 October 1975, the air-raid sirens sounded at Loring Air Force Base in Maine. An unidentified flying object had penetrated the secure air space above the Intercontinental Ballistic Missile (ICBM) installation – one of over two thousand across America that were maintained in a state of constant readiness in case of a Soviet sneak attack. Even though the radar contact had not identified the incoming object as a Soviet missile, the military personnel on the base ran to their emergency stations, ready for the attack that they had spent so long preparing for.

A jet fighter was scrambled to check out the situation. But the pilot, Flight Sergeant Steven Eichner, found that the incoming object was not a Soviet missile. It was something far more exotic. Eichner saw an object that he described as 'a stretched-out football about the length of four trucks, hovering motionless in the air'. It was like nothing he had ever seen before.

It circled around the base for forty minutes then left as quickly as it had arrived. But it returned again the following day. This time it hovered over the base at a height of 160 feet, then landed between two ICBM silos. The military police took charge. They sent vehicles rushing at it in a suicide attack. But instead of retaliating, the UFO shot up into the air and disappeared. The emergency was over, but what no one knew was that this was the beginning of what was to become a sustained campaign of alien intervention at ICBM sites across America.

Sabotage

Just a few weeks after the Loring intrusion, the massive Malmstrom ICBM complex near Lewiston, Montana, played host to a similar but far more baffling UFO encounter. On 7 November, the security alarm sounded, indicating someone had intruded on to the base. The system showed that the problem was in the area of missile silo K-7. A Sabotage Alert Team was despatched. When they reached K-7, they saw a huge disc that was as large as a football field and glowing orange, hovering over the area. As they watched, the UFO sent a beam of light, as brilliant as daylight, down into the silo.

The SAT team was ordered to go in closer but refused. They were armed with machine guns, but none of the team opened fire. Air Force jets went in, but as they neared the object, it vanished. Then when the planes had passed, it suddenly reappeared. Eventually, it shot vertically into the sky until it disappeared from the radar.

A team of technicians was sent down into K-7 to check that everything was okay. They found that the launch and target codes for each of the missiles had been altered. These are the seven-digit codes that prevent the missiles being launched except by direct order from the President. They also fix each missile's target destinations. The codes are the ones that are kept in a black briefcase handcuffed to an officer who always accompanies the Commander in Chief wherever he goes. How these codes came to be altered remains a mystery.

Documents released by Colonel Terence C. James of the North American Defense Command (NORAD) reveal that, during this period, twenty-four UFO sightings were reported over six different missile silos at Malmstrom. Michael Hesemann investigated the incident in his book *UFOs: The Secret History* and concluded: 'If at that moment an atomic war had broken out, the US would have been helpless. Not one rocket could have been started.'

Defenceless

Such incidents were not confined to Loring AFB and Malmstrom. From 27 October to 19 November 1975, there was a wave of incidents during which UFOs targeted a number of America's ICBM facilities. But it does not seem to have ended there.

On 18 January 1978, several witnesses saw a UFO hovering over

McGuire AFB in New Jersey. An MP working for Air Force Security gave chase and found the UFO hovering over his car. Shortly after, the MP saw a three-foot-tall alien, which he said was 'greyish-brown, with a fat head, long arms and a slender body'. He panicked and loosed off five rounds at the alien and one at the UFO hovering above him. The UFO soared vertically and was joined by eleven other craft in the sky.

Afterwards, the body of the alien was found by a runway by a security patrol. A 'bad stench… like ammonia' was coming from it. Later that day, a team from Wright–Patterson came and sprayed the body with chemicals. They then crated it up, loaded it onto a C-141 transport place and left.

Dakota Shoot Out

On 16 November 1977 a UFO encounter took place at Ellsworth Air Force Base in South Dakota, about seven miles south-west of Nisland. A Freedom of Information Act request unearthed the following account:

'At 2059hrs., 16 Nov. 1977, Airmen 1C Phillips, Lt. A. Lims Security Control, telephone WSC. and reported an O2 alarm activation at L-9 and that Lims SAT #1, A-1C Jenkins & A-1C Raeke were dispatched, (Trip #62, ETA 2135hrs.)

'At 2147hrs., A-1C Phillips telephones WSC and reported that the situation at L-9 had been upgraded to a COVERED WAGON PER REQUEST OF Capt. Stokes, Larry D., FSO.

'Security Option 11 was initiated by WSC and Base CSC. BAF (Backup Security Force) #1&&2, were formed. At 2340hrs., 16 Nov. 77, the following information was learned: Upon arrival (2132hrs.) at Site #L-9. LSAT. Jenkins & Raeke, dismounted the SAT vehicle to make a check of the site fence line.

'At this time Raeke observed a bright light shinning vertically upwards from the rear of the fence line of L-9. (There is a small hill approximately 50 yards behind L-9.)

'Jenkins stayed with the SAT vehicle and Raeke proceeded to the source of the light to investigate. As Raeke approached the crest of the hill, he observed an individual dressed in a glowing green metallic uniform and wearing a helmet with visor.

'Raeke immediately challenged the individual, however the individual refused to stop and kept walking towards the rear fence line of L-9. Raeke aimed his M-16 rifle at the intruder and ordered him to stop.

'The intruder turned towards Raeke and aimed an object at Raeke which emitted a bright flash of intense light. The flash of light struck Raeke's M-16 rifle, disintegrating the weapon and causing second and third degree burns to Raeke's hands.

'Raeke immediately took cover and concealment and radioed the situation to Jenkins, who in turn radioed a 10-13 distress to Line Control. Jenkins responded to Raeke's position and carried Raeke back to the SAT vehicle. Jenkins then returned to the rear fence line to stand guard.

'Jenkins observed two intruders dressed in the same uniforms, walk through the rear fence line of L-9. Jenkins challenged the two individuals but they refused to stop. Jenkins aimed and fired two rounds from his M16 rifle.

'One bullet struck one intruder in the back and one bullet struck one intruder in the helmet. Both intruders fell to the ground, however, approximately fifteen seconds later Jenkins had to take cover from a bolt of light that missed him narrowly.

'The two intruders returned to the east side of the hill and disappeared. Jenkins followed the two and observed them go inside a saucer shaped object approximately 20ft in diameter and 20ft thick. The object emitted a glowing greenish light

'Once the intruders were inside, the object climbed vertically upwards and disappeared over the Eastern horizon. BAF> #1 arrived at the site at 2230hrs., and set up a security perimeter. Site Survey Team arrived at the site (0120hrs.) and took radiation readings, which measured from 1.7 to 2.9 roentgens.

'Missile Maintenance examined the missiles and warheads and found the nuclear components missing from the warhead. Col.

Speaker, Wing Cmdr. arrived at the site and set up an investigation. A completed follow-up report of this incident will be submitted by order of Col. Speaker.

'Raeke was later treated at the base hospital for second and third degree radiation burns to each hand. Raeke's M-16 rifle could not be located at the site.'

The Soviet Threat

At first the strange alien craft attacking American air bases were thought to be part of the Soviet threat. But the flight characteristics and eyewitness reports from highly trained Air Force observers led the brass to conclude that these were no terrestrial intruders. It was only years later, after the collapse of the Soviet Union, that they discovered that Soviet missile sites also had their hands full with alien intruders: 124 KGB UFO files were released, revealing that Russian nuclear facilities were receiving similar UFO attention.

On 28 June 1988, a UFO was seen by four witnesses flying back and forth over a military base near the nuclear test site of Kapustin Yar in the lowland of the Caspians for two hours. The KGB report said that the UFO flew over the weapons storage area and beamed a shaft of light down into the missile silo. The report fails to mention whether the missiles in the depot were nuclear.

In March 1993, Colonel Boris Sokolov of the Soviet Ministry of Defence told US TV journalist George Knapp that he had been flown to an ICBM base in the Ukraine. On the way, he had been given a top-secret report describing an incident that took place there in October 1983. The report said that a UFO had come close to triggering World War III after it had penetrated Soviet air space and had hovered over the nuclear missile silos. Attempts to shoot the alien craft down had failed when the automatic mechanism for firing the defensive missiles packed up. This was thought to be due to the influence of the UFO. Again the launch codes for the ICBMs had been scrambled, putting that part of the Soviet nuclear arsenal out of action.

Benign Intent

The Russians are now convinced of the aliens' benign intentions. In February 1997, Italian UFO researcher Giorgio Bongiovanni went to the Russian town of Tever to meet a delegation from the Russian military, headed by General Gennadi Reschetnikov of the Air Force Academy. He said: 'The main attention of UFOs is on all of humanity. But above all it has been the US and Russia, since they have the most powerful nuclear reserves in the world. I think this is the reason the aliens are worried.

Reschetnikov is the highest ranking member of the Russian military to confirm the existence of UFOs and he believes that the aliens are particularly interested in the spiritual condition of humankind. He thinks the aliens are curious about human behaviour and, although they influence us for the good, they expect something in return. That something could be the destruction of nuclear weapons.

Balance of Terror

UFO intrusions at nuclear bases on the continental United States and in the former Soviet Union may explain the aliens' evident interest in USAF airbases in the United Kingdom. One of the security policeman at RAF Woodbridge in Suffolk in 1980 says that he was told by Lieutenant Colonel Charles Halt that a UFO had sent down beams of light over the weapons depot that affected a cache of nuclear weapons that were illegally stored there. The Ministry of Defence was highly concerned when tiny holes were discovered, burned through the walls of the depot.

It is interesting that in none of these cases was the UFO misidentified as incoming ICBMs by either the American or Soviet war rooms, prompting a nuclear response that could have resulted in global annihilation. This is because UFO activity had already forced the two sides in the Cold War to improve their communications, according to UFO researcher Colonel Robert O. Dean.

Between 1963 and 1967 Dean was stationed at NATO's Supreme Headquarters of Allied Powers Europe (SHAPE) in Paris. He was allowed access to the war room there, which was officially known as the Supreme Headquarters Operations Center (SHOC). He says that throughout the 1950s and 1960s NATO defence systems regularly tracked large, circular metallic objects flying in formation over Europe. They appeared to be coming from the Soviet bloc and misidentification of UFOs as Soviet missiles came close to triggering a nuclear exchange.

'On three occasions while I was stationed there,' he says, 'SHAPE went to full nuclear alert.'

Along with other senior military personnel, Colonel Robert O. Dean was shown a number of photographs and videotapes depicting aliens while working at SHAPE.

These brushes with nuclear holocaust prompted the commander of SHAPE, General Lemnitzer, to start a three-year, in-depth study of UFOs. He also established a hotline between SHOC and the Warsaw Pact commander. After the hotline was installed, the situation grew less tense. It led to a direct phone line being established between the White House and the Kremlin. So it was UFOs that led to the thawing of the Cold War and the beginning of *détente*.

Alien Activist

UFOs have intervened elsewhere. In 1986 a number of UFOs were seen hovering over a secret nuclear facility that had been built by the Brazilian government to produce weapons-grade plutonium, in violation of international agreements. Prominent UFO researcher Dr Jim Hurtak investigated the case and discovered that the appearance of the UFOs had attracted the attention of the media, which subsequently discovered the nuclear facility. Because it was built in defiance of treaty commitments, its construction was found unconstitutional and it was closed.

Hurtak believes that events like this show that aliens come with benevolent intentions. Michael Hesemann also believes it is reasonable to extrapolate that extraterrestrials would intervene if human belligerence reached a point where annihilation of the planet became inevitable.

But why are the aliens so interested in our well-being? Dr Hurtak thinks that extraterrestrials are linked with 'ultraterrestrials', or higher spiritual forces, who have intervened before at key moments in history. Indeed, human life on this planet may only be an experiment that aliens have a vested interest in seeing succeed.

Abduction researcher Dr John Mack often hears the aliens' views on human nuclear destructive capabilities from his abductees. He sees their motives for intervention in human affairs as far less altruistic. 'The survival of man figures large in the well-being of creatures we haven't yet met,' he says.

UFO researcher Michael Lindemann also believes that nuclear war on Earth might have untold consequences in other dimensions. Extraterrestrials normally adopt a hands-off approach that allows humans to learn by their own mistakes, he says. They only intrude when it is critically important, not necessarily for their own agenda, but for a larger reason, such as the balance of the cosmos as a whole.

However, much of the information about UFO interest in nuclear installations in the West and in the former Soviet Union is still withheld from the public. It may be some time before we can fully assess its impact.

Target Brazil

Alien attentions are not always so benign. Sometimes they attack for no apparent reason. In the late 1970s, they brought their malevolent attentions to bear on the northern Brazilian states of Maranhao and Para, which together cover an area larger than the state of California. Throughout the decade, there had been a huge wave of UFO reports from this area. But these soon turned out to be no ordinary sighting reports, where the witness sees lights in the sky that perform extraordinary aerobatics before disappearing at an incredible speed. In northern Brazil the UFO fleet had come with hostile intent. Hundreds of thousands of people reported that UFOs fired on them with beams of light. Some people were chased by balls of light that knocked them unconscious and left them with bizarre wounds.

The epicentre of the alien attack was the remote area around the cities of Belem, Sao Luis and Teresina. Manoel Laiva, the mayor of the small town of Pinheiro, estimated that, in just one year, as many as 50,000 people in the area reported UFO sightings. French UFOlogist Jacques Vallee says that UFOs were being seen every night at the peak of the wave in late 1977. Some were seen descending from the sky to hover over houses and probe the interiors with beams of light. Others were seen emerging from the sea, leading to speculation that the aliens had established an underwater base off the coast.

The alien assault was so widespread that it plainly caused the authorities some concern. When amateur UFOlogists turned up to investigate, they found a crack team from the Brazilian Air Force already on the ground. At the time, the Brazilian government would not confirm or deny the attacks, but in July 1987 all was revealed when Brazil's top UFOlogist A.J. Gevaerd interviewed the head of the Air Force team.

Colonel Uyrange Hollanda, who by then had retired, told Gevaerd that the Air Force's top-secret mission to investigate the alien attacks was called 'Operation Saucer'. The investigation began in September 1977 and ran for three months. It had been instigated at the request of the state authorities of Maranhao and Para. They had already begun to investigate hundreds of reports of attacks but soon found they had something on their hands that they were ill equipped to cope with. The civil authorities had sent medical teams out to the remote areas where the reports were coming from. The doctors examined the victims, took statements and sent back their findings. When the civil authorities back in the state capitals read these, they found them so disturbing that they insisted the Air Force take some sort of action.

Stationed at the headquarters of the 1st Regional Air Command at Belem, Colonel Hollanda was ordered to lead a team into the jungle to investigate. At the time, the frequency of the attacks was at an all-time high. Hollanda's team comprised forty specialists. They were a mixture of civilian and military scientists –

doctors, biologists, chemist, physicists and engineers. The team's official mission was to collect eyewitness reports from villagers, ascertain the source of the attacks, and monitor all alien activity using special photographic equipment. Hollanda also had secret orders to attempt to make contact with the aliens to find out what they wanted.

Operation Saucer's primary objective was the island of Colares, just to the north of Belem. The UFO reports were at their peak there. When the UFO team reached the area, they discovered that most of the inhabitants of Colares had fled in panic. Even the schoolteachers, the dentist and the sheriff had turned tail. And they had every reason to flee.

Dr Wellaide Cecin, who was working on the island during the attacks, had treated thirty patients injured by the aliens. Victims had been struck by beams of light that left them with blackened skin, anaemia, loss of hair, inexplicable red patches on the skin, numbness, uncontrollable shaking and puncture wounds. The aliens often attacked after the victims had gone to bed at night. When the beam hit them, they found themselves immobilised and unable to scream. The beam pressed down on their chest like a huge weight and burned them like a cigarette end. Scientists on the Air Force team suggested that the alien energy beam could have been a complex combination of ionising and non-ionising radiation. If such a beam contained pulsed microwaves, it would disrupt the central nervous system, paralysing the victim, cause hallucinations and even affect long-term behaviour.

Aerial observers were deployed each night to film UFO activity. During the first few weeks, they spotted UFOs every other night. They saw balls of light as well as large, structured craft fly directly over their heads. The alien craft did not attack them, but they gradually started moving in closer, as if they were observing the team sent to observe them.

During their investigations, Hollanda's team also encountered large, disc-shaped craft and cylindrical UFOs, as well as much smaller vehicles. Another strange UFO often seen was box shaped. Dubbed the 'flying refrigerator', it made a humming sound that remained at the same pitch despite changes in speed and acceleration.

The balls of light also came in a variety of sizes. When some of these moved close to the Air Force observers, the intensity of their brilliance diminished and the observers were then able to make out the shape of a vehicle inside. They were tear shaped with a transparent canopy, similar to that of a helicopter. Under the canopy a number of alien figures could be seen. The aliens were generally of the classic Grey type, about four feet tall, with big black eyes. Other types were also seen. Hollanda's team took photographs of the craft they encountered, and made a series of sketches of the aliens.

Although the aliens showed no hostile intent towards the Air Force team, their attacks on local hunters and fishermen continued. A variety of craft were involved. Among of the most deadly were large, cylindrical UFOs the villagers called *camburoes*. These would hover over an area and send out powerful beams of light that would sweep back and forth across the ground. One witness, Joao de Brito, related what happened when a friend of his was attacked.

'He felt the light bearing down on his body,' de Brito said, 'and he felt his strength being sucked out of him. He was sure he was going to die. The flying thing was shaped like a cylinder, and he could hear voices coming from it in an unknown language. It left him powerless and he ended up in hospital.'

When the villagers tried to escape the bright beams of light and sheltered in their homes, they found that the alien beams could easily slice through roofs and walls. The local people's only experience of anything similar was the menace of wild animals, so they lit huge fires down by the river and gathered around them. Strangely this seemed to deter the aliens – to begin with. But after a few weeks, they got used to the fires and the attacks resumed.

About seven weeks into Operation Saucer, the UFO activity began to increase dramatically and the aliens appeared more hostile. Each time Hollanda moved his team to a new area of operation, a UFO would already be hovering over their destination when they arrived.

This left Hollanda feeling that the aliens were able to read his thoughts and anticipate his every move. He became increasingly aware that his team had become the object of intense scrutiny. In one extraordinary incident, Hollanda and one of his men set off up one of the Amazon tributaries in a small boat. They were about seventy-five miles from Belem when Hollanda decided to return to camp. A sudden storm meant that the rivers in the area were flooding rapidly, making navigation difficult. As they turned a bend in the river, they saw a huge oval-shaped UFO, around three hundred foot tall, hovering over the bank. As they watched, a door slid open at the top of the craft and a figure emerged. It began to float gently towards them. Without his full force around him, Hollanda decided it was time to make a strategic withdrawal, gunned the out-board motor and made a rapid escape.

Although the Air Force team itself had not been attacked, Holland believed that all of them had been abducted. Hollanda believed that he had undergone multiple abductions himself and all the team members reported experiencing periods of 'missing time'. Hollanda himself had a series of strange dreams. These are common in abductees and are often unconscious memories of the abduction experience.

During his interview, Hollanda told Gevaerd that he had been physically and psychologically examined by the aliens. He said this was for some sort of preparation, but he did not know what for. Hollanda even gave Gevaerd a drawing of one of extraterrestrials holding a pistol-shaped device used in the examination.

It was clear that abduction was part of a long-term alien agenda, as abductions from the area had been going on for quite some time. Sixteen-year-old Antonio Alves Ferreira had been first taken on 4 January 1975. He had heard a buzzing sound in the back yard of his parent's house in the Indigo district of Sao Luis. When he went outside to find out what it was, he saw a small disc hovering over the house. He was not alone. Around five hundred other witnesses reported seeing the same UFO. Since the first encounter Ferreira has been abducted eleven times. Three humanoid aliens are responsible. They told him they were from the planet 'Protu'. They made a clone of him to use and left it as a double on Earth, while he was on their craft. He learned their language and, on one occasion, recorded their conversation. This is the only known recording of on alien speech.

Then on 10 July 1977, a chicken farmer from Pinheiro named Jose Benedito Bogea was on his way on foot to Sao Luis when he was pursued by a bright, bluish-green light.

'I raised my arms,' he said, 'and I saw a bright flash of light. It knocked me to the ground. I felt like I'd had an electric shock. Then I passed out.'

When he came too he found himself in a strange alien city with avenues and gardens. Later he was transported back to Earth and dropped off some seventy-five miles from where he had been abducted. He had been missing for twenty-four hours.

Ninety days after Hollanda's team began their investigation, Operation Saucer was suddenly stopped. Hollanda was ordered to close down the operation and forget about it. This was easier said than done as Hollanda continued to feel the effects years after the operation ended. He said he could feel the presence of the aliens in his home. Sometimes he could see them and sometimes he could just feel they were there.

After Operation Saucer, Hollanda also found that he had acquired paranormal abilities. He was able to read people's thoughts. Later he found he could predict the future. He would know in advance that people were about to turn up at his house and he could tell what was going to happen at work.

Despite these fringe benefits, the abduction experience had a profound and disturbing impact on Hollanda. During the interview with Gevaerd he would often break down and cry. His wife became so concerned that she tried to stop the interview. In an effort to help Hollanda come to terms with the experience, Gevaerd arranged regressional hypnosis for Hollanda. But two days before the first session, Hollanda committed suicide. Gevaerd believes that he was the victim of the profound psychological trauma that can be incurred by exposure to extraterrestrials.

Before Hollanda died, he gave Gevaerd copies of a number of documents that had been included in the detailed report he had submitted to the Armed Forces Headquarters in Brasilia. He also gave Gevaerd copies of some of the five hundred photographs the team had taken in the area. After Hollanda submitted his report, he got no response from the authorities and the outcome of Operation Saucer is unknown.

By the early 1980s, the frequency of UFO sightings and alien attacks in the area had dropped significantly, but they have never stopped completely. Gevaerd believes that aliens have selected remote areas in Brazil where they can go about their activities with impunity. The principal agenda behind the attacks, he says, is some form of biological experimentation. Other investigators have come to the same conclusion.

Fighting Back

Human beings are a resilient species. Even in the face of alien aggression we are not going to give up without a fight. Since 1980 and the beginnings of America's 'Stars Wars' programme, weapons have been under development that can shoot alien craft from the skies.

They had one of their first successes on 28 September 1989, when a mysterious object was shot down over Long Island, New York. According to UFO researchers Brian Levin and John Ford of the Long Island UFO Network, the craft was destroyed using a 'Doppler radar system' built by the III Electronics company in conjunction with the Brookhaven National Laboratories, as part of the Strategic Defense Initiative.

Some three years later, on 24 November 1992, a second UFO was downed in the same area. Around 7 p.m., eyewitness Walter Knowles saw what he described as 'a tubular, dark metallic object with blue lights on each end' moving slowly over South Haven Park. Then he saw a blinding flash of light and the spacecraft crashed into the park. John Ford later obtained a video, shot by Brookhaven Fire Fighters, that shows the charred wreckage of the alien ship.

Over recent years, the number of reports of hostile exchanges between the military and UFOs has risen dramatically. It also appears that military attacks on UFOs have been carried out using exotic technology. Many investigators now believe that much of today's military technology, particularly weapons developed for the Strategic Defense Initiative and now the National Missile Defense programme, has been created with the express purpose of repulsing an alien invasion.

Even more remarkable evidence that this is the case comes from a video shot by one of the TV cameras aboard NASA's Space Shuttle *Discovery* on 15 September 1991. It shows number of strange glowing objects entering the picture. They are seen to respond to a series of flashes from Earth, make a ninety-degree turn – something impossible for a terrestrial craft – then accelerate away. The video comes from the US cable TV channel *NASA Select*, which broadcasts continuous coverage of NASA missions.

The so-called 'STS 48' tape has generated enormous controversy and is regularly screened on terrestrial TV. NASA maintains that the glowing objects were nothing more than ice crystals or space debris being moved about by the thrusts of the Shuttle's altitude adjustment rockets. But this has been discredited by Dr Jack Kasher, a physicist at the University of Nebraska, Omaha.

'NASA claimed they were ice crystals. We proved that was physically impossible,' says Kasher. 'Ice crystals couldn't change direction in the way these objects could.'

According his analysis, he estimates that the objects were at the very least ten miles from the Shuttle. He also calculated that they were able to accelerate from zero to 2,500 miles an hour in just one second. If the objects were a hundred miles away, as Kasher believes, in one second they reached over 15,000 miles an hour. This would have subjected the ship to a force of over 1050 Gs – far beyond the capability of any terrestrial craft. However, there have been plenty of sightings of such extraordinary craft before. What makes the STS 48 video so controversial is that it also shows that the craft made off at these astonishing speeds because they were fired on by some exotic weapons system. Careful analysis of the video shows that a double flash of energy was aimed at one of the craft. Its response is immediate. It changes direction and accelerates away at incredible speed.

Kasher was employed to work on the Star Wars programme until 1996. He points out that, despite the huge amounts of money spent, no anti-ICBM umbrella was ever built. Meanwhile, $35 billion is spent every year in a 'black budget' to develop all sorts of covert technologies.

'It is entirely conceivable that what appears to be a weapon firing at the objects in the STS 48 video may, indeed, be the result of some covert black budget,' he says.

What's more, it backs former Pentagon alien technology expert Colonel Philip Corso's thesis that the US have been secretly fighting a covert war against the aliens for 50 years. He too believes that SDI was developed not only to protect against Soviet ICBMs, but also to defend against alien invaders.

US government policy documents also back Corso's position. In 1967, the National Security Agency – America's largest and most secret intelligence service – produced a study entitled *UFO Hypothesis and Survival Questions*. It recommended 'developing adequate defense measures' against alien invaders. Then in 1978, Michael Michaud, Deputy Director of the US State Department's Office of International Security Policy, said: 'Aliens from other solar systems are a potential threat to us, and we are a potential threat to them. Even if an alien species had achieved true peace within its own ranks, it would still be worried about us and would take the measures it felt were necessary to protect itself. This includes the possibilities of military action.'

Major General Robert L. Schweitzer, a member of the National Security Council, was asked to comment. He said: 'President Reagan is well aware of the threat you document so clearly and is doing all in his power to restore the national defense margin of safety as quickly and prudently as possible.'

It was President Reagan who instigated the Star Wars programme.

Under Attack

The modern military's gung-ho attitude could well be because the armed forces themselves have been under attack since flying saucers first appeared in our skies.

One of the earliest hostile encounters occurred over Kentucky on 7 January 1948. Captain Thomas F. Mantell was flying an F-51 Mustang when he was asked to check out reports of a strange flying object. At 2:40 p.m. he made visual contact at 15,000 feet:

'It appears to be metallic, of tremendous size,' he radioed back. 'I'm trying to close for a better look.'

He followed it up to 30,000 feet where, though he was a very experienced pilot, he lost consciousness due to lack of oxygen and crashed. Richard T. Miller was in the operations room at Godman Air Force Base and heard Mantell's last words.

'My God, I see people in this thing,' he said.

It appears he got too close. Witnesses saw the plane being enveloped in white light. It 'belly flopped' onto the ground, but came off remarkably unscathed – seeing that it had just fallen from 30,000 feet. And Miller said that it had crashed more than an hour after its fuel was supposed to have run out.

An eerily similar encounter took place between a military helicopter and a UFO over Ohio in 1973. On 18 October, Captain Lawrence Coyne and his three crew members were approaching Cleveland Hopkins military airport, when they saw a red light approaching them at high speed on a collision course. Coyne took evasive action and tried to put an emergency call through to the control tower, but it was blocked by interference from the alien craft. Then they saw a cigar-shaped UFO, around sixty-five feet in length. It had a domed top with portholes. It sent out a green beam of energy, which enveloped the helicopter.

Coyne shouted: 'My God, what's happening?'

The beam pulled the helicopter upwards, towards the alien craft. Together they ascended at a rate of around 1,500 feet a minute until they reached 5,000 feet. Then the energy beam flicked out, releasing the helicopter, and the UFO took off at tremendous speed. Numerous eyewitnesses saw the encounter. People stopped their cars on the nearby highway to watch. They described how the green light illuminated the entire area.

Another encounter occurred over pre-revolutionary Iran. When the Shah was still in power, Iran was one of the US's staunchest allies and the Iranian Air Force was equipped with the latest American attack aircraft. At around 1 a.m. on 19 September 1976, Iranian military radar operators detected an unidentified object flying at an altitude of six thousand feet over the Merkabah Tower in Tehran. An F-4 Phantom jet was scrambled from Shahrokin Air Force Base to intercept the mysterious craft. As the interceptor jet sped to within twenty-two miles of the object, the aircraft's instrumentation panel suddenly went dead. The pilot tried to report the malfunction, but the communications equipment was also out. He turned, breaking off the intercept and heading back to base. Then, when it presented no further threat to the UFO, the Phantom's systems came back to life.

In the mean time, a second Phantom had been despatched to intercept the UFO. This time, when the jet got within striking distance, the UFO sped off. The Phantom gave chase, but suddenly the pilot saw 'flashing strobe lights arranged in a rectangular pattern' pulsing in front of his face. Even so, the pilot made another attempt to close in on the UFO. This time a brightly-lit object emerged from the UFO and began moving at high speed towards the jet. This was plainly a hostile act. The pilot automatically retaliated with a Sidewinder. But as he tried to activate it, his weapons system went dead and he lost all communications.

The Phantom was now in imminent danger. The pilot jinked and janked, and banked his jet into a steep dive. Looking around to see if he had shaken the bright object that had been fired at him, he saw it circle around and rejoin the UFO. Almost immediately, the pilot's weapons system was reactivated and his communications returned.

The pilot then saw the UFO fire another missile. This one descended rapidly towards the ground. It made a controlled landing, then cast a brilliant luminescence over an area that the pilot estimated to be around two miles in diameter. While the pilot was watching it, the UFO disappeared.

A fatal encounter took place between the US military and an alien craft above Puerto Rico on 28 December 1988. At 7:45 a.m. hundreds of eyewitnesses saw a huge, metállic-grey, triangular craft, the size of a football field, hovering over Saman Lake in the Cabo Rojo area, which is one of the island's UFO hotspots. 'It was enormous, with many flashing coloured lights,' said eyewitness Wilson Sosa.

Two US Navy F-14 'Tomcats' were scrambled from Roosevelt Road Naval Base to intercept it. When they caught up with it, the alien craft took evasive action. In an attempt to shake them, it spiralled downwards in tight circles. One F-14 nearly collided with the alien craft, but the UFO jinked out of the way. Despite its size, the alien craft was much more manoeuvrable than the Tomcats.

'The jets tried to intercept it three times,' Wilson Sosa said, 'and that's when the UFO slowed down and almost stopped in mid-air.'

Then, in a seemingly suicidal attack, one of the F-14s flew directly at it. The witnesses braced themselves for a collision. Instead, they saw the aircraft disappear as if it had been drawn into the bigger craft. The other F-14 then approached the rear of the craft. It too was swallowed up. Afterwards the huge craft gave out a blinding flash, and split into two smaller triangular ships, which sped away in opposite directions.

Retribution

The aliens may only have been getting their own back. Puerto Rican Professor of Chemistry Calixto Perez said that he examined a dead humanoid being in 1980. It had been killed by Jose Luis 'Chino' Zayas, a Puerto Rican teenage who, with a bunch of friends, had come across a group of small humanoids while exploring the caves at Tetas de

Cayey. One of them turned on Zayas and he battered it to death with a stick, stoving its head in. They kept the corpse as a trophy. It was preserved in formaldehyde by a local undertaker. Later it was seized by officers who said they were attached to NASA, and photographed, before being 'lost' by US officials.

Rules of Engagement

The official policy of the Soviet Air Force was to actively intercept all UFOs and the Russian military established what became the biggest organised effort ever to track and catalogue UFO encounters. Soviet pilots were ordered to get as close to UFOs as possible in an attempt to identify them. However, there were encounters that really scared the authorities. This led to a reversal of policy. Standing orders were issued that pilots should avoid all contact.

Meanwhile, South Africa maintained a 'search and destroy' policy and, in 1990, two South African Mirage FIIG jets, armed with experimental Thor-2 laser cannons, hit a UFO and downed it in the Kalahari desert.

Tony Dodd of Quest was contacted by Captain James Van Greunen, a special investigations intelligence officer with the South African Air Force, who provided Dodd with a small dossier on the case. This contained a report that showed the UFO had been clocked by radar travelling over six thousand miles an hour when it was hit. A special team was sent to the crash site where they found a large silvery disc embedded in the ground. High radiation readings were reported and the craft was carefully shipped back to Valhalla air base.

Once the craft was inside a hangar, a hatchway opened up and out stepped two creatures. They were four feet tall, with grey skin, no body hair, over-large heads and huge slanting eyes. The aliens were taken to a medical unit where they were examined. Passed as fit, they were shipped to Wright–Patterson AFB.

Soon after Van Greunen met Dodd in England, he was ordered home by the South African government. He later fled to Germany where he published his story.

449

Evidence

Photographic Evidence

In the face of official denials, many people refuse to believe in the reality of UFOs and, since the beginning of extraterrestrial visitations, UFOlogists have known that witness reports – no matter how unimpeachable the eyewitness – were not enough. So they have struggled to get convincing evidence on film. The problem is that, in these days of science fiction blockbusters and hi-tech wizardry, almost anything can be faked. The most amazing effects can be produced by even the humblest camera.

'The adage that the camera cannot lie was disproved as soon as it was invented,' says UFO researcher Nick Pope.

The footage showing the alien autopsy and the alien interview were worth hundreds of thousands of pounds. Even a good still picture of a UFO can be worth a lot of money. So no photograph can be taken at face value. It has to be thoroughly investigated by skilled researchers. And even then it might be impossible to prove that the picture is genuine.

In the early days of the UFO sightings, anything went. UFOlogists assumed that if an image looked like a UFO, then it was a UFO. Many photographs of alien 'spaceships' were published in the 1940s and 1950s, fuelling the burgeoning UFO fever. To modern eyes many of these snapshots are obvious, crude fakes made by hanging models from trees or tossing hubcaps in the air. But no one looked too closely. Even fairly dubious pictures were considered good publicity. This naive approach was courting disaster.

The Camera Does Lie

UFOlogy's nemesis came in the form of Alex Birch, a teenage boy from Sheffield. In February 1962, Alex and some friends saw a formation of flying saucers above their garden. Alex succeeded in taking a photograph of the extraterrestrial fleet. Even though no one else in Sheffield had seen the craft, the photograph was taken at face value. Birch and his father were treated like heroes. They were invited to London to file their sighting report in person with officials of the British Air Ministry. And Alex addressed a packed audience at the inaugural meeting of the British UFO Research Association.

Among UFO enthusiasts it was one of the most talked about photographs in years. The problem was that the UFO lobby were so eager to believe that it was genuine that nobody carried out any meaningful investigation. All the picture showed was a smattering of dark blobs on a grainy picture of the sky. Nevertheless, the case entered UFO folklore as an unsolved mystery.

Ten years later, Alex Birch had grown up and he decided to confess. The photograph was a trick. He had painted a few crude flying saucers on to a sheet of glass, propped it up in his back garden and photographed it against some blurred tree branches and the sky. To the uncritical eyes, the result vaguely resembled UFOs hovering in mid-air. Cleverly he had avoided including in the shot any reference point, such as a building, which would give the viewer some idea of the size of the objects and their distance from the camera.

Birch's confession caused a sensation. The general view was that he had set the cause of UFOlogy back years. In fact, in the long run, he probably did it a great service. After his schoolboy hoax, UFO enthusiasts would never be as gullible again. UFO bodies set up guidelines that were to be used when investigating photographic cases. Over the years, these have been constantly refined and improved. These guidelines were used to review old UFO photographs and obvious fakes were thrown up. They also allowed UFOlogists to guard against new hoaxes and helped them weed out what were termed 'accidental fakes'.

Authentication

Just as the human eye can easily be deceived, the camera is open to being fooled. If an eyewitness is willing to believe that a perfectly ordinary light shining through a mist-filled sky is a UFO, a camera will not tell them it's not. In fact, a camera can be a liability when UFO spotting. You experience what you see very differently through the limited frame of a viewfinder than with the naked eye. Because a camera freezes an instant in a single shot, things that looked quite normal in motion can appear as anomalous in a photograph. A common example of an 'accidental fake' can occur when a bird flies through the scene. For just a fraction of a second that the shutter is open, the bird's wings will be caught in a configuration that would not normally be seen by the human eye. And when that is rendered in the two dimensions of a photographic print, instead of the three dimensions of real life, it might look deceptively like a flying saucer – even if the photographer had no intention of producing a fake.

Calling in a photographic expert is now an automatic first step. They can pick out things like lens flare and other aberrations. In all, around five thousand photographic cases have been investigated around the world and a very small number – perhaps only fifty – really seem to be unexplained. Most are a mixture of accidental fakes, common confusion and out-and-out trickery. Even when visual evidence appears irrefutable, few experts would stake their reputation on a picture being genuine.

'Photographs are poor evidence because there are so many things we can do to technically produce images,' says retired USAF colonel and prominent UFOlogist Wendelle Stevens.

Stevens himself goes to great lengths to authenticate the photographs that are sent to him. He interviews the photographer, visits the place where the pictures were taken and takes his own shots from the same spot to use as a reference. By comparing his picture with the original he can usually work out how big the object is and how far it is from the lens. This eliminates the photographs that have been faked using models.

Another technique Steven employs is an evaluation of the 'blur factor'. The amount of blurring on the object, relative to that of other objects in the picture, helps determine whether the object is moving, and if so, how fast. The approximate speed and direction of flight can also be gauged from the 'edge definition'. This exploits the Doppler effect, where light waves from the leading edge are compressed, while those from the trailing edge are stretched.

The distance of an object from the lens can also be judged by 'atmospheric attenuation'. This is caused by moisture in the atmosphere that cuts down the amount of light reaching the lens. Computer analysis also picks up the 'chroma factor'. As red light is more readily absorbed by the atmosphere than blue, the image should contain a greater component of blue the further it is from the camera.

UFO Down

Winnowing out the accidental fake is never easy. One seemingly cast-iron photograph was only discredited after twenty-three years. In November 1966, a famous scientist was driving across the Williamette Pass in Oregon. He had a camera with him and was planning to take photographs of the snow-decked peaks. But as he was driving, he saw out of the corner of his eye a strange object zipping skywards. Reacting instinctively, he fired off a shot.

When the photograph was developed it showed a flat-bottomed disc climbing from the trees, sucking a plume of snow in its wake. More remarkable still was the fact that three separate images of the UFO were on the one print. It was as if the craft had dematerialised and rematerialised several times during the few hundredths of a second that the camera shutter was open. The cameraman was not certain of what he had seen and wished to remain anonymous. He was a big-name biochemist with a PhD and a reputation to lose, certainly not your average hoaxer. Besides, the photograph seemed to speak for itself.

The impeccable credentials of the photographer did play a part in how seriously the case was taken. *Photographic Magazine* conducted an investigation and gave the picture a clean bill of health. The optical and physical characteristics of the camera and image were even used to deduce the approximate shape, size and speed of the mysterious object.

Then in 1993, researcher Irwin Weider announced that the photo was a fake. Everyone was shocked. For years Weider had believed the photograph really did show a UFO. *Photographic Magazine*'s investigation seemed conclusive. But then Weider had taken a trip through the area where the picture had been taken and thought he saw a UFO himself. He drove up and down the road the same stretch of road and found that the 'UFO' only appeared under very specific conditions. This aroused his suspicion. He began conducting experiments, taking pictures from his moving car and using different shutter speeds. He eventually discovered that the UFO was actually a road sign, which appeared to be a flying saucer due to the interaction of the car and camera. He could even reproduce the triple image at the right speeds.

The world of UFOlogy was stunned by this news, but it just goes to show how carefully photographic evidence must be evaluated. However, Weider's tenacious methods do not always bear fruit.

The Genuine Article

There are some UFO photographs that cannot be dismissed. One such picture was taken by farmer Paul Trent, who snapped a flying saucer over his ranch near McMinnville, Oregon on 11 May 1950. The photograph's background and foreground were both clear, allowing the UFO's size and distance to be estimated. Subsequent computer enhancement has revealed that the disc is solid, between sixty and a hundred feet in diameter, and made from a highly reflective material.

Then on 16 January 1958, when the Brazilian naval vessel *Almirante Saldanha* was carrying a team of scientists to a weather station on Trindade Island – an uninhabited rock in the South Atlantic – a UFO appeared low above the ocean and flew past the ship. It circled the island and headed away. More than a dozen people on the ship saw it. One of them was the expedition photographer. He had his camera to hand and took a sequence of shots clearly showing the object.

When the Brazilian captain got back to port, he had the film processed and the resulting pictures were handed over to the military. The Brazilian military's top photo reconnaissance experts examined them and could find no fault. After some deliberation, the Brazilian government released the film and admitted that they were unable to account for what the pictures showed. As the technology has developed, the Brazilian photographs have been regularly reassessed. Even computer enhancement of the photographs has failed to prove them fakes. Even so, sceptics continue to denounce the photographs as a mirage.

Other convincing pictures have come to light more recently. UFOlogist are surprised that, with the growth of camera ownership, they are not inundated with hoaxing and accidental fakes. However, everyone is now so alert to the possibilities that only the genuine cases get left behind.

In 1983 police officer Tony Dodd photographed a UFO near Addingham in Yorkshire. He sent his negatives and prints to Ground Saucer Watch, a UFO research group. They used computer enhancement and a process called 'density slicing' to analyse the pictures and found that the UFO was above the horizon and airborne. The grain of the film was analysed using a technique called 'edge enhancement', which confirmed that there was nothing supporting the flying object. GSW identified vapour come from the craft. This vapour trail blended with the atmosphere, convincing investigators that an image of a UFO could not simply have been matted into a picture of the sky. 'Colour contouring' was used to confirm that the UFO was spherical. GSW concluded: 'The UFO appears structured and thirty feet in diameter. This represents Britain's first confirmed UFO photograph.' Sceptics still doubt the evidence of their eyes.

Even though it seems to be impossible to find that one piece of clinching photographic evidence, that does not mean that UFO photographs as a whole do not tell their own tale. Dr Bruce Maccabee, an optical physicist for the Surface Weapons division of the US Navy, has been called in to investigate numerous cases. He has seen more UFO photographs than most and he has come to some very clear conclusions.

'I believe that UFOs are real and that they are alien in origin,' he says. 'I have established this through my own research and the study of many years of evidence. Photographic cases are often inconclusive and frustrating for the investigator. That final piece of evidence simply may not be available. However, there are sufficient numbers of impressive cases where it can be established with reasonable conviction that some kind of extraordinary craft was photographed. Such evidence provides a case that demands to be answered by the scientific community.'

The Test of Time

Among the UFO photographs that have stood the test of time are those taken by Paul Villa in New Mexico in the 1960s. They were widely published at the time and UFOlogists believe that they are some of the best ever taken. Even so, there are some puzzling aspects to Villa's story that have caused some sceptics to doubt the evidence of their own eyes.

Villa's story began ten years before he photographed his first series of saucers in 1963. While working for the Department of Water and Power in Los Angeles, he had been contacted by extraterrestrials. One day in 1953, he was in the Long Beach area when he was overcome with an urge to go down to the beach. There, he met a strange man nearly seven tall. This spooked Villa. He felt afraid and wanted to run away, but then the strange man addressed him by his name and told him many personal things about himself that only the closest of friends would have known. And he could mind-read. At first Villa was puzzled. Then he realised that the being he was talking to was a very superior intelligence – not just a more than averagely intelligent human being but a super-intelligent extraterrestrial.

'He knew everything I had in my mind and told me many things that had taken place in my life,' Villa recalled. 'He then told me to look out beyond the reef. I saw a metallic-looking, disc-shaped object that seemed to be floating on the water. Then the spaceman asked if I would like to go aboard the craft and look around, and I went with him.'

It was too good an opportunity to miss. Once on board the saucer, Villa met other extraterrestrial beings that were human-like in appearance, though 'more refined in face and body'. They had an advanced knowledge of science and explained to him many things that baffled scientists. They told Villa that the galaxy where the Earth resides was just one among an unfathomable number of galaxies that were inhabited across the entire universe – it was a single grain of sand on a vast beach – and that a superior intelligence governed the universe and everything in it. The aliens had bases on the Moon, but their main base was Phobos, one of the two satellites of Mars. Phobos was actually hollow and had been constructed by the aliens. The alien technology was so advanced that their spaceships could penetrate the Earth's airspace without being detected by radar, unless they wanted to call attention to their presence. Alien craft were regularly visiting Earth and the aliens said that more and more sightings were going to take place to increase public awareness of their existence. They then reassured Villa that they had come to Earth on a friendly mission to help humankind.

Born Apolinar Alberto Villa Jr. in 1916, Villa was of mixed Spanish, Native America, Scottish and German descent. He later came to believe that he had been in telepathic communication with aliens since he was five. Although his formal education did not take him beyond tenth grade, he had a mastery of mathematics, physics, electrical engineering and mechanics. He served as an engineer in the US Air Force and made his living as a mechanic in civilian life.

Ten years after the Long Beach encounter, on 16 June 1963, Villa was contacted telepathically by aliens. He was told to go to a place near the town of Peralta, New Mexico, about fifteen miles south of Albuquerque. He drove there alone, as instructed, arriving at 2 p.m. Soon after, a flying saucer appeared. It was between 150 and 160 feet in diameter. The ship hovered low in the sky and seemed to pose at various distances so that Villa could get good shots of it. He took a series of photographs. In some of them the craft is framed by the trees, and some show his truck in the foreground. This reference is exactly what photographic experts need if they are going to prove a picture genuine.

When the spacecraft first appeared between the trees, the bottom was glowing amber-red, as if it was red hot. The colours changed to shiny chrome, then to dull aluminium grey, then back to amber. At one point it became so bright it was painful to look at it. When it passed over his head, he could feel the heat it gave off and it gave him a tingling sensation all over his body.

The upper half of the craft was domed and could turn independently from the lower half, though during flight it remained stationary while the lower part rotated. When it did this it gave off a whirring sound like a giant electric motor or a generator. At other times the craft buzzed, or pulsed, or was completely silent. It could do complex aerobatics like flipping onto one edge with its bottom half rotating. The aliens later told him that they did this to demonstrate how they had created an artificial gravity-field within the craft. In such manoeuvres, they remained perfectly comfortable inside.

When the spacecraft hovered over his truck, some three hundred feet up, it caused the truck to rise slowly into the air and float about three feet from the ground for a few minutes. When the craft was about 450 yards away, a flexible probe emerged. It bent into different angles and shapes as it probed the trees and the ground. At the same time, a small, shiny orb came flying out of the spacecraft and disappeared behind trees. It suddenly reappeared, this time glowing red in colour, then shot off at incredible speed. Thoughout the whole display Villa took pictures.

After half an hour, the alien craft landed, settling down on three telescopic legs. Then, through a previously invisible door, five men and four women emerged. They were between seven and ten feet tall and beautiful to look at. They were well proportioned, immaculately groomed and wore tight-fitting, one-piece uniforms. The aliens told Villa that they came from 'the constellation of Coma Berenices, many light years distant'. This did not exactly pinpoint their home. Constellations are only patterns of stars in the sky, as seen from Earth, and Coma Berenices is noted for the large number of galaxies it contains.

Although the aliens were perfectly able to communicate with Villa telepathically, they could also speak many Earth languages. During their conversation, which lasted an hour and a half, they spoke to Villa in both English and Spanish, which was Villa's native tongue. Villa noted that when they talked among themselves they spoke in their own tongue which, to his ears, sounded like 'something akin to Hebrew and Indian'.

They told Villa that the spacecraft they travelled on operated as a mothership for nine remotely controlled monitoring discs. Manoeuvred from instrument panels inside the mothership, they picked up pictures and sound and relayed them back to the television monitor panels. This remote-viewing system was remarkably like the one first seen by George Adamski.

Villa returned to New Mexico in April 1965 to take a second series of photographs. This time the aliens appeared to him in several locations. The best photographs were taken at a place about twenty miles south of Albuquerque on 18 April. Again, when the photographic session was over, the ship settled on its tripod landing gear and the crewmen got out for a chat. This time there were only three of them. They had tanned skin and light brown hair, but they were shorter than the ones he had seen before, only about five feet five inches tall. They talked to Villa nearly two hours, discussing both general topics and personal matters.

A third set of photographs was taken on 19 June 1996. These showed some of the mothership's remotely controlled discs and spheres. The discs were from three to six feet in diameter and were photographed both on the ground and in the air. Often they were surrounded by smaller spheres. Larger discs were also launched from the mothership. Villa estimated that these were some forty feet in diameter. Some of them had flexible, probing antennas, which Villa said resembled the antennae of certain insects – though these are not visible in the photos. But in all his meetings with the aliens, although they would let him photograph their ships, they would not allow him to photograph them.

Villa has other photographs showing one of these remotely controlled discs that he made himself – to the exact specifications given by the aliens. It was about three feet across and was photographed during a test flight being monitored by one of the alien spheres. The disc crashed during the test, due a to slight error that Villa had made. However, the problem was soon rectified.

As it is impossible to distinguish the disc made by Villa from the real alien McCoy, this has been taken as proof that Villa made all of them. However, in none of the photographs is there any hint that the objects are suspended or have been superimposed. Atmospheric 'thickening' – the effect that makes distant objects less well defined than those close to – shows that the objects are not models. William Sherwood, formerly an optical physicist for Eastman-Kodak, studied all the Villa photographs and said they are genuine.

Because his pictures were so widely published in the 1960s, Villa was accused of making a fortune from them. He did not. In fact, he spent his own money sending out free copies. He also spent much of his free time writing to world leaders about what the aliens meant to mankind. In 1967, Ben Blaza of UFO International asked Villa's permission to copyright the photographs. Villa granted it, but made very little money himself.

Nor was Villa an attention seeker. His shunned publicity and rarely granted interviews to the media. He has also been threatened. Helicopters seem to follow him and he has been shot at.

British UFOlogist Timothy Good followed up on the Paul Villa case. In correspondence, Good pointed out the inaccuracies in certain prophecies the aliens had made. The aliens had said that seventeen nations would have the atomic bomb by 1966 – there were probably no more than ten by the year 2000. They said that Ronald Reagan would be elected president in 1976, though he did not make it to the White

House until four years later. Worse, they said that there were 'canals' and 'pumping stations' on Mars, and that 'cacti and other plants' grew in certain locations on the red planet.

When asked whether the aliens had lied to him, Villa said no, they just did not tell the whole truth. 'Why should they? People would just make money from that info. Besides, how can humanity appreciate anything if it is beyond their capacity to understand?' he said.

Villa told Good that Walt Disney Studios and the US Air Force had both studied his negatives and found no fault in them. According to Villa, Dr Edward Condon, who headed the University of Colorado's USAF-sponsored investigation team that studied UFOs from 1966 to 1968, said they were the best pictures he had ever seen. But Good could find no mention of Villa or his photographs in Dr Condon's book *Scientific Study of Unidentified Flying Objects*.

In 1976, Villa drove Good around the locations near Albuquerque where he had photographed the alien craft and met their crews. At one of them, Good asked Villa what the other crew members were doing while he was talking to the alien he assumed was the pilot. 'Oh, they were just bathing their feet in the river,' he replied without batting an eyelid.

Like William Sherwood and other researchers who met Villa, Good was impressed and concluded that there was something to his story. Paul Villa died of cancer in 1981.

Scientist's Sightings

Strange lights were seen in the sky over Lubbock, Texas, on the night of 25 August 1951. They were witnessed by an Atomic Energy Commission executive and his wife from their back yard and simultaneously observed by four respected Texas scientists from their vantage point in another part of town.

Approximately three dozen bluish lights were seen. They had the appearance of a giant flying wing, which moved back and forth across the night skies. Several hundred people in the area witnessed the same phenomenon over the next several days.

On 31 August, Carl Hart Jr. photographed the lights, but photo analysis could not prove Hart's pictures were genuine.

Single Exposure

On 24 May 1964, Jim Templeton, a fireman from Carlisle in the North of England, took his young daughter out to the marches overlooking the Solway Firth to take some photographs. Nothing untoward happened, although both he and his wife noticed an unusual aura in the atmosphere. There was a kind of electric charge in the air, though no storm came. Even nearby cows seemed upset by it.

Some days later, Mr Templeton got his photographs processed by the chemist, who said that it was a pity that the man who had walked past had spoilt the best shot of Elizabeth holding a bunch of flowers. Jim was puzzled. There had been nobody else on the marshes nearby at the time. But sure enough, on the picture in question there was a figure in a silvery white space suit projecting at an odd angle into the air behind the girl's back, as if an unwanted snooper had wrecked the shot.

The case was reported to the police and taken up by Kodak, the film manufacturers, who offered free film for life to anyone who could solve the mystery when their experts failed. It was not, as the police at first guessed, a simple double exposure with one negative accidentally printed on top of another during processing. It was, as Chief Superintendent Oldcorn quickly concluded, just 'one of those things... a freak picture'.

A few weeks later Jim Templeton received two mysterious visitors. He had never heard of 'Men in Black' – they were almost unknown in Britain at that time. But the two men who came to his house in a large Jaguar car wore dark suits and otherwise looked normal. The weird thing about them was their behaviour. They only referred to one another by numbers and asked the most unusual questions as they drove Jim out to the marshes. They wanted to know in minute detail about the weather on the day of the photograph, the activities of local bird life and odd asides like that. Then they tried to make him admit that he had just photographed an ordinary man walking past. Jim responded politely, but rejected this suggestion. At this point, they became angry, got back into the car and drove off leaving him there. He then had to walk five miles across country to get home.

Polaroids

Another alien contactee who could back his story with photographic evidence was sign painter Howard Menger, whose alien encounters began in 1932. His alien contacts came from Venus and demonstrated super-human abilities. At 1 a.m. on 2 August 1956, he snapped a series of Polaroids showing a spacecraft landing and a 'Venusian' getting out. The creature had broad shoulders, a slim waist, long, straight legs and long, blonde hair that blew in the soft warm summer breeze. However, Polaroid photography was in its infancy and the photographs are vague and indistinct. Menger only managed to catch the creature in silhouette against the glowing spacecraft. However, Menger explained that the blurring effect around the figure was caused by the electromagnetic flux surrounding the craft.

Menger later found himself employed by the extraterrestrials to help them learn human ways. He had to cut their hair into Earthly styles and introduce the aliens to Earth food. In return, they took him on trips to the Moon. Unfortunately, his photographs of the Moon came out no better than his portraits of the aliens.

Carroll Wayne Watts, a cotton farmer in Loco, Texas, managed to get some Polaroids of the aliens who abducted him in April 1967. As usual, Watts was stripped naked and examined. Just as he was getting dressed, he tried to steal an alien paperweight. He was alone in the room when he pocketed the two-inch-long piece of metal. Nevertheless, one of his captors came marching in, reached into his pocket and removed the paperweight. Watts was then knocked unconscious.

Polaroid shots of aliens served Police Chief Jeff Greenhaw little better. At 10 p.m. on the night of 17 October 1973, Greenhaw received a call from a woman reporting that a flying saucer had landed in a field near Falkville, Alabama. There, Greenhaw encountered a seven-foot-tall metallic humanoid. He tried to communicate with it, but got no response. But he did manage to snap a series of Polaroids before the alien fled – its huge steps allowed it to easily outplace Greenhaw's patrol car.

'He was running faster than anything I ever saw,' said Greenhaw.

The pictures clearly show the outline of a metallic creature. With his position as chief of police on the line, Greenhaw had no reason to fake the photographs, so his evidence had to be taken seriously. His pictures certainly bought him no money and no fame. Within two weeks of the encounter, an arson attack on his house destroyed the original prints, he began receiving threatening phone calls, his car blew up mysteriously and his wife walked out on him. The pictures brought him unwanted publicity. It was said that he had been duped by a prankster wrapped in silver foil and he was forced to resign as police chief. This was hardly the action of a hoaxer.

Polaroids were also unlucky for twenty-three-year-old Filiberto Caponi. Over a couple of months beginning in May 1993, he had taken a series of photos of an extraterrestrial creature in his home town of Ascoli Piceno. He had found it in a sack, but in subsequent shots the sack was gone and the creature seems to have undergone some type of physical development or growth. At first Caponi thought he had stumbled onto some form of bizarre genetic experiment.

In November 1993, his Polaroids were broadcast on the Italian TV station RAI-DUE. Soon after, the Italian police took Caponi in for questioning. He was charged with 'creating panic'. The police confiscated the photographs and he was forced to sign a confession saying he had faked the whole thing.

Big-Nosed Greys

Former US Navy petty officer Milton had access to the famous Grudge/Blue Book Special Report 13 on UFOs, which the US government claims never existed. He also saw a file belonging to Majestic-12, President Truman's secret commission set up to investigate UFOs, while he was a quartermaster under the Commander in Chief of the Pacific Fleet. In the files, Cooper saw a series of photographs of 'big-nosed Greys'. These creatures had struck a deal with the US government. They came from a dying planet that orbited Betelgeuse. Led by His Omnipotent Highness Krill, they had chosen Earth as their new home. The deal was that, in exchange for alien technological secrets, they would be allowed to share the planet and abduct humans occasionally for experimentation. Unfortunately, the deal soon broke down and the aliens went on an abduction spree. But the treaty was patched up and remains in operation to this day.

Undisputed Evidence

On the night of 2 August 1965 fourteen-year-old Alan Smith saw a UFO from his back garden. It changed colour from white to red then to green. The quick-thinking teenager got a camera and photographed the object. He sent the image to the USAF investigation team, who were known as Project Blue Book. They passed it on to the USAF Photo Analysis Division. The analysts concluded that the object was a mile from the camera and thirty feet in diameter. However, in an attempt to debunk the sighting, the report on the photograph concluded that it could have been made by photographing 'a multi-colored revolving filter flood-light'. Twenty-one years later the America UFO group Ground Saucer Watch subjected it to computer analysis which confirmed that it showed 'an extraordinary flying craft of large dimensions'.

Moving Pictures

While it is relatively easy to fake photographs – or produce fakes by accident – it is much harder to falsify moving pictures. Although fifty years ago home movie cameras were comparatively rare, with the advent of video, there has been huge increase in home movie making. These days video cameras are often on hand during UFO sightings and video footage has provided some of the best evidence that UFOs are actually structured flying vehicles, produced by an extremely advanced and non-terrestrial technology.

Despite the abundance of excellent footage in the UFO archives, a film or video fails to carry any real weight unless it has been subjected to a rigorous series of tests. The most exacting professional analysis is extremely expensive though, so it is only possible to submit a small proportion of movie material for specialist examination.

Over the years new technology had provided ways of testing photographs undreamed of when early UFO images were made. NASA has developed powerful computer programs that can rebuild images sent back bit by bit from cameras deep in space. The pictures are scanned electronically then sent to Earth as radio waves. On the way they get mixed up with other electromagnetic radiation. Atmospheric interference further degrades the signal, but when the incoming data stream is picked up on Earth, NASA's computer programmes can rebuilt the original and enhance and sharpen the image. When this technology is applied to ordinary photographs, film and video, it can reveal the most sophisticated trickery. As researchers have become vigilant, the number of UFO photos and video submitted for scrutiny has tumbled.

One of the world's leading experts in UFO film and video analysis is Jim Dilettoso. He has been doing this kind of work since 1977, when he was approached by UFO researcher retired USAF Colonel Wendell Stevens who asked him to look at footage from the controversial Meier case. Stevens chose Dilettoso because he had a background in optical special effects and the latest image processing techniques. With these skills at his command, he pioneered many of the analytical tools that are currently in use to scrutinise UFO footage.

Dilettoso's company – Village Labs of Phoenix, Arizona – is packed with sophisticated equipment. It owns a number of Cray supercomputers along with the most powerful graphics-generating system ever constructed. As well as analysing UFO films, Village Labs uses this equipment to carry out image analysis work for NASA and make the latest specials for Hollywood.

Technology and the procedures Dilettoso has developed over some twenty-five years in the business aside, some footage still passes muster. One video that got the Dilettoso seal of approval was shot by Tim Edwards in August 1995. Edwards was out in the back yard of his home in Selida, Colorado, with his daughter when he saw a large cylindrical UFO hovering in the sky. He got his Hi-8 video camera and filmed it continuously until it disappeared, shooting six minutes in all.

The footage eventually found its way to Dilettoso, who started the laborious process of analysis. When reviewing video or film footage, the job of the analysts is to look for evidence of fakery. There are two principal ways a hoax can be perpetrated these days. It can be done in the old-fashioned way using models, or, these days, an image can be produced digitally by computer.

Discovering if an image has been generated by computer is relatively easy. The first thing Dilettoso does is examine the 'vertical interval' – the black bar that divides one video frame from the next. This acts like a fingerprint, with each video machine producing a vertical interval with slightly different characteristics. Obviously if the footage has been shot on one camera in a continuous sequence, all the vertical intervals will be the same. But if the image has been created digitally or edited by a computer the vertical interval will be altered in the process. If this shows that the footage has been interfered with, Dilettoso looks for evidence that an image has been 'gen-locked'. This is a movie technique whereby one image is superimposed on top of another.

Discovering if a model has been used is far more difficult. The only way to do this is to try and calculate the object's size and distance from the camera. Dilettoso then makes an estimate of its direction of flight and its speed. Taking all these things together should tell you whether the object is small enough to be a model. If possible, Dilettoso likes to go to the location where the footage was shot. Then he shoots a tape on the same camera to use as reference.

In the case of the Edwards' tape, it was easily enough to fly up to Colorado and visit Edwards' backyard. Dilettoso was able to shoot from the same position as Edwards, using Edwards' Hi-8. The process of analysis was made easier because Edwards was standing under the eaves of his house when he shot the video. The camera was pointing upwards so the guttering appeared in the foreground. This was key to Dilettoso's analysis.

'When we survey the unknown, we need to know what the characteristics of the known are,' he says.

Dilettoso could measure the dimensions of the gutter and the distance of the camera from it. He could also establish the brightness of the sun reflecting off other surfaces nearby. Dilettoso then used a computer to create a database from the original footage. He located the darkest object in the shot and the brightest. Then he created a scale showing the relative shades of luminosity of those in between. It was then possible to calculate the approximate distance to the UFO, using the intensity of the reflected light as reference. The quality of reflected light from a large object high in the sky is very different from that reflected from a model a few feet from the lens. This provides a basic test to decide if UFO footage is a fake.

When it has been established that an object is large and some distance from the camera it is then necessary to establish whether it is under intelligent control and not a cloud or some other wind-borne phenomenon. To do this, Dilettoso examines the 'motion blur' of the image. By examining the small differences in the clarity of different parts of an image, it is possible to tell which way the craft is moving and how fast. This must match the speed and direction worked out from the footage as a whole. The motion blur also helps an expert tell whether it is the object that is moving or the camera.

The Edwards footage passed all these tests with flying colours. Dilettoso's conclusion was that the object shown in the video was not a model and was not computer generated. But the really startling result was Dilettoso's estimate of its size. He reckoned that Edwards' UFO was between half-a-mile and a mile in length.

In such convincing cases, UFO researchers ask for a second opinion. In the Edwards' case, the tape was sent to Dr Bruce Maccabee. He agreed that it was not a model but estimated that the object was only between four hundred and eight hundred feet long. 'This was close enough to our estimate to say we were in general agreement,' said Dilettoso.

Case Unsolved

In Britain other footage has withstood the most rigorous examination. On 13 March 1993 Stephen Woolhouse saw a bright light in the sky that drifted silently over farmland behind his house in Bispham, Lancashire. He had a video camera to hand. It was loaded with tape and ready to roll. He filmed the glowing object before it was swallowed up by the darkening skies. The tape was examined by experts from the Northern Anomalies Research Organisation, which confirmed that it showed a flying object. It was neither an airship nor a helicopter according to local air-traffic control. It had no flashing navigation lights and Woolhouse's house was sixteen miles from the nearest airfield. The case remains unsolved.

But in 1996 a spectacular video was released that shows a ball of light creating a crop circle in Wiltshire. A year later evidence was found that indicated that the video was not genuine, merely a sophisticated piece of computerised trickery. But uncovering the hoax took a great deal of time and skill.

Birds on the Wing

At 11:10 a.m. on 2 July 1950 Warrant Officer Delbert C. Newhouse, a veteran Navy photographer, shot about thirty feet of film of ten or twelve strange, silvery objects in the sky near Trementon, Utah. As the objects flew in a westerly direction, one of them veered off from the main group and reversed its course.

After a thousand hours of investigation of the Newhouse film, the Navy Photographic Interpretation laboratory concluded that the objects filmed were not aircraft, birds, balloons or reflections, but were in fact 'self-luminous'.

The 'Robertson Panel' – five distinguished non-military scientists convened by the CIA in 1952 to discredit UFO sightings – concluded otherwise. They decided the objects were a formation of birds reflecting the strong sunlight.

Just Jets

At 11:25 a.m. on 5 August 1950, in Great Falls, Montana, Nicholas Mariana shot nearly twenty seconds of film of two disc-shaped objects as they moved across the sky.

On some of the 250 frames, the objects are seen passing behind the girders of a water tower, which gave film analysts an opportunity to measure the objects' approximate altitude, speed, azimuth, distance and size. It was also a sequence that would have been very difficult to have faked.

Mariana admitted that he had seen two jet fighters on their final approach to a nearby Air Force base just prior to his sighting of the objects, but insisted he knew the difference between the jets and the objects.

The Robertson Panel decided that Mariana did not know the difference – that he had filmed the jets.

The Norfolk Footage

Some of the best UFO footage ever taken was shot in 1997 when Norfolk became a centre of UFO activity. Weird flashing lights were seen in the night sky. Huge cylindrical motherships were floating aloft. And during the day, even when it was clear and sunny, menacing black triangular craft performed seemingly impossible, high-G manoeuvres silently above the broads. Similar sightings had been reported around the world in the 1990s, but what made the Norfolk sightings significant was that they were filmed.

While being open-minded on the subject, David Spoor, a long-time resident of Aulton Broad near Lowestoft in Norfolk, had no interest in UFOs. Then on 19 August 1997, when he was pottering in his back garden, he spotted a cigar-shaped object with a strange strobe light flashing around it in the sky.

'It was a white, self-illuminated cylindrical craft,' says Spoor, 'high in the sky and travelling silently west to east. It seemed to be ringed by bright strobe lights, which flashed randomly but weren't attached to the body of the craft.'

He reckoned that it was forty or fifty feet across, though it was hard to estimate because he could not tell accurately how far it was away. At first it was stationary, then it travelled across the sky at around forty to fifty miles an hour.

As luck would have it, Spoor had recently borrowed a video camera from a friend. He rushed inside to get it. Then, camera in hand, he filmed the UFO as it sailed silently across the sky. Unlike so much UFO footage, the resulting film was clear and unmistakable. But Spoor's coup did not end there. This was just the first of a series of films that would soon make him the Cecil B. De Mille of the UFO world.

In January 1998 he filmed blue beams of light coming at him across a field on the Suffolk border. He could not tell where they were coming from. On 2 February 1998 he shot a number of luminous orbs travelling slowly and silently across the sky. On other occasions he filmed other objects making high-speed manoeuvres that would have generated G-forces no human pilot could withstand. And he filmed numerous black triangles, flying in formation.

Like many people who have seen UFOs, Spoor found his life turned upside down. His house seemed to become the focus for strange forces. Keys bent and twisted in the locks. Lights switched themselves on and off without rhyme or reason. And, most sinisterly, at night, the family's bedrooms were lit up by bright lights which appeared to hover above their yard. Spoor's response was sanguine. He bought a video camera and made his own survey of the skies. Although at first he had questioned his own sanity, by the end of the year, he had shot nearly three hours of footage showing UFO activity over Norfolk. These were backed by his own accounts of the sightings.

Naturally he wanted to find out whether others had witnessed the same thing. A quick check of the local papers told him that others were reporting the odd UFO sighting, but nothing on the scale he had witnessed. However, he made discreet enquiries and found that he was not alone. Another man in the vicinity had also noticed the intense aerial activity. His name was Peter Wrigglesworth. He, too, had filmed the UFOs and had taken his footage to well-known Norfolk UFOlogist David Dane.

Dane was impressed with Wrigglesworth's film and, making enquiries of his own, Dane discovered Spoor and introduced him to Wrigglesworth. This was to become the one of the most productive partnerships in British UFOlogy.

The hours of footage that Wrigglesworth and Spoor had shot was viewed by numerous experts in the field. A number of movie and TV companies in America approached them. At a UFO conference in Laughlin, Nevada, the editor of *UFO* magazine Graham Birdsall offered to authenticate their film for them. He was impressed.

'The object certainly does not conform to any known aerial craft, largely because of the strobe-like features around it,' said Birdsall.

America's leading UFO investigation organisation Quest International had the computer analyst Russell Callahan look at the footage, but he made little progress with Spoor's original film because, apart from the UFO, there was nothing else in the shot to use as a point of reference. For Birdsall this was not a problem.

'All the computer analysis in the world won't tell us where it's from,' he said.

As the UFOlogist most closely involved in the case, Dane, too, believes that the craft are of extraterrestrial origin.

'In all my thirty years' experience of UFOlogy,' he said, 'I've never come across anything quite like this. I still have difficulty taking it in. It is without doubt the best UFO footage I've ever seen.'

Other UFOlogists who have seen the videos are equally enthusiastic, though researcher George Wingfield urges scepticism.

'Something pretty strange is definitely going on above Norfolk,' he said. 'But what it is is another matter. The two men seem genuine and sincere, but that doesn't necessarily mean they're filming what they think they're filming.'

Some have even suggested that the object Spoor filmed on 7 December 1997 was in fact Venus. The planet was visible that night, but it was on the other side of the sky. Others say that Wrigglesworth and Spoor may have filmed aircraft – perhaps experimental ones. The RAF bases at Wattisham, Coltishall, Honington and Marham are nearby. While it is possible that the Jaguars, Tornadoes, air-sea rescue helicopters and conventional military aircraft stationed there may explain some of the sightings in the area, experts say they do not account for all of the objects filmed by Wrigglesworth and Spoor.

In an effort to get to the bottom of the mystery, Dane showed some of the footage to Paul Beaver, a pilot and aeronautical expert who writes for the top military aircraft magazine Jane's *International Defence Review*. At first, he was sceptical.

'My first thoughts were that some of the footage was of kites, or models,' he said, 'but in one sequence, where two black wedge-shape craft are carrying out incredible manoeuvres, I felt that they were more likely RPVs [remotely piloted vehicles] or UAVs [unmanned aerial vehicles] – largely because of their size and the G-forces involved. I wouldn't put it past the military in these areas to be involved in UAV research.'

The RAF said that none of the bases in the vicinity were testing UAVs, but a spokesman at RAF Coltishall explained that, even if they were testing top-secret aircraft, they would obviously refuse to tell anyone. He said that the military carried out very little night flying in the Norfolk area, though, and would offer no opinion on what the craft Wrigglesworth and Spoor had filmed were. But the MoD were adamant.

'No UFOs have penetrated UK airspace, and nothing has been picked up by our detectors,' they said.

Although both Twentieth Century Fox and the BBC have expressed an interest in buying the footage, Wrigglesworth and Spoor have rejected their offers. They say they do not feel that this valuable footage should be exploited for financial gain and they fear that they would be become the centre of a media circus.

'This footage represents the ultimate media scoop, and a lot of people in a position to broadcast it will come away considerably richer for the privilege,' says Dane who is acting as agent for the film. 'Although none of us are "in it for the money", we do want credit to go where it's due. I am not prepared to let footage or individual stills fall into the wrong hands as I believe the whole episode would quickly degenerate into a circus.'

But this stance – however honourable – leaves Wrigglesworth and Spoor open to the charge that they are afraid to open themselves up to proper scrutiny.

Radar Contact

Although photograph and film can be faked, the evidence of trusted and experienced observers is hard to refute. So how can the evidence of highly trained air traffic controllers and military radar operators be dismissed when they see an unidentified blip flashing across their screens?

In the early hours of 21 December 1978 the crew of a Safe Air cargo plane en route from Blenheim to Dunedin, in New Zealand, were requested to search for some explanation for the unusual radar returns that were being tracked at Wellington Airport. Air traffic controller John Gordy said that the targets on his radar screen were unlike any he had ever seen before. As Captain Vern Powell flew his Argosy into the area over New Zealand's South Island, he saw several strange lights. They followed his aircraft for just over eleven miles along the coast before they disappeared. Captain John Randle, also flying an Argosy, on the same route, also diverted into the area and reported seeing UFOs. And at Wellington they were going crazy.

'At one stage our radar controllers had five very strong radar targets where nothing should have been,' said the head of Air Traffic Services at Wellington.

When the Australian TV Channel O from Melbourne heard of this sighting and others in the area, they contacted one of their reporters who happened to be on holiday nearby. The reporter's name was

Quentin Fogarty and, when the TV company gave him the details of the sightings, Fogarty jumped at the assignment. He began his report by interviewing the UFO witnesses. Then he persuaded Safe Air to fly him along the same route to film background footage for the programme on the night of 30–31 December, this time in an Argosy flown by Captain Bill Startup.

Fogarty got lucky. Once again, radar picked up the strange returns. At 12:10 a.m., the crew were filming in the aircraft's loading bay when suddenly they saw a number of strange lights in the direction of Kaikoura on South Island.

They radioed Wellington control for information and were told: 'There are targets in your ten o'clock position at thirteen miles appearing and disappearing, not showing at present, but they were a minute ago.' For some time after that, Wellington radar detected a series of targets that came within five miles of the plane.

At 12:22 a.m., the crew were able to correlate both a visual sighting and a radar contact. A formation of six mysterious lights formed up alongside the plane. 'Let's hope they're friendly,' said Fogarty as he trained the TV camera on the UFOs. They seemed to be around a hundred feet in length and the bright lights seemed to be coming from their domed cabins.

Several seconds of film were shot of the UFOs. During the rest of the flight various other targets were seen and also confirmed by radar. On the return flight, more sightings were made, and more footage was shot of what Fogarty described as 'a sort of bell shape with a bright bottom and a less bright top'. As the flight continued, there were further sightings, again confirmed by radar.

Photographic expert Dr Bruce Maccabee flew out from Washington to New Zealand to study the footage. Maccabee was soon convinced that Fogarty had recorded something truly inexplicable and the Wellington case is widely regarded as one of the most convincing in UFO history.

Nevertheless the sightings have remained controversial, even though they were confirmed by radar. Sceptics have attempted to dismiss Fogarty's pictures as anything from the stars, Venus or Jupiter to the moonlight reflecting off a cabbage patch, and even, somewhat bizarrely, Japanese squid boats. But the air crew, who flew that route regularly, know they saw something extraordinary. Fogarty remains completely baffled by what he encountered that night. And the air traffic controllers are convinced that something strange was out there – something that deserved the official tag 'UFO'.

Bogeys Over Washington

There can surely be no more famous case of radar-detected sightings than those that occurred over Washington, D.C. in 1952. The huge number of radar contacts caused consternation in military circles. Even the US government's own UFO investigation project feared an alien invasion.

The sightings took place over three consecutive weekends: 19–20 July, 26–27 July and 2–3 August. Around 11:40 p.m. on 19 July, Edward Nugent, an air traffic controller at Washington National Airport, spotted seven unidentified blips on his radar screen. They were around twenty-five miles south-west of the city and travelling at around a hundred miles an hour. Over the next few hours, two radar stations covering the airspace above Washington, D.C. detected eight UFOs in the restricted area around the Capitol building and the White House. For security reasons no civil or military planes are allowed to fly through that restricted zone without special orders. But the UFOs took no notice of that. They were moving so fast that their time within the restricted zone passed in the blinking of an eye. They could accelerate to astonishing speeds, stop dead and turn on a sixpence. These anomalous blips appeared on the capital's radar screens throughout the night and into the early hours of the morning and were confirmed by the sightings of pilots and ground observers.

At 3 a.m., two USAF F-94 Lock Starfire all-weather jet fighters were sent up from Newcastle Air Force Base in nearby Delaware. But when they got airborne, the UFOs simply disappeared, only to return again when the jets had landed. The last one left the capital's radar screens at 5:30 a.m.

The alien fleet turned up again the following weekend. They were first spotted by a National Airlines pilot who saw several of them flying high above his aircraft. He described them as looking like the 'glow of a cigarette'. Again, they were picked up on radar and seen by observers on the ground and in the air. At 11 p.m., two Starfires were scrambled from Newcastle AFB, but again the objects disappeared as the jets closed in and reappeared after they left. However, when a second wave of interceptors went in, the UFOs remained where they were and the USAF pilots were able to make visual contact with four of them. One of the pilots, Lieutenant William Patterson, reported the UFOs closing on him rapidly. He was surrounded by blue lights, but they fled before he got permission to attack them.

Civil airline pilots also saw the UFOs. Captain S. Pierman of Capital Airlines was one of several who gave visual confirmation of the radar contacts. But the moment he reported his sighting by radio, the object shot away at an incredible speed.

'In all my years of flying I have seen a lot of falling or shooting stars – whatever you call them,' said Captain Pierman. 'But these were much faster than anything I have ever seen. They couldn't have been aircraft. They were moving too fast for that.'

Air traffic control had seen the UFO's extraordinary retreat too.

'It was almost as if whatever controlled it had heard us, or had seen Pierman head toward it,' said Harry Barnes, the senior air traffic controller that night.

Many people came forward with explanations. Some suggested that the radar contacts were simple radar errors or temperature inversions, where pockets of increased temperature in the lower levels of the atmosphere can cause anomalous radar reflections. To explain the pilots' visual corroboration, it was said that the excitement of the radar flap led them to mistake normal lights for UFOs. But these explanations ignore the fact that the pilots' sightings corresponded exactly to the behaviour of the radar contacts.

Leading UFO researcher Don Ecker has led the investigation into the Washington flap and remains convinced that it presents some of the most important evidence in UFO history. Ecker had discovered that it was not only both civil and military pilots who visually confirmed the radar contacts.

'They were witnessed by some of the radar operators that literally left their scopes and went outside and looked physically into the sky,' he says.

He has also dismissed the idea that the contacts could have come from temperature inversions.

'The radar operators were skilled personnel,' he says. 'They were responsible, literally, for bringing in, and having go out, tens of thousands of air travellers every day. The military radar experts were depended upon to keep our skies safe from enemy intrusions, and these guys had, beyond any shadow of a doubt, dealt with things like temperature inversions.'

Ecker also discovered a cover-up. Edward J. Ruppelt was head of Project Blue Book, the US Air Force's official UFO investigation and as such was the man charged with investigating the flap. But when he looked into the case, he found the authorities less than forthcoming. Ruppelt discovered that the authorities 'were going to great extremes and lengths to get this swept under the rug as soon as possible,' says Ecker.

As the Air Force refused to give information to its own UFO investigator, Ruppelt had to turn to the press. He was bitter about being sidelined and, when asked what the Air Force was doing about UFOs entering restricted airspace, he commented: 'I have no idea what the Air Force is doing; in all probability it's doing nothing.'

Major Donald Keyhoe, who would later become a founder member of the National Investigations Committee on Aerial Phenomena (NICAP), was also involved in the investigation. *True* magazine published his analysis of the sightings in 1953, under the title 'What Radar Tells Us About Flying Saucers'.

In the article, Keyhoe shows just how seriously the Pentagon took the sightings by citing remarks made by Director of Operations Major

General Roger S. Ramey at the time.

'The Air Force, in compliance with its mission of air defence of the United States, must assume responsibility for the investigation of any object or phenomena in the air over the United States,' Ramey said. 'Fighter units have been instructed to investigate any object observed or established as existing by radar tracks, and to intercept any airborne object identified as hostile or showing hostile interest. This should not be interpreted to mean that air-defence pilots have been instructed to fire haphazardly on anything that flies.'

Ramey's remarks demonstrate that the Air Force believed that the radar contacts were very real. Again Keyhoe pointed out that the radar operators would have been very familiar with false returns, such as temperature inversions. Nevertheless they felt that the blips required further investigation to show they were real. In the same issue, *True* magazine quoted an anonymous USAF spokesman who said: 'We don't know what these things were and there's no use pretending we do.'

While the USAF and its investigators were stumped, the US government knew just what to do. Within months of the Washington sightings, the CIA convened the Robertson Panel, which recommended using all means available to allay any public interest in the UFO phenomenon – and the cover-up and the debunking started.

The cover-up continues to this day and it involves not just the US military, but also the military authorities of America's European allies. In the summer of 1998, a four-day workshop reviewed all the physical evidence associated with UFO sightings across Europe that had been accumulated by seven top UFO researchers. They paid particular attention to radar contacts. This presented difficulties, as the workshop's report states: 'The panel concludes from these presentations that the analysis of radar records is a very specialised activity that requires the services of radar experts. The panel also notes that information from military radar can be obtained only with the co-operation of military authorities, and that most military authorities do not offer this co-operation... further study of this phenomenon by means of radar-visual cases may not be feasible unless the relevant authorities recognise the mission of an official UFO research organisation.'

Pacific Panic

In the months after the Japanese attack on Pearl Harbor, America was on tenterhooks. An attack on the mainland, perhaps a full-scale invasion, was expected at any time. On the evening of 25 February 1942, air observers reported aircraft approaching the Pacific coast near Los Angeles. At around 7:20 p.m., lights were seen in the sky near an important defence plant. At 2 a.m., radar reported unidentified contacts out over the sea. Air-raid sirens sounded. Los Angeles was plunged into darkness and anti-aircraft guns filled the skies with flack. A formation of UFOs flew over the city, high and very fast. The guns continued pounding for another hour. When they eventually fell silent, it was found that the city had not been attacked. No bombs had been dropped. No aircraft downed. The only damage done to the city was caused by anti-aircraft shells.

Canadian Contacts

In the later 1940s and early 1950s Goose Bay in Labrador became a UFO hotspot. On 29 October 1948 a UFO was tracked by radar as it streaked across the bay. The following night it returned. This time contact was maintained for four minutes and it was calculated that the object was travelling at over 625 miles an hour.

Two years later, a UFO was seen in the same area by Captain James Howard, a pilot with BOAC. On closer examination, he saw that it was actually a mothership accompanied by a gaggle of other flying objects. They fled when he approached. The sighting received huge press coverage and even prompted Air Chief Marshall Lord Dowding to say that he believed in flying saucers.

The UFO returned to Goose Bay on 19 June 1952, when a strange red light appeared in the sky over Goose Bay Air Base. It was also picked up by radar. Witnesses on the ground saw the light suddenly turn white and increase in brilliance. At the same time, the radar contact seemed to flare. Then it disappeared simultaneously from sight and the radar screen.

Visual Confirmation

On the night of 13 August 1956, multiple radar contacts were made over RAF Bentwaters in Suffolk. Six ground stations and one airborne station independently reported five contacts with objects flying at incredible speeds. Twenty radar personnel confirmed the contacts. Nine visual observers confirmed the contacts with sightings of brilliantly lit objects in the sky.

The first contact was made by Bentwaters Ground Control Approach Radar, which calculated that the object was travelling at a speed of around 4,250 miles an hour. Other slower objects followed in its wake. Bentwaters asked for confirmation from the USAF base at RAF Lakenheath. When it was received, the RAF scrambled two fighters to investigate the intruders. One of them was vectored on an intercept course. It had both visual and radar contact. But suddenly the ground station saw the UFO double back and begin to chase the fighter. The pursuit continued for several minutes before the UFO disappeared. The pilot returned home safely, though shaken and puzzled.

The Guardian

UFOs returned to Canada in 1989. An object was tracked on radar before it fell towards the ground near West Carleton, to the west of Ottawa, on 4 November. The area was immediately sealed off and huge helicopters and military units, specially trained to deal with UFO retrievals, were flown in. The source of this story, who called himself the 'Guardian', also said that the aliens themselves were tracked on radar.

The Guardian said that the alien craft used a pulsing electromagnetic field to fly and was built from a matrixed-dielectric magnesium alloy. It also generated cold fusion radiation. He also said that the alien mission had a malevolent purpose. It was the start of an alien invasion.

MUFON's Bob Oeschler, a former NASA mission specialist, investigated. The Guardian sent him a package in February 1992. The package contained a video, several documents and maps of the area. The tape was thirty minutes long, with the first six minutes showing actual movement, the rest was just stills. The video showed strange lights, movements of 'aliens' around the craft and also a full-frontal shot of an alien's face.

The video was analysed and it had signs of editing, also the scenes of the craft were duplicated by researchers using toy remote controlled helicopters, some flashing lights and some flares. They were also able to purchase an alien mask from a costume shop identical to the one in the video. This case eventually caused Oeschler to resign from MUFON.

Physical Evidence

Not all UFO encounters depend for their credibility on the reliabilty of eyewitnesses, photographs that can be faked or radar contacts that can be withheld by the authorities. Sometimes alien craft leave physical evidence.

One of these cases occurred in the small agricultural settlement of Delphos, Texas. One November evening in 1971, sixteen-year-old farm hand Ronnie Johnson was just finishing his day's work when he suddenly looked up to see a large, mushroom-shaped UFO, hovering just above the ground in front of him. Caught unawares, he was paralysed with fear and the light from the craft was so bright it temporarily blinded him. After a few moments, the craft began to ascend and Ronnie came to his senses and ran off to get his parents. He returned with them in time to see the UFO shooting rapidly up into the sky. But had that been the end of the story, it is unlikely that anyone would have believed them.

However, on the ground in front of them, in the very place the object had been hovering, they saw a circle in the earth about eight feet across that was glowing brightly. It did not appear to be hot and Ronnie's mother bent down and touched the glowing ring. As she did so, her fingers became frozen and numb. They remained that way for several weeks after the encounter.

This case became one of the most thoroughly investigated in the history UFOlogy. But it was far from unique. Thousands of UFO encounters have left behind physical evidence. Investigators call them 'physical trace cases', or encounters of the second kind. They provide the most solid evidence alien spacecraft have visited Earth.

The world's leading expert on physical trace cases, Ted Phillips, investigated the Delphos case. A civil engineer from Branson, Missouri, Phillips has visited four hundred and fifty UFO sites and investigated some six hundred encounters over the past thirty years. From his studies, he says that around the world over five thousand UFO trace cases have been reported.

Phillips first became interested in UFOs when his father told him about a pilot who had been buzzed by a flying saucer. He began to investigate sightings in his home state of Missouri in the 1960s. In 1966, he came across a case in Florida where contactee John Reeves had photographed the footprint of an alien after one had visited his home.

The first case that brought Phillips to prominence occurred the following year. Three men were out hunting when they saw a flying saucer descend into the valley where they had been camping. No only did the men manage to photograph the UFO, they also had physical evidence of it. It swooped so low that it had scorched a tree and damaged the men's camping equipment. Phillips documented the case and took his findings to established UFO researcher Dr J. Allen Hynek of North Western University. Hynek, who is often described as the 'father of UFOlogy', was so impressed that he asked Phillips to work out a methodology for the systematic investigation of physical trace cases. They worked together until Hynek's death in 1986.

According to Phillips' definition, a physical trace case is a UFO sighting where one or more people witness an object, on or near the ground, and once the object leaves the area a number of physical changes to the environment can be found. In the cases Phillips has investigated, these have included impressions left in the ground from landing gear, rings of crushed vegetation and burnt soil, and even alien footprints. He has also come across a number of hoaxes.

'They were very easy to spot,' he says. 'People pour petrol on the ground, ignite it and try to make a ring. Sometimes they simply dig indentations in the soil, but when you've seen hundreds of examples of real traces caused by a UFO, you realise that the effects are very specific and extremely difficult to replicate.'

When he arrives at the sight of a UFO encounter, the first thing Phillips does look for signs of a possible hoax. But at Delphos he was soon satisfied that the case is genuine and began taking soil samples with a cylindrical boring inside and outside the ring. Chemical analysis revealed that the soil from inside the ring had been completely dehydrated down to a depth of fourteen inches. The soil would not even rehydrate when placed in water. But when soil from outside the ring was put in water, it dissolved readily.

The soil in the ring remained affected for quite some time. Six months later, the area was covered by a heavy show fall. When Phillips cleared off the snow and threw a bucket of water on to the soil, the ring reappeared, as the soil there still refused to absorb water.

Phillips carries out most of his work without using professional laboratories. This cuts out the cost of expensive lab work, but Phillips is also suspicious of labs that are directly connected to the government. He believes that they could not be relied upon if his evidence was about to yield significant findings.

'Given the fact that the government is obviously covering up a great deal of information regarding the UFO phenomenon,' Phillips says, 'it would be overly optimistic to think they would help provide evidence for the existence of visiting UFOs.'

But Phillips made an exception in the Delphos case, because there was no other way to find out why soil was so determinedly dehydrated. Phillips called in the help of the leading UFOlogist Stanton Friedman.

They had worked together on a number of UFO cases. Friedman found an independent lab called Agra-Science, which specialised in doing soil analysis for farmers. The lab tested Phillip's soil samples for thermo-luminescence to reveal whether the earth had been subjected to intense heat. According to Friedman, the results showed that the soil had been irradiated by some intense form of energy, possibly microwaves.

The soil samples were also sent to another independent laboratory at Oak Ridge. The scientists there examined them under an electron microscope and discovered that the soil had strange crystalline structures, unlike anything they had even seen before. The soil particles were coated in a mysterious substance, which explained why they could not absorb water.

Phillips tried growing seeds in the affected soil, using soil taken from outside the ring as a control. The seeds would not germinate in the affected soil, though they flourished in the control. Eventually, though, the soil recovered and plants began to grow in it again.

Categories of Evidence

The Delphos case is only one of hundreds of UFO cases where physical traces have been left that have been investigated by Ted Phillips. Phillips has assembled a huge amount of evidence. He has been able to divide physical trace cases into three broad categories. One involves the classic disc-shaped flying saucer, metallic in appearance and thirty to forty feet in diameter. When they land, witnesses often seen humanoid aliens in the area. These flying saucers leave a scorched ring of soil about thirty feet in diameter and indentations thought to be left by the landing gear.

Then there are small circular objects, eight to ten feet in diameter, which often glow brightly. They leave a smaller ring of singed or dehydrated soil. A scorched earth ring of this sort was found in Kofu City, Japan, in 1975, when Masato Kohno saw a UFO land.

Egg-shaped craft leave four indentations, again thought to be made by landing gear. From Phillips' tests of the soil compression in these marks, they would have to be made by an object weighing some twenty-five tonnes.

Phillips has also investigated so-called 'saucer nests'. These are circular areas of flattened crops that appear in fields. They show none of the intricate patterns of crop circles and often show genetic mutations in the plants not normally associated with crop circles. As Phillips' trace cases always involve sightings, he distinguishes 'saucer nest' cases from crop circles – which do not – and believes that they may be two separate phenomena. Similar 'saucer nests' appeared in France in 1990.

Footprints

Some 23 per cent of physical trace cases involve the sighting of the craft's alien occupants and sometimes Phillips is lucky enough to get a photograph or a plaster cast of an alien footprint.

'If we get word of the landing a week or a month after it happened, the chances are that the site would be so beaten down by the weather or local people that any footprints would have been destroyed,' he says. 'In cases where the information has reached us earlier, we have found either a partial footprint or a series of fresh ones.'

He frequently runs into footprints of Greys, who leave footprints like an impression from a moccasin, the size and depth of those left by a small child.

Phillips' work has been officially dismissed and derided. But Friedman maintains that the evidence he presents is indisputable.

'What we are looking at here is empirical evidence that just cannot be dismissed by the "noisy negativists",' he says. 'Hallucinations cannot dehydrate fourteen inches of soil. Nor consistently leave physical, testable and tangible evidence such as phosphorescent rings in the earth.'

Beach Bummer

A UFO crashed on the beach at Ubatuba, Brazil in September 1957. Ibrahim Sued, a journalist with leading Brazilian newspaper *O Globo*, received a letter about it on 13 September. The letter was signed and read:

'As a faithful reader of your column and your admirer, I wish to give you something of the highest interest to a newspaper man, about the flying discs. If you believe that they are real, of course. I didn't believe anything said or published about them. But just a few days ago I was forced to change my mind. I was fishing together with some friends, at a place close to the town of Ubatuba, Sao Paulo, when I sighted a flying disc. It approached the beach at an unbelievable speed and an accident – a crash into the sea – seemed imminent. At the last moment, however, when it was almost striking the waters, it made a sharp turn upward and climbed rapidly on a fantastic impulse. We followed the spectacle with our eyes, startled, when we saw the disk explode in flames. It disintegrated into thousands of fiery fragments, which fell sparkling with magnificent brightness. They looked like fireworks, despite the time of the accident, which was noon. Most of these fragments, almost all, fell into the sea. But a number of small pieces fell close to the beach and we picked up a large amount of this material, which was as light as paper. I am enclosing a small sample of it. I don't know anyone that could be trusted to whom I might send it for analysis. I never read about a flying disc being found, or about fragments or parts of a saucer that had been picked up.'

Sued sent two of the three samples to the Aerial Phenomena Research Organisation, a UFO group in Tucson Arizona, while the third was retained by Brazilian UFOlogist Dr Olavo Fontes for further study.

The three samples looked like pieces of irregular and highly oxidised metal, coloured dull whitish grey. Dr Fontes' sample was tested at the mineral production labs in the Brazilian agricultural ministry. They applied chemical, spectrographic analysis and X-ray diffusion techniques on the metal. These tests indicated that the material was very pure magnesium. The chemist also noted that the normal trace elements expected in magnesium samples were all missing.

Fontes used up all of his sample in a series of further tests. Part of it went to a chemist who conducted an X-ray investigation at the labs of a geology unit. The geology lab determined that the magnesium was of a very high purity, with a reading of 1.87, compared with a normal reading of 1.74. Pieces were also sent to the Brazilian Army and Navy research departments, but both the Army and Navy kept their findings secret.

ARPO sent a sample to the USAF, but the sample they sent met with an 'accident' while they were testing it. The USAF asked for a further sample to be sent. APRO declined. They tried to conduct tests with remaining the sample but it soon became too small to be of any use. APRO still retains one small chunk in their vaults.

Alien Artefacts

Those who have had contact with aliens have often tried to bring back some sort of alien artefact with them as proof of their contact. Betty Hill asked the aliens who abducted her whether she could take one of their books. At first, they seemed to give their permission, then changed their mind. Maybe the aliens have got wary because evidence they have supplied before has been comprehensively derided.

Howard Menger, one of the first alien contactees in the 1950s, was taken to the Moon and brought back a lunar potato. It was sent to the analysts LaWall-Harrisson Consultants in Philadelphia. They found that potato was indistinguishable from the terrestrial variety, however the protein content was some five times higher than that of any Earth potato. At that time, the UFO community was still very trusting and no one suspected that the government was conducting a cover-up, secretly exploiting alien technology for their own ends, or that the military and intelligence agencies were colluding with the aliens. So Menger naively sent his extraterrestrial spud to the Central Intelligence Agency. The CIA jumped at the chance of analysing the specimen. Two weeks later, Menger and his wife visited the CIA laboratories and were allowed to watch the analysis in progress. They were shown pieces of potato under the microscope and other pieces soaking in various fluids in sample jars. Menger was impressed with the rigour of their approach. He never heard from them again.

Alien Implants

Since the Earth was first visited by flying saucers, there have been some people who have doubted the existence of our extraterrestrial visitors. These sceptics have found the idea of alien abduction even harder to swallow. But fortunately, many abductees can prove what they have been saying. They have physical proof in the form of alien implants.

Like many abductees, Pat Parrinello experienced strange phenomena from childhood. It began when he was just six; he was woken by a brilliant light in his bedroom and found himself paralysed. Since then he has had many such experiences. He has been monitored constantly by aliens and visited by the familiar, large-headed Greys.

Unlike most alien abductees, Parrinello has full conscious recall of his experiences and has not had to resort to regressional hypnosis. He clearly remembers every detail of the abduction, including the humiliating medical examinations that most people manage to blank out.

It was after one abduction that Parrinello was convinced that aliens implanted a small device in his hand. It showed up clearly on an X-ray. And in August 1995, he became one of the first abductees to undergo surgery to retrieve an alien implant. This was no simple matter. After Parrinello took the decision to have the implant removed, he suffered weeks of alien intervention designed to stop him. He suffered severe head pains and often found the abductors' UFO following him. Nevertheless he was determined to go ahead.

The operation was done by Dr Roger Leir in his offices in Ventura, California. Parrinello had been taken to Leir by UFOlogist Derrel Sims, who was investigating the case. At the same time Sims was also investigating the abduction case of a woman named Janet, who had an implant in her foot. Leir operated on her at the same time.

The operations had to be carried out under conditions of the strictest security. Dr Leir was afraid that he might risk losing his licence for performing such an unconventional procedure.

'People with credibility who put themselves forward in this field can wind up out of business,' said Leir

Nevertheless Leir risked having the entire procedure videoed. Although the tapes could have been used against him in any medical ethics hearing, he knew they would be vital in establishing the validity of what he was doing.

Leir began the operations with an experiment. With the patient under a strong local anaesthetic, which numbed all sensation in the area of the implant, Leir tapped the implant gently. Both Parrinello and Janet jerked violently in response. It was all Leir could do to prevent Janet leaping from the operating table. There was no doubt that the anaesthetic was working and Dr Leir had no explanation for their reactions.

Next Leir used a meter to detect any magnetic field given off by the implants. It showed a massive reaction. The needle practically went off the scale, indicating a powerful electromagnetic field. This made removing the implant difficult using surgical implements with metal blades. But when the implants were removed the field miraculously dissipated.

An object 4 mm by 2 mm was retrieved from Parrinello's hand. It was dark and covered in a membrane made of keratin and haemoglobin. These are both proteins found naturally in the body. This casing was the sort of covering that builds up around all foreign matter that enters the body and its genetic fingerprint showed a DNA match with Parrinello. But Leir was certain that it was not a cyst or anything else that grew naturally in the body. He had seen nothing like it before. It was so strong that it could not be cut open by a sharp surgical scalpel. It also contained numerous nerve endings. This may explained the Parrinello's response when it was tapped.

'If these objects were actually left in the body by alien beings, it would not be difficult for the aliens to adapt them by forming them along the lines of the body's own chemistry,' says abduction expert

Professor Mack.

Leir had to make a deep incision to remove two objects from Janet's toe. They were of similar composition, were triangular in shape and measured 1.5 mm by 1.5 mm. Sims sent all three to the University of Houston for more detailed investigation. Scientists there discovered that, under the organic membrane, they were made of shiny, black metal strips. Chemical analysis indicated that the implants are metallic and consisted of eleven different elements, including boron, a metalloid substance used to harden steel, which does not occur naturally in the body.

It was also discovered that the implants glowed green when subjected to ultra-violet light. Sims used this property to detect implants under the skin of other abductees. This led to the recovery of another thirteen alien implants from the bodies of abductees in 1996. Sims has collected more than thirty in all.

Despite this concrete evidence, some sceptics are still not convinced. Arch-debunker Philip Klass claims that there is no provable link between the alien implants and extraterrestrials. Although abductees believe that the implants are used by the aliens to monitor them, Klass says that the devices have no obvious purpose and claims that they are mundane growths that can exist inside the body for years without the host noticing because they cause no discomfort or pain. Klass points out that Parrinello had a swelling in the region of the hand where the implant was found as long ago as 1984. However, just because the implant has been in his body for a long time does not mean that it is terrestrial.

What exactly the implants are for, even Sims admits, no one knows. But they had been surgically implanted in people who had no record of surgery, so they must have some purpose, he reasons. Some researchers believe that they are tracking devices – like the transponders not much bigger than a grain of rice programmed with an electronic code that ostrich farmers implant in the neck of their birds to keep track of them. However, Sims does not believe they are tracking devices. He thinks that they are some sort of monitoring

491

device, although they may also be used to control abductees.

Implant Programme

There is a discernible implant programme underway. The earliest reported abduction case occurred in late 1957. No implants were associated with abductions for nearly ten years. Then in 1966, scars began appearing on the bodies of abductees, though they were not recognised in any numbers until the mid-1970s. The vast majority of implant cases seem to have occurred in the US, critics say, pointing out that scars are rarer in abductees in other countries, even where abductions are numerous. However, this is probably because more of an effort is made to look for them in America.

But implants are not unknown in other countries. Social worker and UFOlogist Keith Basterfield investigated the case of 'Susan', a young abductee from Adelaide, South Australia. She had her first contact with aliens when she was ten years old in 1971. Two different species of aliens were involved in Susan's abduction. Tall humanoids were in command, while the small, large headed Greys did all the menial jobs.

A number of encounters ensued over the years. These involved periodical medical examinations to monitor her development. Then in 1991, during a routine visit to the dentist, an X-ray was taken. This showed a shadowy, unidentified object implanted in her mouth. To investigate this, a second X-ray was arranged for a few weeks later. But in the mean time, Susan was abducted again and the implant removed. The second X-ray showed no trace, and meanwhile the first set of X-rays had gone missing.

Surveys have suggested that as many as one in three people can find an unusual scar of unknown origin on their body, if they looked for one. This could mean that a third of the population has been abducted at one time or another. Abductees believed implants were first placed in their bodies in the late 1970s. Most said the devices were being implanted by forcing them up the nose. Abductees often wake from their abduction with a severe nosebleed.

The number of implantation cases rose meteorically in the 1980s.

By the end of the decade, about one in four abductees had implants. The aliens had broadened their scope and were implan ting in the head, via the mouth and the ear as well as the nose. Then in the 1990s, implants were discovered in other parts of the body, such as the foot and the hand – as in the cases investigated by Sims and removed by Leir in 1995. But these cases are still uncommon.

Implant Investigation

The most extensive scientific examination of an alien implant was undertaken by Dr David Pritchard, a physicist from the Massachusetts Institute of Technology. He undertook a full study of an implant recovered from the genitals of a male host, who believes that he was first abducted from his home in New York in 1955. Despite examining the object under an electron microscope and subjecting it to the very latest techniques of mass spectroscopy, he was unable to identify it – although this does not actually prove that it was of alien origin.

'Analysis shows nothing "unterrestrial" about it, quite the opposite,' he says. 'It does not appear to be fabricated, but rather has the overall characteristics of something that grew. [But] it is possible that the aliens are so clever that they can make devices to serve their purposes yet [which] appear to have a prosaic origin as natural products of the human body.'

But American researcher Martin Cannon has a more sinister explanation. He believes that abductees are not being kidnapped by aliens at all, but by some covert arm of the US government, possibly the CIA. The implants are mind control devices that makes ordinary members of the public the unwilling and unconscious slave of the intelligence community. The abduction memories are planted deep in their minds by post-hypnotic suggestion – that's why they usually have to be retrieved by hypnotic regression. The memories of the alien abduction cloak any memory of what really happened. Even if the screen slips and the abductee remembers what really happened, they are easily discredited because they have already claimed that they were abducted by aliens and – in the public's eyes – are already seen as 'kinda flaky'.

Crop Circles

Early one morning in July 1991, Rita Goold got lucky. She and her fellow crop circle investigators were holding vigil near the tiny Wiltshire hamlet of Alton Barnes, where on previous occasions some of the most celebrated crop circles had made an appearance. Shortly after 3 a.m., as the dawn mist crept across the field, a luminous white tube descended from a cloud, slowly at first, pouring forth what the witnesses described as a fluid-like substance. Narrowly missing the field, it hit the ground on a nearby hill.

'As it came down', said Goold, 'it shot out two arms, covering the top of the hill – it must have been eight hundred feet across – and in each arm all this stuff was pouring in, finding rivulets, clouding and making formations, and as it was doing this, the tube was emptying. Then the tube collapsed and vanished.'

The event lasted eight seconds in all.

'It was like something out of a Steven Spielberg movie,' Goold said. Another colleague described it as 'biblical'.

The next day Goold and her friends could find no trace of any disturbance when they visited the hillside in daylight. However, news spread through the crop circle fraternity that Goold and her mates discovered the mechanism behind the crop circle phenomenon.

Dr Terence Meaden was particularly thrilled. He had spent years investigating the phenomenon. But while many insisted that crop circles were caused by flying saucers coming into land, Meaden had consistently argued that there must be a purely scientific explanation.

Meaden had studied tornadoes and put forward the hypothesis that a static vortex of ionised air – similar to a tornado – was responsible for even the most complex patterns. He called the mechanism responsible a 'plasma vortex'. It was, he maintained, a rare but entirely natural effect that occurred only in certain climatic and topographical conditions.

Although crop circles appeared to be a relatively a recent phenomenon, Meaden believed that crop circles had once provided the inspiration for prehistoric stone circles in the area. He also said that his plasma vortices might explain UFO sightings. Blasphemy indeed.

On the other side of the fence, there were those who said that, although the first crude crop circles were caused by UFOs landing, their alien occupants had discovered that they were a good way to announce their presence to humankind. After all, the complex patterns they were producing showed all the hallmarks of intelligent design. A third faction agreed that non-human intelligence was involved, but pointed the finger at Gaia – the notion that the Earth itself is an intelligent entity – or other paranormal entities or psychic energies. To Meaden and his supporters, these theories came from the crankier end of New Age beliefs. But certainly something extraordinary was going on. The pilot of a light aircraft saw an eighty to ninety foot circle formation in a field near Stonehenge, which must have been created in just 45 minutes. It followed the Fibonacci series, forming a highly complex pattern seen in fractal geometry. It had not been there when he flew over the same field three-quarters of an hour earlier.

'At every stage, the circles phenomenon stretches and tests our perception of reality,' said one researcher.

Snowflake patters, spider's webs and the double helix of DNA appeared, along with alien circuit diagrams and star maps, and geometric designs where the flattered crops were brushed in various directions, simulating texture.

'Whatever, or whoever, made them is an artist of genius,' said John McEwen, art critic of the *Sunday Times*. Others compared them to modern-day devotional art that uses mystical symbols and sacred geometry to communicate with the world beyond. Or perhaps it was the world beyond using mystical symbols and sacred geometry to communicate with us.

'This force may be powerful enough to act as a catalyst for the many physiological and psychological effects – both curative and malevolent – that are often attributed to circles,' said investigator Rob Irving.

The Men Who Fooled the World

As the design of the circles became more and more complex, Dr Meaden found it increasingly difficult to explain them using his plasma vortex theory and, privately, he began to suspect there was a simpler explanation. There was. Their names were Doug Bower and Dave Chorley. These two Southampton-based sexagenarians – known as Doug and Dave in the tabloids – claimed to be 'The Men Who Fooled the World'. For fifteen years they had been sneaking into the fields of Hampshire and south Wiltshire and creating complex crop circles with nothing more than a three-foot wooden board and some string. They had all winter to plan the next year's circles and, each summer, they were determined to outdo the previous year's designs. They both had a keen interest in art and sought out inspiration in galleries and libraries. The first design for one of their early efforts – two circles joined by an avenue and flanked by sets of short, parallel bars – was pinched from a book on Russian painting.

Although they were denied recognition, they enjoyed the fact that their creations were being hailed as the work of a higher intelligence. But they got a bit peeved when researchers began publishing books and making money out of their latest alien entity theory. So they decided to reveal all and went to the newspapers, only to discover that few committed researchers accepted their story.

Journalists soon unearthed other groups of covert circle makers. The artist Rod Dickenson also admitted that he had made circles. They used tape measures, balls of string, garden rollers and specially constructed devices made out of pram wheels to flatten the crops. 'I make art for people who don't realise it's art,' he explained. 'What is really an art experience is interpreted as a paranormal experience.' Some journalists also admitted making circles during their investigations of hoaxing, further perpetuating phenomenon. *The Guardian* even sponsored a circle hoaxing competition in 1992, which was won by a team from Westland Helicopters who called themselves 'Masters of the Cereal Universe'.

Were the Hoaxers a Hoax?

While Dr Terence Meaden and his scientific colleagues were happy to cede the field, those who believed in an extraterrestrial author were not. Rumours spread that Doug and Dave – along with anyone else who supported the hoax theory – were merely pawns in a much deeper conspiracy to discredit the circles. And who was behind this conspiracy? Whitehall, the CIA and extreme factions of the church were blamed. Even such distinguished UFOlogists as Jacques Vallee talked of crop circles being caused by the testing of top-secret space-weapons, spun off from the 'Star Wars' programme. The human circle makers were simply being used to muddy the water for serious researchers.

Some more benign souls wondered what mysterious forces inspired Doug and Dave.

'Many human circle makers are, after all, reluctant to claim individual formations as their own work,' said the ever optimistic Rob Irving. 'Perhaps they are aware of a greater force at work, an inherently mysterious guiding hand which shapes and controls their nocturnal efforts.'

By the summer of 1993, the anti-hoax faction knew that they needed hard evidence to support their position. They began applying the strictest scientific methods to their work. They took soil samples and samples of the crops themselves and tested them for evidence of microwave radiation, or intense heat. Some researchers detected changes in the plants' crystalline structures. Others showed differences in the growth rates between seeds taken from the plants flattened in the circles and those taken from the standing crops around them. A wealthy American research team found, in one large formation, minute emissions from radioactive isotopes that do not occur naturally. However, the sceptics were happy to stick with Doug and Dave's story.

The litmus test was to find a way to tell a hoaxed circle from a genuine one. The man who applied his mind to this task was a Michigan-based biophysicist, Dr William C. Levengood. His analysis confirmed that samples displayed anomalous variations. They showed significant differences in their cellular structures when compared to control samples. Both abnormally high and low radiation levels were both found. Most significantly, he found that samples of wheat and the local chalk were covered in a rust-coloured, glaze-like substance he discovered to be meteoric dust. On the other hand, as a scientist, he did not entirely dismiss Terry Meade's work. His conclusion was that crop circles were made by intelligently controlled plasma vortices.

Scientific Encounters

Close Encounters Classified

Things used to be so easy. In olden days, when someone saw a strange phenomenon in the sky, it was an angel or a fiery chariot or a pillar of light or glowing crucifixes. But with the advent of the UFO in the second half of the twentieth century things got altogether more problematic.

For sceptics though, things are still easy. UFO reports fall into just two categories: the misidentifications of a mundane object or the result of some mental aberration. But the fledgling science of UFOlogy began to look for ways to classify real physical flying objects. To quantify and qualify accounts of UFO encounters and to give the subject the gloss of scientific empiricism, UFOlogists began to categorise reports based on the shape of the object, its movement and the witnesses' level of interaction with it. The idea was to find a way to analyse the UFO data statistically and work out whether there were any patterns underlying it.

To start with there was very little interaction between human witness and the craft they saw, but as UFO sighting reports and photographs flooded in, in the wake of Kenneth Arnold's saucer sighting of 1947, 'saucerology' concentrated its attention on what the flying craft looked like and it was discovered that they came in seven essential varieties:

1. **Disc-shaped** – These are the classic flying saucer, flat and round like an ice-hockey puck. Most have a domed upper section, making them more like a hub cap. Some are domed on both the upper and lower surfaces, and some have a broad rim. Disc-shaped UFOs include the flying saucers seen by Kenneth Arnold, the probe ships photographed by Paul Villa, the craft that took George Adamski to the Moon and the 'sports model' that Bob Lazar worked on in Area 51. The most famous photograph of a disc-shaped UFO was taken by Paul Trent over his farm in Oregon in 1950.

2. **Spheroid** – These are globe-shaped craft, although they also appear as elongated or flattened spheres, as ovoid or egg-shaped or as SLOs – Saturn-like objects that are spheroid with a band around the middle. These were particular common in Europe from medieval times and appear in woodcarvings – a fine example comes from Basel, Switzerland in 1566. Almira Baruana photographed an SLO over Trindad in 1958, and Robert Taylor had an encounter with an ovoid craft about twenty feet across in a forest clearing in Scotland in 1979. Two round objects with spikes knocked him to the ground. When he regained consciousness, all three were gone.

3. **Cylinder** – These cigar-shaped objects are almost as common as saucer-shaped craft and may explain the phantom airships that were seen at the end of the nineteenth century. One of the earliest sightings of this type of craft in modern times was made by Ella Fortune, a nurse from the Mescalero Indian Reservation in New Mexico, on 16 October 1957. She saw it hovering over nearby Holloman Air Force Base. Like discs, these craft sometimes have

domed protuberances, tapered or rounded ends, portholes or fins. They are not as common as they used to be. The most famous example is George Adamski's 'mothership', for which he provided detailed specifications.

4. **Flying Triangles** – These triangular-shaped craft have become common since the late 1980s. There is some argument whether they are extraterrestrial craft at all. They are possibly manmade as part of black projects that back-engineer technology from downed alien craft. They are commonly seen at night and are identified by the triangular arrangement of the lights on the underside. They vary in size enormously, from relatively small craft to ones half-a-mile across. They vary in shape, too. Some are conical, like the one Ron and Paula Watson of Mount Vernon, Missouri, saw in 1983, when its occupants were mutilating one of their cows. David Spoor of Norfolk photographed some smaller, more agile triangles in 1998.

5. **Polygonal** – These are craft with more than three sides, such as the diamond-shaped craft that abducted Betty Cash and Vicki Landrum in December 1980 or the five-pointed star seen over Australia the same day in 1978 that Frederick Valentich disappeared. A pentagonal UFO hovered over Shiogama City in Japan in September 1986. It was seen by more than twenty people and photographed by Akira Maezuka.

6. **Balls of light** – These are among the most common UFOs sighted. They occur as a single point of light, but more often come in formations. The most famous example is the 'string of pearls' photographed by student Carl Hart over Lubbock, Texas in 1952. They are often dismissed as a natural phenomenon, such as bolides or 'earthlights' – coloured lights thought to be produced over areas of tectonic stress – and are often seen at Hessdalen, Norway, or over the Yakima Indian Reservation in Washington

State. However, the witnesses often report that the unidentified lights are attached to or surround a solid craft.

7. **Exotic** – This is the category where sightings of UFOs that do not fit into any of the other categories end up. They are usually one-offs. In 1967 RAF Intelligence Officer J.B.W. 'Angus' Brooks saw a huge flying object that took the form of a giant cross. In 1996, a number of witnesses saw a 150-foot high rotating octagonal pyramid over Pelatos, Brazil. One witness, Haroldo Westendorff, was flying his light aircraft when he encountered it. He said that he saw its peak open and a disc-shaped object fly out. The sighting was confirmed by local air traffic controllers. A seventy-one-year-old Polish farmer named Jan Wolski saw a barn-shaped flying object. A family who also saw it said it had multicoloured rotating corkscrews coming out of the corners. And hundreds of witnesses saw a huge boomerang-shape fly over the West Coast.

The first truly scientific attempt at classifying UFOs came from the most influential figure in early UFOlogy, Dr. Josef Allen Hynek. A professor of astronomy at Northwestern University, Hynek was employed in 1948 by the US Air Force to investigate UFO reports. He was consultant to the three major Air Force UFO studies – Projects Sign, Grudge and Blue Book. Although these programmes were largely designed to debunk UFO sightings, Hynek became convinced that there was a real mystery at the heart of the UFO phenomenon. So, after Blue Book was closed, he established the Center for UFO Studies (CUFOS), which remains one of the largest UFO groups in the world, to continue his research.

Hynek's most famous contribution to UFOlogy was his famous 'close encounter' classification system, which was brought to public attention by the Steven Spielberg movie *Close Encounters of the Third Kind* in 1977. Spielberg gave Hynek a walk-on part in the film in recognition of his contribution. Hynek's classification system lent some much-needed scientific weight to the otherwise outlandish UFO reports.

Hynek gave UFOlogy intellectual respectability by recognising that sighting reports were its principal source of data. Rather than dismissing reports because they seemed bizarre, Hynek insisted that witnesses should be listened to. Their reports were real evidence that required proper scientific evaluation. Hynek divided accounts into two types: those where the witness was more than five hundred feet from the object and those where the witness was less than five hundred feet from the object – so-called close encounters.

Within the first category, he identified three different types of report. These were:

1. **Nocturnal lights** – These are lights in the sky that cannot be accounted for by man-made craft, meteorological or astronomical phenomena.

2. **Daylight discs** – These are solid craft, not necessarily disc-shaped, that cannot be accounted for by man-made craft.

3. **Radar visual** – These are anomalous readings on an electronic device, not necessarily radar, that cannot be explained by any man-made phenomena.

The second category – the close encounters – was also subdivided into three types:

1. **Close encounters of the first kind (CEI)** – This is where the witness comes within five hundred feet of an anomalous object, but it has no interaction with the witness or the environment.

2. **Close encounters of the second kind (CEII)** – This is where the witness comes within five hundred feet of an anomalous object that leaves some damage or physical evidence in the

environment.

3. **Close encounters of the third kind (CEIII)** – This is where alien beings are seen inside or close to the object, and who may or may not have some contact with the witness.

Since Hynek first devised this system, the relationship between humankind and aliens has moved on apace, and it has been necessary to add new categories. There are now close encounters of the fourth kind (CEIV). These occur when witnesses experience mental or physical changes due to direct interaction with alien beings. Close encounters of the fifth kind (CEV) involve witnesses who can initiate encounters by contacting aliens physically or mentally. Then there are close encounters of the sixth kind (CEVI), where the witness is 'possessed' by a non-physical alien entity.

Hynek did not include these last three categories in his system because he was sceptical about abduction accounts. He did not feel that there was enough solid evidence in abduction reports to evaluate them scientifically. However, since he died in 1986, a new generation of UFOlogists has made full use of these new classifications.

Although Hynek's system is still the most widely used system of classification, many UFOlogists feel that it is too crude to be useful in investigating modern encounters. Some have tried to devise other systems, but these attempts have usually come to grief. Either they are overly complicated or they rely too much on one or other of the theories of what is happening in UFO encounters. However, one other classification system has been making gains on Hynek's old categories. This is the Vallee Classification System (VCS), devised by the French UFOlogist Jacques Françis Vallee. A graduate of Hynek's astronomy course at Northwestern University, Vallee is one of the leaders of the European 'psychosocial' school of UFOlogy. However, Vallee devised a system that can be used by any of the competing factions within UFOlogy.

Vallee's system looks at three main aspects of UFO reports and classifies them under three categories: Fly-Bys (FB), Manoeuvres (MA) and Close Encounters (CE). Close Encounters is the 'highest' category while Fly-Bys is the 'lowest'. Each of these categories is subdivided into five subcategories:

Fly-bys (FB)

- FB1 – UFO is seen flying in a straight line.
- FB2 – UFO is flying in a straight line that leaves behind physical evidence.
- FB3 – Fly-by with alien beings seen on board.
- FB4 – Fly-by with the witness experiencing a sense of altered reality.
- FB5 – Fly-by that results in injury or death.

Manoeuvres (MA)

- MA1 – UFO seen travelling in an erratic manner.
- MA2 – UFO manoeuvres causing physical effects.
- MA3 – UFO manoeuvring with alien beings seen on board.
- MA4 – UFO seen travelling in an erratic manner with the witness experiencing a sense of altered reality.
- MA5 – UFO manoeuvres that cause injury or death.

Close Encounters (CE)

- CE1 – UFO comes within five hundred feet of the witness, but they feel no effects.
- CE2 – UFO comes within five hundred feet of the witness and leaves traces of landing or injures the witness.
- CE3 – UFO comes within five hundred feet of the witness with alien beings visible.
- CE4 – The witness is abducted.
- CE5 – Abduction that results in permanent injury or death.

Within each of these subdivisions, cases are graded according to their intensity, the amount of detail given and their effects on the witness.

Then each report is also given a credibility score based on three other criteria: the reliability of the source, the thoroughness of the investigation of the sighting, and possible explanations.

The Vallee system is much more complex that Hynek's classification, but this simply reflects the increasingly complicated nature of the UFO phenomenon. And it does have the advantage of retaining the old 'close encounters' category.

Natural Causes

Most UFO researchers agree that the majority of flying saucer sighting reports can be dismissed as misperception, misidentification of unusual aerial events, such as meteorological effects, and downright hoaxes. When those cases are set aside there are still a large number of events in the skies that cannot be accounted for by normal means. But there is now a growing body of UFOlogists, especially in Europe, who seek to explain many of these genuine sightings, not as alien spacecraft, but as the result of a hither-to-unidentified natural phenomenon. Their theory is that these genuinely unidentified objects are so-called 'earthlights', thought to be produced by fault lines in the earth's crust.

For many years, the idea that earthlights – sometimes called balls of light (BOLs) – lies at the heart of the UFO phenomenon has been shunned by mainstream UFOlogy, which concentrated almost exclusively on the idea that UFOs were alien spacecraft. However, the early explorer of the unexplained, Charles Fort (1874-1932), who gave his name to 'Fortean phenomena', was among the first to observe that strange 'meteors' appeared to coincide with earth tremors and earthquakes. Bu it was only in the 1960s, after the discovery of tectonic plates, that several UFOlogists took the next step and began to correlate UFO sightings and geological fault lines.

French researcher Ferdinand Lagarde found that at least forty per cent of low-level flying saucer sightings occurred over, or close to, fractures in the earth's crust. Veteran American UFOlogist John Keel also began to look at the association between the appearance of unusual lights and areas of faulting and anomalies in the earth's magnetic field.

In the 1970s, earth-mysteries researchers Paul Devereux and Andrew York mapped strange phenomena reported over the centuries in the English county of Leicestershire and found that both meteorological anomalies – such as 'strange lightning' – and UFO sightings occurred most often over the fault-line regions of the county.

In 1977 Dr Michael Persinger, a neuroscientist and geologist, then at Laurentian University in Canada, and researcher Gyslaine Lafreniere published a study of the United States that pointed to a correlation between high levels of UFO activity and the sites of earthquake epicentres. Persinger and Lafreniere theorised that UFOs were electromagnetic phenomena arising from magnetic fields in the atmosphere caused by the squeezing of rocks under pressure. This is related to the scientifically respectable piezoelectric effect, by which certain crystals give off electricity when squeezed or distorted. In the run-up to an earthquake, tremendous energy would be generated by tectonic stress distorting the mineral crystals found in the earth's crust.

There could be other natural mechanisms at work here too. Light can be produced when enormous forces crush certain crystals. When the earth's tectonic plates move against each other the friction also generates an enormous amount of heat. Water in the surrounding rock would be vaporised. It would become ionised, collect around the fault and be expelled as luminous plumes of ionised plasma into the air above.

Normally these naturally occurring crustal forces would operate evenly over very large geographical regions and without having a visible effect. But at times of tectonic stress, these forces could become focused in a few small areas of particular geological resistance or instability – such as fault lines, mineral deposits, stubborn rock outcrops, hills and mountains – where the electromagnetic forces generated would produce strange airborne lights. This idea was tested experimentally in Boulder, Colorado, by the US Bureau of Mines, who filmed rocks with high crystalline content as they were placed under stress and allowed to fracture. Prior to this shattering, what looked like mini UFOs were created in the laboratory due to chemical and electrical charges emitted by the rock. This was the first demonstration of what has come to be known in UFOlogy as the Tectonic Strain Theory, or TST.

Devereux has pointed out that, if you scaled up the Boulder experiment to the size of mountains, it would produce enough earthlights to explain the UFO activity you see in 'window areas', which are invariably areas of tectonic stress. In 1982, he applied this theory to his study of sightings in the UK's most active UFO window in the Pennine Hills.

Dr Persinger continued his research and further explored and refined the TST theory. In 1986, he was joined geologist by John Derr in a study of a wave of lights seen over the Yakima Indian Reservation, Washington State. During the 1970s, firewardens on the reservation photographed huge orange balls of light hovering above rocks. They had also seen smaller ping-pong-sized balls of light dancing along ridges. The area had long been prone to unusual meteorological effects, such as glowing clouds.

Derr and Persinger discovered that the lights appeared most often along the ridges that cut across the reservation. These were riddled with fault lines. They also appeared around Satus Peak. Here a fault line broke the surface at the site of one of the strongest earthquakes that occurred in the region in the thirteen years covered by their study. Another wave of sightings occurred in the seven months before a big earthquake that occurred while Derr and Persinger were at work.

The significance of the Yakima study is that the reservation is in the foothills of the Cascade Mountains where, in 1947, Kenneth Arnold saw the first flying saucers –nine glittering objects flying in formation over a mountain ridge. This made a strong tie between 'earthlights' and UFOs.

A second study that made that connection occurred in the remote valley of Hessdalen in Norway. Hessdalen is seventy miles south-east of the remote northern town of Trondheim. The region is rich in copper and other metals. In November 1981 the people in the isolated farms in the valley saw strange yellow and white lights. They appeared just below the summits and ridges of the surrounding mountains. Along with regular balls of light, they saw inverted Christmas trees and bullet-shaped lights with the pointed end downwards. The farmers also heard underground rumblings and saw flashes in the sky.

As the phenomena were clearly linked with UFOs, the Norwegian Defence Department was called in. In March 1982 two Royal Norwegian Air Force officers turned up in Hessdalen to study the situation. By the summer of 1983, sightings had become increasingly frequent. They became big news in Scandinavia, but the Norwegian Defence Department came up with no explanation. Suspecting another official cover-up, Norwegian and Swedish UFO groups pooled their resources and set up Project Hessdalen. From 21 January to 26 February 1984 activity in the valley was monitored twenty-four hours a day with a range of specialist instruments, including radar – even though temperatures dropped as low as minus 30 degrees Celsius. Nevertheless the team managed to capture numerous strange lights on film and pick them up on radar. This sometimes proved baffling. On one occasion, several members of the team noticed a strange undulating sensation in their chests when the lights appeared. In another case, a bright light was seen travelling across the sky. But although it appeared constant to the naked eye, it appeared on the radar screen only every second sweep.

More earthlights were seen in the US when local newspaper reporter John Bennett heard reports that crowds of people were going to watch displays of strange lights at a ranch outside the town of Ada, seventy miles south-east of Oklahoma City. Deciding to investigate for himself, Bennett drove out to the remote ranch that afternoon. He parked his car and waited. As dusk approached, he saw an orange light appear in the middle of some trees. At first, he thought it was the lights of a house. But he changed his mind when the glowing orb started growing steadily larger until it was about three feet across. Then it began darting back and forth, changing colour as it did so. Suddenly a piece broke away and started bouncing across the field in front of him.

'It looked like a luminous basketball,' said Bennett.

After some time, the light went out. Another witness told Bennett that he had seen another light earlier that had come right up to the fence where he was standing.

'I didn't move, and it was like it was looking right at me,' he said.

Light phenomena are frequently reported along the San Andreas Fault in California, and in 1973 a strange streak of light was photographed over the Pinnacles Mountain Monument nearby by physicist David Kubrin. As it moved it created shock waves. Then it stopped dead and began to spin before dissolving. What amazed Kubrin was that it had exhibited signs of having mass – by producing shock waves – but somehow managed to stop without decelerating.

In 1989, geochemist Paul McCartney published his report of his investigation into the appearance of earthlights in north-west Wales in 1904 and 1905. Balls of red light were seen at various sites, but showed up most regularly over the field next to the chapel in Llanfair. He traced the sightings on a map and found that they ran down the course of the Mochras Fault that runs out into Tremadog Bay. Similar lights were seen in many parts of Wales during a wave of earthquake activity that lasted from 1892 to 1906. The area lies next to the Lleyn Peninsula which is one of the UK's most active earthquake areas. In July 1984, it was the epicentre of an earthquake measuring 5.5 on the Richter Scale. The lights reappeared briefly. The evening before the earthquake local people saw a brilliant white light, said to be the size of a small car, float in from the sea and land on the beach.

Then between 1 November 1988 and 21 January 1989 researchers from Quebec University made fifty-two sightings of strange light while on a seismic monitoring expedition to the Saguenay/Lake St John region of south-east Canada. Balls of light, both stationary and moving, were seen several hundred feet up in the air, some persisting as long as twelve minutes. And fireballs up to ten feet in diameter repeatedly popped out of the ground – sometimes only a few yards away from the observer. This research team, again, linked these UFO-type phenomena to rising tectonic strain in the ground that led up to an earthquake in the area.

The link between earthlights and UFOs has split the world of UFOlogy in two. The old-guard UFOlogists continue to advocate the extraterrestrial spacecraft theory and argue that small balls of lights can hardly explain solid-bodied craft that are seen in daylight – or, indeed, the sixty per cent of UFO sightings that do not occur near fault lines. On the other side of the fence are the new model earthlight researchers who point out that the phenomenon is not confined to small balls of light. With an appropriate build up of energy, earthlights can reach the size of a conventional flying-saucer. And they contend that, if earthlights are made from some kind of plasma – hot, electrically charged gas – they would also appear shiny and metallic in daylight, explaining the 'silvery discs' reported by Kenneth Arnold and many other witnesses.

To resolve the argument one way or the other, more data is required. A new Project Hessdalen has been set up in Norway and an expedition is planned to the Australian outback, where there has been persistent earthlight activity. Meanwhile, a research group headed by Paul Devereux has shown that geomagnetic anomalies and sightings of dancing lights around the increasingly active volcano, Popocatapetl, in Mexico have coincided with that country's recent prolonged UFO 'flap'.

'The fact is that the vast majority of UFOs are described as balls of light,' says Devereux. 'But it's only subjective interpretation that turns them into the lights of an alien craft.'

However, some consider this research, no matter how fascinating, as a diversion from the real business of UFOlogy – finding aliens.

More Windows

Paul Devereux's work on UFO window areas has opened the way to even more exotic theories. It has long been noted that window areas tend to feature not only UFOs but also other sorts of strange phenomena, including monster sightings and time anomalies. This has led John Keel to suggest that windows are portals between our reality and a supernatural dimension. He believes these represent points of weakness in the boundary between the two realities that allow strange phenomena to flow into our world – and possibly take us in the opposite direction. This would explain alien abduction and mysterious disappearances. If a window is the result of natural physical energies induced into the atmosphere by local geological factors, then they should remain relatively constant across time. So a window area would not only produce modern-day UFO sightings, but also reports of strange phenomena down the centuries. Deveraux's study of the historical records shows that the Pennine Hills is just such a window.

At the centre of the window on the Yorkshire–Lancashire border is the UK's most UFO-plagued town – Todmorden. It boasts dozens of sightings and six alien contact cases – out of just a hundred in the whole of the UK. In one case, a policeman from Todmorden was being abducted, but while he was being dragged into the UFO his boot caught on something and split.

Another case involved children's home worker Jenny, who was on her way home after horseback riding on the hills around Walsden. As she walked down the steep path from the moors to the town, she noticed that her dog was looking up into the sky. She look upwards to see what it was looking at and saw a lens-shaped object with coloured light under it floating silently at around roof-top height. As she stood and stared there was a telepathic exchange of information between her and the occupants of the UFO.

'It was like being plugged into a computer,' she said.

Contact ended when the UFO split into three separate glowing pieces and shot off in different directions.

UFOlogist Peter Hough has spent over twenty-five years studying the Pennine window and has come to the conclusion that we live in a multiverse, where other dimensions intersect with our own.

'Certain areas act as access points,' he says.

However, there may be a more prosaic explanation. Fiery balls of light appeared above the ancient church in the village of Linley,

Shropshire. At the same time, the locals reported the presence of a poltergeist. Metal door latches opened themselves, crockery moved by itself and chairs were hurled across the room. Dr Michael Persinger says that earthlights might also be triggered by a localised increase in the Earth's magnetic field, which would explain these other bizarre happenings.

Abductions Experts

Although there have been numerous well-documented cases of alien abductions since the 1960s, many UFOlogists refuse to believe then. So in an attempt to discover whether they were really happening, in June 1992, the first Abduction Study Conference was held at the Massachusetts Institute of Technology. Three of the world's leading experts attended. They included Budd Hopkins, a pioneering investigator in this field, and Dr David Jacobs, associate professor of history at Temple University, who had been investigating UFOs for twenty-five years.

Chairing the conference was Dr John E. Mack, professor of Psychiatry at Harvard Medical School and a Pulitzer Prize winner. He was also a founder of the psychiatry teaching department and Cambridge Hospital, Harvard, and director of the Program for Extraordinary Experience Research at the Center for Psychology and Social Research.

The conference concluded that, although people from a whole cross-section of society had been abducted, their reports showed a remarkable consistency. The same type of aliens were involved in most cases. The abduction procedures were the same and abductees reported similar details of what they were subjected to. If alien abduction was some form of delusion, the accounts should differ wildly. Yet they showed consistent and repeated patterns. This was strong evidence that victims really were being abducted.

Greys were almost always responsible, though in some cases they are directed by taller humanoid aliens. Victims found themselves under the total control of the aliens. Inside the craft, they were forced to strip, made to lie on a table and subjected to intimate examinations and invasive surgery. Victims were then returned, though usually their memories had been wiped clean of the events, which could only be accessed through regressional hypnosis.

Added to that, Professor Mack pointed out, the victims often had hard physical evidence of their abduction. People returned with scars on their bodies that were fully healed though they were not been there before the abduction. Strange implants have been located on X-rays and CAT scans. Some have been removed and examined.

Chemical analysis of the implants has shown that they were usually made from elements found on Earth. But one of Professor Mack's colleagues, a nuclear biologist, ran tests on an implant taken from the nose of an abductee and discovered that the implant was not a naturally occurring biological structure. It was made from manufactured fibre. Leir's work on isotope ratios had not been done at this time.

The leading sceptics also turned up at the conference. They dismissed the physical evidence provided by Professor Mack and others, and claimed that no reliable evidence for abduction exists outside the victim's imagination. The villain of the piece, according to the sceptics, was the use of regressional hypnosis techniques to recover hidden memories. The Society for Psychical Research's Kevin McClure claimed that the abduction researchers using hypnosis are not qualified psychologists. When they did use qualified ones, McClure said, they implanted memories. He alleged that, under hypnosis, victims were encouraged to recount details that support the abduction scenario by asking leading questions. McClure also argued that False Memory Syndrome may also be to blame. This is a disorder where the subconscious creates a bogus memory to cover up some painful childhood trauma such as sexual abuse. Abductees may be subconsciously creating false memories of an alien abduction to protect themselves from the real memories of a more traumatic experience.

Professor Mack, a psychologist by training, dismissed this theory.

'There is not a single abduction case in my experience or that of other investigators that has turned out to have masked a history of sexual abuse or any other traumatic cause,' he said. 'In fact, the reverse has frequently occurred – that an abduction history has been revealed in cases investigated for sexual or other abuse.'

Psychologist Susan Blackmore of the University of the West of England had another theory. She claimed that an abduction experience could be induced artificially by stimulation of the temporal lobes – the part of the brain where memories are stored. A Canadian research team under Dr Michael Persinger from the University of Sudbury, Ontario, supported this thesis. They had designed a helmet that generated a magnetic field. Dr Persinger claimed that, when this field was applied to the back of the brain, it could produce an alien abduction experience in people who have never previously claimed to have had one. But when the device was tried out on Dr Susan Blackmore, she said she felt 'someone pulling my arms and legs' and 'sudden and uncontrollable emotions'. This is hardly an alien abduction experience.

The author of *Allergies and Aliens*, Albert Budden, also said that electromagnetic fields create memories of alien abductions. He was convinced that the wave of abduction reports over the last forty years is caused by electromagnetic pollution. Electromagnetic radiation in the atmosphere is strong enough to affect the temporal lobes of abductees' brains, he says, causing abduction-like experiences. All abductees are electrically hypersensitive, he believes, and their experiences are a symptom of their allergic reactions to electromagnetic fields in the environment.

But Hopkins, Jacobs and Mack pointed out that over-active imaginations, false memories and electromagnetic simulation of temporal lobes cannot explain physical scars on abductees' bodies or the implants taken from them.

Dr Sue Davidson, a psychotherapist, thinks all abductees are raving mad. 'I have not come across the phenomenon of abduction by aliens except as a delusional belief of someone suffering from schizophrenia,' he says. But how does that explain cases like that of Travis Walton, where there were other witnesses to the 'spacenapping'? Are they all mad? If they are then it is an insanity that is widespread in society. In 1995, Robert Durant compiled the statistics on alien abductions. He discovered that some five million Americans had reported having been abducted over the previous fifty years. That works out at about 274 a day. Assuming that it takes six aliens to abduct a human – abductees rarely report that they have seen more than six – and that each six-alien team abducted twelve humans a day, you would need just 137 to cover the whole of America.

And UFOlogists have now tied the alien abductions to the mutilation of livestock as further evidence that aliens are conducting genetic experiments planet-wide. Again, bizarrely butchered carcasses are not caused by hallucinations, delusions or false memories.

Alien of the Soul

So how do the earthlight theorists explain the phenomenon of alien abduction? It might not be as hard as you think. Let's look at one of the most celebrated alien abduction cases in the whole of UFOlogy – that of Travis Walton, whose abduction formed the basis of the 1993 movie *Fire in the Sky*.

Walton was abducted one November evening in 1975, from a forest track near his home in Heber, Arizona. A lumberjack, he was travelling home with the rest of the wood-cutting crews in the truck, tired after a long day's work, when, in a clearing up ahead, they saw a strange, glowing ball of light. As the truck came closer, Walton jumped out and rushed towards the mysterious object, which cast a ring of light on the ground. It was about twenty feet across and floated in the air unsteadily, emitting strange beeping and rumbling sounds.

A blue-green bolt of light zapped out of the object. Walton heard a crackling sound and felt 'a numbing shock... like a high-voltage electrocution'. It lifted him up and flung him to the ground. The rest of the crew fled. By the time they returned to the scene, the mysterious ball of light was seen shooting skyward, and Walton had disappeared.

Five days later, Walton turned up naked in a phone box. He was seriously dehydrated, delirious, dazed, distraught and half-dead. He had been knocked out by the bolt of light. Later he recalled regaining consciousness in some sort of spacecraft, surrounded by 'foetus-like' aliens, with large dark eyes and marshmallowy skin.

It certainly seemed that something odd had happened in the woods the evening he went missing. But had Walton had an encounter with an earthlight rather than an alien spaceship? Certainly what Walton and his workmates saw was the right size and shape to be an earthlight. And reports from around the world of earthlights mention that they make strange sounds, just like the ones Walton and his workmates had heard.

As earthlights are an electromagnetic phemonemon, one could easily have zapped him with a bolt of electricity. If Walton had suffered a massive electric shock, he might have been left in a confused mental state. He could have wandered off into the forest and lost himself there for days. In that case, what were the strange aliens Walton recalled?

According to Canadian neuroscientist and earthlight proponent Dr Michael Persinger, an individual exposed to enormous electromagnetic fields is likely to experience a number of effects on his or her body, brain and mind. These effects could include impaired memory and vision. At its most extreme, an electromagnetic field might put a victim into a trance-like state where the boundaries between waking and dreaming become blurred and they might suffer intense hallucinations.

The area of the brain most sensitive to changes in magnetic and electrical fields is the area of the temporal cortex. Under the cortex proper lie the amygdala and hippocampus. Stimulation of the amygdala produces intense emotional feelings, while alterating the function of the hippocampus can modify memory and release dreams into the waking state.

In an effort to explain alien abductions, Michael Persinger has been running a series of experiments in which volunteers have the temporal cortex of their brains subjected to magnetic fields. Subjects sit in a darkened soundproof cubicle, wearing a helmet that creates magnetic 'vortices'. Computer-controlled electrodes directed these into various areas of the temporal cortex with great precision. During the course of the experiment, subjects see visions or feel some sort of presence. One even said the cubicle was haunted by the devil himself.

Persinger has found that when a subject has undergone several of these sessions, it takes little to trigger what he calls 'the mystical state of mind'. The magnetic helmet often induced vivid scenes from infancy and childhood.

Journalist Ian Cotton tried this out. He found himself sitting in a darkened cubicle with a magnetic helmet on. The first thing he was conscious of was a strange noise, then he went into a lucid dream state. He said that it was as clear as if his 'inner eye' was a video camera, and he saw vivid scenes from his childhood. He saw the pattern of the wallpaper in his bedroom and the red roses on the tablecloth in his childhood home, along with other long-forgotten details, with lifelike clarity.

In one particularly telling experiment, the subjects were asked concentrate on a single light in front of them. It was a normal sixty-watt electric light bulb, but many subjects described seeing slit-mouthed, grey-skinned aliens and horrific medical probes – images common to the typical UFO abduction scenario.

Medical researchers who have conducted experiments with psychedelic substances such as dimethyltryptamine (DMT) and LSD have had similar effects. Drugs induce vivid hallucinations and infantile regression with some people even claiming to have re-experienced their own birth trauma. As well as occurring in certain vegetables and seeds, DMT occurs naturally in the body. Native American tribes take it as a means of seeing spirits, contacting dead ancestors or communicating with the gods. Modern users of the drug find themselves in a deep mental state, where they see primitive creatures not dissimilar to Grey aliens. One research subject also reported being escorted by alien entities to a kind of landing platform at a space station. There he met android-like creatures that were 'a cross between crash dummies and the Empire troops from *Star Wars*'.

Another said they saw a 'giant, complex control panel' and creatures that were 'bipedal and roughly human size'. These are all familiar images from abductions.

According to UFO researcher Alvin Lawson, the archetypal image of the Grey alien inhabits this very realm of our imagination. It is a kind of primal template of the mammal. Lawson says that the Grey, with it large eyes, tiny features and a small, wasted body, is essentially an elaborate image of the human foetus and as such is an archetype lodged deep within our minds. Certainly, the image of a baby is closely associated with the Greys, who are the most common abductors. Women regularly report that the aliens take their babies and, more commonly, their foetuses. Many abductees, men as well as women, report aliens probing their reproductive organs. And UFOlogist Dennis Stacy says that the Grey abduction motif is associated with the trauma surrounding abortion.

A number of researchers now believe that the alien abduction experience can be triggered by a variety of temporal lobe stimuli in those with sufficient sensitivity. This sensitivity can have been induced by trauma – either a physical trauma such as an electric shock or a psychological trauma such as an incident of child abuse. Such stimuli sensitise the temporal cortex. What's more, they are cumulative, each one leaving the subject more susceptible the next time.

British investigator Albert Budden has interviewed numerous abductees, and found that virtually all of them have suffered such trauma. Electrical sensitivity is common among them. When such people come within the influence of high-tension wires, for example, the electromagnetic field can precipitate hallucinations of such vividness that they think they really have encountered a UFO or aliens.

Abductees usually end up back in their own bed. Companions are not aware that they have been missing and abductees often feel that they have been abducted in some abstract or spiritual sense, while their body has been left behind in bed. Finnish abductee Rauni-Leena Luukkanen-Kilde said that during her abductions it was her 'astral' body that boarded the spaceship. The scars that manifested themselves on her physical body later appeared as a result of the trauma to her spiritual self, she thought.

Alien Races

The Grey alien became the best known species of extraterrestrial when alien abductee Whitley Strieber put the picture of one on the cover of his 1987 best-seller *Communion*. However, despite the enduring fame of the Grey, on the night he was first abducted, 26 December 1985, Strieber actually encountered three other types of creature.

One was the robot-like being that initially led him out of the bedroom of his country home in upstate New York. Then, in the forest outside, he encountered a large number of short, stocky beings in dark blue overalls. They had wide, blue faces, 'glittering, deep-set eyes', pug noses and broad, human-like mouths, he said. It was only later, when he found himself inside the circular room, that he encountered Grey-like beings – but their eyes, although black, were not almond shaped but 'as round as buttons'.

Strieber's case is by no means unique. While virtually every abduction case involves Greys, abductees regularly see a variety of aliens during their experiences. Dutch therapist Hilda Musch made a survey of abductees in the Netherlands and found that 85 per cent of them reported encounters with aliens other than Greys. Numerous different types have been reported since contact with extraterrestrials began. Sceptics say that there are as many types of alien as there are people who report them. But that is not entirely true. Contact reports do show some degree of consistency. In fact, all the aliens reported being seen over the past century can be categorised into one of four classes:

1. **Humanoid** – These are essentially human in shape, though witnesses have the strong sense that they are not human. This class includes Greys.
2. **Animalian** – These are animal-like creatures, including reptilian aliens and Chupacabras.

3. **Robotic** – These are entities that have a distinctly mechanical appearance.
4. **Exotic** – This is a catch-all category for those that do not fit into any of the categories above, and makes up just five per cent of the sightings.

Each class of alien can be further divided into types. The most recognisable type of Humanoid is called the Human. This is simply because it is nearly impossible to tell 'them' from 'us' – except they are usually better looking with blond hair and blemish-free complexions. These 'Nordic' types used to be very common visitors to Earth. They were the aliens who visited George Adamski first on 20 November 1952, landing somewhere between Desert Center, California and Parker, Arizona. They had long blond hair, high foreheads and seemed to radiate great love, warmth and understanding.

Then there are the familiar 'Short Greys', which are the main alien type seen on Earth. Before they were made famous by Whitley Strieber, they had made an appearance at the end of the movie *Close Encounters of the Third Kind*. This, UFO sceptics said, would spark a rash of copycat sightings. It did not happen. Short Greys had already appeared in movies in the 1940s and 1950s. They were the pilots of the flying saucers that crashed at Roswell in 1947. But in the literature they predated that, first appearing on the cover of the magazine *Astounding Stories* in 1935.

Greys are often not very nice. But as astronomer Carl Sagan once remarked: 'I would love it if there were aliens here, even if they are a little short, sullen, grumpy and sexually preoccupied.'

Closely related are Short Non-Greys. They are like Greys but they are very hairy or have green skin and are common visitors to Latin America. It was a pair of the Green race that geologist Rapuzzi Johannis encountered when out studying rock formations in northern Italy on the night of 14 August 1947. They were about three feet tall and had green faces. When they came within six feet of him, Johannis noticed their hands. They had eight jointless, opposable fingers. Small green Short Non-Greys appeared in the movie *Invasion of the Saucermen* in 1957.

The Animalians also include some creatures that are not formally thought of as extraterrestrials – such as Yetis, swamp creatures and goblins. Bigfoots, for example, show all the characteristics of being alien. Some even have spaceships. Stephen Pulaski and two boys came across a dome-shaped craft that had landed near Greensburg, Pennsylvania, on 24 November 1973. Suddenly, two large, bear-like creatures appeared. They were eight feet tall with glowing, yellow-green eyes. Being a good American, Pulaski pulled a gun and shot at them. It had no effect. The boys then fled. Pulaski gave them covering fire, to no avail.

Abductee Betty Andreasson saw an entirely different type of Animalian. When she was abducted from her home in South Ashburnham, Massachusetts, on 25 January 1967, she was taken on a saucer-shaped craft to some other world where she saw three-feet high lemur-like creatures. They were headless and had eyes on the ends of prehensile stalks.

Robotic aliens come in just two types. The most common is the Metallic, which is mechanical and made totally out of metal. Lee Parish of Prospect, Kentucky, saw three machine-like beings on 27 January 1977. Under hypnosis, he said that two of the slab-like creatures were six foot tall. One of them was bulky and white, the other slim and red. The third towered above the others. It was around twenty feet tall and black. Scottish forester Bob Taylor is also thought to have encountered Robotic aliens in 1979 when he was attacked by two metal beach balls around a foot in diameter with six legs that emerged from a UFO. He smelt a pungent odour before passing out. There is also a rare type of Robotic alien that has parts made out of a substance that resembles flesh. They are called Fleshy Robots.

The Exotic category of aliens again has two main types. The Apparitional are at least partially transparent, while the Physical are completely solid. Hans Gustafsson and Stig Rydberg encountered a Physical Exotic while out driving near Domesten in Sweden on the night of 20 December 1958. They noticed a glow in the woods and stopped to investigate. In a clearing, they saw a spacecraft with four odd-shaped creatures jumping around the landing site. The amorphous, blue-green blobs were six feet tall and hostile. The two men barely escaped the suction force of the blobs' onslaught.

Aliens are a mixed bunch and several types often appear together. In May 1969 Brazilian soldier Jose Antonio was abducted by two short aliens in silver suits. On board their craft he met another alien who was about four feet tall with wavy, waist-length hair, large eyes, a mouth like a fish and deep-set greenish eyes. And in July 1983, Ron and Paula Watson encountered four aliens in Mount Vernon, Missouri – two silver-suited humanoids, a Bigfoot with shaggy hair all over its huge body and a 'lizard man'.

That there is an enormous variety of aliens is no real surprise. After all, there is a huge variety of life on earth. And alien visitors are hardly a rarity. Huge numbers of aliens have dropped in. An American survey found that some five million people have been abducted by aliens over the past fifty years – almost three hundred a day. It is estimated that the average abduction team comprised six aliens. From the length of time each abduction takes, it has been worked out that they can perform a maximum of twelve abductions per day. That means that 140 aliens have to be at work day and night to cope with the workload in the US alone.

Lizard Men

The lizard man Ron and Paula Watson saw was six foot tall, with green reptilian skin, webbed hands and feet, and glowing, cat-like eyes with vertical pupils. This was a sighting of a reptilian alien. Indeed these 'reptoids' are the most common species of alien after the Greys, and, for that reason, the most fascinating.

One was seen in Italy on 6 December 1978. Twenty-six-year-old night-watchman Fortunato Zanfretta saw four bright lights moving behind a house at Marzano in Genoa. He went to investigate and was confronted by a nine-feet-tall bipedal reptoid, which pushed him to the ground and then vanished. Zanfretta picked himself up and ran to his car. On the way, he felt a sudden heat, heard a loud whistling sound and saw a huge triangular craft soaring up into the sky. He radioed his colleagues for help and, when they arrived, he took them to where the craft had taken off. There, they found a depression the ground. It was twenty-five feet across and shaped like a giant horseshoe.

Under hypnosis, it was discovered that Zanfretta had been abducted by the reptoid and taken on board its craft for a time. He could not remember much about the spacecraft's interior, but he gave a vivid description of the alien. It had horn-like projections on its forehead above luminous-yellow, triangular eyes, pointed spines on either side of its head and a stocky body. Its skin was dark green and marked by a series of horizontal folds or ribbing.

Numerous UFOlogists have collected reports of similar sightings. 'When a so-called reptilian is repeatedly described as having the same scaly skin, claws for fingers, and extreme interest in sexuality, one must pay attention,' said Dan Wright at MUFON's 1995 symposium in Seattle.

In the autumn of 1938, near the town of Juminda in Estonia, two eyewitnesses saw a three-foot high creature with greenish-brown skin. It had slit-like eyes and month and looked like a giant frog, they said. It had some trouble walking on dry land; even so, it managed to outpace the witnesses when they chased it.

On 29 June 1988 seventeen-year-old Chris Davis was driving home past Scape Ore Swamp, near the village of Bishopville in South Carolina, at around 2 a.m., when his car had a puncture. He pulled over and changed the tyre, and was about to get back in the driver's seat, when he saw a figure running towards him across a field. As it drew closer, he saw that it was not human. Over six feet six inches tall and standing upright, it looked like a giant lizard, with green scaly skin, and slanted, red glowing eyes. It had three digits on its feet and hands, each of which had a four-inch-long black claw.

Terrified, Davis jumped back into his car. When the creature reached the vehicle it wrenched the wing mirror off in an attempt to open the door. When Davis drove off, the lizard man leapt on to the car's roof and clung on as the terrified teenager drove through the swampy wilderness at up to fifty miles an hour. Fortunately, the creature eventually lost its grip and fell off.

Davis reported the encounter to the police, and the local sheriff, Liston Truesdale, investigated. 'We checked out his reputation, and he's a pretty clean-cut kid,' said Truesdale. 'He's also agreed to take a polygraph test or go under hypnosis.'

Davis's father, Tommy, told the newspapers: 'All I can tell you is that my son was terrified that night. He was hysterical, crying and trembling. It took a while before he was calm enough to tell us what happened.'

In the weeks that followed, numerous other sightings were reported and Scape Ore Swamp became a media circus, with TV crews battling it out for prime filming sites. A local radio station offered a reward of $1 million for the capture of the lizard man. They kept their money. However, a number of three-toed footprints, each fourteen inches long, were later discovered in the swamp, and casts were taken. Meanwhile, numerous Fortean researchers stepped forward to offer speculative theories. Others said that Davis had been attacked by a drunken tramp who and crawled out of a ditch, and dismissed the footprints as the work of a prankster. Some later sightings indeed proved to be hoaxes and, soon, the lizard man fell out of the headlines. The enigmatic entity itself was, like so many other anomalous creatures, never identified, let alone captured.

In veteran Fortean investigator Loren Coleman's *Curious Encounters*, he reports encounters with a 'creature from the black lagoon' – named for the 1954 sci-fi cult movie – in Ohio in 1972. At around 1 a.m., on 3 March, police officer Ray Schocke was driving down a riverside road towards the town of Loveland, when his headlights lit up what he initially took to be a dog. But the creature then stood up on its hind legs and he could see that it was a three-foot tall reptilian with leathery skin and a frog-like face. The frog-man looked at him for a moment, then jumped over the guard rail, slithered down the embankment and disappeared into the river. Schocke drove to the police station and returned with fellow officer Mark Matthews. They searched the area. Although they did not find the creature, they did find scrape marks leading down to the river along the course the fleeing creature took.

Two weeks later, Matthews was driving along the same river when he saw what he took to be a dead animal lying in the road. He stopped to move the carcass. When he got out of his patrol car, the creature got up and moved to the guard rail without taking his eyes off Matthews. Matthews took a pot shot at it but missed. The creature climbed over the guard rail and made off. Other witnesses in the area reported seeing a strange frog-like creature.

That same year there were other reptilian encounters at Lake Thetis, near Colwood in British Columbia. On two separate occasions in August 1972, two sets of witnesses saw a humanoid reptile-man with a silver body covered in fish-like scales emerge from the lake. One witness said the creature had a monstrous face, huge ears, and at least one large spike projecting from its head. It was a biped, with three-pronged flippers for feet, a fish-like mouth, and very large fish-like eyes. This description fits other reptoid sightings that date back to the nineteenth century and beyond.

In 24 October 1878 a Kentucky newspaper, the *Louisville Courier Journal,* reported that a strange creature captured alive in Tennessee was on exhibit in Louisville. According to the article, the entity was around six feet six inches in height, had eyes twice as large as a human's and was 'covered with fish scales'.

Sighting reports of these creatures shows such consistency that researcher John Carpenter has been able to piece together a detailed morphology of these scaly creatures and, in MUFON's journal of April 1993, he provided an identikit so that you will recognise one if you see one. These are its characteristics:

- **Height** – six to eight feet.
- **General appearance** – grotesque, repulsive.
- **Skin** – lizard-like scales, smooth in texture.

- **Colour** – greenish to brownish.
- **Head** – central ridge running down to the snout.
- **Face** – cross between a snake and human.
- **Eyes** – cat-like with golden iris and a vertical slit for a pupil.
- **Hands** – four-fingered claw with brown webbing.
- **Chest** – external ribbing often visible.
- **Manner** – intrusive, forceful, insensitive.
- **Behaviour** – intrudes, assaults and rapes.
- **Method of communication** – none.
- **Physical evidence** – large claw marks photographed.

Some researchers have suggested that the reptoids are not newcomers to our planet. While UFOlogists speculate that Greys are a future stage in human evolution who travel back through time to visit us, some have suggested that reptoids may be a remnant of humankind's distant past. Another theory concerns human evolution. Whereas DNA shows that humankind is closely related to the higher apes, the theory of evolution cannot explain the great intellectual and cultural gap that separates *Homo sapiens* from other species. Some suggest this is because human development was spurred on by higher beings visiting our planet from outer space. During his study of reptilian aliens, UFOlogist Dr Joe Lewels turned to the Bible and other, more obscure, religious texts. He found that there are myths and religions from around world that tell of an ancient race of scaly super-beings who descended from the sky to give humankind a helping hand. Take the biblical Creation, for example. An ancient Jewish document called the *Haggadah* says that, physically, Adam and Eve were originally very different from humans today and, when they ate the forbidden fruit from the Tree of Knowledge, it says: 'The first result was that Adam and Eve became naked. Before, their bodies had been over-laid with a horny skin and enveloped with the cloud of glory. No sooner had they violated the command given them than the cloud of glory and the horny skin dropped from them, and they stood there in their nakedness and ashamed.'

The *Haggadah* also says that the snake who tempted Eve was humanoid in form. 'He stood upright on two feet, and in height he was equal to the camel.' Only after Adam and Eve's disobedience was found out was the serpent condemned to crawl on its belly. Indeed, in fifteenth century Christian art, the serpent is depicted standing on two legs and proffering the apple with an extended arm.

So the first two humans were initially covered in a shining, scaly skin, and their punishment for eating the forbidden fruit was to lose their scales. If Adam was created in the image of his maker, then his maker must have been reptilian. Support for this radical theory is found in other early documents. The *Nag Hammadi* texts, a series of ancient scrolls found inside a clay jar in a small Egyptian town of that name in 1945, contains a passage which describes what Adam and Eve did next: 'When they saw their makers, they loathed them since they were beastly forms.'

In his book *Flying Serpents and Dragons: The Story of Mankind's Reptilian Past*, reptilian researcher R.A. Boulay concludes: 'The sad fact is that in the West we have created God in our image and not the other way around. In this way we have hidden the true identity of our creators.'

Numerous researchers have also noted that the Western image of a humanoid creator is in stark contrast to the Eastern beliefs that humanity is descended from reptilian ancestors. Chinese emperors claimed lineage from a race of dragons, and certain noble Indian families claim descent from Indian serpent deities or 'nagas'. Then there is the Dogon tribe of Mali, whose astounding astronomical knowledge came from a race of reptilian extraterrestrials known as the 'Nommo'.

In his book *The Dragons of Eden: Speculations on the Evolution of Human Intelligence* Carl Sagan recalled the pioneering brain studies of Dr Paul MacLean, head of the Laboratory of Brain Evolution and Behavior of the United States' National Institute of Mental Health. MacLean's work led him to propose that the three distinct regions of the forebrain in higher vertebrates – mammals, birds and reptiles – was each acquired during a different phase of evolution. According to MacLean, the most ancient of these regions is the one that surrounds the midbrain and is known as the reptilian R-complex. This, he says, evolved several hundred million years ago and is shared by reptiles, birds and mammals. Surrounding this are the limbic system and neocortex, which both evolved later and are more highly developed in mammals. Humans experience emotions with the limbic system and think with the neocortex. But in his book *The Dreams of Dragons* biologist Dr Lyall Watson suggests that when we dream, it is our long-suppressed reptilian complex that takes over. This archaic portion of human minds might contain memory remnants of the time when, more than 65 million years ago, our ancestors, the first mammals, were tiny, shrew-like creatures that ran around the feet of the dinosaurs. It is unlikely that memories of what it was like to be a tiny creature in a world inhabited by giant reptiles would be entirely lost, even after millions of years of evolution. As our cultural memories of such things were handed down the generations as oral traditions, they would inevitably become distorted. Both Sagan and Watson suggest that this is the key to the intriguing morphological similarities between real dinosaurs and unreal dragons – and why both of these reptilian groups hold such a grip on our imaginations.

Dinosaurs Live

Some researchers believe that the reptilian aliens are not extraterrestrial in origin. They are the descendants of an intelligent race of dinosaurs. One such is researcher and writer John Rhodes. In his book *Dragons of the Apocalypse* he gives a detailed morphology of the reptoids. His researches have led him to conclude that the reptilian race includes a royal elite called 'Draco' – who are also reportedly working at Dulce, according to Thomas Castello. Although rarely seen, Draco are much taller that your average reptoid – up to eleven feet tall. They have cranial horns and leathery wings. He speculates that Draco may be responsible for the outbreak of sightings of 'Mothman' in West Virginia in the 1960s.

On 24 August 1995 Rhodes told the First International UFO Congress in Mexico City that reptoids were responsible for the recent outbreak of UFO sightings there.

'They may be preparing the way for the prophesied return of the Feathered Serpent god of Mexico – Quetzalcotl,' he said.

Another believer in the survival of dinosaurs is David Barclay. But his theory is slightly different. He points out that, in the fossil records, humankind dates back only a few million years, but during that time we have evolved into an enormously intelligent species. The dinosaurs were around for 150 million years – how much higher might they have developed?

According to Barclay's book *Aliens the Answer?*, a species of humanoid dinosaurs provoked some global catastrophe at the end of the Cretaceous Period some 65 million years ago and wiped out most of its own kind, along with the more familiar species of dinosaur. But some survived. The original human beings were their pets and were bred like we breed dogs. While we evolved into *Homo sapiens* through this process, the humanoid dinosaurs evolved into Greys. This is why, Barclay says, the Greys take such an enormous interest in us.

Alien Motives

Alien abductions are widely seen as the most intriguing twist in the evolution of the UFO phenomenon. Since the first recorded case, involving the forcible abduction of Antonio Villas-Boas in 1959, an increasing number of people around the world have reported being abducted by alien entities and often subjected to humiliating medical examinations. At first their motives were puzzling, but gradually researchers are coming to understand the phenomenon.

One of the first attempts to identify the common features of the abduction experience was made by researcher Dr Thomas 'Eddie' Bullard, who began a comparative analysis of abduction cases from around the world. From his studies, he was able to identify a distinct pattern. Most abductees' experiences, he said, had eight distinct components: capture, examination, conference, tour, other worldly journey, theophany, return, and aftermath.

However, since Bullard finished his initial studies, a wealth of new abduction cases have come in and new components have been identified that may help open the way for a deeper understanding of the abduction phenomenon. One of these new components is the feeling that many abductees have that they are being controlled prior to the abduction itself. Many find themselves being attracted inexplicably to a particular place or destination by an urge they are powerless to resist.

Under regressional hypnosis, Jill Pinzarro recalled an abduction she had experienced at the age of nine in 1958. She was pushing her bicycle home from the library one afternoon, but instead of walking directly home, she found herself drawn inexplicably towards some trees. 'I didn't feel as if I could resist,' she said. Inside the trees, there was a spacecraft with a ladder. She climbed up it into an alien spacecraft where she was stripped and examined.

When she got back to the park bench, it was already dark. She was scared, put her books in the basket on her bike and set off home. It was late and her parents were frantic. They had already called the police who were out looking for her. But when she arrived back, her parents were so relieved that they were not even angry with her.

When she was abducted again, at the age of eleven, the aliens were particularly interested in a scab on her knee she had got after falling of her bike. A tall alien stared into her eyes. She found this reassuring. The alien, she thought, really cared about her and would not let her come to any harm. But for Jill this was not accompanied by any sexual feelings. She thought the alien was a female. However, when the alien touched her on the forehead, she felt calm and had the sensation that she was willing to surrender sexually to the creature.

When she was abducted in 1980 at the age of thirty-two, she was given a baby to hold. It was about two-and-a-half-months-old, she reckoned. It had little hair and its skin was light. The alien nursemaid said that the child needed nurturing, but they were not very good at it and they needed her to do it. The baby was quiet and seemed to enjoy

Jill holding it. When she had to give it back, Jill felt an acute sense of loss. She had bonded with it. She thought this was strange because she did not consider herself a very maternal person. She had only ever wanted one child, which she had – back on Earth.

Many abductions reportedly involve the abductee being taken against their will from their house by aliens who first move them into an open area from which they are lifted at high speed by some extraterrestrial elevator into a UFO hovering overhead. Again the victim has no control over the matter.

In 1982 Barbara Archer was abducted by aliens from inside her own home. She was sixteen. One night, she had just been getting ready for bed when she noticed a light coming in through the window. She drew the curtains, but still the light seemed to illuminate the whole room. She peeked out but could see no source for the light. She checked the other window too, then got the strangest sensation that there was someone in the room with her.

By the closet she saw a small creature, which she took to be male. Although she was puzzled by the light, she was not shocked to see him there. He touched her on the wrist, which reassured her. Then she began to float straight up out of the window.

'When we went out the window, we went straight in between my house and my next door neighbour's,' she recalled. She said it was like being in a lift with no walls. She could clearly see the driveway, her house, then the rest of street, below her. She was scared of heights. It made her feel nauseous and she hoped she would not be sick.

'Up there, I could see everything. I could see all the rows of houses on my street,' she said.

She floated up underneath some sort of flying saucer. It was dark grey, metallic. Then she noticed the light was coming out of it. But the elevation continued. 'We just went right in through the bottom,' she said.

The alien she saw in her bedroom was still with her. More were waiting inside.

She also recalled being abducted when she was twelve. That time

531

she found herself in a room with forty or fifty tables. After the regular physical examination, a tall alien came over to her and looked deep into her mind. This made her feel happy and she lay back. She did not feel sick anymore, just a little cold. Although she was scared of the smaller aliens, she liked the taller one and thought that he liked her. Again there was a very sexual element to this. Although she was only twelve, Barbara suddenly felt very womanly, very grown up. She got the feeling that the alien could read her mind and really understood her.

She was abducted again at the age of sixteen in 1982 when she was suffering from anorexia. This annoyed the aliens because she had stopped menstruating.

When she was twenty-one, Barbara went on holiday to Ireland where she was abducted again. This time the aliens got cross with her because she did not take her clothes off quickly enough. Later she was taken to a nursery on board the spacecraft, where there were about twenty babies in cribs. Some were in nappies. Others were slightly older and dressed in simple smocks. They looked kind of scary. They did not have much hair and their skin was an unnatural grey colour.

The aliens told her she could hold one and picked out a baby girl for her. The child had big eyes. They were shaped like an alien's but they were not as ugly. Barbara remembered feeling very protective and maternal. The alien nurse then told her to feed it and Barbara put the baby to her breast. Afterwards they took the baby away from her. When Barbara was told she had to leave, she felt bad leaving the baby behind. She asked the aliens whether she could see it again. They did not give her an answer.

However, it was in what the abductees observe on board the abductors' craft that researchers find the most consistency. For example, the aliens on board the UFO usually answer to the same description. Often, there is very noticeably a leader, sometimes described as a 'chief doctor' or 'captain', who seems to direct the abduction and who is generally described as a 'he'. The leader is usually described as more cold and clinical or more authoritarian than the other aliens on board. In almost all cases, he is taller than the other creatures. This started way back in 1961 when Betty Hill struck up some rapport with the taller leader.

Almost all abductees describe their captors as having large, compelling eyes. Their impenetrable blackness makes them somehow hypnotic. Some abductees feel that the aliens' eyes are a means of telepathic communication; others fear that the aliens use their eyes to exert control over abductees. However, looking into the eyes of an alien is often said to bring a soothing calmness or diminish any pain the abductee might feel.

Abduction expert David Jacobs believes that when abductees feel they have been profoundly affected by alien eyes in this way, they have, in fact, been subjected to a 'mind scan'. The aliens stare deeply into the abductee's eyes and monitor all their thoughts.

One abductee, Karen Morgan, allegedly felt the effects of 'mind scan' during her abduction in 1981. She remembered entering a UFO and being taken to a waiting area with a number of benches in arched alcoves. She sat in one and there were other men and women waiting in the others. Some wore nightclothes. One young man was slumped, as if he was not at all well. Other women looked very frightened.

They were strapped in. Karen told herself not to panic. She got the curious feeling that she had been through this before. Then the aliens came. There were two per person. The first woman was stripped. The humans were then herded into the examination room. The sick man had to be helped. Karen tried to resist but the aliens push her along anyway.

Karen was last into the examination room. There were four operating tables in the room. A shelf ran around the room with instruments on it. Karen was stripped and strapped to the table. Karen had braces on her teeth at the time and the aliens were fascinated by them. They asked her to take then out, but she refused. Next morning when she awoke, she found them on her belly.

The aliens also cut off a sample of her gum for analysis. This made her fighting mad. She asked how much more of her they were going to take and how long it took to study someone. Their answer was, it could take years.

The tall 'leader' alien asked her to look into his eyes. She did and felt that she was being overwhelmed, as if she was falling into them. Her will power was sapped. She could not look away or fight the alien in any way. It was as if she no longer had a mind of her own.

'Once you look into those eyes, you're gone. You're just gone,' she said.

Later, Karen got angry at the gynaecological procedures the alien was performing on her. She cursed the creature in her mind. The alien read her thoughts and reassured her that she would come to no harm. They performed something resembling a smear test on her, but she believed they were inserting an embryo into her, implanting it in her womb.

She found this idea repulsive and told the alien that he was not going to get away with this. He told her that she had no choice. It was part of a very important programme. But still Karen protested. She said that, back on Earth, she would have an abortion. The alien said that she would not, because she would not remember the embryo being implanted in her. She kept protesting that she would, but felt the alien's hypnotic suggestion that she would forget the incident overwhelming her mind. There was nothing to worry about, the alien said reassuringly, they had done this many times before.

Karen then remembered that she had indeed been through this procedure many times before and felt sick. The embryos, she knew, were hybrids; part human, part alien. She felt like an animal that was being experimented on. Sometimes the procedure was quick. This time it took longer because she resisted. When the alien was finished, he pulled the instruments out and patted her on the stomach. Karen was disgusted and told the alien to take his hands off her. Reluctantly, he did, but shook his head as if bewildered by her uncooperative attitude. In the morning, Karen woke back in her own bed. She found a mysterious gooey substance between her legs, took a shower and washed it off.

There are of course similarities in the events that occur on board abductors' craft as well – especially in reports of sexual and reproductive experimentation. During abductions, orgasms have reportedly been induced in both men and women, and sperm and ova have also been removed. Many female abductees claim to have been made pregnant by their captors, and then forced to carry the human–alien hybrids until the foetus is removed later, during another abduction.

Twenty-one-year-old musician Tracy Knapp recounted an experience of this nature. Knapp was driving from Los Angeles to Las Vegas with two girlfriends in 1978; she was abducted after seeing a light appear above the road and move down on top of her car. As it whizzed by them, the car started spinning. All three of them starting screaming and crying.

The car was being lifted up into the sky. Then Tracy remembered hands coming in through the window. When they touched her, she went limp. Then they lifted her out of the car. From then on, she lost sight of the other women. She did not see them again until they were back on the ground. When she returned home, she found that she was pregnant.

A few months later she was abducted again; she recalls lying down with her legs up. Two creatures were pressing on her and someone cutting her internally with long handled scissors that had very small blades. They doused the wound with a fluid that burned her. The procedure continued for a long time. The aliens seemed to be cutting threads. Then they pulled out their instruments and removed a sac with a tiny foetus in it.

'They removed something out of me. They removed a little baby or something,' she said.

This was put in a small, silver cylinder about three inches wide. The cylinder in turn was put into a drawer in the wall, along with numerous other live foetuses.

While some cases involve physical after-effects, most abductions involve some psychological disturbance. The most common is the sensation of missing time. Many abductees notice a time discrepancy between how long they perceived the encounter to have taken, and how long it had lasted in reality. These periods last maybe just a few minutes, or hours, or even, as in the case of famous abductee Travis Walton, days.

In October 1979, Luli Oswald and a companion were driving from Rio de Janeiro to Saquarema in Brazil when they saw a number of UFOs, which seemed to interfere with their car. Later, when they stopped at a service station, they found that two hours had mysteriously elapsed. Luli suffered some bad after-effects. Regressional hypnosis later revealed that they had both been abducted.

Another element regularly experienced after abductions is so-called 'screen memory'. These were first highlighted by celebrity abductee Whitley Strieber in his book *Communion*. A screen memory involves a disguised version of reality. These are used by aliens to prevent abductees remembering what actually happened. These disguises take the form of false memories or substitute images.

Debbie Jordan, the subject of UFOlogist Budd Hopkin's book *Intruders*, had a catalogue of screen memories as a result of her many abductions. On one occasion, she remembered leaving her house to visit the local store, but she was somehow 'steered' into a UFO which she saw in the store. The sales assistant in the store was a screen memory for the alien, she thought.

Professor Alvin Lawson believes that the abduction experience is a screen memory itself. It is a falsified account of the victim's birth trauma. All the elements are there, he points out. There are foetus-like creatures, obstetrics, medical equipment, even tools such as forceps. Some leave down long corridors; while some are helped out by the aliens or forcibly ejected, which he compares of a forceps birth. He compares some of the more traumatic ejections to Caesarean birth. Professor Lawson also points out the phenomenon of 'doorway amnesia'. Few abductees remember how they got into the alien craft, he says, just as no child could have any memory of how it got into the womb. The problem for Professor Lawson's thesis is that some abductees have a very clear idea of how they were conducted into the

UFO.

All the elements described above occur regularly in abductions and researchers have been able establish a consistent pattern to abductions. But what light does this shed on the abduction phenomenon itself?

For some time, it has been noted that the UFO phenomena often echo ancient legends and beliefs. Instead of being abducted by gods or goblins as people were in former time, we are now taken by UFOs and aliens as if this is somehow more in keeping with the technological world that surrounds us. Following this logic, the idea has been advanced that the abduction phenomenon taps into ancient fears and concerns of human beings, expressed in the terms of today's increasingly technology-driven society. A clear parallel here can be drawn between the idea of 'alien implants' and the modern-day fear expressed in films such as *Terminator* and *Westworld* that human beings can be turned into machines.

Researcher John Rimmer argues that the recognition of authoritative figures, the feeling of being controlled and the sexual experimentation that regularly feature in the accounts of abductees all spring directly from the culture in which we live. In his book *The Evidence For Alien Abductions*, he says: 'Abduction cases grow from our own culture and social background and reflect our fears and preoccupations, both on a personal level... [and] a social level...'

Rimmer believes that the abduction experience is psychological in origin. Far from being the result of extraterrestrial intervention, abduction, he says, is a symptom of personal crisis in the life of the individual concerned. However, for abductees it is all too real.

In 1977, Professor Alvin Lawson conducted a unique experiment. He got a number of people who had no reason to believe that they had ever been abducted to write a fictional account of an imaginary abduction. When these were compared to the accounts given by real abductees there was no discernible material difference between them. This led him to conclude that the accounts of the real abductees were also fiction. Others have pointed out that this conclusion is bogus. By 1977, the major elements of the abduction experience were already well publicised and Lawson himself had given the subjects some direction. Even Lawson himself conceded that there was one huge difference between the fictional accounts and the reports of real abductees – the amount of emotion expressed. The abductees truly believed that they had undergone the abduction experience.

Bud Hopkins, who has interviewed hundreds of abductees over more than twenty years of research, performed a similar experiment. He asked subjects to imagine an abduction that involved a medical check-up. Their descriptions were nothing like abductees' reports.

'What we got was ninety per cent their last medical check-up and ten per cent *Star Trek*,' he said.

Hopkins also points out that the medical examinations reported in alien abductions are not a projection of people's health fears. Alien examinations concentrate on the reproductive system and sperm and ova extraction. Surveys show that most people are more concerned with the working of their heart and stomach.

The UFOlogists

Stanton Friedman

Nuclear physicist Stanton Friedman is one of America's leading UFOlogists and has been researching the subject for over forty years, ever since a one-dollar book he bought in 1959 sparked his interest. He co-wrote *Crash at Corona* – the definitive study of the Roswell incident –with Don Berliner. In *TOP SECRET/MAJIC*, he investigated the Majestic-12 documents and US government efforts to conceal evidence of alien spacecraft from the American people. He has lectured around the world. He says that he silenced all but a handful of sceptics who refuse to believe that the Earth is being visited by intelligently controlled extraterrestrial spacecraft.

Curiously, Friedman has never seen a flying saucer himself. Instead he is a critical judge of other people's reports. Nevertheless, he says that seeing UFOs is much more common than most people imagine. At his lectures, he asks people whether they have seen a flying saucer. The hands go up reluctantly, he says, 'but they know I'm not going to laugh'. Typically, ten per cent of the audience admit to seeing a UFO. Then he asks how many of them reported it.

'I'm lucky if it's ten per cent of the ten per cent,' says Friedman. 'Sightings of flying saucers are common, reports are not.'

Friedman became interested in the world of UFOs by accident when he was twenty-four. He was ordering books by mail and needed to buy one more to avoid paying shipping charges. The one he chose was *The Report On Unidentified Flying Objects* by Air Force Captain Edward Ruppelt, former director of Project Blue Book. Friedman read the book and was intrigued. He figured that Ruppelt had to know what he was talking about. So he read fifteen more books on UFOs and spent a couple of years digging up as much information as he could.

His conclusion was that there was overwhelming evidence that Earth is being visited by intelligently controlled extraterrestrial spacecraft. However, he believed that, while some flying saucers are alien space ships, most are not. He believes that since July 1947, when two crashed saucers were recovered in New Mexico along with alien bodies, the government has back-engineered spacecraft of its own. Only a few insiders know that this has been done and he calls the cover-up the 'Cosmic Watergate'.

He began investigating the Roswell incident in 1978 after being put in touch with one of the witnesses. He has now interviewed over two hundred witnesses – of those some thirty were involved with the discovery and recovery of the alien craft and the subsequent cover-up of the two crashes. On top of that he has news cuttings from Chicago to the West Coast newspapers on 8 July 1947 and FBI memos that back the story. He also believes that these show that there was a second UFO crash in New Mexico in 1947, 150 miles to the west of Corona, the first crash site, in the plains around San Augustin. He has found eyewitnesses who saw 'a large metallic object' stuck in the ground there.

He is not convinced by Ray Santilli's alien autospy film though, seeing nothing in it that was associated with a crashed saucer at Roswell or anywhere else. He is also concerned that Santilli has refused to have the film verified. Nor has he released details of the cameraman so that they can be checked out. Friedman likes to look at the evidence.

Friedman is not flattered by being called a UFOlogist. He says that it is supposed to mean a person who has studied the science of UFOlogy, but there are no standards.

'Anybody who reads two books and carries a briefcase thinks he qualifies,' he says.

A big part of the problem of proving that flying saucers really exist is that people make wild claims that cannot be substantiated by the evidence. But he is more annoyed at the failure of the media to do their job. They have failed to dig into what Friedman considers to be the biggest story of the millennium. He believes that the media pay too much attention to what he calls the 'noisy negativists', none of whose arguments stand up under careful scrutiny, he says. 'They sound good, until you look at the evidence and they collapse of their own weight.'

He points out that there have been five large-scale scientific studies on UFOs, ten doctoral theses have been published and hundreds of papers have been produced by scientists. But most people, especially the debunkers, seem to be totally ignorant of this enormous amount of information. In his lectures he goes through the five scientific studies and asks how many people have read them. Less than two per cent of these people, who are plainly interested in the topic, are familiar with even one of the studies.

Friedman is also invited to speak to government bodies and gets a good response. But he finds that the question-and-answer sessions with the government people are a one-way street. They ask him a lot of questions but they do not reveal anything. He has spoken at Los Alamos National Laboratory and pulled a huge crowd. He has also given testimony to Congressional hearings in 1968 and at the United Nations in 1978.

Friedman finds being trained as a scientist is very useful in his work as a UFOlogist. It has meant that his approach is objective, painstaking, honest and scientific. Much of what he worked on as a scientist was classified. He wrote classified documents and had a security clearance. This gave him the opportunity to find out how security works and was good training for searching government archives for classified material later. Now he now lives in Canada and works on less sensitive science research projects such as pollution control and food irradiation.

He believes that the Majestic-12 documents prove President Harry Truman set up a super-secret group of top people from the fields of science, the military and intelligence to learn about alien spacecraft. He has spent over twelve years trawling through fifteen government archives, checking out whether these documents are real. Repeatedly, he has found confirmation of details in the documents that no one but insiders could have known. Friedman has even collected $1,000 from one critic who claimed one of the typefaces used in one of the MJ-12 documents was wrong.

'It was an absurd challenge, since I'd spent weeks searching through the government archives and he hadn't,' says Friedman. 'It also typifies the intellectual bankruptcy of the pseudo-science of anti-UFOlogy. I've yet to see a good anti MJ-12 argument.'

Friedman has had no chance to check out the data on alien abductions, but believes that every abduction story should be taken on its own merits. He has faith in abduction researchers because of his dealings with them and thinks that some people have been abducted.

According to Friedman's theory the government used five major arguments for withholding evidence from the public. The first is that it wants to figure out how flying saucers work because they make wonderful weapons delivery and defence systems. Secondly, it needs to do this before any potential enemy does. Thirdly, if this information was released, the younger generation would see humankind merely as 'earthlings' – which is what we are from an alien point of view. Friedman thinks this would be a great benefit. The problem with that is that there is no government on earth that wants its citizens to owe their primary allegiance to the planet rather than their country. Fourthly, there are certain religious fundamentalists who maintain humankind is the only intelligent life in the universe – that means that UFOs must be the work of the devil. These fundamentalists have huge political influence and their religions would be destroyed if they were proved wrong. Fifth, any announcement that the aliens were here would cause panic. Some people would believe that the aliens were here to slaughter us. Others would reason that the aliens were obviously more technologically advanced than us and would bring with them new energy sources, new transportation systems, new computers and new communication systems. So the stock market would crash and there would be untold economic consequences.

However, Friedman still believes that the public is ready to hear the truth about UFOs. There would, of course, be some people who did not want to know – just as there are five per cent of the American public who do not believe that man has been to the moon. But the evidence about UFOs could be presented honestly and openly.

'I certainly don't think we should put technical data about flying saucers out on the table,' he says. 'But our planet is being visited by intelligent aliens. It's time we grew up.'

Jaques Vallee

Steven Spielberg's movie *Close Encounters of the Third Kind* made Jacques Vallee the most famous UFOlogist in the world. The François Truffaut character is based on the French researcher. Although he became a computer scientist for the Department of Defense, Vallee began his career as an astrophysicist. As a young man, it was curiosity that led him to study astronomy, but that same curiosity led him on into the world of UFOs. He does not find studying anomalous phenomena unscientific, pointing out that Nobel prize winner Niels Bohr said that all science starts with an anomaly.

He was working at the Paris Observatory when he first got interest in UFOs. They had observed a number of 'unidentified satellites'. However, when the scientists there were ordered to destroy the data concerning these 'anomalies' instead of sending it to their colleagues for further study, he rebelled.

This was during the early 1960s when the idea that UFOs were connected to alien intervention was widespread. Back then, he found that the 'extraterrestrial hypothesis' seemed to match witnesses' accounts. But since then, thousands more cases have been reported and statistical models could be used to analyse them. This has forced Vallee to take another, more critical look at the extraterrestrial hypothesis.

Vallee already had a passion for religious history, myths, occultism and parapsychology and, around 1968, he realised that many aspects of the UFO phenomenon were also present in the folklore of every culture. By 1975 he got the idea of combining these disciplines by considering the UFO phenomenon, not as simply a manifestation of extraterrestrial visitors, but as a control system that had been in existence since the beginning of humankind. He points out that UFO sightings did not start with Kenneth Arnold in 1947. Elements of the phenomena existed before. He believes that the wheels of Ezekiel, cherubim and burning bushes seen in Biblical times, the flying goblins in luminous chariots of the Middle Ages, the phantom airships of the nineteenth century, the 'ghost rockets' of 1946 and the extraterrestrial spacecraft seen today are all essentially the same phenomenon.

As we learn more about the history and geographical distribution of the phenomenon, the standard extraterrestrial hypothesis leads to glaring contradictions, Vallee says. He believes that objects and beings connected to the UFO phenomenon are symbolic, or even theatrical, manifestations, rather than a systematic alien exploration where abductions are conducted for the purposes of so-called 'biological studies', as other UFOlogists suggest.

'We are also looking at some form of non-human consciousness,' he says. 'However, one must be wary of concluding that we are dealing with an "extraterrestrial race".'

Vallee aims to shatter the assumption that 'UFO' means 'extraterrestrial spacecraft'. He believes that behind these enigmatic luminous phenomena is a form of intelligence capable of manipulating space-time and influencing human evolution. In his best-selling book *Confrontations*, published in 1990, he analysed over a hundred UFO encounters using scientific methods, and concludes that the aliens visiting us come from another dimension.

Vallee is the champion of a bold new speculative physics. He believes that objects capable of gradually appearing and disappearing on the spot are modifying space-time topology. This validates the multidimensional models of the universe that theoretical physicists have been working on in recent years.

But he does not totally reject the extraterrestrial hypothesis, just the hard-nosed American approach to it. He believes that we share our existence with other forms of consciousness that influence the topology of our environment and affect the human mind psychically. Vallee has been accused of contradicting himself, because at times he emphasises the physical and material aspects of UFOs, while at others stressing the psychic and paranormal side. But this contradiction is in the data, he says.

Vallee is a believer in alien abduction, but believes that hypnotising abductees as practised in America is unethical, unscientific and perhaps even dangerous. He has investigated over seventy abduction cases. From his interviews with witnesses he has no doubt that the large majority of abductees have had a close encounter with an object emitting electromagnetic radiation, pulsed at hyper-frequencies. The effects on the human brain of these are unknown, so hypnotising the victims could put them at risk. He points out that UFO encounters are dangerous enough to humans as it is, with large amounts of energy confined to a restricted space.

One of the abduction cases Vallee studied was that of Franck Fontaine, who was abducted on 26 November 1979 from the Parisian suburb of Cergy-Pontoise after seeing a bright light in the sky. Vallee was particularly interested in the case because he was born in Pontoise and went to the same school as Fontaine. Although Fontaine admitted, two years later, that the abduction was a hoax, Vallee does not believe the explanations that have been given. They do not correspond to his knowledge of the area or the psychological state of the witnesses.

'I don't believe it was a UFO, but I do think that Franck was actually abducted,' he says. 'Someone is hiding something.'

The dozen or so 'implants' he has examined have not been mysterious in nature. Analysis showed that many of them were the tips of rusty needles, fragments of insects or other natural material embedded in the flesh. However, Vallee was the first to draw attention to the subject of animal mutilations over twenty years ago in his book *La Grande Manipulation* ('The Great Manipulation'), but he has not published research because he was unable to prove the link between the mutilations and the UFO phenomenon. He does believe that the link exists, though.

Vallee finds the USAF's latest explanation of the Roswell incident – that it was the crash of a balloon carrying a basket full of mannequins – laughable.

'The most recent report from the Air Force is even more absurd than all the other "explanations" given previously,' he says. 'The fact that an extremely strange object came down near Roswell and that the military made every effort to discourage research into the incident and continues to do so is beyond doubt. However, this doesn't mean that the object in question was a UFO.'

For Vallee, the jury is still out on the Roswell incident. He believes that the idea of a crash is only plausible if you believe it to be a deliberate demonstration on the part of an external intelligence. In the meantime he is investigating nineteen other different crash cases.

Vallee believes that every country's armed forces uses the UFO phenomenon to cover up operations involving advanced or illegal weapons. This started in the USSR as early as 1967, when the KGB spread rumours about UFOs in a region where the inhabitants had seen rockets being launched that were carrying satellites in violation of international agreements. UFO rumours also cloak remotely controlled rigid airships that the military use to gather electromagnetic data. An American soldier he knows approached one of these craft standing in a clearing in Germany during manoeuvres before the Gulf War and he has read US patent applications describing them.

Generally Vallee's scientific colleagues are open-minded about UFOs. They have no time for grandiose conspiracy theories, but they do admit the existence of a 'non-standard phenomenon'. During his forty years of UFO investigations, he has discovered that the UFO phenomenon is considerably more complex than he used to think. It cannot be explained simply by an extrapolation of current human technology.

'We are faced with a phenomenon that underlies the whole of human history, manipulates the real world and seems to obey laws that bear no relationship to those we hitherto imagined,' he says. 'I believe we're entering a particularly exciting period in the phenomenon's history, since we now have the opportunity of re-examining all the various hypotheses.'

More recently, Vallee has published a memoir of his years in

UFOlogy called *Science Interdite* ('Forbidden Science'). This also examines the validity of the US Army's secret 'Memorandum Pentacle'.

Bob Lazar

Soft-spoken physicist Bob Lazar is one of the most controversial figures in UFOlogy. A man with a strong scientific background, he has been involved in the 'back-engineering' of alien spacecraft at the notorious Area 51 in the Nevada desert.

In 1982 he was a member of a scientific team at the US military's Groom Dry Lake installation. There he worked on a top-secret project to unravel the technology used by alien spacecraft that had been recovered from various crashes. Nine disc-shaped craft were held under armed guard in an underground section of the base known as 'S4'. The job of Lazar's team was to find out what made these flying saucers tick and whether their components could be replicated with materials found on Earth.

Many people have poured scorn on Lazar's story since it was first aired in a TV interview in 1989. As a child he was eccentric. His resumé includes bankruptcy and an association with a Las Vegas brothel. Lazar is easily discredited. Officials at Area 51 deny that anyone named Robert Lazar ever worked there – just as they once denied that Area 51 itself existed. But a salary statement issued by the United States Department of Naval Intelligence proves that Lazar did work in Area 51 for the five months as he claimed.

And when it comes to engineering, it is plain that Lazar knows what he is talking about. He has an impressive list of technical qualifications and is a scientist with a pedigree. In the early 1980s he was employed on several projects at the Los Alamos National Laboratory, New Mexico, where the first atomic bomb was developed. At Los Alamos he conducted experiments with proton-scattering equipment and worked with high-energy particle accelerators. The work he did there was on the cutting edge of the new physics and could open the way to faster-than-light travel. As a prominent member of the town's scientific community, he earned himself an appearance on the front page of the *Los Alamos Monitor* when he installed a jet engine in a Honda CRX.

Despite the efforts made to paint him as slightly cracked, Lazar's account of what went on in Area 51 is lucid and concise, clearly not the ramblings of a disturbed mind. With his scientific background, his observations have a solid foundation. His specific task at Area 51 was to investigate the propulsion system of a small flying saucer dubbed 'the sports model', which was kept in one of the S4 hangars built into the side of a mountain. He witnessed a brief, low altitude test flight of the disc.

The sports model was some forty feet in diameter and fifteen feet high. It had three levels. The top level was an observation deck nine feet across, with portholes. Below that were the control consoles and seats, which were too small and too near the floor for adult humans to use comfortably. The main cabin had a headroom of just six feet. Also in the central level was an antimatter reactor and, located directly below it on the lower level, were the three 'gravity amplifiers', connected to the reactor by wave guides. He worked on this propulsion system both in situ in the craft and on the bench in the lab.

The power source for the sports model and the eight other discs in S4 was an 'antimatter reactor', Lazar says. These reactors were fuelled by an orange-coloured, super-heavy material called 'Element 115'. This mysterious element was the source of the 'Gravity A' wave as yet undiscovered by terrestrial science. It also provided the antimatter radiation required to power the saucer in interstellar flight.

The flying saucers in S4 have two modes of travel. For local travel, near the surface of a planet, they use their gravity generators to balance the planet's gravitational field and ride a Gravity A wave like a cork on the ocean. During interstellar travel, covering distances that would take aeons even travelling at close to the speed of light, the Gravity A wave from the nucleus of Element 115 is amplified. This bends space and time in the same way it is bent in the intense gravitational field generated by a black hole. As the saucer travels through space, time is 'bent' around the craft. By distorting space and time in this manner, the disc can travel across vast expanses of space at incredible speeds. This is the same principle used by the *USS Enterprise*'s 'warp drive' in *Star Trek*.

Terrestrial rockets push the craft towards their destination by blasting jets of hot gas in the opposite direct, while alien craft 'pull' the destination towards them. Lazar explains how this works with the analogy of a rubber sheet with a stone, representing the spacecraft, on it. To go to any particular destination, you pinch the rubber sheet at that point and pull it towards the stone. Then, when you let got, the rubber sheet springs back, pulling the stone – or spacecraft with it.

'In a spacecraft that can exert a tremendous gravitational field by itself,' he says, 'you could sit in any particular place, turn on the gravity generator, and actually warp space and time and "fold" it. By shutting that off, you'd click back and you'd be at a tremendous distance from where you started.'

Although this type of propulsion appears to be the stuff of science fiction, many scientists believe that faster-than-light travel may be possible. Cambridge University's Lucasian professor of mathematics Stephen Hawking has suggested that interstellar travel might be achievable via natural or manmade 'worm-holes' in the fabric of space-time. Understanding how this works in practice is a bit more taxing, of course.

Inside the flying saucers' antimatter reactor, Lazar says, Element 115 is transmuted into another esoteric material called 'Element 116'. This is highly unstable and decays, releasing antimatter. The antimatter then reacts with matter inside the reactor in a total annihilation reaction, where one hundred per cent of the matter–antimatter is converted into energy. This energy is used to amplify the Gravity A wave given off the Element 115 and the heat generated by reaction is converted to electricity via a solid state thermo-electric generator.

The alien craft were saucer-shaped to diffuse the electrical charges generated by the antimatter reactor. In flight, Lazar says, the bottom of the alien craft glowed blue and began to hiss like a high voltage charge does on a sphere.

'It's my impression that the reason that they're round and have no sharp edges is to contain the high voltage,' says Lazar. 'If you've seen a high voltage system's insulators, things are round or else you get a corona discharge.'

The craft's high voltage makes them hiss when they take off. Otherwise they are silent. And the hissing stops when they have climbed to twenty or thirty feet. 'There are just too many things that Lazar knew about the discs that can't be explained in any other way,' said George Knapp, the TV journalist who first interviewed him.

Lazar says that, at one time, there were Soviet scientists and mathematicians working at Area 51, alongside the Americans there. He did not know whether they were actually allowed to work on the alien craft, but believes that they were employed on the scientific and mathematical theory that underpinned his group's practical work.

They were kicked out after a major breakthrough had been made in understanding how the discs and their propulsion systems worked. They were none too happy about this. Lazar says that in the aftermath of their exclusion, paranoia at the base soared. Employees were issued with firearms, in case the Soviets tried to kidnap them.

During his time at Area 51, Lazar had to read a document the size of a telephone directory, which revealed that the top-secret base at Groom Lake was not the only US government facility back-engineering ET technology. The US government's admission that other secret bases do exist lent weight to Lazar's story. However, what goes on in them is still beyond top secret. Since Lazar's Area 51 security clearance was mysteriously revoked at the end of the 1980s, he has been subjected of intense harassment. His house and car have been broken into and he has been shot at by unseen snipers in an attempt to discourage him from divulging the secrets of S4.

Edgar Fouche

Like Bob Lazar, Edgar Fouche worked at Area 51 and has since spent his time telling the world about what is going on there. Fouche is a true insider who spent twenty-eight years with the US Air Force and

Department of Defense. During that time, he was stationed at top-secret sites, including the nuclear test site in Nevada, the Nellis Test Range and the Groom Lake Air Base, home of Area 51. Fouche's work in intelligence, electronics, communications and a number of black programmes has given him inside information on some of America's most classified technological developments, including the super-secret SR-71 and SR-75 spy planes and the TR-3B, which many people believe is sometimes mistake for the 'Flying Triangle'.

However, during the 1980s when President Reagan was in power, he became completely disenchanted with the defence industry. It was full of fraud and abuse of power and he decided that he could not be associated with it anymore. He was suffering serious medical problems at the time and did not think he was going to live much longer. So he decided to speak up.

In this, he was helped by five friends who served with him in Vietnam. One was a former SR-71 spy plane pilot. Two of them went on to work for the National Security Agency. A fourth friend's father had worked for the NSA for twenty years and the fifth worked for the Department of Defense. He also gleaned information about the TR-3B by talking to pilots.

His buddy who was the SR-71 pilot told him that once, when he was flying back across the South China Sea, he saw a shadow fall across the cockpit. The aircraft started to nose down and the avionics went crazy. When he looked up to find out what was happening, he saw a UFO that was so big it completely blocked out the sun. It was oval and surrounded by a shimmering energy field, and he reckoned that it was three hundred feet across.

What really amazed Fouche was that all the pilots he spoke to reported encounters with UFOs. Some had seen circular UFOs, others had encountered plasma balls that seemed to dance around the craft. These reports were all the more impressive because the SR-71 can fly at over 60,000 feet. This gives it enormous visibility. If something is up there, an SR-71 is going to see it.

Fouche's contacts told him that the development of the TR-3B started in 1982 as part of a top-secret project named 'Aurora', whose aim was to build and test advanced aerospace vehicles. He discovered that around 35 per cent of the US government's 'Star Wars' budget had been siphoned off to finance it. The TR-3B is a triangular nuclear-powered aerospace platform and is undoubtedly the most exotic aerospace programme in existence. Its designation 'TR' stands for tactical reconnaissance. This means the craft is designed to get to the target and stay there long enough pick up information on the enemy's deployment and send it back. The advantage of being powered by a nuclear reactor is that it can stay aloft for a long time without refuelling.

Its advanced propulsion system also allows it to hover silently for long periods. The circular crew compartment is located at the centre of TR-3B's triangular airframe. It is surrounded by a plasma-filled accelerator ring, called the Magnetic Field Disrupter, which generates a magnetic vortex and neutralises the pull of gravity. The MFD does not actually power the craft; what it does is effectively reduce its mass. Propulsion is achieved by three multi-mode gas-propelled thrusters mounted on each corner of the triangle. But MFD makes the aircraft incredibly light. It can fly at Mach 9 speeds vertically and horizontally, and can outmanoeuvre anything except UFOs.

One of Fouche's sources who worked on the TR-3B told him that they were working on the possibility of developing the MFD technology so that it not only reduces mass but also creates a force that repels gravity. This would give the TR-3B a propulsion system that would allow it to routinely fly to the Moon or Mars. This anti-gravity system is how UFOs work and Fouche is convinced that the TR-3B has been developed through the back-engineering of alien technology.

Fouche believes that the black triangles tracked by the Belgian Air Force in the late 1980s and early 1990s were TR-3Bs. He has a simple rule: if it is triangular it is terrestrial, if it is circular or tubular it is extraterrestrial. He says that the US government could easily get round treaty agreements that prohibit testing advanced aircraft over Europe. These agreements, he points out, say that they cannot fly an aircraft over a friendly country without that country being informed. It would be easy enough to inform the Belgian government on the sly. After all, the US is not supposed to have nuclear weapons in the UK or Japan, but they do.

Groom Lake's six-mile-long runway is the longest in the world. Fouche says that it was built to accommodate the CIA's latest super-hi-tech spy plane, the 'Penetrator' or SR-75; 'SR' stands for strategic reconnaissance. It can exceed Mach 7 with speeds of over 28,000 miles an hour at an altitude of 40,000 feet and can reach any point on the Earth within three hours. This plane is so secret that the US government does not even admit to its existence. After the SR-71 Blackbird was retired in 1990, the US Air Force said that it would not be replaced because satellites provided all the military's high-level reconnaissance needs. But Fouche's sources say that the SR-75 has been designed to service spy satellites in orbit. It acts as a 'mothership' and launches unmanned SR-74, or Scramp, craft. Operated by remote control, these can place satellites in space, reaching altitudes of 95 miles and speeds of 6,250 miles an hour, or Mach 15.

Fouche was assigned to Groom Lake in 1979 because he was one of the few people who had the necessary top-secret clearance. He was certified to work with particular equipment which, even years after the event, he was not prepared to discuss. He had been working at Nellis Air Force Base at the time and was told that he was being temporarily reassigned, but was given no idea of where he was going to be sent. Some thirty technicians were herded onto a blue bus with blacked-out windows. There were two guards on board, armed with M16 rifles. They told the passengers not to speak unless spoken to. This is how Fouche ended up at Groom Lake.

The conditions were extremely oppressive. He was issued with heavy glasses, like welders' goggles. These had thick lenses that blocked peripheral vision and prevented the wearer seeing further than thirty metres ahead. Everywhere he went, he was escorted by a soldier carrying an M16 who would never talk to him. He could not even go to the lavatory alone.

According to Fouche, the military used sinister mind-control techniques on employees. One of his five collaborators named Sal was a victim of this. A former NSA electronic intelligence expert, he had helped develop Magnetic Field Disruption. After two-years at a top-secret NSA facility, he came down with what he thought was the flu. He went to see the facility's doctor, who gave him some medication and told him to go home and rest. The next day, Sal had no memory of where he worked or who he worked for. When his brother contacted the NSA, he was told that Sal's contract had been terminated. Sal's memory has not returned and the only evidence he has that he worked at the NSA facility at all is a few scribbled notes and his pay slips.

Security at Area 51 was so tight that a key card and a code were needed for every door. Fouche is very sceptical about people who claim to have been at Groom Lake and accidentally stumbled into a hangar with a UFO inside. His twenty-eight years with the Department of Defense and the US Air Force taught him that anything that was top-secret was protected by numerous levels of security.

However, in Area 51 there is a facility on the Papoose Lake site called the Defense Advanced Research Center, which extends for ten storeys underground. It was built in the early 1980s with Strategic Defense Initiative money. The DARC is the centre for what is officially designated 'Foreign Artefacts' – this means alien artefacts. Crashed and recovered alien technology is stored there. The DARC is where all the analysis of 'extraterrestrial biological entities' – alien creatures – and back-engineering takes place.

Fouche says that the reason the US government cannot come clean about what they are up to at Area 51 is because, since the birth of the UFO phenomenon in 1947, it has consistently violated people's constitutional rights. The government considers anything that it cannot control a threat, he says. It cannot control the alien agenda, so it tries to control any information surrounding it. People who find out too much about UFOs or aliens either disappear or have been killed, he says. The government would be held accountable if the facts got out and it could not handle that.

David Adair

Another witness to what is going on at Area 51 is space scientist David Adair. He became involved in the world of UFOs through his lifelong passion for science and rocketry.

Adair was a child prodigy. He built his first rocket at the age of eleven. This was no fourth-of-July firework. He fashioned it from sophisticated alloys, using tools and fuels from his father's machine shop.

Then, in 1968, he set out to build a new type of rocket which used powerful electromagnetic fields to contain and harness the thermonuclear energy from a fusion reaction. Although this sounds exotic, it was not his original idea. He got the plans from the long-range planning division of NASA's Marshall Space Flight Center in Huntsville, Alabama. They had come up with the theoretical designs for fifty different types of engine. Only two of them used conventional liquid fuel or solid propellants, so fusion was the obvious the way to go. The one that Adair decided to build was a remarkable design. At the time he wondered why NASA had never made it themselves. Later he realised that they probably chose not to develop it for political reasons. If you developed an efficient fusion-based propulsion system, oil and gas would be redundant. Nevertheless the fourteen-year-old Adair saw the design's potential and, through Republican Congressman John Ashbrook, he got a $1-million grant to build it.

But the grant came with strings attached. The Department of Defense were involved. He was prohibited from telling anyone about what he was building. And for Adair the outside world ceased to exist as he worked on the rocket day and night for the next three years. In 1971, when Adair was seventeen, the rocket was ready to be tested. General Curtis LeMay, the project manager, decided that the rocket was too powerful to be tested outside a secure military facility, so he scheduled a test at White Sands Missile Range in New Mexico.

When Adair was at White Sands preparing for the test, a black DC-

9 arrived. It was carrying Dr Arthur Rudolph, one of the designers of the Saturn-5 moon rocket. Originally Rudolph had worked on the Nazi German V-2 programme, but after the war he had been taken to America. Adair told Rudolph that, proportionately, his rocket was a thousand times more powerful than the Saturn-5, and Rudolph was furious.

When Adair was programming his rocket's guidance system, his military bosses gave him a precise location for the landing. The coordinates they gave him specified a place four hundred miles away in an area called Groom Lake in Nevada. This puzzled Adair as all the maps showed there was an empty dry lakebed.

After the rocket was launched successfully, Adair was told to get on board the DC-9. They flew him to Groom Lake and, as they came in to land, he could see the huge runways and a huge base that had not appeared on the map. This, he was informed, was Area 51.

When he arrived at Groom Lake, Adair thought he was there to collect his rocket. But he was bundled onto an electric golf cart and driven over to three large hangars. As he got close to the buildings, he could see that they were new, but they had been painted to look much older. The middle hangar was the area of two football fields. Once he was inside, warning lights began flashing, guard rails sprang up and an area of the floor about seven hundred square foot started to descend. Adair realised they were on a huge lift. It went down through solid rock and, when it stopped, Adair found himself the biggest underground space he had ever seen. It contained a lot of aircraft. Most of them were covered up, but he recognised one as the XB-70, an experimental aircraft. It was huge. But he also noticed a number of craft that were a strange teardrop shape with their surfaces perfectly smooth in all directions. The most peculiar thing about them was that they did not have any of the intake or exhaust ports that are needed by jet engines. In fact, they had no visible means of propulsion, yet they were surrounded by support equipment and looked quite capable of flying. Looking back, he now thinks that they used some kind of electromagnetic or flux-field propulsion.

Still in the golf cart, he was driven over to a big set of doors. The driver jumped out and put his hand on a panel. It flashed and the doors opened. We know these things now as optical hand-print scanners, but in 1971 they were the stuff of science fiction. Inside the air was cold and the lighting was strange. There was plenty of light, but nothing seemed to cast a shadow. He was then shown a huge engine that was about the size of a bus. It looked like two octopuses linked together by their tentacles. When Adair examined it, he realised it was some kind of giant version of the motor in his rocket.

His companions explained that this engine used a fusion reaction similar the one he had designed and they wanted his opinion on the firing mechanism. The whole situation struck Adair as bizarre. Why didn't they ask the people who built it, he enquired. He was told they were on leave. So Adair asked to look at their design notes. This seemed to annoy the people who had brought him there.

'Look son, do you want to help your country or not?' they said.

Adair believes that the engine was extraterrestrial in origin. Although it was huge, he could not see a single bolt, rivet or screw holding it together. The surface was perfectly smooth and, although the room was cold, it felt warm to the touch. Whenever he touched the surface, bluish white waves swirled out from his hands and disappeared into the material. They would stop each time he moved his hand away. He climbed up on top of the engine and looked inside. He saw a large container holding bundles of tubes. These were filled with some kind of liquid. Adair's overall impression was that it was organic – part mechanical, part biological. He realised it had been made using non-terrestrial techniques and materials.

He shrugged his shoulders and told his companions that he had no idea how the thing worked. The manufacturing techniques used were very different from anything he had ever seen before. He reasoned that it could not have been built by American engineers or by the Soviets. As it dawned on him that it must have been built using extraterrestrial technology, he got angry. Flying saucers had landed and the government were keeping it a secret. When Adair expressed his outrage at this, his companions shouted at him to get away from the device.

Adair does not think that the engine was working too well, though they have had three decades to work on it since then and he hopes they have been successful. He could certainly see the potential. Adair's own rocket was puny by comparison but it channelled enormous amounts of energy out of the back of the rocket for propulsion. He believes that the alien engine could have managed to contain all the incredible energy generated by the fusion reaction inside the propulsion system, producing a 'field effect' outside the craft. This would create a huge 'gravitation well' which would break through the fabric of space-time. Space would be folded back on itself, allowing the craft to travel vast distances in an instant, without exceeding the speed of light.

However, he is still angry that this device and other exotic craft are in government hands and all their amazing technology is hidden from the rest of the world. Meanwhile people at NASA are struggling to send small spacecraft to Mars. The fact that the US government are withholding knowledge of their contact with other civilisations he also finds incredible.

'These are ET civilisations we could learn so much from,' Adair says. 'When I think of all the ways that we could advance with this knowledge of ET contact, it makes me sick that this information is hidden.'

Since his visit to Area 51 in 1971, Adair has worked as a technology transfer consultant, redesigning space-programme technology for commercial applications. He has an office in Ventura, California. But he has not forgotten what he saw.

On 9 April 1997, Adair testified to a Congressional hearing in Washington, D.C. as part of the campaign for full UFO disclosure. The hearings were organised by the Center for the Study of Extraterrestrial Intelligence and gave key witnesses, including military personnel and pilots, the opportunity to lobby the US government. David Adair was under oath when he told the Congressional panel what he had seen in Area 51 and, unexpectedly, the Congressmen immediately got confirmation that he was telling the truth.

During his testimony, Adair mentioned that the device he had seen was covering in strange markings. He remembered what they looked like and drew them for the panel. Also giving testimony was an attorney from North Carolina named Steven Lovekin, who had top-secret clearance when he worked as a cryptologist at the Pentagon in the 1950s. As a military aide, he had given regular briefings to President Eisenhower on UFO activity. In that capacity, he had been shown a piece of metal that he was told came from a downed flying saucer. It was covered in strange markings – the same markings Adair had seen in Area 51.

Wendelle Stevens

Wendelle Stevens' involvement with UFOs began in 1947 when he was assigned to the Air Technical Intelligence Center at Wright Field in Dayton, Ohio, home to the USAF's various in-house UFO study programmes, Sign, Grudge and Blue Book. That year, Stevens was sent from Ohio to Alaska to supervise a squadron of B-29 bombers that were being used to map the Arctic. However, he discovered there was a hidden agenda behind their polar mission. The B-29s were equipped with cutting-edge electronic detection technology and cameras to detect and film 'foo fighters', as UFOs were then known.

Stevens's security clearance was not high enough to allow him to see the footage the B-29s had shot before it was sent to Washington, but the pilots told him of their UFO encounters. Many of his pilots saw UFOs soar rapidly into the sky and fly off as the B-29s approached. In most cases, they caused electromagnetic disturbances to the plane's instrumentation, often affecting the engines. On one occasion a UFO approached a B-29 head on. Then, before they collided, it slammed into reverse, manoeuvred itself around next to the wing and stayed there.

Astounded by these revelations, Stevens asked his superiors if he could pursue an investigation into the UFO phenomenon. He was told he could do so only outside of official military channels. So, in 1963, after twenty-three years' active service, he retired and began a new career as a UFO researcher.

He began collecting newspaper clippings of UFOs from all over the world. Where photographs had been printed, he would write to the people who had taken them and ask for a copy. Now he boasts the world's largest collection of UFO photographs – over three thousand images in all – along with a vast library of UFO film and videos.

To establish the authenticity of the photographs, he visits the people who took them and investigates their encounter. He also examines their camera equipment and takes his own photographs from the same spot, so that he can compare relative scale and distances. After these preliminary checks, he subjects the photograph to a series of analytical procedures. Today he uses computer techniques. It was easier in the old days, he says, when all a photographic expert had to do was to make a large-scale blow-up and examine it with a magnifying glass.

Stevens is one of the few UFOlogists who had has made a career of studying contactees. In 1976, he was the first researcher to investigate the claims of Swiss contactee Eduard 'Billy' Meier, who was in telepathic contact with aliens and photographed their spaceships coming into land. At Stevens' behest, Meier submitted his evidence for analysis to scientists at McDonnell Douglas, IBM and NASA's Jet Propulsion Laboratory. Their results were inconclusive. However, computer analysis of one of Meier's pictures reveals a model next to a fake tree and models of flying saucers were found in Meier's home. Nonetheless, Stevens believes Meier is genuine.

Stevens decided to specialise in contactees because they presented a unique opportunity to learn about extraterrestrials and their possible agendas. If possible, he sets up a two-way dialogue, asking contactees to pose questions to the extraterrestrials for him next time they meet. Sometimes he gets an answer.

One of the most important contactee cases he investigated was that of Bill Herrmann, who lived in Charleston, South Carolina, near the Air Force base there. He and his wife repeatedly saw a UFO, which flew in a darting motion with sharp, angular turns, unlike the smooth turns of a plane. One night in 1977, when he was try to get a closer look at it through binoculars, Herrmann was abducted. He was enveloped in a beam of blue light, which drew him up inside the UFO. The extraterrestrials he encountered inside the craft were friendly. They came from one of the twin stars in the Reticulum system. When he asked them questions, he would hear their replies in English inside his head. They told him that the darting movements of their craft were made to avoid any radar lock-on. Radar-guided weapons had previously been responsible for the crashes of three of their ships. They also told Herrmann that they wanted their downed ships back and were prepared to negotiate, but the US government was too hostile to deal with. After this first abduction experience, Herrmann was invited back onto the craft another five times.

When Stevens began investigating the Herrmann case, he discovered that the Reticulans were sending Herrmann vast amounts of information when he was in a trance-like state. He transcribed the transmission in automatic writing. The result was numerous pages of text in a totally unknown alphabet, along with schematic diagrams of their propulsion system. The complex technical information he was provided with was way beyond current human scientific knowledge and Herrmann could never have acquired it from any terrestrial source.

From his work with contactees, Stevens has discovered that there are many different kinds of extraterrestrials. They come from different places and have different languages, morphologies, technologies and agendas. The largest group are the various humanoid species who often tell contactees that they come from the Pleiades star system. The next largest group are the well-known 'Greys', which again comprise a number of different races.

Stevens has also carried out research on Area 51 and tracked down Derek Hennesy, a former security guard who worked on level two of S4, the famous underground complex where Lazar had worked on alien propulsion systems. During his time there, Hennesy saw nine bays for flying saucer bays on level one. There were a further seven bays on level two with three identical alien craft in the first three bays.

Hennesy also saw large tubes that contained the preserved bodies of dead Greys. After Stevens first interviewed Hennesy, Hennesy disappeared for a while. When he re-emerged he claimed to have no knowledge of what he had previously seen or said.

However, Stevens had another friend who works as an engineer at Area 51 and says it is engaged in bridging the gap between alien technology and our own. He has built simulators to train human pilots to fly flying saucers. There are two extraterrestrials at Area 51 who can fly alien craft. They have been trying to train humans to do this, but not very successfully. So far they are limited to flights within the atmosphere. They have not yet mastered flight in deep space, but they can hover using some kind of gravity propulsion.

Stevens thinks that there is little chance that the curtain of official secrecy surrounding UFOs will be lifted in the near future. The government have kept what they know a secret for fifty years and he expects them to do so for another fifty. Governments have far too much to lose from any official disclosure, he reckons. The impact on society would be incalculable. The only way the world's governments would admit to the reality of alien visitations is if a group of extraterrestrials makes its presence visible on a massive scale, he says. Stevens believes that there are signs that this may be about to occur in Mexico, where there was an explosion in the number of sightings in the 1990s.

Peter Gersten

For twenty years, New York criminal defence attorney Peter Gersten specialised in murder and drug cases. But then, in 1977, as the lawyer for the UFO group Ground Saucer Watch, he took the CIA to court and won. It was a historic victory for UFOlogy.

The suit was filed under the Freedom of Information Act. Ground Saucer Watch were trying to force the CIA to release just five UFO-related documents the agency had in its possession. But Gersten expanded the case. Under the FOIA it was as easy to create a lawsuit to get the CIA to release all the UFO document it had as it was to get just five. As a result, in 1979, the CIA was forced to release nine hundred pages of UFO-related documents – the first time that any US intelligence agency had ever released previously classified UFO information to the public. A further fifty-seven documents were withheld. But the case showed beyond any doubt that the CIA, which had previously denied any involvement in UFOs, had been studying them for years.

The documents not only confirmed the reality of UFOs and gave detailed descriptions of them, they also gave researchers access to numerous reports from credible witnesses – scientists, military personnel and law enforcement officers. Some of the documents released originated from other agencies. This confirmed that every other US agency had also been studying the UFO phenomenon and that the military had been involved in UFO research even before 1947.

Bolstered by this success, Gersten formed Citizens Against UFO Secrecy (CAUS), an organisation dedicated to breaking down the wall of secrecy surrounding the UFO phenomenon. Its aim is to force the government to come clean on what it knows about contact with extraterrestrial intelligence, and it believes that the public has the absolute and unconditional right to know.

In the early 1980s, Gersten continued his legal assault on the US intelligence community, taking the National Security Agency to court after the NSA refused an FOIA request for UFO-related documents that CAUS knew they had in their possession. In court, the judge asked the NSA's attorney how many documents had surfaced when they had processed the CAUS's FOIA request. He was told that it was classified information. Gersten told the judge that the CIA had told him that the NSA had at least eighteen documents. The judge then insisted that the NSA come up with a figure. The agency finally admitted that there were 135. But that was as far as it went. The NSA invoked the National Security Exemption, one of twelve exemption clauses built into the FOIA. To argue their exemption, the NSA used a twenty-one-page affidavit that was itself classified, and the case was dismissed.

Although Gersten was unsuccessful in obtaining the UFO

documents, he did succeed in getting the NSA to admit that they held them. He took the appeal to the Supreme Court and, when it was dismissed, it made headline news. Even though he did not get the documents, he had succeeded in drawing great attention to the issue of UFO secrecy and highlighted the US Supreme Court's role in this cover-up.

In further court actions, Gersten succeed in forcing the release of a heavily censored version of the NSA exemption affidavit and, in due course, most of the documents they withheld have been released.

Gersten is not optimistic about the efforts of various organisations – such as Dr Steven Greer's Center for the Study Of Extraterrestrial Intelligence – to get US Congress to hold open hearings on the subject of UFOs. He says that the idea of open hearings is inherently ridiculous because any discussion of UFOs involves a discussion of advanced technology. This is an area that the military keeps secret by invoking national security, while the corporations protect their developments by using patents. The elected officials of Congress are always up for re-election – every two years for Representatives and six years for Senators. They need money and are always vulnerable to the demands of special interests.

Getting Congress to grant immunity to people who may have to break secrecy oaths to testify would not help. Gersten points out the problems: 'Let's say you have a general who wants to testify in a Congressional hearing even though he is sworn to secrecy. He will naturally expect Congress to grant him immunity. However, the military will then question Congress's right to grant immunity and they would then have to fight it out in the courts, which could take years.'

Gersten finds it more effective to work through CAUS where he can protect the privacy of any informant, through client–attorney privilege, at the same time getting the information out.

He used the Freedom of Information Act to try and pressurise the US Army into releasing documents relating to statements made by Colonel Philip J. Corso in his book, *The Day After Roswell*. Corso was willing to testify that he had seen the bodies of dead aliens in 1947 and that he had read alien autopsy reports in 1961. Gersten was ready to take the issue to court, so he filed an FOIA request with the US Army for the release of any documents they may have had supporting Corso's claims. The Army claimed it could find no documents and Gersten took them to court. But Corso died and, on 26 April 1999, the case was dismissed. Gersten decided not to take that matter any further. Instead he filed a suit against the Department of Defense over Flying Triangles, in an attempt to find out what these mysterious craft actually are. While Gersten concedes that some of the sighting reports clearly describe advanced US experimental aircraft such as the TR-3B, which researcher Ed Fouche claims was built at Area 51, many of the reports could not possibly be the TR-3B. People have seen triangular craft that are half-a-mile wide. Some are seen at treetop level and over populated areas, shining beams of light on the ground. Witnesses also report seeing orb-shaped lights detach from these craft, fly around and re-attach. None of this can be explained in terms of advanced military technology.

Gersten sued the US government for damages after Betty Cash, Vickie Landrum and her grandson were abducted in Texas on the night of 29 December 1980. Gersten argued that as the UFO concerned was escorted by twenty Chinook helicopters it must have been part of a military operation. The case was dismissed on the grounds that the government denied all knowledge of the UFO and Gersten could not prove that it belonged to them.

Gersten is also bringing an unprecedented FOIA lawsuit against the CIA, the FBI and Department of Defense on the grounds that alien abduction can be viewed legally as a form of invasion. Article 4, section 4 of the US Constitution requires that the Federal Government protect the individual states against invasion, a provision that was enacted to persuade the original colonies to abandon their independent militias and join the Union. However, the Federal government are plainly failing in their duty to protect citizens of the States if those citizens are being abducted.

CAUS and Gersten have even more ambitious plans. As it is

unlikely that the President is likely to open up all the files on UFOs in the foreseeable future, they want to find out for themselves. They are planning a privately funded mission to the Moon, to send back pictures from the Sinu Medi regions where some UFOlogists have locateed alien structures. Using existing technology, they estimate that their 'Project Destination Moon' would cost $12 million – small change to the likes of Bill Gates and Ted Turner.

'Think of all the money sponsors would make from the publicity if they funded the first civilian mission to the Moon, especially if alien artefacts were discovered,' says the ever-optimistic Gersten. 'The space programme is in the hands of the government and the military. We are all like virtual prisoners on this planet. This is a project that is just waiting to happen.'

Derrel Sims

Alien implant expert Derrel Sims is a former CIA operative and got involved in UFO research after being abducted himself. He has conscious recollections of multiple abductions between the ages of three and seventeen. He started researching in this field at the age of sixteen and has been at it for more than twenty-seven years. After leaving the world of covert intelligence, he rose to become chief of investigation for the Houston-based Fund for Interactive Research and Space Technology. There he concentrated on collecting physical evidence, as he believes that this is the best way to prove that UFOs and alien abductions actually exist.

He has investigated hundreds of cases of alien implants, some of which have been inside the body for up to forty-one years. Despite being foreign bodies, they trigger no inflammatory response. He says that the devices found are 'meteoric' in origin. Although some labs have said that this is impossible, 'double blind' tests had proved this to be the case.

Dr Roger Leir

For years, people doubted the reality of alien abductions. This was largely because abductees had no physical evidence to back their stories. One man changed all that – Dr Roger Leir. A podiatrist from south California, he was the first doctor surgically to remove an alien implant. Until his first operation in August 1995, they had been seen only on X-rays and CAT scans.

Leir had a long interest in UFOs and was a long-standing member of the Mutual UFO Network, where he gained an investigator's certificate. As an investigator, he attended a UFO conference in Los Angeles in June 1995, when he met Derrel Sims. Sims showed Leir a number of X-rays. One of them showed a foreign object in the big toe of an abductee. Leir was sceptical, but Derrel produced the abductee's medical records, which showed that she had never had surgery on her foot. Leir offered to remove it and this led to a series of operations on abductees.

He selects candidates for surgery by strict criteria, which were developed when Leir was working at the National Institute for Discovery Science. Anyone undergoing surgery had to be a suspected abductee – they had to have experienced missing time or, at the very least, seen a UFO. They had to fill out a form that determined how deeply they were involved in the abduction phenomenon. They also had to have an object in their body that showed up on an X-ray, CAT scan or MRI.

Some of Leir's patients would have a conscious memory of the object being implanted into their bodies during the abduction. But, more often, implants are discovered by accident. Some abductees find unusual lumps and scars that have suddenly appeared and go to their doctors to get them X-rayed. In one case, an implant was discovered during treatment following a car crash.

All Leir's patients are given a psychological examination before and after the implant is removed. Some of them experience a new-found sense of freedom after surgery. One abductee went straight back to her family, saying she wanted nothing more to do with UFOs.

Leir has, so far, operated on eight individuals and removed a total of nine objects. Seven of them seem to be of extraterrestrial origin. Five were coated in a dark grey shiny membrane that was impossible to cut through even with a brand new surgical blade. One was T-shaped. Another three were greyish-white balls that were attached to an abnormal area of the skin. Leir found that patients would react violently if the object was touched and often suffered pain in that area in the week before the implant was surgically removed.

During surgery, Leir discovered that there was no inflammatory response in the flesh around the implant. He found this surprising as any foreign object introduced into the body usually causes an inflammatory response. In this case, there was no rejection. He also found that the surrounding tissue also contained large numbers of 'proprioceptors'. These are specialised nerve cells usually found in sensitive areas, such the finger tips, which sense temperature, pressure and touch. There was no medical reason for them to found where he found them, clustered around the implant. In two cases, Leir found 'scoop mark' lesions above the implants. In each case, Leir found that the tissue there suffered from a condition called 'solar elastosis'. This is caused by exposure to ultraviolet light, but it could not have been due to sunburn as only a tiny area was affected.

Leir found that the membrane surrounding the implants was composed of protein coagulum, hemosiderin granules – an iron pigment – and keratin. All these three substances are found naturally in the body. However, a search of the medical literature revealed that they had never been found together in combination before.

The implants themselves would fluoresce under ultraviolet light – usually green, but sometimes other colours. In one case, Leir found that an abductee had a pink stain on the palm of her hand. It could be removed temporarily, but would seep back under the skin. Derrel Sims uses this fluorescent staining, which cannot be removed by washing, to detect implants. Leir believes that it is caused by a substance given off by the implant to prevent rejection.

A wide range of tests have been carried out on the implants Leir has removed. They are submitted to routine pathology tests to see if they are human in origin. When that draws a blank, they are sent for metallurgical testing and they have been examined under optical microscopes and electron microscopes, and analysed using X-ray diffraction techniques that tell which elements they are made of.

When the T-shaped implant that Leir had removed from one patient was magnified one thousand times under an electron microscope, a tiny fishhook could be seen on one end of the crossbar of the T, which Leir believes anchored the implant to the flesh. The other end was rounded off like the nose of a bullet, while in the middle there was a tiny hole into which the shaft of the T fitted perfectly. One of the rods had a carbon core, which made it electrically conductive. The other had an iron core, which was magnetic. An attractive force between them made them cling together. The shaft was encircled by a band of silicate crystals. Bob Beckworth, an electrical engineer who works with Leir, likened this to an old-fashioned crystal set, where a quartz crystal and a copper wire were used to pick up a radio signal.

Specimens were sent to some of the most prestigious laboratories in North America – Los Alamos National Laboratories, New Mexico Tech and Toronto University, among others. The samples were found to contain rare elements in the same isotopic ratios that are found in meteorites. When the labs were told that the specimens had been removed from body tissue, they did not believe it. For Leir, this is the smoking gun.

When you mine an element on Earth, the ratio of the various radioactive isotopes it contains always falls within a certain range. If you mine uranium, for example, it will always contain a certain ratio of uranium 234, 235 and 236. This will be roughly the same anywhere on Earth. But rock samples from the moon or meteorites contain completely different isotopic ratios. The isotopic ratios in the implants showed clearly that they were not of earthly origin.

Leir is not sure what the implants are for. They could be transponders or locating devices that enable alien abductors to track those they have abducted. They might be designed to modify behaviour – some abductees exhibit unexplained compulsive behaviour. They might detect chemical changes caused by pollution, or be used to detect genetic changes in the body.

'If researchers such as Zachariah Sitchen are correct,' says Leir, 'and the human race is a genetically altered species, then it's possible that this genetic manipulation may still be going on and is something "they" wish to monitor closely.'

But whatever the implants are for, it is quite clear that they are extraterrestrial in origin. As Leir points out, if you find people who have been abducted by aliens and then find implants in them that have an isotopic ratio not found this planet, what other sane conclusion can you draw?

Tony Dodd

Ex-Sergeant Tony Dodd became interested in UFOs after having an encounter with one himself in 1978, when he was a police officer in North Yorkshire. He saw an object hovering about a hundred feet away. It had a domed top with four doors it. There were flashing lights around the sides, and three large spheres protruding from the underside. The whole structure was glowing bright white and it was silent. Dodd was sure this strange object was homing in on him, though it eventually floated off and landed nearby.

After he reported his sighting, his superiors told him not to talk to the press. This was standard procedure in the police.

Since then, he has seen seventy or eighty UFOs. Some of them are simply balls of light, anything from a couple of feet to thirty feet across. However, they seemed to contain some kind of mechanical device. He could often see a small, red pulse of light inside them, which created the aura of light. He has received had hundreds of reports of these balls of light, which apparently fly in formation. That must mean they have intelligent controls, he reasons.

After retiring from the police force, Dodd took the opportunity to speak out. He devoted himself to UFO research full-time and became Director of Investigative Services for Quest International, one of the world's leading UFO societies, and he oversees the publication of their high influential *UFO Magazine*. For part of his time in the police, he was a detective and he uses police investigation techniques on UFO cases. His police background has taught him which lines of enquiry to pursue and how to encourage witnesses to come forward and talk. It has also given him contacts in intelligence and the military. This is not always an advantage. Dodd's mail is tampered with, even the registered packages that turn up. And the CIA have threatened to kill him, though he remains stoically unintimidated.

Dodd is the foremost expert on animal mutilations in the UK and believes the government know all about it. He also believes that elite forces in America and Britain had adopted a hostile attitude towards a certain type of alien because the aliens out there do not resemble us very closely. Aliens, he points out, do not necessarily have two legs and two arms. Indeed, in human eyes some are quite grotesque. This is the reason the aliens are abducting people and creating hybrids. The aliens, apparently feel the same way about us. When people are abducted, they are treated the way we treat animals on game reserves.

Abductions are never one-off incidents, he says. Dodd has never come across a victim who has been abducted in childhood and never abducted again. Once it has happened, it tends to occur throughout the victim's life. Dodd believes that abductees are being conditioned until they reach puberty. After that the visitors start taking sperm and eggs. Part of the alien's agenda, Dodd believes, is a genetic experiment to create human–alien hybrids. He has investigated cases where aliens have impregnated female abductees. The conception is not natural. It is performed with a needle that it inserted through the navel. Human babies can be conceived using similar methods, but our medical profession is years behind. Three months into the pregnancy, the abductee is picked up again and the foetus is taken from the womb. The resulting 'star children' have thin limbs, large heads and alien eyes and faces, though they have hair on their heads and small human noses.

One woman he knows has been impregnated twice and both times the aliens have taken the baby. When the woman was three months pregnant, she was out walking her dog and a strange light appeared in the sky. She knew they had come to take her baby. She also saw jars containing embryos, which were suspended in liquid, as if in an artificial womb. These jars were all around the walls of the room she was in.

In many of the cases that Dodd has investigated, the abductees seem to have a sixth sense. They get a feeling when they know the abduction is about to take place. However, people generally do not know that they have been abducted. The clue is when they know things that they would not normally know about.

He uses lie detectors in his investigations. But he also uses his knowledge of the subject and his police background to sniff out the hoaxers. He also uses hypnosis and always employs the same hypnotist. This is because the man does nothing more than put the subject under hypnosis. Dodd himself asks all the questions. This is vital because he does not want the witnesses to be led or have them given guides or pointers.

In abduction cases, Dodd also looks for physical evidence. Some abductees have strange marks on their bodies. In one case he investigated, a woman saw strange balls of light in the bedroom at night, and she had an inexplicable burn mark on her arm. The woman had contacted him after he had made radio broadcast about alien abductions and, although many of the things he had mentioned had happened to her, she wanted to be reassured that she had not been abducted.

He has also come across a case where an abductee set off a camera flash near an alien implant in his head. Something under his skin glowed green. It was about a quarter of an inch wide, but it did not seem to cause the man any pain.

On several occasions, Dodd has had a person under hypnosis who has ended up speaking as somebody else – one of the aliens, Dodd believes. When he asked them what right they had to abduct people, the alien voice replied: 'We have every right to do this, you do not understand the nature of things.' Dodd concluded that he was talking to a highly intelligent being.

Dodd has tried to develop this as a method of communication with the alien race and has come to believe that extra-terrestrial beings are involved in a collect-and-analyse experiment to study the human race. He is in regular communication with them, but they only divulge things piece by piece. When he gets impatient, they tell him that they have to take things slowly because the human race is not able to handle the truth. We have to be educated as if we are in infant school. Dodd finds this very spiritual.

This is why they are not communicating with all of us. We are not ready for the knowledge they possess. That is why Dodd himself is here. His role is to disseminate information, to learn from the aliens and to give what he knows out to humankind. His alien contacts have told him that he is some form of teacher. Apparently this was decided before he arrived on Earth as a child and it is why they are making contact with him. They have explained humankind's place in the universe and have told him that we are immortal spirits that go on and on.

'Every flower has its seed and every creature its destiny,' Dodd has been told, 'weep not for those who have fulfilled their earthly obligation, but be happy that they have escaped that charge of material suffering. As the flower dies, the seed is born and so shall it be for all things.'

Dodd's contact with the aliens has religious aspects. He believes they are a higher force and that they are responsible for us being here.

Jaime Maussan

Latin America is one of the world centres of UFO activity, and Mexican TV investigative journalist Jaime Maussan became interested when a huge wave of UFO sightings occurred in Mexico in 1991. He quickly became the country's leading UFOlogist. Since then he has gone on to investigate the semi-legendary, blood-sucking vampiric entity known as the Chupacabra, or 'goat-sucker'. These have attacked livestock throughout Mexico, leaving their carcasses drained of blood, and they are thought to be extraterrestrial in origin.

This first Chupacabra attack that Maussan investigated occurred on 17 July 1994. Official records that show that, around this time, people were going out into the mountains to search for a mysterious creature that had been seen sucking the blood from cattle. At that time the name 'Chupacabra' had not been coined. Maussan believes that this is important, because it shows that the attacks are a real phenomenon, not something created by the media. The media did not become interested until 1996.

Maussan's interest grew out of his UFO research. From the start they seemed to be related. When Chupacabra attacks started to happen, he began to look into them and soon found that they were a real phenomenon. This became his main area of research because it inspired even more fear in people than the UFOs.

His research has taken him to the places where the attacks have occurred and he has interviewed eyewitnesses. This led him to build up a network of investigators across the country and he corresponds with other researchers outside Mexico.

Chupacabras mostly attack sheep, sometimes chickens and goats. Rarely, they attack larger animals such as donkeys or cattle. But at least 80 per cent of the attacks Maussan has investigated were on sheep.

The animals concerned are domesticated and live close to humans. There have been no reports of attacks on deer or other large wild animals in Mexico, though Maussan has read a report of deer being attacked over the border in San Antonio. On that occasion, ten deer were attacked. However, even though they were wild animals, they were in a controlled situation. It seems that wild animals are somehow more protected from this kind of presence. Maybe they can escape and hide from the predator more easily.

The creatures in the first attacks were described as some sort of big cat with wings. The witnesses had all seen the creature close to, sometimes from just a few feet away. Then the press began reporting what was happening in Puerto Rico. In 1996 the name 'Chupacabras' was imported and hundreds of reports began.

The recent sightings are consistent. People are reporting an animal about three feet tall with a face like a kangaroo or a mouse. It has a small, spiny back, wings, little hands and very thick feet. Some people have seen it flying. Footprints have been found and samples of what appears to be the creature's excrement have been taken. Maussan's problem is that these incidents take place far out in the country where there are no facilities to carry out an investigation. When he finds out about an attack, it is usually two, three or even four days after it has happened. By then it is too late. You need to be there straight away, he says.

Rural communities are terrified of the attacks. In one town, local people painted crosses on the walls of the buildings around the site of the attack, hoping that they would given them some form of protection. After an incident in the town of Sinaloa, the whole community was so frightened that people could not sleep. There were so many attacks that people became afraid for their children. They figured that if the creature could attack animals with impunity their kids would be next. Animals were disappearing every night and people thought that it would soon take a child. They had to call in the army to get some protection. Interestingly, the attacks always took place at night. Maussan does not have any reports of attacks in Mexico that have happened during daylight.

Maussan has linked these attacks with UFO reports. Elements of the Chupacabra phenomenon suggest that creatures responsible for the attacks are coming from another world. Some people have suggested that they come from another dimension or reality. After having investigated this phenomenon, Maussan concludes that the creatures responsible are no known terrestrial species.

Humans have been attacked by Chupacabras both in Mexico and Puerto Rico. Maussan believes this may be related to the Mexican version of vampires. In Mexican folklore, people are turned into animals that suck blood from their victims. In one modern-day case a man managed to fight off a Chupacabra and escape. The struggle was witnessed by his wife and his brother. Their three accounts match. Apparently, the creature smelled very bad. The victim was left in a state of shock with two small, bloody holes in his arm.

To Maussan, this suggests that the same creature is responsible for old-fashion vampire tales and modern-day Chupacabra attacks.

'Perhaps these vampires were not human,' he says, 'and it is the same old creature that has been with us for a long time but we have never been able to discover exactly what it is.'

He has come across some cases where animals have survived for several hours after having been drained of blood. Maussan has found some strange substance left in the holes in the victims' carcasses which allows the blood to flow rather than coagulate normally. A proper chemical analysis of this substance might indicate what kind of creature is responsible for these attacks.

Maussan investigated the 1996 case, where there was an attack on some sheep in the small town of Puebla. A farmer, Dom Pedro, called the local vet, Soledad de la Pena. When she arrived she was amazed to see one of the sheep still alive, twelve hours after the attack, even though it had been drained of blood. Maussan thought this could be crucial.

'If we could find out what chemical was secreted to keep the animal alive after being drained of blood, it could be a very real and major breakthrough in medicine that could benefit mankind,' he says.

But Maussan has not been able to get this sort of work done in Mexico. Although some doctors and some universities have expressed an interest, none have come forward publicly.

Meanwhile, the authorities have been unable to explain these attacks, so they have chosen to ignore the whole phenomenon – another parallel with UFOs. And the church has refused to comment. Maussan is a little stumped about what to do next. When the Chupacabra attacks first started in Mexico, everyone was taken by surprise. By the time the media were interested, and Maussan had everything set up in order to investigate the attacks, the main spate was over. However, if the attacks start again, Maussan will be ready for them.